Preface

I nstructing Students Who Have Literacy Problems is the second edition of a book originally titled *Remedial and Clinical Reading Instruction*. This title change reflects the evolution in remedial programs from an exclusive focus on reading to a coalescence of reading and writing in order to advance overall literacy attainment with low-achieving readers. Much that was popular with instructors and students in the first edition has been retained in the revision, but plainly, as can be seen from an examination of this volume, there also is much that is new.

This book is intended for upper-level undergraduates and graduate students in courses on corrective, remedial, and/or clinical reading instruction. It also is suitable for use in courses focusing on instruction of individuals having learning disabilities since the educational dilemmas of these students center more frequently on reading problems than on any other academic area.

Many available texts concentrating on literacy difficulties primarily consider the elementary school child. However, few colleges offer separate courses in remedial reading assessment and instruction for elementary and secondary preservice and inservice teachers. As a result, secondary teachers enrolled in these courses frequently complain that the text they must use gives little attention to their specific problems when working with older disabled readers. Although the needs of elementary school children are discussed extensively in this book, it also offers information in every chapter for secondary teachers. In addition, a comprehensive section in Chapter 15 addresses illiterate and functionally illiterate adults.

After completing this book, students will be familiar with techniques grounded in cutting-edge research. One of the most important features of *Instructing Students Who Have Literacy Problems* is that principles for assessment and instruction presented in every chapter are based on current theories of the reading process and, very significantly, on the most up-to-date research available about each topic. Upper-level college students should be familiar with research in their field. However, the research evidence presented in this text has been integrated within an understandable discussion that also highlights practical teaching recommendations based on the findings. In short, to promote the goal that these research-based procedures actually be applied in schools, much of the research information presented in the text has been blended with case studies of students and within descriptions of lessons that can be implemented in real classrooms. Thus, by relating teaching suggestions to sound theory and to research, this text serves the practicing teacher's need for specificity in regard to program planning and instructional procedures.

Advising teachers what *not* to do, as well as what *to* do, is important. Literacy instruction, like much of education, has at times fallen prey to cyclical movements during which old ideas are resurrected and prove to be as unsuccessful the second and third times around as they were the first. For most topics in the text, ill-advised practices of the past and present are specifically noted, with research findings cited to substantiate these points.

Several organizational features have been added to this second edition that should be helpful:

- The book is divided into 15 chapters, as opposed to the 23 in the first edition. This organization fits better the number of weeks in a typical college semester.
- Case studies are interspersed throughout. Inservice and preservice teachers can read about application of suggested assessment and instructional techniques with actual or hypothetical students.
- Each chapter now ends with a section titled "Reflections," which focuses on questions and activities to prompt college students' reflective thinking about the chapter content. Some require the preservice or inservice teacher to apply to his or her own learning the principles and/or procedures discussed for aiding their pupils.
- Key terms defined in text are printed in **bold**.

Some of the many content changes and additions in this second edition include the following.

- There is discussion of the present trend for inclusion of special programs within regular classrooms, including suggestions and considerations.
- The well-received chapters on causation in the first edition have been updated and expanded (for example, to include research on phonemic awareness and on effects of an individual's reading history).
- The four chapters on assessment each have been extended to reflect the growing advances in assessment procedures. A few of many examples include elaborated sections on performance-based assessment and on use of portfolios in remedial reading and learning disabilities programs; a delineation of ways to use listening comprehension to judge reading potential; a discussion of preferred methods for assessing writing; descriptions of use of running records; discussions of tests of phonemic awareness; a depiction of varied tests of metacognitive strategy use; and others.
- New research on the value of oral reading is cited.
- Data supporting the principles of early intervention, one-to-one tutoring, and collaborative learning in special programs is included.
- Instructional details of learning systems such as Reading Recovery and Success for All are given.
- Findings of motivational theory research are reported and ways are suggested for implementation of these findings by reading teachers.
- New views on emergent literacy are explained and implications for prevention of literacy delays are considered.

- Current high-quality literature and other new materials for remedial instruction are described.
- One of the most exciting areas of inquiry at the moment consists of explorations of developmental phases of word learning. In an enlarged chapter on *word recognition*, new understandings of these phases and their instructional significance are related to important concerns of remedial teachers.
- Views of the best pedagogical procedures for increasing *word identification* strategies also are in a period of rapid change. The changing convictions, based on recent research offerings, are highlighted in a second chapter on word study. The chapter includes explanations of research-based approaches for improving phonemic awareness; discussion of the controversies related to phonic analysis and context as word identification cues—along with recommendations about these instructional strategies; ways to employ writing activities to enhance both word recognition and word identification; and other critical topics.
- Innovative methods for increasing students' understandings of word meanings, which can positively affect their text comprehension, are added to the chapter on vocabulary knowledge.
- As was previously the case, the entire text reflects the positions that (a) the purpose of reading is to gain meaning, and (b) that one gains skill in other facets of literacy (for example, word identification) in order to facilitate comprehension. Yet it is true that students are able to identify words appropriately and adequately, but still have serious difficulties understanding overall and important meanings of text. Because of the centrality of meaning in all literacy instruction—to help focus on the needs of students with comprehension problems—there are two chapters that specifically provide research findings in relation to comprehension instruction. In the new edition, one is devoted to the understanding of narrative text, and the other highlights comprehension of expository selections, including the understanding of content area materials. In both chapters, the best that research has to say about methods of comprehension instruction is thoroughly described for teachers.
- Reviewers of the first edition particularly valued the chapter on severely disabled readers because the subject is skirted in many texts on remedial and clinical reading instruction, as well as in most books directly addressing learning disabilities. In the second edition, this chapter details many more data-based procedures for instructing these students. In addition, the discussion is augmented with specific methods for working with the most critical reading disability cases of all—nonreaders.
- Discussions of reading instruction with students having linguistic and cultural backgrounds that differ from the mainstream, likewise, have been amplified. Increased attention has been given to those individuals traditionally considered at risk for educational failure, and descriptions are provided of family literacy programs.

In this short preface, all modifications in the new edition cannot be described, but a review of the book will disclose other changes that should be beneficial to preservice and inservice teachers. Although this book presents important background details, it also provides teachers and prospective teachers with specific, practical assessment and instructional strategies for use with students having literacy problems.

ACKNOWLEDGMENTS

My thanks go to my many professional colleagues across the country who reviewed this work and whose helpful criticisms guided me in preparing the final version of the manuscript: Carole L. Bond, Memphis State University; Deanne Camp, Drury College; Kathleen A. Gormley, Russell Sage College; Michael W. Kibby, University at Buffalo; and Grace Nunn, Eastern Illinois University. I also thank those literacy researchers who continue to devote many arduous hours to understanding and explicating instructional procedures that will help educators assist students with literacy difficulties. Finally, my special thanks are offered to Linda Scharp, my editor, for her unusually understanding and helpful attitude, and to editors Louise Sette and Janet Battiste for their efficiency and competence.

I look forward to receiving comments, questions, and suggestions from the students and instructors who use this book.

Sandra McCormick

Brief Contents

Contents

2

Causes and Correlates of Individual Differences in Reading Ability: Part I   33

3

Causes and Correlates of Individual Differences in Reading Ability: Part II   57

UNIT TWO
ASSESSMENT   75

4
Assessment for Identification of Reading Problems   77

5
Assessment for Verifying General Reading Level   105

6

Assessment for Identifying Specific Strengths and Weaknesses in Reading: Part I   131

7

Assessment for Identifying Specific Strengths and Weaknesses in Reading: Part II   165

UNIT THREE
INSTRUCTIONAL INTERVENTIONS   203

8
Important Principles of Remedial and Clinical Reading Instruction   205

9

Word Recognition   249

10

Word Identification   295

FOUNDATIONS OF REMEDIAL AND CLINICAL READING INSTRUCTION

1

Basic Concepts and Definitions in Reading

A developmental reading program should include many opportunities to read narrative and informational materials, to learn strategies, and to practice study skills.

L iteracy is not just an issue for our contemporary society: it has long been a concern in many societies. For example, in 17th century Sweden, being literate in order to be able to read religious books was considered so important that parents were fined if they failed to teach their children to read, and marriage was denied adults until they could demonstrate some level of literacy (Venezky, 1991). In the 1800s, members of the ruling classes in Western countries promoted literacy so that the general population could participate more effectively in politics and in the military. In addition, learning to read was encouraged as a means of improving a nation's overall economic condition—as a consequence of having a better educated and more skilled workforce.

Being able to read is even more critical in contemporary life. For individuals, reading provides access to employment, increases educational opportunities, promotes social adjustment, offers entertainment, and serves as a means for lifelong learning. In addition, a literate population is recognized as crucial for generating ideas that lead to social change and improvement—so much so that today many governments, including our own, mandate universal education, with literacy as one of the prime objectives.

Reading is seen as an indispensable skill for both the individual and society. See Table 1–1. Most students do attain reading skill; in fact, data from several sources show that students in U.S. schools exhibit reading achievement that reaches or surpasses that of students from any other period in American education. Nevertheless, many elementary and secondary schools have large numbers of students who are disabled readers despite years of reading instruction. Why is this so, and what can *you*, as a teacher of reading, do about it? The answer is, you can serve as a superior teacher of reading in one of several types of programs.

TYPES OF READING PROGRAMS

Developmental Reading Programs

A **developmental reading program** is a regular classroom program designed for most school-aged students.[1] A developmental program should be well balanced and provide students with many varied opportunities to read stories and informational material, as well as include specific activities for students to develop word identification, comprehension, and other reading strategies. There are eight major components of developmental reading programs:

1. *Promoting emergent literacy.* Emergent literacy activities facilitate the initial stages of reading acquisition and prepare students for the next steps in learning how to read.

2. *Developing automatic recognition of words.* Procedures help students enlarge the number of words they recognize immediately and accurately.

3. *Developing word identification strategies.* Students learn several word identification strategies to use alone or in combination when they encounter unknown words.

---

[1]Most definitions in this text conform to those given in *A Dictionary of Reading and Related Terms* (T. L. Harris & Hodges, 1981), commissioned by the International Reading Association to bring consistency to meanings of terms used in the field of reading. In the past, lack of consistency has been prevalent (for example, see the numerous conflicting definitions for the term *dyslexia* listed later in this chapter); this has prevented clear communication. The present text supports the effort to agree on meanings for reading terminology.

TABLE 1–1

Reading levels of a sampling of items and materials encountered in adult life

Items and Materials	Approximate Grade Level of Reading Ability Needed
Help-wanted ads in newspapers	6–7
Front-page stories in newspapers	9–12+
Dosage and symptom information on aspirin bottle labels	10
Preparation directions on boxes of frozen dinners	8
Directions for filling out the 1040 income tax forms	9–10
Training materials for military cooks	7–8
Articles in *Reader's Digest, Saturday Evening Post, Ladies' Home Journal, Popular Mechanics,* and *Harper's*	12+
Articles in romance, TV, and movie magazines	8
Recent presidential inaugural addresses	9
Information on financial statements	11–16+
Life insurance policies	12
Apartment leases	College

Sources: Bargantz and Dulin (1970); Bittner and Shamo (1976); Bormuth (1973–74); Felton and Felton (1973); Hirshoren, Hunt, and Davis (1974); Hoskins (1973); Kilty (1976); Kwolek (1973); Pyrczak (1976); Razik (1969); Sticht (1975); Worthington (1977).

4. *Enlarging the student's meaning vocabulary.* Students are helped to increase the number of words whose meanings they understand.

5. *Increasing comprehension.* Many different strategies help students comprehend material effectively. Since the only reason to read is to comprehend, this is the most important component of any program. All other components assist comprehension.

6. *Reading orally.* Adequate oral reading is sometimes needed for good communication. More often, however, oral reading is used as an informal assessment tool so that the teacher can determine if a student is employing sound reading strategies.

7. *Promoting appropriate rates of reading.* Students learn to read at a rate appropriate to the specific purpose and material.

8. *Developing study skills and content area reading skills.* Because all reading material is not narrative (story-type) material, students develop the special types of language and reading skills they need to deal with content area materials and other informational writing.

A developmental program that inadequately or inappropriately treats any of these eight components or does not provide students with large amounts of time for reading to practice strategies may lead to mild or moderate reading disabilities for some students. Developmental reading programs exist through the end of sixth grade in some school systems; however, more districts are including developmental reading as a regular part of the curriculum in their middle schools and high schools. These secondary level developmental reading programs are for average, and even above-average readers, and are designed to help students continue to perfect reading skills and attain advanced ones.

Since the only reason to read is to comprehend, this is the most important component of any program. All other components assist comprehension.

Corrective Reading Programs

A **corrective reading program** is carried out in a regular classroom by the classroom teacher. It is designed to help a student with a mild reading disability who needs special attention in one or more of the eight major reading components. Despite the need to provide a general developmental reading program for the class as a whole, the classroom teacher can still support appropriate and adequate remediation for students with mild disabilities. A corrective reading program has been described as "more specific than developmental instruction, but less intensive than remedial reading instruction" (T. L. Harris & Hodges, 1981, p. 71). Some students who need corrective reading may not have a specific weakness; rather, they exhibit a general, slight weakness in all areas.

Remedial Reading Programs

A **remedial reading program** is one in which students with moderate to severe reading disabilities receive specific instruction from a specially trained reading teacher. Often this instruction is conducted in small groups of about 5 to 8 students outside of the regular classroom. More comprehensive assessment of students' reading problems is undertaken than in most developmental or corrective programs to determine students' specific weaknesses and the reasons for these weaknesses, as well as any strengths that may help alleviate their problems. The teacher adjusts instruction to the special needs of the students, and the students are usually grouped according to common needs in order to attend the remedial class at the same time. At the end of a class period (often about 45 minutes), students return to their regular classrooms, and another group of students with reading problems comes to the reading room for special instruction. Since students are grouped according to common needs, some instruction may be carried out with all members of the small group participating. At other times, students may work in a one-to-one situation with the teacher. The special training of the teacher and the small size of each class make possible in-depth assessment, more frequent ongoing assessment, and flexibility in adapting instructional techniques to individual differences.

Clinical Reading Programs

A **clinical reading program** is designed for students with severe reading disabilities, and the clinician works with only one student at a time. Assessment is usually more extensive than in other programs and often includes referrals to other professionals or agencies, such as physicians, speech and hearing specialists, and psychologists, for evaluation. Diagnostic procedures include formal testing and informal observation. Remediation is specialized, intensive, and highly individualized. A case study report is usually developed for the student; it includes the results of assessment and the student's responses to various instructional techniques. Some school systems have centrally located reading clinics to which students from all over the district are transported. Universities and colleges frequently have educational clinics that serve students with severe reading disabilities. Hospitals and other social agencies may also sponsor reading clinics.

Other Reading Programs

Other programs in which teachers of reading work are learning disability programs and programs for the developmentally disabled (mildly retarded) student. Research has consistently shown that the largest percentage of students in learning disability (LD) programs are enrolled because of difficulties in learning to read. Likewise, a major task of teachers of developmentally disabled (DD) students is dealing with student difficulties in attaining an acceptable degree of literacy.

The school psychologist may also deal with reading disabled students. The psychologist is often requested to assess students as the result of a suspected learning disorder. In most cases, the possible learning problem is first noted because students are not progressing as they should in reading. School psychologists need to understand the reading process so they can assess students according to current thinking in the field and make appropriate recommendations to teachers.

Although there may be some differences between developmental, corrective, remedial, clinical, LD, and DD reading programs in degree of individualization, intensity, and pace of instruction, they are all based on the same basic principles of learning and learning to read, and all deal with the eight major components of reading instruction. Finally, all must deal with the affective domain. Teachers often positively affect learning by capitalizing on students' interests as these relate to feelings and attitudes. Feelings and attitudes can also have a negative influence on learning, however. Infused throughout the chapters of this book are discussions of the role that reading problems play in a student's emotional outlook, of the influence emotional distress has on reading disability, and of ways to observe student interests and attitudes, as well as suggestions for promoting self-esteem among poor readers. Attention to the affective domain is important for all students, but it is particularly crucial for students with learning problems.

So, although there are differences among the various types of reading programs, there are more similarities. Most techniques suggested in this text are equally useful in all programs, and teachers in all programs need to know how to deal with basic reading problems and promote acquisition of reading strategies.

ROLES OF READING TEACHERS

A teacher trained in reading education may serve several roles. A **reading teacher** can be loosely defined as anyone whose work includes reading instruction, but more often the term means a teacher with special training who works with students who have reading problems and who teaches in a setting other than the regular classroom. The term *reading specialist* is used synonymously with that of *reading teacher.*

Currently there is a trend for reading teachers to work cooperatively with the teacher in the regular classroom, rather than having classes of their own with children who are "pulled out" of the regular classroom for special reading instruction (e.g., see McAloon, 1993). In such an arrangement, the reading teacher and the classroom teacher may work as a team with all students, or the reading teacher may focus his or her attention on the problem readers in the class. Some LD teachers also are working under this arrangement.

In many cases, the presence of the reading teacher in the regular classroom has proved to be quite advantageous. Part of the reason is that the "dead" time in which students move from one classroom to the other is eliminated. This may seem a minor issue on the face of it, but may actually be more significant than it appears. Allington (1993) determined that the amount of time required for students to leave one room, move down the hall, and get settled down to learning in another averages about 12 minutes; in the course of a week, then, an hour of instructional time could be wasted.

This arrangement (sometimes called a "push-in" program) has not worked well in other cases, however. Its effectiveness depends a good deal on whether the classroom teacher and the reading teacher share similar perspectives on teaching and classroom management strategies.

For many years, there has been a debate about whether special education students fare better in pull-out or push-in programs. Research in this area has shown that the critical variable is that excellent teaching in either type of arrangement results in better achievement than mediocre teaching in the other (see Dunn, 1973; Gottlieb, 1974; Mullen & Itkin, 1961; Payne, Polloway, Smith, & Payne, 1981). This finding is not too great a surprise and likely may be the best conclusion that can be made on the controversy of whether instruction for poor readers is better provided inside or outside of the regular classroom.

When successful push-in programs occur, certain factors seem to be in place. A case in point is the Rights Without Labels (RWL) program in Pittsburgh, Pennsylvania (R. Bean, 1992). This push-in program was carefully planned to include (a) inservice instruction for regular and special teachers before the program was initiated; (b) special assistance to teachers throughout the school year, when needed; and (c) piloting of the program in one grade only in order to address difficulties before it was implemented schoolwide. Furthermore, the teachers who would be working in RWL were involved in its design during a full year of preplanning, which included not only attention to teaching philosophy but also to consistency across teachers in classroom management policies. During the program, participating teachers had a daily planning period. At the end of the first year, regular education students and those with low literacy levels achieved as well as they had when there had been a pull-out program, serious discipline problems subsided somewhat (by 7%), and students seemed to receive more direct instruction (probably because there were two teachers—the regular classroom teacher and the special teacher—in the room at the same time). While RWL is viewed as a successful push-in program, participant teachers still had certain concerns: (a) how to meet the special and varied needs of all students when additional assistance from resource teachers was not available, and (b) how to cope with the unfamiliar role of team teaching with another teacher, in the same room, alternating responsibilities and ensuring appropriate instructions for all students.

A compromise to the pull-out versus push-in issue is the close integration of the content covered in regular classrooms with that covered in pull-out programs. Regulations that guide the federally funded Title I programs in the United States now compel the coordination of special reading programs and the student's classroom reading instructional program in some way (Allington, 1993).

One program linking all of a student's reading instruction that has been very effective in several urban communities is the Success for All program (Wasik & Slavin, 1993). Both classroom and special teachers receive training in the reading instruction adopted for use in the program—a broad-based, well-balanced approach following the tenets of current research. Furthermore, a systematic form of communication is used between both of a student's reading teachers (classroom teacher and special teacher); a tutor-teacher contact form is completed each day to communicate to the special teacher what the student is working on in the regular room.

There are other roles for reading teachers. The terms **reading consultant** and **reading resource teacher** usually define the same role. These are specialists who use their skills and knowledge to work with other teachers; they do not serve students directly, but devote their time to providing inservice training programs, classroom consultation, demonstrations, and other services designed to improve reading instruction in all types of programs within a school district (E. James, 1994).

An **LD resource room teacher** serves a different function. Unlike the reading teacher, the LD teacher works with other learning disorders in addition to reading problems. Although some teachers in LD programs have self-contained classrooms where students remain most of the day, many LD teachers have a role similar to the reading teacher's in a pull-out program: they serve a number of small groups of students with moderate or severe problems in settings outside the regular classroom at different times during each day. LD teachers are now working in push-in programs, as well.

The designations **reading coordinator** and **reading supervisor** are used synonymously. Both may oversee and coordinate all the reading programs within a school system or may be in charge of one specific program and the teachers within it.

OTHER IMPORTANT DEFINITIONS

Reading teachers, LD teachers, DD teachers, and school psychologists should be able to define important terms used often in the profession. Many are used incorrectly or imprecisely by nonprofessionals. You should understand their meanings and correct uses.

Disabled Reader

Who is a disabled reader? A **disabled reader** is anyone reading significantly below his or her own *potential*. However, there has been a good deal of controversy about how to determine the *discrepancy* between an individual's present reading achievement and his or her potential—and, subsequently, in determining if the discrepancy is severe enough to warrant special instruction.

Sometimes the criterion to label a student as a "disabled reader" has simply been whether a student is reading below grade level. This criterion has been criticized for several reasons. First, very intelligent students actually should be reading above grade level; if not, they are not reading up to their potentials. Conversely, students with significantly lower than average IQs may be reading below their assigned grades, but still be reading up to their own potential.

In other cases, various mathematical formulas have been used to specify the degree of discrepancy between actual reading achievement and potential reading achievement. These take into account a number of factors, but particularly intelligence as specified by IQ scores. This method, too, has come under fire because of lack of consensus about the concept of intelligence and the failure of intelligence test scores to provide precise, accurate measures (Stanovich, 1991a).

Most authorities suggest that use of a measure of listening comprehension may be the soundest procedure for measuring discrepancy that is currently available (e.g., Spring & French, 1990). In this measure, a comparison is made between students' understanding of material when they read it themselves, in contrast with their understanding after listening to material read to them. For example, suppose Annie attains a reading instructional level of only 4.0 (fourth grade) on a standardized test she reads by herself, but attains a score of 6.0 (sixth grade) on a test of listening comprehension. It can be said that her reading potential is sixth-grade level. A difference of 2 years exists between the level at which Annie should be reading according to her potential and the level of her present reading achievement. With a discrepancy of 2 years, Annie likely would be considered a disabled reader and would receive special reading instruction.

Learning Disability

The term **learning disability** was adopted in 1963 as a generic description to replace the many different labels applied to students who had difficulty in listening, mathematics, reading, speaking, spelling, thinking, or writing. See Table 1–2.

In most states, eligibility for services in learning disability (LD) programs is determined in the same way that eligibility for remedial or clinical reading programs is determined. The levels at which students should be achieving are compared to the levels at which they are achieving. If the difference is significant, students are considered learning disabled and receive remedial instruction from an LD teacher or an LD tutor.

During the early years of the LD movement, students designated as learning disabled were believed to be perceptually disabled or brain injured or to have processing dysfunctions in their central nervous systems. Even today the term *learning disability* is used differently by individuals with different theoretical biases. However, generally in the current use of the term, a large number of students labeled as learning disabled have no discernible brain injury or other neurological problems. For students labeled as learning disabled, just as for those labeled as reading disabled, there may be a number of different underlying causes for the learning difficulty (discussed in Chapters 2 and 3)—not necessarily physical ones—and whatever the origin of the problem, a student may be considered learning disabled if he or she manifests significant discrepancy between estimated academic potential and actual academic performance.

It is generally assumed that the reading teacher works with students with less serious reading problems, while the LD teacher works with students who require more intensive and specialized instruction. In fact, the original intent of the law that requires services for LD students was to provide aid only to those with the most profound disabilities (an estimated 2 to 3% of the student population). In practice, LD teachers work with students who have moderate and severe reading disabilities, as do reading teachers. For this reason, and because criteria for assigning the labels *learning disabled* and

TABLE 1–2

Terms used to describe students with learning disabilities

Prior to 1963	After 1963
brain-injured	learning disabled
childhood aphasics	
children with cerebral dysfunctions	
children with chronic brain dysfunctions	
congenitally word-blind	
developmentally dyslexic	
dyslexic	
disgraphic	
minimally brain-damaged	
children with minimal brain dysfunctions	
minimally brain-injured	
neurologically disordered	
neurologically impaired	
perceptually disabled	
perceptually handicapped	
children with perceptual-motor handicaps	
psychoneurologically disabled	
Strauss-syndrome children	
children with strephosymbolia	

reading disabled are the same in most programs today, the label students receive and the program they enter may be largely a matter of chance: the school psychologist who tests the student may be more familiar with reading programs than LD programs and so may suggest placement in the remedial reading class; or if the reading class is full but there is room in the LD program, the principal may suggest that the student be tested to determine if he or she is eligible for LD services.

In contemporary LD programs, the instruction a student receives in reading is no different from instruction received in remedial and clinical reading programs. This was not true in the early days of the LD movement. Because initial work in this field was conducted by professionals who had worked with brain-damaged and severely mentally retarded persons, their theories of what caused difficulty in learning to read had a neurological or physiological orientation. In those days, many methods employed with students labeled *learning disabled* were far removed from techniques that have more recently been shown to improve reading ability. For example, students in LD programs were required to engage in body management activities (such as walking on balance beams), complete perceptual exercises, and undergo training meant to improve defective brain processing functions.

Professionals in the LD field became disillusioned with perceptual-motor techniques and assessment during the early 1970s, when numerous studies began to show that direct teaching of reading was effective for students with learning disorders while treating "underlying psychological processes," such as visual-perceptual, visual-motor, and auditory-perceptual problems, was not (Batemen, 1971; Black 1974; Bryan 1974; Hammill & Larsen, 1974; Masland & Cratty, 1971; Saphier, 1973). Although a few LD programs still display this process training orientation, most now employ direct teaching, that is, teaching directly what students need to learn rather than hoping their disabilities will be remediated in some roundabout fashion. For example, if a student has a reading disability, instruction should involve reading activities, not physical activities; if a student has a math disability, instruction should employ math activities, not perceptual activities. A reading teacher and an LD teacher teaching reading in programs based on current research use no significantly different methods in their classes.

Dyslexia

The term **dyslexia** elicits many conflicting definitions and contrary hypotheses regarding its causes and symptoms. Some, for example, define dyslexia as a reading disability of *unknown origin*:

> [Dyslexia is] an inability to read when no specific causes are evident. (Hittleman, 1978, p. 407)

> Originally the word [dyslexia] was used to identify a form of brain damage that deprives the patient of his ability to recall words, letters, and symbols. By extension, it has come to refer simply to a disorder of reading, without specific regard to what might lie behind that disorder and how it should be treated. (Calkins, 1972, cited in M. M. Evans, 1982, p. 576)

> [Dyslexia describes one] whose reading ability is grossly impaired and in whom no difficulty of basic visual or auditory receptive apparatus, amentia, dementia, neurological disease or injury, or serious psychiatric illness exists. (Drew, 1955, p. 247)

Certain definitions retain aspects of the original definition used in the late 1800s by Hinshelwood (1896) in which the cause is specified as a *brain defect or of other neurological origin*:

> [Dyslexia is] a rare but definable and diagnosable form of primary reading retardation with some form of central nervous system dysfunction. (Abrahms, 1980, cited in T. L. Harris & Hodges, 1981, p. 95)

Other definitions refer to *brain and neurological disorders but include other causes as well*:

> Among the causes suggested for dyslexia are brain damage and inherited neurological abnormalities not associated with brain damage. Environmental factors, such as poor teaching, are also regarded as possible causes. (S. A. Cohen, 1969, p. 516)

Some deny that defects of a neurological origin contribute in any important way but do agree that dyslexia has *a constitutional origin*:

> Sometimes it [dyslexia] implies a constitutionally based reading disability in an individual who is free from mental defect, serious neurotic traits, and gross neurological deficits. (A. J. Harris & Sipay, 1980, p. 137)

Certain definitions indicate that dyslexia may be *genetically determined* rather than being caused by damage to the brain or central nervous system:

> [Dyslexia is] a constitutional and often genetically determined deficit in written language skills such as reading, writing, and spelling. (Ekwall & Shanker, 1983, p. 316)

Others not only *deny the association of brain damage with dyslexia, but specify that perceptual difficulties are also unrelated*:

> To . . . criteria [for dyslexia] may be added: the absence of serious brain damage or of perceptual defects. (Critchley, 1970, p. 11)

While for some, *perceptual deficiencies are central* to the definition:

> [A dyslexic is] the kind of child who cannot unscramble auditory and/or written symbols which reach the brain so that they have the same order-pattern and meaning which they have for others. (Zedler, 1969, cited in M. M. Evans, 1982, p. 577)

Many definitions include the criterion that the reading disability must be *serious*:

> [Dyslexia is] a *severe* reading disability of unspecified origin. (T. L. Harris & Hodges, 1981, p. 95)

Others use the term to indicate *any type of reading problem:*

> [Dyslexia is] a popular term for any difficulty in reading of any intensity and from any cause(s). (T. L. Harris & Hodges, 1981, p. 95)

> [Dyslexia is] a synonym for reading disability. (Money, 1962, & Klasen, 1972, cited in A. J. Harris & Sipay, 1980, p. 137)

One of the oldest definitions of dyslexia even suggested substance abuse as a cause; Hinshelwood (1896) described a form of dyslexia that he claimed to be of a "toxic origin" after he studied an alcoholic who could not read, but whose reading disability gradually improved when alcohol was withheld from him.

In addition, several terms that have been used synonymously with dyslexia include *congenital word blindness, dyssymbolia, word amblyopia, specific reading disability,* and *primary reading retardation.* This variety of terms compounds the prevailing confusion.

Professionals in education, genetics, neurology, ophthalmology, psychiatry, and psychology often define *dyslexia* differently; even specialists in reading explain the term in many different ways; and the lay press uses numerous uninformed definitions of the term. One writer makes this suggestion: "Put all the definitions in a line and then pick every 73rd word. This would be your definition. It couldn't be any worse than what we have now" (Inouye, 1981, p. 3).

Perhaps the best definition of dyslexia currently used is the one described by Stanovich (1991a): *a reading deficit that is domain specific, is at the word recognition level, and which shows a qualitative difference from that of other poor readers.* "Domain specific" simply means the problem is specific to *reading* tasks (there are no problems in math, for instance). Furthermore, the deficit, most often, is related to a lack in phonological processing ability—ability to hear and use sounds to identify words. "Qualitative differences" means discrepancies between potential reading achievement and actual achievement are more severe than they are for other poor readers. However, even Stanovich points out that the validity of this description has not yet been confirmed.

Because the term *dyslexia* has so many different meanings, many professionals avoid its use and substitute the term *severe reading disability.* T. L. Harris and Hodges (1981) state this point of view:

> Due to all the differing assumptions about the process and nature of possible reading problems, dyslexia has come to have so many incompatible connotations that it has lost any real value for educators, except as a fancy word for a reading problem. . . . Thus, in referring to a specific student, it is probably better that the teacher describe the actual reading difficulties, and make suggestions for teaching related to the specific difficulties, not apply a label which may create misleading assumptions by all. (p. 95)

Additional Definitions

Here are other definitions with which you should be familiar:

Reading deficiency.   A mild reading disability in which the individual lacks a specific skill necessary for effective reading.

Reading retardation.   Reading below grade level. *A Dictionary of Reading and Related Terms* (T. L. Harris & Hodges, 1981) prefers the term *reading disability* because reading achievement below grade level often is considered an inappropriate criterion for assigning students to remedial programs.

Reluctant reader.   An individual who can read but does not like to. At times, the term *alliterate* is applied to such persons.

Underachiever.   An individual whose achievement is below the level expected according to intelligence tests.

Slow learner.   An individual with an IQ between 76 and 89. (While these individuals may have an intellectual functioning level below the average range of 90 to 110, they are not considered retarded.)

Developmentally disabled.   An individual with an IQ between 50 and 75[2] who also manifests deficits in adaptive behavior. (The term *mildly retarded* is sometimes used synonymously.)

Nonreader.   An individual who has been unable to learn to read (or has attained *unusually minimal* success at doing so) despite normal intelligence, adequate instruction, and absence of gross neurological or sensory defects.

Illiterate.   An individual who is unable to read and/or write; the illiterate person may have had little or no instruction or may not have learned from the instruction received.

Functional illiterate.   An individual who has some reading ability, but it is so limited that he or she cannot read basic information needed to function in daily life.

Preliterate.   A person who is not yet reading simply because he or she has had no reading instruction; for example, a preschool child.

THE INCIDENCE OF READING DISABILITY

Accurate estimates of the number of individuals with reading disabilities are difficult to obtain, largely because of the differences in the amount of discrepancy used to determine if students should receive remedial or clinical reading services. Some programs include any student whose discrepancy is at least 1 year. Other programs alter the requirements according to grade level. For example, a program may require a 6-month discrepancy for primary grade students; a 1-year discrepancy for intermediate grades; a 1-year, 6-month discrepancy for middle or junior high school students; and a 2-year discrepancy for high school students. To be eligible for remedial instruction in federally funded Title I programs, students usually must score in the lower third (by percentile) on tests of reading achievement. Because of this and similar variations, reports of the number of disabled readers differ from school district to school district.

Spache (1981) and others believe that the following are the most useful discrepancies for determining if a student has a reading disability serious enough to warrant instruction in a remedial or clinical program: primary grades, 1 year; intermediate grades, 2 years; secondary level, 3 years. If these criteria are used, about 15% of students in the United States need remedial and clinical reading services; and about 3% of all students have severe problems. Because classroom teachers may have insufficient

---

[2]The IQ range for this designation may vary somewhat depending on the organization making the designation, the state or individual school district providing services, and even the IQ test administered (e.g., the American Association of Mental Deficiency specifies the IQ range for mild mental retardation at 68 to 52 on the Stanford-Binet Intelligence Test but 69 to 55 on the Revised Wechsler Intelligence Scale for Children).

training and time to plan special reading instruction, students with discrepancies of less than those cited by Spache are often included in remedial reading programs.

The problem of reading disabilities does not end when students complete high school. It is estimated that 1 to 2% of college students have reading problems for which special remediation is warranted. In the U.S. adult population, the most reasonable estimates of functional illiteracy have ranged from 18 million (Peck & Kling, 1977) to 31 million (Cook, 1977). Among young adults, ages 21–25, in a 1987 National Assessment of Educational Progress (NAEP), 3.2% scored at the lowest (or rudimentary level) (Kirsch & Jungeblut, 1987).

In recent years, there had been a large increase in the number of students designated as learning disabled. However, many states are now taking steps to ensure that students are not being classified as learning disabled erroneously and, therefore, the rate of increase is slowing.

MILESTONES IN THE HISTORY OF REMEDIAL AND CLINICAL READING INSTRUCTION[3]

Teachers working with reading instruction need a sound perspective about why we are doing what we are doing today in the field of reading. Present practice is based on years of investigation and practical application by our professional predecessors. Reading instruction, like much of education, has been subject to cyclical movements. The prospective teachers should be familiar with previous points of view so that when ideas or procedures reappear they can be recognized as ones that have been suggested before. Many old ideas still have validity. Some do not. Certain concepts that seem nonsensical in current thinking were once accepted as genuinely useful. Old ideas resurface and often prove to be as unsuccessful the second or third time around as they were the first time. In short, being familiar with the history of the field can help teachers examine questionable notions that arise in the present.

Then, too, theories of reading tend to swing from one extreme to another. For example, after criticisms of the exclusive emphasis on oral reading that was prevalent in the last century and the early part of this one, many teachers allowed students to engage *only* in silent reading in their classrooms, instead of using the method appropriate to specific objectives. Either-or positions deny students adequate instruction. Understanding the past helps us avoid such extremes.

We have moved forward in our understanding of how to help disabled readers, but at times, it appears as if for *every* three steps forward, we move one step backward. We must be careful not to repeat the mistakes of the past but to capitalize on what was good and what we have learned. Table 1–3 provides an overview of some important milestones that have affected or still do influence our field.

MODELS OF THE READING PROCESS

How do reading teachers choose what to do? Even though they may not be consciously aware of it, their choices are based on beliefs and assumptions they hold about how people learn to read.

---

[3]Before his death, Dr. Edgar Dale critiqued a good portion of this section summarizing the history of the reading field—a large part of which he lived through and contributed to. The author is grateful for his assistance.

TABLE 1–3
Some trends and issues in remedial and clinical reading instruction

Time Period	Instructional Approaches	Suggested Causes of Reading Disability	Prevalent Assessment Techniques and Tools	Milestones
Prior to the 1800s	• The alphabetic method of reading instruction is used almost exclusively until the 1700s; students spell out words letter by letter and reading is mainly oral. • The whole-word method is introduced in the 1700s.			
1800s	• Phonics methods become popular.	• Kussmaul suggests "word blindness" as a cause of reading disability.		• Research in reading has its beginnings in Europe with Valentius' work on perceptual processes.
1900–1909		• Perinatal difficulties, such as injuries during birth, are postulated by Bronner as causal factors.		
1910–1919	• The "non-oral" method, consisting of an exaggerated emphasis on silent reading, is introduced. • Russell and Schmitt suggest a method for teaching nonreaders consisting of elaborate phonics stories and the acting out of action words.	• "Congenital word-blindness" is popularized as *the* cause of reading disability.	• The first edition of the Gray Standardized Oral Reading Paragraphs is published; it provides teachers with the opportunity to observe and analyze students' reading errors. • The first standardized reading achievement tests are used.	• The first journal article on reading disabilities is published (Uhl, W. L. [1916]. "The use of the results of reading tests as bases for planning remedial work." *Elementary School Journal, 17,* 266–275).

1920–1929	• The kinesthetic method is introduced. • A swing away from phonics and an emphasis on the whole-word approach reemerges. • An emphasis on silent reading is prevalent.	• Lack of cerebral dominance is believed by some to be the major etiological factor in reading disability. • Inappropriate eye movements are postulated as a cause.	• The first Informal Reading Inventory is developed. • Diagnosis usually involves compiling a case history.	• The first reading clinic is begun at UCLA. • The first remedial reading textbook is published in the United States (Gray, C. T. [1922]. *Deficiencies in reading ability: Their diagnosis and remedies.* Boston: D. C. Heath.)
1930–1939	• The language experience approach (LEA) is developed.	• Emotional disturbance is suggested as a cause. • The concept of *multiple causation* is introduced.	• Machines begin to be used in diagnosis (e.g., eye-movement cameras).	• Monroe writes *Children Who Cannot Read*, a classic book advocating a phonic-kinesthetic approach to remediation.
1940–1949	• Both oral and silent reading are advocated. • Interest in LEA subsides.	• Much emphasis is given to emotional disturbance as a cause. • Interest in eye defects (myopia, astigmatism, and so on) as causes of reading disabilities is seen. • The concept of multiple causation gains popularity after Robinson publishes *Why Pupils Fail in Reading*, a classic interdisciplinary study that examines etiology of reading disability.	• Use of Informal Reading Inventories is popularized by Betts. • The notion of independent, instructional, and frustration levels of reading is introduced.	• The work of Strauss and Lehtinen forms the roots of the LD movement.

TABLE 1–3 *(continued)*

Time Period	Instructional Approaches	Suggested Causes of Reading Disability	Prevalent Assessment Techniques and Tools	Milestones
1950–1959	• Interest in LEA revives. • There is a trend away from the whole-word method and back toward phonics again.	• Emotional disturbance as a cause continues to receive attention in the beginning part of the decade; reading problems begin to be attributed to neurological impairments and brain processing deficiencies in the latter part. • The concept of multiple causation is considered to be most viable by many.		• Many universities begin programs to train reading specialists.
1960–1969	• Body management activities (e.g., walking balance beams) are suggested as remedial activities. • The linguistic approach gains some popularity. • The training of students' visual perception skills is advocated. • Interest in teaching to the "strongest modality" emerges.	• Brain damage is thought by many to be a major causal factor. • Belief in multiple causation continues.	• The Illinois Test of Psycholinguistic Abilities (ITPA) is introduced and influences the focus of instructional interventions in many reading and LD programs for the next decade. • Prediction of reading failure before it occurs (called "early identification") is advocated.	• Title I programs begin. • Goodman's model of the reading process is introduced. • Certification of reading teachers begins in many states. • The term *learning disability* is suggested to replace many diverse labels for the same general condition. • Research begins on differences in mental processes in the left and right brain hemispheres.

1970–1979	• There is strong interest in reading instruction based on psycholinguistic research, with an accompanying emphasis on LEA. • Another major interest is diagnostic/prescriptive teaching. • There is a movement away from training visual, auditory, and motor processes.	• Inappropriate diet is purported to be a causal factor in lay press articles. • An interest in the role of defective memory processes as etiology in reading disabilities is seen. • There is a deemphasis on brain damage as a cause. • The concept of multiple causation continues to be supported by most authorities.	• Criterion-referenced tests are widely used. • The Reading Miscue Inventory (RMI), devised to promote qualitative as well as quantitative judgments about reading errors, receives much attention and use. • The cloze procedure is considered an important diagnostic technique.	• The National Right-to-Read Effort is begun. • The Education for All Handicapped Children Act is passed; this increases the number of LD classes in public schools. • An interactive model of the reading process is proposed by Rumelhart.
1980–1989	• There is a heavy emphasis on techniques for improving comprehension. • Computer-based instruction is being used and its value debated. • There is interest in how reading and writing are linked.	• The concept of multiple causation continues to be the causal theory most widely accepted.	• Investigations into improved ways to assess comprehension are undertaken. • The RMI and cloze technique continue to be used.	• There is a growing closeness of the reading disability and learning disabilities fields.
1990–present	• There is an interest in whole-language and literature-based instruction. • Interest in word recognition processes revives. • The Reading Recovery Program shows success with at-risk first graders.	• Research demonstrates that a strong characteristic distinguishing good and poor readers is the latters' lack of phonemic awareness.	• Portfolio assessment is popular.	• Marilyn Adams publishes *Beginning to Read: Thinking and Learning about Print*, providing a research base supporting phonics instruction.

Sources: Table 1–3 draws upon numerous sources. Some of the most useful are listed here: Cook (1977); Critchley (1970); M. M. Evans (1982); Hall (1970); Hildreth (1965); A. J. Harris (1968, 1976, 1981); Matthews (1966); Ribovich (1978); H. A. Robinson (1966); Schreiner & Tanner (1976); N. B. Smith (1965); L. J. Thompson (1966).

DeFord (1985) developed an instrument to determine teachers' beliefs about practices in reading. This instrument is shown in Figure 1–1. *Note:* At this time, pause and answer the questions on this instrument based on your own current views about what teachers and students should do during reading instruction. Plan to return to the questionnaire after completing this textbook to see if any of your answers change.

Based on their beliefs, teachers make judgments about whether to use, modify, or reject ideas from other sources, such as teacher's manuals, traditional practice, or how-to books of reading activities. Good reading teachers are critical thinkers who make decisions based on research, the opinions of authorities, and their own knowledge of the world of reading. Either-or thinking, that is, complete reliance on either authority or personal knowledge alone, does not make a good teacher.

Where do teachers of reading obtain knowledge of the world of reading? From working with students in real classroom settings and engaging in a lot of good, hard thinking about what is helpful and what is not. Sometimes critical thinking results in instructional procedures that contradict common practice.

Most researchers and reading authorities have also done a lot of good, hard thinking about the reading process and have had experience working with students. Good theories and good practice go hand in hand. Being aware of their conclusions helps us develop our own ideas, saves us time, and helps us accept new ideas. It prevents us from having to reinvent the wheel.

During the early part of this century, many reading professionals attempted to find out just what our brains must do to recognize words, combine them into sentences and paragraphs, and understand the meanings of the written language. They also attempted to identify which skills must be learned to read proficiently and which objectives are important to meet all of our lifelong demands for reading. Those early twentieth-century educators proposed theories and conducted research to determine if the theories were correct. After a time, however, the interests of reading professionals began to move in another direction; researchers tried to determine which methods of instruction were best. Their research has helped us identify and weed out many spurious techniques, but numerous important questions about how to promote reading achievement have remained unanswered. Recently, interest has returned to studying the act of reading, and many believe we will not be able to solve the persistent problem of poor reading until we understand the overall process better.

As researchers have studied reading they have developed *models* to explain their conclusions about the reading process. In this context, **model** means "a structure or design intended to show how something is formed, or how it functions, by analyzing the relationships of its various parts to each other and to the whole. A reading model is a theoretical representation of reading processes" (T. L. Harris & Hodges, 1981, p. 200). The phrases *reading model* or *model of reading* can mean either a verbal explanation presented to explain a conception of reading or a diagram prepared to accompany and clarify the verbal explanation.

We do not entirely understand the complex act of reading, although in recent years some progress has been made. Since 1953, many different models or explanations of reading have been proposed. These models are of two kinds.

1. Some models describe reading **skills** (that is, what a person must learn to be a proficient reader).
2. Other models describe the reading **process** (that is, the functions that must occur in our brains, *eyes, ears,* and so on for us to read printed symbols).

FIGURE 1–1

The DeFord Theoretical Orientation to Reading Profile (TORP)

The DeFord
Theoretical Orientation to Reading
Profile (TORP)

Name _____

Directions: Read the following statements, and circle one of the responses that will indicate the relationship of the statement to your feelings about reading and reading instruction. *SA* 2 3 4 *SD*

Select *one* best answer that reflects the strength of the agreement or disagreement.

1. A child needs to be able to verbalize the rules of phonics in order to assure proficiency in processing new words.	*1* SA	*2*	*3*	*4*	*5* SD
2. An increase in reading errors is usually related to a decrease in comprehension.	*1* SA	*2*	*3*	*4*	*5* SD
3. Dividing words into syllables according to rules is a helpful instructional practice for reading new words.	*1* SA	*2*	*3*	*4*	*5* SD
4. Fluency and expression are necessary components of reading that indicate good comprehension.	*1* SA	*2*	*3*	*4*	*5* SD
5. Materials for early reading should be written in natural language without concern for short, simple words and sentences.	*1* SA	*2*	*3*	*4*	*5* SD
6. When children do not know a word, they should be instructed to sound out its parts.	*1* SA	*2*	*3*	*4*	*5* SD
7. It is a good practice to allow children to edit what is written into their own dialect when learning to read.	*1* SA	*2*	*3*	*4*	*5* SD
8. The use of a glossary or dictionary is necessary in determining the meaning and pronunciation of new words.	*1* SA	*2*	*3*	*4*	*5* SD
9. Reversals (e.g., saying "saw" for "was") are significant problems in the teaching of reading.	*1* SA	*2*	*3*	*4*	*5* SD
10. It is a good practice to correct a child as soon as an oral reading mistake is made.	*1* SA	*2*	*3*	*4*	*5* SD
11. It is important for a word to be repeated a number of times after it has been introduced to ensure that it will become a part of sight vocabulary.	*1* SA	*2*	*3*	*4*	*5* SD
12. Paying close attention to punctuation marks is necessary to understanding story content.	*1* SA	*2*	*3*	*4*	*5* SD
13. It is a sign of an ineffective reader when words and phrases are repeated.	*1* SA	*2*	*3*	*4*	*5* SD

FIGURE 1–1 *(continued)*

		1	2	3	4	5
14.	Being able to label words according to grammatical function (nouns, etc.) is useful in proficient reading.	SA				SD
15.	When coming to a word that's unknown, the reader should be encouraged to guess meaning and go on.	SA				SD
16.	Young readers need to be introduced to the root form of words (run, long) before they are asked to read inflected forms (running, longest).	SA				SD
17.	It is not necessary for a child to know the letters of the alphabet in order to learn to read.	SA				SD
18.	Flashcard drills with sightwords is an unnecessary form of practice in reading instruction.	SA				SD
19.	Ability to use accent patterns in multisyllable words (pho' to graph, pho to' graphy, and pho to gra' phic) should be developed as part of reading instruction.	SA				SD
20.	Controlling text through consistent spelling patterns (The fat cat ran back. The fat cat sat on a hat) is a means by which children can best learn to read.	SA				SD
21.	Formal instruction in reading is necessary to ensure the adequate development of all the skills used in reading.	SA				SD
22.	Phonic analysis is the most important form of analysis used when meeting new words.	SA				SD
23.	Children's initial encounters with print should focus on meaning, not upon exact graphic representation.	SA				SD
24.	Word shapes (word configuration) should be taught in reading to aid in word recognition.	SA				SD
25.	It is important to teach skills in relation to other skills.	SA				SD
26.	If a child says "house" for the written word "home," the response should be left uncorrected.	SA				SD
27.	It is not necessary to introduce new words before they appear in the reading text.	SA				SD
28.	Some problems in reading are caused by readers dropping the inflectional endings from words (e.g., jumps, jump*ed*).	SA				SD

Skills models are of less interest to educators today because it is believed that once we understand the process of reading, the necessary skills, strategies, or conditions to attain proficiency will be evident. Accordingly, this chapter describes *process models,* emphasizing those currently considered most important.

The Goodman and Smith Models

Although Kenneth Goodman called his explanation of the reading process a *psycholinguistic model* and Frank Smith called his an *information-processing model,* both their models were based on the same basic principles. Goodman presented his model in 1967 and Smith proposed his in 1971. Both attempted to explain how we use various brain and language processes when we read.

Their two models were highly influential in the field of reading for well over a decade. Many instructional procedures and programs during the 1970s and 1980s were rooted in principles suggested by these models—and in fact, some still are. Interest in these models has begun to subside, however, because as sometimes happens with theories, later research findings have been contrary to certain ideas the theories proposed.

For example, an important tenet of these theories suggested that during *word recognition,* attending to all of the visual information on a page (that is, to the ink marks that convey letters and words) was not only unnecessary, but impossible. Rather, it was argued that good readers selected only the most helpful visual information through a sampling process and predicted (guessed) the other information based on knowledge of language and the world. Subsequent research on eye movements has refuted this supposition. Instead, it has demonstrated that good readers not only attend to almost every word on a page (although relatively instantaneously and unconsciously), they attend to almost *every* letter! (For example, see Rayner & Pollatsek, 1989; Zola, 1984.)

Furthermore, according to the Goodman and Smith theories, the better the reader, the more that prediction is used and the less that visual information is employed. This was believed to increase fluency in reading. However, it has been shown in eye-movement research that when good readers can easily predict a word, they do not, but rather wait until their eyes are fixated directly on the word before pronouncing it (e.g., Balota, Pollatsek, & Rayner, 1985). In addition, it has been found that if even a single letter is removed from a word, reading fluency is slowed significantly because information contained in *every* letter is important to proficient reading (Bertera & Rayner, 1979). Certain other implications of these models also have not held up under scrutiny.

On the other hand, some assumptions of the Goodman and Smith theories do appear to be supported by research evidence, for example, the use of prediction (or context) based on knowledge about the world to assist in *comprehending* text. Also, their notions about *redundancy,* that is, that a written message can be picked up through a variety of means—through spelling pattern cues, sentence pattern cues, and meaning cues—are part of the currently accepted models.

The LaBerge and Samuels Model

In 1974, David LaBerge and Jay Samuels proposed a reading model (that Samuels revised in 1977). Their model emphasizes the need for automatic information processing, or as they put it, the need for "automaticity." They describe the steps a reader must go through to transform written language into meaning. According to their theory, first, the brain uses *visual memory* to detect the features of the ink marks on the page that allow the reader to identify letters—that is, the brain's memory recognizes letters by remembering that certain lines put together in certain ways indicate a specific letter. The visual memory system then identifies (in sequence) letters, then spelling patterns, and then the word.

Identification of a word activates the *phonological memory system.* For example, according to this model when visual memory identifies a word such as *pretty,* the phonological memory system becomes conscious of its sound equivalent; however, if visual memory does not identify a word, the phonological system scans the word by letters or syllables then blends these sounds to identify the word.

Finally, identification of a word activates the *semantic memory system,* which attaches a meaning to a word. Semantic memory can also engage attention in comprehension of longer passages by combining word meanings, organizing words into grammatical units, and determining relationships among meanings. LaBerge and Samuels theorized that these steps occur *sequentially,* with the information being processed in one stage before it moves on to the next.

A proficient reader or an individual who is reading easy material may skip one or more of the stages. Nonetheless, according to this theory, all readers must go through several stages of information processing. On the other hand, if a reader must spend too much time on every step, the memory and attention limits of the brain will be exceeded. Therefore, LaBerge and Samuels suggest it is important for responses to the many subcomponents of reading to become automatic. If correct responses to all or most words in a passage are spontaneous then the reader can focus his or her attention on understanding the message conveyed by the words. Conversely, if a reader places too much attention on decoding words, comprehension suffers. Or, if he or she must consciously attend to the meanings of many individual words then understanding and recall of the overall information will be adversely affected.

Practical Implications.   Advocates of this model believe that teachers should emphasize letter-sound correspondences and other decoding subskills early in a reading program and that teachers must teach reading subskills directly, especially to poor readers. They believe that students need practice so their responses become automatic and quick.

However, practice should not be confined to the letter and word identification level only. An important way to improve reading ability is to do a great deal of reading in connected text. Students also need frequent exposure to meaningful arrangements of material so their responses to phrases become automatic.

Developing **automaticity** depends on practicing correct responses. The teacher must provide feedback so the student does not practice incorrect responses.

The Rumelhart Model

David Rumelhart proposed an *interactive* model of the reading process in 1976. He contended that most previous process models explained reading as occurring in separate, sequential steps with no interaction (called **sequential processing**). Such models are designated as **serial models.** He cites research evidence supporting his view that serial models may be based on incorrect assumptions. In contrast to former theories, Rumelhart's model shows how various processes work simultaneously when a person reads. This is called **parallel processing.** Since the processes also work with each other, this model is designated as **interactive.**

Serial models are divided into two types: bottom-up and top-down. **Bottom-up models** suggest that the reader goes from smaller elements of language (such as letters

An important way to improve reading ability is to do a great deal of reading.

and words) to larger portions and meaning. **Top-down models** suggest that the reader first predicts meaning and then identifies words. In contrast, Rumelhart's interactive model proposes that reading occurs as the reader simultaneously initiates word identification and predicts meaning; the lower-level processes (word identification) and higher-level processes (meaning) help each other at the same time. The reader may rely more or less on the lower- or higher-level process depending on the difficulty of the material—using more low-level cues if the material is difficult and more high-level cues if the material is easy.

Rumelhart illustrated the interactive nature of the reading process in the diagram seen in Figure 1–2. In this model, ink marks on the page (*graphemic input*) are registered in the brain's visual information store and are acted on to determine the features that will identify them by the *feature extraction device*. The *pattern synthesizer* (the model's most important feature) then uses **syntactical knowledge** (knowledge of sentence patterns), **semantic knowledge** (knowledge of meaning), **orthographic knowledge** (knowledge of letters, spelling patterns, and sounds), and **lexical knowledge** (knowledge of words) to extract the message (that is, the most probable interpretation) from these distinguishing features. The reader can use these four types of knowledge sources to hypothesize, seek information, confirm or reject predictions, add new hypotheses, and reach decisions because of information stored in what Rumelhart calls the *message center* of the brain. Hypotheses and predictions can be confirmed or rejected by any one of the knowledge sources. Diehl (1978) gives an example of this process in action:

> A reader picks up a book and begins to read. Immediately, the syntactic knowledge source hypothesizes that the first meaning unit will be a noun phrase (since most sentences begin with a noun phrase). The lexical level knowledge source might hypothesize that the first word is "the". The feature level, detecting certain lines, might hypothesize that the first letter is *t*, and this hypothesis would be carried on to the letter-level knowledge source. All the various hypotheses generated—whether or not they are in agreement—are entered in the message center. Each of the knowledge sources continually scans this message center for hypotheses relevant to its own sphere of knowledge. (For example, once the letter-level source has hypothesized that the first letters are *t, h, e*, the lexical level knowledge source reviews the hypothesis to confirm that such letters do form a known word.) (p. 17)

FIGURE 1–2

A stage representation of an interactive model of reading

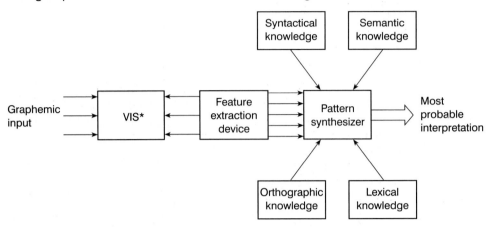

Source: From "Toward an Interactive Model of Reading" by D. Rumelhart in *Theoretical Models and Processes of Reading* (3rd ed., p. 736) by H. Singer and R. B. Ruddell (Eds.), 1985, Newark, DE: International Reading Association. Copyright 1985 by the International Reading Association. Reprinted by permission of the International Reading Association.

*VIS = Visual information store

Many reading professionals agree with Rumelhart that bottom-up and top-down models do not explain many things we know to be true about the reading process, and certain experimental findings seem to confirm that the process is interactive.

Practical Implications.   Instructional programs should emphasize both word identification and meaning since lower-level processes aid higher-level processes and vice versa. The interactive model not only shows that the reader uses many kinds of information, but also suggests that the reader must be flexible in use of strategies. Teaching just one strategy—for example, to use in word identification—is inappropriate. Students should not only have the opportunity to learn a variety of strategies, but also have many chances to practice them. If one strategy doesn't work, students should be able to ask themselves, "What could I try next?" "What other information could help me?" Help students see that print is predictable. For example, use cloze exercises (see Chapter 5), or, in the early stages of reading, highly predictable books.

Students have syntactical knowledge (knowledge of sentence structure). Emphasize the need to use it, instead of relying exclusively on orthographic and lexical knowledge. For semantic knowledge to be accessible for use, meanings must be stored in the brain's message center. Help students add to their store of meanings by providing direct experiences, discussions before reading, and vicarious experiences, such as opportunities to view pictures and other audiovisuals. Use teaching strategies that lead students to apply their background knowledge (semantic knowledge) when they are reading.

Written syntactic structures do vary from oral language patterns, although there are more similarities than differences. Increase your students' knowledge of written language patterns by reading aloud to them. Since some decisions are made based on prior knowledge of print structures, students themselves also need to read as much as possible. The more students read, the more efficient their predictions will be.

The Stanovich Model

Keith Stanovich (1980) proposes an *interactive-compensatory* model. He believes reading processing involves interactions of several knowledge sources, as does Rumelhart. However, the word *compensatory* was added to Stanovich's description to indicate that, when there is a deficit in any of the processes theorized in interactive models, then the reader relies more heavily on other processes—in other words, the reader *compensates* by using other knowledge sources. For example, poor readers deficient in automatic word recognition may turn to context cues to identify words, that is, they may guess unknown words based on known words in a sentence or surrounding text.

One important feature of this proposal is that higher-level processes can help lower-level processes, as in the example just given: use of context (a meaning-level or higher-level process) compensates for limited word knowledge (a recognition-level or lower-level process). Stanovich believes that this model explains individual differences in the development of reading fluency.

Stanovich cited a large body of research confirming the principles of his theory. For example, many studies were offered showing that poor readers make greater use of context than good readers and therefore have slower word recognition times. On the other hand, good readers are more proficient in context-free word recognition (that is, they recognize a word automatically without having to resort to guessing the words from context), and further, have more effective phonological decoding skills (use of letter sounds to identify words). Both these factors produce rapid word recognition and fluent reading. In turn, these may account for the superior comprehension seen in good readers since less attention must be directed at word identification.

Practical Implications.   Research cited in support of the Stanovich model suggests that readers may necessarily rely, to some extent, on context clues during early stages of learning to read. However, this is a compensatory word identification strategy. If poor readers are to become good readers they must become skilled at context-free word recognition—in other words, they must learn the identities of words well so that these may be recognized automatically and rapidly without resorting to the assistance of context. During early reading stages in which many words are still unknown, having knowledge of phonic and structural analysis strategies, and being able to use these skillfully and quickly, is an aid to fluent reading. Since comprehension is the purpose of reading, teachers should help students gain mastery of these strategies so that undue attention to word recognition tasks does not deflect from gaining meaning.

The interactive-compensatory model also suggests that readers need a wide variety of knowledge sources to call upon, as is implied by Rumelhart's interactive model.

The Just and Carpenter Model

Just and Carpenter (1987) have given their model the name READER. A diagram of this currently popular model is seen in Figure 1–3.

In this reading process theory, a set of *actions* (seen in the first column of the diagram) acts on information in the brain's *working memory* (seen in the middle box). This occurs when each "action" recognizes from print an element also present in working memory. This system of actions takes information *from* working memory to assist in word recognition and understanding, but also puts new information *into* working memory as the actions carry out the recognition process. During this process, the information in working memory can be assessed *simultaneously* by all the action features. The

FIGURE 1–3

The Just and Carpenter (1987) model of reading

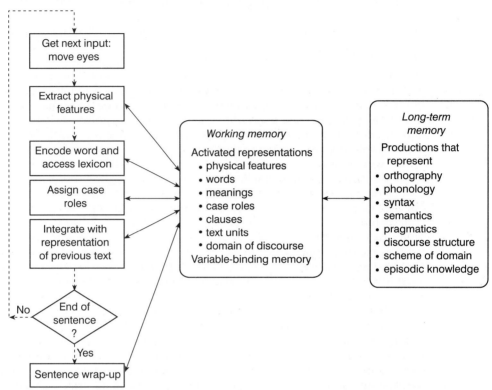

Source: From *The Psychology of Reading and Language Comprehension* by M. Just and P. Carpenter, 1987, Needham Heights, MA: Allyn & Bacon. Copyright 1987 by Allyn and Bacon. Reprinted by permission.

actions that have their conditions satisfied can simultaneously complete their functions. The actions also can change the information in the brain's *long-term memory.*

The actions depicted by this model are described as "cascadelike" because later actions begin while earlier actions are still continuing. Therefore, there is a good deal of parallel processing. However, there are some restrictions to parallel functioning in the Just and Carpenter model. For example, integration of words into text cannot occur until word meaning is identified.

Practical Implications.   Like all current models, both lower-level processes and higher-level processes show some mutual dependence in this model. The reader must be able to recognize words, or know strategies that allow identification if the word is not immediately recognized, in order to access text meaning.

Because being able to decode and assign meanings to words is important to comprehension, proponents of this model reject the notion that reading instruction should be an either-or proposition. Both a focus on skills to the detriment of meaning and a focus on meaning to the detriment of skills are repudiated. Specific instructional attention to word recognition is necessary because the model suggests that the initial steps in identifying words cannot occur based simply on expectations from stored oral language knowledge.

Vygotsky's Learning Theory

Although not specifically a reading model, Vygotsky's (1978) theory of learning has assumed increasing importance among literacy educators. Of particular interest has been Vygotsky's notion of a **zone of proximal development**. In his model, this "zone" is a developmental area that lies between (a) what a child can achieve unassisted and (b) what the child can achieve with assistance.

Vygotsky proposed that by providing a particular kind of guidance called **scaffolding**, teachers (or parents) can help children cultivate more advanced learning behaviors. In scaffolded instruction, the adult assesses the child's present level of performance on a given task and then furnishes support to lead the child to accomplishments just slightly above what the child can do unaided; the child is guided gradually upward to a higher level of *independent* achievement. The child's independent achievement is enhanced when such collaborative interactions occur frequently, with the adult increasingly releasing more and more responsibility to the child. Throughout these interactions, the adult must make decisions about how much help is needed and at what point the child can be drawn forward to a step just beyond his or her present status.

In scaffolded assistance, specific solutions to tasks are not usually supplied by the adult, but rather, the adult gives prompts and backing that lead children to discover the solution themselves. As a simple example, a teacher would not tell a student an unknown answer, but would ask questions and give cues until the child is able to produce the answer himself or herself. When this combination of support and independence is present, the child is said to be operating in his or her zone of proximal development—the developmental area where Vygosky contended that the most learning can occur.

In scaffolded instruction, children are taught interim steps necessary to autonomously develop conclusions. To do so, the teacher may (a) model appropriate performances for the student; (b) invite student participation during teacher modeling; (c) contribute clues about specific elements; (d) give clues about specific strategies; and (e) urge students to think through general plans of action for approaching a problem (Beed, Hawkins, & Roller, 1991). One or several of these prompting tactics may be employed, depending on the student's level of development in relation to a specific task.

This view of learning suggests that levels of development are not predetermined by the age or intellectual ability of a student, but careful child-adult interactions can advance the levels at which a student operates. Vygotsky's theory is in opposition to those positions that suggest that one should wait until children are developmentally "ready" so that they will progress on their own.

Throughout this text you will learn of instructional procedures based on Vygotsky's views.

A Summary of Reading Models

Process models attempt to explain just how our brains can accomplish complex reading tasks. There are other models that have not been described in this chapter, but those discussed will give the prospective reading teacher an orientation to currently accepted concepts of how we read.

Although there are some similarities in the theories outlined in this section and in their practical implications, model makers also show some variation in their views. Table 1–4 summarizes contrasting features of the models presented here.

TABLE 1–4
Contrasting features of process models

Nature of the Models	LaBerge & Samuels	Rumelhart	Stanovich	Just & Carpenter
Information is processed sequentially.	X			
Information is processed in parallel steps.		X	X	sometimes
The process is always interactive.		X	X	X
The process is interactive when the reader encounters difficulty.	X			
The reader goes from print to meaning.	X			X
The reader simultaneously uses meaning and identification of print.		X	X	
Unskilled and skilled readers process materials differently.	X	X	X	X
Background information already stored in the reader's brain is important for obtaining meaning from print.	X	X	X	X
The reader uses as little printed information as possible to obtain meaning.		sometimes		
Accurate identification of small printed units (letters, words) is necessary to obtain meaning.	X	sometimes	X	X

Implications of the Models	LaBerge & Samuels	Rumelhart	Stanovich	Just & Carpenter
Direct and intensive practice on subskills of reading is important.	X		X	X
Whole language activities are important; readers internalize subskills through exposure to regular connected material.		X	X	X
Some attention to subskills of reading is helpful.		X		
All word identification errors should be corrected.	X		X	X
Only word identification errors that affect meaning should be corrected.		X		
Beginning reading instruction should emphasize word identification.	X			
Beginning reading instruction should treat both word identification and meaning.		X	X	X
Proficiency in word identification helps the reader obtain meaning.	X	X	X	X
Meaning helps the reader identify words.		X		

CONCLUSION

This chapter presented background information about important reading terms and concepts for prospective teachers of reading.

But this is just the beginning: reading teachers must have knowledge and skill related to causes of reading problems, assessment, instructional techniques, organization and management of reading programs, and materials. To use just one job role as an example of this, let's suppose you chose to work as a reading clinician. Bader and Wiesendanger (1986) reported the following methods and materials plus their frequency of use in U.S. reading clinics: the language experience approach, 87%; linguistic patterning, 52%; the Fernald approach, 37%; DRTA, 31%; basal readers, 6%. (These and other approaches are discussed in later chapters.) The researchers found that clinics provided sight word instruction, taught word identification strategies that stressed analytic phonics, and emphasized silent reading with a focus on comprehension. The clinics also provided instruction on study skills and content area reading for students aged 10 through 17.

Teachers preparing to be reading clinicians would, of course, need to be familiar with all of these techniques and should know the strengths and weaknesses of each. Bates (1984) reported that diagnostic services provided by clinics included, among others, assessment of silent and oral reading proficiency, word recognition, intellectual development, study skills, and general achievement. He also found that 66% of clinics offered consultant services to schools.

There is clearly wide diversity in organizational patterns and materials used in clinics; as a result, it can be seen that the reading clinician needs a broad perspective of knowledge and some specialized competencies. The same is true for reading teachers, consultants, resource teachers, coordinators, and supervisors, as well as for LD and DD teachers, and for school psychologists. Throughout the remainder of this book, many important topics related to reading instruction are discussed, accompanied by research data to support suggestions and practical ideas for applying research.

📖 REFLECTIONS

This section, titled Reflections, is found at the end of each chapter of the book. It is designed for instructors to involve students in decision-making activities related to the chapter content.

Understanding models that provide explanations of how we process text in order to read is important—it is also difficult for those to whom the concepts behind the models are new. Cognitive research indicates that *collaborative learning* may be helpful when concepts are novel and complex. This is a technique you may want to use with students in your own classroom. For now, try this yourself. Divide into teams of 2 (sometimes called "dyads"). Each team should discuss one of the reading process models presented in this chapter. Do the following.

1. Review the text to determine what the model suggests about the steps a reader must go through to transform written language into meaning. Together with your partner, make a list of these steps.
2. Examine *each* step. Do you understand it? Engage in peer tutoring—discussing and questioning—to explain each step until both partners understand each of the steps.
3. Finally, what are the overall assumptions of the model—in other words, what are the main ideas or issues the model maker(s) believe underlie or are associated with reading processes? Develop a short list of these with your partner.

2

Causes and Correlates of Individual Differences in Reading Ability: Part I

Research has shown that in successful schools in low-income neighborhoods, there is a wide variety of library books available to students.

A common question asked of reading and learning disability teachers is "What *causes* a student to have reading problems?" Parents frequently worry that delayed reading development is due to a child's lack of intellectual ability. Some parents believe a simple intervention such as getting glasses for a child will solve a reading problem. Teachers have sometimes told parents that a child is simply not ready to read and that as the child develops socially and emotionally he or she will catch up and learn to read as well as other students. Frustrated parents may place the blame for their children's reading problems on poor teaching or other educational inadequacies. Popular magazines and newspapers frequently feature articles that attribute reading or other learning disabilities to diet, emotional disorders, allergies, brain damage, hyperactivity, lack of sensory integration, and many other factors.

What actually does cause reading disabilities? How much truth is there in commonly held beliefs about the causes of reading problems?

To answer these questions, one must first understand the difference between *correlation* and *causation*. Although two events may be correlated, one does not necessarily *cause* the other. For example, suppose a particularly silly researcher decided to undertake a study to determine the relationship between reading achievement and facial hairiness in school-age boys. The researcher probably would find a higher degree of reading achievement in those males with more facial hair because, of course, in general, students who have more facial hair are also older and normally have had more reading experience. Although a correlation between hairiness and reading achievement could be shown, it certainly would not mean that hairiness results in increased reading ability. Nor does it mean that if lack of hairiness could be "corrected" (for example, by giving hormonal treatments to all fourth-grade boys in remedial reading classes), reading achievement could be increased. Misunderstanding the difference between causation and correlation has led to incorrect interpretations of research on the causes of reading disabilities and to many fruitless teaching procedures.

Reciprocal causation must be considered in relation to reading disabilities. For example, failure to read large amounts of text hinders development of automatic recognition of large numbers of words. Without automatic recognition of large numbers of words, the student cannot read large amounts of text.

Another important concept in understanding etiology (that is, causes) of reading differences is the notion of **reciprocal causation** (Stanovich, 1993–94). This term refers to instances when lack of attainment with one factor important to achievement causes failure with a second factor also important to learning, and failure with the second factor, in turn, has a negative effect on the first factor. An example of this would be a student who fails to read large amounts of text that, as a result, precludes the student's development of automatic recognition of a large number of words; without automatic recognition of large numbers of words, the student cannot read large amounts of text. As we will see later, this and other reciprocal causation cycles may have a very important bearing on reading disability.

Third, we now know that what may be reading difficulties common in students of one age (or grade level) may differ from the difficulties associated with a different age. Understanding these developmental differences also is important when trying to sort out the various causes of serious reading problems.

A final general consideration in understanding causes and correlates of reading disabilities is the teacher's knowledge of research methodology. Teachers working with students who have learning disorders should take courses that provide information about research procedures and as well have opportunities to critique existing research. Much research about the causes of reading disabilities is so poorly constructed that the results are simply not credible. Learning to identify faulty research procedures will help teachers avoid accepting fallacious research results. This text points out instances when faulty research has been the only support for a supposition, or when no evidence at all supports a hypothesis. However, since no text can provide all information that a remedial teacher needs, teachers must learn to evaluate research critically themselves.

The remainder of this chapter and all of Chapter 3 present information about factors that are (and are not) causes or correlates of reading disabilities. Eight general areas are discussed:

1. Physiological factors
2. Hereditary factors
3. Emotional factors
4. Sociocultural factors
5. Educational factors
6. Cognitive factors
7. Language factors
8. Reading history factors

The first four topics are treated here, in Chapter 2; the remaining four are discussed in Chapter 3.

PHYSIOLOGICAL FACTORS

Sensory Impairments

A slight sensory impairment may have no effect on a student's reading achievement, but certain more severe impairments may contribute to a reading disability. This section explores sensory impairments (e.g., sight, hearing, speech) and what research shows about how they affect reading ability.

Vision.   For certain visual problems, research does show a relationship with reading difficulties, while for other defects the majority of the research shows there is none. Usually when a correlation has been shown, it has been related to **fusion difficulties,** that is, impairment in using the two eyes together (Dearborn & Anderson, 1938). One example is aniseikonia, in which the images of an object as formed by each eye appear unequal in size and shape. Fusion difficulties occur much more rarely than refractive errors such as nearsightedness, farsightedness, or astigmatism.

Some visual abnormalities interfere more directly with reading than others. For example, some may make it difficult for readers to identify written symbols, while others may simply lead readers to experience discomfort, such as fatigue and headaches, when they engage in any intensive visual activity. However, the discomfort may reduce the amount of time an individual can or will read. Since a large amount of reading practice is highly related to reading success, eye defects may then become an indirect cause of a reading problem.

The most prevalent visual problem among school-age individuals, *myopia* (near-sightedness) has no positive relationship to reading difficulties, according to most research (e.g., E. A. Taylor, 1937). This is also the case with astigmatism (blurred vision resulting from lack of a clear focus of light rays in one or more axes of the retina) (e.g., H. M. Robinson, 1946), as well with amblyopia (a condition in which the image from one eye is not transmitted to the brain) (A. J. Harris & Sipay, 1980). This is important information for teachers who counsel parents. It means that simply obtaining glasses for a child may not solve the child's reading problems. Correcting visual problems may make it possible for students to see printed information more easily, but once the visual difficulty is corrected, instruction is still necessary to help students learn new reading strategies. This is also true in relation to other visual difficulties that have been associated with reading disability.

Another area that has been explored in attempting to explain individual differences in reading ability has involved *eye movements.* A prevailing hypothesis at one time was that reading difficulties occurred because of inefficient control of eye movement; that is, that poor readers fixate longer on words and make more eye-movement regressions than do individuals who have more adequate reading skills. In actuality, this is true. However, much research over an extended period of years has laid to rest the assumption that this is a *cause* of reading disabilities. Rather, these eye-movement patterns are a *result* of poor word recognition skill (Rayner & Duffy, 1988).

Likewise, it has been suggested that poor readers have a smaller *perceptual span*—in other words, that they can recognize fewer letters and words in a single fixation of their eyes. Using computer technology, recent researchers have shown this to be a faulty assumption (e.g., Underwood & Zola, 1986). Their studies demonstrate that the perceptual spans of skilled and unskilled readers do not differ.

A further important concern for teachers, especially those counseling parents, is the need to know about the effects of visual training exercises on improving reading ability. Many ophthalmologists and optometrists hold opposing views on the value of such training. (**Ophthalmologists** are medical doctors who specialize in the diagnosis and treatment of eye diseases and abnormalities and have passed the examinations of the American Board of Ophthalmology; **optometrists** are nonmedical vision specialists trained to diagnose vision defects and prescribe glasses or contact lenses.) Some optometrists advocate visual training as a corrective measure in treating reading problems, while most ophthalmologists believe the training has no value.

Recently a joint statement was prepared by the American Academy of Pediatrics, the American Academy of Ophthalmology and Otolaryngology, and the American Association of Ophthalmology, stating their position on the relationship between learning and visual function. This statement is reproduced in Figure 2–1, which should be read in its entirety. The third point in the statement indicates that these medical special-

FIGURE 2–1

The eye and learning disabilities

The problem of learning disability has become a matter of increasing public concern, which has led to exploitation by some practitioners of the normal concern of parents for the welfare of their children. A child's inability to read with understanding as a result of defects in processing visual symbols, a condition which has been called dyslexia, is a major obstacle to school learning and has far-reaching social and economic implications. The significance and magnitude of the problem have generated a proliferation of diagnostic and remedial procedures, many of which imply a relationship between visual function and learning.

The eye and visual training in the treatment of dyslexia and associated learning disabilities have recently been reviewed with the following conclusions by the American Academy of Pediatrics, the American Academy of Ophthalmology and Otolaryngology, and the American Association of Ophthalmology.

1. Learning disability and dyslexia, as well as other forms of school underachievement, require a multidisciplinary approach from medicine, education, and psychology in diagnosis and treatment. Eye care should never be instituted in isolation when a patient has a reading problem. Children with learning disabilities have the same incidence of ocular abnormalities, e.g., refractive errors and muscle imbalance, as children who are normal achievers and reading at grade level. These abnormalities should be corrected.

2. Since clues in word recognition are transmitted through the eyes to the brain, it has become common practice to attribute reading difficulties to subtle ocular abnormalities presumed to cause faulty visual perception. Studies have shown that there is no peripheral eye defect which produces dyslexia and associated learning disabilities. Eye defects do not cause reversals of letters, words, or numbers.

3. No known scientific evidence supports claims for improving the academic abilities of learning disabled or dyslexic children with treatment based solely on visual training such as muscle exercises, ocular pursuit and glasses, or neurological organizational training such as laterality training, balance board or perceptual training. Furthermore, such training has frequently resulted in unwarranted expense and has delayed proper instruction for the child.

4. Excluding correctable ocular defects, glasses have no value in the specific treatment of dyslexia or other learning problems. In fact, unnecessarily prescribed glasses may create a false sense of security that may delay needed treatment.

5. The teaching of learning disabled and dyslexic children is a problem of educational science. No one approach is applicable to all children. A change in any variable may result in increased motivation of the child and reduced frustration. Parents should be made aware that mental level and psychological implications are contributing factors to a child's success or failure. Ophthalmologists and other medical specialists should offer their knowledge. This may consist of the identification of specific defects, or simply early recognition. The precursors of learning disabilities can often be detected by three years of age. Since remediation may be more effective during the early years, it is important for the physician to recognize the child with this problem and refer him to the appropriate service, if available, before he is of school age. Medical specialists may assist in bringing the child's potential to the best level, but the actual remedial educational procedures remain the responsibility of educators.

Source: This statement was prepared by an ad hoc committee of the American Academy of Pediatrics, the American Academy of Ophthalmology and Otolaryngology, and the American Association of Ophthalmology with the assistance of the President and the Past President of the Division for Children with Learning Disabilities. Reprinted by permission of the American Academy of Pediatrics.

ists do not support visual training procedures; educators agree with this position. A review of the research on the effects of visual training in remediating reading difficulties shows that the research methodology used in these studies has been inadequate. Consequently, these studies also provide no evidence for the value of visual training (Keogh, 1974).

Visual Perception. The role of visual perception problems in contributing to reading has been much discussed in past years. Allegedly, students with poor visual perception are plagued by confusions and distortions when they look at visual symbols. Some *supposed* symptoms are listed here.

1. A word appears as a meaningless mixture of letters. The word *music,* for example, might appear a *msuci.*
2. Letters and words are reversed. For example, *b* appears as *d,* or *was* as *saw.*
3. If the type of print or size of a word is changed, students may not be able to identify it.
4. A word may appear as its mirror image.
5. Students who, for example, pronounce *where* as *when* may be unable to see a word as a whole, so they guess at the parts they cannot perceive.
6. Students may respond to small details of a letter, such as the curve in a lowercase *r,* to the detriment of seeing the letter as a whole.
7. Students may attend to the white spaces between letters in a word instead of the letters themselves.
8. Students may see a sentence such as *Marie likes to ski* as *Mar i eli kest os ki.*
9. Students may perceive spots or flaws in the paper as parts of words and respond to these.

Some optometrists claim to be able to alleviate visual perception problems by visual training exercises. Others believe these alleged difficulties are of a neurological origin and, therefore, retraining of brain processing is necessary.

In looking at the list of symptoms ascribed to students who purportedly have visual perception problems, teachers might ask how one can know a student is responding to the printed page in this manner. What behavior would students exhibit if they were reading the white spaces between the words? What response would students make if they were reading only the curve in the lowercase *r?* When students read *where* as *when,* how can teachers know they do so as the result of not being able to perceive a word of that length? If a student reads *I don't know where you are* as *I don't know when you are,* is it not more likely that the student has failed to learn to read for meaning?

While it is true that some students with reading disabilities do reverse letters and words, research also indicates that many average readers make letter and word reversals during preschool and early primary grade years. Spache (1976) examined 35 studies related to reversals and found that 80% of these showed no difference in the occurrence of reversals in good readers and poor readers. D. A. Brown (1982) makes an important point:

> Although the perceptual centers in the brain invert the scene reported to it by the optic nerve . . . they cannot invert some small portion of that scene. If, for example, a person looks out the window onto a beautiful panorama of mountains, trees, and greenery, it is not possible for him to see one tree in an inverted position while all the rest of the landscape is right side up. . . . Although the optic nerve reports everything to the perceptual centers upside down and backward to what is actually there, the entire scene is interpreted right side up and in proper left and right relationship based on the perceptual center's past expe-

rience of what is real. The perceptual center cannot interpret all of a page as right side up but leave one small word such as *was* or *saw* upside down and backward. It would be even further beyond belief to imagine that the perceptual center of the brain would interpret sensations received from the optic nerve right side up with the exception of the word *was*, which it would interpret in reversed right-to-left order but not inverted. Such perception would be completely incredible. (pp. 63-64)

When students continue to make reversals beyond the primary years, it is because they fail to use directionality in making discriminations (Moyer & Newcomer, 1977) or fail to read for meaning (F. Smith, 1978), not because they have problems with visual perception.

Very little that has been suggested about reading problems resulting from visual perception is observable or measurable. Most is merely conjecture. A "visual perception problem" is one of the many scapegoats used to explain a problem that seems to defy explanation. At a certain time, everything from reading difficulties to discipline problems may be blamed on a student's "minimal brain damage." A few years later the scapegoat in vogue may be "neurological disability" or "lack of sensory integration." Similarly, reading disabilities have been blamed on visual perception problems at various times, on a cyclical basis.

A variety of educational programs have been proposed for training students with supposed visual perception problems. However, both research and practice have shown that visual perception training does not increase reading ability or remediate other learning disabilities.

One well-known program designed to improve students' visual perceptual skills has been the Frostig program, which requires students to match shapes, draw lines within printed lines from one picture to another, and engage in other similar activities. Buckland's (1970) investigation of the influence of this program on the word recognition ability, visual perception skills, and reading readiness of low-achieving first-graders failed to prove its usefulness in any of these areas. Other studies have confirmed the findings of Buckland's research.

Another type of training advocated for remediating visual perception difficulties is the use of visual tracking exercises. Such exercises have no value in increasing reading skills of any kind. For example, D. K. Cohen (1972) investigated the use of the Visual Tracking and Word Tracking workbooks of the Michigan Tracking Program with 75 remedial readers and concluded that such exercises did not increase reading achievement.

Visual perception is indeed involved in reading, but there are no specialized kinds of perceptual skills required. As F. Smith (1978) states,

[t]here is, in fact, nothing unique about reading. There is nothing in reading as far as vision is concerned that is not involved in such mundane perceptual activities as distinguishing tables from chairs or dogs from cats. (p. 2)

Based on research evidence, it is logical to conclude that visual perception "difficulties" do not contribute to reading disabilities.

Hearing. Students who are severely hearing impaired frequently have difficulties learning to read.

The degree of hearing loss that individuals experience varies greatly and can have more or less of an impact on reading ability. Students with a slight hearing loss may need special attention to vocabulary development and require special seating in order to hear more easily. Students with a somewhat greater loss may miss much of class discussion, have limited vocabularies, and need special instruction in reading. A marked hearing loss may result in problems with language production and understanding; these students will need special help in reading and all language skills. Students with even more severe losses may be able to discriminate vowel sounds but unable to discriminate consonants; since speech does not develop spontaneously for these students, they may need a special program designed for developing language skills. Students suffering the most extreme losses have difficulties with speech and require special training in oral communication, concept development, and all reading and language skills. It should be noted, however, that there is some evidence that students with profound hearing impairments have a different language base—rather than a deficient one—from which to process written language (Ewoldt, 1981). The depressed reading scores of those with profound hearing impairments may result from conventional reading instruction methods that require them to use the same types of language processing that hearing readers use.

Because of the possible effects of a hearing disability on an individual's language and concept development, it is important to determine the age of onset of a hearing loss. If the child experiences a serious loss before developing language—as with a congenital loss—the effects on learning are more detrimental than if the loss occurs afterward.

Although many individuals with severe hearing impairments reach a high level of educational attainment, some do not, even though they may have normal intelligence. In general, students with severe hearing impairments have more difficulty in learning to read and progressing in reading than any other group. Since the reading skills of students with severe hearing impairments are often atypical, special national norms have been developed for interpreting their reading scores on certain tests.

Even students with a mild hearing loss may be handicapped in some instructional tasks involving reading, especially if they cannot hear sounds in the high frequency range (i.e., certain consonant sounds). These students may also have less advanced oral language development than their hearing peers and be unable to learn as much from class discussions. When a student has a mild hearing loss, the teacher needs to make instructional adaptations. If these adaptations are made, a mild hearing loss should not contribute to a student's reading disability.

A relatively low incidence of hearing problems occurs in the school-age population in the United States. About 0.6% of students have a severe to profound hearing loss. Approximately 4.5% may have a mild hearing loss. Impairments in auditory acuity are a possible cause of a reading disability in only a small number of cases.

Speech.   The causes of a speech disorder (such as distortions of sounds, stuttering, problems of pitch, spastic speech, and others) include emotional problems, developmental delay, inadequate hearing, imperfectly developed vocal cords, cleft palate, and brain damage.

When a speech problem results from a brain lesion, it is not unusual to find that the affected individual also has a reading disability. Because one of several areas of the brain involved in reading is located near the language center, injury to the language center may also affect the reading area. An individual may exhibit both speech and reading disorders, but the speech disorder does not cause the reading problem. Rather, typically both result from a common cause.

Most speech problems, such as poor articulation (which accounts for about three fourths of all speech disorders), stuttering, lisping, and problems of pitch, have no direct relationship to reading disabilities. However, if a teacher evaluates reading ability inappropriately, for example, on the ability to pronounce sounds of letters in a manner consistent with standard speech or on the basis of "good" oral reading ability, then it may appear that students' speech disorders are hindering their reading progress. Sometimes checklists that help teachers evaluate students' reading ability include items that have nothing to do with ability to read. For example, they may include such questions as these:

- Does the student enunciate distinctly?
- Does the student have a pleasant voice quality?
- Does the student use a suitable voice pitch?

In contrast, when reading ability is evaluated appropriately, no direct relationship between speech and reading ability is evident. Speech defects are no more prevalent among disabled readers than among average readers.

It is possible that speech problems are an indirect cause of reading disabilities, as the result of the effect that the disorder has on students' personal adaptation to the school environment. If students must concentrate on how to say something rather than on what they are saying, this can be detrimental to learning and to performance of many school-related tasks. Although a speech disorder in itself does not cause a reading disability, students with a speech problem should be referred to a speech therapist as soon as it is noted.

Neurological Difficulties

Neurology is the study of the nervous system. The human nervous system comprises the brain, spinal cord, nerves, ganglia (masses of nerve tissue), and parts of receptor organs. Several types of neurological difficulties have been related to reading disabilities—most of them associated with the brain. See Figure 2–2 for a brief description of the workings of the human brain.

Some general terms used synonymously with *neurological difficulty* are *neurological involvement, neurological impairment, neurological disorder,* and *deviations in brain functioning.*

Brain Damage.   Brain damage can result from injuries, disease, or toxic substances. Complications during pregnancy can cause some types of neurological damage in the child. Brain damage may also occur at birth. Neurological difficulties related to pregnancy and birth are called **perinatal neurological disorders**. High and prolonged fevers or poisoning (for example, lead poisoning) can also damage brain tissue. Stroke is the most common cause of brain damage in adults. These various injuries, diseases, or toxins may cause a **lesion**, that is, an abnormal change in the structure of the brain. Lesions may be mild, moderate, or severe and may occur in areas of the brain that do not affect learning to read, as well in those that do.

Some educators have attempted to distinguish between diagnosed brain damage and what they call *minimal brain damage*. A neurological examination by a medical doctor, including an electroencephalogram (an EEG), can often determine the existence of brain damage. An EEG records the electrical activity of the brain. This record is displayed as a tracing of the brain waves. However, even when an EEG is accompanied by a careful study of the perinatal and developmental history of the individual, the diagnosis of brain damage may not be definite. Physicians admit that findings from an EEG are not always conclusive. In addition, the distinction must be made between major abnormalities in the EEG and those that, even though they vary from the normal read-

FIGURE 2–2

Information about the operation of the brain

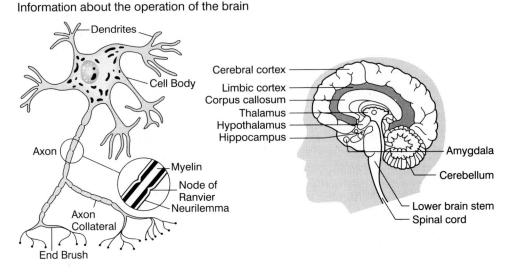

Schematic of a neuron   Cross-section of a brain

Parts of the Brain
1. *Neuron.* A cell consisting of a cell body, dendrites, and an axon.
2. *Dendrites.* Wispy, fingerlike parts surrounding the neuron cell body.
3. *Axon.* A single, taillike portion attached to each neuron cell body.
4. *Neurotransmitter.* A chemical that carries a message from one neuron to another.
5. *Synapse.* A gap between neurons.

Brain Processes
This is a simplified version of what is presently known about how the brain works.
1. Sensory receptors all over the body (e.g., in the eyes, ears, and so on) send messages to the brain.
2. When the initial message reaches the brain, neurons further process it in the following way:
   a. Dendrites receive the message and expel an electrical impulse.
   b. This impulse is moved to the axon, which releases a chemical called a neurotransmitter.
   c. The neurotransmitter moves across a synapse to the dendrite of the next neuron.
   d. This process is repeated over and over through many of the 5 to 25 billion neurons in the brain, each of which is as complicated as a computer.
   The brain comprises many areas including the cerebral cortex, limbic cortex, corpus callosum, thalamus, hypothalamus, hippocampus, amygdala, and cerebellum, plus the lower brain stem, which is connected to the spinal cord. Specific sections specialize in specific activities, but often more than one brain area is involved in functions and behaviors. Scientists still do not understand the neural codes that translate sensory perceptions into the processing performed in the brain.

Interesting Facts
1. The outer covering of the brain, the cerebral cortex, is only about one tenth of an inch thick, but controls all higher level mental functions.
2. Memory is stored in cells all over the brain; although in the long run, it may end up in the cortex.
3. There are more than 50 chemical substances that make up the different neurotransmitters that carry messages.
4. An electroencephalogram (EEG) measures the electricity expelled by the brain's neurons.
5. There is white matter as well as gray matter in the brain. Gray matter consists of clusters of neuron cell bodies. White matter consists of bundles of nerve fibers.
6. When a neuron is damaged, a new one does not replace it; it simply ceases to function.

ings, have no significance. If a diagnosis of brain damage is made after proper procedures are followed, it is said that there are "hard signs" that brain damage does exist.

In some cases, when brain damage is not indicated by an EEG and a person's developmental history, educators may insist that minimal brain damage (MBD) exists as evidenced by certain "soft signs." They infer from an individual's behavioral patterns and certain psychological tests that brain damage is present. Behavioral patterns believed to be indicative of minimal brain damage are inattention, poor motor coordination, difficulty in left-right discriminations, overactivity, underactivity, and distractibility. Actually over 100 symptoms have been described as indications of MBD. Poor performance on the Bender-Gestalt test, certain subtests of the Wechsler Intelligence Tests, the Draw-a-Person test, and others administered by psychologists have also resulted in labeling students as minimally brain damaged. Labeling an individual as brain damaged as the result of certain behaviors and results on psychological tests is misleading. Poor motor coordination, hyperactivity, lack of left-right discrimination, and other supposed symptoms may have many causes other than the assumed medically undetectable brain damage. Further, Reed, Rabe, and Mankinen (1970) warn that

> results from psychological tests cannot be accepted as evidence of brain damage in the present state of knowledge. . . . To report distortions in Bender-Gestalt drawings as evidence for brain damage is naive and reveals a lack of appreciation of the complexities of obtaining neurological criterion information. (p. 398)

In summary, MBD is a catchall term used to refer to widely differing problems. There is definite danger in labeling a student with this term without a medical examination. The concept of "soft signs" as an indication of brain damage is not helpful to educators.

The consequences of brain damage that has been medically diagnosed vary. Although some students with diagnosed brain damage may have reading disabilities, most have no difficulty at all in learning to read. For example, Byers and Lord (1943) reported a study of 13 students with medically determined brain damage caused by lead poisoning; all were making adequate progress in reading. On the other hand, Balow, Rubin, and Rosen (1975–76) found a statistically significant (although low) correlation between perinatal neurological disorders and reading disabilities. In any case, the consensus holds that only in severe cases of reading disability is brain damage a possible factor, and even in these cases an infrequent one.

Even if a neurologist may diagnose mild or moderate brain damage in students with reading disabilities, the diagnosis in itself provides little useful information for the teacher. In the past, special instructional techniques such as training in perceptual-motor coordination, manipulation of visual-spatial configurations, left-right discrimination, and memory for designs were used with students who had suffered brain damage. It has since been found that these activities have no positive influence on learning to read for brain-damaged students or any other students. After reviewing the research on teaching brain-damaged students, Reed et al. (1970) found little evidence to indicate that these students require or benefit from teaching procedures different from those useful for other disabled readers.

Recent studies in neurology may have some implications for educators working with students with severe brain damage. From studying adults who have suffered brain damage, scientists have learned that different parts of the brain control different cognitive activities, even activities that seem closely related. There are brain-damaged adults who cannot read, but nevertheless can write—even the same words they cannot read. These patients may be able to recognize numerals, such as 1, 9, 2, but not letters such as R, T, Z. Because there appear to be similarities in behaviors of brain-damaged adults and certain students with learning disabilities, some educators use techniques employed with these adults for young people with learning disabilities who also have indications of severe brain damage. They may have students use their sense of touch (for example, by feeling three-dimensional letters) as an aid to recognizing letters. This technique has been employed successfully to help adult stroke victims regain reading skill. A reading or learning disabilities teacher may try this technique for a young student in the rare cases where severe brain damage may be a causal factor in a reading disability.

Some cautions should be noted, however, before the educational community advocates a wholesale adoption of techniques used with adults having **alexia** (the loss of previously established reading ability). When damage occurs in the brains of young children, undamaged portions of the brain may take over the functions of the damaged portions—even though these functions may not normally be linked to those parts of the brain. Older children and adults do not respond in this manner. Therefore, some techniques useful with brain-injured adults may or may not be helpful with severely brain-damaged younger children.

Neurological Dysfunctions.   Neurological dysfunctions from causes other than brain damage have been studied in relation to reading disabilities. Some of these may result from **atypical maturation of the brain** (one area may develop more slowly than others) or from a **congenital brain defect** (an individual is born with an underdeveloped area of the brain). Individuals with such problems are very rare, however, and in addition, these abnormalities may not always cause a reading disability. Ackerly and Benton (1947) reported the case of a man who had very good reading skills, despite a serious congenital defect—part of a brain lobe was missing.

Some authorities believe that one of three situations may exist in regard to brain dysfunction and severe reading disability: (a) the reading disabled student has no brain dysfunction; (b) there is specific brain damage, that is, a lesion in the occipital-parietal areas of the brain; or (c) there is a general defect in the central nervous system. Their position is that although individuals are born with the capacity to develop the basic perceptual and associative processes needed for learning, these processes develop in the central nervous system. If there is a central nervous system defect, learning may not occur as it should or when it should. But they also point out that not all individuals with a central nervous system disorder have reading or other learning disabilities.

One unfortunate notion related to neurological dysfunction is that of "lack of neurological organization." Delacato (1963) and others have proposed a theory based on the premise that development of neurological functions progresses from lower to higher levels. They theorized that the central nervous system may sometimes bypass certain normal developmental stages, resulting in a lack of neurological organization. To remediate irregular neurological organization, the Delacato program proposes a series of motor and other sensory stimulation activities purportedly based on the evolutionary stages of motor development in humans. Clients engage in such activities as cross-pattern creeping and walking (extending the right foot while pointing to it with the left hand and vice versa), one-sided crawling, visual pursuit activities, and sleep patterning. (Sleep patterning requires a child to sleep in specific positions; parents check throughout the night and readjust the child's position if necessary.)

Delacato contended that these motor activities cause proper neural connections to occur in the central nervous system because of the stimulation to the sensory system. This program is supposedly useful in treating individuals with reading and other learning disabilities, assisting brain-damaged individuals, and increasing IQ. In four separate studies (R. W. Anderson, 1966; Foster, 1966; O'Donnell & Eisenson, 1969; Robbins,

1966), the program was not shown to increase reading achievement. In addition, there is no evidence that any type of stimulation activities can remediate neurological deficits that have already occurred. Educational research has refuted the effectiveness of Delacato's system and disproved his theory. His claims have been censured by major educational organizations such as the International Reading Association and the National Association of Retarded Children. Medical and health organizations such as the American Academies of Neurology, Orthopedics, Pediatrics, Physical Medicine and Rehabilitation, and Cerebral Palsy have accused Delacato of making undocumented claims of cures. Interest in Delacato's theory had begun to diminish, but recently commercial clinics employing methods similar to Delacato's have opened. These should not be recommended to parents of children with reading disabilities, learning disabilities, or mental retardation.

On the topic of brain dysfunction, it is important to clarify the term *word blindness*. **Word blindness** is a loss of the ability to read; it is an acquired condition in adults, often caused by stroke. This loss of ability may be temporary, and adults may be able to read again with retraining. In the late 1800s and early 1900s, however, the term *word blindness* was applied to individuals who had never learned to read despite a great deal of instruction. In many cases, this inability to read was labeled *congenital word blindness* (Hinshelwood, 1917) since it was believed that a congenital brain defect made individuals unable to recognize words. The term *word blindness* still occasionally appears, incorrectly, in relation to young nonreaders. Word blindness is a rare defect that may be acquired by adult stroke victims; it is not a congenital defect.

Mixed Cerebral Dominance.   In 1928, Samuel Orton proposed a theory of reading disabilities based on the premise that individuals who have difficulty in learning to read have mixed cerebral dominance. Orton believed that normal readers have an established dominance of one side of the brain, which can be determined by the side of the body the individual prefers for hand, eye, ear, and foot use. That is, if individuals are right-handed and also show clear preferences for use of the right eye and right foot, this is an indication that **lateral dominance** has been established for one side of the body, in this case, the right side.

Orton proposed that students with reading disabilities have not established cerebral dominance. Such lack of dominance is indicated if they are right-handed and left-eyed, or left-handed, right-eyed, and left-footed, and so forth. His premise was that mixed cerebral dominance resulted in a condition he called *strephosymbolia,* which means "twisted symbols." Since supposedly neither side of the brain was dominant, Orton believed that students perceived words or letters appropriately on one side of the brain and at the same time perceived them as their mirror images on the other side. According to this theory, readers with mixed cerebral dominance would sometimes respond to the appropriate image and sometimes to the mirror image. Orton believed that when they responded to the mirror image, they made reversals of letters or words, for example, calling the letter *b* the letter *d* or calling the word *on* the word *no.*

Much research with young beginning readers, adolescents, students with reading and other learning disabilities, and individuals with mental retardation has shown that lack of established lateral dominance has nothing to do with reading ability (e.g., Belmont & Birch, 1965; Benton & McCann, 1969; Capobianco, 1967; Gates & Bennett, 1933).

Attention Deficit Disorder.   Attention deficit disorder (ADD) has been divided into two categories: (a) ADD and (b) ADD with hyperactivity (Sawyer, 1989). The former may be diagnosed when a student exhibits behaviors such as distractibility, impulsiveness, inattentiveness, short attention span, and instances of being easily frustrated. The second may be diagnosed if there is an accompanying unusual degree of motor activity. It has been proposed that neurological difficulties may be one source of ADD, and, in fact, there is question if ADD is actually a valid diagnosis if there is no evidence of neurological damage (Bohline, 1985).

Determination of the presence of either form of ADD should be made by a medical professional. There has been much criticism of use of rating scales by nonmedical personnel to apply this label, with studies showing that far too many students are misdiagnosed with such a procedure.

Because behaviors associated with ADD also are typical of students who have severe difficulty in learning, the "chicken and egg" question is increasingly being asked, "Does ADD prevent students from learning, or do difficulties in learning simply result in frustration and avoidance tactics such as off-task behaviors and restlessness?" It is believed that in the vast majority of instances, the latter is the case.

Contrary to certain notions, most students with learning disabilities do not exhibit behaviors that have been associated with ADD. In addition, all students with "discipline" problems do not have ADD, and neither are all these students in need of drug or other therapy; many may simply be taking advantage of a teacher who has poor classroom control.

Three types of dietary interventions have been suggested for controlling behaviors associated with ADD: (a) elimination of foods containing certain additives, (b) megavitamin therapy, and (c) elimination of refined sugar. The National Advisory Committee on Hyperkinesis and Food Additives (1975) and the Committee on Nutrition of the American Academy of Pediatrics (1976) have found that claims for the efficacy of eliminating additives and of treatments using megavitamins lack objective foundation. They have discounted the effectiveness of these therapies in reducing ADD-like behaviors.

The suggestion that refined sugars be eliminated from the diet is based on the notion that after eating large amounts of sugar, hyperactive individuals secrete too much insulin, which consequently induces hypoglycemia; the resulting hypoglycemia supposedly interferes with the functioning of the brain. A number of arguments refute this theory. For one, Sieben (1977) points out that no research has shown that abnormal amounts of insulin are secreted in hyperactive or learning disabled students. In addition, Sieben says that "since the body sees to it that the brain has first claim to whatever sugar is available, a truly hypoglycemic person would not be able to sustain the muscular effort required to be hyperactive" (p. 138). In sum, reducing ADD-like behaviors through dietary control has not been effective.

In contrast, drug therapy and behavior modification techniques can be helpful in controlling behaviors associated with ADD. Because drugs have been overused with some students in the past, there has been a reaction against using them at all. Using certain drugs, such as dilantin and phenobarbital, discriminately is helpful with some students, however, and can effectively eliminate hyperactive behaviors that prevent learning. Behavior modification techniques also provide a promising avenue for working with students who exhibit hyperactive behaviors. For example, such behaviors have been reduced by rewarding students for on-task behavior—and by rewarding classmates for not encouraging off-task behavior. This dual procedure deprives students of reinforcement they receive from peers for inappropriate behaviors and substitutes reinforcement for behaviors conducive to learning. That hyperactivity can be controlled in this fashion indicates that, regardless of its original source, many of its associated behaviors are learned and increased by environmental conditions.

Motor Coordination.   Some educators have proposed that poor motor coordination is linked to reading disability. This is not the case, nor does training to improve motor development assist in eliminating reading or other learning disabilities.

Many programs have been proposed to promote sensory-motor development with the belief that they will increase academic achievement. A widely known example is Kephart's (1960) program of motor activities and body management. Kephart advocated such activities as balance beam walking, performing "angels in the snow" routines on the classroom floor, jumping on trampolines to get a feeling for the body's "position in space," and tracing circles on a board to practice crossing the body's "midline."

Hammill, Goodman, and Wiederholt (1974) reviewed 76 studies relating to the Kephart procedures. They concluded that the effect of this training on achievement in academic skills or on intelligence was not demonstrated. Class time spent on perceptual-motor activities is wasted time that would better be spent on reading practice. Balow (1971), after an extensive review of the research, stated that

> in numerous searches of the literature . . . no experimental study conforming to accepted tenets of research design has been found that demonstrates special effectiveness for any of the physical, motor, or perceptual programs claimed to be useful in the prevention or correction of reading or other learning disabilities. (p. 523)

Sensory Integration.   While most neurological problems suggested as possible causes of reading disability originate in the brain itself, problems of sensory integration purportedly originate in the brain stem. Ayres (1972) has theorized that learning disorders result from deficient integration of the brain stem functions. Her program for treating learning problems is to stimulate the position awareness and balancing systems of the body, which supposedly will help the brain stem make better neurological connections. Sieben (1977) points out several flaws in Ayres's theory. First, medical researchers have contended that such stimulations cannot improve neurological connections. Second, there is no evidence that the brain stems of students with learning disabilities malfunction in any way. Finally, it is difficult to see how good balance can aid reading ability.

Hyperlexia.   One rare condition that may be a result of a neurological difficulty is hyperlexia. **Hyperlexia** is a syndrome in which individuals have a significant delay in both oral language and cognitive development, yet begin to recognize written words, even though they have had no reading instruction.

Hyperlexic students have been described by Healy (1982), Huttenlocher and Huttenlocher (1973), Mehegan and Dreifus (1972), and Silberberg and Silberberg (1967). A number of consistencies in the behaviors of these students have been identified.

1. The child exhibits an early (ages 2-4) and *dominating* preoccupation with words to the exclusion of other activities.
2. The child encounters words—even complex words—in reading and then uses them in oral language, although the child may have little understanding of their meanings.
3. When comprehension necessitates abstract thinking, the child's understanding is extremely deficient, nonexistent, or bizarre.

Studies have made other significant findings about the behaviors and characteristics of hyperlexic children. Their IQs have varied from the mentally retarded range to above-average intelligence. In the Silberberg and Silberberg study (1967), over one half of the students had been previously diagnosed as autistic, as having some form of neurological dysfunction, or as retarded. Severely delayed oral language development is exhibited, in some cases, with total lack of speech but ability to respond to written materials.

In at least two cases, this rare condition was found in sets of brothers, one set of which was twins (Silberberg & Silberberg 1967). Some behaviors exhibited by hyperlexic students appear similar to those of adults with alexia (Gardner, 1975) or children with neurological dysfunctions attributed to atypical maturation of the brain. As yet, no one has identified the underlying cause of this rare syndrome.

New Frontiers.   Attention to neurological correlates of reading disabilities began to wane in the late 1970s. By the mid-1980s, interest had resumed somewhat because of work investigating abnormal brain structures, cerebral blood flow during reading, and mapping of electrical activity in the brain. New and unusual techniques are being used in studies, such as computerized topographic (CT) scans of the brain and analyses of brains of severely reading disabled individuals during autopsies (Hynd, 1986). While this research appears to support the existence of neuroanatomical abnormalities in severe reading cases (Hynd & Hynd, 1984), as well as differences in the electrical activity in the brains of average readers versus readers with severe disabilities, many authorities consider the work controversial (e.g., Otto, 1986). At this time, however, there is considerable interest in the findings of this research.

HEREDITARY FACTORS

Some studies have suggested that reading disability is inherited. A number of these have compared the differences in reading ability between identical twins and fraternal twins. Identical twins often share almost identical personal characteristics; fraternal twins, on the other hand, do not necessarily do so. Bakwin (1973) believes his research with reading disabled twins supports the theory of the genetic origin of the disabilities: his study showed a significantly higher proportion of both twins exhibiting a reading disability when they were identical rather than fraternal. The research of Matheny, Dolan, and Wilson (1976) supports these findings. However, most educators have long believed that both biological and environmental influences affect academic learning. Since one fraternal twin may be male and one female, each may be subjected to different environmental influences, and this may account for some of the differences in the research findings from the studies of identical versus fraternal twins.

Other studies have identified family groups in which there is a high incidence of reading disability. One group of researchers investigated the reading abilities of the family members of 20 problem readers and found that siblings and parents of these students also had a high percentage of reading problems (Finucci, Gutherie, Childs, Abbey, & Childs, 1976). In Hallgren's study (1950), only 1% of his 122 reading disabled subjects did not come from homes where there was a family history of reading difficulties. Results of studies by Bettman, Stern, and Gofman (1967), the Institute of Behavioral Genetics, and others seem to support the genetic interpretation of reading problems. However, Coles (1980) provided an extensive critique of these studies and pointed out major procedural problems in many of them.

There does seem to be a genetic predisposition to certain aptitudes. For example, musical ability appears to run in some families, or unusual mathematical facility may be found in a student with a parent having a strong mathematical aptitude. It may be that parents genetically transmit a stronger or weaker aptitude for learning to read, just as they transmit other characteristics to their children. Phonemic awareness, for instance, which has a clear link to reading success, may have a genetic as well as an environmental base (Stanovich, 1986). A student with a weak inherited aptitude for a skill may face greater difficulties in acquiring it.

Some families do seem to have a higher incidence of reading disorders. The genetic transmission of an aptitude, or lack of aptitude, may indeed be a tenable explanation for the success or failure of some individuals. However, in some cases what may appear to be a hereditary cause may be an environmental one. Some of the best predictors of students' success in reading are the parents' academic guidance of their children, the intellectual atmosphere in the home, parental aspirations for children, and parental language models, praise, and work habits. This means that parental behavior and the environment they create for their children may have as significant an impact on their children's reading success as genetic factors.

EMOTIONAL FACTORS

The 1940s and 1950s witnessed great interest in the effects of emotional disturbances on reading disability. Despite the cautions of leading educators, emotional maladjustment was considered by many at the time to be the most frequent cause of students' reading problems, and research designed to verify this hypothesis was common. Results of the research showed, however, that rather than emotional disturbances being a contributing factor to reading disabilities, in most cases, the converse was true—that is, reading disabilities contributed to emotional disorders.

Admittedly, a small number of students have emotional problems so severe that their problems have a debilitating effect on their social behaviors and, consequently, on all aspects of their academic learning. However, for most students who are reading disabled and emotionally disturbed, the reading problem is at the root of the emotional disturbance, rather than the other way around. These students come to school with emotionally healthy outlooks, but when they have difficulties in learning to read while their peers are progressing normally, they begin to exhibit mild to moderate emotional problems. A circular effect usually occurs, that is, emotional problems stemming from difficulties in learning to read, in turn, contribute to lack of further progress in reading. Problems of motivation become evident. Students may come to believe that they *cannot* learn to read—believing that something is wrong with them. The students' motivation to read continues to erode further over time, as does their confidence. This state has been referred to as **learned helplessness** (Johnston & Winograd, 1985). Learned helplessness then may lead to poor performance in cognitive processes and tasks other than reading (Stanovich, 1986). For these students, once the reading problem is remediated, the apparent emotional disturbance disappears. A case that illustrates this phenomenon is Brian. (See Figure 2–3.)

In those rare cases where a student's emotional problems are the initial underlying cause of the reading disability, therapy or psychological counseling is called for. For example, if the student comes from a home environment characterized by stress, conflict, and lack of security, neurotic symptoms may block learning. In these cases, an integrated effort similar to that in the combined project of the Family Therapy Program and the Reading Clinic at Lehigh University (Garrigan, Kender, & Heydenberk, 1980) may be needed. Such programs recognize the need for involving the total family in treating a student's emotional problems and recognize that this is best carried out in conjunction with reading remediation efforts.

FIGURE 2–3

Brian: A brief case study

Brian, a fourth-grade boy labeled as having learning disabilities and behavior disorders, was able to read almost nothing when he was enrolled in a university reading clinic. When Brian's tutors attempted to engage him in any type of reading-related activity, he would spend only a few minutes on task. Then he would engage in a variety of avoidance behaviors, such as putting his head down, saying he was too tired to read, stating that his eyes hurt (although no visual problems of any kind existed), attempting to climb on the desk (even though he was quite large) to peer at students being tutored in other carrels, talking in a loud voice about off-the-subject topics, making abusive comments to his tutor, crawling on the floor, hiding under the desk and grabbing his tutor's legs when she came in, and simply refusing to engage in any planned activity. After five months of patient work, during which many instructional techniques were tried, and even the smallest bit of progress was praised and visually demonstrated to him, Brian began to read. An almost immediate change in his behavior was seen. He remained on task for the entire one-hour tutoring session; he asked to engage in specific reading activities; he became eager to demonstrate his reading skill to other clinic personnel; he was quiet, pleasant, and attentive in dealings with his tutor; and before and after tutoring sessions, he wandered about the clinic attempting to read everything in sight. On the day Brian came into the clinic wearing a badge he had received at school that day, a cheer went up in the clinic — the badge said that he had been chosen as the good citizen of the month for his entire elementary school. As soon as Brian began to read, his other inappropriate behaviors disappeared. When these behaviors were eliminated he was able to focus on tasks necessary in learning to read, and his progress in reading increased rapidly.

SOCIOCULTURAL FACTORS

Sociological factors are those related to human social behaviors. Cultural factors relate to patterns of behaviors and values characteristic of a population or community. In 1932, Bartlett conducted a classic study that showed how beliefs or values can affect learning. Some sociocultural factors that may affect a student's reading ability are socioeconomic status, ethnic identification, and culturally determined gender roles.

Socioeconomic Status

There are differences in reading achievement when comparing students from high, middle, and low socioeconomic status (SES) backgrounds. Studies have shown the incidence of reading disability increases as SES decreases (Gutherie & Greaney, 1991).

Many Americans tend to associate low socioeconomic status with race or ethnicity, although in many cases this association does not hold true. For this reason, it should be emphasized that low school achievement is linked with low socioeconomic status only, not with race or ethnic background. Also, traditional ways of viewing SES (education, income, occupation) may be less useful in examining variations in reading achievement than looking at differences in specific practices within homes at any SES level. Some home factors correlated with high achievement are the following:

1. Preschool experiences with books (Feitelson & Goldstein, 1986)
2. Parents' interest in reading themselves, thus providing a model for the child (Neuman, 1986)
3. High-quality parental verbal interactions with the child (Hess & Holloway, 1984)
4. Provision of space and opportunity for the child to read (Gutherie & Greaney, 1991)

Some home factors correlated with lower achievement also have been shown:

1. Fewer books in the home (Spiegel, 1981)
2. Hearing books read to them less frequently by parents (Spiegel, 1981)
3. Unstructured lifestyles regarding home activities such as bedtime, television viewing, and others (Fielding, Wilson, & Anderson, 1986)

While some of the practices correlated to lower achievement do seem to be associated with certain SES levels, they are not necessarily so.

Wachs, Uzgiris, and Hunt (1971) found intellectual deficiencies in African-American and Caucasian low SES children in the United States as early as 7 months of age. They believed this to be the result of several aspects of home environment, such as lack of intellectual stimulation. Other causes of poor reading achievement may be family environmental patterns that are unresponsive to school-dictated requirements such as homework, as well as social behaviors and values of self-discipline different from those of the mainstream culture. Because of low educational levels of parents, children may not be encouraged to deal with conceptual problems: children are not asked questions to make them think independently and to develop strategies for learning and problem solving. Low SES preschool children may have less access to opportunities that lead to school success. No one purposely stimulates their interest in reading; therefore, they do not come to school eager to learn to read. Because fewer books are read to them at home they lack the familiarity with book language and the larger, richer oral language vocabularies of children who have been read to regularly. Shirley Brice Heath (1991) points out the differences in these homes and those in which mainstream parents engage in book reading and game playing with their preschool children to encourage thinking skills. All of these factors put the students from low SES homes more at risk for having problems in learning to read. In addition, students from low SES backgrounds may have poor health care and inadequate diets, leading to health problems and poor school attendance.

Some school-related factors can also cause poor reading achievement in students from low socioeconomic backgrounds. Lower teacher expectations seem to be a variable leading to lack of success. Variations in teacher beliefs about whether at-risk students *can* learn have been shown in some inner-city schools (e.g., Winfield, 1986). Teachers must be trained to assess students' abilities independent of their socioeconomic status. R. C. Anderson, Hiebert, Scott, and Wilkinson (1984) have reported on successful schools in low-income neighborhoods where reading levels of students were equal to those of students from middle-class backgrounds. Classrooms were described as quiet and conducive to learning, there was a high degree of teacher-directed instruction, teachers had high expectations, and a wide variety of library books was available to students.

Administrative regulations may be another contributor to lack of reading success for low SES students. Governmental programs, such as Title I—which is designed to provide remedial instruction for low-income students—have required that services be provided only to students having the lowest percentiles in reading scores. Students who are eligible one year may not be eligible the next since, because of effective instruction, they are no longer in the lowest percentile of their school population. Although they may not yet be reading up to their potentials or to the grade norm, and although they both need and have shown they can benefit from special instruction, they are no longer allowed services in the program.

Another school-related factor thought to be a possible contributor to low achievement is the apparent mismatch between the cultural and linguistic experiences of low SES students and the language, settings, and activities in standard reading materials. Several studies have shown that this mismatch does not affect reading achievement. Ratekin (1978), for example, compared reading abilities of Caucasian, African-American, and Hispanic-American children instructed in identical reading material—a standard basal reader series. All children in the study were from low socioeconomic backgrounds and were at similar reading levels at the beginning of the study. There were, however, linguistic differences among the groups: the African-American children spoke an inner-city Black dialect, and the majority of the Hispanic-American children were bilingual, speaking Spanish in their homes. In addition, the cultural experiences conveyed in the stories in the basal readers were for the most part representative of middle-class life and did not reflect the lifestyles of any of the groups. Despite the linguistic and cultural differences embodied in the reading materials, all groups of children made equal and excellent gains, as a result of the reading instruction. Ratekin believed that an important factor in these gains was that the teachers in the study were prepared to accept and understand language and cultural differences. The results of this and other studies indicate that a mismatch between the cultural experiences and the language of students and their textbooks does not contribute to reading disability if teachers are sensitive to, and handle, the mismatch appropriately. The discussion in Chapter 15 of this text suggests ways to accommodate linguistic and cultural differences.

Ethnic and Racial Identification

The culture that a student comes from apparently can have an effect on the ways the student learns best. For example, Au and Mason (1981) reported that verbal interactions in a classroom that were similar to their everyday cultural patterns resulted in Hawaiian children exhibiting more achievement-related behaviors than when interactions were dissimilar. For example, in one classroom, children were required to wait to be called on by the teacher before speaking in a reading group and were required to speak one at a time—behaviors typical in classrooms of the mainstream culture. In contrast, in another classroom, reading group interactions were allowed to assume the characteristics of a Hawaiian talk story—students took turns responding to the same question or engaged in joint responses. Children allowed to respond in the second manner had more academically engaged time and made more reading-related responses during group time.

Similar studies have been reported with Native American populations. Children at the Warm Springs Indian Reservation were less willing to participate in school activities if they were directed at individuals, and more willing to participate in group activities (Phillips, 1972). Many Native American Indian cultures are family- or group-centered, and students from these cultures are often uncomfortable if required to compete. This culturally determined trait contrasts with the requirements of mainstream-culture classrooms, where individuals are singled out to exhibit their understanding of a topic. Many Native American students respond to singling out by remaining silent rather than by trying to excel over their peers; their silence as a response to a question may be incorrectly interpreted by a teacher as lack of knowledge.

Heath (1991) described similarities in ways some African-American and Hispanic-American working class communities use language in learning:

1. Children learn from daily, real situations rather than from specific information and questions presented by adults.
2. Questions are not asked of children when the answers are already known by adults.
3. Stories are developed by groups and interruptions are a standard feature of this process.

All of these ways in which learning occurs and is displayed differ from characteristics of mainstream school-based learning.

Bicultural students often appear to lack competence and intelligence in school settings, while they more than adequately demonstrate these traits in their own communities and homes. Good teachers adapt instruction to the ethnic experiences and values of their students and at the same time help them adjust to the mainstream culture. When teachers fail to adapt, their students may not achieve to their potentials.

Culturally Determined Gender Roles

Gender differences have been demonstrated in relation to reading achievement. In the United States, girls have superior attainment in early reading progress, although in the general school population these differences tend to disappear by age 10. In addition, more boys than girls have reading difficulties that necessitate a remedial or clinical program. Males enrolled in university-based reading clinics outnumbered females 3 to 1 in a recent national survey (Bader & Wiesendanger, 1986).

Although these differences may be partially explained by biological reasons, they may also have a sociocultural basis. One premise has been that the content of stories used in reading instruction reflects interests consistent with the culturally determined gender roles of girls rather than boys—and that this in turn affects boys' motivation and achievement. Studies of stories in the most widely used basal reader series have found

Although low school achievement is linked to low socioeconomic status (SES), it is not linked with race or ethnicity.

this assumption to be untrue. Stories do not favor girls' interests over boys', nor do they more frequently describe activities thought of as feminine.

A second premise has been that boys' achievement is adversely affected because schools have predominantly female staffs. Some have suggested that women teachers provide instruction that requires learning styles unnatural for boys and that they have lower expectations for boys. A review by Lahaderne (1976) of 22 studies related to this issue laid this myth to rest. What Lahaderne did find was that both men and women teachers seem to operate from the same cultural biases. There were no differences between the perceptions of male and female teachers—they both perceived boys as having more problems than girls; there were also no differences in the grades they assigned for academic performance. There were no differences between male and female teachers in regard to their treatment of boys and girls: boys received more inter-actions of all types (approval and disapproval) from both groups, and both groups were more directive with boys. Finally, there were no differences in student outcomes between the boys or girls who had male teachers and the boys or girls who had female teachers, and no differences in student adjustments.

A third premise is that general cultural expectations related to gender roles exist that are reflections of larger societal norms. These expectations come from parents, peers, and society as a whole. Specific factors that can affect perceptions of gender roles vary from cultural group to cultural group. In North America, preschool boys and girls view reading as a masculine activity (May & Ollila, 1981), but school-age boys and girls view reading and books as feminine. Culturally determined appropriateness of reading in relation to gender roles may influence the amount of reading done by boys and girls, as well as their motivation to become good readers. Girls seem to have more positive attitudes toward reading than do boys (Greaney & Hegerty, 1987).

CONCLUSION

Chapter 2 has provided information about the prevailing thought related to physiologi-cal, hereditary, emotional, and sociocultural causes of reading disabilities. New hypotheses are frequently offered as explanations for reading problems. Some of these hypotheses have merit, but some have proved to be spurious. Teachers who deal with reading disabled students need to be critical readers and thinkers when they confront these issues. Coles (1980) offers the following warning:

> An examination of the response to ideas in their historical context reveals that it is fre-quently difficult to judge the merit of social and scientific theories in one's own time. For example, the late 19th- and early 20th-century theory of craniology, with its guiding tech-nique, the "cephalic index," claimed that humans could be classified as roundheads (brachycephalics), longheads (dolichocephalics), and in-between heads (mesocephalics), and that these physical classifications correlated with fundamental social and intellectual characteristics. . . . From this theory came illuminating conclusions, such as the tendency of urban residents to be more long-headed because they "showed a stronger inclination to city life and a greater aptitude for success" . . . than did roundheads. Craniology remained part of the prevailing wisdom of anthropology for decades, even after Franz Boas conclu-sively repudiated it. . . . [W]e look back on the simplistic, reductionist explanations of a problem that is sociological in origin and are appalled, angered, and perhaps amused by the investigations, conclusions, and statements made under the guise of "scientific thought." Yet at the time, these ideas were presented and received largely as credible and worthy of consideration. (p. 379)

To continue to learn about the topic of causes of reading disabilities, teachers must study professional journals, but they must also carefully evaluate what they find there. Most of all, they must be careful to evaluate critically what they read in the popular press.

📖 REFLECTIONS

Some educators believe that understanding a *cause* of a student's reading disability is not important. They say, for example, if a fifth-grade student uses inefficient word identification strategies, one must simply teach the student efficient strategies.

Discuss this view. In doing so, consider some of these issues.

1. Is it or is it not important for a teacher to know that a particular student's reading problem may have *begun*, for example, because of an undetected auditory acuity problem or an impoverished preschool background (or any other possible cause)?
2. Should our concerns as reading teachers be focused only on remediation? Should we or should we not be concerned with prevention? Is there anything teachers can do in regard to prevention? If so, are there things we can do and things we cannot?
3. If or when (depending on your conclusions for 2 above) we cannot prevent a reading problem, are there adaptations in instructional programs we can make to accommodate learning needs resulting from the "unpreventable" cause? If so, what kinds of adaptations might be possible and effective? If we are unaware of the causes of the problem, would or would not the needed accommodations be evident anyway? Discuss specific examples to substantiate your view.
4. Consider the following: In other fields, research into etiology of disabilities has led to an almost complete elimination of certain factors. For instance, when a woman contracts rubella (German measles) during the first month of pregnancy, the fetus has a 50% risk of being born with abnormalities in intelligence. Programs of immunization against rubella are eliminating this cause of mental retardation. Does this example point to any potential for research in our own field?

3

Causes and Correlates of Individual Differences in Reading Ability: Part II

Phonemic awareness is an important prerequisite to reading, spelling, and writing.

Chapter 2 provided information about four general factors— physiological, heredity, emotional, and sociocultural—that have been studied to determine their connections with reading problems and disabilities. This chapter discusses four other areas: educational factors, cognitive factors, language factors, and reading history.

EDUCATIONAL FACTORS

Educational factors may contribute to a mild or moderate reading disability, but are not usually an *initial* cause of a *severe* disability. They may, however, lead to a worsening of the condition if appropriate interventions are not undertaken. Although many people believe that poor teaching is the predominant educational factor contributing to reading problems, sometimes the teacher is at fault, but sometimes not.

Lack of Research Information

We do not yet entirely understand the reading process, and until we do, all answers teachers need to help students learn best are not available. Instead, teachers must rely on existing research and their own judgments to make instructional decisions. Nonetheless, as we come to understand more about the reading process, procedures commonly used by teachers that once seemed entirely appropriate, as well as procedures suggested by authorities in literacy education, have sometimes later proved to be wrong. This lack of certainty occurs in many other fields as well.

We do have some research evidence about the behaviors and skills of teachers that seem to lead to good reading achievement. This body of research has come to be known as "teacher-effectiveness literature" or the literature on "teacher instructional actions" and deals with such topics as time on task, management skills, grouping, and pacing (Allington, 1984; Brophy, 1983; Gambrell, 1984; Rosenshine & Stevens, 1984). Among other findings, these studies show that (a) direct instruction is important for low-achieving students, (b) effective teachers avoid wasting time, (c) students learn more when instruction is paced so their success rates are high, and (d) teachers who spend larger amounts of time on reading produce greater gains. Although we do not know all of the teacher behaviors necessary to help students increase achievement, these findings can guide teachers in structuring their attitudes and developing their own skills. Teachers can also continually increase their learning by subscribing to professional journals. Figure 3–1 lists some journals that can help teachers of reading.

Lack of Time on Task

Sometimes administrative policies prevent good teaching. Teachers may be required to carry out so many tasks unrelated to the academic needs of students that they do not have time to treat academic areas as comprehensively as necessary. Many studies show that the amount of time students spend directly engaged in the actual skill the teacher wants them to learn is significantly related to their achievement. For example, the amount of instructional time is positively related to reading gains, whether or not the teacher employs small- or large-group instruction; in addition, this relationship is strongest for students reading below or at grade level.

Some nonacademic tasks required of teachers are unnecessary. Administrators should carefully examine what they ask teachers to do and eliminate as far as possible those tasks not directly related to students' learning. Of course, some nonacademic

FIGURE 3–1
Selected journals with articles on reading instruction

Subscribing to journals and reading an article or two in each monthly issue can help teachers to stay abreast of new teaching developments.

Two Journals for Elementary Teachers

The Reading Teacher
International Reading Association
800 Barksdale Road
Post Office Box 8139
Newark, Delaware 19711

Language Arts
National Council of Teachers of English
1111 Kenyon Road
Urbana, Illinois 61801

A Journal for Secondary Teachers and Teachers of Adults

Journal of Reading
International Reading Association
800 Barksdale Road
Post Office Box 8139
Newark, Delaware 19711

Some Journals for Both Elementary and Secondary Teachers

Teaching Exceptional Children
The Council for Exceptional Children
1920 Association Drive
Reston, Virginia 22091

Reading Horizons
Reading Center and Clinic
Western Michigan University
Kalamazoo, Michigan 49008

RASE: Remedial and Special Education
5341 Industrial Oaks Boulevard
Austin, Texas 78735

Learning Disability Quarterly
c/o The Council for Learning Disabilities
Post Office Box 40303
Overland Park, Kansas 66204

tasks *are* necessary. Teachers with good management skills can structure the time needed to carry out these tasks so they impinge on students' learning as little as possible. For example, an elementary teacher who is required to collect students' lunch, milk, and snack money each morning might plan to have students engage in sustained silent reading during the 15 or 20 minutes it takes to collect money. While one student at a time comes to the teacher's desk to deposit money, the other students read. By eliminating what is usually educationally dead time, a teacher can add 1 to 1½ hours of learning time during a school week. Perceptive teachers at all levels can turn nonlearning time (such as homeroom in middle schools and high schools) into times of academic engagement. Stallings (1986) promotes a self-analytic approach for teachers to determine if they are using time effectively. She encourages them to use a checklist to carefully analyze duration of activities, on-task rate, intrusions from outside, type of activities, and those who took part. Teachers are to examine the results and use problem-solving skills to make thoughtful adjustments.

Another administrative policy that causes problems of time is the continually increasing number of subjects teachers must cover in a school day. In the 1800s, more than 90% of school time was devoted to reading, writing, and arithmetic. Since then, time allotments for these subjects have decreased markedly. Not only has time devoted to other basic academic areas increased, but also driver's education, consumer education, sex education, values clarification, productive use of leisure time, and other worthwhile, but time-consuming topics are subjects included in today's school curriculum.

Since a school day has only a specified number of minutes, each new area added to the curriculum means additional minutes must be taken from existing subjects. Judicious decisions must be made about the value of each proposed addition in relation to existing programs. The value of different school programs may also vary with the individual. Although the quality of life may be enhanced by learning ways to use leisure time, a nonreader or functionally illiterate individual's quality of life may be more critically affected by increasing his or her reading skills. Teachers must set priorities as to what they teach and how much time they devote to each subject.

Sometimes the teacher is at fault when school time is not used for instruction. Durkin (1978–79) reported a study conducted to determine the amount of instruction in reading comprehension received by students in grades 3 to 6. She found that almost no instruction occurred; what little time was spent on comprehension was primarily used for assessment; that is, students were tested to determine *if* they had comprehended material but had no direct instruction on how to do so. In addition, large portions of instructional time were spent giving and checking assignments rather than helping students learn strategies for comprehension. Many teachers need to rethink how they organize and use time during a school day.

Inappropriate Instructional Materials and Techniques

Administrative policy may also be the culprit when teachers are required to use out-of-date materials and nonproductive techniques. Occasionally when administrators do not have in-depth understanding of current practice in an area for which they establish instructional policy, teachers are forced to use methods that are not as productive as they should be. On this issue, the role of reading specialists is important; they must inform administrators about effective reading instruction techniques through inservice training sessions and one-to-one discussions.

Another educationally caused problem can occur when teachers uncritically follow the dictates of publishing companies. Many reputable companies that publish reading materials use editors who are reading authorities and who screen materials and evaluate the value of suggested activities. Other publishers do not follow this policy and may publish outdated or unsupported suggestions based on a layperson's ideas about what is helpful in reading instruction. When teachers follow such programs uncritically, they waste student learning time. Teachers try to instruct students not to believe everything they read, and we need to adopt the same healthy skepticism. Because a suggestion is made in a teacher's manual or an activity is found in a workbook does not necessarily mean the suggestion or activity is useful.

Teachers should question *every* procedure they carry out and *every* activity they assign. We need to ask, "What does this activity really do to help increase this student's learning?" "Is this an activity that recent evidence says is not helpful?" "Although this is an activity used for many years, do we now know better ways to accomplish this goal?" "Is this an activity leading to learning of such minor importance that I should substitute an activity that will be of greater value to this particular student with a reading disability?" "Is this activity designed correctly? Does it really teach rather than test? Is it just a time filler rather than a learning experience?" These and other questions will help a teacher plan lessons so that learning can occur. Using hours and days of valuable instructional time having students engage in nonuseful activities prevents them from using the time productively. Over weeks and months, this inefficient use of time can contribute to a student's reading problem. The decisions teachers make about instructional planning do affect student learning. It is important to become a reflective teacher.

Teachers sometimes feel that if they could find just the right method, or just the right set of materials, or adopt just the right classroom organization, their students would learn more. Methods do not teach; materials do not teach; classroom organizations do not teach. Teachers teach. Good teaching is the major key to eliminating educational causes of reading disabilities.

Features of Successful Reading Programs

After a review of successful reading programs, Samuels (1981) identified the characteristics of exemplary programs. They fall into two categories: administrative factors and teacher characteristics.

Administrative Factors in Successful Programs. Here are the characteristics of effective reading programs:

1. Exemplary programs had administrators who provided time for teachers to plan and carry out instruction.
2. Teachers were allowed to participate in making decisions.
3. Teachers' instructional behaviors were supervised.
4. Regular inservice sessions were part of the program, and they focused on real problems.
5. Teachers were allowed to observe other successful teachers to use them as role models.

Characteristics of Teachers in Successful Programs. The following are the qualities that distinguish teachers in effective reading programs:

1. Teachers devoted large amounts of energy and time carrying out the program.
2. Teachers had had practical training.
3. Teachers employed direct instruction, that is, when the goal was to have students learn to read, they gave them the opportunity to practice *reading* and *reading strategies.* They did not ask students to walk balance beams, match shapes, or engage in other activities not directly related to the goal.
4. Teachers provided large amounts of instructional time and used time efficiently.

Direct, teacher-guided instruction often is important with low-achieving students.

5. The level of complexity of instruction was kept low.
6. Teachers used ongoing evaluation to measure student progress frequently and determine immediate needs.
7. Classes were structured, but teachers maintained a friendly atmosphere.

These characteristics offer some specific clues for establishing educational programs that will not contribute to students' reading failure.

COGNITIVE FACTORS

Cognitive factors sometimes linked to reading disabilities include intelligence, cognitive style, left and right hemispheric functions, and memory. Each will be examined in this section.

Intelligence

There is a relationship between intelligence and reading achievement. Generally, an individual whose intelligence quotient, or IQ, is higher needs less practice to learn anything than an individual whose IQ is lower. In addition, proficient reading requires anticipation of meaning, association of ideas, and perception of relationships—all of which require some degree of abstract thinking, a trait more common in students with higher IQs. Students with lower mental ages, or MAs, tend to have more specific, or concrete, reactions to words and written text.

The relationship between intelligence and reading ability is variable, however. For instance, the correlations between reading ability and IQ vary at differing grade levels. These correlations are relatively low for children in the primary grades but become higher in intermediate grades and at secondary school and adult levels. This is undoubtedly due to the increasing complexity of reading tasks at these higher levels—tasks that require higher-order thinking. In addition, although higher intelligence is generally associated with higher reading achievement, this is most true when we are considering a fairly wide difference in intelligence. For instance, if all other factors are equal, we would expect a student with an IQ of 108 to be a better reader than a student with an IQ of 79. If, however, we are comparing two individuals with IQs of 108 and 99, and all other factors are equal, there should be little significant difference in reading ability.

Does low intelligence cause a reading disability? While a student of low intelligence may be expected to have a lower reading achievement than a student of average intelligence, a lower intellectual functioning level does not necessarily cause a reading disability. Today, expectations of reading achievement are based on an individual's potential, not on grade-level expectancies. A student with a significantly lower than average IQ is not expected to read "on grade level," as might be expected of the student's intellectually average peers. For example, let us consider Jamie, who has a chronological age (CA) of 13.5, but an MA of only 10.9. Using an appropriate manner for determining potential, we might find that Jamie should be reading at approximately a sixth-grade reading level. Although at age 13.5, Jamie may be in an eighth-grade class, she would not be expected to be reading at eighth-grade level, and she would not be considered a disabled reader if her reading achievement was at or near sixth grade.

Sometimes less intelligent students do become reading disability cases, usually when appropriate adaptations are not made in their instructional programs. Students of less-than-average intelligence need more opportunities to practice, as well as introduction of new material at a slower pace. If adjustments are not made, these students' reading achievement levels may not reach their own individual potentials. In such cases, the contributing cause to the reading disability is an educational one and is not due to intelligence. Almost all students can learn to read, even educable mentally retarded individuals. Today, even some institutionalized persons with mental retardation are being taught functional reading skills.

That there is not a simple cause-and-effect relationship between intelligence and reading is evident from the number of students of normal intelligence who have difficulty learning to read. In Monroe's (1932) classic work, she found an IQ range from 60 to 150 in reading disability cases she studied. A student or researcher examining a population of clients enrolled in a reading clinic can expect to find that the subjects' IQs conform fairly closely to a standard bell-shaped curve, with the largest number of students having IQs in the average range, a smaller and approximately equal number with IQs slightly above and slightly below average, and a very small and approximately equal number with very high and very low IQs. (See Figure 3–2). While there are undoubtedly more disabled readers with very low IQs than are typically enrolled in a reading clinic, the reason for the fairly small size of the enrollment of this population is that these students are usually receiving services through other special programs (such as classes for the developmentally disabled).

An additional confirmation that no simple cause-and-effect relationship between intelligence and reading achievement exists is that the correlation between IQ and reading improvement gains for students enrolled in remedial reading programs and clinics is not high—in other words, IQ scores are not good predictors of the amount and rate of progress a student enrolled in such programs will make.

Cognitive Styles

Recently there has been interest in the effects of cognitive styles on learning. **Cognitive style** refers to an individual's personal manner of processing perceptions and conceptions. Sometimes cognitive styles are called **learning styles.** Various cognitive styles have been described and contrasted. Research related to some cognitive styles has been undertaken to determine the effects on reading achievement.

FIGURE 3–2
Bell-shaped curve showing IQ range of students typically enrolled in a reading clinic

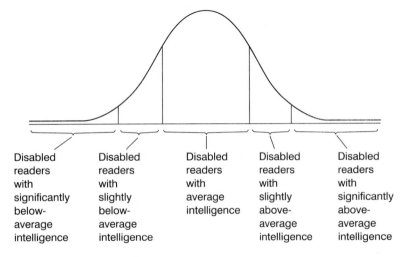

| Disabled readers with significantly below-average intelligence | Disabled readers with slightly below-average intelligence | Disabled readers with average intelligence | Disabled readers with slightly above-average intelligence | Disabled readers with significantly above-average intelligence |

Stein and Prindaville (1976) and Kagan (1965) examined the reading behaviors of students with reflective and impulsive learning styles. A **reflective style** is characterized by thoughts formed as a result of careful and calm consideration, while an **impulsive style** is marked by spontaneous choices and by unpremeditated action. Results indicated that reflective readers were superior to impulsive readers in acquiring word discriminations earlier; in addition, reflective readers made fewer errors in word recognition and were better at correcting their errors. However, in contrast, good readers and poor readers in a study by C. S. Hayes, Prinz, and Siders (1976) showed no differences in reflectivity and impulsivity.

Field independence is defined as the ability to distinguish relationships when analyzing material, while **field dependence** is the inability to do so. Newsome (1986) conducted two experiments that measured effect of field dependence on remembering information from text; in one, there was evidence of effect, but in the other there was none.

As apparent from these studies, presently available information does not provide teachers with definitive answers about the importance of the relationship of cognitive styles to reading achievement. Research is meager and inconclusive; even authorities have contradictory opinions. An important question that remains to be answered is, Do cognitive styles really affect reading behavior, or is an interaction of a number of variables producing the effect?

Preferred Learning Modality.   The concept of a **preferred learning modality** is a topic that falls under cognitive styles. A **modality** refers to a sensory channel through which information is received. Some educators have hypothesized that individuals have a specific sensory channel through which they learn best; that is, they benefit most from a visual, auditory, kinesthetic, or tactile presentation of material.

It has been postulated that matching the type of instruction to an individual's preferred modality will enhance learning. This is called **aptitude-treatment interaction.** A study by Ringler and Smith (1973) shows how aptitude-treatment interaction research is often carried out. The New York University Learning Modality Test (I. L. Smith, Ringler, & Cullinan, 1968) was administered to 128 first-graders. The results of this test indicated that 33 children had visual aptitudes, 30 had auditory aptitudes, 28 had kinesthetic aptitudes, and 37 had no preference. Children were randomly assigned to treatment groups to learn word recognition. Children in the *visual treatment* group matched words to models or words to pictures, selected one word from among others, and pointed out salient characteristics of words printed on overhead projector transparencies. Children in the *auditory treatment* group compared and contrasted word parts, listened to words in context and isolation as presented orally by the teacher and by audiotape, associated graphemes with phonemes, matched sounds of words, and selected a written word when it was spoken. The children in the *kinesthetic treatment* group traced words outlined in pipe cleaners or cut from sandpaper and wrote words on newsprint with crayons. The children with *no preference* pointed out salient visual characteristics of words, associated pictures with words, compared and contrasted word parts, listened to words in context, and traced words. However, the results of this study showed that matching the reading treatment to children's assessed modality preferences made no difference in increasing their reading achievement. Other research with students having learning or reading disabilities has reached the same conclusion. Similar studies also have been conducted with students who have mental retardation and, again, when instruction has been matched to the students' stronger modality, no significant differences have been found in their reading scores.

The folk wisdom that a contributing factor to reading difficulties may be a mismatch between a student's preferred modality or learning style and the instruction provided in the classroom is not supported by research evidence (Johnston & Allington, 1991).

Left and Right Brain Hemispheric Functioning

In times past, reading specialists were interested in the influence of **lateral dominance** (the preference for use of one side of the body). As discussed in Chapter 2, research has shown that lateral dominance is not related to reading ability. Not to be confused with this older concept, however, is a newer idea that involves hemispheric dominance and is based on recent work of neuroscientists exploring the functions of the left and right hemispheres of the brain. Their research indicates that each side of the brain has discrete functions. As a result, some have hypothesized that certain individuals appear to be more "left-brained" and others more "right-brained" and consequently have different aptitudes and skills.

Although brain research is far from being complete, the functions of the *left hemisphere* of the brain apparently include these:

1. Dealing with complex verbal ideas and complex or abstract uses of words
2. Dealing with difficult mathematical calculations
3. Engaging in inductive reasoning, that is, determining whole principles based on observation of parts
4. Dealing with fine motor coordination
5. Segmenting patterns
6. Carrying out analytical thinking, sequential thinking, and symbolic thinking
7. Perceiving conceptual relationships

The evidence presently indicates that the *right hemisphere's* functions include these:

1. Dealing with nonverbal ideas
2. Dealing with spatial concepts, including depth perception and sensitivity to geometric forms
3. Dealing with simple uses of words and simple mathematical concepts
4. Visualizing
5. Engaging in deductive reasoning, that is, inferring specific instances based on known general principles
6. Engaging in holistic thinking
7. Dealing with gross motor coordination
8. Making sensory discriminations, such as recognizing environmental sounds and detecting tactile patterns
9. Performing mechanical types of information processing
10. Perceiving perceptual relationships

Some educators have looked at these findings to determine if there are implications for instructing students. Based on the functions of each hemisphere as described above, they have postulated that a "left-brained" person would be more academic and well organized and that a "right-brained" individual would be more successful in creative and physical endeavors. These educators are more concerned about "right-brained" students because they believe that typical instruction favors the types of learning in which a "left-brained" individual is more proficient. They have even raised the question whether reading or other learning disabilities may be the result of teaching students with a dominant right hemisphere in ways inconsistent with the way they learn best.

Although neuroscientists have made major advances in understanding brain functions, complete and definitive evidence about many neurological functions does not exist, and many scientists hold contrasting views. Furthermore, understanding the implications these findings have for education is little more than speculation. Even though it may eventually be established that certain functions do indeed occur in one hemisphere or the other, the notion that one hemisphere works more efficiently than the other in some individuals is only a guess.

While the concept of "left-brained" versus "right-brained" is an interesting idea, well-constructed neural research is needed to support this hypothesis. Further, if research does show that certain individuals have a strong hemispheric dominance, then well-controlled educational research, confirmed by many replications of the studies, is needed to determine if specific types of educational experiences enhance learning for individuals with a specific hemispheric dominance. Some suggestions made for teaching "right-brained" students are

1. Provide many exposures to the material to be learned.
2. Teach in a one-to-one situation so the student can focus attention on the task at hand.
3. Use dramatization to aid learning.
4. Use stories, puppets, and poetry.
5. Use audiotapes, films, and pictures.
6. Teach students to finish a task.
7. Allow students to manipulate materials.
8. Use peer modeling.
9. Have students deal with real situations.
10. Provide many opportunities for correct responses; do not let students practice errors.

As can be seen, these suggestions would enhance the learning of *any* student and simply reflect good teaching practice. Teachers should not regard unresearched suggestions for matching teaching activities to an inferred hemispheric preference as representing a panacea for reading problems. Indeed, many reading educators believe that reading is a "whole brain" activity. For example, as Zutell (1985) states,

> Reading is primarily a means of communicating through written language. As such, it is best understood as a "whole brain" activity. While disconnection of particular cortical regions may disrupt reading ability in some cases, effective reading requires the integration of both sequential and parallel, holistic processes. Consequently, fluent reading and learning to read are activities which depend on perceptual and conceptual relationships. (p. 37)

Neuroscientists also agree that many activities require an integration of hemispheric functions; that is, each hemisphere must use part of the other side's knowledge to solve certain types of problems.

Memory

Theorists postulate the existence of three stages in acquiring information. First, information is contained in a perceptual stage, called *sensory store;* after the eye picks it up, information theoretically remains in sensory store for 1 or 2 seconds while the brain makes some decisions about it. Next, information from sensory store is selected and stored in *short-term memory*, which is also called *working memory*. Working memory processes information, holds it until it is stored in *long-term memory*, or sometimes loses information (if it is not important enough to store in long-term memory, or because short-term memory is overloaded). Finally, information is transferred from short-term memory to long-term memory by being associated with previously stored information. The information in long-term memory is our continuous knowledge of the world (F. Smith, 1982).

A number of researchers have investigated whether aberrations in memory processes may be a cause of difficulty in learning to read. Daneman and Carpenter (1980), for example, suggest that differences in reading comprehension abilities may stem from differences in facility of use of short-term memory. Their research showed that poor readers' short-term memories were less *efficient* than good readers'; the poor readers processed and stored less information.

Another difference between good and poor readers may be the *speed* with which they can remember graphic information. In Jackson's (1980) study with young adults, better readers had better memory reaction times than poor readers. However, the speed with which readers can retrieve the pronunciation (and meaning) of a word from long-term memory has been correlated with reading fluency, but not with comprehension (Daneman, 1991).

Furthermore, some research seems to indicate that poor readers have less available *capacity* in their working memories than better readers (Daneman & Green, 1986). This may occur because the poor readers have not developed automatic use of certain reading processes, and, therefore, working memory must divide its actions among several processing functions. For example, reading educators today recognize the importance of automatic word recognition so that processing efforts can be freed for comprehending the messages in a text.

The lower a student's mental age, the less able is the student to handle the memory tasks required in reading. Of course, a low mental age may simply be correlated to a low chronological age—an average 7-year-old is expected to have an MA of 7, not 9 or 10. If classroom expectations are not reasonably matched to students' MAs, the students may have difficulties remembering what is taught.

Students with lower-than-average IQs will have MAs lower than their chronological ages; basing reading requirements for these students on those generally expected of students of their chronological age may result in failure. Many researchers have shown that short-term memory facility, in particular, varies with intelligence. Students with lower than average IQs need to be taught how to use rehearsal strategies, such as verbal association and labeling, to help them retain information in short-term memory long enough to process it for long-term memory. Interestingly, long-term memory facility appears to be less affected by intelligence; if teaching is geared to students' abilities, students with lower-than-average intelligence will forget no more than their average peers.

There is a major hindrance for the practitioner in determining if a student's reading disability is caused by faulty memory: many tests purporting to assess memory are only partially related to the memory requirements of reading. Many test batteries available to reading specialists and school psychologists assess only short-term auditory and visual memory. Short-term memory is necessary to reading, but long-term memory is also of importance. Commonly used published tests do not provide any insight into problems of storage and retrieval in a disabled reader's long-term memory.

What is more, results from short-term memory tasks may not provide any useful information to shed light on a reading disability. A case in point would be certain tests of auditory memory. The term **auditory memory** has been used to describe the ability to store in the brain what is heard and then to later recall this (Lerner, 1981). In IQ tests and some reading tests, assessment of auditory memory is conducted by having students repeat the *order* of a series of numerals, nonsense syllables, words, or sentences after they have been stated orally to the students. The Detroit Tests of Learning Aptitude includes such a subtest. Well-known intelligence tests, such as the Stanford-Binet Intelligence Scale, the Wechsler Intelligence Scale for Children–Revised (WISC-R), and the Wechsler Adult Intelligence Scale, also employ such tasks and refer to them as tests of digit span or auditory memory span. Most research investigating the relationship between these subtests and reading ability has shown the correlations are usually low or nonexistent. For example, certain studies have shown that poor readers have performed better than good readers on the memory subtests of the Stanford-Binet, and disabled readers have scored high on the WISC-R digit span test. In addition, attempts to improve scores on auditory memory tasks have resulted in improved scores on the tests, but with no accompanying improvement in reading ability. Although specific students with reading disabilities may score low on such tests, this is clearly a case of correlation, not causation.

Much of the research that discusses the role of memory in reading is based on a **stage model** of cognitive processing, a model in which the brain (mind) processes information through several stages from the time of input to the time of output or storage. Analyzing the acquisition of information into sensory store, short-term memory, and long-term memory is an example of a stage model. Others might diagram the stages in this way: (a) feature analysis; (b) short-term memory mechanism; (c) additional processing, such as determining underlying meaning; (d) decision making; and (e) response (D. A. Norman, 1984). But psychologists, like reading educators, hold many opposing views, and other models of memory are available. Criticisms of the stage model include the manner in which information is supposedly encoded (Kroll, Parks, Parkinson, Bieber, & Johnson, 1970), the view of effects of recent learning and retention (Bjork & Whitten, 1974), and assumptions about the storage capacity of short-term memory (Craik & Lockhart, 1972). Some of these memory theories may have important applications to reading. Other researchers will probably continue to explore these areas.

Other Cognitive Processes

Deficits in some other cognitive processes have been proposed as candidates for causing reading disability: *associative learning* (the ability to associate one thing with another); *pattern analysis* (noting that a pattern remains the same in more than one place); *attention* (the ability to attend to distinguishing features, dependent on acquired knowledge and motivation); and *serial memory* (retaining the order in which things occur). However, because disabled readers do not have difficulties in applying these general processes to types of learning other than reading, the notion of reading disability as caused by difficulties in these areas has been discounted (see Vellutino & Denckla, 1991).

LANGUAGE FACTORS

Reading is a language-based activity. The three major aspects of oral language are **phonemes** (sounds), **syntax** (sentence structure), and **semantics** (meaning). In written language, a fourth is added, namely, **graphemes** (letters). Deficits in syntactic and semantic aspects of language processing have been associated with reading disability. For example, poor readers more often than skilled readers fail to distinguish between syntactically appropriate and inappropriate sentence structures (Vellutino & Scanlon, 1987), and lack of knowledge of word meanings (semantic knowledge) has been suggested as causing reading difficulties at the comprehension level (Vellutino & Denckla, 1991). However, the area most strongly associated with reading problems is phonological. Differences in **phonological recoding skill** (or more simply put, skill in using letter-sound relationships to identify unknown words) have been shown to account for individual differences in reading ability for readers of all ages (Fredrickson, 1982; Stanovich, 1986), affecting not only their word recognition, but often their comprehension as well.

Phonemic Awareness

Our writing system in English is based on the **alphabetic principle**: written words are made up of letters that have approximate matches with the sounds heard in these words when we speak. One important aspect of learning to read is to understand how written language and oral language correspond in this way.

To understand the alphabetic principle, first one must recognize that *spoken words consist of a sequence of sounds;* this understanding is called **phonemic awareness** (Ball & Blachman, 1991). The concept that words are made up of sounds is not necessarily an easy one for students to grasp because when we speak we only rarely pay conscious attention to the sounds we make; rather, we are simply concerned with getting our messages across. Phonemic awareness is not really very important to our purposes in spoken language, but it becomes central in learning to read.

There is direct evidence that lack of phonemic awareness is a major cause of word identification difficulties (Vellutino & Denckla, 1991). Phonemic awareness permits students to use letter-sound correspondences, employ phonic strategies, and identify unknown words more quickly (Griffith & Olson, 1992; Treiman & Baron, 1983). Phonemic awareness also may have a bearing on whole-word learning as well (Tunmer, Herriman, & Nesdale, 1988). In addition, phonemic awareness is a prerequisite to *spelling and writing,* which also require hearing and matching sounds. Phonemic awareness is now viewed as a critical variable in emergent literacy (Sulzby & Teale, 1991) and beginning reading acquisition (Juel, 1991). Recognizing that words can be broken into phonemes and syllables, and being able to manipulate these, has a high correlation with reading achievement (Lundberg, Frost, & Petersen, 1988; Perfetti, Beck, Bell, & Hughes, 1987). Research has shown that phonemic awareness is a more powerful determiner than intelligence in predicting whether students will be successful in reading; it is also a stronger predictor than "general" language proficiency (Lomax & McGee, 1987). The importance of phonemic awareness holds regardless of the type of instructional methodology employed. For example, Klesius, Griffith, and Zielonka (1991) compared a whole-language reading instructional program with a traditional first-grade program and found that neither produced hoped-for results with children who lacked phonemic awareness; likewise, when phonemic awareness was sufficiently developed, students achieved equally well in either program.

It is not surprising, then, that a large body of research recently conducted in the United States and in other countries indicates that one of the most significant discriminators between good and poor readers is poor readers' lack of phonemic awareness (for example, see L. Bradley & Bryant, 1985; Cossu, Shankweiler, Liberman, Katz, & Tola,

1988; Juel, 1988; Juel, Griffith, & Gough, 1986; Morais, Cluytens, Alegria, & Content, 1984; Pratt & Brady, 1988; Stanovich, Nathan, & Zolman, 1988; Torneus, 1984; Vellutino & Scanlon, 1987; J. Williams, 1984). Moreover, this holds true regardless of the intelligence level or socioeconomic status of the students.

On the strength of this research, there is little doubt that lack of phonemic awareness is a cause of reading disabilities in a large portion of students whose difficulties lie with word recognition. Phonemic awareness is a *prerequisite* to adequate word recognition abilities, but, also, more advanced understandings about phonemic awareness develop as a *result* of reading and writing. Because low-achieving students usually read and write less than other readers, the effects are cyclical.

Yopp (1988) has identified two levels of phonemic awareness: (a) *simple phonemic awareness* and (b) *compound phonemic awareness.*

The knowledge that words can be broken into phonemes and syllables is evident when students can perform these simple phonemic awareness tasks: (a) **isolation of a sound** (e.g., being able to give the first sound in *camel* after hearing the word pronounced); (b) **blending** (being able, in oral language, to combine separate sounds into a word, e.g., when given the sounds /h/ /a/ /m/[1] being able to produce *ham*); (c) **segmentation** (being able to tell the sounds heard in a word, e.g., after hearing the word *bat* pronounced, and being able to identify the *sounds* in the word). Simple phonemic awareness is an important *prerequisite* to reading and writing.

Compound phonemic awareness involves two operations. Examples of compound phonemic awareness tasks are (1) **phoneme deletion** (being able to isolate a sound in a word and blend the remaining sounds, e.g., responding correctly when asked, "What word would be left if the /r/ were taken away from the middle of *brake?*") and (2) **word-to-word matching** (being able to isolate a sound in a certain position in two words, and, compare the sounds, e.g., responding correctly when asked, "Do *dog* and *dime* begin the same?"). Compound phonemic awareness seems to *result* from reading experience, but may be important for *further* advancement in reading and writing.

For disabled readers who are experiencing serious difficulties in developing word recognition and in acquiring word identification strategies, it is important that teachers assess their phonemic awareness. Tests of phonemic awareness are discussed in Chapter 6. Although phonemic awareness is considered a linguistic (i.e., language) skill, it also clearly requires cognitive skill. However, there is evidence that phonemic awareness does not simply occur with maturation or age, but, instead, results from certain experiences. Furthermore, research indicates that phonemic awareness *can* be trained. This is good news! Chapter 10 presents suggestions from research for providing instruction that will enhance phonemic awareness.

Oral Language Knowledge

Readers use knowledge of oral language when they read. They determine if what they have just read "sounds right." If it does not, that is, if it is not syntactically or semantically correct, the good reader usually rereads and self-corrects. Although all readers can use oral language knowledge when reading, many poor readers do not. When students

---

[1]The convention that has been adopted in several fields is to indicate *sounds* by placing the letter between two parallel lines like this: / /

Children who are read aloud to on a regular basis have greater knowledge of the syntactic patterns of written language than those who have not had the benefit of such experiences.

lack the intuitive use of this strategy or receive no direct instruction to make up for this lack, they may demonstrate reading difficulties. Grammatical sensitivity (both syntactic and semantic) has been found to be significantly related to reading skill (Willows & Ryan, 1986).

There are more similarities than differences between oral and written language. If this were not so, a reader would not be aided by knowledge of oral language in reading. However, there are also important differences that have implications for teaching reading. Written language is not simply "talk written down," as some teachers have told their students. Certain types of sentence patterns encountered in written language are seldom, if ever, used in oral language. Making this point, McCormick and Moe (1982) give examples of dialogue structures that are found only in written language.

"There's a hole in my pocket," laughed Joey.

"In the morning," Pete yelled up to his brother, "I'll show you how to throw a fast ball." (p. 49)

Because patterns like these are not employed in oral language, students are less able to use their oral language knowledge in self-correction. To deal with problems caused by the incongruency between oral and written language, students must gain as much familiarity with written language as they have with oral language. This is best accomplished by reading aloud to children. Young children who have had books read aloud to them frequently and regularly during the preschool years come to school able to respond to written language structures, as well as to oral language. Students who have not been exposed to the more elaborate formal code of written language lack an important experience, which may contribute to a reading disability.

A study previously cited in Chapter 2 indicated that differences between the oral language dialects of nonstandard English speakers and of standard English do not affect reading achievement. Other studies have also shown this to be true. At one time, there was much interest in preparing reading materials in the nonstandard dialects of the students who were to use them, and a number of publishers developed materials of this type. In the end, the materials proved not to be useful in increasing the reading achievement of nonstandard dialect speakers.

Many reading materials actually do contain language that is divergent from the oral language of any speaker. For example:

> See me. See me go. See me go up.
>
> Dan, the big man, has a fan.

Furthermore, divergences between oral and written language will always exist whether a speaker's dialect is standard or nonstandard, as was shown in the McCormick and Moe work cited above.

A student's nonstandard dialect may not contribute to reading difficulties if language differences are handled appropriately. Too often, however, teachers mistake a language difference for a reading error. Teachers' misperceptions of what constitutes reading skill can lead to erroneous evaluations of students' true abilities if teachers do not take into account language differences.

Some researchers have attempted to change the language of students to "correct" the mismatch between oral language and the language of texts, for example, programs in use of standard English with Black dialect speakers. These programs have not brought about an increase in *reading* achievement. Some commercial language development programs are designed to teach students to speak only in complete sentences. These programs assume that the failure of students, particularly low socioeconomic status (SES) students, to do so makes it difficult for them to contend with the more formal sentence structures they encounter in written material. However, teaching students to use written language structures in their oral language is unnecessary, since, for all speakers, oral language patterns are more informal. Short phrases or even single words appropriately serve as complete communication exchanges in oral language. For example, a friend might say, "What did you have for lunch today?" and you might simply respond, "Chili." It is unnecessary to say, "I had chili for lunch today." Incomplete sentences occur frequently in oral language, even the language of well-educated adults. Oral and written language patterns are well suited to their special purposes, and it is unnatural and inappropriate to train students to speak in atypical ways. Furthermore, to do so does not help their reading ability.

Other myths have developed about the relationship of language problems and their effect on reading ability. One myth is that low SES students are poor readers because they are less verbal. Sometimes this does appear to be so in formal testing situations because students are unfamiliar with the examiner and the testing environment; but when they are tested in more familiar settings, low SES students are found to be highly verbal. Another myth is that low SES students have deficient oral vocabularies that interfere with learning to read in the early grades. Although research does indicate that low SES children have more limited vocabularies than middle-class children, it is believed that this research may be an underestimate of students' true abilities. Even if these underestimates are correct, it has been shown that low SES students do have the oral vocabulary knowledge necessary to deal with the words found in the most widely used beginning books.

READING HISTORY

There is strong research suggestion from a multiplicity of areas that a student's reading history is a major source of poor reading ability.

If a young child experiences difficulty in learning the strategies that allow for word identification, this prevents the child from reading ample amounts of connected text, which is important to reading success. For example, able readers in the middle of first grade may read almost five times as much during a reading instruction session as the poorest readers in the class (Allington, 1984a). This greater volume of reading practice permits automatic word recognition to develop more readily, improves knowledge of the complex syntactic structures of written language, and contributes to acquisition of broader background information, development of word meanings, and improved comprehension. Students who do not learn word identification strategies early do not have these advantages and fall further and further behind their peers. Small differences between individual children develop into larger and larger differences. Educators now use the term **Matthew effects** (e.g., Stanovich, 1986) to describe this occurrence, based on reference to a biblical text in the book of Matthew alluding to the "rich getting richer and the poor getting poorer."

The following tracing of events illustrates the series of interrelated, negative cycles in the history of many disabled readers:

- Genetic factors and/or environmental factors in the preschool years may lead to low phonemic awareness.
- Low phonemic awareness leads to difficulty in establishing word identification strategies.
- Lack of word identification strategies leads to less volume in text reading.
- Less text reading leads to lack of development of automatic word recognition.
- Lack of automatic word recognition leads to slow and laborious reading.
- Slow and laborious reading leads again to less text covered when students are required to read in instructional settings, *and* to lack of motivation to engage in independent reading (and therefore, again, to less text covered).
- Less text covered also means fewer word meanings learned from the context of reading material, less understanding of written syntactic structures, and less background knowledge base built from information found in texts.
- Excessive attention to decoding words because of lack of automatic word recognition distracts concentration from comprehending the text. Limited knowledge of word meanings inhibits comprehension. Lack of familiarity with written syntactic structures inhibits comprehension. Lack of a sufficient background knowledge base detracts from comprehension.
- Less text covered leads to slower progress in general reading achievement.

Slower progress in general reading achievement also appears to lead to more generalized cognitive and linguistic deficits (Stanovich, 1986). Many students who enter school with no measured deficiencies in memory, intelligence, or language begin to show evidence of deficits in these areas as the time goes on during which they make limited progress in reading. Stanovich (1986) describes these deficiencies as "behavioral/cognitive/motivational spinoffs from failure at . . . reading" (p. 389). The longer the enfeebling reading history continues without successful remediation, the more these other areas are affected. Therefore, a number of authorities today believe that many of the deficient cognitive and language factors shown to be associated with reading disability are actually *results* of limited reading progress and are not initial *causes* of this difficulty. This is particularly true of memory factors (Brainerd, Kingma, & Howe, 1986), verbal intelligence (Bishop & Butterworth, 1980), and knowledge of meaning vocabulary, written syntactic structures, and background information (Stanovich, 1986).

Stanovich (1986) suggests prevention and amelioration of the serious reading history problem should be undertaken through (a) early identification and remediation of severely underdeveloped phonemic awareness in beginning readers and (b) large amounts and extended practice of connected text reading. It is predicted that incorporation of these two features into reading programs will counter the cumulative disadvantage that is one of the major causes of reading disability—that is, debilitating reading histories that progressively weaken an individual's ability to develop.

CONCLUSION

Chapters 2 and 3 have discussed possible causes and correlates of reading difficulties. Obviously this is a complex topic, and we still lack many answers about the roots of reading disabilities, as well as other learning disabilities. However, it should be clear that those who propose simple hypotheses for the causes of reading difficulties are unfamiliar with all of the issues involved.

REFLECTIONS

Suppose you have been asked to deliver a short presentation to the PTA or PTO at your school about the causes of reading disability. As a group, decide on main points to be made. Have someone write these on the chalkboard as suggestions are offered by the group. Consider the following: (a) What do you believe will be the parents' major questions? (b) What do *you* think is important for them to know? and (c) What common misconceptions—for example, such as often presented by the media—will you want to address?

This activity will require that you select important concepts and summarize the somewhat lengthy discussions of topics found in Chapters 2 and 3. Summarization aids understanding and promotes recall. Summarization is an activity you should also use with your own students in comprehension instruction.

ASSESSMENT

4

Assessment for Identification of Reading Problems

Assessment should be carried out over time, in various settings and social contexts, and while students are reading for different purposes.

Assessment is the total process of collecting information to make instructional decisions. Testing is one part of assessment. Technically, the terms *testing, measurement,* and *assessment* have different meanings. According to Calfee (1993 pp. 3–5), *testing* relates to whether items are known by a student; *measurement* refers to assigning numbers to a performance based on an established standard; and *assessment,* while also having to do with student performance, is thought to influence curriculum and instruction. In common practice, however, the terms are often used interchangeably.

Formal assessment uses **standardized tests.** One common kind of standardized test is called *norm-referenced.* These are published tests for which norms based on the performances of large numbers of students have been developed. Norms allow educators and others to compare the performances of students with those of a sample group. Sometimes *criterion-referenced* also are standardized. You will learn about criterion-referenced testing in a later chapter.

Informal assessment employs many types of nonstandardized measures, such as teacher-prepared tests; daily, ongoing observations; published informal inventories; checklists; interest inventories; measurements of attitudes or habits; interviews with other teachers, the student, and parents. More and more often teachers are helping student engage in self-evaluations of their reading and writing products and performance (Afflerbach & Kapinus, 1993; Rauch & Fillenworth, 1993). Currently many of these measures are assembled into a student *portfolio,* allowing assessment of *change* over time. Unfortunately, there has been less research on these informal measures than on formal assessment procedures, but currently more studies are being undertaken.

Table 4–1 shows the general characteristics of formal and informal assessments.

Examples of formal and informal assessment procedures are interspersed throughout all chapters in Unit 2. The examples are placed to reflect the pattern and sequence that teachers in real school or clinic settings generally use. Introducing the assessment procedures in order of need seems more useful than discussing formal and informal tests in separate sections (as is often done). The organization in this book, therefore, provides both a scope and a sequence for diagnostic procedures. Unit 2 has the following organization:

TABLE 4–1
Types of reading assessment

Formal Assessment/ Standardized Tests	Informal Assessment/ Nonstandardized Procedures
A. Group tests	A. Group procedures

1. Used for determining reading levels
   2. Used for determining specific strengths and weaknesses in strategies, knowledge, and skills
	1. Used for determining reading levels
	   2. Used for determining specific strengths and weaknesses in strategies, knowledge, and skills

B. Individual tests	B. Individual procedures

1. Used for determining reading levels
   2. Used for determining specific strengths and weaknesses in strategies, knowledge, and skills
	1. Used for determining reading levels
	   2. Used for determining specific strengths and weaknesses in strategies, knowledge, and skills

- This chapter presents information about assessment techniques that are often used *before* students enter a special reading program. These techniques are employed to determine eligibility for placement in a Title I or other remedial reading class, an LD program, or a reading clinic.
- Chapter 5, the next chapter, discusses the first type of assessment usually conducted once students are enrolled in a program—assessment to determine or confirm reading level.
- Chapters 6 and 7 present a variety of tests that are often used next in the assessment process. These are used to determine specific reading and writing strengths and weaknesses. Chapters 6 and 7 also discuss measures of interest and attitude so that teachers can structure environments that facilitate learning.

SOME GENERAL ISSUES RELATED TO ASSESSMENT

Formal Testing Versus Informal Testing

Periodically there are tensions between educators who advocate formal testing and those who prefer informal testing. For most authorities, however, what is desired is a "reasonable and appropriate balance" between the two (Afflerbach & Kapinus, 1993; Calfee & Hiebert, 1991); a recognition of the weaknesses—and strengths—inherent in each type; and selection of those tests that are best in their category, whether that category be formal or informal. A recent publication by the U.S. Department of Education (Sweet, 1993) endorses the notion that the most useful assessments of literacy assessment, regardless of category, reflect our present understandings of the reading and writing processes and approximate authentic literacy tasks. Assessment procedures that are selected must reflect the complexity of literacy learning (Johnston, Nolan, & Berry, 1993).

In addition, there must be an understanding of the specific purpose for which each category of test is best suited. For example, Figure 4–1 presents Farr's (1992) description of assessment audiences—that is, what it is that different groups or individuals legitimately need to know from tests and what types of tests are most suitable for providing that information.

The Appropriate Interpretation of Test Scores

Teachers using any type of assessment must realize that scores provided by tests are generally approximations. For example, a student who receives an IQ score of 94 on an intelligence test may have an intelligence quotient close to 94, ranging a few points above or below this obtained score, but the obtained score should not be viewed as exact. An important concept that educators must understand when using any formal assessment procedures is that of **standard error of measurement.** This term refers to the principle that scores provided by tests are only estimations of an individual's "true" score, and that there is a range of scores in which a student's true score lies. For example, if the standard error for a specific test is 5, then the true score for a student taking this test probably lies somewhere in a range between a score 5 points *below* and 5 points *above* the score actually obtained on the test. Let's take this hypothetical case: Jerry's computed score on a standardized reading test is 3.5. However, since the standard error of measurement for this particular test is 7, his "true" score could lie anywhere between 2.8 (7 points below 3.5) and 4.2 (7 points above 3.5). Test manuals

FIGURE 4–1
Assessment audiences

Audiences	The Information Is Needed to	The Information Is Related to	Type of Information	When Information Is Needed
General public (and the press)	Judge if schools are accountable and effective	Groups of students	Related to broad goals; norm- and criterion-referenced	Annually
School administrators/staff	Judge effectiveness of curriculum, materials, teachers	Groups of students and individuals	Related to broad goals; criterion- and norm-referenced	Annually or by term/semester
Parents	Monitor progress of child, effectiveness of school	Individual student	Usually related to broader goals; both criterion- and norm-referenced	Periodically; 5 or 6 times a year
Teachers	Plan instruction, strategies, activities	Individual student; small groups	Related to specific goals; primarily criterion-referenced	Daily, or as often as possible
Students	Identify strengths, areas to emphasize	Individual (self)	Related to specific goals; criterion-referenced	Daily, or as often as possible

Source: From "Putting It All Together: Solving the Reading Assessment Puzzle" by R. Farr, 1992, *The Reading Teacher, 46,* p. 29. Copyright 1992 by the International Reading Association. Reprinted by permission of Roger Farr and the International Reading Association.

report (or should report) the standard error of measurement for their test. For example, the publishers of the Gates-MacGinitie Reading Tests (3rd ed.), a group survey standardized reading test, include error of measurement data in their *Technical Report*, provided with the test.

Remembering that test scores are estimates also is important when using informal measures. For example, when the reading potential (also called reading expectancy) for a student is determined to be 6.0 based on an informal listening comprehension test, this means it is *approximately* sixth-grade level, and so forth. Assigning numerical scores to human abilities is not an exact science by any means. A score derived from an assessment instrument represents a good "ballpark" figure and is helpful because it gives us a place to begin when making instructional or placement decisions. It should never, however, be interpreted as definitive.

Especially in regard to informal assessment, MacGinitie (1993, pp. 556–558) highlights several common types of biases that come into play in appraisals of human performance:

When students take either formal or informal tests, teachers should be aware that assigning numerical scores to human abilities is not an exact science by any means.

1. *Assimilation bias.* The tendency to base judgments on early evidence and ignore evidence obtained later
2. *Category bias.* Once we believe a person fits into a category because of some attributes, the tendency to assign all attributes ascribed to the category to the person
3. *Confirmation bias.* The tendency to hold to beliefs, thus failing to look for other possibilities
4. *Contrast bias.* The tendency to exaggerate the differences between earlier and later findings
5. *Negativity bias.* The tendency to allow negative statements or information to take a disproportionate influence over positive.

In addition, sometimes scores obtained from a single test may simply be wrong (Farr & Carey, 1986; P. H. Johnston, 1983). When Stephanie receives a score of 75 on an IQ test, but all her academic behaviors indicate she is functioning above the mildly retarded range, it is likely that factors other than intelligence have depressed her test score. Perhaps she was feeling ill the day she was tested, or perhaps the examiner was not skillful in administering the test. Sometimes teachers say something like, "Juan's standardized test score indicated he is reading at fourth-grade level and I don't understand this because he is having no difficulty handling fifth-grade material in my class." They seem reluctant to rely on their own observations if these do not agree with results of formal testing. Tests are helpful starting places when selected and administered properly, but their scores should be interpreted in light of other available evidence, especially teacher observation.

Because of limitations of tests and other assessments procedures, MacGinitie (1993) emphasizes the need to be tentative in our decisions. Decisions should be reappraised periodically, recognizing the biases inherent in both formal and informal evaluations. Furthermore, achievement should not be confused with ability (Cooter, 1993); in remedial students in particular, the two often are not synonymous.

Furthermore, reading assessment should be carried out over a period of time, conducted in various settings and social contexts, and undertaken while students are

TABLE 4–2
Types of scores provided by common standardized tests

Raw Score	**Grade Equivalent**
The number of questions a pupil has answered correctly on each subtest or on the total test. Raw scores mean little, but provide the basis for determining more helpful scores.	The grade equivalent score obtained is the score expected of the average student at the grade level designated. For example, a score of 4.2 indicates that the student scored at the same level as the average student in the group used for norming who was in the second month of fourth grade.
Percentile Score	**Stanine**
Tells the percentage of students in the norming group who had scores lower or higher than this student's score. A percentile score of 55, for example, means that 55% of the group on which the test was normed scored lower. Should not be used for determining growth.	A statistical interpretation of percentile score useful in examining an individual's score.
Normal Curve Equivalent (NCE)	**Extended Scale Score**
A statistical interpretation of percentile score useful in examining group performance. Unlike percentile scores, these scores have been transformed into equal units of achievement. Often used in Title I programs.	Scores that can be used to follow a student's achievement over an extended time—even for several years. Not provided by all standardized test manuals.

reading for various purposes. Interpretations often are different and more accurate when this is done, and frequently are in contrast to interpretations that rely merely on a single measure. It is especially important that students' behaviors be assessed while they are engaged in real reading in authentic texts, and not just when they are taking tests.

ISSUES RELATED TO FORMAL ASSESSMENT

The first assessment task of a reading teacher is to identify those students who warrant remedial services. This is called *assessment for identification*. Since a good deal of assessment for identification involves use of formal measures (that is, use of standardized tests) teachers should be aware of limitations of these tests, as well as advantages if they have been properly selected, administered, and interpreted.

Judging the Merits of Test Quality

Two types of standardized tests are frequently administered to students with reading problems.

1. **Survey tests** are designed to determine students' general reading levels.

2. **Diagnostic tests** are used to analyze a student's specific strengths and weaknesses in reading strategies, knowledge, and skills.

Teachers need to consider many factors when they choose a standardized survey or diagnostic test. Some factors are practical ones. For example, a teacher may ask, "Is the time needed for administration reasonable since I have many students to assess?" Issues related to the technical acceptability of tests also are of crucial importance. If a test has not been properly devised, the results may be meaningless, and consequently, valuable time may be wasted—and, even more serious, a student's instructional program may be based on incorrect information.

The technical acceptability of a test is built on three factors: norms, validity, and reliability.

Norms. **Norms** are scores that represent an average and are used for comparing one student with other students. Test makers develop norms by administering their test to a large sample of individuals. To develop adequate norms, they must use a sample of students who are similar in age, IQ range, and general characteristics to the group with whom the published test is to be used. Most test publishers also try to select their sample from urban, suburban, and rural areas—and if they are attempting to develop **national norms,** that is, norms based on a nationwide sample, from all regions of the country. (**Local norms,** based on data from certain schools or certain areas, are occasionally used instead of national norms.) Based on the performances of students in the sample, **grade norms,** that is, the average score of students from a given grade level, are determined. Test manuals should report the characteristics of the sample on which the test was normed so teachers can determine if the test is appropriate for their students. In addition, norms must be revised at least every 15 years to remain current.

Validity. The **validity** of a test is the degree to which it measures what it claims to measure. **Content validity** is the extent to which a test assesses the whole class of subject matter about which conclusions will be made.[1] An example of a test sometimes used in reading assessment that lacks content validity is one consisting simply of a list of isolated words that students read orally. These tests purport to specify a student's instructional level based on this performance and claim to measure general reading ability. However, they obviously do not measure all factors involved in real reading. Some other types of validity are **construct validity** (the degree to which performance on a test actually predicts the extent to which an individual possesses a trait), **concurrent validity** (the degree to which performance on a test predicts performance on a criterion external to that test), and **predictive validity** (the extent to which a test predicts future performance in an area). Test manuals should report evidence of validity.

Reliability. The **reliability** of a test relates to the degree of consistency of its scores. In other words, if a student took the same test more than once, would he or she make approximately the same score every time? Test makers can determine a reliability coefficient for a test by such methods as computing a coefficient of correlation between two alternate forms of the test or between scores obtained from repeated administration of the same test. Adequate reliability coefficients for a test used to compare groups should be above 0.60, but should be *above 0.90 if used for diagnostic purposes with individual students* (Salvia & Ysseldyke, 1982). Reliability coefficients should be reported in test manuals.

---

[1]Definitions obtained from Farr & Carey (1986)

Before administering a test, teachers should examine the accompanying manual for information on norming procedures, validity, and reliability. Buros, who edited the Mental Measurements Yearbooks for 40 years, stated that one of his goals was "to make test users aware of the importance of being suspicious of all tests—even those produced by well-known authors and publishers—which are not accompanied by detailed data on their construction, validation, uses, and limitations" (Mitchell, 1985, p. xiv). Table 4–3 details some of the flaws in well-known published reading tests.

Advantages of Standardized Tests

Generally, standardized tests save time since they may be administered to many students simultaneously. Group tests may also be used with individual students. In addition, if a standardized test has been properly devised, the test passages and questions have been tried out with numerous students. Some items are discarded in this process, and new items are tested until a final group of suitable items is chosen. Most teachers do not have the time to prepare tests they design themselves with such thoroughness. In addition, many test makers now monitor **passage dependency,** that is, they take care

TABLE 4–3
Technical inadequacies of some published reading tests

Norms Inappropriately Developed or Information on Norming Group Inadequately Reported	Lack of Validity or Evidence of Validity Inadequately Reported	Low Reliability or Reliability Inadequately Reported
Illinois Test of Psycholinguistic Abilities	Slosson Oral Reading Test	Illinois Test of Psycholinguistic Abilities
Diagnostic Reading Scales	Illinois Test of Psycholinguistic Abilities	Gilmore Oral Reading Test
Gates-McKillop-Horowitz Reading Diagnostic Tests	Gates-McKillop-Horowitz Reading Diagnostic Tests	Durrell Analysis of Reading Difficulty
Silent Reading Diagnostic Test	Gilmore Oral Reading Test	Frostig Developmental Test of Visual Perception
Gilmore Oral Reading Test	Wide Range Achievement Test	
Wide Range Achievement Test	Durrell Analysis of Reading Difficulty	
Wepman Auditory Discrimination Test	Frostig Developmental Test of Visual Perception	
Durrell Analysis of Reading Difficulty		
Frostig Developmental Test of Visual Perception		

Source: Adapted from *Assessment in Special and Remedial Education* (2nd ed.) by J. Salvia and J. E. Ysseldyke, 1982, Boston: Houghton Mifflin. Copyright 1982 by Houghton Mifflin. Adapted by permission.

FIGURE 4–2
Sample test comprehension passage

Level 3

"We're going to have a baby," Lizzie's mother said. "A little brother or sister for Lizzie. The baby will share your room. We'll move out your toy box to make a place for the <u>crib</u>."

"I don't think there's room for a baby," Lizzie said. "Couldn't we have a turtle instead? He'd sleep in a little box under my bed."

1. Who told Lizzie about the baby?

○ Lizzie's father.

○ Lizzie's mother.

○ Lizzie's brother.

○ Lizzie's sister.

2. Lizzie thought that a baby would need too much

○ food. ○ sleep.

○ time. ○ space.

3. Where will the baby's <u>crib</u> be?

○ In Lizzie's room.

○ In Lizzie's mother's room.

○ Outside.

○ Next to the toy box.

Source: From the Gates-MacGinitie Reading Tests (3rd ed.), Level 3 comprehension practice questions 1–3: From *Couldn't We Have a Turtle Instead* by Judith Vigna. Reprinted with permission of Curtis Brown, Ltd. Text and illustrations copyright 1978 by Judith Vigna. Chicago: Riverside Publishing Company. Copyright 1987–88 by the Riverside Publishing Company. Reprinted by permission.

to ensure that a student must actually read a passage to answer the questions, rather than being able to answer the questions based merely on previous knowledge. Finally, standardized tests are usually available in two or more equivalent forms so that students can be retested to measure growth.

Survey Tests. The general reading achievement levels obtained on survey tests can be used for comparative purposes. Some reasons for comparing students' reading performances with others' are to evaluate the effectiveness of specific instructional procedures and to compare and evaluate programs from different school systems. Group standardized tests can also be used to select students who require remedial programs by comparing their performances with the performances of others. In fact, administration of a standardized test is required for determining eligibility for most LD classes and Title I remedial reading programs.

Diagnostic Tests.   If the grade scores from standardized diagnostic tests are ignored and substituted with an analysis of student performance on specific reading tasks, some helpful diagnostic information may be obtained. As indicated above, grade scores from standardized tests are not very reliable. However, a teacher, with careful reflection about each error and its possible causes, may occasionally find them useful.

Disadvantages of Standardized Tests

There has been an increase in use of standardized tests every decade since the 1950s. Although standardized tests provide useful information if they are applied to the appropriate purpose, there also are disadvantages in using them.

Survey Tests.   Survey tests provide some information about how well a student is performing in reading, for example, specifying an approximate reading *level*. But they do not provide an analysis of *why* the student is performing well or poorly. Although survey tests are usually divided into subtests, the subtests contribute only very general information about individual students' strengths and weaknesses in reading and writing strategies, knowledge, and skills. Diagnostic profiles cannot be developed from students' performance on types of items (e.g., inferential comprehension questions or questions that require recognizing directly stated main ideas), because not enough items of each type are provided to make adequate judgments. In addition, since test passages become increasingly difficult as the student moves from the beginning to the end of the test, some students may miss items simply because the overall difficulty of some passages is above their reading levels, not because they lack the specific skill tested by the items answered incorrectly.

Furthermore, most standardized survey tests do not measure all understandings a student needs in order to perform well on every reading task; for example, the special skills necessary for reading content area texts or for appreciating an author's style may not be included in such tests. Moreover, because passages used are only brief excerpts, the reading task necessary for these tests often does not approximate that of authentic text reading.

Finally, using the grade-level scores obtained on survey tests alone for planning instruction is of somewhat questionable value since both research and practice have shown that scores are often an overestimate of the reading level at which a student can actually function in instructional material.

Diagnostic Tests.   Grade-level scores obtained on many standardized diagnostic tests commonly used in remedial programs vary from test to test and do not provide an accurate index of reading level. One reason for this variance is that criteria for evaluating students' errors differ from test to test (Farr & Carey, 1986).

New Horizons.   To answer some concerns voiced about standardized tests, certain groups recently have directed much effort toward overhauling test instruments in terms of (a) content and (b) *how* students demonstrate their knowledge, strategies, and skills.

Two notable examples are the states of Illinois and Michigan (Pearson & Valencia, 1987; Wixson & Peters, 1987). In these cases, university-based reading authorities, leaders in professional reading associations, and classroom teachers have teamed to develop what may be better assessment instruments. In many circumstances, the typical multiple-choice or similar format items have been retained, but students are required to answer in atypical ways—for example, marking all plausible answers or ranking answers (e.g., 1, 2, 3) according to plausibility. Passages are lengthier than is common in most currently published standardized tests, and, therefore, they more closely resemble authentic texts. Narrative (story-type) selections as well as expository (informational) selections are included, and often each selection is followed by many test items. An emphasis is placed on demonstrating reasoning, and some questions are designed to measure **metacognition**—that is, students' own awareness of the text-processing strategies they are using. Tryouts and changes in formats of these new tests continue. Use of these atypical instruments has been most successful when inservice training has helped teachers understand the rationale and appropriate interpretation of results. These tests may be one step toward improving formal test instruments.

Using Standardized Tests With Students Who Speak Nonstandard Dialects and Those With Limited English Proficiency

Reading Tests.   Another issue about which there has been much concern is the degree to which standardized reading tests are suitable for students who speak nonstandard dialects. Some argue that students should not have to take tests in a dialect they do not speak. Educators voicing this view emphasize the differences between sounds (the phonological system) of standard English and those of nonstandard dialects, believing this puts certain students at a disadvantage. For example, some sound discrimination items found on primary-grade standardized tests are not differentiated in the oral language of a variety of nonstandard dialect speakers. It should be noted, however, that this argument is applicable only to primary-level assessment instruments. Above this level, tests usually do not include items designed to measure how well students can identify letter sounds. Instead, they typically contain components that require whole-word recognition and passage comprehension.

Those who favor use of standardized tests with these students assert that students from nonmainstream cultures are really bidialectal; that is, although they speak a nonstandard form of English, they understand standard English when they hear it. These students obviously grasp standard English sentence structures (the syntactical system) and standard English vocabulary (the semantic system), because they can obtain meaning from standard English utterances in everyday situations.

A further point in the favor of standardized tests is that the overall objective of reading tests and reading programs should be taken into consideration. The material students read in school, and later throughout life, is written in standard English. Therefore, it seems reasonable to test students in standard English to determine just how well they can handle this task and to plan instruction if tests show they do not handle it well.

Finally, a substantial amount of research has shown that in reading testing, as in reading instruction, nonstandard English dialect differences do not play a major role in affecting performance. For example, Hochman (1973) compared African-American and Caucasian third-, fourth-, and fifth-graders' performances on two forms of the California Reading Test. One form was written in standard English; one was written in a Black vernacular dialect. No differences were found in test scores of African-American or Caucasian students on either form; if students did well on one form, they did well on the other, and, likewise, if they did poorly on one, they did poorly on the alternate form.

While variations seen in standardized test performance may be relatively minor for students who speak a nonstandard form of English—with the one exception being those subtests administered in primary grades that tap into phonological aspects of language—there may be greater difficulties for limited English proficient students, especially when comprehension is evaluated. Garcia (1991) examined effectiveness of Hispanic fifth- and sixth-graders of limited English proficiency on a standardized test written in English (the California Tests of Basic Skills). These students performed poorly because they lacked knowledge of vocabulary used in the questions. They also had incomplete background information about a number of topics addressed in the test passages, and this adversely affected their ability to answer inference questions (questions that rely on an individual's prior knowledge, as well as on statements provided in the text). In a follow-up interview with the students in which questions were asked orally, and in which performances were examined on passages with culturally familiar topics, it was found that the standardized test seriously underestimated comprehension abilities of limited English proficient students. This study provides evidence that caution should be taken in using tests for placement and assessment decisions with students not yet proficient in English as a second language, and for whom cultural experiences are inconsistent with those targeted by test makers preparing test passages for students in the educational systems of the United States.

Writing Tests.   Because of the growing recognition of the connections between reading and writing in many of today's classrooms, *standardized* writing tests sometimes are being used to evaluate students and make placement decisions. Care should be taken in interpretation of standardized tests of writing when these have been administered to non-native English speakers. These tests place a relatively heavy emphasis on measuring knowledge of the English syntactical system—knowledge of which limited English proficient students may lack adequate control (S. W. Freedman, 1993). Indirect measures of writing seen on some standardized writing tests, such as multiple-choice items of grammar and other mechanics of English, will not well predict abilities of the limited English proficient students (nor for many others) to express ideas, logically sequence thoughts, and engage in other skills important to producing interesting and effective writing. Many states are now replacing indirect (standardized) measures of writing with direct measurement of students' actual writing samples.

STEPS IN ASSESSMENT FOR IDENTIFICATION

In Chapter 1 of this text, you learned that the most common method for identifying students who need corrective, remedial, or clinical reading services (or placement in an LD program) is to assess a student's *potential* and then to compare this with the student's *present achievement* to determine the degree of discrepancy between the two.

Assessing Potential

Various means have been used to estimate a reading disabled student's **potential** (sometimes called **reading expectancy**)—that is, where the student *should* be achieving if the reading problem did not exist. To understand the concept of potential, let's

A measure of students' understanding after they have listened to material read to them is currently a preferred method for assessing potential.

consider a hypothetical case, Teddy, who is in the fourth grade, has average intelligence, no neurological difficulties, and no sensory deficits (e.g., he has no hearing or visual impairments). One might expect, given this information, that Teddy would be reading at the level of other average fourth-graders—or, another way to say this is that his *potential* would be fourth grade (sometimes expressed as 4.0).

But, what of students who have significantly less-than-average intelligence? It would be atypical for such students to be reading at a level similar to students of average ability who are at their same grade levels. And, what of intellectually gifted youngsters? Their potentials surely are greater than the typical student; that is, a student with an intelligence quotient 30 points above the norm, for example, would certainly be expected to be reading *above* grade level—this student's potential would be higher than that of the average student. What would a good estimate of that potential be? Should we expect a seventh-grade student with an IQ of 140, for example, to be reading at eighth-grade level? ninth? tenth? Or, what would be a useful estimate of potential for the student with an intelligence quotient 15 or 20 points below the average?

Intelligence seems to come into the question often when the problem of determining an individual's potential for achievement is addressed. For this reason, several different mathematical formulas for estimating potential have been developed using an individual's intelligence quotient (IQ) score, or a numerical representation of a related concept such as mental age (MA), in the equation. For example, until recently it was common practice to use the Horn formula (e.g., see Burns, 1982) in which MA plus chronological age were the two factors considered to determine **learning expectancy level** (yet another name for *potential*). In the Bond and Tinker (1979) formula, IQ and number of years in school are used instead. In a number of states today, students' eligibility for learning disability programs is predicated on a discrepancy of two standard deviations or more between their intelligence levels and their present achievement levels.

However, lately, there has been serious question about the wisdom of basing estimates of potential so heavily on scores obtained from intelligence tests, a concern voiced both by authorities in the LD field (Siegel, 1989) and in the literacy profession (Stanovich, 1991a). The arguments made against use of IQ scores include (a) the lack of consensus about appropriate means for measuring intelligence; (b) the growing conviction that scores on presently available intelligence tests reflect only *current* intellectual functioning, and not what this functioning might potentially be; (c) the fact that being a poor reader seems to cause poor performance on IQ tests (even when the individual is not required to do any reading), because reading, itself, promotes various cognitive abilities; and (d) the recognition that different types of IQ tests (e.g., verbal versus nonverbal) tend to identify different students as those with the greatest discrepancy between achievement and potential.

A measure of students' *understanding after they have listened to material read to them* is the currently preferred method for assessing potential (Spring & French, 1990). This measure of **listening comprehension** tells us the level of material students could understand if they were able to read the material themselves. Stanovich (1991a) and others contend that listening tests are sounder reading aptitude measures than use of mental age or IQ scores.

Assessing listening comprehension is quite simple. The teacher reads a series of graded passages to each student, beginning with the easiest passage. Questions are asked after the passage is read aloud, and the process continues until the students are able to answer so few questions that it is evident that their frustration levels have been reached. Graded passages in an informal reading inventory (IRI) may be used for this purpose, and the scoring criteria employed for IRIs to determine frustration level based on comprehension may be used. (You will learn more about IRIs and how to score them in Chapter 5.) Or, you may use published measurement instruments that include subtests designed specifically for assessing listening comprehension. Some of these are the Basic Reading Inventory, the Diagnostic Achievement Battery, the Stanford Achievement Test, Listening Comprehension Tests, the Analytical Reading Inventory, the CTB/McGraw-Hill Listening Test, and the Ekwall/Shanker Reading Inventory (3rd ed.).

An Assessment Case Study

Throughout the four chapters of Unit II, we will follow a student who has been referred to a remedial reading program. We will name this hypothetical student, David Adams. In this chapter, we will assume that tests must be administered to determine if David does indeed warrant remedial services. At this stage, the teacher begins an **assessment information form** for him, a form on which diagnostic information is systematically recorded to aid in decision making. Refer to Figure 4–3 and you will see the beginning notations the teacher has placed on this form. As you will observe, David is in the fourth grade and is 9 years old, information which the teacher places on the assessment information form. Further, you will note that at this time, the teacher has already administered a test of listening comprehension, employing graded IRI passages, and that David's potential based on this test appears to be fourth grade. This result may be interpreted to mean that he *should* be able to read at a level commensurate with his present grade placement. The questions now are, "Does he?" And if not, "How serious is his delay?" Further testing will provide some answer to these queries, and we will continue to follow David's test performances to see what the outcomes will be.

FIGURE 4–3
A partially completed record form of assessment information for a hypothetical student

---

Assessment Information Form

Student's Name: ___David Adams___

Grade Level: ___4th___

Chronological Age:

    1) Birthdate ___February 19, 19—___

    2) Age ___9.0___

Listening Comprehension Level:

    1) Method of determination ___use of graded IRI passages___

    2) Level ___4th grade___

Assessing Present Reading Achievement

After determining a student's listening level and recording it on the record form, the teacher must determine the student's present reading achievement. Informal procedures are usually unacceptable for designating present achievement level when the purpose is to verify eligibility for programs. Federal or state regulations frequently require that a standardized test be administered for this purpose.

Entry-Level Assessment. It is becoming common practice to administer **out-of-level** standardized tests to students with reading problems. With out-of-level assessment, a test that has been designed for students at the grade level that is equivalent to a student's suspected *reading* level, rather than that student's actual *grade* level, is administered. For example, if we suspect Donna, a fifth-grader, is reading at about third-grade level, we would administer the test the publishers have specified for third-graders rather than the one prepared for students in fifth grade. Fisher's (1962) study of over 1,000 students showed that, for both poor and gifted readers, this procedure provided a more accurate measure of reading achievement than using the on-grade-level test. Long, Schaffran, and Kellog (1977) refer to use of out-of-level tests as *instructional-level testing.*

If the purpose of administering a standardized survey test is to determine a student's reading achievement level, how can we decide that level beforehand to administer an appropriate out-of-level test? **Entry-level tests,** quick screening devices that provide a rough approximation of a student's reading ability, are used for this purpose. Although entry-level tests should never be used as the definitive specification of a student's reading level, they are useful in pinpointing the level of test to be administered for two reasons: they prevent students from possible demoralizing experiences, prevent wasted time, and allow selection of a formal measure that will provide an accurate estimate of reading.

Consider this example: Joseph, a 16-year-old, is enrolled in a reading clinic by his parents. They are quite unsure of his present reading level and only know he is behind the level needed to adequately meet expectations in his 10th-grade class. A call to Joe's school by the clinician, Mr. Doughty, results in the same information—Joe is apparently behind the other students in reading because he is having difficulty with all assignments involving reading, but neither the counselor nor the classroom teachers have an idea about what his approximate reading level might be. What should the clinician do? Should he choose a test designed for seventh- or eighth-grade students since there is at least agreement that Joe is behind the average readers in his classes? Let's suppose this is the choice. Joe sits down to begin this test only to find he cannot read the first passage. Embarrassed, he tries to hide this deficiency from the clinician and begins putting on a fair imitation of a student reading and marking the answers, although he is marking them randomly since he cannot read the passages or the items. As passages become successively more difficult and Joe begins to see many more words in a passage that he doesn't know, frustration takes over and he gives up any pretense of reading. He pushes the test a bit to the side, takes the answer sheet in front of him and marks any square on which his pencil happens to fall. As a result, he completes a 27-minute section of the test in 8 minutes. Mr. Doughty, who has been observing Joe from the corner of his eye, realizes that any score obtained from this test is obviously worthless in specifying an accurate reading level. He decides that the next day he will have Joe take the form of this standardized test designed for fourth- to sixth-graders since he is sure from Joe's behavior that the previous test was too difficult for him and that his test-taking performance was not because of laziness or perverseness.

When Joe sees the test being handed to him the next day, it looks very little different from the one with which he had such a frustrating experience the day before. He becomes tense and makes up an excuse for what he expects will be his similarly poor performance today ("I've got a terrible headache, Mr. Doughty."). But, because he's a cooperative student, he reluctantly and with feelings of great distress tries again. This time he is able to read the first passage, can handle the second passage somewhat, but after that it is all uphill again. Today he makes no pretense of reading. When the third passage turns out to be totally undecipherable to him, he uses yesterday's strategy. He pushes the test away and marks answers randomly—without having set eyes on passages 4 through 9. The result is that a 24-minute section of the test is completed in 10 minutes. Having again observed Joe surreptitiously, the clinician, also feeling frustrated, decides he must administer a primary-level test so Joe can read the test, and so that some meaningful measure of Joe's ability can be obtained.

On the third day, Joe is given the second-grade form of the same standardized test. The clinician has to provide many words of comfort and encouragement to get Joe to begin, but when he starts, Joe finds he can read and answer almost all parts of the test. He works thoughtfully and when clinician calls "time" at the end of 20 minutes, he has completed all but the last question. If the clinician had administered an entry-level assessment before choosing the first form of the standardized test much wasted time and feelings of futility could have been avoided.

The developers of the 3-R's Test: Achievement have provided directions in the teacher's manual for out-of-level testing with their test battery. Other publishers have established special norms for using out-of-level testing; for example, this has been done with one of the more widely used series of standardized tests, the Gates-MacGinitie Reading Tests (3rd ed.). In addition, the Comprehensive Tests of Basic Skills (CTBS) provides entry level tests called "locator tests" and overlapping levels (e.g., 2.6–3.9 and 3.6–4.9) to facilitate out-of-level testing.

Entry-level tests usually consist of graded word lists. Students read the words orally, and teachers estimate reading levels from their performances. In addition to those supplied with some standardized tests, many published informal reading inventories contain such lists. Specific directions for obtaining an estimated level vary according to the test used. The published informal inventories described in Chapter 5 furnish good sources for acquiring a graded word list. If our hypothetical student David Adams scored second grade as his entry level on such a test we would select a second-grade form of a standardized test to administer to him.

Administering a Standardized Test. A teacher needs to select a standardized test with care and, before tests are purchased, request a specimen set from the publishers. A specimen set usually includes one copy of each level of a test, plus a teacher's manual and technical manual. The technical manual should be examined meticulously for information on the norming population, reliability, and validity. Most teachers do not relish the thought of reading a technical manual for a test, but doing so is a necessary and critical part of a reading teacher's job.

Furthermore, it is wise to take an important additional step before making decisions about which tests will be used in an assessment program—that is, to read published reviews of any tests under consideration. These reviews are written by experts in both assessment procedures and literacy instruction. Reviews of tests can be found in many professional journals, but probably the most valuable resource is the Mental Measurements Yearbook (MMY). This important reference book provides descriptions of reading and other tests currently in print, addresses of the publishers, and critiques of the tests. The critiques are especially helpful in selecting tests for a remedial program. Even though a test has been published or it is widely used, this does not necessarily mean it is a good test. The MMY lists strengths and weaknesses of specific tests. The usefulness and adequacy of many tests are discussed in the chapters of Unit II of this book, but because there is an extensive number of tests from which a teacher may choose, it is impossible to describe them all. The MMY can provide information about many tests of potential interest. This reference book is found in most college and university libraries. All school systems should purchase at least one copy of the most recent edition for use by teachers and administrators. The most recent edition is The Eleventh Mental Measurements Yearbook. It is published by the Buros Institute of Mental Measurements and distributed by the University of Nebraska Press. (See Figure 4–4 for an example of a typical entry in the MMY.)

The Buros Institute of Mental Measurements also publishes a volume called Tests in Print III (TIP). Inclusion of a test in the MMY is based on whether the test is new or has been revised since the last edition, while TIP includes all tests currently available for purchase. TIP does not provide critiques of tests, as does the MMY, but only a listing and description; therefore, TIP cannot be used when questioning whether a test is worthwhile or not—only to determine if it is still published. Another helpful resource produced by the same institute is Reading Tests and Reviews II, which contains lists, references, and critiques of reading tests that have appeared in all Institute publications since 1938.

When considering test selection for the purpose being discussed—determining a student's eligibility for a special program—a teacher should select a survey test; a ***survey test*** provides information about students' general reading levels, rather than specific

FIGURE 4–4

A test review in the Mental Measurements Yearbook

Informal Reading Comprehension Placement Test.

Purpose: Assesses the instructional and independent comprehension levels of students from pre-readiness (Grade 1) through level eight plus (Grade 8).

Population: Grades 1–6 for typical learners and Grades 7–12 remedially.

Publication Date: 1983.

Scores, 3: Word Comprehension, Passage Comprehension, Total Comprehension.

Administration: Individual.

Price Data, 1989: $49.95 per complete kit including 1 diskette, 1 back-up diskette, management, and documentation (15 pages).

Time: (35–50) minutes for the battery, (15–20) minutes for Part 1 and (20–30) minutes for Part 2.

Comments: Test administered in 2 parts; Apple II or TRS–80 microcomputer necessary for administration.

Authors: Ann Edson and Eunice Insel.

Publisher: Educational Activities, Inc.

Review of the Informal Reading Comprehension Placement Test by GLORIA A. GALVIN, School Psychologist, Dodgeville School District, Dodgeville, WI:

This test consists of two types of tasks: word analogies and a series of eight graded paragraphs. The paragraphs were developed using readability formulas to control for vocabulary and sentence length. Each paragraph is followed by four multiple-choice questions (each with three one-word answer choices) designed to test comprehension of each of the following: detail, main idea, inference, and vocabulary from the context. The major purpose of the test is to enable a student to be placed in curricular materials at the appropriate reading comprehension level. The authors' rationale for the test is "to use the findings to prescribe a developmental, corrective, or remedial reading program for the individual student."

The main advantage of this test over other commercial tests or typical teacher-made tests of this type is the computer format that lets the child take the test largely independent of a test administrator. However, this advantage is limited because there are points within the program where the student may be given the instruction, "Please call your teacher," so that an examiner must be available to advance or terminate the program appropriately. Further, there is a fundamental problem in having beginning or poor readers do a reading test independently when the instructions are printed on the screen and must be read and comprehended to be executed correctly. Children whose reading comprehension is at the lower reading levels may not be validly tested because they do not understand the printed program commands, and not because they cannot comprehend the lower level paragraphs. This limits the usefulness of the test with many young children and also with older children with reading problems.

A major problem with this test is the complete lack of reliability, validity, and normative information. Although the test is claimed to have been used with 3,000 children, no data are presented. Furthermore, how well this test places children into various curricular materials at various grade levels is not known. For the purpose of placing children accurately into reading materials, teachers would be better served by their own teacher-made materials that fit their specific curricula.

A second problem with this test is the authors' failure to fully utilize the computer technology. Although the variety of comprehension questions accompanying each paragraph is laudable, greater

FIGURE 4–4 *(continued)*

---

numbers of questions could have been incorporated to make the measurement more reliable. For example, questions could have been arranged so that a student answering 100% of the four basic questions would be given some higher level inferential questions, whereas the student falling below the criterion would be given additional easier questions. The process should lead to a fuller understanding of the student's level of comprehension. In addition, qualitative information on the student's test performance should be made available using computer technology, rather than limiting the output to a few summary scores. Given the rationale for the test by the authors as a way of helping plan for prescriptive and remedial help for the individual student, information on the (*a*) number and types of errors made, (*b*) amount of rereading the student did (each paragraph can be recalled once per question), and (*c*) rate at which the student completed the test should also be made available. Such information would be available in many, typical paper-and-pencil, examiner-administered tests.

In summary, this test offers some positive features such as the variety of comprehension questions uniformly applied to each paragraph, minimum examiner time per student, and a test that ends smoothly without showing the student how many items were not presented. However, this test lacks the basic foundation for adequate measurement by ignoring the concepts of reliability and validity. Further, the test fails to utilize the computer format to provide analysis of student errors and actually is more limited in the information it provides and the flexibility with which it can be used than a well-constructed teacher-made test for a specific curriculum. Therefore, although time is saved in administration of this test, the information gleaned is much less than it could have been. This test may be useful for a quick screening of reading placement level, but does not have much to offer the educator who has the goal of remediation for the individual student.

Review of the Informal Reading Comprehension Placement Test by CLAUDIA R. WRIGHT, Assistant Professor of Educational Psychology, California State University, Long Beach, CA:

The Informal Reading Comprehension Placement Test was developed by two educators with backgrounds as reading specialists in elementary and secondary school settings who also have worked as curriculum development consultants for public school districts located in New York. This test was designed to serve as a computer-facilitated screening and placement test providing a measure of reading comprehension levels for students in grades 1 through 6 who may range in reading ability from prereadiness through eighth-grade levels and beyond. In addition, the test has been employed for remediation purposes with secondary and special education students.

The Informal Reading Placement Test is divided into two parts. The first section, identified as the Word Comprehension Test (Part 1) is made up of eight sets of eight word-meaning analogies for a total of 64 test items in a multiple-choice response format. Approximately 15 to 20 minutes is required for testing. Vocabulary levels for this part of the test have been validated, in part, by the employment of the EDL and Dolch Word lists as referents in the selection of words for each level. The second section, the Passage Comprehension Test (Part 2), is composed of eight reading passages which range in reading difficulty from prereadiness to eighth-grade plus levels. Vocabulary and sentence length have been controlled for each level using Spache, Frye, and Dale Chall readability formulas. Each of the eight passages is followed by four multiple-choice test items that purportedly measure comprehension of detail, main idea, inference, and vocabulary. Completion time for Part 2 is 20 to 30 min-

FIGURE 4–4   *(continued)*

utes. In addition to the two reading comprehension components, estimates of a respondent's total instructional level, independent reading level, and frustration level are also provided.

The entire test is administered and scored on the microcomputer. The test manual provides the teacher with clear instructions for the operation of the program through a sample testing session. The process is facilitated further by illustrations of the sequence for several test segments. The computer displays are personalized with the student's name, the content is easy to read and hierarchically organized, and the program is well suited for independent or teacher-assisted testing. In addition, explicit directions are provided for the interpretation of student performances. Teachers have access to five types of information for each student: (a) a word comprehension score that identifies the number of incorrect responses at each of the eight reading levels; (b) a passage comprehension score for each of the eight reading levels; (c) the total instructional level, which is a composite indicator made up of a comparison of the word comprehension and passage comprehension levels to determine by how many levels the two scores differ; (d) a total independent level that identifies the level at which the student can read independently (operationally defined as that level at which the student correctly identifies words with 99% accuracy and passes the comprehension items at the 95% level); and (e) the total frustration level, which signifies the lowest level of comprehension (less than 90% word accuracy and 50% or below in correct responses to the comprehension items) and is thought to indicate the extent to which the reading material is too difficult for the student. This reviewer assumes that conventional mastery-learning rationales have been employed for the selection of these particular percentages as cutoff scores, even though no rationales have been cited.

No reliability or validity information has been provided with the test materials. The authors acknowledge that the psychometric properties of the instrument are "undoubtably not the same as a typical standardized reading test," however, they fail to report what information may have led them to this conclusion. Further, a relatively thorough search of the literature revealed that very little, if any, research has employed the Informal Reading Placement Test to support the validity of the instrument.

As noted in the test manual, the Informal Reading Placement Test has been used with over 3,000 students enrolled in grades 1 through 6 as a tool for the classroom teacher to assess reading comprehension for placement and to provide information for remedial instruction. It would appear that with such a broadly based usage of the instrument, some data from standardized achievement tests could be made available for estimating construct and criterion-related validities.

The authors are encouraged to incorporate within the test manual any additional information that may be obtained from empirical studies to establish the reliability of the instrument as well as the construct and criterion-related validities of the Informal Reading Placement Test. These data could serve to support the placement and remedial functions for which the test was developed. Even though a test has been designed to afford a "quick" assessment of behavior, the brevity of the assessment does not reduce the demand for an instrument with sound psychometric properties.

Overall, the Informal Reading Placement Test as a computer-assisted assessment device would appear to provide a promising approach for classroom applications. Caution, however, should be exercised in the use of this instrument if it is employed as the only criterion for placement or remediation purposes, particularly in light of the absence of reliability and validity data.

Source: From *The Eleventh Mental Measurements Yearbook* by J. J. Kramer and J. C. Conoley (Eds.), 1992, Lincoln, NE: The Buros Institute of Mental Measurements. Reprinted by permission.

information about strengths and weaknesses in strategies and skills. Some standardized reading survey tests are the Iowa Tests of Basic Skills, the Metropolitan Achievement Tests, the Iowa Silent Reading Tests, the Nelson-Denny Reading Tests, the Stanford Achievement Test, the Gates-MacGinitie Reading Tests, the Comprehensive Tests of Basic Skills, the California Achievement Tests, and the Nelson Reading Skills Test. The Curriculum Referenced Tests of Mastery is a standardized instrument that provides grade levels based on national norming, as well as an evaluation of mastery of specific skills. See Test Bank A for information on these and other standardized survey tests.

The content of different survey tests varies, but most include a section on vocabulary and one on comprehension. Most survey tests also have alternate forms at the same level so that one form may be used as a pretest and another as a posttest to measure student growth at the end of an instructional program.

A caution is in order about certain tests that purport to measure general reading achievement level, but which, in fact, do not. These tests usually consist entirely of lists of isolated words that are read orally by the student. Two such tests are the Slosson Oral

Test Bank A
Norm-Referenced Survey Tests

Name	For Grades	Type of Administration	Time for Administration	Publisher
California Achievement Tests—Forms C & D (CAT)	K–9	Group	Varies by level	CTB/McGraw-Hill
CAP Achievement Series	Preschool–12	Group	Varies by level	American Testronics
Comprehensive Tests of Basic Skills—Forms U & V (CTBS). Spanish edition available	K–9	Group	Varies by level	CTB/McGraw-Hill
Curriculum Referenced Tests of Mastery. Also provides criterion-referenced scores.	1–12	Group	Varies by level	Psychological Corporation
Educational Development Series (EDS)	K–12	Group	Varies by level	Scholastic Testing Service
Gates-MacGinitie Reading Tests, 3rd edition.	K–12	Group	Varies by level	Riverside
Iowa Silent Reading Tests (ISRT)	6–16	Group	Varies by level	Psychological Corporation
Iowa Tests of Basic Skills (ITBS)	K–9	Group	Varies by level	Riverside

Test Bank A (cont.)

Name	For Grades	Type of Administration	Time for Administration	Publisher
Metropolitan Achievement Tests (MAT). A "Survey Battery" and "Reading Instructional Tests" are available; the latter are used most often in reading programs.	K–12	Group	Varies by level	Psychological Corporation
Nelson-Denny Reading Tests (NDRT)	9–12, college, adults	Group	50 minutes	Riverside
Nelson Reading Skills Test—Forms 3 & 4 (RST)	3–9	Group	Varies by level	Riverside
SRA Achievement Series	K–12	Group	Varies by level	Science Research Associates
Stanford Achievement Test: Reading Tests	1–9	Group	Varies by level	Psychological Corporation
Stanford Test of Academic Skills	8–13	Group	Varies according to subtests used	Psychological Corporation
Tests of Achievement and Proficiency. This test battery includes subtests on using sources of information, as well as on reading comprehension.	9–12	Group	Varies according to subtests used	Riverside

Reading Test–Revised and the Wide Range Achievement Tests–Revised (WRAT-R). These tests cannot be used to determine general reading achievement level, even though they claim to do so, because of the limited type of reading behavior they measure—they measure only the ability to pronounce words in isolation. These tests include no assessment of a student's understanding of the meanings of the words, no measure of general comprehension ability after silent reading, nor any appraisal of the ability to read words in context (as found in authentic reading situations). The WRAT-R has been normed by age rather than grade and the publishers indicate that grade scores given by this test are only rough clues to instructional level.

A number of studies have been conducted to determine if there is congruency between the grade-level scores obtained on certain short tests of isolated word recognition and students' reading abilities as seen in actual classroom performance. The results of many of these have not been favorable. J. M. Bradley (1976), for example, found that 90% of the 150 students in his study were given incorrect instructional placement by the WRAT. Many standardized tests tend to overestimate the reading achievement level of students, but overestimates by the WRAT in this study were extreme—the reading levels of approximately 38% of the students were overestimated by 3 or more grade levels. If these tests measure only a limited type of reading behavior and the scores obtained are often widely divergent from students' actual functioning levels, why are they used? Primarily because they are quick and simple to administer. Spache (1981) has said "judging from such tests as the WRAT or the Slosson, which require about 3 to 5 minutes, it appears that school personnel want the shortest, most superficial measures they can find" (p. 288). Time is a major problem for teachers, but, since these tests have been inappropriately devised to measure general reading achievement and since the results are often questionable, they should not be used.

Administering a survey test correctly is essential. If a teacher does not follow directions in the teacher's manual exactly, the norms will not be applicable because the test was standardized using these directions. Directions include exact specifications for the length of time a student may work on each section of a test. Allowing more or less time, even by a minute or two, invalidates the results. At times, teachers feel they should permit a student with learning problems to have more time than specified in the manual, but this is inappropriate and should in no case be allowed. However, other strategies might ease the test-taking task for a poor reader. It is often possible to allow the student to have a break between sections of the test, that is, after the teacher has called "time" on one section, to engage in some other activity for a while before beginning the next timed section. The poor reader might also be permitted to mark answers directly on the test rather than on an answer sheet. This can eliminate a possible source of errors since some students have difficulty finding the correct answer space when they must look back and forth between the test and a separate answer sheet. Most sections of survey tests require silent reading. Even though direct teacher involvement is unnecessary while the student reads and responds to questions, the teacher should remain close at hand to unobtrusively observe the student's reading and test-taking behaviors and to quietly prompt if the student should give up or lapse into periods of daydreaming. Survey tests are designed to be administered to groups of students during the same time period. In a remedial situation, tests can be administered in this way if several students need to take the same level tests. If not, tests can be administered individually.

Scoring a standardized test is easy since an answer key is provided. Raw scores for each section (which are simply the number of correct responses) are combined for all sections to obtain a total raw score. The teacher then consults a table in the teacher's manual that indicates the grade-level equivalent of the total raw score. For example, after combining the number of correct answers for all sections of a test, the teacher may find that David Adams's total raw score is 24 and that the table indicates this is equivalent to 3.0 or beginning third-grade level.

Standardized Test Scores: To Convert or Not to Convert? Once a teacher has obtained a grade-level score from a standardized test, what should be done with it before comparing it to the student's potential (as indicated by the listening test score)? Since a grade-level score on the standardized survey test is the average score made by all students at that level on whom the test was normed, if a hypothetical student named Robert receives a raw score of 52 and the test manual tells us this is equivalent to 6.0 grade level, this means that the average raw score of all students at the 6.0 grade level who took this test during the norming procedure was 52. This helps us to compare Robert's performance with that of other students. It does not necessarily tell us what level of instructional materials Robert is able to handle in real classroom situations. Sometimes this standardized test grade-level score is a fair estimation of a student's instructional level, but sometimes it is not. The **instructional level** is the level at which a student can handle material in an instructional situation with normal teacher guidance, that is, with the typical amount of assistance with new vocabulary, help with small comprehension difficulties, and so forth.

Because teachers have often noticed that the scores on a standardized test overestimate the instructional level of many students, a number of studies have been undertaken to determine how valid these scores are for specifying the level of functioning of students with actual classroom materials. The data are conflicting. In research with students in grades 4 through 7, several investigators have found that these scores do overestimate the actual instructional levels of students by about a year, with the overestimations particularly seen with poor readers (Betts, 1940; Glaser, 1965; Killgallon, 1942; McCracken, 1962). J. L. Williams's (1964) study with fourth-, fifth-, and sixth-graders, however, found standardized test scores to be relatively close to students' instructional levels, and Sipay (1964) found that whether these test scores provided a good estimate depended on which standardized test the teacher used and the criteria used to determine actual classroom functioning level.

Teachers who work with poor readers often find that standardized test scores do indeed overestimate instructional levels for the majority of students, although not for all. For this reason, it has become common practice to consider the score obtained from a standardized test to represent a student's frustration level. **Frustration level** is the level at which the material becomes too difficult for a student. For example, if 4.0 is specified as Elaine's frustration level, material at the fourth-grade level and above should not be selected for her. To determine the student's instructional level based on a standardized test score, common practice is to subtract 1 year from that score; for example, if Elaine's standardized test score is 4.0, her approximate instructional level would be 3.0. Further, the student's independent level is estimated by subtracting an additional year. The **independent level** is the level at which a student can easily handle material without teacher guidance; this material is easy enough for the student to read independently. If Elaine's instructional level is 3.0, her approximate independent level is 2.0. (One standardized test, the Metropolitan Achievement Tests, provides a table for converting grade-level equivalent scores to instructional levels.)

There is some argument, however, against subtracting a constant of 1.0 (1 year) from the obtained standardized test score to derive an estimate of instructional level. MacGinitie (1973) argued that the practice is statistically incorrect. Also, as noted above, the standardized test score is not an overestimate of actual functioning levels for all students. In fact, it may be an underestimate for those students whose reading ability is adequate but whose test-taking skills are poor. Thus, there are two choices when using a standardized test score.

1. *Do not convert the score.* That is, do not subtract a constant of 1 year from the standardized score, but rather, use the score exactly as obtained. Some program regulations may require this approach because administrators are unaware that these scores overestimate the actual functioning level of most students, or MacGinitie's (1973) objections may be cited, or, since the scores are relatively accurate estimates for some poor readers, it is feared that subtracting a year from the score will result in an underestimate of instructional level for a few students.

2. *Do convert the scores.* That is, subtract a constant of 1 year from the standardized test score. The author of this text prefers this practice since it provides a better estimate for most students with less-than-average reading abilities.

Although either choice can result in error, the first choice may result in many students' being denied eligibility for programs they need, while the second choice can result in a few students being placed in special programs they do not need. The second choice seems to be the lesser of two evils. If students in a program are found not to require special help, it is easy enough to report this happy finding and dismiss them from the program. On the other hand, if a student is denied placement, it may be a long time before this student is considered for eligibility again—time during which the student may slip even further behind. Because of this difficulty with grade equivalent scores, some programs require use of a percentile rank instead. If a student scores at the 63rd percentile, this means the score is better than 63% of the students at that grade level who have taken the test. It is common practice in many Title I programs to enroll only students who score below the 33rd percentile or the 25th percentile, for example.

Computing the Discrepancy Between Potential and Achievement

Computing the discrepancy between measured reading potential and measured achievement is easy. The teacher simply compares the student's potential (as indicated by the score on the listening comprehension test) and the present reading instructional level. The result for one student might be

$$
\begin{array}{ll}
4.0 & \text{(listening score)} \\
- \ 2.0 & \text{(present reading instructional level)} \\
\hline
2.0 & \text{(discrepancy)}
\end{array}
$$

In considering our hypothetical student David Adams, whose partial assessment information form was seen in Figure 4–3, we will assume that David received a grade equivalent score of 3.0 on a standardized test and we have computed his present reading achievement instructional level to be approximately 2.0. David's discrepancy, therefore, indicates he is approximately 2 years behind the level at which he should be reading according to his estimated potential (which, as you remember, was fourth grade). Using the criteria specified in Chapter 1 of this text (1 year discrepancy in primary grades; 2 years discrepancy in intermediate grades; 3 years discrepancy at the secondary level), we can see that David, an intermediate-grade-level student, does warrant special remedial services.

Additional information can now be added to David Adams's assessment information form. See Figure 4–5. The teacher has recorded David's entry-level assessment results, which indicated the level of the standardized test to be administered to him. The name, level, and *form* of the standardized test that was used is noted for future reference, and his score on this test, the estimate of his approximate instructional reading level, and the discrepancy seen between his estimated potential and approximate reading level are included on the form.

Because David will be placed in a program for special reading services, additional assessment will be undertaken to determine *why* he is not reading up to his potential, or, in other words, to discover his present strengths and weaknesses. This further information will help his reading teacher plan an effective program to meet David's needs. We will see David Adams again in the next chapter, and learn the results of these additional evaluation procedures.

FIGURE 4–5
Continuation of a partially completed record form of assessment for a hypothetical student

---

Assessment Information Form

Student's Name: ___David Adams_____

Grade Level: ___4th_____

Chronological Age:

　1)　Birthdate ___February 19, 19—_____

　2)　Age ___9.0_____

Listening Comprehension Level:

　1)　Method of determination ___use of graded IRI passages_____

　2)　Level ___4th grade_____

Entry Level Assessment Results: ___2nd grade_____

Standardized Survey Test:

　1)　Name of test ___Gates-MacGinitie Reading Tests, Level 2, Form A_____

　2)　Grade score obtained ___3.0_____

Present Reading Instructional Level (based on standardized test results): ___approximately 2.0___

Discrepancy Between Listening Level and Present Achievement: ___2.0_____

CONCLUSION

Although the most common practice for determining eligibility for special programs is to compute discrepancy between potential and achievement, other factors should also be kept in mind.

　1.　Does the discrepancy indicate that remedial reading or LD services are required, yet the student has made very little progress in such programs previously? A clinical reading program should then be considered.

　2.　Is the student's classroom functioning level well above or below test performance level? Remember, there can be error in even the best test estimates. All available information should be considered before placement in a special program is accepted or denied.

TABLE 4–4
A teacher checklist for conducting assessment for identification

	Yes	No
1. Has a listening test been administered and a score obtained?		
2. Has an entry level assessment been administered?		
3. Has a standardized group survey test, at the appropriate level, been administered?		
4. Has the constant of 1.0 been subtracted from the grade equivalent score obtained from the standardized test?		
5. Has discrepancy between potential and present achievement been computed?		
6. Have other factors been considered before a final placement decision is made?		

3. If a corrective reading program in the regular classroom is deemed sufficient to meet a student's needs, does the classroom teacher have the skills and the time to provide a special program for the student?

4. If more students are eligible for a special program than can be accommodated, have you considered all students' needs before making the final selection so that first priority may be given to students with the greatest need?

Determining discrepancy between potential and achievement is an important, and often required, first step in assessment for identification of students for special literacy instruction, but good teacher judgment must also enter into the decision-making process. Table 4–4 suggests some questions a teacher might ask when conducting an assessment for identification.

📖 REFLECTIONS

Discuss these questions.

1. What is the value of assessment?
2. Since appropriate norming procedures as well as measures of validity and reliability are important if a standardized test is to offer believable information, why do some test producers fail to provide this information?
3. What do *you* see as the major advantage to using standardized tests in reading assessment? the major disadvantage?

5

Assessment for Verifying General Reading Level

Ongoing, daily observation of reading and writing behavior is an important part of assessment.

After completing the assessment procedures described in Chapter 4, teachers will have information available about students' reading ability and will have identified students with reading problems. Refer to Figure 4–5, found at the end of the last chapter, and as a review, note the types of information already recorded for David Adams, our case study student. The tests administered measure the students' potential reading ability and their reading achievement.

Now the teacher must gather further data—information for designing an intervention plan for each student. Two major types of assessment must be undertaken: (a) assessment for determining the student's general reading level (or, at this point, verifying the level obtained on the standardized test) and (b) assessment for determining the student's strengths and weaknesses in reading strategies, knowledge, and skills. This chapter describes procedures for verifying students' general reading levels.

Literacy educators know that determining a student's reading level is an important instructional consideration. However, certain other individuals have refuted this view, saying the only task of consequence is determining the specific skills students lack so these can be taught. The focus on skills may be valid for certain subject areas, for example, in math. A level in math may only represent some comparison with the scores of a norm group and, therefore, provide little value in helping the teacher decide what to do when a student is performing poorly. However, this is decidedly not the case in reading.

If students are to increase their reading achievement, it is essential that they read a great deal in regular, connected material; that is, reading complete stories, chapters, articles, books, and so forth. To assign texts or to help students select materials to read, teachers must know the students' instructional reading levels and their independent reading levels. Texts at a student's approximate instructional level should be used when the teacher plans to provide some assistance as the student reads. On the other hand, teachers should assign material at students' independent levels if they are going to read independently at home, in study hall, or in any situation where there will be no instructional support. Placing students in texts that are too difficult is a major hindrance to their

Research has shown that using several measures of achievement (both formal and informal) provides the best estimate of actual reading level.

progress and should be carefully avoided. As a result, determining students' functioning levels is a key step in reading assessment.

As previously noted, there is a question about the accuracy of instructional level scores obtained from standardized tests. If teachers subtract 1 year from the grade equivalent score to obtain instructional level, the resulting instructional level will be a reasonably good estimate in many cases. However, in others, it may be an overestimate or underestimate. In addition, research has shown that using several measures of achievement provides the best approximation of actual reading level (Farr, 1992; P. H. Johnston, 1983). Therefore, it is common diagnostic practice to use an informal reading inventory, or sometimes a cloze procedure, to verify general reading achievement level. (Some programs use an informal reading inventory in place of a standardized test, rather than in combination with it.)

INFORMAL READING INVENTORIES

An **informal reading inventory** (IRI) is a series of graded passages, each of which is followed by a comprehension check. One of two types of IRIs may be used: one based on the specific instructional material the student will be using or a published IRI designed for general use.

IRIs Based on Specific Instructional Materials

IRIs based on actual materials students will be using render the most valid measure of the level appropriate for instruction, if these IRIs have been carefully developed and are correctly administered and scored.

IRIs Furnished by Basal Reader Publishers.   Teachers using a basal reader series may find the publishers have produced an IRI based on their texts. Although it is important to determine if appropriate steps (described later) have been used in developing the IRI, properly devised published IRIs can save teachers preparation time.

Teacher-Prepared IRIs.   When teachers choose to use materials that have no accompanying IRI, they may develop their own. These assessment instruments can be highly valid if they are based on the texts of instruction, but preparing an IRI properly is quite time consuming. Time devoted to producing an IRI is well worthwhile, however, if the teacher plans to use the same basic materials over a period of time with many students. Also, this instrument can be reused with students throughout the year for periodic, ongoing assessment. Since this test must be carefully developed and since the information it is to provide is of critical importance, it is often helpful for two or more teachers to work together to prepare an IRI that will be available for all teachers who are using the same materials. Listed here are recommended procedures for preparing, administering, and scoring a teacher-made IRI.

Here are the steps necessary for *preparing* an IRI:

1. For every book in the series of reading materials, select 5 passages. The length of each passage should vary according to the grade level of the book as follows.

Preprimer-primer = 100 words
First grade = 125 words
Second-third grade = 150 words
Fourth-sixth grade = 175 words
Above sixth grade = 200 words

When selecting passages, do not stop in the middle of a sentence since a few words over the specified number will cause no problem. If whole stories in books at the lowest levels (for example, in preprimers) do not contain 100 words, use two or more stories. Keep each story separate and develop questions for each.

2.   Use a readability formula to check the reading level of each of the passages from each book. Choose 2 of the 5 passages that are most representative of the reading level of the stories in that book. Include these passages in your completed IRI, one to be read orally and one to be read silently at each level.

3.   Label the passages in the following manner: The first passage from the easiest book should be designated "Level A–Oral." The second passage from the easiest book should be designated "Level A–Silent." The first passage from the second book should be designated "Level B–Oral," and so on.

4.   Type each passage on a separate page, and label each page ("Level A–Oral" and so on). Use a primary typewriter, if available, for typing passages for the first preprimer through second grade levels; or if a computer with a printer capable of producing fonts in various sizes is available, use a large-size font of 16 to 18 points. Spacing between lines should be 1½ spaces. For the remaining levels, use pica type and double spacing. Here is a sample of how a portion of two pages might look.

Level G—Oral

The stork had made a nest on the roof
of the farmer's house. Everyone in the family
had . . .

Level G—Silent

Mr. Pott was the dog's name. We thought that
was the silliest name we . . .

---

5.   Make several copies of the stories. Students will use one set; the teacher uses the other copies for marking errors.

6.   Place the pages to be used by students in a sequence from easiest to most difficult, with the passage for oral reading preceding the passage for silent reading at each level. Store the teacher's sets so that multiple copies of each story are placed in separate file folders.

7.   To assemble the IRI from which students will read, first type a cover sheet like the one shown here. Place the cover sheet on top of the sequenced pages. Staple these inside a manila folder.

```
Informal Reading Inventory

Based on: [Which series?]

Date this series was published _____

Level A = 1st preprimer
Level B = 2nd preprimer

[etc.]
```

8. Next, devise 10 questions about each passage. Be certain to include higher-level questions, as well as literal ones. Write the same number of questions for both the oral and silent passages at any given level Type the questions for each passage on a file card, and title the file card (for example: Level C—Silent). Specify the type of question in front of each one. Then type the answer to the question. Here is a brief example.

```
Level D—Oral

(factual)     1. Why was the dog sad?
                 (He was going to be sold.)
(inference)   2. Why do you think the rabbits wanted to help?
                 (He was the only dog who did not chase them.)
```

Instead of asking specific types of questions, a teacher may choose to have students retell the information they have just read. If you prefer this alternative, prepare a retelling outline that lists the major points to be retold.

9. Using masking tape and a piece of another manila folder, make a pocket inside the front cover of the manila folder in which you have stapled the selected passages. Place the questions on file cards or the retelling outline in this pocket.

10. With a marking pen, print "Informal Reading Inventory" on the outside front cover.

11. A word about pictures: Some stories in the lowest level books make little sense unless pictures appear in conjunction with the text to help students follow the story line. A comprehension check over such a passage without the accompanying pictures will not provide accurate information. If this is the case, make some provision for students to use the pictures with the passage as they read by drawing the pictures on the IRI page containing that passage, by photocopying (with permission) necessary pictures and affixing them to the page, or by allowing students to read that passage directly from the textbook.

Authorities do not agree on all procedures for *administering* an IRI, but research and the opinion of the majority of authorities suggest the following steps.

1. Steps in preparing for the test
   a. Select a place where no other students can overhear the reading or responses to the questions.

    b. Plan about 30 minutes of testing time for each student.

    c. Set up a tape recorder to record students' responses.

    d. Select the first passage by using the entry-level score obtained during assessment for identification.

2. Before testing

    a. Allow the student to play with the tape recorder for a minute or two (by talking into it, listening, turning it off and on, and so on, so that the student feels comfortable with its presence).

    b. Begin with a motivating statement, saying something like, "Read this passage to find out what funny thing a girl's pet raccoon did."

    c. Be certain to tell the student ahead of time that you will ask questions after he or she has read the passage.

    d. If the passage is to be read orally, do not allow it to be preread silently.

3. During oral reading

    a. If the student cannot pronounce a word, tell the student to do anything he or she knows how to do to figure it out and, if the student still cannot pronounce it, to skip it and continue reading.

    b. Do not mark the student's oral reading errors (often called miscues)[1]; instead follow along and keep a mental count of them.

4. For silent reading

    a. Usually no time limitations are imposed.

    b. It is wise to remain with the student to observe whether *all* of the passage actually is read and to ensure that he or she does remain on task.

5. After student reading

    a. Remove the test before checking comprehension.

    b. Allow the tape recorder to continue to run and ask the questions previously prepared or ask the student to retell the information in the passage.

    c. Provide careful prompting if the student is having difficulty with a question (taking care not to divulge the answer); if employing the retelling procedure, use the retelling outline to prompt the student if important information has been omitted (the retelling outline is for teacher use and is not shown to the student).

    d. Note the number of questions the student answered correctly.

    e. Have the student read passages until you identify his or her frustration level.

Score an IRI when the student is not present. For the oral reading test, use the duplicate sets of passages and mark word identification miscues as you listen to the tape recording of the student reading. Some commonly used marking procedures appear in Table 5–1 and Table 5–2. For both oral and silent tests, determine comprehension of each passage based on responses to the questions or during the retelling. Finally, determine if each passage is at the student's independent, instructional, or frustration level based on percentages of correct word identification and correct comprehension. To determine percentage of correct word identification, note the difference between the

---

[1]The term *miscue* is often used instead of the term *error*. The term *error* applied to a student's deviation when reading orally seems to imply that the deviation is a random response. However, we know that these deviations are cued by the language and thought processes of readers as they interact with the printed text and are not random at all. When the student's oral response is not the one the author intended, it is therefore called a miscue.

TABLE 5–1
Marking procedures used with IRIs for miscues that are both recorded and scored

Type	Example	Marking Procedure
1. Substitutions	The student says *when* although the text word is *where*.	Write the word the student said above the text word: *when* "I don't know where the cat went."
2. Omissions	The student leaves out a word that is in the text.	Circle the word: "The tall, (old) man was sitting on the bench."
3. Insertions	The student adds a word that is not in the text.	Insert the word with a caret: *big* "That black dog bit the boy." ^
4. Use of nonwords	The student substitutes a nonsense word for a real word.	Phonetically write the nonword above the text word for which it was substituted: *pauk* "He sat on the back porch."
5. Word reversals	The student pronounces the word *no* as the word *on*.	Code this as a substitution.

miscue types listed in Table 5–1 and those shown in Table 5–2. Miscues described in Table 5–1 are recorded and scored; that is, the teacher marks these on the duplicate copies of the passages while listening to the tape and considers them when determining percentage of correct word identification. Miscues shown in Table 5–2 are recorded but not scored; that is, the teacher marks them on the duplicate passages to analyze later for the student's reading strategies, skills, and knowledge but does not include them when scoring passages to determine percentages of correct word identification. Silent reading performance is based on ability to answer the comprehension questions for each passage.

If the student repeatedly makes a miscue on the same word, count it only the first time. Pronunciations that differ from the expected response due to a student's oral language dialect should not be counted as miscues.

Authorities have suggested various criteria for determining whether a passage is at a student's independent, instructional, or frustration level. Some have also suggested different criteria for different grade levels. Research has been undertaken to determine

TABLE 5–2
Marking procedures used with IRIs for miscues that are recorded but not scored

Type	Example	Marking Procedure
1. Repetitions	The student repeats the same word or phrase one or more times.	Draw a wavy line under the text portion the student repeated: "We saw an elephant at the zoo."
2. Self-corrections	The student makes an error, but then corrects it.	Code the original error in the usual manner, but then place a "C" above it: "His chemistry set is going to get him in trouble."
3. Hesitations	The student hesitates for a long time before pronouncing a word.	Place a slash in front of the word: "Please hand me my/glasses."
4. Ignoring punctuation	The student appears not to have noticed a period, comma, or other punctuation mark.	Code as an omission, i.e., circle the omitted punctuation mark.

which of these criteria provides the most accurate estimates. For example, Fuchs, Fuchs, and Deno (1982) reported that their analyses support the criterion of 95% accuracy in word identification as a standard for determining instructional level. Powell's (1971) research, on the other hand, suggested the following range of criterion levels for determining instructional level based on word identification miscues: preprimer through second grade (87% to 94%); third through fifth grades (92% to 96%); sixth grade and above (approximately 96%).

Both word identification and comprehension accuracy must be taken into account to determine a student's reading levels. Based on the best available research evidence and the opinions of authorities, the following criterion levels are suggested:

Level	Word Identification	Comprehension
Independent	100%–96%	100%–90%
Instructional	95%–90%	89%–70%
Frustration	below 90%	below 70%

Published IRIs Designed for General Use

The best choice for many teachers is a commercially published IRI designed for general use. In most remedial reading classes, reading clinics, LD classrooms, and other similar programs, more than one set of reading texts is employed. Students read a variety of materials such as books of high-quality literature, easy-to-read, high-interest level books, their own dictated experience stories, stories selected from a number of different authentic texts to meet their interests, and books from a variety of kits designed especially for remedial programs. For teachers to prepare an IRI specifically related to each of these certainly is not practical, and to develop an IRI based on only one set loses the advantage of the test being directly related to all instructional materials used. A published IRI designed for general use is a satisfactory alternative.

There are many commercially prepared IRIs from which to choose. Most contain graded word lists that are used to determine the level at which testing should begin and also for assessing word knowledge. The core of the IRI, however, is a series of graded passages to be read orally and silently. These are designed to help the teacher further assess a student's word knowledge, to examine a student's word identification strategies and comprehension, and, as well as, to determine a student's independent, instructional, and frustration levels.

Some commercially prepared IRIs include the Analytical Reading Inventory (ARI), the Basic Reading Inventory (BRI), the Classroom Reading Inventory (CRI), the Contemporary Classroom Reading Inventory (CCRI), the Diagnostic Reading Inventory (DRI), the Diagnostic Reading Scales (DRS), the Edwards' Reading Test (ERT), the Ekwall Reading Inventory (ERI), the Flynt-Cooter Reading Inventory for the Classroom, the Informal Reading Assessment (IRA), the McCarthy Individualized Diagnostic Reading Inventory–Revised, the Standard Reading Inventory (SRI), the Sucher-Allred Reading Placement Inventory (SARPI), and the Qualitative Reading Inventory (QRI). A third edition of the Ekwall test is now available, titled the Ekwall/Shanker Reading Inventory. A number of IRIs include additional supplementary tests, and some are standardized (e.g., the Diagnostic Reading Scales). Most IRIs, although not all, have passages from first-grade through middle school levels, and an IRI of interest to secondary teachers is the Advanced Reading Inventory, which is designed for grade 7 through college. Only some of these inventories have passages as low as preprimer or primer levels; therefore, if these lower levels are needed, the teacher should check before purchasing an inventory to determine if tests at these levels are available in the IRI. See Table 5–3 for important characteristics of many of these tests, including range of grade levels covered. Also see Test Bank B.

How Did Our Case Study Student Fare on the IRI?

Now let's return to David Adams, the hypothetical student for whom we have been gradually completing an assessment information form. To verify general reading levels, we will suppose his teacher has chosen to use a published IRI, and that David's performance on this test indicates his functional reading levels to be:

Frustration Level	Approximately 2.5 and above
Instructional Level	Approximately 2.0
Independent Level	Approximately 1. 0

If we compare David's present reading achievement level based on the results of the previously administered standardized test with the instructional level obtained from this IRI, we find they are similar indeed (see Figure 5–1). This means we can feel relatively confident that placing David in material at approximately the beginning of second-grade level will be appropriate for his initial instruction. Scores obtained on an IRI to

TABLE 5-3
Important features of 11 published IRIs

Informal Reading Inventories

Features	ARI	BRI	CRI	CCRI	DRI	DRS	ERI	ERT	IRA	SARPI	SRI[a]
Contents											
No. of forms	3	3	3	3	1	2	4	2	4	1	2
Range of passages	P–9	PP–8	PP–8	P–9	1–8	1–8	PP–9	6–13 yrs.	PP–12	P–9	PP–7
Graded word lists	P–6	PP–8	PP–6	P–7	1–8	1–6	PP–9	6–13 yrs.	PP–12	P–9	PP–7
Separate student passages	Yes	Yes	Yes	Yes	Yes	Yes	Yes	Yes	Yes	Yes	Yes
Student summary sheet	Yes	Yes	Yes	Yes	Yes	Yes	Yes	Yes	Yes	Yes	Yes
Class summary sheet	Yes	Yes	No	No	No	No	No	No	No	Yes	No
Pictures/illustrations	No	No	Yes	Yes	No	No	No	No	No	No	No
Motivation/purpose statement for each passage	Yes	No	Yes	Yes	Yes	No	No	No	Yes	Yes	Yes
Supplementary features[1]	B	B	ST	B, ST	ST	CL, ST	ST	B, ST	B	TT	CL, RS
Passages											
Length (words)	50–339	50–100	24–174	47–316	224–361	29–221	31–202	25–100	61–217	51–191	47–151
Content[2]	N, E	N, E	N, E	N, E	N	N, E	N, E	N, E	N, E	N, E	N, E
Readability estimates given	Yes	Yes	No	Yes	No	No	No	No	No	Yes	No
Readability formulas used[3]	HJ, SP	DC, FR, SP	DC, FL, SP	BG, DC, FR, HJ, SP	NI	DC, SP	DC, HJ	E, SM	FR, SP	DC, SP	DC, SP
Same format student/teacher copies	No	Yes	No	No	No	No	No	Yes	No	No	Yes

Questions

No. per passages	PP-2:6 3-9:8 3-9:8	PP:4 P-8:10	5	P-1:5 2:6 3:7 4-9:8	1-3:12 4-8:20	1-2:7 3-8:8	PP:5 1-9:10	4-10	PP-2:8 3-12:10	5	PP:5 P-7:13-15
Types of questions[4]	L, I, CE, MI, V	L, CE, MI, V	L, I, V	L, I, CE, MI, S, V	L,I,CE,V	NI	L, I, V	NI	L,I,CE, MI, S, V	L,I,CE, MI, V	L, I, V
Suggested answers given	Yes	Yes	Yes	Yes	No	Yes	Yes	Yes	Yes	Yes	Yes

Administering

Oral	Yes	Yes	Yes	Yes	Yes	Yes	Yes	Yes	Yes	Yes	Yes
Silent	Optional	Optional	Optional	NI	Yes	Yes	Yes	Yes	Optional	No	Yes
Listening comprehension	Yes	Optional	Optional	Optional	Yes	Yes	Optional	Yes	Optional	No	Optional
Directions given for—											
Starting/stopping	Yes	Yes	Yes	Yes	Yes	Yes	Yes	Yes	Yes	Yes	Yes
Marking miscues/errors	Yes	Yes	Yes	Yes	Yes	Yes	Yes	Yes	Yes	Yes	Yes
Aid given in oral reading	Yes	No	Yes	Yes	Yes	Yes	Yes	Yes	Yes	Yes	Yes
Probing of comprehension recommended	NI	Yes	NI	Yes	No	Yes	Yes	NI	Yes	NI	Yes
Timing of rate	NI	Optional	Optional	NI	NI	Yes	NI	Yes	Optional	NI	Yes

Scoring

Types of miscues/errors counted[5]	A, I, I/R, O, R, S	"Sig. Mis-cues"	A, I, O, R, S	A, I, I/R, M, O,R,S	A, I, O, S	A, I, I/R, M, O,R,S	A, I, I/R, M, O,R,S	A, I, I/R, M, I, O, S	A, I, I/R, M, O,R,S	A, I, M, O,R,S	A, I, M, O, P,R, S, SC
Partial credit for comprehension questions	NI	Yes	Yes	Yes	No	Yes	Yes	Yes	NI	Yes	Yes

TABLE 5-3 *(continued)*

Informal Reading Inventories

Features	ARI	BRI	CRI	CCRI	DRI	DRS	ERI	ERT	IRA	SARPI	SRI
Criteria for levels											
Independent											
Word recognition	99/more	99/more	95/more	97/more	98/more	NI	99/more	95/more	99/more	97/more	97/more
Comprehension	90/more	90/more	NI	80/more	90/more	60/more	90/more	70/more	90/more	80/more	NI
Instructional											
Word recognition	95/more	95/more	95/more	92/more	92/more	NI	95/more	90/more	85–95/more	92/more	92/more
Comprehension	75/more	75/more	75/more	60/more	60/more	60/more	60/more	70/more	75/more	60/more	NI
Frustrational											
Word recognition	90/less	90/less	NI	91/less	90/less	NI	90/less	90/less	90/less	92/less	92/less
Comprehension	50/less	50/less	NI	60/less	50/less	NI	50/less	70/less	50/less	60/less	60/less
Listening											
Comprehension	75/more	75/more	75/more	60–75/more	60/more	60/more	70/more	70/more	75/more	NI	NI 40 unaided / 70 aided
Interpreting											
Suggestions for diagnostic interpretation	No	Yes	Yes	Yes	Yes	Yes	Yes	No	Yes	No	Yes
Sample cases demonstrated	No	Yes	Yes	Yes	Yes	No	Yes	No	Yes	Yes	No
Teaching suggestions offered	No	Yes	No	No	No	No	No	No	No	No	No
Guidance for handling discrepancies in performance	Yes	Yes	Yes	Yes	Yes	Yes	Yes	No	Yes	Yes	Yes

KEY:
NI = Not Indicated
[1] Supplementary Features: B, Bibliographies; CL, Checklists; CS, Case Studies; RS, Rating Scales; ST, Additional Student Tests; TT, Teacher Test
[2] Content: N, Narration; E, Exposition
[3] Readability Formulas: BG, Botel-Granowsky; DC, Dale-Chall; E, Edwards; FL, Flesch; FR, Fry; HJ, Harris-Jacobson; SM, SMOG; SP, Spache
[4] Types of Questions: CE, Critical-Evaluative; I, Interpretive-Inferential; L, Literal-Factual; MI, Main Ideas; S, Sequence; V, Vocabulary
[5] Types of Miscues/Errors: A, Aid; I, Insertions; I/R, Inversions/Reversals; M, Mispronunciations; O, Omissions; P, Punctuation; R, Repetitions; S, Substitutions; SC, Self-Corrections
[a] See text for indication of name of test represented by these initials.

Source: From "Test Review: Commercial Informal Reading Inventories" by K. Jongsma and E. Jongsma, 1981, *The Reading Teacher, 34*, pp. 700-702. Copyright 1981 by the International Reading Association. Reprinted by permission of Kathleen S. Jongsma and the International Reading Association.

Test Bank B
Informal Reading Inventories

See Table 5–3 for comprehensive information about many published informal reading inventories. Other IRIs are listed here.

Name	For Grades	Type of Administration	Time for Administration	Publisher
Advanced Reading Inventory (ARI)	7 through college	Group	Varies according to subtests used	Wm. C. Brown
Ekwall/Shanker Reading Inventory (3rd ed.)	Preprimer through 9	Individual	Varies with student	Allyn and Bacon
Flynt-Cooter Reading Inventory	1 through 9	Individual	Varies with student	Gorsuch Scarisbrick
McCarthy Individualized Diagnostic Reading Inventory— Revised Edition	K–12	Individual	35–60 minutes	Educators Publishing Service
Qualitative Reading Inventory	1 through junior high	Individual	Varies with student	HarperCollins

verify general reading levels should be recorded on the student's assessment information form, as was done for our case study student, David Adams, in Figure 5–1.

However, such close agreement between two tests, as is the case with David, is not always found. Consider, instead, other students for whom you see significant contradictions between the conclusions of the two tests: as an illustration, presume a student's present achievement level according to a standardized test is 4.2, but the instructional level based on an IRI corresponds to sixth-grade level; or for another student, for example, the standardized test results indicate an instructional level of 3.0 and the IRI outcome specifies an instructional score of primer (i.e., about middle of first-grade level). In instances such as these, you should carefully review any circumstances during administration of the tests that might have resulted in a score not accurately reflecting the student's reading level. For example, did the student work conscientiously only during the first part of the standardized test, then appear to become bored and rush through questions during the last part? Did you tend to be particularly lenient or stringent in scoring comprehension checks on the IRI when there was doubt about the correctness of a student's response? After answering questions such as these, if the incongruities cannot be resolved, you would do best to place the student in materials at a level consistent with the lower of the two scores. Follow placement with careful daily

FIGURE 5–1

Continuation of a partially completed record form of assessment information for a hypothetical student

---

Assessment Information Form

Student's Name: David Adams

Grade Level: 4th

Chronological Age:

1) Birthdate   February 19, 19—

2) Age   9.0

Listening Level:

1) Method of determination   Use of graded IRI passages

2) Level   4th grade

Entry Level Assessment Results: 2nd grade

Standardized Survey Test:

1) Name of test   Gates-MacGinitie Reading Tests, Level 2, Form A

2) Grade score obtained   3.0

Present Reading Instructional Level (based on standardized test results):   approximately 2.0

Discrepancy Between Listening Level and Present Achievement: 2.0

Verification of General Reading Levels:

1) Name of test   Analytical Reading Inventory

2) Grade scores obtained   Frustration level—approximately 2.5 and above

Instructional level—approximately 2.0

Independent level—approximately 1.0

---

monitoring and if it appears the lower test score was indeed too low, move the student up through successively more difficult material until you find an appropriate level for instruction. It is better to place the student in material that is too easy at the beginning of a program rather than in text that is too difficult.

Using an IRI to Analyze Specific Strengths and Weaknesses

Although the major purpose of this chapter is to describe procedures for verifying students' general reading levels, some information about specific strengths and weaknesses may also be gained from IRIs, if miscues and behaviors are *analyzed,* as well as counted to obtain a score. Let's suppose a teacher is now going to go back through David Adams's IRI and do just that. She or he takes the teacher's copy of each passage from the IRI on which his miscues were marked and some blank paper and then begins to appraise David's performance on each passage. Her written comments are found in Figure 5–2.

From the teacher's analysis, as it unfolds in Figure 5–2, we may examine David's performance with material that is easy for him, on material that is at what we now estimate to be his instructional level, and in material at his frustration level, and we can contrast his reading behaviors in text at these varying levels of difficulty.

We observe from the information provided by the teacher, for example, that David finds no obstacles with comprehension at the preprimer and primer levels (the easiest levels of first-grade text), has only minor problems on the first-reader-level passages (a level often used by students near the end of first grade), and that, although understanding becomes more challenging for him on the beginning second-grade selections, his effectiveness is still within an acceptable range at that level. We are also able to compare comprehension after oral reading versus silent reading and can note that his confusions at these levels are associated with higher-level comprehension rather than with literal questions. However, a decided difference is detected in his comprehension responses after reading the passages designed for the second semester of second grade. There is a breakdown in understanding after both oral and silent reading, and for both literal and higher-level questions.

Some clues to this deterioration in grasping the text message are found when David's word recognition and word identification abilities are studied from the teacher's written analysis. Looking again at Figure 5–2, we perceive the same kinds of changes *across* levels as were seen with comprehension—word knowledge skill becomes increasingly less satisfactory from the first to the last passages he read. However, we also observe some pervasive difficulties in *all levels,* even the easiest. It appears that David does not have accurate recognition of basic high-frequency words (words that occur often in all text). He confuses many of these with words that look similar, or he is unable to pronounce them at all. The result is that the meaning of the text is changed.

There is also evidence of deficient word identification strategies. David appears not to know all strategies he might employ when encountering an unknown word and is ineffective in using those of which he is aware. All of this has caused him to focus considerable attention on word identification, which can divert concentration from the sense of the selection. What is more, David makes no attempt to self-correct errors, even when the consequence of these word confusions and omissions is the production of sentences that are meaningless. In the easiest test passages, though word recognition miscues do appear, they are relatively infrequent, and therefore, the printed message remains sufficiently intact so that understanding is not interrupted. But as numerous problems with words emerge in the more demanding passages, comprehension is adversely affected.

Based on this analysis, the teacher can already reach some conclusions about what is needed in David's instructional program and can make decisions about further testing that should be conducted. Finally, the teacher adds these conclusions in a summary statement at the end of the written comments (this summary can be found in the next figure, Figure 5–3) and attaches these to the student's assessment information form.

FIGURE 5–2
An analysis of a hypothetical student's IRI performance

Analysis of David Adams' IRI Performance

Preprimer Level

Oral Reading

Word Identification: One sight word confusion (*there/where*); even though the resulting sentence did not make sense when he made this miscue, David read on with no attempt to self-correct.

Comprehension: All responses were correct.

Silent Reading

Comprehension: All responses were correct.

Primer Level

Oral Reading

Word Identification: 1. One sight word confusion (*get/got*); David did not self-correct although the resulting sentence did not sound like normal language.
2. There was one basic word David could not read at all (*first*). He immediately attempted to "sound it out" when he could not recognize it. However, he was unsuccessful, repeatedly producing the sound of the first letter of the word, but then giving up, omitting the word, and reading on.

Comprehension: All responses were correct.

Silent Reading

Comprehension: All responses were correct.

First-Reader Level

Oral Reading

Word Identification: 1. Four confusions of basic words (*of/off*; *this/these*; *black/back*; *soon/some*). No attempts at self-correction, although in no case did the resulting sentence make sense or sound like normal language.
2. Did not know one basic word (*are*) at all; again attempted to sound it out, saying /ă/ several times and then abandoning attempt and reading on. No attempt to use context, which would have cued the word in this passage.

Comprehension: Missed 1 question out of 10 (a question that required the reader to draw a conclusion).

Silent Reading

Comprehension: All responses were correct.

2₁ Level[1] (First Semester of Second Grade)

Oral Reading

Word Identification: 1. Five confusions of basic words (*everything/everyone*; *came/come*; *that/what*; *eat/ate*; *because/become*). No attempts to self-correct, although some of the resulting sentences made no sense.

FIGURE 5–2   *(continued)*

	2. Two basic words he did not know at all (*were; show*). Attempted to sound them out by using the first one or two letters; did not use context along with these cues. Omitted both words after unsuccessful attempts.
	3. After a brief hesitation before the word *doesn't*, omitted it with no obvious attempts to work it out using any word identification strategy.
Comprehension:	Missed 2 out of 10 questions (one requiring him to identify the main idea of the passage; the other requiring him to make an inference).

Silent Reading
Comprehension: Missed 1 out of 10 (a question requiring him to draw a conclusion).

2_2 Level (Second Semester of Second Grade)

Oral Reading

Word Identification:	1. Confusions of 11 words (*have/had*; *their/they*; *stay/start*; *slid/slide*; *skin/sky*; *which/with*; *something/someone*; *like/let*; *soup/soap*; *when/then*; *I'll/It's*). No attempts at self-correction.
	2. After hesitations before *chipmunk* and *remember*, omitted these with no obvious attempts to use any word identification strategy.
	3. On eight other words (*people, smart, stood, birds, waiting, knows, rider, seeds*), he attempted unsuccessfully to sound them out, only producing sounds of the first one or two letters of the word before abandoning attempt; no attempts to use context clues.
	4. Two words were pronounced as nonsense words (*gravel*/"gratel"; *wheels*/"we-les").
Comprehension:	Missed 5 out of 10 questions (two of those missed were literal level questions; one required him to make an inference; one required him to follow a sequence of events; and one required him to draw a conclusion).

Silent reading

Comprehension:	Missed 4 out of 10 (one literal level question; one required him to draw a conclusion; one required him to select main idea of passage; and one required him to make an inference).

[1] Numbers with subscripts are used conventionally to denote grade and semester. 2_1, for example, denotes first semester of second grade.

ISSUES RELATED TO INFORMAL ASSESSMENT USING IRIs

For determining reading levels and specific strengths and weaknesses in reading, informal procedures often can provide more reliable information than standardized tests because they may be carried out more frequently and, therefore, provide a larger sampling of the behaviors for teachers to use in instructional planning (Farr & Carey, 1986). IRIs are one of the most widely employed of the many types of informal assessments. (See Figure 5–4, for an example of a test passage from an IRI.)

FIGURE 5–3
A summary of a hypothetical student's IRI performance

Summary of David Adams' IRI Performance

Implications for Instruction

David must be taught to use a variety of word identification strategies along with use of the beginning letter(s)/sound(s) of a word (a strategy he already employs). He must be taught to read for meaning and to self-correct when what he reads does not make sense or sound like normal language. Attention should be given to eliminating his many sight word confusions; he substitutes words that look similar (e.g., *of/off*; *because/become*), even when they make no sense in that passage. He must be taught to use meaning as an aid in word identification.

David appears to need more work in higher-level comprehension tasks rather than in literal-level ones. On this test, he had difficulty with literal-level questions only when he reached his frustration level. He also had slightly more difficulty with comprehension after oral rather than silent reading. Since oral reading requires more attention to word identification than silent reading, increasing his efficiency in word identification strategies also appears to be important for the purpose of allowing him to attend more to comprehension of the material.

Advantages of Informal Inventories.   IRIs may serve the functions of both a survey test and a diagnostic test: as seen above, they can be used to determine a student's reading level and also provide evidence of specific strengths and weaknesses in reading strategies, knowledge, and skills. In addition, research shows that grade scores obtained on IRIs are often closer to the actual classroom performance of students than scores from standardized survey tests. Informal reading inventories with graded passages taken directly from the actual materials a student will be reading have high content validity. Finally, since IRIs are individually administered, the teacher is able to observe students directly while they are responding to reading tasks; direct observation of reading behaviors informs teacher decisions in ways not possible when merely obtaining scores from standardized tests.

Disadvantages of Informal Inventories.   Accurate results on an IRI depend on the competence of the teacher administering the test. Scoring IRIs requires more skill than scoring standardized instruments. Also, despite a teacher's efforts to be objective, evaluating a student's performance on an IRI always involves some subjectivity. For example, when the accuracy of a student's response to a comprehension question is in doubt, one teacher may decide the answer is more right than wrong and score it correct; another teacher might apply more stringent criteria to the same answer and score it as incorrect. Therefore, as research has shown, interpretations of informal measures may not be consistently reliable since some teachers construe results in one way and others draw different conclusions from the same results; but fortunately, training on scoring IRIs apparently can alleviate this problem (Visonhaler, Weinshank, Polin, & Wagner, 1983).

The type of comprehension check used also affects the results; in teacher-prepared IRIs, questions must be planned carefully ahead of time. Accuracy of results also

FIGURE 5–4
An example of a typical IRI

Level 2 (118 words   13 sent.)

Examiner's Introduction
(Student Booklet page 33):

Imagine how you would feel if you were up to bat and this was your team's last chance to win the game! Please read this story.

Whiz! The baseball went right by me, and I struck at the air!

"Strike one," called the man. I could feel my legs begin to shake!

Whiz! The ball went by me again, and I began to feel bad. "Strike two," screamed the man.

I held the bat back because this time I would kill the ball! I would hit it right out of the park! I was so scared that I bit down on my lip. My knees shook and my hands grew wet.

Swish! The ball came right over the plate. Crack! I hit it a good one! Then I ran like the wind. Everyone was yelling for me because I was now a baseball star!

Comprehension Questions
and Possible Answers

(mi) 1. What is this story about?
(a baseball game, someone who gets two strikes and finally gets a hit, etc.)

(f)   2. After the second strike, what did the batter plan to do?
(hit the ball right out of the park)

(inf) 3. Who was the "man" in this story who called the strikes?
(the umpire)

(t)   4. In this story, what was meant when the batter said, "I would kill the ball"?
(hit it very hard)

(ce) 5. Why was the last pitch a good one?
(because it went right over the plate)

(ce) 6. What did the batter do after the last pitch?
(The batter hit it a good one and ran like the wind.)

Miscue Count:

O___ I ___ S ___ A ___ REP ___ REV ___

Scoring Guide	
Word Rec.	Comp.
IND 1	IND 0
INST 6	INST 1–2
FRUST 12 +	FRUST 3 +

Form A / Teacher Record / Graded Paragraphs

Source: From *Analytical Reading Inventories* (4th ed., p. 63) by M. L. Woods and A. J. Moe, 1985, Columbus, Ohio: Charles E. Merrill. Copyright 1989 by Macmillan College Publishing, Inc. Reprinted by permission of Macmillan College Publishing Company.

depends on careful selection of the passages to be read. For example, if the "sixth-grade" passage in an inventory is actually much easier or much more difficult than typical sixth-grade material, the teacher may incorrectly evaluate a student's performance. In published IRIs the criteria used for measuring performance varies; when tests employing different criteria are used, different results may be obtained. Since IRIs must be administered individually, they are more time consuming than group-administered standardized tests. Alternate forms of many published IRIs are not equivalent; therefore, these IRIs cannot be used as pretests and posttests to measure student growth. And, like most standardized tests, passages on many IRIs are quite short and, therefore, may not provide the same task demands as those of authentic reading (Calfee & Hiebert, 1991).

Nonetheless, despite some disadvantages, IRIs are an excellent assessment tool, if used for appropriate reasons and if prepared, administered, and interpreted correctly.

CLOZE TESTS

The cloze procedure has been used for three purposes: (a) to determine readability levels of texts, (b) to instruct students in use of context clues, and (c) to test students to determine placement. This third use is called a **cloze test,** and such testing is sometimes employed for verifying general reading levels obtained on a group, standardized survey test. A cloze test consists of a passage from which words have been systematically deleted. The student is asked to supply the missing words, and an estimate of reading levels is based on performance on this task.

Preparing a Cloze Test

Here are instructions for preparing a cloze test. First, select 2 passages from each book in a series for which the reading levels are known. The passages should be ones students have not previously read, and each should be about 300 words in length. Usually the first sentence in the passage is left intact (i.e., no words are omitted from it). Beginning with any of the first five words in the second sentence, delete every fifth word in the passage until 50 words have been omitted. Fifty words must be deleted to have a reliable measure. Typically one additional sentence is included after the 50 deletions, and this last sentence is kept intact.

Every fifth word should be deleted, even though a specific deletion may be judged difficult for students. (The criteria of omitting every fifth word is not applied when the cloze procedure is used for instructional proposes; rather, specific key words are deleted to fit the objective of that lesson.) If numerals appear in a passage and are to be deleted, the whole numeral is considered as one word. For example in the sentence, "Native Americans lived in this area 350 years ago," *350* would be treated as one word. When the passage is retyped, blanks indicating missing words are to be the same length.

Administering a Cloze Test

Students can write responses in the blanks or respond orally. Give the following directions to students:

1. Read over the whole passage, and then go back and fill in words.
2. Try to use the exact word you think the author would have used.
3. Write one word on each line, or tell me one word.

4. If you have trouble guessing a word, skip it, and go back after you have finished the whole passage and try again.

A practice passage is used to be sure students understand the task and they are
given as much time as needed to work on it.

Scoring a Cloze Test

On a cloze test, only the *exact* words deleted from the text are scored as correct. Synonyms are not accepted. (This requirement is not used when the cloze procedure is
employed for instructional purposes; instead, any word conveying the same meaning
intended by the passages is accepted as correct.) Misspellings of correct words are not
considered incorrect. To determine the percentage of correct words for each passage,
the number of correct responses for that passage is divided by 50 (the number of deletions). For example, if Dale had 32 correct responses on one passage, his percentage of
correct responses is 64% (that is, 32 divided by 50 =.64). Average the student's percentage of correct responses for the two passages selected for each reading level. If, for
example, Brian scored 58% correct on one third-grade passage and 50% on the second
third-grade passage, his average percentage of correct responses at the third-grade level
is 54 percent. The following criteria are used to determine a student's reading levels
(Bormuth, 1968):

Independent Level	Over 57%
Instructional Level	44% to 56%
Frustration Level	43% or less

These criteria are based on the deletion of every fifth word from the text and on accepting as correct only responses identical to the deleted word.

Advantages of Cloze Tests.   Use of cloze tests is controversial. Some authorities point
to their advantages, and others to disadvantages.

As far as advantages, cloze tests are easier to prepare, administer, and score than
IRIs. Cloze tests also assess a student's ability to use knowledge of language and to
comprehend text at the sentence level. In addition, there is some measure of word
knowledge inherent in these tests, and they probably furnish a reasonable appraisal of
literal understanding. On these bases, studies have shown cloze tests to be valid and
reliable measures for determining students' reading levels (Cziko, 1983; Jones & Pikulski, 1974; Paradis, Tierney, & Peterson, 1975; Rankin, 1978; Ransom, 1968; Warwick,
1978). Furthermore, relatively high correlations (between approximately .60 and .80)
have been shown when comparing evaluations from cloze tests and scores obtained
from standardized tests featuring multiple-choice questions (Shanahan & Kamil, 1984).
Considering that reading levels obtained for students are approximate on any test, these
correlations seem more than sufficient to proponents of cloze tests.

Disadvantages of Cloze Tests.   The major criticism of cloze tests is that they do not
provide a good evaluation of interpretive (or higher-level) comprehension. This asser-
tion is based on a fairly large number of studies showing that these tests do not measure
the type of comprehension that goes *across* sentences—that is, comprehension
processes that employ information in one sentence to assist with understanding of
another (called *intersentential comprehension*) (e.g., see Kamil, Smith-Burke, &
Rodriguez-Brown, 1986; Shanahan, Kamil, & Tobin, 1982). Using information across

sentences makes reading more efficient and aids recall as well as inferential understanding. Because cloze tests do not gauge intersentential comprehension, many authorities warn against their use on the basis that they are incomplete assessments of comprehension.

A second disadvantage is that cloze tests do not provide a reliable and valid measure for students reading below the third-grade. A modified cloze procedure used with students reading below third-grade level is called a *maze test*. Suggested by Gutherie, Seifert, Burnham, and Caplan (1974) as an easier task for younger children and poorer readers, the maze test provides 3 alternatives for each deleted word. In a maze test, every fifth word is omitted from a passage of about 125 words so that there are 20 deletions. The first and last sentence remain intact. The 3 alternatives always include the correct word, one incorrect alternative that has the same grammatical function as the deleted word (e.g., if the deleted word is a verb, this alternative is also a verb), and one incorrect alternative that has a different grammatical function. See the example in Figure 5–5.

Criteria for determining reading levels based on percentage of correct responses on a maze test are

Independent Level	Over 85%
Instructional Level	50% to 84%
Frustration Level	49% or less

All other procedures for preparing, administering, and scoring maze tests are the same as those for cloze tests.

DAILY ONGOING OBSERVATIONS

One of the most powerful forms of informal assessment is daily observation, which provides teachers with a chance to reflect on what students can and cannot do in authentic reading tasks. Most teachers make judgments about the ability of students to handle material in daily work, and in fact, after a review of assessment research, Johnston, Afflerbach, and Weiss (1993) contend that teachers are the main assessment "instruments" in judging students' needs and growth. However, while research may accept teachers as evaluation "instruments," many teachers feel hesitant to assume that their judgments and observations are a legitimate form of assessment.

Johns (1982) proposed the name *innerocular technique*, or IOT, be used for observations during daily lessons. His tongue-in-cheek suggestion for using this pseudo-scientific term is an attempt to legitimize an important diagnostic procedure. Teachers sometimes believe their own judgments lack the value of real tests. This is simply not

FIGURE 5–5
Example of a maze procedure

The queen told her _____ to go into
(servants, friends, sleeping)

the _____ and pick all vegetables
(woods, dark, fields)

_____ saw lying above the _____
(they, that, he)   (clouds, ground, wet)

true. Careful and thoughtful decisions based on students' daily work provide a highly useful form of evaluation that can help the teacher verify (or disprove) test results, note when growth has occurred, provide clues for changing instructional materials when daily performance does not conform to test performance, and highlight *patterns* of behavior—all of which have more important implications for instruction than do single or infrequent measures of reading. As such, the "IOT" can be used to refine decisions about students' reading levels. Keeping graphs and charts provides a permanent record of daily performance that lends credence to the decisions based on this type of informal assessment.

It is false to assume that the only assessment information that should be used in planning remedial instruction comes from formal or informal tests. Consistent reflection after observing students' responses during day-to-day instruction is important, and behaviors noted should be included in the written diagnostic workups of students if these behaviors conflict with those exhibited on tests.

It should be noted, though, that research suggests observation is more reliable and reflection more productive with experience (Berliner, 1986). Or, as K. P. Wolf (1993) puts it, assessment must be informed as well as informal, conducted systematically by a knowledgeable teacher. Preservice teachers need many opportunities to work directly with students to increase their expertise in observational assessment.

Oral Reading

Since daily observation has frequently meant observing students during oral reading, a few words about oral versus silent reading performance are in order. Today, reading educators recognize the need for both oral and silent reading, and avoid using one to the exclusion of the other. Silent reading does have a place in remedial and clinical programs, but there are several reasons why oral reading also must be given attention.

Silent reading practice is important, first, because in most real-life situations, and in most school settings as well, students must read material silently. Poor readers need

Students need opportunities for both oral and silent reading.

practice in sustaining attention and gaining ideas during silent reading. Second, some students of low-reading ability comprehend better after reading silently because they can concentrate on the message rather than pronunciation. This may be particularly true when the task involves understanding higher-level concepts. Third, some poor readers, especially older students, are self-conscious about reading aloud in front of others; they may be nervous because their oral reading performance reflects less skill than they actually possess. Finally, students reading silently may move through the material at their own pace, perhaps regressing if an idea or word presents difficulty; for this reason, students with reading disabilities often feel less pressure during silent reading.

On the other hand, although many poor readers comprehend more adequately after silent reading, research as shown that some have greater understanding of the material after reading orally (e.g., Swalm, 1972). Many poor readers seem to need to hear the language they are reading since this additional input provides a link between spoken and written language. Others try harder during oral reading because they are demonstrating their abilities to someone else. Furthermore, many have less difficulty sustaining attention in oral reading (during silent reading they are on their own to choose whether to attend to the page or not). And some poor readers simply prefer oral to silent reading—it is fun because they have captured the teacher's attention. Finally, several research studies suggest that time spent in oral reading may be more directly tied to increases in reading attainment than are silent reading activities (Reutzel, Hollingsworth, & Eldredge, 1994; Stallings, 1980; Wilkinson, Wardrop, & Anderson, 1988).

When oral reading is used in remedial programs, teachers should understand appropriate (and inappropriate) objectives. Figure 5–6 shows an exercise from McGuffey's Fifth Reader designed to provide practice in correct expression for young readers at the turn of the century. Even today, some teachers worry about lack of expressiveness in poor readers' oral reading. However, recent understandings of the reading process indicate that good expression is a reflection of students' understanding and is not an important objective in itself. When students comprehend material (and no longer have to laboriously concentrate on word identification), good expression follows naturally as the student absorbs the message rather than attending consciously to the ink marks on the page.

Oral reading affords one avenue for the important practice students need in contending with connected text. However, in regard to assessment, the main purpose for oral reading in remedial or clinical programs is to serve as a frequent, informal, and ongoing diagnostic tool for the teacher. Oral reading provides a window to students' reading behaviors so that teachers can identify and stress needed strategies.

CONCLUSION

It is common practice to evaluate the progress students have made after a period of remedial instruction. Comparing performance on pre- and post-measures is one customary method for judging growth. To make this comparison, the teacher uses as a posttest the same form or an alternate form of the standardized survey test employed for preassessment, or asks the student to read a form of an IRI for the posttest that contains passages not read during the initial appraisal. The teacher then compares the student's original test to the posttest to determine the student's gains.

There is some question as to whether using the *same* form of a test is appropriate for measuring progress. If the same test is used, some believe that "practice effects" will cause students to receive higher scores even if they have not progressed. On the other

FIGURE 5–6
Exercise to provide expression in oral reading from McGuffey Fifth Reader

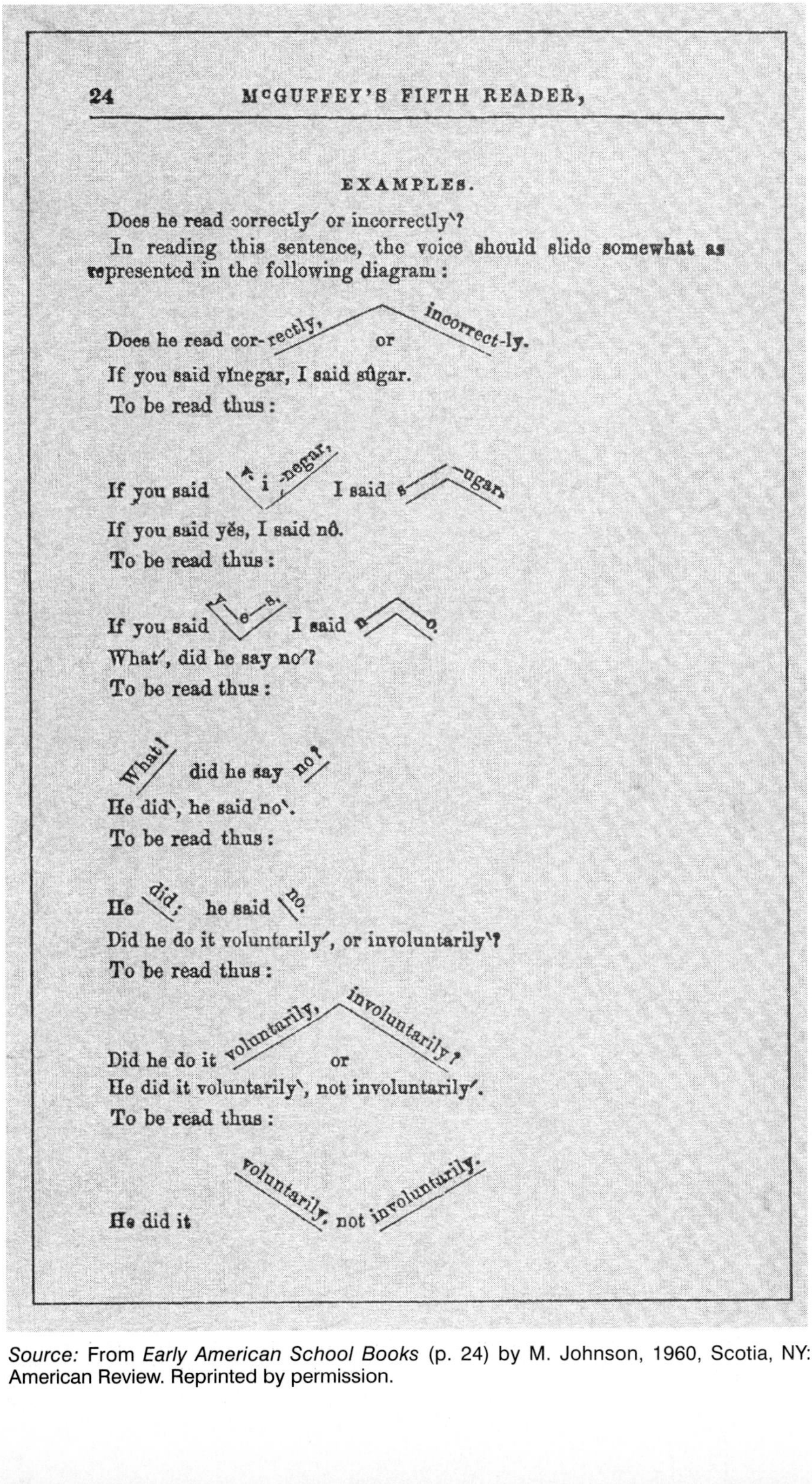
24 McGUFFEY'S FIFTH READER,

EXAMPLES.

Does he read correctly′ or incorrectly‵?

In reading this sentence, the voice should slide somewhat as represented in the following diagram:

Does he read cor-rectly, or incorrect-ly.

If you said vĭnegar, I said sûgar.

To be read thus:

If you said vinegar, I said sugar.

If you said yĕs, I said nô.

To be read thus:

If you said yes, I said no.

What′, did he say no′?

To be read thus:

What! did he say no?

He did‵, he said no‵.

To be read thus:

He did; he said no.

Did he do it voluntarily′, or involuntarily‵?

To be read thus:

Did he do it voluntarily, or involuntarily?

He did it voluntarily‵, not involuntarily′.

To be read thus:

He did it voluntarily, not involuntarily.

Source: From *Early American School Books* (p. 24) by M. Johnson, 1960, Scotia, NY: American Review. Reprinted by permission.

hand, others have noted that test results sometimes indicate a student has made no progress even when growth is obvious; this may occur because the student remembers answers he or she gave on the original test and marks them again, rather than applying the new skills and strategies developed in the remedial program.

There are also problems with using an *alternate* form of a standardized test or IRI. Although authors of some tests may be able to claim statistical equivalency of their alternate forms, it is doubtful that real equivalency exists between all of the many variables that make up the test. For alternate forms to be exactly equivalent, test makers would have to control factors such as the content of test passages, the length and complexity of all sentences, word length, vocabulary difficulty, and a large number of other factors (Farr & Carey, 1986). Though they may attempt to regulate some of these, it is impossible to control every component.

Of the two procedures—using the same form of the test versus using an alternate form—it is probably best to use the alternate form, but in doing so, teachers need to remember the previous admonition that all test scores are approximate. In addition, pre- and postmeasures should be coupled with teacher observation when student development is assessed. Finally, to obtain an accurate picture of student improvement and to determine if the student has maintained the gain, teachers should conduct posttest measures not only at the end of a remedial program but also 3 to 6 months after the student has left the program.

An alternate method of assessing growth that is being viewed with increasing favor is the use of portfolios. Portfolio assessment is discussed in Chapter 7.

📖 REFLECTIONS

1. Are formal assessment measures better than informal measures? Are informal measures better than formal? After reading the pros and cons of different assessment types in the last two chapters, what do *you* think?
2. There are no perfect assessment procedures. Why is this the case?

6

Assessment for Identifying Specific Strengths and Weaknesses in Reading: Part I

Having students engage in a probed retelling of a story after they have read it is one procedure used for some assessment measures.

After verifying a student's approximate instructional level for reading, the teacher must next determine the student's specific strengths and weaknesses in reading strategies, knowledge, and skills. The purpose is that special teachers be able to direct their instructional procedures efficiently; that is, as Winograd (1994) says, these "assessments should be administered with an eye on learning" (p. 421). To be most useful, the findings of assessment must be tightly linked with instruction (Graue, 1993). Some indications of the tests that should be used to determine strengths and weaknesses can be obtained from a student's IRI performance, as illustrated in Chapter 5.

Further assessment tools and procedures that are needed vary according to the instructional level of the student—for example, assessing the dictionary skills of a student reading at early first-grade level normally would be a waste of time; a child at such a beginning level of literacy acquisition typically would not be expected to have advanced skills, such as using a dictionary. Likewise, a student reading at sixth-grade level almost certainly would have knowledge of basic high-frequency vocabulary taught in primary grades; otherwise, this student could not be reading at sixth-grade level, and, therefore, testing basic sight vocabulary would be unnecessary.

The diagnostic process should include only necessary assessment. Although assessment should be thorough, it should also be completed as quickly as possible so that instruction to alleviate problems can begin. The time needed to conduct a thorough assessment will vary from student to student. In a few uncommon instances, some students may require tests not typically necessary for students reading at a particular level. Figure 6–1 lists a general outline of basic tests to administer at each reading level; it provides teachers with a starting point, but adjustments should be made for individual students. Both this chapter and Chapter 7 describe some tests that may help a teacher assess a student's specific needs.

ASSESSING PREREADING CONCEPTS

An assessment of prereading concepts should be conducted with nonreaders and beginning readers. For students whose standardized test or IRI scores indicate that preprimer material is at their frustration level—that is, that they cannot adequately read material even at this easiest level—one of the tests listed in Test Bank C may be used.

A test that is particularly recommended for nonreaders and beginning readers is Concepts About Print. For this test, booklets titled *Sand* or *Stones* are read to the students. During the reading, the teacher asks questions to assess the student's knowledge of several concepts about printed language, such as (a) where the front of a book is found; (b) that the words, not pictures, convey the message; (c) where to begin reading on a page; (d) that it is necessary to move from one line to another; (e) what a "letter" is; (f) what a "word" is; and (g) that the left page should be read before the right. This test also measures student knowledge of letter names, which is important prerequisite information, since letter recognition is critical for word recognition and word identification strategies.

ASSESSING PHONEMIC AWARENESS

In Chapter 3, research was cited demonstrating that phonemic awareness (also called phonological awareness) is important to reading achievement. Studies show that tests of phonemic awareness are better indicators of students who are at risk for low reading performance than any other commonly assessed factors such as oral language

FIGURE 6–1
General outline of basic tests to administer at each reading level

For students whose scores on a standardized test or IRI indicate that material at the preprimer level is at the student's frustration level:

1. Administer a test of prereading concepts
2. Administer tests of phonemic awareness
3. Use the student's own dictated story for assessment
4. Administer tests of knowledge of basic sight vocabulary
5. Administer a test of knowledge and use of word identification strategies
6. Assess writing
7. Orally administer an interest inventory
8. Assess background information

For students whose instructional levels are at the preprimer level:

1. Use an informal test to determine if the student's approximate instructional level is first, second, or third preprimer level
2. Administer tests of phonemic awareness
3. Use the student's own dictated story for assessment or use a running record
4. Administer tests of knowledge of basic sight vocabulary
5. Administer a test of knowledge and use of word identification strategies
6. Assess comprehension
7. Assess writing
8. Orally administer an interest inventory
9. Assess background information

For students whose instructional levels are at the primer level:

1. Administer tests of phonemic awareness
2. Use the student's own dictated story for assessment or use a running record
3. Administer tests of knowledge of basic sight vocabulary
4. Administer a test of knowledge and use of word identification strategies
5. Assess comprehension
6. Assess writing
7. Orally administer a measure of attitudes toward reading
8. Orally administer an interest inventory
9. Assess background information

processes (e.g., Uhry, 1993). This research indicated that a large proportion of poor readers whose difficulties lie with word recognition are particularly lacking in phonemic awareness.

Phonemic awareness has been assessed in a number of ways. Yopp (1988) conducted a comprehensive study to determine which method of assessing phonemic awareness produced the most valid and reliable results. Her study investigated both

FIGURE 6–1 *(continued)*

For students whose instructional levels are at first-, second-, or third-grade levels:

1. Administer tests of phonemic awareness
2. Administer tests of knowledge of basic sight vocabulary
3. Administer a test of knowledge and use of word identification strategies
4. Administer a reading miscue inventory or use a running record
5. Assess comprehension
6. Assess writing
7. Orally administer a measure of attitudes toward reading
8. Orally administer an interest inventory
9. Assess background information

For students whose instructional levels are at fourth-, fifth-, or sixth-grade levels:

1. Administer selected portions of a test of knowledge and use of word identification strategies
2. Administer a reading miscue inventory
3. Assess knowledge of word meanings
4. Assess comprehension
5. Assess writing
6. Administer an attitude scale
7. Administer an interest inventory
8. Assess background information

For students whose instructional levels are above the sixth-grade level:

1. Administer a reading miscue inventory
2. Assess knowledge of word meanings
3. Assess comprehension
4. Assess reading rate
5. Assess writing
6. Administer an attitude scale
7. Administer an interest inventory
8. Assess background information

published instruments and common tasks used to test students' sensitivities to phonological aspects of words. Results of this analysis showed that use of two of these tests together provides a good indication of phonemic awareness levels. Using the following two may be an efficient way for teachers to carry out assessment of phonemic awareness: the Yopp-Singer phoneme segmentation test (Yopp, 1988) and the Bruce phoneme deletion test (D. Bruce, 1964).

Test Bank C
Tests of Prereading Concepts

Name	For Ages	Type of Administration	Time for Administration	Publisher
The Brigance Screens	2–6	Individual	12–15 minutes	Curriculum Associates
Croft Readiness Assessment in Comprehension Kit	Students for whom early diagnostic information is needed	Individual	Varies according to subtests used	Croft
Gates-MacGinitie Reading Tests— Levels PRE & R	5–7	Group	Varies according to subtests used	Riverside
Inventory of Early Development— Revised	birth–7	Individual	Varies according to subtests used	Curriculum Associates
Sand: Concepts About Print Test	5–7	Individual	5–10 minutes	Heinemann Educational Books
Stones: Concepts About Print Test	5–7	Individual	5–10 minutes	Heinemann Educational Books
The Test of Early Reading Ability	3–8	Individual	15–30 minutes	Pro-Ed
Test of Kindergarten/ First Grade Readiness Skills	3½–7	Individual	20 minutes	Academic Therapy Publications

The Yopp-Singer Phoneme Segmentation Test

The Yopp-Singer phoneme segmentation test is administered individually and takes from 5 to 10 minutes. It should be conducted in the following way (Yopp, 1988, p. 166). First, tell the student: "I will say a word and I want you to break it apart. Tell me each sound in the word, in order. If I say *old,* you would say /o/ /l/ /d/."[1] (In this test, please note that students are being asked to give the *sounds,* not the letter names.) Give three other examples, using *ride, go,* and *man.*

---

[1]As you probably remember from a previous chapter, when letters are placed between slashes, as is done with /o/ /l/ /d/, this indicates that the *sound* that the letter represents is being referred to, not the letter name.

Assessing knowledge of pre-reading concepts is important with some students. These concepts include what a word is, what a letter is, and that we move from left to right when reading print.

Next, use the word list found in Table 6-1 to administer the test. Keep track of the number of correct answers that the student gives. When the student answers correctly, indicate this. Consider as correct only those words for which the student gives the right answer without teacher assistance. When the response is wrong, provide the student with the correct answer before moving on.

This test assesses **simple phonemic awareness** (see Chapter 3 for a review of the definition of this term).

The Bruce Phoneme Deletion Test

The Bruce phoneme deletion test is individually administered and takes about 10 minutes. Students are asked what word would remain when a specific letter is removed

TABLE 6–1

List of words for the Yopp-Singer Phoneme Segmentation Test

dog	lay	keep	race
fine	zoo	no	three
she	job	wave	in
grew	ice	that	at
red	top	me	by
sat	do		

Source: From "The Validity and Reliability of Phonemic Awareness Tests" by H. K. Yopp, 1988, *Reading Research Quarterly, 23,* p. 177. Copyright 1988 by the International Reading Association. Reprinted by permission of Hallie K. Yopp and the International Reading Association.

from a word. Yopp (1988, p. 164) suggests using the following practice examples before beginning the test. Ask, "What word would be left if the /c/ in *cat* were taken away?" Follow with these example items: *bright* (remove the /r/); *cried* (remove the /d/). (The teacher should be certain to pronounce the *sound* of the letter to be removed, not the letter name.)

Then use the word list found in Table 6-2 to administer the test. The Bruce phoneme deletion test assesses **compound phonemic awareness** (refer to Chapter 3 for a definition of this term).

Phonemic Awareness Tests That Are Not Useful

There were two assessments evaluated in Yopp's (1988) investigation that proved to be ineffective as indicators of phonemic awareness abilities. One of these was use of rhyming tests in which students do not have to *perform* an operation on the test items; in other words, they are simply asked to state if two words *do rhyme*. The other was a published test, the Wepman Auditory Discrimination Test (Wepman, 1973), which, likewise, only asks students to say whether a pair of words is the same or different. Based on her study, Yopp concluded that the best assessments of phonemic awareness require students to operate on and/or manipulate speech sounds within words.

In Chapter 10, which provides details on instruction to increase phonemic awareness, additional tasks for ongoing assessment are suggested.

TABLE 6–2
List of words for the Bruce
(1964) phoneme deletion test

1. *s-t-and* (middle)	16. *c-old* (first)
2. *j-am* (first)	17. *part-y* (last)
3. *fair-y* (last)	18. *we-n-t* (middle)
4. *ha-n-d* (middle)	19. *f-r-og* (middle)
5. *star-t* (last)	20. *n-ear* (first)
6. *ne-s-t* (middle)	21. *thin-k* (think)
7. *f-rock* (first)	22. *p-late* (first)
8. *ten-t* (last)	23. *s-n-ail* (middle)
9. *lo-s-t* (middle)	24. *b-ring* (first)
10. *n-ice* (first)	25. *pin-k* (last)
11. *s-top* (first)	26. *le-f-t* (middle)
12. *far-m* (last)	27. *car-d* (last)
13. *mon-k-ey* (middle)	28. *s-p-oon* (middle)
14. *s-pin* (first)	29. *h-ill* (first)
15. *for-k* (last)	30. *ever-y* (last)

Source: From "An Analysis of Words Sounds by Young Children" by D. Bruce, 1964, *British Journal of Educational Psychology, 34,* p. 170. Copyright 1964 by Scottish Academic Press (Journals) Limited. Reprinted by permission.

USING A STUDENT'S OWN DICTATED STORY FOR ASSESSMENT

It is difficult to test in normal contextual materials those readers who are in the very beginning stages of learning to read, because they can read so little. By using a student's own dictated story for assessment, a teacher can examine reading behaviors and knowledge while the student is reading *connected* text, rather than simply measuring isolated behaviors. Basing assessment processes on student-dictated text has been a successful procedure in many reading clinics (McCormick, 1981; Waugh, 1993) and with illiterate students (Waugh, 1993). Directions for employing student-dictated stories for this purpose are given in Figure 6–2.

One helpful suggestion to assess reading growth after this initial assessment is to tape students reading their own stories (or published materials) several times throughout the year. Keep these on file for comparison and for reports on student growth to parents. The tapes and analyses can be placed in a portfolio with other assessment information.

ASSESSING KNOWLEDGE OF BASIC SIGHT VOCABULARY

The term **sight vocabulary** (or sight words) is used in three ways:

1. It is used to refer to words a student recognizes instantly.
2. It has been used to mean phonetically irregular words that must be recognized at sight rather than identified through use of letter-sound correspondences.
3. It is often employed synonymously with the phrases **high-frequency words** or **basic vocabulary** or **core vocabulary words**—that is, those words that occur frequently in all written material.

In the following section, the term *sight vocabulary* refers to high-frequency vocabulary. Mastery of basic words is important to fluent reading because they occur so often in any material that a student reads. A student who has to focus on each individual word or identify every word with a word identification strategy usually loses the sense of the material. Immediate recognition of basic words allows students to focus on meaning. Also, because these words appear often, they provide much of the context for other words.

Lists of high-frequency words have been compiled for teacher reference. Some of these include the *Harris-Jacobson Core Lists* (A. J. Harris & Jacobson, 1972), *A Basic Vocabulary for Beginners* (D. D. Johnson, 1971), the Ekwall list (Ekwall, 1975), *The New Instant Word List* (Fry, 1980), the *Dolch Basic Sight Word List* (Dolch, 1936), and the Durr list of high-frequency words in primary level library books (Durr, 1973).

The first two hundred words on all of these lists are about the same because they are basic function words such as *the, and, of, but, for, in, a, that, be, is, to, are, so, it,* and *this.* (See how many and how often each of these basic function words occur on the page you are reading right now.)

A test of knowledge of basic sight vocabulary, that is, high-frequency words, should always be individually administered with the student reading to the teacher. Some published tests of sight word knowledge have been devised so that 3 or 4 words are printed by each item number, the teacher pronounces one of these, and the student circles the word. This procedure does not provide an accurate measure because stu-

FIGURE 6–2
Using student-dictated stories for assessment

1. Materials Needed:
   a. Tape recorder with microphone
   b. Blank tape
   c. Object or picture to stimulate discussion
   d. Paper and pencil
   e. Index cards
2. Initiating Procedures:
   a. At the beginning of the session, allow the student to talk into the tape recorder, listen to the tape, turn the recorder on and off, and engage in any other activity that will help the student feel at ease with the subsequent taping procedures. Temporarily put the tape recorder aside.
   b. Use an object or picture to stimulate discussion.
   c. Have the student dictate a short "story" based on the previous discussion. For some students, the story may consist of no more than two or three sentences. Other students will dictate a longer narrative. Write down the story for the student exactly as it has been dictated.
3. First Taping Procedure:
   a. Turn on the tape recorder.
   b. Have the student read the dictated story.
   c. If the student has difficulty, encourage him or her to
      1. use any procedure known to figure out the unknown word
      2. guess what word would "sound right there" or
      3. skip the word and go on

   Student success during the first taping procedure must be assessed subjectively by the teacher. In general, the attempt may be judged successful if the student is able to read back the sentences within the dictated story in a reasonably meaningful manner. The successful student may not be able to pronounce correctly every word as was originally dictated, but the majority of each sentence will remain intact.

   The behaviors of unsuccessful students may consist of any of the following: the student simply cannot read back any of the dictated story; or the student will focus on isolated words in the story, pointing out only those few which are known; or the student may attempt to scan sentences in correct left to right progression, but can only pronounce an occasional word, thus rendering the story meaningless.

   d. Turn off the tape recorder. Write each word from the story on an individual card. Shuffle the cards and present the words to the student in a random order. Record the student's responses by placing a check or an X on the back of each word card to indicate a correct or incorrect response. When one word is substituted for another, write the substitution on the back of the card.
4. Second Taping Procedure:
   a. If the student had relative success during the first taping procedure, repeat the taping procedure after a short interval (approximately 30–60 minutes) using the *same* story.
   b. If the student has been decidedly unsuccessful during the first taping procedure, do not engage in the second and third taping procedures.

FIGURE 6–2 *(continued)*

5. Third Taping Procedure:

    a. If the student has had relative success during the second taping procedure, repeat the procedure *the next day* using the *same* story.

    b. If the student has been decidedly unsuccessful during the second taping procedure, do not engage in the third taping procedure.

6. Analysis:

    Make one, two, or three copies of the story, depending on the number of taped readings you have obtained. On these copies of the story write information as you listen to the tapes. As you listen, write down words the student substitutes for other words and whether the student subsequently corrects the substituted words. Indicate words that are omitted or added.

    Analyze the student's reading behaviors by responding to the following questions, and by making other observations and statements that are applicable to a specific student's performance.

    a. How does the student's performance in reading the story compare with his or her performance in reading the isolated words printed on the cards? Are there differences between these two performances during the first, second, and third sessions?

    b. Does the student seem to understand correct directional movements in reading connected printed material (i.e, does he or she attempt to read from left to right across a line of print)?

    c. When the student has substituted words in reading the story, do the words

        1. look similar?

        2. mean about the same thing?

    d. Did the student's behavior in substituting words in the story differ from any substitutions he or she made when reading the isolated words from the cards? What differences were seen?

    e. Each time the student omitted or added words within the story, did the sentence

        1. still make sense?

        2. retain its general meaning?

    f. When the student has read aloud a rendition that changes the meaning of the original text, does the student self-correct? If so, how did the student determine that a correction should be made?

    g. When reading the story, what strategies did the student employ when faced with an unknown word? Did he or she attempt to sound out the word letter by letter? Did he or she use the first one or two letters of the word only, and then pronounce any word that begins with those letters? Did the student pronounce any word that has a general configuration similar to the text word? guess wildly? use context to make a choice?

    h. What reading knowledge did the student's performance indicate he or she possessed at the time of the first taping procedure?

    i. What differences were noted in the student's reading behaviors and knowledge when comparing the results of the first, second, and third tapings?

Source: From "Assessment and the Beginning Reader: Using Student-Dictated Stories" by S. McCormick, 1981, *Reading World, 21,* pp. 29-39. Copyright 1981 by the College Reading Association. Reprinted by permission of the author and the College Reading Association.

dents can often recognize a word when it is pronounced, but are unable to identify it when they must read it for themselves. Published tests that take this approach should not be used.

There is some controversy over whether, for tests of knowledge of sight vocabulary, the words should be read in context or in isolation. Those who argue for a contextual presentation correctly point out that in most reading tasks, words do not occur in isolation and that other words in the sentence or passage provide context clues that aid in word identification. While some words in real-life do appear in isolation (such as the word *Stop* on traffic signs or *Men* and *Women* on restroom doors), there is an environmental context that aids identification in these cases. Certainly many high-frequency words, such as *of* or *that*, do not occur in isolation in authentic reading tasks. Have you ever found a sign with the single word *of* printed on it, or found the single word *that* all by itself on a door, or wall, or book page?

On the other hand, those who argue for presenting words in isolation during assessment of sight vocabulary point out, also correctly, that although the context provided by other words in a text often aids word identification, it does not do so in many cases. For example, suppose Don is often confused by the words *was* and *saw*; in the following example, context would not provide any clue to eliminate his confusion.

I_____ a witch on Halloween.
        (was, saw)

Although the longer the selection, the more likely that context will provide clues, it certainly does not always do so. Since instant and accurate recognition of frequently occurring basic words is so important, proponents of an isolated presentation of words during assessment contend that we must determine a student's ability to recognize basic words in any situation, including those where context does not help. One indicator of expert reading performance is the ability to recognize words rapidly (Royer, Cisero, & Carlo, 1993).

A further issue in the debate is offered by research that shows the helpfulness of context depends on a student's familiarity with the word (e.g., M. J. Adams & Huggins, 1985; Frederiksen, 1981). Of course, when students have *much familiarity* with the word, context is unnecessary as an aid to recognition because they know the word so well they can pronounce it automatically without resorting to use of other words in the text for clues. Conversely, this research shows that when students are *very unfamiliar* with a word—that is, they do not have any usefully complete stored memory of the word's identity—they most often do not pronounce it correctly even with the aid of context. The latter finding has held true for both poor readers and good readers, as well as across all grade levels. However, at the *intermediate stage of familiarity*, context does appear to be helpful. When a word is at this intermediate stage, some functional knowledge of the word has been stored in memory, but not to the extent that recognition is automatic. The student may have to use partial letter-sound decoding to determine the word, or may hesitate significantly before recognition, or may not recognize it at all if context does not provide a sufficient hint as to what the word is. At this stage, word recognition may be markedly assisted when the word is in context.

A Contextual Test of Sight Vocabulary

One resolution to this problem is to test sight vocabulary both ways—in context and in isolation. Poor readers often have particular difficulty with the high-frequency words because many are **function words,** such as prepositions and conjunctions. Function words are more abstract than **content words,** such as nouns. Can you define the word *of,* for example? Other than saying it is a preposition, probably not. Function words are more difficult for poor readers to learn initially because they lack the concrete meaning of content words; and at the same time, they are easier to confuse with similar words for the same reason. Therefore, the teacher may wish to test function words in context initially. Words the student is unable to read, even in context, should have the first priority for instruction. Once a student's basic core vocabulary has been assessed in context, it can be tested in isolation. Words recognized in context but not in isolation can be taught after the first priority words are learned.

You can use the following procedure to test basic sight vocabulary in context.

A.   To develop a contextual test of basic sight vocabulary

1.   Use all words from one of the lists of basic high-frequency words. Or select all words from the first preprimer of the material to be used for instruction to compose section 1 of your test; then do the same for the second preprimer to compose section 2; and so on.

2.   Write sentences that include each word; other words in the sentences should be words the student can identify so that they provide a context for the target word you are testing. In constructing these sentences, you will probably use some of the basic high-frequency sight words several times; that is, they will probably occur not only as a target word but also in the context of sentences for other target words. In this way, you will have several opportunities to observe the student's response to the same word.

B.   To administer a contextual test of basic sight vocabulary

1.   Have the student orally read the sentences into a tape recorder.

2.   If a word is not known, tell the student to do anything he or she can to figure it out; if the student still cannot identify it, tell the student to skip it and continue reading.

3.   If a student begins to exhibit great difficulty as the test progresses, discontinue testing. Plan to provide instruction for those words missed up to the point when you stopped testing. After the student has mastered these words, you can administer the test again to identify further words to be learned.

C.   To score a contextual test of basic sight vocabulary

1.   When the student is not present, listen to the tape and mark miscues on a duplicate copy of the test.

2.   Do not mark words only as right or wrong; rather, write down what the student said when a word was mispronounced. For example, if *when* is read as *then,* write *then* above the word *when.*

3.   Circle any word the student is unable to pronounce at all.

4.   Consider correct only those words for which there was "instant" recognition. If there is a long pause before the student can say a word or if a word identification strategy must be used, then there is not instant recognition.

5.   Prepare a list of words the student cannot recognize at all, and another list of words confused with similar words (such as *on* for *no, here* for *there,* and so on). On the second list, note the test word and the similar word.

6.   No grade score is obtained from this type of assessment. Instead, it is used to determine if the student does or does not need instruction on basic sight vocabulary and how much instruction is required. A contextual test also informs the teacher about the kind of instruction needed: is initial instruction needed with most words because the student cannot identify them at all, or is the main problem that the student is confusing words with ones that look similar? A contextual test provides lists of specific words for which instruction is needed.

A Context-Free Test of Sight Vocabulary

Testing basic high-frequency words in context should be followed by a test where context provides no clue to their identification; that is, sight words should also be tested in a context-free situation, or in other words, in isolation. It is preferable to have each word printed on a separate index card rather than presenting the student with one long list. An extended list of words can overwhelm some poor readers and they may feel defeated before they begin.

A.   To develop a test of basic sight vocabulary in isolation

1.   Use a typewriter that has large or primary type; type one word per card. Alternatively you may simply print each word on a card, using correct manuscript writing.

2.   Divide the word cards into sets of 10. In each set, number the cards on the back from 1 to 10.

3.   Make copies of sheets to be used during scoring, with each word in each set listed on the sheet. One example of such a sheet is shown in Figure 6–3.

FIGURE 6–3

Example of a scoring sheet for a sight vocabulary test

Student's Name _____   Date _____

1. on _____	1. have _____	1. is _____
2. of _____	2. go _____	2. go _____
3. the _____	3. if _____	3. now _____
4. for _____	4. and _____	4. know _____
5. with _____	5. red _____	5. never _____
6. some _____	6. so _____	6. no _____
7. where _____	7. every _____	7. from _____
8. because _____	8. a _____	8. off _____
9. to _____	9. have _____	9. which _____
10. it _____	10. had _____	10. said _____

B. *To administer the test of sight vocabulary in isolation*

1.   Have students read from one set of word cards at a time, following the same three procedures as for administering a contextual assessment of sight vocabulary (see p. 142).

2.   Always present the words within a set in the same order (card 1 first, card 2 second, and so on) so that they will match the sheets you have prepared for scoring.

C. *To score the test of sight vocabulary in isolation*

1.   Use scoring sheets

2.   Follow the same procedures described for scoring the contextual test of sight vocabulary (see p. 142).

ASSESSING KNOWLEDGE OF WORD IDENTIFICATION STRATEGIES

Although we hope that students will eventually recognize most words instantly, they will undoubtedly encounter some words they do not know during the developmental stages of learning to read. Even skilled adult readers occasionally find unknown words as they read. Therefore, readers must learn strategies to identify words they do not recognize on sight. An assessment of a student's knowledge of word identification strategies should include tests of phonic analysis, structural analysis, and possibly use of context clues— although the latter is not as crucial as once was believed, or at least appears to be important in a different way. (This will be discussed in a later section.) Analysis of student performance on an IRI provides some incidental information about use of word identification strategies, but there are several ways to obtain more in-depth information. See Figure 6–4 for a diagram that summarizes several approaches.

Formal Measures

The formal measures for assessing word identification strategies, using published tests, discussed in this section provide specific diagnostic information, in contrast to the general reading levels that are obtained from the survey tests discussed in Chapter 4.

Diagnostic tests assess the student's specific strengths and weaknesses in reading. There is no perfectly adequate published diagnostic test, and a variety of problems may occur with those that are available. The tests may not assess all important areas, or they may test areas that research has shown to be unimportant for reading achievement. Some only sample sets of knowledge; for example, they may test only a few consonant sounds instead of them all.

Certain tests measure skills and strategies inappropriately. For example, some authorities question the use of nonsense words to test word identification strategies. The argument for use of nonsense words is that students may recognize real words at sight, and, as a result, their performance on the test then would not be a true reflection of their knowledge of word identification strategies. Using nonsense words may, nonetheless, be inappropriate for several reasons. Even though students may be told that the "word" they are to pronounce is a nonsense word, many attempt to pronounce a real word and, as a result, incorrectly pronounce the sounds in the nonsense word. This is, of course, an indication that they are attempting to use knowledge of the world and lan-

FIGURE 6–4

Methods of assessing knowledge of word identification strategies

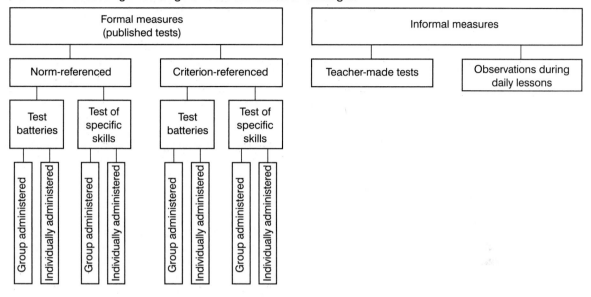

guage to identify words, a strategy we, in fact, want them to employ. In addition, research has shown that pronouncing a nonsense word may require greater skill than pronouncing a real word (Cunningham, 1977), and is, therefore, an inappropriate test of what a student needs to know in authentic reading situations.

Certain tests do not measure what they say they do. For example, some test the ability to use letter-sound correspondences by presenting a picture instead of a word and the student is to circle a letter representing the sound heard at the beginning. This is a test of auditory discrimination rather than of the ability to produce the sound represented by the letter and use this in order to identify unknown words.

To be fair to test designers, it must be said that some of these problems are difficult to resolve. For example, those who employ nonsense words to test word identification strategies are correct in saying that using real words presents the possibility that a student will know the word at sight, and selecting real words that no student will know is a difficult task. Today many teachers attempt to get around the problems of assessing knowledge of letter sounds by having students write words from the teacher's dictation. When doing so, the teacher is not concerned with misspellings, but only with the use of letters that represent the sounds heard. For example, if the student is asked to write *hammer* and writes *hamer*, the teacher knows this student can correctly match the sounds heard in the word with letters or letter combinations that commonly represent those sounds. If the student is asked to write *can* and writes *kan,* again the student has correctly matched sounds with common letter representations and the teacher can extend the assessment by saying "Yes, that's one way you can write the sound heard at the beginning of *can*; now do you know another way?" When using this procedure, however, the teacher must remember that if the student already knows how to spell the word, this method is not a test of the ability to match sounds with letters. In addition, it does not test whether the student uses this knowledge when reading.

There are no simple solutions to some of these problems in preparing published or teacher-made tests, and sometimes a teacher may need to select a test procedure that is the lesser of two (or more) evils. Because of these and other problems, it is necessary to carefully analyze published tests and select the most adequate. In some cases, a teacher may choose to use certain subtests within one test battery and reject others. In many circumstances, it will be necessary for parts of several different published tests to be combined and used along with some teacher-developed subtests to appropriately assess all word identification strategies. Even so, teachers should verify results of all formal assessments through daily observations during instruction.

Some formal, diagnostic tests are *norm-referenced* (i.e., standardized with reference to a norm group). However, providing grade scores, as norm-referenced tests do, is not very important information on a diagnostic test since grade levels do not tell the teacher specifically what a student needs to learn. In addition, grade scores obtained from various published diagnostic tests are generally not comparable (Farr & Carey, 1986); that is, a student can achieve one grade-level score on one published diagnostic test, but on another published diagnostic test administered immediately afterward, achieve a different grade-level placement. Grade-level scores obtained on norm-referenced *diagnostic* tests should be ignored. Diagnostic tests should be used only for determining a student's specific strengths and weaknesses in various areas related to reading.

Some norm-referenced formal assessment instruments consist of diagnostic test batteries. A **test battery** contains many subtests that assess different skills. Most test batteries provide better tests of word identification strategies than of comprehension.

A few norm-referenced test batteries may be group-administered. One such battery is the Basic Skills Inventory. Another is the Stanford Diagnostic Reading Test designed for levels 1.5 to 3.5, 2.5 to 5.5, and 4.5 to 9.5. Subtests for the first level of the

Individually administered tests often provide a more accurate assessment than group-administered tests.

Stanford include auditory vocabulary, auditory discrimination, phonic analysis, word recognition, and comprehension; the second level also includes a test of structural analysis and measures inferential as well as literal comprehension; the third level adds a measure of reading rate.

While they do save time, the problem with *group-administered* diagnostic tests is that they often do not require the same types of performance needed in actual reading tasks. For example, the student's test paper may include a list of numbered items with three or four consonant blends listed beside each; the teacher says a word, and the students circle the blend they hear in the word. This task is easier than, and different from, encountering an unknown word in reading and producing a blend sound to aid in identifying the word. In addition, some group-administered tests include multiple-choice items so that the student may score a correct response by guessing. As a result, group-administered diagnostic tests provide only a "ballpark" notion of the student's needs. As such, they are usually more suitable for planning corrective reading instruction; the information gained is not specific enough for remedial or clinical reading or LD programs.

Other norm-referenced test batteries are *individually administered.* Two of these are the Diagnostic Reading Scales and the Durrell Analysis of Reading Difficulty; both of these tests have undergone recent revisions. If individually administered diagnostic tests have met other standards for test construction, they provide a more accurate assessment than a group-administered one because the student can be required to perform tasks that are closer to those necessary in authentic acts of reading. For example, students can be asked to read a response to you rather than circle a letter or item number in a multiple-choice question. See Test Bank D for a listing of some norm-referenced diagnostic test batteries.

In addition to norm-referenced test batteries, there are also *norm-referenced tests of specific skills.* These tests furnish detailed information about one specific area, rather than incorporating a number of subtests assessing many diverse areas. For example, one test of specific skills may assess only concepts related to word identification, while another may assess only comprehension. Some norm-referenced tests of specific skills may be *group-administered.* Two tests that assess word identification strategies are the Primary Reading Profiles and the Silent Reading Diagnostic Tests. One norm-referenced test of specific skills that may be *group-administered or individually administered* is the McCullough Word Analysis Test. Designed for grades 4 to 6, this test assesses eight phonic and structural analysis skills, namely, (a) initial consonant blends, (b) initial consonant digraphs, (c) phonetic discrimination of vowels, (d) matching letters to vowel sounds, (e) sounding out whole words, (f) interpreting phonetic symbols, (g) dividing words into syllables, and (h) identifying root words and affixes. This test provides an adequate sampling of items in most categories and requires about 65 minutes to administer. See Test Bank E for some available norm-referenced diagnostic tests of specific skills.

Some published diagnostic tests are **criterion-referenced.** Criterion-referenced tests do not compare students' performances with a norm group, but are designed only to provide information about whether students have mastered certain knowledge, strategies, or skills. They often give more specific and comprehensive information about a student's strengths and weaknesses than norm-referenced tests. There are some problems with published criterion-referenced tests, however. For example, enormous numbers of different skills are often tested. One criterion-referenced test has 302 separate objectives, another 343, another 367, and another 518. Many skills tested are unnecessary; they represent rules and principles of low utility. In other cases, basic word identifi-

Test Bank D
Norm-Referenced Diagnostic Test Batteries

Name	For Grades	Type of Administration	Time for Administration	Publisher
Basic Skills Assessment (BSA)	7 and up	Group	40–60 minutes	CTB/McGraw-Hill
Basic Skills Inventory. The reading subtest of this battery may be ordered separately.	K–12	Group	45 minutes per subtest	Los Angeles County Office of Education
Biemiller Test of Reading Processes (BTORP)	2–6	Individual	Varies according to subtests used	Guidance Centre, University of Toronto
CIRCUS	Nursery school–3	Group	30–40 minutes per subtest	CTB/McGraw-Hill
Diagnostic Achievement Battery (DAB)	Ages 6–14	Group or Individual	Varies according to subtests used	Pro-Ed
Diagnostic Reading Scales (DRS)	1–7 and disabled readers in grades 8–12	Individual	60 minutes	CTB/McGraw-Hill
Diagnostic Screening Test: Reading. For preliminary screening, not in-depth assessment	1–12	Individual	5–10 minutes	Facilitation House
Durrell Analysis of Reading Difficulty	1–6	Individual	Varies according to subtests used	Psychological Corporation
ERB Comprehensive Testing Program II	1–12	Group	Varies by level	Educational Testing Service
Gates-McKillop-Horowitz Reading Diagnostic Test	1–6	Individual	Varies according to subtests used	Teachers College Press

Test Bank D (cont.)

Name	For Grades	Type of Administration	Time for Administration	Publisher
Iowa Tests of Educational Development—This battery measures a broad area of achievement and includes a subtest on general vocabulary.	9–12	Group	Varies according to subtests used	Science Research Associates
Primary Reading Profiles	1–3	Group	95–100 minutes	Riverside
Sequential Tests of Educational Progress, Series III (STEP). Includes tests of listening and study skills.	3–12	Group	Varies by level	CTB/McGraw-Hill
Stanford Diagnostic Reading Test (SDRT)	1–13	Group	Varies by level	Psychological Corporation
Tests of Academic Achievement Skills	Ages 4–12	Individual	15–25 minutes	Academic Therapy Publications
Test of Individual Needs in Reading (and Red Fox Supplement). The three forms of this test were designed for students in the Western United States and Canada, American Indians, and Western Australians.	1–6 and older poor readers	Individual (Red Fox Supplement is group-administered)	25–50 minutes	Council for Indian Education
The 3-Rs Test	K–12	Group	Varies by level	Riverside
Woodcock-Johnson Psycho-Educational Battery	Ages 3–80	Individual	Varies according to subtests used	Developmental Learning Materials

Test Bank E
Norm-Referenced Diagnostic Tests of Specific Skills

Name	For Grades	Type of Administration	Time for Administration	Publisher
Assessment of Reading Growth. Consists of tests of literal and inferential comprehension	Ages 9, 13, or 17	Group	42–50 minutes	Jamestown
Degrees of Reading Power. Assesses comprehension	3–14	Group	Varies by level	The College Board
McCullough Word Analysis Tests	4–6	Group or Individual	70 minutes in 7 sessions	Chapman, Brook, & Kent
Standardized Oral Reading Check Tests	1–8	Individual	1–30 minutes	Pro-Ed
Stanford Achievement Test: Listening Comprehension Tests	1–9	Group	25–35 minutes	Psychological Corporation
The Test of Reading Comprehension: A Method for Assessing the Understanding of Written Language (TORC)	Ages 6–14	Group	90–180 minutes	Pro-Ed

cation strategies are divided up into tiny splinter skills, while other skills that are tested are overlapping. Needless to say, an entire test would be very time consuming and, for some skills tested, simply a waste of time since no information of significant relevance for instruction would be obtained.

On the other hand, some criterion-referenced tests do not include enough items. For example, the Reading Yardsticks test uses only 3 to 5 items to measure each skill. Reliability of tests with so few items per skill is usually very low. Criterion levels set for supposed mastery of a skill are subjective and questionable on some tests (Hittleman, 1983). For important word identification knowledge, 100% mastery may be necessary if the student is to be proficient in using that knowledge when encountering an unknown word. Yet, many criterion-referenced tests specify levels of only 80% to 90% to indicate mastery. If student knows only 80% of the consonant sounds, he or she will encounter problems with unknown words that contain the other 20%.

As with all published tests, the teacher should carefully analyze criterion-referenced tests to determine which are worth purchasing. In many cases, the teacher may choose to use only certain subtests and may adapt mastery levels set by publishers to more appropriate standards.

Published *criterion-referenced tests,* like norm-referenced tests, include test batteries. One test of this type, which may be either *group administered or individually administered,* is the Reading Diagnosis Test. A *group administered* criterion-referenced test battery is the PRI Reading Systems. Examples of test batteries that are *individually administered* are the Assessment of Basic Competencies, the Diagnostic Reading Test Battery, and the Brigance Diagnostic Comprehensive Inventory of Basic Skills. The Brigance has sections for spelling, handwriting, math, and English usage, as well as reading. The reading section includes 19 subtests of word identification skills, plus subtests in other reading areas. This test is designed for grades kindergarten through 6. Time needed for testing varies according to the number of subtests administered. Although a popular test, especially in learning disability programs, unfortunately the Brigance provides no information on the reliability or validity of the test scores.

A recently developed individually administered diagnostic test battery is the Diagnostic Assessments of Reading with Trial Teaching Strategies (DARTTS). DARTTS includes subtests for word recognition and word analysis, as well as for oral reading, silent comprehension, spelling, and word meaning. There are levels of this test suitable for administration in grades 1 through 12. See Test Bank F for a listing of some criterion-referenced diagnostic test batteries.

Certain *criterion-referenced* tests are *tests of specific skills.* One example which is primarily *group administered* is the Cooper-McGuire Diagnostic Word-Analysis Test. This test has a section on readiness for word analysis, plus 17 subtests of phonic analysis and 10 subtests of structural analysis. Two other tests of this type that are group administered are the Doren Diagnostic Reading Test of Word Recognition Skills and the Group Phonics Analysis test.

Criterion-referenced tests of specific skills that are *individually administered* are the Decoding Inventory and the Sipay Word Analysis Tests. The Sipay Word Analysis Tests, commonly called the SWAT, has 17 subtests to measure word identification skills, each of which requires 10 to 15 minutes to administer. Students respond to all items orally. Teacher materials for each subtest of the SWAT include a "Mini-Manual," a group of test cards, an answer sheet, and a report form for recording the student's correct and incorrect answers.

Bench Mark Measures is a criterion-referenced test of specific skills that has some *individually administered and some group-administered parts.* It tests general phonic knowledge and has some useful sections; one feature, however, is that certain portions require producing sounds in nonsense words, which is sometimes viewed as inappropriate. Some criterion-reference diagnostic tests of specific skills are listed in Test Bank G.

In conclusion, then, there are some problems with published diagnostic tests of word identification strategies; however, they can be helpful in assessing students' abilities if used judiciously.

Informal Measures

Many teachers find developing their own tests of word identification strategies preferable to using published tests. To develop a teacher-made test for this purpose, follow these steps:

1. List the areas to be assessed within the broader areas of phonic analysis, structural analysis, and use of context clues.

Test Bank F
Criterion-Referenced Diagnostic Test Batteries

Name	For Grades	Type of Administration	Time for Administration	Publisher
Achievement Tests	1–8	Group	Varies according to subtests used	Macmillan
Assessment of Basic Competencies (ABC)	Ages 3–15	Individual	120 minutes; given over 3 or 4 sessions	Scholastic Testing Service
Assessment of Basic Skills—Spanish Edition	K–6	Individual	Varies according to subtests used	Curriculum Associates
Basic Achievement Skills Individual Screener	1–post-high school	Individual	50–60 minutes	Psychological Corporation
Bench Mark Measures	Ungraded	Some parts group; some parts individual	30–60 minutes	Educators Publishing Service
Botel Reading Inventory (BRI)	1–12	Individual and group	Varies according to subtests used	Follett
Brigance Diagnostic Comprehensive Inventory of Basic Skills	K–9	Individual	Varies according to subtests used	Curriculum Associates
Brigance Diagnostic Inventory of Essential Skills	4–12	Individual and group	Varies according to subtests used	Curriculum Associates

2. Examine published tests for appropriate ways of assessing various strategies you can adapt and improve upon in your test.
3. Carefully consider the problems of published diagnostic tests to avoid those faults in your own teacher-made instrument.
4. Carefully develop items for each subarea within your test.
5. Divide the test into logical sections so you have the choice of administering the entire test or only selected sections.
6. Prepare typed copies of the test for your students, a typed set of directions for the teacher for consistency in administration, and duplicate copies of student record sheets for indicating students' responses to items.

Test Bank F (cont.)

Name	For Grades	Type of Administration	Time for Administration	Publisher
Clarke Reading Self-Assessment Survey. Self-administered and self-scored.	11–college	Individual	60 minutes	Academic Therapy Publications
Corrective Reading Mastery Tests	4–adult	Group	Varies according to subtests used	Science Research Associates
Criterion Test of Basic Skills	1–6	Individual	10–15 minutes per subtest	Academic Therapy Publications
Diagnostic Assessments of Reading with Trial Teaching Strategies (DARTTS)	1–12	Individual	50–60 minutes	Riverside
Diagnostic Skills Battery. Also provides norm-referenced information.	1–8	Group	150–200 minutes	Scholastic Testing Service
Distar Mastery Tests (DMT)	Preschool–3	Group	30–60 minutes per subtest	Science Research Associates
IOX Basic Skill System	5 and 6, and 9–12	Group	40–50 minutes	IOX Assessment Associates
Multilevel Academic Skills Inventory: Reading and Language Arts	1–8	Individual	Varies according to subtests used	Psychological Corporation
Pope Inventory of Basic Reading Skills	Reading levels 4 and below	Individual	Varies according to subtests used	Book-Lab

7. Be prepared to revise and improve sections if you note inadequacies in the original version when you actually administer and interpret the test.

Context Clues.   Context clues can be used by developing readers to *identify* some words and by more proficient readers to *confirm* the correctness of words they have attempted to identify through analysis of sounds and letter sequences. Since only a few published diagnostic tests include an assessment of context use, even those teachers who employ published tests to assess phonic analysis and structural analysis knowledge may wish to prepare an informal test of this word identification strategy.

Test Bank F (cont.)

Name	For Grades	Type of Administration	Time for Administration	Publisher
Prescriptive Reading Performance Test	1–12, and adults	Individual	Varies according to subtests used	Western Psychological Services
PRI Reading Systems (PRI/RS)	K–9	Group	Varies according to subtests used	CTB/McGraw-Hill
Reading Skills Diagnostic Test III	2–12	Group	40–60 minutes	Brador Publications
Reading Yardsticks	K–8	Group	Varies by level	Riverside
Roswell-Chall Diagnostic Reading Test of Word Analysis Skills, Revised and Extended. Also includes tests of high-frequency words, letter naming, and spelling	1–4	Individual	10–15 minutes	Essay Press
Spadafore Diagnostic Reading Test	1–12	Individual	30–60 minutes	Academic Therapy Publications
Task Assessment for Prescriptive Teaching (TAPT)	Ages 6 and up	Individual and group	20–40 minutes per subtest	Scholastic Testing Service
Test Lessons in Primary Reading, Enlarged and Revised Edition	Reading levels 1–3	Group	Varies according to subtests used	Teachers College Press
Zip Scale for Determining Independent Reading Level	6–12	Group	Varies according to subtests used	J. Weston Walch

There are two major ways to assess a student's use of context clues. The first procedure requires the teacher to select several paragraphs, or one longer passage, for each reading level. (Since students must be tested at their instructional levels, develop test passages for all levels so you have a selection suitable for any student you test.) For each passage, leave the first sentence intact; thereafter, periodically omit words that *can be determined from the context* of the selection. (Some words can be identified from the syntactic context; that is, sentence structure clues help the reader identify unknown words. Other words are identified from semantic clues; in this case, meaning supplied in the passage is used in concert with the reader's background knowledge to provide clues to the unknown word.) Finally, when omitting words, retain the first letter (or letters, if

Test Bank G
Criterion-Referenced Diagnostic Tests of Specific Skills

Name	For Grades	Type of Administration	Time for Administration	Publisher
Alphabet Mastery	K and up	Group	Varies by age level	Ann Arbor Publishers
Cooper-McGuire Diagnostic Word-Analysis Test	1 and up	Group	Varies according to subtests used	Croft
Decoding Inventory (DI)	1 and up	Individual	Varies according to subtests used	Kendall/Hunt
Diagnostic Word Patterns Test	3 and up	Group	15–30 minutes	Educators Publishing Service
Doren Diagnostic Reading Test of Word Recognition Skills	1–4	Group	60–180 minutes	American Guidance Service
Group Phonics Analysis	Reading levels 1–3	Group	10–15 minutes	Jamestown
Informal Evaluation of Oral Reading Grade Level	Ages 5–11, plus older individuals with reading problems	Individual	Varies by level	Book-Lab
The Instant Words Criterion Test. Measures sight-word knowledge.	1–6	Individual	15–20 minutes	Jamestown
The Instant Words Recognition Test	1–3, plus poor readers	Group or Individual	10 minutes	Jamestown
The IOX Basic Skills Word Lists. Teachers devise their own tests from these word lists.	1–12	Individual	Varies according to student's ability level	IOX Assessment Associates

the word begins with a consonant blend or consonant digraph). The latter is done since the most efficient strategy to employ when using context is to combine the graphic and/or sound cues provided by the first letter(s) of the word with the clues furnished by the context.

Figure 6–5 is a brief example of a fourth-grade level test passage using this first procedure for assessing use of context clues. The scoring of such an assessment gener-

		Test Bank G (cont.)		
Name	*For Grades*	*Type of Administration*	*Time for Administration*	*Publisher*
Listening Comprehension. Uses game format for testing.	1–3	Group	Varies according to subtests used	Educators Publishing Service
The McGuire-Bumpus Diagnostic Comprehension Test	1–6	Group	30–40 minutes	Croft
McLeod Phonic Worksheets	3 and below	Individual	Varies with student	Educators Publishing Service
Phonovisual Diagnostic Tests. Assesses phonics skills.	3–12	Group	Varies according to subtests used	Phonovisual Products
Signals Listening Tests	3 and 5	By tape recording	35 minutes	Project SPOKE
Sipay Word Analysis Tests	1–adult	Individual	Varies according to subtests used	Educators Publishing Service
Wisconsin Tests of Reading Skill Development: Comprehension	K–6	Group	Varies by level	NCS Interpretive Scoring Systems
Wisconsin Tests of Reading Skill Development: Study Skills	K–6	Group	Varies by level	NCS Interpretive Scoring Systems
Wisconsin Tests of Reading Skill Development: Word Attack	K–6	Group	Varies by level	NCS Interpretive Scoring Systems

ally involves subjective judgment, with the teacher noting the consistency (or lack of consistency) with which the student is able to use contextual clues.

A second procedure for assessing context use has been described by Timian and Santeusanio (1974). First, compile a list of words believed to be in the student's oral language vocabulary, but not in the student's reading recognition vocabulary. In the first

FIGURE 6–5

A sample passage for assessing use of context clues

Black Barney was the captain of a small, rickety whaling ship. He wore a black p_____ over his right eye and a pair of old, brown b_____ on his feet. When at sea, he stomped about the d_____ of his ship and watched for wh_____ through a very long brass spyglass.

If many days passed without spying a whale, Barney became angry and would scr_____, "I'm the best whaling man on the seven s_____. Why can't I spot a whale to harpoon and slice and boil down for its o_____?" When Barney got mad at the whales for not appearing, his stomping and shouting made his small ship sh_____ like it was going to break apart and send the sailors to the b_____ of the sea. The other sailors became sc_____ when this happened and one day decided they must do something to help Black Barney find and harpoon a whale.

Pegleg Sam, so called because he had one w_____ leg, was the oldest sailor on Barney's ship, and he was not only the oldest, he was also the w_____. He had learned many things during his y_____ at sea and he thought he had a good i_____ for helping Barney find a whale.

session, test the student's sight recognition of these words when they are presented in isolation; discard those words the student is able to recognize automatically. Following the first test session, write sentences using the words the student did not recognize in isolation, being certain that the other words in each sentence (the context) do indeed provide clues to the unknown word; for example, if the student does not know the word *audience,* you might write the following sentence:

> Henry thought he'd like being in the school play, but he got scared when he stepped out on the stage and saw how many people were in the *audience.*

In the second session, have the student read each sentence to determine if the student can use context to identify each word that was unknown when it was presented in isolation; if the student does not readily pronounce the word with use of the available context, say "Use the other words in the sentence to decide what it is."[2]

Tests, whether formal or informal, provide a guide for instructional programs that are designed to eliminate weaknesses in word identification strategies. Although there are no perfect tests, it is more efficient to administer tests and use the results for initial program planning than to rely exclusively on incidental information. Ongoing daily observations are important for verifying and extending these test findings. At times, students perform better during instruction than they did during assessment. In addition, needs not identified through administration of tests may become evident as daily instruction progresses. In these circumstances, modifications of original instructional goals are necessary.

---

[2]The Biemiller Test of Reading Processes includes one subtest that assesses how quickly a student uses context to facilitate word identification. The Decoding Inventory also has a test of context use, as does Level R (first grade) of the 3rd edition of the Gates-MacGinitie Reading Tests.

Using the Reading Miscue Inventory

The Reading Miscue Inventory, commonly called the RMI, offers insights about two significant areas: (1) it helps teachers determine if students' reading miscues *are* preventing them from obtaining meaning from a passage, or, in contrast, if their miscues are relatively inconsequential; and (2) it helps in deciding if a student is using knowledge of language and the world as an aid in reading. It is one of the more productive appraisals for obtaining indications about how specific students are processing print. The RMI assessment procedures are based on the following ideas:

1.   The purpose of reading is to gain meaning.

2.   Some miscues are "better" than others. Compare, for example, these two student responses to the same sentence:

wiggling

Ralph ran wildly about the room trying to catch his pet mouse before his mother found it was loose.

madly

Ralph ran wildly about the room trying to catch his pet mouse before his mother found it was loose.

The miscue in the second sentence does not change the essential meaning of the sentence as the first one does, and therefore, is considered a better miscue.

3.   Reading is not an exact process. Even proficient readers change words, omit words, and insert words, with no change in the author's intended meaning.

4.   Teachers should not treat all miscues the same way. Miscues should be evaluated according to how much they change meaning; that is, an analysis of a student's reading performance should be qualitative as well as quantitative.

The RMI is different from an IRI in several ways. No reading level is obtained from an RMI, but instead, it provides information about strengths and weaknesses in the use of specific reading strategies. During administration of an RMI, the student reads a complete selection, that is, a whole story or a complete selection of informational material. In comparison to an IRI, which uses relatively short passages, these longer selections present greater opportunity for the teacher to see how a student interacts with text when more language cues and more meaning clues are available. Also in contrast to an IRI, an RMI bases analysis on oral reading performance only.

Although modifications of the original RMI procedures are sometimes seen, those described here are the ones established for the primary instrument, the Reading Miscue Inventory developed by Y. M. Goodman, Watson, and Burke (1987). Seven items are needed to administer this test: (a) a test manual, (b) a passage for students to read, (c) a worksheet copy of the passage, (d) a Coding Sheet, (e) a Profile Sheet, (f) a tape recorder, and (g) a blank tape.

To administer the RMI, the teacher first selects a passage that is demanding enough so the student will make at least 25 miscues, but not so difficult that it cannot be handled at all. Next, the student reads the selection into the tape recorder, and then, while the tape recorder is still running, retells what has been read. An outline is used by the teacher in guiding the retelling. Following this, the teacher asks questions, being careful not to cue answers so that the student's responses reflect his or her actual comprehension and recall. Later, when the student is not present, the teacher listens to the tape and marks the student's miscues on the worksheet copy of the passage, and in addition, determines the student's retelling score. Then the teacher codes 25 of the student's miscues on the Coding Sheet and transfers a summary of that to the Profile Sheet. Finally, the teacher plans instruction based on an analysis of the student's performance. Clear and specific directions for marking and coding miscues, for determining a retelling score, and for all necessary procedures are found in the test manual. (See the sample Coding Sheet in Figure 6–6.) Directions for preparing materials also appear in the test manual. It takes approximately 15 minutes to administer the RMI and about 1 hour to analyze a student's responses.

RUNNING RECORDS

With the assessment technique called a *running record*, the evaluator uses many strategies similar to those employed with an RMI. This is a "record" the teacher makes as a student reads orally; the record is taken by using check marks to indicate every word read correctly, and, for errors, employing a marking system similar to that described in Tables 5–1 and 5–2 in Chapter 5 for use with an IRI.

A running record differs from an RMI or an IRI in a rather notable way, though—no copy of the story is used for recording the teacher's markings. Rather, the marking is done on a plain piece of paper so the running record can be taken spontaneously with any story, if desired. This means, however, that when an error is made the teacher must record the text word, as well as the student's incorrect response. See Figure 6–7 for a partial sample of a running record.

According to Clay (1985), teachers can learn to take a running record with about 2 hours' practice and can become proficient enough to do so without audiotaping the student's reading. Still, Clay's research also has shown that running records for poor readers characteristically are more complex than those for average readers; therefore, with poor readers, use of a tape recorder may, at times, be advisable.

For a preplanned (nonspontaneous) assessment, the teacher often arranges to take a running record with three stories of 100 to 200 words each—one story that will be easy for the student who is to be evaluated, one of average difficulty for the student, and one that will be hard. This allows a range of strengths and weaknesses to be identified. From a calculation of error rate (number of errors *divided* by all words), as well as an analysis of the errors and of other reading behaviors (including nonverbal ones), a teacher may obtain data about whether a particular book is too hard for a student (less than 90% accuracy), the degree of match between a student's oral language skill and

Test Bank H				
Test of Reading Strategies				
Name	*For Grades*	*Type of Administration*	*Time for Administration*	*Publisher*
Reading Miscue Inventory (RMI)	1–8	Individual	Approximately 15 minutes with pupil; 1 hour for analysis	Richard C. Owen

FIGURE 6-6
Reading miscue inventory coding sheet

MISCUE ANALYSIS PROCEDURE I CODING FORM

READER Betsy   DATE Nov. 3

TEACHER Mrs. Blau   AGE/ GRADE 3   SCHOOL York Elem.

SELECTION The Man Who Kept House

(Goodman, Watson, Burke)

LINE No./MISCUE No.	READER	TEXT	1 SYNTACTIC ACCEPTABILITY	2 SEMANTIC ACCEPTABILITY	3 MEANING CHANGE	4 CORRECTION
1	so	some	P	P	–	Y
2	start	stay	P	P	–	N
3	house	home	P	P	–	N
4	keeping	keep	P	P	–	N
5	we'll	well	Y	P	–	N
6	bread	butter	P	P	–	Y
7	all		Y	Y	N	N
8	well	we'll	Y	Y	P	N
9	you		Y	Y	N	N
10	day	morning	Y	Y	N	N
11	job	work	Y	P	–	N
12	@and	.As	Y	N	–	N
13	$churn	churn	Y	P	–	N
14	•He	he	Y	Y	N	Y
15	the	this	Y	Y	–	N
16	So	Seen	Y	Y	N	N
17	•buttermilk	butter	Y	Y	P	Y
18	Couldn't	could not	Y	Y	N	Y
19	There	She	N	N	–	Y
20	is	was	Y	P	–	Y
21	into	to	P	P	–	Y
22	forest	far	P	P	–	N
23	in	to	P	Y	N	N
24	†the	his	Y	P	–	N
25	heard	had	P	P	–	Y
		COLUMN TOTAL				
		PATTERN TOTAL				
		PERCENTAGE				

Right-hand columns:

MEANING CONSTRUCTION (See 2, 3, 4)	No Loss / Partial Loss / Loss
GRAMMATICAL RELATIONSHIPS (See 1, 2, 4)	Strength / Partial Strength / Overcorrection / Weakness
5 GRAPHIC SIMILARITY	H / S / N
6 SOUND SIMILARITY	H / S / N

a. TOTAL MISCUES ____
b. TOTAL WORDS ____
a ÷ b × 100 = MPHW ____

Source: From *Reading Miscue Inventory* (p. 96) by Y. M. Goodman, D. Watson, and C. L. Burke, 1987, New York: Richard C. Owen. Copyright 1987 by Richard C. Owen Publishing. Reprinted by permission.

FIGURE 6–7
A sample running record from
four pages of sample text

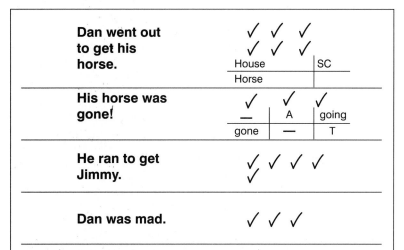

In this sample the student read most words correctly, as indicated by
checkmarks. At first he miscalls horse as house, but then self-corrects (SC).
On the second page, he does not know gone and appeals to the teacher (A);
the teacher asks the student to try the word, but he miscalls it as going,
whereupon the teacher (T) tells him the word. Complete details on marking
procedures for running records, as suggested by Clay, can be found in the
3rd edition of The Early Detection of Reading Difficulties (Clay, 1985); also
found are proposed analyses of pupils' reading behaviors based on the
errors exhibited during a running record.

the text, reading fluency, the cues and strategies a student uses, and self-correction
behavior. Much of this information depends upon the teacher examining *every* error
and asking *why* that error occurred (Clay, 1985, p. 24).

A great deal about a running record seems analogous to both IRIs and the Reading Miscue Inventory. However, since running records can be undertaken with any
story, with no preparation, this may mean that a teacher can examine a student's reading behaviors more frequently with a running record and thus have a thorough and
ongoing set of information to guide instruction.

For more description on running records, see *The Early Detection of Reading Difficulties* (Clay, 1985); this book contains suggested marking procedures, although Clay
believes teachers also can develop their own marking systems or implement those they
are familiar with from IRIs, as long as a consistent system is maintained. Also provided
in this book are proposed analyses and likely conclusions about what error types and
behaviors mean.

ASSESSING KNOWLEDGE OF WORD MEANINGS

Knowledge of the meanings of words is one indication of the background information a
student can apply to the understanding of reading material. As such, vocabulary knowledge is an important aspect of comprehension.

Although most standardized survey tests administered to groups during assessment for identification contain subsections on meaning vocabulary, for several reasons, these subtests do not provide an adequate measure of students' knowledge of word meanings for diagnostic purposes. First, because time limits are used, a teacher cannot always determine whether a student who scores poorly lacks vocabulary knowledge or is merely reading slowly and methodically. In addition, because of poor sight vocabulary knowledge or inadequate word identification strategies, the student may not recognize many words in written form, even though this student knows their meanings when they are heard in oral language. Then, too, most of these tests measure only common meanings of words, and ignore knowledge of multiple meanings of the same word. Finally, vocabulary items tested represent only a very small sample of words.

Even though a student's general performance on these survey tests is not definitive enough for explanatory purposes, it can provide clues about the necessity of administering a diagnostic test of knowledge of word meanings. If the student has performed poorly on a group standardized survey test, the teacher may wish to read words from this test *to* the student and informally check his or her knowledge of their meanings. If, under these conditions, the student performs well, the original poor performance probably has a different basis (for example, lack of adequate word identification strategies, or inability to work well when speed is required). However, if the student performs poorly during this oral probe, more in-depth assessment is advisable.

Some published diagnostic tests of specific skills are available for assessing knowledge of word meanings. One is the Test of Reading Comprehension (TORC). This test is suitable for use with grades 2 through 12 and tests vocabulary related to common concepts, words related to several content areas (science, social studies, and math), and vocabulary necessary for reading directions for school work. The Nelson Reading Skills Test, as well as the 3rd edition of the Gates-MacGinitie Reading Tests, assesses some vocabulary words in context. Assessing words in context is a positive feature for a standardized test.

Informal tests of word meaning knowledge can also be devised. To do so, teachers may compile a file of test forms for each grade level. To develop such a file, the first step is deciding on the content for *every* level. The *general content* of word meaning tests should involve assessment of these items:

1. Knowledge of synonyms
2. Use of precision when encountering words with similar meanings (for example, one person saved money but another hoarded it—what is the difference?)
3. Knowledge of multiple meanings of words (D. D. Johnson & Pearson, 1984)

Decisions about the *specific content* involves selecting the words to be tested. A sample of words may be obtained from one or more of the following sources:

1.   The book titled *The Living Word Vocabulary* (Dale & O'Rourke, 1976), which provides a listing of approximately 44,000 words with a grade level specified for each indicating the level at which the meaning of that word is known by most students

2.   Word lists from basal readers beginning at grade 4 (Words introduced in basal readers prior to grade 4 are generally selected because they are words that are in the oral language meaning vocabularies of most children; the task in these early years is one of getting students to recognize these known words in printed form.

Beginning at grade 4, an additional objective is to introduce words for which meanings must also be learned.)

3.   Lists of frequently occurring affixes and roots. One such source is Stauffer's (1969) list of the 15 most frequently occurring prefixes in the English language

4.   Lists of content area words, such as the Carroll, Davies, Richman list for grades 3 through 9 (Carroll, Davies, & Richman, 1971)

The next step in developing an informal assessment instrument is to choose a method of assessing the words. Kelley and Krey (cited in Farr, 1969, p. 34) suggested one or more of the following methods:

I. Unaided recall
  A. Checking for familiarity
  B. Using words in a sentence
  C. Explaining the meaning
  D. Giving a synonym
  E. Giving an opposite
II. Aided recall
  A. Recall aided by recognition
    1. Matching tests
    2. Classification tests
    3. Multiple-choice tests
      a. Choosing the opposite
      b. Choosing the best synonym
      c. Choosing the best definition
      d. Choosing the best use in sentences
    4. Same-opposite tests
    5. Same-opposite-neither tests
    6. Same-different tests
  B. Recall aided by association
    1. Completion tests
    2. Analogy tests
  C. Recall aided by recognition and association
    1. Multiple-choice completion tests
    2. Multiple-choice substitution tests

Beck and McKeown (1991) have expressed concern about use of multiple-choice items, only, to assess meaning vocabulary. It appears that such items measure best those words students have only in their "partial range" of knowledge. That is, there are different degrees of "knowing" a word—a student may not know its meaning at all, may have partial knowledge of it, or may know it so there is depth of understanding and can *use* it. Although a word may seem to be known as a result of performance on a multiple-choice item, the most helpful knowledge—in-depth understanding—may not have been attained. Beck and McKeown suggest that words should be tested in ways that show learners recognize *uses* of the word, can contrast it with a word having a related meaning, can give multiple meanings of the word, can explain what a word means in a specific sentence, and in other tasks that measure completeness, precision, and richness of vocabulary knowledge.

Formal or informal tests should be supplemented with observations during daily work to determine a student's need for remediation in the area of meaning vocabulary.

FIGURE 6-8
A checklist of adequacy for diagnostic tests

	Yes	No
1. Is the test valid?		
2. Is the test reliable?		
3. Are all important areas covered?		
4. Does the test do more than merely sample a few items within a skill or knowledge area?		
5. Does the test refrain from assessing areas that research has shown to be unimportant to reading achievement?		
6. Does the test or each subtest within the test assess what it purports to test?		
7. If information is needed to plan programs for moderately or severely disabled readers, is the test individually administered?		
8. As much as is possible, is the required performance on the test like the performance required during the real act of reading?		
9. Does the test provide detailed, comprehensive information about a student's knowledge and skills rather than merely a "ballpark" notion of needs?		

CONCLUSION

This chapter has discussed several procedures for determining a student's specific strengths and weaknesses in reading. Some of these involve using formal, published tests and others informal, teacher-constructed instruments. In either case, assessment procedures should be evaluated with the checklist found in Figure 6–8 before use. This checklist should also be kept in mind as you read about additional assessment procedures in the next chapter.

📖 REFLECTIONS

1. Three hallmarks of exemplary assessment are
   a. Use of multiple and diverse procedures to assess knowledge/strategies/skills
   b. Thoughtful inspection of reading behaviors
   c. Merging of results to obtain as accurate and as complete a picture as possible

These three could serve as guidelines for your own undertakings in reading assessment. Based on the tests and procedures described in this chapter, give examples of each of these.

2. What fourth guideline for high-quality assessment might *you* add?

7

Assessment for Identifying Specific Strengths and Weaknesses in Reading: Part II

Talking with students about their interests and attitudes is a part of assessment.

C ontinuing the topic of Chapter 6, this chapter further describes assessment procedures for determining specific strengths and weaknesses in reading.

ASSESSING COMPREHENSION

Comprehension assessment can be conducted with conventional tests (both formal and informal) or teacher-constructed instruments and procedures. Each approach has advantages and disadvantages.

Using Conventional Tests

Conventional tests that have some utility for measuring comprehension are survey tests, group-administered or individually administered diagnostic tests, IRIs, and the RMI.

Formal Assessments.   When a student exhibits poor reading performance on the standardized group survey test employed during assessment for identification, the comprehension section is often examined to determine if comprehension difficulties exist. This is deemed to be an appropriate means of appraisal since survey tests measure comprehension after silent reading—the type required in most "real-life" reading tasks.

However, sometimes use of group survey tests for measuring comprehension has been criticized because these tests are timed. Some researchers have questioned, therefore, whether they measure speed of comprehension rather than power of comprehension. That is, they are concerned that a student having a slower than average rate of reading (because of word recognition difficulties or for other reasons) may be penalized, even though the student's comprehension is adequate when the student has all the time needed to complete a reading task. In such cases, it is contended that these tests would not give a true reflection of the students' comprehension abilities.

Nevertheless, if other diagnostic tests have indicated that a student has no difficulty with word recognition and word identification strategies, then the time limits of these tests should be sufficient for students to complete them. So, if the student cannot complete the comprehension subtest, that likely indicates comprehension difficulty. If, on the other hand, a student has poor word knowledge skills, after completion of the group survey test, an alternate form at the same level can be administered for diagnostic purposes. This time the student is asked to orally read the test and answer the questions. The teacher can then determine whether poor performance results from word recognition and identification difficulties, from comprehension problems, or from both. Additional insights into the student's thinking processes and background knowledge are obtained if students are asked *how* they arrived at their answers.

Another criticism of group survey tests is that they do not measure retention. During these tests, students can refer to a relevant passage to find an answer; because of this, the tests are said to measure immediate recall. Retention of comprehended material is often vital, especially in schoolwork, and the ideal test probably would include certain sections where students could refer to a passage and others where they cannot. Yet some research seems to demonstrate that performance on test passages where students *can* look back to find answers more accurately measures reading achievement.

Other criticisms of group survey tests for determining comprehension ability are these:

1. Answers are generally written in a multiple-choice format, which allows for guessing and may provide clues that are not available when students must resort to unaided recall.
2. Most measure comprehension of only short excerpts of material (for example, single paragraphs), which is not representative of most authentic reading tasks.

Standardized group survey tests are only the beginning point in assessment since the results provide only a general measure of understanding.

Formal, *group*-administered *diagnostic* tests are also available for assessing comprehension. Most are subtests in larger *test batteries*. Some batteries that include comprehension subtests are the Sequential Tests of Educational Progress, the Basic Skills Assessment test, and the Stanford Diagnostic Reading Test. Comprehension subtests of test batteries should be examined to determine if they measure what they say they do. For example, the "comprehension" subtest of the Botel Reading Inventory tests only a student's ability to recognize word opposites. An example of a group-administered diagnostic test of specific skills that does assess comprehension is the Test of Reading Comprehension (TORC) for grades 2 through 12. In addition to paragraph comprehension, the TORC includes subsections on sequencing sentences and on determining whether sentences have similar meanings, although they are syntactically different. Because standardized, group-administered diagnostic tests are usually timed and read silently, a follow-up in which students orally reread the test or an alternate form, as suggested above, yields more specific diagnostic information.

Some *individually* administered *diagnostic test batteries* that incorporate subtests of comprehension are the Brigance Diagnostic Comprehensive Inventory of Basic Skills, the Diagnostic Reading Scales, the Basic Achievement Skills Individual Screener, the Durrell Analysis of Reading Difficulty, and the Diagnostic Achievement Battery.

An advantage of individually administered tests is that students can be observed while they are responding. Some of these tests assess comprehension only after silent reading, some after oral reading, and some after both. Most these tests stipulate an oral reply to questions or a retelling of the passage, rather than a written response. This method is advantageous when evaluating students with poor academic skills. Remember, however, that subtests of test batteries do a better job of assessing word identification strategies than of measuring comprehension. In addition, basic information on norming, reliability, and validity should be obtained by checking the technical manual for the test to ensure that the test is suitable for the intended purpose and group. For example, the validity of the Basic Achievement Skills Individual Screener has been questioned for students beyond eighth grade (Conley, 1986), although the test may be suitable for younger children. The questions suggested for critiquing diagnostic tests which are found in Figure 6–8 at the end of Chapter 6 should also be used before selecting a formal test for reading comprehension.

Informal Measures. An informal reading inventory (IRI), usually administered to verify students' general reading levels, also supplies some knowledge about a student's comprehension abilities—if the teacher goes beyond merely counting the number of correct and incorrect responses and looks at the *types* of questions that have been difficult for a specific student. An IRI also enables the teacher to analyze the degree to which comprehension is affected by word recognition and word identification difficulties. In addition, with many IRIs, the teacher can compare comprehension levels after oral versus silent reading. If a student's comprehension is better after oral reading, for example, this may mean one of several things. Students with lower-than-average intellectual functioning levels often comprehend better after oral reading, perhaps because oral responses keep the student's attention focused on the material. This characteristic is also observed in some severely disabled readers, as well as in some students with specific learning disorders despite their having average or above-average intelligence. The need to hear what they are reading is also typical of average beginning readers, but this need usually disappears with experience.

If comprehension is better after silent reading, that finding may mean that during oral reading the student is focusing on word pronunciation rather than meaning. If comprehension after both oral and silent reading is substantially lower than the student's word identification performance on the IRI, instruction in comprehension strategies is almost certainly needed. Another advantage in using an IRI to assess comprehension is that the test is untimed. The teacher can thus feel confident that power of comprehension is being considered rather than speed of comprehension.

The results of a Reading Miscue Inventory (RMI) also help to estimate comprehension abilities. Because complete selections (whole stories, whole articles) are read, the RMI enables the teacher to measure student comprehension of longer passages than those found in survey tests, diagnostic tests, or IRIs. In addition, analysis of individual miscues provides data about the degree to which students use sentence structure and background knowledge to gain meaning, and the extent to which miscues may affect comprehension. The RMI also affords a look at student self-correction. Analysis of students' self-corrections provides information about the propensity to read for understanding. It also indicates what clues they are using to comprehend material.

Let's consider, for example, Tim, a student who initially reads:

pleasant

Long ago, a peasant boy who lived with his family in a poor hut went sullenly every day to work in the king's fields.

Suppose Tim self-corrects the word *peasant,* which he had read as *pleasant,* immediately after reading the word *sullenly.* This self-correction may be prompted because the expression *sullenly* seems to conflict with the description *pleasant.* In this case, Tim is using a meaning clue at the word level as a prompt to reexamine his original response. On the other hand, suppose he self-corrects after reading the whole sentence. In this instance, background information may have been evoked to cue the author's intended word—for example, familiarity with other stories or history material may cause him to think it logical to find a *peasant* boy in a poor hut working in the fields of a king. An analysis of many self-corrections furnishes details about cues a student does or does not use, and this is beneficial in planning instruction. A disadvantage in attempting to capitalize on self-correction data in assessing comprehension strategies is that some students mentally self-correct a miscue but do not do so orally.

Performance during the retelling of a *story selection* for the RMI demonstrates the student's proficiency in literal recall of characters and events, understanding of character development, grasp of overall plot, and ability to infer a theme. Effectiveness during retelling of an *informational selection* assesses memory for specific details, skill in forming generalizations based on stated facts, and ability to abstract major concepts from the text.

Developing Teacher-Constructed Instruments and Procedures

Obviously, preparing tests is more time consuming than using published instruments, but doing so has the advantage of allowing teachers to devise assessments that do not contain some of the flaws found in conventional measures. Teachers can improve upon traditional comprehension tests by doing the following:

1. Making multiple-choice questions more diagnostically relevant
2. Determining the types of prompts a student needs to comprehend material
3. Designing questions that assess higher-level comprehension of many types
4. Using free recall measures followed by probes

Designing Diagnostically Relevant Multiple-Choice Questions.   One way to improve on traditional comprehension tests using multiple-choice questions is to write the questions so that each alternative reflects a certain response behavior. For example, in a series of multiple-choice questions, one of the incorrect alternatives could always be written so that it reflects an answer for which the inference drawn is too broad or too narrow; another alternative could always be written so that it is a literal response to an inference question; and so on. Because many alternatives of the same type would appear through the series of questions, a pattern of student response strategies should emerge to provide suggestions for future instruction.

The second way to strengthen the diagnostic value of multiple-choice questions is to ask students to rate each alternative answer on its probability of correctness, rather than selecting only the best answer. For example, students could use a rating scale of 1 through 4, with 1 indicating the answer that is most likely correct and 4 indicating the answer least likely so. Here is an example of a question in which both multiple-choice procedures have been used:

The reason the fairy let Pinocchio cry about his nose was that

_4_ A. the fairy let Pinocchio cry for an hour about his nose.
_2_ B. she didn't notice he was crying because she was thinking about his lies.
_1_ C. she wanted to teach him a lesson.
_3_ D. she liked to hear people cry.

Note that alternative A is simply a literal statement taken directly from the question stem. It does not answer the question. A student who consistently selects an alternative of this type as the most probable correct response needs a different type of instruction than does the student who usually chooses alternatives like D. Alternative D was written so that its choice indicates a student who is not integrating text information with background knowledge to draw an inference. Examination of the ratings a student gives to each alternative allows the teacher to note thinking processes and the test-taking skills a student practices.

Assessing Types of Prompts Needed.   It is also helpful for teachers to know the types of prompts a student needs to correctly answer comprehension questions. To investigate this, an assortment of selections is chosen, and questions for them are written in a multiple-choice format. Students read some passages orally and others silently. After reading, they orally read the alternative answers and attempt to designate the correct one. On those passages where an incorrect answer is picked, the teacher asks questions and gives prompts as would be done in an instructional situation. The student's responses and the teacher's comments are tape-recorded for later analysis. The appraisal is then

To determine the types of assistance students need to answer comprehension questions correctly, the teacher works with the student during an assessment session, asking questions and giving prompts as would be done in an instructional situation.

used to determine flaws in background knowledge or thinking strategies and the types of prompts needed.

Let's look at an example of this technique. The student is asked to read the passage and then to choose the most appropriate response to the multiple-choice item.

> In 1849 when gold was discovered in California, many men in other parts of the country left their jobs and families to travel there. The journey to California was often long and hard, but they thought it was worth it. They believed they would strike it rich once they reached California. When these men, called forty-niners, arrived in California one of the first things they did was to buy supplies needed for mining gold. The most important of these was a mining pan. The miners would take this pan when they went out to try their luck at finding gold in streambeds. They would put water from the stream and sand from the streambed into the mining pan and shake it. Gold can be found in this way because it is heavier than sand and settles to the bottom of the pan while the sand still floats in the water. If the miners did find gold, it was usually in the form of fine particles called gold dust, but sometimes they found a larger piece that was called a nugget. Many miners stayed in California for years and years before returning to their families. Some of these determined men did find gold, but only a few found enough to become very rich.
>
> What is the main point of this paragraph?
>
> A. It is written to tell you some things about the forty-niners.
> B. It is written to tell you why gold settles to the bottom of a pan.
> C. It is written to tell you the year gold was discovered in California.
> D. It is written to tell you two forms in which gold can be found.

Here is a typescript of a student's responses after reading this passage and a teacher's prompts and questions.

>   STUDENT: I think the answer's B.
>   TEACHER: Why do you think so?

STUDENT: It says it in the story.

TEACHER: It does say that, but I want you to read the question to me again.

STUDENT: "What is the main point of this paragraph?"

TEACHER: When you read the question the first time, did you notice the word *main*?

STUDENT: *(Pause)* Not really.

TEACHER: *Main* is a key word in the question. Often when you have to answer questions about what you've read, there's a key word that helps you get the correct answer. Did you know that, Tommy?

STUDENT: *(Laughter)* No.

TEACHER: In this question, *main* is the key word. Do you know what the question is asking you when it asks for the *main* point?

STUDENT: *(Pause)* Important?

TEACHER: Right. *Main* can mean important. So what is the question asking you to tell if it asks you for the main point?

STUDENT: The important point?

TEACHER: Right! Or another way to say it is the major point.

STUDENT: But it says that right here about the gold settling.

TEACHER: You're right. It does. That *is* one thing that the passage tells you, but there are many other things the author told you, aren't there?

STUDENT: Yes.

TEACHER: That's just one small point that was made. When the question asks you for the main point, it wants you to figure out what the whole thing was about. Or, in other words, you could ask yourself, "What was the *main* reason the author wrote this? What was the overall idea he wanted me to learn from this?" What do you think it was?

STUDENT: About those men, I guess, about what they did.

TEACHER: Great! Now you've got it. Okay, read the answers to yourself again. Now which one do you think is right?

STUDENT: None of them say anything about the men.

TEACHER: Well, let's work on each answer together. Maybe I can help you. Read the first answer out loud to me.

STUDENT: "It is written to tell you some things about the forty-niners."

TEACHER: Do you understand that answer, Tommy?

STUDENT: I guess so.

TEACHER: Do you remember the paragraph saying anything about the forty-niners?

STUDENT: *(Pause)* Yes . . .

TEACHER: Well, let's find the part in the paragraph that mentions the forty-niners and you read it out loud to me.

STUDENT: "When these men, called forty-niners, arrived in California one of the first things they did was buy supplies needed for mining gold."

TEACHER: What does the term *forty-niners* mean in that sentence?

STUDENT: *(Long pause)* The men!

TEACHER: Right! When you read the sentence the first time, did you realize the sentence was telling you the men were called forty-niners?

STUDENT: No.

TEACHER: What did you think it meant when it said, ". . . these men, called forty-niners, . . ."?

STUDENT: They called it. They said it.

TEACHER:	You mean you thought the men called something out? They called out, "Forty-niners"?
STUDENT:	Yeah.
TEACHER:	Okay, I tell you what, let me write a sentence for you that's almost like that, but is about something you're more familiar with. Watch what I write. *(Teacher writes sentence on paper)* Read that to me.
STUDENT:	*(Reads sentence teacher just wrote)* "Our school football team, called the Tigers, is the best team in town."
TEACHER:	What does *called* mean in this sentence?
STUDENT:	*(Rereads sentence silently)* Named!
TEACHER:	Right! Look back at the sentence about forty-niners. Could *called* mean the same thing there?
STUDENT:	*(Reads sentence silently)* Yeah. It does.
TEACHER:	Okay, let's look at answer A again. What do you think? Is it the right or wrong answer?
STUDENT:	*(Reads alternative A silently)* Yeah. It's the right one 'cause the story's about the men.
TEACHER:	It seems to me you're right, but let's look at the other answers just to be sure there's not a better one. We've already decided B is not correct. Read C out loud to me.
STUDENT:	"It is written to tell you the year gold was discovered in California."
TEACHER:	What do you think? Right or wrong?
STUDENT:	Wrong, 'cause . . . *(Long pause)*
TEACHER:	Why?
STUDENT:	Well, it's just a small point.
TEACHER:	Super. It *does* tell when gold was discovered, doesn't it? But you're right. It's not the overall or major idea the author wanted you to learn about in this paragraph. What about D? Read that one to me.
STUDENT:	"It is written to tell you two forms in which gold is found."
TEACHER:	What do you think?
STUDENT:	It tells you those and I think that's important, but it tells more than that and it's mostly about the men and what they did. *(Rereads alternative D silently)* So D isn't the right answer.
TEACHER:	Excellent. And what happened to them? What did it say happened to the men in the end?
STUDENT:	Some got rich and some didn't.
TEACHER:	Right. Did more of them get rich or more not get rich?
STUDENT:	*(Has to reread last sentence of passage)* More didn't.
TEACHER:	Super. Okay, now read this next passage silently and when you get done, I'll ask you to answer a question about it.

When a teacher uses questions and prompts in this fashion, it is possible to learn much about students: their approaches to the comprehension task, their test-taking skills, the background knowledge they do or do not possess, the types of prompting necessary to help them understand material, their skills in dealing with written language structures, their abilities to generalize from familiar knowledge to the unfamiliar, and how readily they pick up on instructional cues provided by the teacher. In short, the teacher can determine rather specifically what is preventing comprehension.

A variation of assessing prompts that are needed is suggested by Sammons and Davey (1993–94). Some clues about students' comprehension of expository material in content books (such as history, geography, and science) can be gained through an interview procedure they call the Textbook Awareness and Performance Profile (TAPP). In the first portion, students are asked what strategies they use to learn from a book they have been assigned to read in their regular classroom. Next, they are given specific tasks to carry out, such as summarizing, note taking, scanning, underlining, using headings and graphics, using the Table of Contents and index, and defining vocabulary. TAPP was designed as an assessment measure to be used in clinical and remedial classes so that comprehension instruction in those settings could complement the students' typical daily literacy needs. The complete profile is printed in the *Journal of Reading* in the December 1993/January 1994 issue.

Using a Variety of Types of Higher-Level Questions.   As a solution to the failure of many formal tests to measure higher-level thinking processes except in a limited manner, Spache (1981) suggests that teachers develop a series of questions based on the question categories proposed by Sanders (1966) and apply these to graded selections. Sanders's categories were derived from Bloom's *Taxonomy of Educational Objectives* (1956, p. 3) and are listed here.

1. *Memory.*   Recognizing and recalling information directly stated in the passage. Example: The story states that Susie had to wait after school for her mother to pick her up. The teacher asks, "Why did Susie wait after school when the rest of the children went home?"

2. *Translation.*   Paraphrasing ideas. Example: The teacher asks the student to put into his or her *own* words the moral stated at the end of an African folktale.

3. *Interpretation.*   Seeing relationships among facts or generalizations. Example: The teacher asks, "Based on what you have read so far, what evidence is there that this is a work of historical fiction?"

4. *Application.*   Solving a problem that requires the use of facts or generalizations. Example: The teacher says, "Taking into account the information provided in this science passage, list the steps you would want to be certain to carry out if you wanted the bean seed you planted to grow."

5. *Analysis.*   Recognizing and applying logic to a problem; analyzing an example of reasoning. Example: The teacher asks, "What do you think of Mafatu's solution to his problem of fear of the sea? Why?"

6. *Synthesis.*   Using original, creative thinking to solve a problem. Example: The teacher asks, "What are some other ways Mafatu could have overcome his problem?"

7. *Evaluation.*   Making judgments. Example: The teacher asks, "Now that you've read several of Chris Van Allsburg's books, which character do you think he has portrayed in the most interesting way? Why?"

Using Sanders's question categories extends the measurement of comprehension beyond responses to literal questions.

Using Free Recalls, Plus Probes.   Use of **free recalls** (sometimes called **retelling**) is another means for assessing comprehension. To use this method, the teacher prepares an outline of significant information about the text students will read. The outline is available to the teacher, but not to students. After reading, students are simply asked to retell what they remember. When asking for free recalls, the teacher should carefully specify the task demand, that is, students should be directed to tell everything they remember. Failure to delineate this expectation often results in superficial retellings during which students do not relate all information gained. To further minimize the problem of a cursory retelling, the teacher can follow up with the retelling outline by asking about significant understandings the student has omitted. The follow-up questions are called **probes.** The student's free recall and answers to probes are tape-recorded. Later, the retelling outline is used in conjunction with the audiotape to analyze the student's performance.

There are several advantages to using free recall measures. They aid the teacher in determining whether students have noted important information, whether they can reproduce it in a manner that makes sense, and whether their background knowledge has an effect on the way they interpret the substance of the text.

These procedures also provide some insights about a student's short-term retention. In addition, if there is a delay between the time when students read some selections and the time when they are asked to retell, a measure of long-term retention can also be obtained. Another advantage is that the teacher's preparation is minimal.

One disadvantage to free recalls is that students who do understand the material may nevertheless have difficulty adequately retelling the selection: they don't know where to begin or what sequence to follow in the retelling. This results in a disorganized retelling in which major details are overlooked, conveying the false impression that the student did not comprehend or recall the material. This problem usually can be overcome if students receive some practice and training in retelling. Production problems can also result if students are asked to write their responses during a free recall. Although they may understand the material, they may have trouble producing the information in written form. When assessing students with poor academic skills, asking for oral responses is usually preferable.

Probes are important. A second disadvantage is seen when relying on free recalls, without probes, since this often does not enable assessment of higher-level comprehension. Students tend to report only facts and information directly stated in the selection. For example, it would be highly unusual for students during their retellings to say,"Oh, by the way, the theme of this story is _____," or, "Incidentally, an important generalization I drew from the information in this article is that _____." Therefore, using probes to follow up student retellings is important so that higher-level comprehension can be assessed.

Another problem is that greater demand on memory is required of the student during free recall than with multiple-choice questions, which provide some clues for remembering the material. Because of this problem, students should always be told prior to reading a selection that they will be asked to retell it afterward. Four published tests that employ free recalls are The Reading Miscue Inventory (RMI), the Basic Reading Inventory, the Bader Reading and Language Inventory, and the Durrell Analysis of Reading Difficulty.

It is suggested that teachers extend free recall procedures beyond the ways in which they are commonly used in published instruments, however, to incorporate these suggestions:

1. Include assessment after silent reading, as well as after oral reading.
2. Include methods for measuring long-term retention, as well as short-term recall.

A Final Word.   As with other areas, the best measure of a student's comprehension is gained through a combination of assessments. As Johnston (1983) states,

The object of much past development of reading comprehension assessment has been a single test which will tell us all we want to know. It is my contention that pursuing this objective is futile. Given the complexity of the reading task and the number of variables to be assessed and/or taken into account, I believe that a potentially more reasonable approach would be to refine and use the variety of approaches to measurement which we have available already, in the light of our knowledge of the skills and abilities involved in each, though we might want to add some supplementary approaches. By appropriately selecting combinations of these measures, we may gain a clearer picture of what and how a reader comprehends under a given set of circumstances. (p. 54)

ASSESSING METACOGNITION

Experts have studied comprehension rather intently over the past several years to learn what teachers can do to help students better understand what they read. In doing so, they have learned that it is important for readers to engage in metacognitive activity. **Metacognition** can be defined as thinking (consciously) about one's own thinking (Garner, 1992). Metacognition is important in all aspects of reading, but has been explored most often in relation to comprehension.

Metacognitive activity has three major facets: (a) metacognitive awareness, that is, conscious knowledge about one's own thinking processes, about the specific demands of the task at hand, and about reading strategies; (b) monitoring, that is, self-appraisal to judge when understanding has broken down; and (c) strategy use, that is, knowing when and why to match specific strategies to specific reading tasks—and doing so (R. Barr, Sadow, & Blachowicz, 1990).

Metacognitive Awareness

Interviews have been suggested (e.g., Paris, Wasik, & Turner, 1991) for determining students' knowledge about their own *thinking* (e.g., what is hard for a specific student or what is easy) and knowledge about the nature of reading and writing *tasks* (e.g., what is important in text and what is not). Garner (1992) proposes the following types of questions for a metacognitive awareness interview:

1. Are any sentences in a paragraph more important than others?
2. Is it easier to retell a story if you tell it in your own words, or if you use the author's exact words?
3. Are reading to study and reading for fun the same thing?
4. What things does a person have to do to become a good reader?
5. What makes something difficult to read?
6. How do you answer a question in your textbook if you remember that you read about the topic, but you do not remember the answer?
7. How can you tell what an author thought was important in a passage?
8. How do you write a short summary of a long piece of text?
9. What do you do if you come to an unfamiliar word in something you're reading for homework?
10. How do you put something "in your own words"? (p. 239)

The Metacomprehension Strategy Index (MSI), developed and validated by Schmitt (1990), measures *awareness* of reading strategies. This instrument, organized in multiple-choice format, asks students to select statements that indicate important things they should do to aid understanding:

1. Before They Read

Example: Before I begin reading, it's a good idea to:

A. See how many pages are in the story.
B. Look up all the big words in the dictionary.
C. Make some guesses about what I think will happen in the story.
D. Think about what has happened so far in the story. (p. 459)

2. While They Are Reading

Example: While I'm reading, it's a good idea to:

A. Read the story very slowly so that I will not miss any important parts.
B. Read the title to see what the story is about.
C. Check to see if the pictures have anything missing.
D. Check to see if the story is making sense by seeing if I can tell what's happened so far. (p. 460)

3. After They Have Read

Example: After I've read story, it's a good idea to:

A. Count how many pages I read with no mistakes.
B. Check to see if there were enough pictures to go with the story to make it interesting.
C. Check to see if I met my purpose for reading the story.
D. Underline the causes and effects. (p. 461)

The MSI has 25 items and is published in its entirety in the March 1990 issue of *The Reading Teacher*. Although designed for examining awareness of strategies to be implemented with narrative material (i.e., stories), it can be adapted for assessing knowledge of strategies critical for use with expository text (i.e., informational selections).

Garner and her colleagues have also assessed strategy awareness by having students tutor others during reading and helping others during the answering of questions (Garner, Macready, & Wagoner, 1984; Garner, Wagoner, & Smith, 1983). This procedure allows the evaluator to determine strategies readers possess by observing those they encourage other students to use.

A commercial test for measuring strategy awareness is Strategy Assessments, available from D. C. Heath Publishing Company.

Comprehension Monitoring

To ascertain students' abilities to judge when understanding has gone awry, Paris et al. (1991) and others advocate error detection tasks. Students are given paragraphs containing nonsense statements, sentences that are inconsistent with other information in the paragraph, or statements incompatible with common background knowledge. They are asked to underline anything that does not seem sensible to them. Paragraphs such as these are used:

> The cat seemed yellow when you first saw her, although after looking carefully you could see one stripe of orange down her back. She was a good cat and we liked everything about her, except when she began to shed. At those times it was not pleasing to find tufts of black hair on the furniture and on our clothes.

> While most people don't like turnips, I love them. Mashed and cooked with butter, I think they make a delicious dish. I always serve chopped turnips with our Thanksgiving turkey and my guests sometimes try to hide their dislike for them as they sip them from their coffee cups.

This comprehension monitoring task can be taken a step further by asking students to edit the paragraphs to make sense.

A self-appraisal of answer correctness also provides an evaluation of ability to monitor comprehension. Manzo and Manzo (1993) advise having students reinspect their answers after completing any test and to display confidence in the appropriateness of their responses by using this marking key:

(+)   I'm fairly certain that this is correct.
(0)   I'm uncertain of this response.
(–)   I'm probably wrong on this item. (p. 120)

They call this "the response self-appraisal method."

Strategy Use

While evaluation of metacognitive awareness may shed light on whether students have *knowledge* of helpful reading strategies, it is, of course, important to know if they take this knowledge to a higher stage and actually *use* the strategies to foster understanding of text. The assessment technique most frequently cited for judging strategy use is the "think-aloud" (e.g., Marzano, Hagerty, Valencia, & DiStefano, 1987; Wixson & Lipson, 1991). A *think-aloud* is a routine in which readers self-report their thinking processes during reading. Sometimes this verbal report is made while they are reading (an *introspective report*); other times it is made immediately after they have read (a *retrospective* report). Wade (1990) has delineated procedures for administering and scoring a comprehension think-aloud; these can be seen in Table 7–1. Think-alouds have some limitations (as is true with all assessment procedures), and these include the difficulties some students may have in expressing the strategies they use; in addition, others may use strategies about which they are not consciously aware.

In a later part of this chapter, you will read a section on *performance assessment*, which includes additional methods useful for measuring metacognitive strategy use. Especially beneficial are the process assessment approaches developed by Paratore and Indrisano (1987), described in that section, for evaluating comprehension behaviors.

ASSESSING READING RATE

An unusually slow rate of reading or an excessively rapid one can hinder comprehension. If it is suspected that an inappropriate reading rate is compounding a student's reading problems, an assessment of reading rate may be included in the diagnostic procedures.

Formal Measures

Beginning at the fourth-grade level, many group survey tests include a test of reading rate along with the usual vocabulary and comprehension subtests. Some IRIs also contain a rate measurement, such as the Informal Reading Assessment. These tests require students to answer comprehension questions after reading passages so that rate of comprehension is determined. Checking comprehension is important since any measure of rate is useless without information on whether students understand what they read at that rate. Rapid word recognition is not helpful if the student does not comprehend the information.

TABLE 7-1
Procedure for administering and scoring a comprehension think-aloud

---

I. Preparing the text

Choose a short passage (expository or narrative) written to meet the following criteria:

1. The text should be from 80 to 200 words in length, depending on the reader's age and reading ability.
2. The text should be new to the reader, but on a topic that is familiar to him or her. (Determine whether the reader has relevant background knowledge by means of an interview or questionnaire administered at a session prior to this assessment.)
3. The text should be at the reader's instructional level, which can be determined by use of an informal reading inventory. Passages at this level are most likely to be somewhat challenging while not overwhelming readers with word identification problems.
4. The topic sentence should appear last, and the passage should be untitled. Altering the text in this way will elicit information about the reader's strategies for making sense of the passage and inferring the topic.
5. The text should be divided into segments of one to four sentences each.

II. Administering the think-aloud procedure

1. Tell the reader that he or she will be reading a story in short segments of one or more sentences.
2. Tell the reader that after reading each section, he or she will be asked to tell what the story is about.
3. Have the student read a segment aloud. After each segment is read, ask the reader to tell what is happening, followed by nondirective probe questions as necessary. The questions should encourage the reader to generate hypotheses (what do you think this is about?) and to describe what he or she based the hypotheses on (what clues in the story helped you?).
4. Continue the procedure until the entire passage is read. Then ask the reader to retell the entire passage in his or her own words. (The reader may reread the story first.)
5. The examiner might also ask the reader to find the most important sentence(s) in the passage.
6. The session should be tape-recorded and transcribed. The examiner should also record observations of the child's behaviors.

III. Analyzing results

Ask the following questions when analyzing the transcript:

1. Does the reader generate hypotheses?
2. Does he or she support hypotheses with information from the passage?
3. What information from the text does the reader use?
4. Does he or she relate material in the text to background knowledge or previous experience?
5. Does the reader integrate new information with the schema he or she has already activated?
6. What does the reader do if there is information that conflicts with the schema he or she has generated?
7. At what point does the reader recognize what the story is about?
8. How does the reader deal with unfamiliar words?
9. What kinds of integration strategies does the reader use (e.g., visualization)?
10. How confident is the reader of his or her hypotheses?
11. What other observations can be made about the reader's behavior, strategies, and so on?

Source: From "Using Think-Alouds to Assess Comprehension" by S. E. Wade, 1990, *The Reading Teacher, 43*, p. 445. Copyright 1990 by the International Reading Association. Reprinted by permission of Suzanne E. Wade and the International Reading Association.

Informal Measures

Informal tests of reading rate also may be used. To do this the teacher asks the student to silently read a story or informational selection of appropriate instructional level. At the end of a specified time—for example, 5 minutes—the teacher calls "stop," and the student places a slash mark after the last word read. Rate (words per minute) is determined by dividing the total number of words read by the number of minutes:

$$\text{Number of minutes} \overline{\left) \begin{array}{c} \text{Words per minute} \\ \hline \text{Total number of words read} \end{array} \right.}$$

Comprehension should also be checked.

Because good reading requires that students vary their rates of reading according to the material and purpose, informal rate assessments should be conducted with different types of material with readers given different purposes for reading. For example, 5-minute rate samples could be taken when the student is asked to read narrative material, read various selections from content area materials such as history or science texts, skim an article to determine its overall purpose, or read to answer several factual questions.

WRITING ASSESSMENT

Because reading and writing instruction increasingly are being linked in classroom instructional programs, reading teachers may wish to make particular effort to assess students' writing. Large-scale testing of writing to evaluate school programs is expanding, but these endeavors do not adequately supply the kinds of information teachers need to

For writing assessments, multiple samples of a student's work should be collected over time.

follow student development. Many published tests use **indirect measures** of writing such as multiple-choice items, which do not estimate well students' true writing abilities (S. W. Freedman, 1993). And some published tests using **direct measurement,** that is, examining actual student writing samples, ask students to produce these samples under conditions that are atypical from authentic writing situations.

The most widely recommended manner of evaluating writing levels and abilities is to collect examples of student writing when it is done in ways advocated by good writing instruction principles and in a fashion consistent with that used by proficient writers. That is, students should have an opportunity to (a) choose their own topics for writing, (b) write under untimed conditions, (c) elicit feedback from others, and (d) revise. What is more, after initial evaluation, teachers should collect chronological samples (dated and over time), not only to measure ongoing skill, but also using these to involve students in self-evaluation of their writing *processes* as well as their writing *products.*

To adequately judge patterns of behavior and growth, teachers should collect selections of various types of writing (stories, informational writing, and so on), along with several revisions of single pieces of work. This collection of samples is often brought together into a **portfolio,** a large folder used to collect and organize student products. Calfee and Perfumo (1993, p. 533) suggest that the portfolio include rough drafts, memos from student-teacher conferences, final drafts, and "published" versions of students' writing, with some of these assigned and others student-selected projects. The length of these may vary from substantial pieces to those that are relatively brief. (See a later section of this chapter for more information on using portfolios in literacy assessment.)

Teachers' written observations also should be maintained over time to document students' learning histories, and most important, to guide instruction for individual students. Many teachers in Britain are now using The Primary Language Record (1989) to structure this type of writing assessment. This assessment tool is also available in the U.S. and Canada (see Test Bank I). On this record, teachers' written observations include, but are not limited to, responses to the following types of questions:

1. The student's willingness to become involved in writing and to maintain this involvement
2. The student's independence and confidence when writing
3. The student's understanding of written language conventions and the spelling system
4. The student's willingness to write collaboratively and to share and discuss his or her writing
5. The range and variety of the student's writing
6. The student's pleasure and interest in writing (paraphrased from p. 44)

Heller (1991) advises teachers to employ analytical checklists to evaluate a student's composing process during prewriting, writing, and postwriting phases. She recommends the checklist pictured in Figure 7-1 for use with children in kindergarten through grade 8. These written observations from different points in time may be maintained in the student's portfolio to provide another basis for judging maturation and need.

Writing also supports opportunities to estimate spelling development. Studies (e.g., Beers & Henderson, 1977; Read, 1975; Zutell, 1978) have shown naturally occurring stages in most children's spelling behaviors. Examination of writing samples over time allows the teacher to systematically note changes in these. Gentry (1981) has described the following spelling stages:

Test Bank I
Tests of Writing Skills

Name	For Grades	Type of Administration	Time for Administration	Publisher
Integrated Literature and Language Arts Portfolio Program (ILLAPP)	2–8	Group	Three 45–minute sessions	Riverside
The Primary Language Record (A handbook and record sheets)	Primary grade levels	Individual	Varies	Heinemann
Writing Process Test	2–12	Group	45 minutes	Riverside
Written Language Assessment	Ages 8–18+	Group	15–20 minutes per writing task	Academic Therapy Publications

1. *Stage 1.* Often called the *random* or *deviant* stage. Example: Child spells *dinosaur* as *WSA*. Occurring when the child is in earliest development of writing within our alphabetic system (prior to this "writing" may have consisted of scribbling) and is characterized by a random selection of letters, showing no knowledge of letter-sound relationships. Diagnostically, some questions the teacher might ask are: Which letters does the student know how to form? Which must still be taught? Does the student discriminate letters from numerals? (At the random stage, some children combine numerals and letters to write "words," e.g., L6T.) Can the child give names for the letters written? Are the "words" written from left to right?

2. *Stage 2.* Often called the *prephonetic* stage. Example: Child spells *rabbit* as *RBT.* At this stage, the child begins to show an emerging realization that sounds heard in words are associated with letters—though some sounds heard may not be used, with only a few of the most salient represented in the student's written form of the word.

3. *Stage 3.* Often called the *phonetic* stage. Example: *Ghost* spelled *gost* or *jumped* spelled *jumpt.* A much closer association between letters and sounds is seen, with all sounds heard being represented in the child's written form of the word, although some vowel sounds may be substituted for others. At times, letter names also are substituted for letter sounds. Gentry (1981) gives this example of the latter: *ADE LAFWTS KRAMD NTU A LAVATR*—which should be read as "Eighty elephants crammed into a elevator." Inflectional endings (e.g., *-ed*) are spelled as they are heard.

4. *Stage 4.* Often called the *transitional* stage. Example: Child spells *airplane* spelled *arplane.* At this stage, vowels appear in all syllables and the student shows recognition of correct spellings of inflectional endings. Common letter patterns

FIGURE 7–1
An analysis of the composing process (K–8)

Prewriting
How does the student determine a purpose (topic and form) for writing?

_____ from a personal experience?

_____ from listening to and talking about a story, poem, or nonfiction?

_____ from reading a story, poem, or nonfiction?

_____ by taking the teacher's suggestions literally?

_____ by imitating a friend's ideas?

_____ by first drawing a picture or creating a piece of art?

Writing
While writing does the student

_____ need absolute quiet?

_____ talk quietly with peers about the content of the work in progress?

_____ appear to maintain a relatively relaxed posture in the use of pen or pencil and paper?

_____ seek help in a reasonable way with spelling, grammar, punctuation?

_____ comfortably use invented spelling?

_____ revise and edit while writing, as evidenced by scratched out words and phrases, arrows, erasures, and so on?

_____ use a word-processing program with ease?

_____ consider the initial draft to be the final draft?

Postwriting
After finishing what the student feels is the final draft, does the student

_____ readily share the work with teacher, parents, and friends?

_____ express a desire to move on to other reading and writing projects?

_____ articulate opinions about the writing process previously completed?

_____ exhibit a positive attitude about the written work?

Optional legend: A = always, S = Sometimes, N = Never.

Source: From *Reading-Writing Connections: From Theory to Practice* (p. 247) by M. F. Heller, 1991, New York, Longman. Copyright 1991 by Longman Publishing Group. Reprinted by permission.

begin to show up in words (e.g., the final *e* on *arplane*), but not always correctly (e.g., *He ackted bad.*)

5.   *Stage 5*. Often called the *correct* stage. Most words are spelled correctly. Of course, the student's age and grade must be taken into account, and the likelihood of the amount of exposure to a specific word. Even college students and professors occasionally misspell words when they have had limited exposure to the word in printed form!

Knowing this typical evolution in spelling growth prevents misinterpretation of spelling behaviors. For example, at times when students with learning disabilities have exhibited spellings at the random or deviant stage or at other stages consistent with spelling behaviors of younger students, their spelling attempts have been erroneously construed to mean that they have some bizarre neurological anomaly affecting their auditory or visual perception. While it is true that such students must be assisted to move to higher stages of spelling development, quite obviously, these misjudgments about causes of nonstandard spellings are made by persons unaware that all students follow natural spelling growth patterns. The correct interpretation of such spelling behaviors is simply that these students are moving through the stages more slowly than the norm, and not that peculiar mental processes are occurring.

A student's stage of spelling development is directly related to understandings of critical importance in reading progress as well. For example, an evaluation of spelling development can help teachers answer these questions: Does the student know that (a) letters have names and form words? (b) letters must be written in left-to-right order to form words in English, as well as recognized and read in the same order? (c) sounds one hears are represented by letters in words and that there is some consistency to these relationships that helps one write and read words (i.e., understands the **alphabetic principle**)? (d) it is the *sounds* representing letters that are written in words—not the *names* that portray those letters? (e) there are common letter patterns often found in words, which are pronounced in relatively consistent ways?

ASSESSING ATTITUDES AND INTERESTS

Conducting an assessment of students' attitudes about reading and their interests in general can help in planning instruction.

Measuring Attitudes Toward Reading

An important principle for helping students increase their reading proficiency is to have them engage in a great deal of reading. Teachers should schedule time to include this critical component in their programs, but also, students who do additional reading outside of class usually improve in reading performance more rapidly than those who do not. Attitude toward reading has a high relationship with amount of voluntary reading (Greaney & Hegerty, 1987).

Several reading attitude scales are available. On the Estes Attitude Scale (Estes, 1971), which has been validated for students in grades 3 through 12, students rank a list of statements from A to E to indicate attitudes ranging from "strongly agree" to "strongly disagree." (See Figure 7–2 and Test Bank J.) This scale may be readministered after a period of remediation to determine if a change in attitudes has occurred.

For students reading at third-grade level and below, Johns (1982) suggests that statements be read orally to them and that they mark their responses on an answer sheet by circling the appropriate face:

Statements he suggests for use with primary students are

Test Bank J
Measure of Attitude

Name	For Grades	Type of Administration	Time for Administration	Publisher
Estes Attitude Scales: Measures of Attitudes Toward School Subjects (EAS)	2–12	Group	20–30 minutes	Pro-Ed

I can read as fast as the good readers.
I like to read.
I like to read long stories.
The books I read in school are too hard.
I need more help in reading.
I worry quite a bit about my reading in school.
I read at home.
I would rather read than watch television.
I am a poor reader.
I like my parents to read to me. (p. 5)

These two procedures measure attitudes by having students rank statements. Attitudes can also be measured through direct observation by the teacher.

Measuring General Interests

Knowing areas of student interest can help teachers select material that the students will enjoy reading. When students are allowed to read something that interests them, substantial reading growth often can be seen. **Interest inventories** consist of statements for students to complete or questions to answer so that they can express their likes and dislikes. Sample questions for an interest inventory might include

What do you like to do most after school and on the weekends?

What things do you think you do well?

What do you like best in school?

What do you like least in school?

What is your favorite TV program?

Do you have any hobbies?

What do you like to do with your family?

What is your favorite sport?

Are there any kinds of animals you like?

Do you have any pets?

Do you belong to any clubs?

What is your favorite activity during recess?

What do you and your best friend do together?

FIGURE 7–2
The Estes Attitude Scale

A = Strongly agree   C = Undecided   E = Strongly disagree
B = Agree   D = Disagree

1. Reading is for learning but not for enjoyment.
2. Money spent on books is well-spent.
3. There is nothing to be gained from reading books.
4. Books are a bore.
5. Reading is a good way to spend spare time.
6. Sharing books in class is a waste of time.
7. Reading turns me on.
8. Reading is only for grade grubbers.
9. Books aren't usually good enough to finish.
10. Reading is rewarding to me.
11. Reading becomes boring after about an hour.
12. Most books are too long and dull.
13. Free reading doesn't teach anything.
14. There should be more time for free reading during the school day.
15. There are many books which I hope to read.
16. Books should not be read except for class requirements.
17. Reading is something I can do without.
18. A certain amount of summer vacation should be set aside for reading.
19. Books make good presents.
20. Reading is dull.

Items	Response Values				
	A	B	C	D	E
The negative items: Nos. 1, 3, 4, 6, 8, 9, 11, 12, 13, 16, 17, 20	1	2	3	4	5
The positive items: Nos. 2, 5, 7, 10, 14, 15, 18, 19	5	4	3	2	1

Source: From "A Scale to Measure Attitudes Toward Reading" by T. H. Estes, 1971, *Journal of Reading, 15.* Copyright 1971 by the International Reading Association. Reprinted by permission of Tom H. Estes and the International Reading Association.

If you could have anything you wanted for your birthday, what would it be?

If someone granted you three wishes, what would you wish?

Has your family ever taken a vacation? Where did you go?

Have you traveled to any other states? Where?

What do you like to read about most?

What do you like to read about least?

An interest inventory is an excellent way to break the ice between teacher and student. Questions and responses should be given orally. Using a tape recorder and simulating a radio or TV interview can be fun. An interest inventory also may be administered in brief written form. The written inventory seen in Figure 7–3 can convey details on both attitudes and interests. It can also yield a brief sample of spelling behaviors early on in the assessment process. Many teachers administer an interest inventory in their first meeting with a student because information obtained can help in planning subsequent sessions.

FIGURE 7–3
A written interest inventory

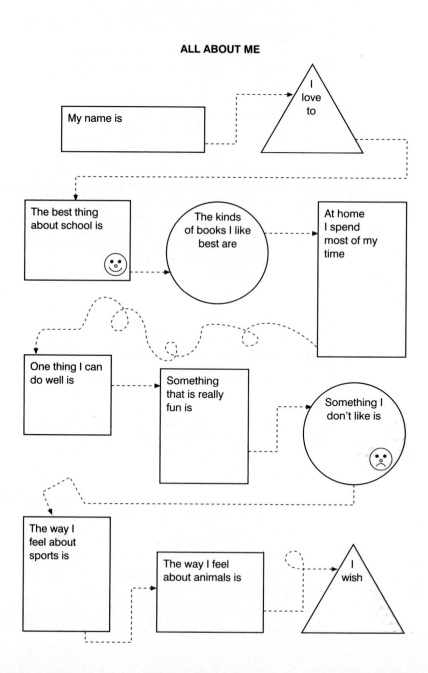

ALL ABOUT ME

OBTAINING BACKGROUND INFORMATION ABOUT THE STUDENT

Early in a student's program and as a part of the assessment process, it is valuable to obtain background information about the student in order to consider variables outside, as well as within, the learner that may have a bearing on progress. It is common practice for teachers working in reading clinic settings to obtain this information by interviewing parents and by talking with other teachers who also work with a student they are assessing and instructing. This is a routine that should be adopted widely by all reading teachers.

Parent interviews can contribute information on a number of relevant factors such as the student's home experiences with literacy events (hearing stories read, activities involving writing, and so on), parents' attitudes toward schooling and the amount of support given to academic requirements or pursuits, types of free-time interests, as well as amount of concentration and effort the student exhibits on these. The parent as informant can furnish many clues to consider in decision making for structuring remediation programs.

Conversations with other teachers who work with the student, likewise, can be productive for understanding what must optimally occur so that students may achieve up to their potentials. Interviews with other teachers may confirm assessment results obtained by the reading teacher and may prompt collaborative effort to alleviate a student's problems. They may, conversely, show that reading behaviors in a regular classroom setting are different from those seen in a small group or one-to-one situation, and the realization of these differences may initiate informative discussion as to why this is so—discussion helpful to all teachers involved, and most particularly to the student. Among the information to be shared are types of instruction to which a student has not responded, as well as topics, activities, and materials that foster the student's motivation. Observation of the student at work within his or her regular classroom also is highly recommended.

Obtaining information from parents and other teachers early on is fundamental to efforts to understand a student's needs.

PERFORMANCE ASSESSMENT

An increasingly favored type of informal evaluation called **performance assessment** seeks to make assessment tasks authentic, that is, for the content and format of the measures to be as close as possible to real reading situations (Spiegel, 1992). Several of the *specific* tests and procedures discussed in the present chapter and in Chapter 6 may be categorized as types of performance assessment. The following section considers performance assessment generically, that is, in terms of *general* assessment approaches that may be used throughout a program to gain perspective about *all* forms of reading behaviors. Most often performance assessment involves informal techniques; however, some published measures are available based on this evaluation perspective. Two such examples are seen in Test Bank K.

Classroom Observation

Observations that are undertaken systematically and are carefully analyzed to identify *patterns* of a student's significant reading behaviors can serve as a form of performance assessment.

Test Bank K
Published Performance-Based Assessments

Name	For Grades	Type of Administration	Time for Administration	Publisher
Integrated Literature and Language Arts Portfolio Program (ILLAPP)	2–8	Group	Three 45-minute sessions	Riverside
Diagnostic Assessments of Reading with Trial Teaching Strategies (DARTTS)	1–2	Individual	50–60 minutes	Riverside

Recently there has been a resurgence of interest in a slightly more organized type of observation than Johns's innerocular technique (IOT), which was discussed in Chapter 5. This type of firsthand assessment is called **ethnographic observation.** It is defined as "on-site, naturalistic study of classroom teaching/learning situations" (T. L. Harris & Hodges, 1981). In other words, the teacher directly observes students' natural behaviors in their natural environment, recording the behaviors and later analyzing them. Ethnographic observation is based on the premise that a teacher cannot really understand all facets of a student's academic or social performances unless the individual is studied holistically.

Through attentive observation and interpretation of classroom events, the teacher can learn more about students. This may promote students' academic development for several reasons. In the first place, the teacher can formulate questions directly related to difficulties a particular student is having and structure observation to answer those questions. Secondly, this type of assessment may be more valid than some conventional assessments because students are behaving and responding naturally in real-life situations (e.g., a student may respond one way during a formal test and quite differently when reading a funny passage to a friend during a free period). Finally, observing a student may help teachers generate new ideas about why a student is having difficulty—ideas that do not fit in the typical pattern of the assessment data as usually gathered.

Irwin and Bushnell (1980, p. 64) offer these guidelines for ethnographic observation:

1. Make a clear distinction between your observation and your interpretation of the event (although ultimately both are important).
2. When appropriate, take down exact words and behaviors, including the type of body language exhibited.
3. Make an attempt to interpret what was observed from the student's point of view (or in other words, ask *Why?*).

Some tools teachers use during ethnographic observation are checklists, participation charts, and rating scales. **Checklists** consist of statements used to record specific behaviors; the teacher simply checks off or writes *Yes* or *No* to indicate their presence or

FIGURE 7–4

Example of a checklist used in ethnographic observation

Reading Checklist

Name: _Jenny_

Date: _Dec. 6_

Situation: _Oral reading individually to me_

_No_ 1. Omitted words after *inspecting* them

Yes 2. Omitted words because of *rapid reading*

_No_ 3. Self-corrected when omissions caused a change in meaning

_No_ 4. Appeared to be relaxed during the activity

absence during a particular observation. (See the example in Figure 7–4.) Cartwright and Cartwright (1984) suggest a variation of a checklist, called a **participation chart,** which can be used when several students are being observed. (See Figure 7–5.) Unlike a simple checklist, **rating scales** (like the one in Figure 7–6) allow the teacher to record quality or frequency of behavior.

FIGURE 7–5

Example of a participation chart used in ethnographic observation

Reading Participation Chart

Situation: _Teacher-directed group of four students; expository passage_

Date: _October 11_

	Karen	Marc	Bob	Al
1. Participated in prereading discussion	✔	✔		✔
2. Made attempt to predict story or passage events	✔			✔
3. Began reading when directed to do so	✔	✔		✔
4. Read attentively without obvious mind wandering	✔	✔	✔	✔
5. Volunteered information in follow-up discussion	✔	✔		✔
6. Appeared uncomfortable when asked to answer questions			✔	

FIGURE 7–6

Example of a rating scale used in ethnographic observation

Reading Rating Scale

Name: _____Sara_____

Date: _____May 6_____

Situation: _____Oral reading of first story in a new book; group situation_____

_____

	Yes	Most of the Time	Sometimes	No
1. Did the student make miscues on words already known to him or her?			✔	
2. Did the student self-correct?		✔		
3. Did the student use appropriate word identification strategies when a word was unknown to him or her?			✔	
4. Did the student appear to be interested in the story/passage?	✔			

The observation form seen in Figure 7–7 has yet another advantage; it allows teachers to record observations across *settings*. This is useful because students' literacy behaviors may vary from one context to another. This specific **across-contexts observation form** could be employed in primary-grade reading classes or LD classes. Using it, the teacher might make written notation of Shawna's highly motivated responses during Story Time when the teacher reads to the children, noting her intelligent interpretation of the story line. During Independent Reading Time, he may observe that Shawna chooses books readily, especially fairy tales and folktales, but only looks at the pictures. During Writing Time, the teacher might note that Shawna willingly participates but exhibits spelling behaviors at a level more consistent with those typically found in preschool children. In Reading Group Time, the teacher's written observation may reveal that while Shawna shows extreme reluctance to read orally before the group, she offers astute comments in interpreting meanings underlying the message of the story, gained from careful listening while other students read. During Reading-Related Activities/Tasks, the teacher might note that Shawna's fear of taking risks in oral reading activities subsides a great deal when gamelike activities are used for practicing letter-sound correspondences or for learning new words. In Informal Settings, he may record that Shawna's oral language development seems well developed, even advanced, and she is outgoing and confident. In the category of Using Books and Print as Resources, the teacher may indicate that he sees little evidence of this in Shawna's case.

Examination of the teacher's comments from this sample observation form begins to build a picture of a bright little girl, interested in books, with excellent oral language skills, who is self-possessed and well adjusted in situations *other than* those in which she is required to read. The teacher's written notations here indicate no difficulties with comprehension, but rather that Shawna's problems lie with word recognition and word identification, as seen both in reading and writing activities. Clues to interests and moti-

FIGURE 7–7
Across-contexts observation form

Description of child's work and behavior for each context
(cite specific indications of skills or knowledge)

Settings and Activities   *Examples of Child's Activities*

Story Time: Teacher reads to class
(responses to story line; child's comments,
questions, elaborations)

Independent Reading: Book Time
(nature of books child chooses or brings
in; process of selecting; quiet or social
reading)

Writing (journal stories; alphabet; dictation)

Reading Group/Individual (oral reading
strategies: discussion of text; responses
to instruction)

Reading-Related Activities/Tasks
(responses to assignments or discussion
focusing on word letter properties, word
games/experience charts)

Informal Settings (use of language in play,
jokes, storytelling, conversation)

Books and Print as Resource (use of
books for projects; attention to signs,
labels, names; locating information)

Other

Source: From "Assessment of Young Children's Reading: Documentation as an Alternative to Testing" by E. Chittenden and R. Courtney in *Emerging Literacy: Young Children Learn to Read and Write* (p. 110) by D. Strickland and L. E. Morrow (Eds.), 1989, Newark, DE: International Reading Association. Copyright 1989 by the International Reading Association. Reprinted by permission of Edward Chittenden and the International Reading Association.

vators also are evident in her choice of books (fairy tales and folktales) and in the lessening of feelings of stress when activities take on a gamelike character.

Chittenden and Courtney (1989) believe that across-contexts observational recording is important because literacy assessment should not be confined to one simple reading activity, such as degree of competence during group reading instruction or performance on an informal reading inventory (IRI), for example.

Because observing students in natural settings allows a teacher to say more about real world behaviors, some reading educators favor ethnographic observation over formal testing. This type of assessment also generally focuses on qualitative, and not mere quantitative, information.

Integrated Assessment

Integrated assessment (Farr, 1992) also is considered a promising type of performance assessment. Some publishers now are developing instruments that test reading and writing within the same measurement procedure. In these tests, for example, students might be required to read a story and then write an extension of the story that reflects understanding of information inferred from it. In this way, the teacher can rate comprehension as well as several facets of writing ability within the same test task—and do so in an activity closely tied to what might be seen in typical high-quality classroom instruction.

One example of such an assessment package available in published form is the Integrated Literature and Language Arts Portfolio Program (ILLAPP). ILLAPP assesses student's interests, attitudes, and experiences, as well as their performances in various reading and language arts strategies, all within the context of reading, writing, and listening related to authentic narrative and expository literature selections.

Process Assessment

Process assessment (also called **dynamic assessment**), when viewed in progress, seems a coalescence of testing and teaching. If a student is unable to respond correctly to a test item, the teacher presents the item differently or gives additional information. If the student remains unsuccessful, then, yet a different manner of presentation is tried or even more information added until the correct response is forthcoming. The purpose of process assessment is to determine more than the student's immediate functioning level, but also to ascertain conditions under which this individual learns best. Popularized by an Israeli psychologist, Reuven Feuerstein (1979), process assessment is also being explored in Europe, North America, and Australia as an assessment alternative.

Paratore and Indrisano (1987) have described ways in which process assessment can be used to evaluate comprehension behaviors. Students are asked to demonstrate important strategies such as predicting before reading, inferring relations between ideas, and showing knowledge of passage structure (p. 779). If they are unable to do so, the test examiner models the behavior, and the student is asked to apply the strategy to another reading selection. Similar types of testing procedures can be used for word identification or other areas targeted for exploration. Process assessment provides insights into degree of guidance needed, type of guidance needed, and the student's needs for further intervention. It is conducted as a collaborative effort between examiner and examinee (Johnston, 1992).

One published, individually administered test battery that employs a form of process assessment is the Diagnostic Assessments of Reading with Trial Teaching Strategies (DARTTS). With this test battery, after assessment of six areas of reading and language, the teacher seeks to determine through a set of trial teaching methods and materials those suitable for students who have previously failed to achieve adequately. For some time, clinical teachers have employed somewhat similar strategies, calling this process *diagnostic teaching*. An example of diagnostic teaching is seen when the teacher presents new words to a student through two or more instructional methods and then notes which produces the most accurate and/or rapid learning. Another example is illustrated by the teacher who gives a tryout to two or more general instructional approaches, for example, indirect versus direct instruction, and determines the effectiveness of each with a specific student before finalizing an overall instructional plan.

Portfolio Assessment

Using portfolios is another example of performance assessment. As you may remember from an earlier section, a **portfolio** is a large folder containing frequently collected samples of student's work. A literacy portfolio might contain daily work from school (or home), tapes of oral reading, or even computer disks that provide samples of writing performance.

The notion of collecting samples of student's work is not a new one. William S. Gray, an early and noted authority on reading disabilities, suggested in the very first issue of the *Journal of Educational Research* (Gray, 1920) that a monthly sampling of students' oral reading behaviors be accumulated to make possible the identification of (a) patterns of need and (b) patterns of growth. Today the portfolio has become a popular idea and is one that can be valuable for teachers of students with literacy problems because it allows *ongoing assessment* and documentation of *progress* from the beginning to the end of a program.

Teachers use the portfolio to plan future work, as well as in conferences with parents, the student's regular classroom teacher, and others. For example, playing a short tape from the portfolio on which oral reading behaviors have been recorded over the course of time can dramatically demonstrate a student's development. Moreover, it also can show the direction in which instruction must subsequently move in order for growth to continue.

An important part of portfolio assessment is to involve students in *self-evaluations* of their own products. This leads to highly desirable interactions among assessment, instruction, and learning. Teachers schedule brief, but regular, conferences in which "reflective interviews" about the samples of work are undertaken. Paris et al. (1992) suggest these types of general questions in student-teacher conferences:

> Here is a sample of your writing that you did this week. Are you finished with it? What do you like about this piece? What would you change to make it better? Did other students in the class help you to write or revise it?
>
> What book have you read this week? Tell me about it? How did it make you feel? Was there anything surprising in the book?
>
> Do you think you are a good reader and writer? What makes someone a really good reader? When you think of yourself as a reader, what would you like to do differently or better? (p. 95)

Interviews should focus on both products and processes. Records of the conferences often are maintained in the portfolio.

Frequently students, along with the teacher, make decisions about which samples of work will be included in the portfolio. This adds the extra advantage of student motivation to do well in areas targeted for inclusion. Sometimes students even voluntarily do extra work at home because they want to add to their portfolios.

In many cases, there should be *multiple samples* of the same targeted area, systematically acquired *across time*, so processes, as well as products, can be evaluated. Materials should have recorded on them, in some manner, the date on which they were placed in the portfolio.

Because objectives for individual students in remedial programs vary, so, too, may the types of samples collected for different students show a range of diversity. See Table 7–2 for a listing of some of the many items a literacy portfolio might contain.

TABLE 7–2
Samples of items that might be found in a literacy portfolio

- Audiotapes of oral reading or of story conferences
- Computer disks containing writing samples
- Comments by student, reflecting self-evaluation
- Different forms of student writing (stories, poems, informational pieces, and so on)
- Several revisions of the same piece of writing, as well as the final product
- Informal reading tests
- Literature logs (lists of books read)
- Charts showing number of pages read
- Journals
- Teacher's notes from reading/writing conferences
- Student's opinions about stories and nonfiction material (written or taped)
- Story discussions that reflect degree of understanding and types of prompts needed (audiotaped)
- Student-dictated stories, written by the teacher

Based on the portfolio, the teacher can evaluate amount of reading, changes in oral reading strategies, ease of understanding (comprehension), growth in word knowledge, students' perceptions of their own growth and needs, skill in various types of writing, types of books enjoyed, and other areas crucial for instructional decisions. Research indicates that teachers who keep records focus more on critical details related to academic growth than teachers who do not (Fraatz, 1987).

A helpful source for teachers wishing to know more about portfolio assessment is *Portfolio Assessment in the Reading Writing Classroom* by Tierney, Carter, and Desai (1991).

FINAL NOTATIONS ABOUT THE CASE STUDY STUDENT

At this point, let us assume that initial evaluation procedures with our hypothetical student, David Adams, for whom we have been developing an assessment case study, have been completed using several of the appraisal processes described in Chapters 6 and 7. Examine the additional notations placed on his assessment information form, illustrated in Figure 7-8.

Details in this figure indicate that two tests of knowledge of high-frequency words were administered to David—one with the words assessed in context and one in which recognition was tested in a context-free task. Both substantiated the brief, preliminary evidence from the IRI given to him earlier, with all three tests pointing to David's need to develop more accurate and automatic recognition of words.

In addition, a word identification strategies inventory was administered. It directed attention to many areas where instruction is essential, also confirming the results of the IRI, but extending those findings in a way useful for planning instruction. David's performance on this latter test allows the teacher to determine areas of phonic analysis and areas of structural analysis where David demonstrates strengths and others where intervention is indicated. Note in the teacher's written comments in the figure just what these specific areas are. The RMI results, also recorded there, corroborate other findings: David's miscues apparently disrupted his comprehension of several important elements as he read the story, and he showed a propensity to substitute graphically similar words for the actual text words in many cases, with no self-correction attempts in evidence.

As can be seen, the teacher applied an informal measure of comprehension by having David orally read many of the passages that he had previously read silently on the standardized reading test. In doing so, she noted trouble he had in recognizing words in the test selections, in the questions, and in the alternative answers. When assisted with recognizing the words he had trouble with, David was able to answer many questions correctly that he had missed in the original administration of the test. This again leads to the conclusion that the major stumbling block preventing David from reading at grade placement is not with comprehension, but with word recognition and word identification strategies. There were signs, however, that some attention to higher-level comprehension would be useful.

The measures of interests and attitudes reported in Figure 7–8 show that David is aware of his reading difficulties, but that serious problems of motivation have not yet come into play: he does want to learn to read better, and this will likely assist the teacher in her efforts to move him along quickly to realizing his potential. In addition, many of the pastimes and pursuits David says interest him will guide the teacher in selecting materials in which he will be willing to invest effort.

David's assessment information form is concluded with background information that the teacher has obtained from his parents, from other teachers, and from her observations of David while he is in his regular classroom. One conclusion from this part of the data-gathering process is that David's parents can be a source of assistance in the efforts to provide a program of high-quality remediation. Their sensitivities in exposing David to good books by reading aloud to him and enrolling him in a summer library program may be one reason why David remains interested in reading despite his problems. The teacher can enlist their help by asking them to continue to provide time for David to read short, easy books to them each day at home.

Reflections by his classroom teacher reveal a concern for David and, in addition, that many important adjustments are being made for him, but also that this teacher does not have time to furnish adequate individual instruction to meet requirements for

FIGURE 7–8

A record of assessment information for a hypothetical student

---

Assessment Information Form

Student's Name: ___David Adams___

Grade Level: ___4th___

Chronological Age:

   1) Birthdate ___February 19, 19—___

   2) Age ___9.0___

Listening Level:

   1) Method of determination ___Use of graded IRI passages___

   2) Level ___4th grade___

Entry Level Assessment Results: ___2nd grade___

Standardized Survey Test:

   1) Name of test ___Gates-MacGinitie Reading Tests, Level 2, Form A___

   2) Grade score obtained ___3.0___

Present Reading Instructional Level (based on standardized test results): ___approximately 2.0___

Discrepancy between Listening Level and Present Achievement: ___2.0___

Verification of General Reading Levels:

   1) Name of test ___Analytical Reading Inventory___

   2) Grade scores obtained ___Frustration level—approximately 2.5 and above___

                           ___Instructional level—approximately 2.0___

                           ___Independent level—approximately 1.0___

Specific Strengths and Weaknesses in Reading Knowledge, Strategies, and Skills:

  A. An analysis of strengths and weaknesses determined from David's IRI performance is attached to this Assessment Information Form, along with implications for instruction.

  B. Knowledge of basic sight vocabulary

    1. On a contextual inventory, David confused 24 words with similar words.

    2. On a test of words in isolation, David was unable to pronounce 5 words and confused 37 others with similar words.

    3. Specific words from both tests which David did not know and those he confused with others are listed on a sheet attached to this Assessment Information Form

C. Knowledge and use of word identification strategies
   1. An informal assessment confirmed the finding from the IRI that David does not use context clues to identify unknown words, nor does he seem to have any concept of this strategy.
   2. On a teacher-prepared instrument, strengths in phonetic analysis knowledge were seen for
      a. consonant sounds
      b. blends (clusters)
      c. consonant digraphs
      d. naming of vowels
      e. long vowel sounds

   Weaknesses were seen for

      a. short vowel sounds
      b. sounds of r-controlled vowels
      c. combinations with silent letters
      d. use of consonant substitution in combination with phonograms
      e. special vowel combinations
   3. On a teacher-prepared instrument, strengths in structural analysis were seen for
      a. use of inflectional endings
      b. reading contractions and matching these to the words from which they were derived

   Weaknesses were seen for

      a. identifying compound words
      b. identifying words when their spellings were changed before adding an inflectional ending
      c. dividing words into syllables
      d. recognizing prefixes
      e. recognizing suffixes

Specific phonetic and structural analysis information David did and did not know is listed on a sheet attached to this Assessment Information Form.

D. Performance on the Reading Miscue Inventory
   1. Most of David's miscues resulted from substituting a graphically similar word for the text word. In many of these cases, words were used that did not have the same grammatical function as the text word and, therefore, syntactically and semantically unacceptable sentences were produced.
   2. David self-corrected only 2 of the 25 miscues that were analyzed, even though 15 of these resulted in a loss or partial loss of the intended meaning.
   3. Percentage scores for comprehension were
      a. No loss—40%
         Partial loss—14%
         Loss—46%
   4. Percentage scores for use of grammatical relationships were
         Strength—24%
         Partial strength—30%
         Weaknesses—46%
         Overcorrection—0%

FIGURE 7–8 *(continued)*

---

5. Retelling
   a. Score ___59___
   b. Strengths were seen in recall of characters and remembering events.
   c. Weaknesses were seen in stating the overall plot of the story and identifying the theme.
   d. He had some difficulty stating information related to character development because of two miscues he made throughout the story, which caused a misinterpretation of important information.

E. Comprehension assessment

   In addition to analysis of comprehension performance on the IRI and RMI, two additional assessments were carried out.

   1. David was asked to orally read passages and answer questions from the comprehension subtest of the group standardized survey test that had been used during assessment for identification. This oral assessment showed that the majority of his difficulties on this test had stemmed from word recognition and identification problems. Questions were answered incorrectly because he confused words or could not identify many of them. When the teacher told him the correct word, he was usually able to answer the question. On a few questions, he was unable to respond correctly, even with this assistance. When asked why he responded as he did on these latter questions, he appeared confused by the task of being asked to draw an inference and was attempting to find the answer directly stated in the passage.
   2. David was asked to read silently a story selected from a basal reader at his instructional level and then retell it. His retelling was followed by probes. This assessment was used to compare his performance with his retelling after oral reading on the RMI. His performance was somewhat better after silent reading, but only slightly.

F. Measures of attitudes and interests

   1. An informal measure of reading attitudes was conducted. David believes he is a poor reader and needs more help in reading, but still says he likes reading and being read to.
   2. An interest inventory revealed that
      a. David loves anything having to do with football—playing it, reading about it, watching it on TV. He hopes to be a football player, like his brother, when he gets to middle school.
      b. He likes animals of all kinds. He owns two cats (Scruffy and Stripes) and two ducks (Sally and Ronald). He says he likes to write stories about his animals and likes to look at books that have pictures of animals from Africa.
      c. If he could have three wishes they would be
         1) to get a 10-speed bike
         2) for his sister to leave his stuff alone, and
         3) to have muscles.
   3. On Saturday mornings he loves to watch cartoons on TV.
   4. In school he likes math, gym, music, and studying about "people of long ago" best.
   5. His family takes summer vacations and he loves going to the beach and going fishing.

G. Background Information

1. *From David's parents:* David's parents report that there have been no serious illnesses during his preschool and early school years. They have routinely read aloud to David, on most nights providing a bedtime story. In summers since age 4, he has belonged to a library book club where experiences with high-quality children's literature are provided to small groups of children once a week. Mr. and Mrs. Adams try to help David with work sent home from school, but recently he has been reluctant to accept their help, balking and exhibiting avoidance behaviors. The lack of concentration seen during these attempts to assist with most homework is not seen when they read to him or when he is looking at or reading easy books related to topics of great interest to him.

2. *From other teachers:* David's classroom teacher says he has had a reputation in the school for having a nice disposition. Though he has a lively nature, he previously has been cooperative. At present, however, she is noticing many off-task behaviors and little effort in many reading-related activities. Her literature-based reading program provides the class much exposure to good books that David enjoys when this involves listening activities, but he is increasingly unable to use many of the books the other students are enjoying in independent activity because of his limitations in word recognition and identification. Because these problems are not characteristic of other pupils in the class, the teacher does not provide time for direct instruction in these areas. She would like to furnish David with individual help, but has difficulty finding time considering the numbers of students in her class. She gives him some extra attention but worries that it is not enough. The results of her assessments of his reading abilities are similar to ours and she says when she is occasionally able to find suitable books for their current literature theme which are about two years below the level the other students are reading, David is able to participate more fully. He does engage in writing activities, but she notes that his spelling behaviors are characteristic of those of a younger child.

   Observation of David during one morning in his classroom confirmed much of this information. During that time he engaged in no actual reading of text himself, but listened avidly when others were reading favorite parts of the book on which the class was currently focusing. He wandered aimlessly about the room quite a bit, but was diligent in his efforts during a 20-minute math lesson.

   Examination of his school records revealed notations by previous teachers indicating slow progress in letter recognition, in gaining control of letter-sound correspondences, and in developing an adequate knowledge of basic words. Although progress was seen in all grades, every teacher had indicated his advancement in these areas was not commensurate with that of other students.

David that are untypical of most other students in her class. The special attention David will receive in these areas in the small-group situation of the reading class will, therefore, be especially critical. By observing David in his regular classroom and by examining notations from previous teachers in his school records, the reading teacher has confirmed her own observations as well as those reported by the present classroom teacher. David does have many strengths (for example, his interest in writing stories and in listening to stories read aloud), and these can be built upon in planning his program. The information provided by other teachers, as well as the on-site observation, also provide additional clues to weaknesses that must be alleviated (see the information in the figure).

ASSESSMENT PROCEDURES THAT ARE NOT USEFUL

As has been noted, there are no perfect assessment instruments or procedures for evaluating reading. Even the best ones available have shortcomings. But when employed judiciously and in combination with other measures, most of these do provide helpful information.

TABLE 7–3
Some tests and their inadequacies

Published Tests	Inadequacies
Visual Motor Gestalt Test (Bender)	1. Ability to copy designs is not related to reading. 2. Scores do not differentiate average readers, readers with learning disabilities, and those with reading disabilities. (See studies by Chang & Chang, 1967, and Robinson & Schwartz, 1973.) 3. There are unacceptable problems with reliability and validity.
Motor-free Visual Perception Test	Ability to visually discriminate geometric figures does not transfer to visual discrimination of letters and words.
Developmental Test of Visual-Motor Integration (Beery-Buktenica)	Ability to copy geometric designs is not related to reading. (See also the review of this test in Bush and Waugh, 1982.)
Frostig Developmental Test of Visual Perception	1. Visual perceptual factors measured by this test are not related to reading. 2. Scores do not discriminate between good and poor readers. 3. There are inadequate norming procedures. 4. There is inadequate reliability. (See Robinson & Schwartz, 1973; Ysseldyke & Algozzine, 1982).
Illinois Test of Psycholinguistic Abilities (ITPA)	1. All subtests but one are uncorrelated with reading ability. 2. Scores are correlated with intelligence. 3. Scores do not distinguish between good and poor readers. 4. Norms are based only on middle-class students. 5. There is questionable retest reliability. 6. Students who speak a nonstandard dialect may be penalized. (See a review of this test in Newcomer & Hammell, 1975.)

However, there are other tests and assessment procedures that, although sometimes suggested for reading programs, simply are not useful.

One reason that these tests lack value is that they are based on faulty ideas or theories about reading and the reading process; their procedures and interpretations are in conflict with research evidence. Another reason they lack utility is that they are so poorly constructed that they do not provide valid information.

In previous sections of this text, some tests have been discussed that should be avoided. Other tests to bypass are listed in Table 7–3, with reasons for their inadequacies.

MEASURING GROWTH IN SPECIFIC STRATEGIES, KNOWLEDGE, AND SKILLS

Measurement of students' growth in specific strategies, knowledge, and skills may occur at various times after a remedial program has been instituted, including at the end of the program. If *formal* tests are used for this purpose, care should be taken to select tests that measure the same areas treated in instruction. For instance, if stress has been

TABLE 7–3 *(continued)*

Published Tests	Inadequacies
Peabody Individual Achievement Test—Revised (PIAT-R)	1. Reading Recognition subtest involves only letter knowledge and word pronunciation in isolation; therefore, it lacks content validity. 2. Reading Comprehension subtest consists only of reading *single sentences;* therefore, lacks content validity. 3. The standard error of measurement is large for both subtests.
Woodcock Reading Mastery Tests—Revised	1. Word identification subtest only assesses words in isolation. 2. Word Attack subtest employs only nonsense words. 3. In the Passage Comprehension subtest, one third of the "passages" consist of only one sentence. 4. A cloze task is used to assess comprehension, a questionable procedure for measuring higher-level comprehension.
Test of Nonverbal Auditory Discrimination (pitch, timbre, duration, loudness, rhythm)	Nonverbal auditory discrimination is not related to the auditory discrimination demands of reading.

Observational Tests	Inadequacies
Tests of visual tracking of a moving object	Ability to visually track a moving object is unrelated to reading ability.
Tests of balance	Balance is unrelated to reading ability.
Tests of eye-hand coordination	Eye-hand coordination is not related to reading ability.
Tests of left-right discrimination	Ability to distinguish between left and right is unrelated to reading ability.
Tests of lateral dominance	Lateral dominance is not related to reading.

placed on developing higher-level comprehension strategies, a test that predominantly assesses literal-level comprehension would be an inappropriate choice. Furthermore, one must remember the concept of standard error of measurement discussed in Chapter 4. If this measurement index is ignored when comparing scores obtained at the beginning of a program with those at the end, interpretation may be seriously faulty.

More often, *informal* procedures are used to assess growth in reading. Teacher-made tests of strategies, knowledge, and skills similar to those used during the initial assessment procedures are appropriate and should be combined with judgments made during daily teacher observations. Portfolios, too, can, of course, add an effective dimension in measuring growth.

A more structured version of using informal testing to measure growth is called **curriculum-based assessment** (Fuchs, Fuchs, & Hamlett, 1989). With this assessment plan, teachers set instructional goals, and tests are devised to monitor subsets of learning along the way toward meeting these goals. If progress is not forthcoming, teaching procedures are changed. Some programs have computerized the testing and monitoring procedures associated with curriculum-based assessment. Certain special education classes have made rapid gains in achievement under this plan in which assessment is based directly on the planned curriculum, but in which assessment also is the basis for *changing* the curriculum (Fuchs, Fuchs, & Hamlett, 1989).

Finally, an attempt should be made to determine whether students are employing newly gained strategies, skills, and knowledge in the regular classroom. If newly gained learning has not generalized to other settings and is not serving to bring about overall academic improvement, the remedial teacher must make efforts to assist the student in applying skills to other settings.

CONCLUSION

As can be seen from the four chapters in this unit, assessment is a complex process. One must not only evaluate students to determine their competence in a variety of abilities related to reading proficiency, one must also consider factors outside the learner, such as home and school background, and methods as well as learning tasks and materials that produce understanding and a favorable rate of learning for each *specific* student. Teacher skill in assessment is predicated on knowledge of test instruments, familiarity with testing procedures, and conclusions based on careful reflection after many observations of students. Because adequate instruction of students having literacy problems is based on valid conclusions from assessment, it is a major responsibility of professionals working with these individuals to be well informed.

📖 REFLECTIONS

- - - - - - - - - - - - - - - - - - - -

1. Valencia, McGinley, and Pearson (1990) say portfolio assessment should be (a) authentic, (b) collaborative, (c) conceptually grounded, (d) continuous, and (e) multifaceted. What do each of these mean? Compare each of these criteria to the description of portfolio assessment provided in this chapter. How do they apply to portfolio assessment as discussed here?
2. Using the same five criteria cited in number 1, above, consider other assessment procedures you have read about in this and the three preceding chapters. Which tests or procedures would meet one or more of these criteria?

- -

INSTRUCTIONAL
INTERVENTIONS

8

Important Principles of
Remedial and Clinical
Reading Instruction

Research on cognition indicates cooperative learning has potential for all learners.

T his chapter presents instructional principles that should be considered by reading educators in order to promote successful reading growth. It also discusses the logistics of organizing and managing remedial and clinical reading programs. It focuses on those teacher tasks, decisions, and behaviors necessary to arrange the learning environment to ensure effective learning.

PRINCIPLES

Principle One: Begin Early

Early intervention is important for students who are displaying difficulties and delays in learning to read. In times past, this was not considered the critical principle that it is today. Previously it was believed that certain young students simply were not "ready" to learn to read and that given the curative of time, they would mature into a "readiness" to read. This conventional wisdom has not been borne out by research, however (e.g., Juel, 1988; Lundberg, 1984). While it is certainly true that students do begin reading acquisition on slightly variable schedules, if delays appear to be outside the normal *range*, simply waiting for students to catch up is not effective (Clay, 1979; Johnston & Allington, 1991).

A number of the most successful current programs dealing with children who are not progressing adequately in reading have as a central tenet the plan to intervene *as soon as* a lag is apparent. One such example is the productive Reading Recovery Program begun in New Zealand (Clay, 1979) and adopted widely with first-grade children throughout the United States (Pinnell, 1989). The Reading Recovery Program initiates instruction with first-graders who are below the average of their classes, before inappropriate reading behaviors can be firmly entrenched. Reading Recovery, which is undertaken with children who are in the lowest 20% of their classes, is viewed as a *preventive* tutoring program. The components of this early instruction are described in Figure 8–1, as seen from the point of view of a child—and, as is shown in the figure, involve connected text reading, development of multiple reading strategies, and writing. (Lee and Neal [1993] describe an adaptation of the Reading Recovery Program with a middle school student who was seriously lacking in reading skill, which they call Reading Rescue—a program that was successful for the student.)

Principle Two: Consider the Benefits of One-to-One Tutoring

Working with students individually has many advantages because teachers are able to give undivided attention to the student. This total concentration on a single student allows instruction to mesh exactly with student needs at any given time. The reader's confusions are readily noted, immediate feedback is possible, and the instructional curriculum can be woven around a specific reader's strengths, weaknesses, and interests. As Johnston and Allington (1991) say, "Accommodating individual learner differences is at the root of remediation" (p. 994).

A further value of individual work consists of the increased opportunities for response. That is, an individual reader is doing all of the responding during a lesson rather than sharing the response opportunities with others in a group. Research has shown the number of occasions a student has for response is correlated with achievement (e.g., C. R. Greenwood, Delquadri, & Hall, 1984).

Studies conducted to compare the efficacy of one-to-one tutoring with more conventional group instruction have consistently found large differences in learning in favor

FIGURE 8–1
Reading Recovery lesson

HI! WELCOME TO MY READING RECOVERY LESSON

Fluent Writing Practice

Before my 30 minute lesson begins, I get to write some words on the chalkboard. I'm learning to write little important words as fast as I can so I can write them in my stories. It's fun to write on the chalkboard!

Rereading Familiar Books

In every lesson every day I get to read lots of little books. I get to pick some of my favorite stories that I have read before. This is easy for me. I try to read my book like a story and make it sound like people are talking. My teacher says "That's good reading; that's how good readers read."

Taking a Running Record

Now I have to read a book all by myself! My teacher will check on me and won't help me unless I have a hard problem. If I just can't figure out a word or I get all mixed up my teacher will tell me the word or say "Try that again." I read this book yesterday. My teacher helped me work hard to figure out the tricky parts. Now I think I can read it pretty good all by myself!

*Letter Identification or
Word Analysis (optional)*

Sometimes I need to do work on learning about letters or important "chunks" of words. My teacher knows all about the things I need to learn. I like to move the magnetic letters around on the chalkboard; they help me understand what I am learning.

FIGURE 8–1 *(continued)*

Writing a Story

Every day I get to think up my own story to write in my writing book. I can write lots of the little words all by myself. My teacher likes my stories and helps me work to figure out how to write some of the words. We use boxes and I say the word I want to write slowly so I can hear the sounds and then I write the letters in the boxes all by myself. I like to read my story when I'm done.

Cut-up Sentence

I read the story and my teacher writes it on a long strip of paper. My teacher cuts up my story so I can put it back together. I have to think real hard to get it all back together, then I have to check myself to see if I got it right. Most of the time I do!

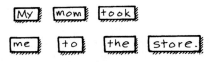

New Book Introduced

I like this part of the lesson the best! My teacher picks out a new story just for me and tells me what the story is all about. We look at the pictures and think about what the people and animals say in this book. My teacher also helps me think about some new, important words in my story. Isn't it fun to hear about the story and look at the beautiful pictures before you read it? I think it helps me read the story too!

New Book Attempted

Now it's my turn to work hard again but I like this story and I know my lesson is almost over. When I come to a hard part my teacher will ask me questions to help me think or might show me what I should try to think about or do. My teacher is trying to teach me to do all the things that good readers do. If I have to work real hard on this story we will probably read it again together so I can just think about the story but I'm not sure there is enough time.

Didn't I do lots of work in my lesson today? I hope you learned something too. Bye!

Source: Mary Fried, Coordinator, Reading Recovery Program, Columbus, Ohio, City Schools

of the students who are tutored. For example, Anania (1982) and Burke (1984) found that students in grades 4, 5, and 8 who had one-to-one instruction, on the average, scored 98% (or two standard deviations) higher than the group-instructed students. Tutored students also ended the program with more positive attitudes. Similarly, in a review of five one-to-one tutoring programs, each having different curricula, Wasik and Slavin (1993) found that all had high success rates—although there were some differences among the five, with those having the most comprehensive and balanced programs and the most highly trained teachers producing the greatest gains.

Some school districts have attempted to address the need for more personalized instruction by reducing class size substantially. As Allington (1993) has noted, if instruction does not change along with class size, then enhancement of learning cannot be expected; however, if teachers use smaller class size to give more and individualized guidance to low-achieving students, then more positive results can occur. Small class size has indeed helped, but the growth seen for students still is not as great as with one-to-one teaching (Wasik & Slavin, 1993).

Two notable reading programs that feature one-to-one instruction are Reading Recovery (discussed under Principle One) and Success for All (Madden, Slavin, Karweit, Dolan, & Wasik, 1991). In a comparison of Reading Recovery with three other instructional models for educationally at risk first-graders, it was found that one of the three variables leading to the success of the Reading Recovery Program was the one-to-one lessons (along with intensive training of the teachers and the framework of the lessons themselves) (Pinnell, Lyons, DeFord, Bryk, & Seltzer, 1994). Success for All is a program that has been initiated in several inner-city communities for kindergarten through third grades. In this program, group instruction is undertaken, as well as one-to-one tutoring to meet readers' needs.

It is likely that one-to-one reading instruction will be *most* profitable and have the most enduring effects if it is based on students' assessed needs, focusing on knowledge, strategies, and skills that are missing from each student's repertoire, with sizable amounts of student time apportioned to connected text reading—using materials at a level of difficulty appropriate for the reader. It is likely that tutoring will be *less* effective when the one-to-one instructional time is allotted to helping the student carry out class assignments. When teachers or tutors primarily assist the student by supplying guidance with homework and other assigned exercises undertaken by the regular class as a whole, the student does receive a benefit. However, such an approach does not allow the student to fill the gaps in basic learning; eliminating these could solve the learning problems and special instruction would no longer be needed.

Principle Three: Take into Account the Effects of the Teacher's Instructional Actions During Group Learning

Remedial instruction may be conducted through one-to-one tutoring, or with groups of students, or in situations where students work individually on their own. Because one-to-one instruction is not always feasible, many reading teachers work with small groups. Even in these conditions, however, there are times when the teacher instructs only one student while others in the group go about assigned tasks independently. Individualized instruction can take place in all—or none—of these instructional arrangements. Individualized instruction does not necessarily imply working with just one reader at a time. Rather, **individualized instruction** (sometimes called **personalized instruction**) is the tailoring of teaching to a student's specific needs. Where more than one student has the same educational requirements, grouping students is appropriate: individualized instruction can still occur. Conversely, a teacher can work on a one-to-one basis with a student and yet personalized instruction can fail to take place, if the learning requirements of that particular student are not addressed.

Deciding how and when to group students is based on assessment, not only those judgments preceding the instructional program, but also during informal daily ongoing evaluation of students' reading progress. This means that the decision to have a student participate in a group, or to work individually with the teacher, or to operate independently can vary from day to day as class members' needs change because of their different learning rates.

Grouping for instruction does have some advantages. One of these is efficient use of teacher time. A second benefit is that students often learn from each other by hearing the responses of their peers and by sharing in problem-solving experiences. One current program that has proved effective is the Boulder Project (Hiebert, Colt, Catto, & Gury, 1992), a specially modified Title I program in which students are instructed in small groups of 3.

Despite some positive features of group instruction, the teacher must be certain that readers in the group do not receive unequal treatment. Explanations, prompts, opportunities for response, reassurance, and support should be directed to all students in a balanced manner to guarantee equitable student participation in learning endeavors. Bloom (1984) contends that teachers are frequently unaware that they supply more occasions for active engagement for some students than they do for others. Studies have shown that the readers who need the most help are the ones who are often ignored (Brophy & Good, 1970).

The influence of teacher expectations, discussed in a previous chapter, must also be kept in mind. When teachers *expect,* and plan for, students' success, beneficial effects are more probable. High—but reasonable—standards for all lead to favorable consequences.

Principle Four: Provide Opportunities for Collaborative Learning

When group instruction is implemented, important positive outcomes can result if readers are allowed at times to engage in collaborative learning. In **collaborative learning,** peers work together in pairs or small groups to write (compose, revise), discuss answers to questions about text, find solutions to problems, share information, and take turns in leading group discussions. Although students lead and share responsibility for learning, teacher guidance precedes—and is available when needed throughout—collaborative learning occasions. Palincsar and Brown's (1984) research on reciprocal teaching showed that learning of strategies to foster and monitor comprehension was effective when students worked collaboratively. Heath (1991) has suggested that collaborative learning opportunities may be particularly valuable with students from ethnic and racial communities who highly value group cooperation, but she also points out that research on cognition indicates cooperative learning has potential for all learners.

Cross-age collaborations also have merit. When older and younger students have been paired to work together on reading and writing tasks, gains have been seen, including improvements in cognitive objectives and attitudes toward literacy activities (e.g., Leland & Fitzpatrick, 1993–94; Rekrut, 1994).

Principle Five: Consider the Implications of Independent Work

Secondary teachers find that students in the age groups they teach sometimes prefer independent practice rather than group activities. Therefore, secondary reading or LD classes at times are managed so that readers carry out assignments independently, with the teacher moving from student to student to provide some direct, individual instruction for a part of each period.

It should be noted, however, that research has shown that independent endeavors *without teacher supervision* are negatively related to academic gains. (See, e.g., Sinde-lar & Wilson, 1982). This implies careful planning if students are to spend the maximum amount of time on academically relevant tasks when functioning alone. Independent practice can be effective if it follows these principles:

1. It immediately follows teacher-directed instruction.
2. It is at the appropriate instructional level.
3. It is engaged in for short periods of time.
4. It is interspersed with either group or individual teacher-directed instruction.

One way to facilitate good use of time during independent exercises is to prepare personalized assignment sheets for each student (like the one in Figure 8–2) and have students check off responsibilities as they are completed.

Group instruction and individual (one-to-one) instruction make maximum use of teacher-directed activities, while independent work does not. Teacher-directed instruction is an important feature of productive programs (M. J. Adams, 1990a, 1990b; Duffy & Roehler, 1987). It appears that more *teacher-directed* time is necessary for delayed readers. For example, Stallings (1980) found that when low-achieving students made high achievement gains, 72% of their instructional time had been spent in teacher-directed experiences, while average readers made high gains when only 49% of their time was spent in teacher-led instruction. In addition, although the number of occasions

FIGURE 8–2
Example of an individual assignment sheet

Mike

✔ 1. Reread by yourself the story you read with my help yesterday.

✔ 2. Go to the learning center and complete the two activities on recognizing prefixes that have been placed there.

____ 3. Write a one-paragraph "story" about your basketball practice last night. I'll be by after you have finished to hear you read this to me and to talk to you about any problems you may have had with sounds of letters. We'll also add words from your story to your word bank. Be thinking of which ones you want to choose.

____ 4. There is an activity for sequencing a story in your folder. Do this.

____ 5. Choose a new story from the book I have placed on your desk. Begin reading it. I'll come by to work with you on this story at about 10:40.

for student response is correlated with growth in learning, not all response opportunities have the same impact. Sindelar and Wilson (1982) reported that their studies showed that the opportunities to respond during teacher-directed instruction were more likely to lead to learning than responses made during independent performance. This is probably due to the lack of immediate feedback about correctness of responses when students function alone.

Principle Six: Consider Time on Task

Time on task is a concern closely related to several of the preceding principles. An advantage to group work or individual instruction in contrast to arrangements in which students work on their own is that high rates of academically engaged time are possible. That is, the teacher can ensure that students are working more of the time on academically relevant enterprises. Monitoring students is more difficult when readers have been assigned to complete tasks independently. Rosenshine (1980), for example, found rates of academic engagement to be 84% during teacher-led instruction as opposed to only 70% during independent assignments. The amount of time students are actually engaged in academic projects is an important variable in learning.

Analysis of the value of group and individual instruction versus independent work should take into account the differences between *allocated time* and *engaged time*. In discussing the amount of time they have allocated for instruction, teachers will often say something like, "In Nicole's daily schedule, I have 20 minutes planned for sustained silent reading," or, "I'm having Scott work on higher-level comprehension for 25 minutes of each period." But what too often occurs is that Nicole is sent to a desk to read on her own while the teacher has responsibilities with other students; Nicole then spends 3 minutes looking through her purse, 5 minutes glancing at pictures elsewhere in her book, 4 minutes daydreaming, and only 8 minutes really reading. Or, during Scott's 25 minutes of independent work, he may read an assigned article for a while, then he watches what another student is doing, then reads a bit more and writes answers to a question or two, then plays with his pencil for a few minutes, then reads and thinks about a couple more answers, then draws a picture on his paper, then writes any answer without reading the remainder of the questions. Obviously, he has really devoted considerably less than 25 minutes to genuine learning ventures. Allocated time has no impact on learning. Engaged time does.

In remedial programs, independent performance often is necessary so that teachers can meet the diverse needs of all students, but teachers must take care in planning and monitoring students' independent work to ensure that they spend adequate academically engaged time. It should be said, however, that the nature of teacher behaviors and instructional guidance during teacher-directed instruction also determines the ultimate value of academically engaged time. For example, if the teacher chooses projects that have little relevance to skills students need in authentic reading or if the teacher allows students to waste instructional time with constant off-task behaviors, students will not grow in reading ability. In other words, the quality of instruction is as critical as the quantity.

Another issue related to time on task is the predetermined length of group sessions. If students are scheduled to participate in a special reading class for only limited time each day (e.g., 20 minutes or 30 minutes), substantial increases in learning should not be expected. When group rather than one-to-one instruction is necessary, more appropriately conceived plans organize time in 40- to 45-minute periods, *every day* of the school week. Reading clinics commonly allow for tutoring of students for 1 hour per session several times per week. This expanded allotment of academic time, along with one-to-one tutoring, plausibly are two important factors accounting for the significant growth in learning of students who have shown little improvement in other instructional arrangements. School programs wanting to seriously address students' reading difficulties and hoping to realize major gains should consider these more favorable conditions. While it is true that some programs have had notable successes when working with students in time frames as short as a half hour a day, typically in these situations, instruction is conducted on a one-to-one basis and by highly trained teachers (e.g., the Reading Recovery Program).

Some schools where the importance of time on task is now realized have adopted practices of extended schooling. Students attend special remedial classes before or after school or on Saturday mornings, as well as receiving instruction during the regular school day (Allington, 1993). Others have moved to year-round programs with all students attending during the summer months as well as during the traditional school year.

Principle Seven: Let the Students Read

Teachers who work with poor readers often are so concerned about the skills and strategies these students lack that they allocate the majority of instructional time to specific exercises related to such inadequacies. Yet, while there can be no question that instructional time must be spent on skill and strategy acquisition (M. J. Adams, 1990a, 1990b; R. C. Anderson, Hiebert, Scott, & Wilkerson, 1984; Chall, 1987), it is inappropriate to require that students spend all of their class time on developing specific reading skills while never being given the occasion to practice such skills in meaningful material.

It is now generally recognized that the single most helpful way to promote growth in reading competence is the processing of large amounts of regular, connected reading material. A. J. Harris and Serwer (1966), for example, found that one of the most important variables positively correlated with reading success was the amount of time spent "actually reading." In their study, "actually reading" did not mean carrying out supportive activities such as drawing a picture to accompany a language experience story, discussing objects the teachers had brought in to furnish background for a story, or completing other language arts activities. Although the teacher may choose to include these types of experiences in a remedial reading program, time spent on such pursuits should not be counted as part of actual reading time.

In many regular classrooms, time spent reading is shockingly small—as little as 7 to 8 minutes a day in elementary classes and 15 minutes a day in middle school programs! (See Dishaw, 1977; Durkin, 1984). Such restricted practice in actual reading is detrimental, especially for students with low aptitudes for literacy learning.

In those remedial and clinical programs in which maximum reading growth is seen, students spend a large portion of each class period reading regular, connected authentic texts. In those programs in which the majority of time is allotted to skills and strategy practice, readers do improve in these specific skills, but the degree to which the skills are generalized to, and applied in, real reading functions remains limited. For example, suppose a criterion-referenced test reveals that Kimberly lacks knowledge of consonant sounds. Based on the test results, the teacher plans instruction so that most of each class session is apportioned to drill, games, worksheet assignments, and so on, to help her learn consonant sounds. After a time, it is very likely that if the test is readministered, Kimberly will show marked improvement in knowledge of these sounds. However, it is also likely that when asked to read in her regular classroom, she will not perform significantly better than she had before the remedial instruction—because she has not had sufficient chance to practice or transfer the new skills to an authentic reading situation.

Teachers should carefully determine the number of minutes any given student spends engaged with regular, connected reading material under teacher-directed guidance, as well as in independent work. The teaching plan should furnish the student with ample time for reading every day. In addition, teachers should not forget that one of the most valuable independent or seatwork assignments is *reading a book.*

Principle Eight: Encourage Outside Reading

Research has frequently reported a significant correlation between amount of free time reading and reading growth (e.g., Greaney & Hegerty, 1987). There is no question that poor readers who regularly spend some time outside of reading class reading books, magazines, newspapers—or anything (even comic book reading has been related to gains in reading competence [Greaney, 1980])—make more substantial and rapid progress than those who do not. The teacher should have interesting, easy-to-read materials in the classroom and encourage students to check out some of these each time they leave the class. Parents should be asked to turn off the TV and have their child read for 15 or 20 minutes daily.

Cooperating with regular classroom teachers to set up programs of **sustained silent reading** (SSR) in their rooms is also urged. During SSR, all students, including those from the remedial program, read anything they choose for a designated period every day. Effects of SSR have been particularly positive when the program has been carried out for a year or more (Gutherie & Greaney, 1991).

Principle Nine: Model Effective Reading Behaviors

If students have difficulty accomplishing a task when told what to do, add another dimension: *demonstrate* how to do it. For example, during oral reading, take turns reading with them. It is surprising how quickly a student's oral reading will begin to take on characteristics of the teacher's reading when this is done.

Role-playing in reading situations can also help. For example, the teacher can pretend to come to an unknown word and then talk through strategies to identify it. For example, let's suppose the teacher pretends difficulty identifying the word *bridge*:

> On Sunday our family went for a drive. As we drove along we came to a bridge we had to cross. It went over a small river.

When the teacher comes to *bridge,* he or she could say, "I'm not sure what that word is, so I'll use some strategies to figure it out." The teacher might continue reading out loud to the end of the sentence and then state, "Well, I know it's something you can cross in a car. It may be a highway or a street or a bridge. I'll look at the beginning letters of the word. They're *br. Bridge* begins with the sounds of those letters, so it's probably *bridge.* I'll read on and see if I can tell if I'm right." After reading the next sentence, the teacher would then say, "Yes, I must be right because it would make sense for a bridge to be over a river." In this kind of role playing, it is best to choose a word unknown to the student.

Modeling the strategies needed in comprehension is also effective (Duffy & Roehler, 1987). If a student has difficulty responding to a question, the teacher may take over the student's role and demonstrate the thinking processes one would go through to arrive at the appropriate answer, showing how to select clues, rejecting some answers because of the text information, testing possible answers against background knowledge, and so on. Modeling effective reading behavior shows students *how* to learn, not just what to learn.

Investigations have confirmed that when teachers improve their use of cues, explanations, and modeling, students' final achievement is substantially higher than that of students not receiving enhanced cues (e.g., Bloom, 1984).

Principle Ten: Provide Feedback and Correction

Instructional feedback is consistently and strongly related to student learning (e.g., Lysakowski & Walberg, 1982). Teachers must monitor students' responses, inform them in a positive manner of those that are correct and those that are not, and provide immediate assistance in correcting strategies that lead students to inappropriate interpretations.

Feedback to students and instituting corrective procedures necessitates formative evaluation. **Formative evaluations** are the specific assessment procedures a teacher undertakes periodically throughout instruction to aid in identifying immediate needs. Formative evaluation allows teachers to determine the readers' grasp of what Bloom (1984) refers to as "initial cognitive prerequisites"—that is, what the student still needs to know before being able to move to a subsequent level of learning. This permits teachers to plan lessons that will avoid students' becoming confused and will increase their knowledge at the present level in order to facilitate understanding at a higher stage. Formative evaluation also includes the daily ongoing appraisals made "on-line" as a student reads and those reflections on student performance immediately after daily lessons that furnish teachers with instructional guidance to meet students' learning requirements. (This type of evaluation is in contrast to **summative evaluation,** which occurs at the end of a program of learning to assess achievement gain.)

For feedback to have an impact on student understanding, the teacher must be a sensitive observer—one who understands the reasons why a student makes miscues or offers erroneous explanations of text. For example, when observing students during daily reading, teachers often look for patterns of miscues with the hope that these patterns will suggest remediation procedures. This is a sound process if the focus is on what is *causing* a given problem. When the focus is on the *symptom,* however, remedial procedures sometimes go awry.

For instance, suppose the teacher notices that a student makes many repetitions of words when reading orally. Remedial procedures suggested when the focus is on the *symptom* (repeating words) might be use of a controlled reader (a machine that projects words at a given speed) so the student must keep reading forward and cannot repeat; or use of a tape-recorded story, having the student read along with the tape to prevent him or her from repeating. The intent here is to eliminate the repetition itself. Perspectives based on recent reading research, however, would suggest a different approach. The question should be asked, "*Why* is the student making repetitions?" The focus is then on the *cause* rather than the symptom.

Imagine that Phillip reads:

We saw a big, fat hippopotamus at the zoo.

He reads *fat* once, then repeats it twice before reading on. It is likely that Phillip repeated *fat* to give himself time to work out the word *hippopotamus* or to recall it. He used the repetitions as a time-holder to provide the chance to remember the word or to use phonic or structural analysis strategies to figure out how to pronounce it, or to read silently to the end of the sentence in an effort to employ context as an aid. There is no reason for the repetition itself to be eliminated in this case. Actually, Phillip's reading behavior is a positive one. It indicates that he is using word identification strategies to distinguish unknown words, or that he is taking time to try to recollect a word to which he has previously been exposed.

Another example is Ted, whose reading is impulsive, excessively rapid, and characterized by numerous omissions of words. Here is a partial typescript of a story he read. (The circled words are omissions.)

> The boy and his dog (ran) to play. They found their friends in the ball (park.)
>
> "Give me (the) bat," yelled Timmy. His (little) dog was very excited.

If the focus were on the symptom (excessive omissions), the teacher might immediately call attention to each one, perhaps by saying, "You skipped a word" each time this occurred. On the other hand, if the focus is more appropriately on the cause, the teacher will first let Ted know that very fast reading is often not good reading and that when reading orally one must communicate meaning. Then the teacher will consider each omission in light of its unique implications for instruction. Looking at this sample, it is obvious that Ted is not applying his knowledge of language patterns to reading performance. The teaching model below exemplifies more useful instructional procedures.

1. The boy and his dog (ran) to play. (The teacher should ask, "Did that make sense?")

2. They found their friends in the ball (park.) (The teacher should ask, "Did that make sense?")

3. "Give me (the) bat," yelled Timmy. (The teacher should ask, "Did that sound like language?" or "Does that sound the way we would talk?")

4. His (little) dog was very excited. (Perhaps the teacher will choose to ignore this omission since it does not cause a significant change in meaning.)

If we examine what was done when the focus was on the cause rather than the symptom, it can be seen that these procedures may help Ted establish self-monitoring behaviors that will remain useful when he is reading independently. Establishing self-monitoring and self-correction behaviors is critical for all aspects of literacy learning.

Similar questions should be asked for each variety of miscue: "Why did the student make this particular substitution (or omission, or insertion, and so on)?" It is not helpful to simply count the number of various kinds of miscues and then decide that instruction is needed to eliminate the most frequent types. Teachers need to determine why the miscue was made in order to decide what to do to eliminate it—or to conclude that instruction to eliminate it is unnecessary.

This same model of reflective decision making must be used when helping readers unravel comprehension confusions, as well. We should ask, "What is the *reason* for the lack of understanding?" and allow the answer to this question to guide our feedback and our correction activities.

Sensitive observation and reflective decision making usually develop from extensive training and, to a degree, from experience. This calls into question the use of untrained paraprofessionals to work with students who have serious reading problems. Wasik and Slavin (1993) reviewed research on five tutoring programs and found that students enrolled in the three in which instruction was conducted by trained teachers had larger and more consistent gains than those in the two using tutors who were not certified teachers; they also reported that having aides work in the classroom has not been effective in terms of increasing student achievement.

Principle Eleven: Stimulate Motivation

Motivation is learned. From infancy, children are selectively rewarded for their behaviors. The child learns to crawl, and the movement feels good. Children begin to talk, and their parents reward them with responses and praise. As a result, during the preschool years, natural motivation to achieve and learn new things is established. When some children begin school, however, they fail to develop many of the skills that get rewards in the academic environment. By the time many students are identified as needing special instruction and are placed in a remedial or clinical reading program (or in classes for the learning disabled or the developmentally disabled), their desire to participate in learning experiences has been stifled. As Ignoffo (1993–94) has pointed out, these students "tire of the frustration, lose enthusiasm, and do not relish attempting a similar task again" (p. 315). For many of these children, then, the teacher in the special program must make definite plans to reestablish motivation so that academic learning can occur.

Just as researchers analyze ways to teach reading most effectively, other investigators study ways to increase students' motivation to achieve in all academic areas, including reading. These studies have shown two crucial variables that affect achievement motivation:

1. Whether or not the individual *expects* to be successful in the activity
2. The *value* the individual places on a successful outcome (Wigfield & Asher, 1984)

The amount of persistence a student is willing to deliver for any given pursuit is highly dependent on these factors.

Another important concept related to achievement motivation is that of **attributions,** that is, to what individuals attribute successes or failures—or, in other words, what they think makes them successful when they are or what they think has caused them to fail when they do. Most individuals credit their successes or failures to one of three basic factors: (a) their personal abilities, (b) the amount of effort they have expended, and (c) luck (Weiner, 1979; Wigfield & Asher, 1984). Research has shown that different students make these attributions differently. Table 8–1 shows the attributions often made by persons with high motivation versus those with low motivation. As can be seen from this table, students with high motivation seem to have self-confidence and an attitude that they can take charge of their own successes and failures ("I should have worked harder at this and then I would not have failed"). In contrast, students with low motivation do not evidence this same spirit of self-esteem.

To be certain, there may be reasons why lack of confidence is displayed by the students with low motivation. After students have repeatedly experienced failure, they may come to believe that they are *incapable* of being successful through their own competence or efforts. Dweck and Goetz (1978) described such an outlook as one of "learned helplessness" because this fatalistic attitude has been developed, or *learned,* from negative events. Other researchers have shown, however, that such pessimism may be overcome if the two critical variables enumerated above—expectancy of success and value of outcome—can be arranged in the learning environment (Covington & Omelich, 1979; Wigfield & Asher, 1984). Furthermore, training to extricate students from the perspectives of learned helplessness should include (a) providing actual success experiences; (b) training students to ascribe success or failure to *effort;* and (c) teaching students needed skills, strategies, and knowledge so they do not continue to fail (G. R. Andrews & Debus, 1978; Schunk, 1981; Wigfield & Asher, 1984).

There are many ways teachers may apply the findings from achievement motivation research. Plans to stimulate motivation can be classified into two types: (a) those that deal with antecedent conditions and (b) those that deal with consequences.

Antecedents. **Antecedents,** that is, conditions planned prior to the learning exercise, are important. It is not enough to merely shore up poorly planned or dull programs by rewarding students' performances after a learning endeavor. Students must see value in the outcomes of the tasks they are asked to attempt. Here are six approaches to arranging antecedent conditions that are designed to motivate students to read.

1. *Instill a need for reading.* Help students recognize how reading can assist them in achieving personal goals. If Randy's ambition is to play Little League football, find an easy-to-read book on how to be a football player and use this as his material for regular, connected reading.

    If Harrison wants to obtain a driver's license, help him learn to read traffic signs as part of your word identification strategy lessons. In fact, an easy way to capture interest in reading with many older students is to use the state's driver's license manual as the instructional material in remedial classes. Obtain several copies and work through the manual section by section over a period of time. Plan lessons to focus on the strategies and skills the readers need to handle the manual. If, for example, students need to enlarge their recognition vocabularies, make a cumulative card file, selecting new words for it from each day's lesson; review all the words each day. If meaning vocabulary is the need, write definitions of the words on the backs of the cards. Have the students study these and discuss how the words relate to questions that might occur on the written driver's test. If word identification strategies are deficient, select some words for preteaching before each lesson. In one lesson, have students examine structural elements (pre-

TABLE 8–1
Attributions for success or failure

	Attributions for Success	**Attributions for Failure**
Students with High Motivation	Ability ("I'm smart." "I'm good at doing this." "I can do things well.")	Lack of effort ("I should have worked harder at this and then I would have done better.")
Students with Low Motivation	Luck ("I was lucky. I got a good grade.)	Lack of ability ("I'm not smart." "I'm not good at this." "I can't do things well.")

fixes, suffixes, base words); in another, ask them to divide multisyllabic words into syllables, or to guess words from the context of the sentence or paragraph in which they are embedded. Engage the readers in comprehension tasks after each section.

There are, of course, many other ways to instill a need for reading. Teachers must be attuned to the aspirations and pastimes of readers to develop lessons that meet the unique demands of each student.

2. *Understand that a reward for practice can exist within the activity itself.* For example, if the action or plot in a story is intrinsically interesting to a particular student because of its suspense, excitement, humor, or characters, he or she will be impelled to finish it. (**Intrinsic motivation** refers to motivation that comes from within an individual. **Extrinsic motivation** refers to motivation that has been arranged from an outside source, such as providing a reward for participating in an undertaking.)

Teachers should find out what interests their students. It should be noted, however, that studies have shown when materials are too difficult, interest alone will not provide adequate incentive to sustain the attempt at reading (G. Anderson, Higgins, & Wurster, 1985); students must expect to succeed. Interesting material not only motivates students, it also seems to increase their understanding. Theorists believe this is so because they attend more closely to the text, and, also, because they may have more prior knowledge to bring to a topic. No long-term studies have been conducted to examine the influences of consistent use of high-interest materials on students' reading achievement and their enduring desire to read, but use of such material has been advocated (Wigfield & Asher, 1984). The results of longitudinal studies of this type would be quite informative to reading professionals.

In nonfiction material, reading for a definite purpose gives students a reason to complete the endeavor, or even to undertake it in the first place. Some examples are reading and following directions to cook, or to construct an item, or to play a game, or reading to satisfy curiosity (sometimes piqued by the teacher).

The point is to use materials and routines that are responsive to the unique or group interests of the students because learning can then become its own reward. See Teachers' Store A for books and materials that may have particular appeal for secondary students.

3. *Use student-prepared materials.* Have students dictate books about themselves. Even students who initially pretend to be interested in nothing usually find "self" to be a compelling topic. A day's dictation can make up one chapter of the book. The various chapters may be used for connected reading and the focus of strategy lessons. Dictating books is made even more intriguing to secondary students if a machine is involved: interview the students with a microphone and tape recorder to get stories from their lives, or have them type their own chapters on a classroom computer.

Students also enjoy reading stories written by their peers. Establish a classroom mailbox system: a student writes a story and places it in a manila envelope addressed to someone else in the class; the student who receives the story reads it, then writes a reaction, and mails a story to someone else. Or, simply have students write letters; these, too, provide text to read. Watkins (1993) found that writing and receiving letters provided high incentives to produce words accurately and to be concerned with content.

TABLE 8–2
Positive reinforcements

Primary Reinforcers

Unconditioned reinforcers are an integral part of life and are effective without any history of specific events, for example, food, water, sex. Sometimes food (e.g., candy) is used as a reinforcer in academic programs, but this is usually inappropriate because students can become satiated and then the food is no longer reinforcing. There are also other practical problems with using edibles as reinforcers—a student may be allergic to a particular food and have an undesired reaction, or parents may object because it interferes with good nutritional habits.

Learned Reinforcers

Conditioned reinforcers acquire value as a result of experiences.

1. *Tangibles.* The student is given tangible items as a consequence of desired performances. Examples of items sometimes used are inexpensive books, stickers, or collectibles.

2. *Tokens.* The teacher prepares small cards or pieces of construction paper and gives the student one of these "tokens" for correct responses. When a specified number of tokens have been collected, they may be exchanged for a tangible item, activity reinforcer, or natural reinforcer.

3. *Activity Reinforcers.* As a result of a change in academic behavior a favored event is scheduled— pupils may have extra gym time or may view a cartoon, for example.

4. *Natural Reinforcers.* A privilege is given in relation to a naturally occurring classroom event, for instance, being allowed to (a) choose the story the teacher will read to the class on that day, (b) sit at the teacher's desk during sustained silent reading time, (c) have an extra turn at the class computer, (d) write a story on the chalkboard instead of paper, or (e) design this week's class bulletin board.

5. *Knowledge of Progress.* Instead of merely telling students they are doing well, a visual display, such as a chart or graph, is used to demonstrate growth.

6. *Praise.* The teacher praises effort as well as accomplishment. Praise is frequent and sincere. Labeled praise is best, that is, the teacher specifies why the praise has been given. For example, instead of saying "Good job!", the teacher says "Good job! You tried to use what you know about letter sounds on every hard word today, instead of just guessing wildly." Praise can also be administered nonverbally, for example, with a wink or a smile.

---

result of improved performance, or *effort,* can make the task more palatable. ("A spoonful of sugar makes the medicine go down in the most delightful way.") It is important, however, to use the least intrusive reinforcer that is effective for a specific student. If Brian will expend more effort as a result of keeping a graph of his own progress, it is inappropriate to set up a token system to grant him activity reinforcers (see Table 8–2). If Scott is motivated to try to learn more basic high-frequency words simply by being told that for each day he shows improved performance, he may sit at the teacher's desk for silent reading, it is inappropriate to give him tangibles as reinforcers. Reinforcers should be gradually faded from the more intrusive to the least as the student moves toward the ultimate goal of intrinsic motivation.

Here are some additional specific suggestions for planning positive consequences:

1. *Give positive recognition.* For example, incorporate a student's name into bulletin boards, stories, and so on, as a form of praise. (See Figure 8–3.) What student wouldn't love to walk into a classroom and see that he or she is the focus of the class bulletin board, or that one of the group events that day is reading a short story complimenting him or her?

2. *Visually demonstrate progress.* Use charts, graphs, add-to puzzles, or color-in puzzles. An add-to puzzle is made by cutting a picture into many puzzlelike shapes. For each correct answer the student selects and lays a piece of the puzzle on the desk, slowly developing the complete picture with each subsequent correct response. A *color-in puzzle* has a shape embedded in the puzzle. (See Figure 8–4.) The student colors in one section for each appropriate response until he or she has a complete picture.

3. *Help students get through all the tasks of a lesson.* Even when students work directly with the teacher, concentrated effort and on-task behavior can be a problem for unmotivated, unskilled readers. Devise a system in which students can observe their own progress by marking off each responsibility as it is completed. A simple checklist may be sufficient for older students, but an attractive picture to color works well with elementary school children. See the example in Figure 8–5. The student colors in each figure in the picture as each activity ends. They can thus see what has been accomplished and where the lesson is going.

4. *Inform parents about the student's learning.* Some teachers have had success by using daily report cards to motivate students. Each day a report is sent to parents indicating progress their child is making. Most parents praise students

FIGURE 8–3
A colorful bulletin board display to recognize a student in a positive way

FIGURE 8–4
Example of a color-in puzzle

when growth is evident; thus children receive reinforcement at home as well as at school. In addition, on-task behavior may be increased with daily report cards. For instance, a card can be devised on which the teacher places a check mark for each assignment completed during a class period. Parents then may award the student privileges at home based on the number of check marks received.

5. *Use contracts to spell out goals and rewards to the student.* A contract is a written agreement between the teacher and the student designed as both a prompt and a reminder to help the student meet an objective. The contract delineates the task very specifically and specifies the reward when the goal is accomplished. An example of a contract is seen in Figure 8–6.

FIGURE 8–5
An imaginative checklist for younger readers

FIGURE 8–6
Example of a contract between a student and a teacher

I, _____Paul_____ , agree to ___study the title and pictures___
         (student's name)   (what)

of stories and make a prediction about each story before I read_____ , to do this for

1 story a day_____ , to do it ___everyday for one week___ ,
        (how much)   (when)

and ___not to put my head down and say I don't want to___
                            (under what conditions)

I, _____Mrs. Daly_____ , agree to ___let Paul take home my tape___
         (teacher's name)   (what)

recorder and dictate a story onto tape_____ , to do this for

one night_____ , to do it ___the day after he completes all___
        (how much)   (when)

5 stories as agreed to above_____ ,

and ___to provide the tape, which he may keep.___
                            (under what conditions)

Signed ___Paul Hill___

Signed ___Mrs. Daly___

Principle Twelve: Cooperate With the Classroom Teacher

Whether the teacher of reading or special education teacher operates within what has been called a "pull-out" program or a "push-in" program, close working relationships with the student's regular classroom teacher bodes well for successful learning outcomes. Sharing insights, professional knowledge, and plans for intervention is productive.

Principle Thirteen: Enlist Parent Involvement

Often when parents learn their child is having difficulty with reading they seek a teacher's advice, asking "What can I do to help with my child's reading problem?" Teachers can offer a variety of practical suggestions to parents who want to help their children. You may wish to make the following recommendations:

1. *Read aloud to your child.* One of the best way parents can assist is by reading aloud, *every* day if possible. Because reading to their child is such a simple task, parents are often skeptical about its value. For this reason, the research specifying the positive effects of these interactions can be cited. Reviews of research on reading aloud (McCormick, 1977, 1983) say that children who are read to on a *regular* basis have a larger quantity of vocabulary awareness, a higher quality of vocabulary knowledge, and better comprehension of text. It also introduces print information to children, helps students view reading as a pleasurable act, acquaints them with syntactic (sentence) patterns found in "book language," increases attention span, and motivates the desire to read.

It is beneficial to recommend books and other materials that are good choices for reading, and to suggest places where these may be easily obtained. Scholastic Publishing Company sells "Parent Book Bags" at a low price; each of these plastic bags includes a paperback book, a letter to parents, and an activity card for you to send home with their child. Because these packages are inexpensive, they may be a worthwhile investment for a school, or teachers could make a similar kit with plastic food storage bags. You may also suggest that parents read material already in the home, such as comic strips in the newspaper.

2. *Have your child read something orally to someone every day.* Remedial students also need to process large amounts of print themselves. Oral reading is often the best way to initiate at-home reading because when students are reading *aloud,* parents can be sure reading is going on.

Encourage parents to allow the child to read easy material. Oral reading at home should not be a task that demands a lot of effort. The intent is that readers be exposed to many and varied language structures and gain confidence in their ability to handle print. Permitting students to do their at-home reading in easy material accomplishes these purposes without the pressures of an instructional-level lesson. Because students are less likely to make errors in easy material, parents are less prone to become impatient and the lesson is less apt to result in tension and frustration on the part of parent and child.

Students should also be encouraged to read highly appealing books during these reading sessions. Good children's and adolescent literature is distinguished by its high interest, of course, but if students prefer reading magazines or newspapers or any books on a topic stimulating to them, they should be permitted to do so. Encourage parents to be positive, to use praise, and to remain patient during these short sessions.

3. *Try assisted reading.* Hoskisson, Sherman, and Smith (1974) suggest **assisted reading** as one technique for parents to help children overcome reading difficulties. Assisted reading is conducted differently according to the ability of the student.

With severely disabled readers, parents read to the student, having the child read each sentence immediately afterward as the parent points to the words. After several books have been completed, students have often acquired a sight vocabulary large enough to read beginning books. Hoskisson et al. (1974) report that after one year of interactions during assisted reading, one nonreader scored at a high second-grade level on a standardized test.

For somewhat better readers, parents listen to their youngsters read, but no attempt is made to engage them in word identification strategy lessons; parents simply tell them any word they do not know. In another study by Hoskisson et al.

(1974), after 4 months in which parents used assisted reading for 15 to 20 minutes, 3 to 5 times each week, students self-corrected more miscues, made fewer miscues of all types, increased their reading rate, and scored higher on tests that measured word recognition, paragraph meaning, and vocabulary. They also willingly checked out library books, although they had not previously done so.

Assisted reading is basically a language immersion technique. Although no specific help is given on word identification strategies, these strategies generalize somewhat from the large amount of connected text youngsters process. They actually read more words because they are not slowed down to figure out unknown words.

At times parents' good intentions to supply a helping hand can go awry after initial enthusiasm has diminished. Here are some ways to remedy the "parent drop-out" problem.

1. *Establish a communication system.* If a parent has agreed on an agenda that she or he will attempt at home, establish a communication system to ensure that it will be implemented. Suppose, for example, that Mrs. Adkins has agreed to have her son, Mark, read aloud to her every night for 10 minutes after supper. The teacher can produce a form (like the one in Figure 8–7) that Mark delivers back and forth between the school and Mrs. Adkins. Mrs. Adkins writes in the date and the name of the book each evening and Mark returns it to school the next day. The teacher then uses the column at the right to deliver some sort of reinforcer. For example, she may place a sticker there or draw in a happy face. Similar communication systems can be adapted to whatever transactions the parents are conducting.

2. *Send home a newsletter.* A newsletter can be prepared and sent home on a regular basis. What can be written in newsletters? Specific information about what the class is working on is helpful, but suggestions for at-home activities should be emphasized. The newsletter does not have to be long; on the contrary, it is more likely to be read if it is not.

3. *Distribute pamphlets, booklets, and book lists.* Occasionally teachers may wish to supplement their newsletter by sending home short pamphlets, booklets, or lists of good books for students to read. Such materials can often be obtained free or inexpensively from a variety of educational organizations.

FIGURE 8–7
A sample form for reinforcing parent-child activities at home

Date	Name of Book Read	
3-15-94	Amigo	
3-16-94	The Murder of Hound Dog Bates	
3-17-94	Emma's Dragon Hunt	
3-18-94	Alistair in Outer Space	

Principle Fourteen: Let Research Guide Your Instruction

Research evidence is not available to answer all questions we have about student's literacy learning, but still there is an enormous database on which we can rely. Topics related to reading instruction have been investigated more than any other area of education! When presented with new ideas for stimulating students' reading education, teachers should ask the question, "Is the advocacy of this method or procedure based on opinion or on research?" Students in remedial programs need the highest quality instruction that it is possible to provide. When faced with an educational problem, the teacher should ask, "What does *research* have to say about this issue?" Many leading authorities in the literacy field today are concerned that this question is not being asked (e.g., Stanovich, 1993–94).

When you seek counsel from a physician about a medical problem, you do not want your doctor to prescribe treatment based on a "seat-of-the-pants" decision or a personal bias—you want the doctor to make judgments reflecting knowledge of current research. So, too, must teachers who earnestly care about promoting the learning of seriously delayed readers distinguish between opinion, suppositions, speculations, biases, beliefs, feelings, convictions, zealotry, ideas, views, and sentiments versus *research*. Your watchwords might be "In God we trust, but all others must present data."

ORGANIZING AND MANAGING REMEDIAL AND CLINICAL   READING PROGRAMS

Teachers who employ the 14 principles outlined above would certainly be well on their way to offering a superior program to students who are most in need of excellent reading instruction. The following section makes recommendations to assist with day-to- day organizational and management concerns.

Selecting Instructional Materials and Equipment

Materials can influence instruction and, as such, may positively or negatively affect readers' progress. There are hundreds—even thousands—of reading materials from which to choose. Only a few are described in this text. To locate others, teachers can write to publishers and ask for free catalogs. Many professional journals also list recommended materials, and, on request, publishers' representatives will call on teachers and demonstrate their products.

Teachers should not assume, however, that commercially published materials necessarily suggest sound teaching processes. It is a teacher's professional responsibility to carefully evaluate materials before they are used. The checklist in Figure 8–8 is helpful in appraising the effectiveness of products designed for reading objectives.

Individual Books.   Books are the most important element in any program for remediating reading problems. They should be available for direct instruction, for independent practice, and for students to take home to increase their out-of-class reading. A permanent collection should be kept in the classroom and supplemented by books brought in periodically from the school or public library. The permanent assortment should include informational books, as well as books of fiction. Picture books of high literary and artistic quality also are important; although many of these are intended for young students, others are suitable for older readers. Using **predictable books** (books in which words

FIGURE 8–8

Checklist for evaluating reading materials

	Yes	No
1. Does the material provide much opportunity for the student to read in regular, connected material?		
2. Is it based on current research and not on outdated notions?		
3. Does it really teach what it says it teaches?		
4. Does it teach anything important?		
5. Does it teach anything at all?		
6. Is the instructional level appropriate?		
7. Is the interest level suitable for students in terms of topic, pictures, and type size?		
8. Is it better for initial learning, practice, or review?		
9. Is it attractive and appealing rather than shoddy or dull?		
10. Are directions easy for students to understand?		
11. Is it well organized rather than difficult to follow?		
12. Are lessons of an appropriate length for your students?		
13. Is it reusable rather than consumable?		
14. Is it durable?		
15. Would something less expensive do the job just as well?		

or phrases are consistently repeated) is excellent for students with limited knowledge of basic vocabulary. Also for beginning readers are **big books,** which are large enough for a group to see; students can read these with the teacher or chorally in unison with one another. A nice way to integrate reading and writing is use of Stick-on Storybooks (DLM); these are wordless picture books accompanied by stick-on/peel-off paper on which students write their own original story lines to accompany the pictures.

Knowing students' interests is important for having appropriate books available. For instance, high-quality children's literature about adventure, animals, fantasy, humor, mystery, and games and sports generally appeal to elementary school children (Gutherie & Greaney, 1991). Some examples are *Martha Speaks* (Houghton Mifflin), a very funny book in which a family's dog begins to speak after eating alphabet soup, and *Old Turtle* (Pfeifer-Hamilton), a beautiful fantasy that won a national children's book award for its story and illustrations. Intermediate grade students begin to show an interest in nonfiction, for example, *Tales Mummies Tell* (Crowell), in which the secrets of mummies are revealed, and *Zooming In: Photographic Discoveries Under the Microscope* (Harcourt, Brace, Jovanovich), an informational book about microphotography with fascinating photographs to intrigue even the student who does not like books.

Children's poetry preferences include poems with humorous themes or those relevant to real-life experiences, for example, those in the poetry anthologies by Shel Silverstein such as *A Light in the Attic* (Harper & Row) or by Jack Prelutsky, such as *The New Kid on the Block* (Greenwillow). Teachers' Store B lists a selection of high-quality chil-

"It's a book, dear. It's what they use to make movies for TV".
(Reproduced by permission of the artist, Clem Scalzetti)

dren's literature (fiction, poetry, and informational books) that can be used with less able elementary school readers.

Secondary students often are interested in adventure, humor, and mystery. Students particularly like romance and historical fiction and like science fiction and sport (Wenedelin & Zinc, 1983). Some examples that may be suitable for older students who are having reading difficulties are *Sarah, Plain and Tall* (Harper & Row), about the life of a mail-order bride at the time of the opening of the American prairie; *Star Lord* (Harper & Row), a science fiction tale of an unwilling visitor to earth when his spacecraft crashes; and *Dirt Bike Racer* (Little, Brown), in which a boy finds a dirt bike at the bottom of a lake, but has problems on the job he takes to earn money to restore it for use in a race.

Copious use of authentic texts improves the caliber of remedial instruction. Some high-quality literature that can be used with secondary students who are poor readers is listed in Teachers' Store C; some quite easy and some slightly more challenging narratives, poetry anthologies, and informational books are included in the list.

High-interest, low vocabulary books are another worthwhile material in remedial programs. These books are easy to read, but have stories and topics that appeal to students with more mature interests. One example is *Disasters!* (Jamestown), a booklet of 21 articles about famous calamities such as the Hindenburg blimp disaster, the San Francisco earthquake, Krakatoa, the Black Death, and Pompeii. This booklet is written at sixth-, seventh-, and eighth-grade levels, but is designed for high school students and adults. A popular set of easy-to-read, high-interest books is the *Tom and Ricky Mystery Series* (High Noon Books), written at advanced first-grade level but with two 14-year-old boys as the major protagonists so that stories are attractive to intermediate and middle school students. A monograph titled *Easy Reading: Book Series and Periodicals for Less Able Readers* (International Reading Association) lists many others.

Teachers may also purchase special books likely to "turn on" turned-off readers. A good example is *Slugs* (Little, Brown), a wild and crazy book describing many things you can do with slugs; with wonderful illustrations, this is the kind of book that makes readers say "Yuk-k-k. Let me read some more!" and is probably more appreciated by middle school students than by teachers.

Teachers' Store B

**Some High-Quality Literature Suitable for
Less-Able Elementary School Readers**

Note: Authors' names are given in parentheses.

Where's Spot? (Hill)
Brown Bear, Brown Bear, What Do You See? (Martin)
The Teeny Tiny Woman (Galdone)
The Cat Sat on the Mat (Wildsmith)
A Very Busy Spider (Carle)
Whose Mouse Are You? (Kraus)
Truck (Crews)
The Cat in the Hat (Seuss)
Little Bear (Minarik)
Frog and Toad Are Friends (Lobel)
Mouse Tales (Lobel)
Owl at Home (Lobel)
Uncle Elephant (Lobel)
A Dark, Dark Tale (Brown)
The Chick and the Duckling (Ginsburg)
The Space Ship Under the Apple Tree (Slobodkin)
Danny Dunn and the Anti-Gravity Paint (Williams & Abraskin)
Busybody Nora (Hurwitz)
Superduper Teddy (Hurwitz)
Ramona the Pest (Cleary)
Cornrows (Yarborough)
Amelia Bedelia (Parish)
Tales of a Fourth Grade Nothing (Blume)
How to Eat Fried Worms (Rockwell)
The Secret Three (Myrick)
Something Queer at the Lemonade Stand (Levy)
Encyclopedia Brown Takes a Case (Sobol)
When I Was Young in the Mountains (Rylant)
The Paper Crane (Bang)
Where the Buffaloes Begin (Baker)
Ben's Trumpet (Isadora)
Shadow (Brown)
The Snowy Day (Keats)
My Friend Jacob (Clifton)
A Lion to Guard Us (Bulba)
The First Year (Meadowcroft)
The Courage of Sarah Noble (Dalgliesh)
The One Bad Thing About Father (Monjo)
Benny's Animals and How He Put Them in Order (Selsam)
Wild Mouse (Brady)
I Did It (Rockwell)

Teachers' Store C

Some High-Quality Literature for Less-Able Secondary School Readers

Note: Authors' names are given in parentheses.

Bargain Bride (Sibley)
The Matchlock Gun (Edmonds)
Sounder (Armstrong)
The Philharmonic Gets Dressed (Kuskin)
Journey to Topaz (Uchida)
The Secret Soldier: The Story of Deborah Sampson (McGovern)
Rosa Parks (Greenfield)
Jim Thorpe (Fall)
Cesar Chavez (Franchere)
Sally Ride, Astronaut: An American First (Behrens)
Ol' Paul, the Mighty Logger (Rounds)
The Gorgon's Head (Hodges)
Cupid and Psyche (Barth)
Sir Gawain and the Loathly Lady (Hastings)
Bunnicula (the Howes)
Slaves of Spiegel (Pinkwater)
The Haunted Mountain (Hunter)
Sweet Whispers, Brother Rush (Hamilton)
Playing Beatie Bow (Park)
Cave Beyond Time (Bosse)
The White Mountains (Christopher)
Where the Sidewalk Ends (Silverstein)
Why Am I Grown So Cold? Poems of the Unknowable (Livingston)
Of Quarks, Quasars, and Quirks: Quizzical Poems for the Supersonic Age (the Brewtons)
Sprints and Distances, Sports in Poetry and Poetry in Sports (Lillian Morrison)
I Am the Darker Brother: An Anthology of Modern Poems by Black Americans (Adoff)
Songs of the Dream People (Houston)
Call It Courage (Sperry)
Chernowitz! (Arrick)
The Human Body (Miller)
Commodore Perry in Land of the Shogun (Blumberg)
Castle (Macaulay)
Wolfman: Exploring the World of Wolves (Pringle)
Strange Footprints on the Land (Irwin)

Book Series.   Some series of books contain selections to read, accompanied by follow-up activities located directly in the student materials. One of these, designed for intermediate grades through high school, is *Reading for Concepts* (McGraw-Hill), in which books ranging from 1.9 through 6.4 reading levels consist of one-page informational articles followed by a page of comprehension questions, with an emphasis on higher-level responses. Another series is *Superstars* (Steck-Vaughn), comprised of six softcover books containing 90 minibiographies of superstars of rock, soul, and country music, plus superstars of sports, movies, and TV. Each short biography in the *Superstars* books is followed by vocabulary and comprehension exercises; the reading levels are grades 4 through 6.

Other series of books consist primarily of stories, with the suggestions for practice activities found only in the teacher's manual. The *Monster Books* (Bowmar) and *The Best in Children's Literature* (Bowmar) contain stories highly appealing to children. *Giant First-Start Readers* (Troll) is a series in which each book is written with very few words (for example, one uses only 34 different words, another 37, and another 47). Another well-liked set of books is the *Attention Span Series* (Jamestown), written at approximately second–to–third grade levels but with topics of interest to intermediate and middle school youngsters; at the end of each page the last sentence is a "cliffhanger" and readers choose the direction the story will take by selecting a page number from three possible scenarios, each of which leads to a different adventure.

Many basal reader series today include absorbing, high-quality selections and attractive formats (Chall & Squire, 1991). One of these is the *Sounds of Language Readers* written by Bill Martin (Holt, Rinehart, & Winston; also available from DLM). However, basal readers are used differently in remedial and clinical reading lessons than in classroom developmental programs. In remedial classes, students are not asked to read all stories in a book; instead, certain stories are selected because they complement student interests.

Kits Containing Reading Materials and/or Skills and Strategy Lessons.   Many attractive kits for poor readers are on the market. *The NFL Reading Kit* (Bowmar) entices students who are interested in football. It contains 150 cards with colorful photographs and short articles about actual National Football League players and teams, with selections written at 2.0 through 4.0 reading levels. Each article is followed by a series of questions to develop vocabulary and comprehension. *Story-Plays* (Harcourt, Brace, Jovanovich) consists of a primary and an intermediate kit of play booklets. Four copies of each play are included so that groups of students can work together. *The Supermarket Recall Program* (William Orr) is three kits of cards, each of which has a label for students to read taken from a real supermarket product. Reading objectives related to the vocabulary found on each label also appear on the card.

Multimedia Kits.   Multimedia kits include audiovisual materials in addition to strategy lessons and reading selections. One kit popular with secondary students is the *Action Reading System* (Scholastic). Although stories are written at second-grade level, the books are mature-looking and invite teens to read. The kit includes action stories, romance, science fiction, mysteries, and plays. Participation pages help students with word identification, vocabulary, and comprehension; audiocassette tapes are included. The *Double-Action* kit, a part of the same series, has stories written at levels 3.0 through 5.0.

A kit suitable for students reading at primary levels is *Breakthrough to Literacy* (Bowmar). Books in this program are based on stories told by children and are accompanied by audiovisuals. There are two *Interaction* kits (Houghton Mifflin), one for primary reading levels and one for reading levels 4.0 through 6.9. Components include booklets supplemented by audiocassette tapes, photo stories, nonsense stories, and activity cards. The *Power Reading Series* (Gamco) holds the attention of many reluctant readers because each of its seven kits is composed of ten 20-page comic books and one audiotape on which the comic is read word for word. Written for reading levels 3.0

through 6.0, the comic books are used to develop vocabulary and comprehension strategies. Each of the following is available: "Beneath the Planet of the Apes," "Batman," "Captain America," "Star Trek," "Superman," "Wonder Woman," and "Spider Man."

Workbooks.   Educators have been criticized for using workbooks in reading programs. Workbooks have received a bad reputation partly because certain teachers have overused them until no time remained for the most important literacy activity—reading authentic texts. In addition, many workbooks are poorly prepared and dull. Nevertheless, workbooks can be helpful if they are thoughtfully selected and used. Thoughtful use includes employing workbook pages *occasionally* as part of a much wider variety of materials, and selecting *only* those pages directly related to a strategy or skill on which the student needs specific instruction. Carefully choosing workbooks with useful and appealing activities is also important. One interesting workbook is *Using the Want Ads* (Janus), designed to teach reading strategies and a survival skill at the same time; this workbook is written at the 2.5 reading level.

Activity cards may be substituted for workbook pages. These are individual cards on which a single lesson is printed. Boxes of activity cards are available from various companies, such as the sets for practicing use of context clues developed by Frank Schaffer Publications.

Duplicating Masters.   The same admonition concerning selection and use of workbooks applies to duplicating masters. Occasional use of well-developed activity sheets is appropriate. One example is *Super Survival Skills for Reading Activity Sheets* (Kids & Co.), which includes exercises for reading bus schedules, TV guides, menus, and other practical items. Another is *Cartoon Comprehension* (Frank Schaffer); each page presents a 6-frame cartoon to be read and followed by vocabulary and comprehension tasks.

Games.   Games, carefully selected and appropriately implemented, are good materials for remedial programs. Because most students enjoy games, they attend carefully and often expend more effort to determine correct responses than during more traditional school activities. Games are most advantageous in a *directed lesson*, with the teacher present to prevent students from practicing errors. Teachers can also model correct responses and solution-seeking behaviors by playing the games with the students.

One caution about games: in most cases they provide few chances to read in connected text. Therefore, devoting a whole class period to playing games is never suitable.

Whether bingo games, card games, domino-type games, puzzles, or board games, the majority of games published for school use emphasize rehearsals with words and applications of word identification strategies. One publisher with a series for comprehension study is Learning Well Corporation. This series includes board games for participation in drawing conclusions, getting the main idea, distinguishing fact from opinion, identifying cause and effect, reading for details, drawing inferences, and following written directions.

Teacher-Made Materials.   Teacher-made materials can include books, strategy lessons, games, and audiovisuals.

For example, teachers may write their own classroom books or short stories stressing specific words with which certain students need practice. Other books can be developed from student-dictated stories; some teachers type these directly onto a classroom computer as students dictate so the stories can be reproduced for distribution to everyone in the group. When several stories have been produced, they can be bound together and placed in the class library.

Teachers also compose their own strategy lessons. These take the form of reading-development sheets for practicing a single word identification or comprehension strategy. A strategy lesson that has demonstrated success in helping one student can be easily photocopied and placed in a file for future use with students displaying the same need.

Many teachers enjoy constructing learning games and other manipulative tasks for students. If any of these are to be used independently, they can be designed to be self-correcting so that students discover immediately whether they are responding correctly. Teachers' stores, now found in many communities, are sources of materials for teachers who like to make their own games. They sell inexpensive items such as blank bingo boards, spinners, and game markers to be used with teacher-prepared projects. A practical booklet for this purpose is the *Classroom Reading Games Activities Kit* (Center for Applied Research in Education).

Teachers can also make audiovisuals. For example, preparing filmstrips is simple if outdated commercial filmstrips are available. These old filmstrips can be dipped in common household bleach, which quickly removes all photographed and printed matter. On the now-clear filmstrip, new frames are drawn with a ruler and marking pen. Sight words, contractions, consonant letters, or similar brief text can be written in the frames. Kits for creating filmstrips from clear film are available from Barry Instrument Corporation. A professional book with directions for creating several other types of audiovisuals is *Making and Using Inexpensive Classroom Media* (Professional Educators Publications).

Magazines and Newspapers.   Some students find magazines or newspapers more appealing and less intimidating than books. This appears to be especially true of secondary level readers (C. James, 1987). That attitude may exist because selections are shorter, or because, unlike books, magazines and newspapers may not be associated with failure in the classroom. One newspaper written especially for lower-achieving secondary readers is *Know Your World, Extra* (Weekly Reader Secondary Periodicals). With a subscription, multiple copies of this newspaper can be received weekly in the classroom. A magazine popular in elementary classes is *Ranger Rick* (National Wildlife Federation). The monograph *Easy Reading: Book Series and Periodicals for Less Able Readers* (International Reading Association) lists many periodicals pertinent for remedial classes.

The community's daily newspaper also can be used as a learning tool. An inexpensive booklet, *Teaching Reading Skills Through the Newspaper* (International Reading Association), has many suggestions for employing newspapers in a reading class. Readability levels of newspapers have risen in recent years, although these vary from newspaper to newspaper and even from section to section within the papers. Some research has found that front-page stories range from ninth- to twelfth-grade levels, and that many help-wanted ads (important to secondary students) are written at about sixth- to seventh-grade levels. Obviously, certain students may have difficulty if asked to read many newspapers without assistance. However, the easy-to-read newspapers available for remedial classes could be substituted for a community's daily paper.

Newspapers may serve many educational goals, a number of which are listed here.

1. For vocabulary study, read a feature story to the students. Then ask them to work collaboratively to change *every* adjective to a synonym.

2. To address critical reading skills, read an editorial with the students. Ask them to underline facts and circle opinions.

3. Cut apart news stories and their pictures. After students have read the stories, ask them to match the pictures with the corresponding story as a comprehension check.

4. To have students focus on evaluation skills, have them read newspaper stories for one week. Then as a group venture, on the chalkboard, list stories that would fit under two categories, good news and bad news. Discuss why.

5. Have students cut out bar, circle, line, and pictorial graphs. Have them describe how to read each one.

6. To deal with content area vocabulary, ask students to search for math words (sales tax, square feet, metric measurements, pints, math words found in recipes, percentages, and so on).

7. To increase skimming skills, have a scavenger hunt. Provide a list of items found in one daily paper. Students must list page numbers on which items are found. The first one with a complete (and correct) list is the winner.

8. For one week, as a class, collect and read all articles on the President of the United States or other newsworthy individual. At the end of the week, collaboratively summarize the selected person's activities. The second week, do the same, but have students write individual summaries. Discuss and evaluate the summaries as a group.

9. To stimulate inferencing skills, have students study editorial cartoons. Discuss their meanings. Also, consider how one can learn from pictorial material.

10. Ask students to use the travel ads to plan a vacation. Have them list all information they can cull from the ads—climate, recreational opportunities, sports attractions, and so on.

11. Read book reviews. Classify the books as fiction, nonfiction, biography, and so on.

12. To focus on word meanings, have teams devise crossword puzzles using words from the newspaper and exchange them for other teams to complete.

13. To practice classification skills, have students read the sports section. With students, list the sports under various categories (Activities That Took Place in Our Community versus Those in Other Communities, Team Sports versus Individual Sports, Spectator Sports versus Participation Sports, and so on). Which sports may be listed under more than one category?

14. Ask students to study comic strips. Have students infer from their actions each character's personal characteristics and list vocabulary describing each one.

15. Help students to use headlines to generate predictions about articles before they are read.

16. Select an article and have students act out what was reported.

17. Ask students to read feature and sports articles to find these figures of speech:
    - alliteration—several words in a row beginning with the same letter
    - simile—a comparison using *like* or *as*
    - metaphor—a comparison that does not use *like* or *as*
    - personification—giving human characteristics to something that is not human.

    The teacher should list two or three examples of each of these on the board before students begin.

18. White-out the dialogue in a comic strip. Make photocopies to give to each student. Have students write their own dialogues.

19. Give readers several articles to skim. Next, ask each to make up one question for every article, using the *W* words: *who, what, where, when,* and *why.* Then hold a news contest: two students are the contestants and are asked questions by the others; when a student gives an incorrect answer, he or she is replaced by another student as a contestant.

Technology and Equipment. A tape recorder and sets of headphones are integral to many remedial classes. Students can listen and read along silently or orally with books, follow prerecorded teacher directions for completing an activity, or use recording and playback equipment in many other productive ways.

A number of publishers offer cassette tapes of well-known children's and young adult literature with accompanying read-along books. One such company is Jabberwocky, with titles including *Hansel and Gretel, The Fisherman and His Wife, Beauty and the Beast, Sherlock Holmes,* and *Tales of Poe*; these tapes are also available in Spanish.

A Language Master (Bell & Howell) is another serviceable teaching aid. This machine is accompanied by cards with an audiotape running along the bottom of each. Teachers write words, sentences, and so on, on each Language Master card and then record on audio on each one what has been written. Students attempt to read each card, then place it in the machine, and press a button to hear what the teacher recorded. Thus, students can determine if their own responses are correct or incorrect. This device provides the immediate feedback so important during the independent work of low-achieving readers.

A filmstrip projector is also a useful addition to remedial classes. A number of excellent filmstrips are available to provide an interesting route to learning. (See the media section on p. 240.)

Microcomputers are the latest major advance in equipment to assist the reading teacher. They are the outgrowth of a technology that began with large mainframe computers, such as PLATO, used in initial attempts at *computer-assisted instruction* (CAI). As early as 1965, Stanford University and a few other educational institutions were experimenting with CAI in the teaching of reading. Most of these computer programs were designed for primary students and emphasized decoding skills.

Computer programs can assist the reading teacher with management of classroom instruction and assessment as well as provide students with drill and practice, instructional games, simulation learning, or tutorial experiences.

Since the mid-1980s computers have been widely used in schools. Computer programs are now available to assist the teacher with management of classroom instruction or to provide students with drill and practice, instructional games, simulation learning, or tutorial experiences, among other uses. Several publishers also have devised programs usable for assessment.

Computer technology requires students to learn specialized terminology. Of interest to reading teachers is the list of words Dreyer, Futtersak, and Boehm (1985) suggest students must read to use computers, based on a sample of 35 programs. (See Table 8–3.)

Of course, the computer itself must be accompanied by *software,* the informational component comprising the individual lessons used in the computer. Educational software is often categorized in the following ways:

1. *Programs for instructional management.* These help teachers track student progress and monitor accomplishments.

2. *Drill and practice programs.* The purpose of these is to reinforce basic skills and strategies through independent application.

TABLE 8–3
Essential words for computer-assisted instruction in the elementary grades

activity	complete	end	lesson	play	selection
adjust	command	*enter	letter	player	*sound
again	computer	erase	level	*please	*spacebar
another	*continue	*escape or \<esc\>	list	point	speed
answer	control or \<cntrl\>	exit	load	practice	start
any	copy	find	*loading	*press	team
*arrow	correct	finished	match	print	text
audio	correctly	follow	memory	problems	then
bar	cursor	format	*menu	*program	try
before	delete	*game	[module]	quit	turn
begin	demonstration	good	monitor	rate	*type
bold	description	help	move	ready	up
button	different	hit	*name	regular	use
[cartridge]	directions	hold	need	remove	video
[cassette]	disk	incorrect	no	repeat	wait
catalog	diskette	incorrectly	*number	*return	want
change	display	indicate	off	[rewind]	which
choice	document	insert	on	rules	win
*choose	down	instructions	options	save	word
colors	drive	joystick	paddle	score	work
column	edit	*key	password	screen	yes
compete	effects	keyboard	picture	select	your

* Words present in at least 10 of the 35 programs
[] Additions—not in any of the 35 programs

Source: From "Sight Words for the Computer Age: An Essential Word List" by L. G. Dreyer, K. F. Futtersak, and A. E. Boehm, 1985, *The Reading Teacher, 39,* pp. 14–15. Copyright 1985 by the International Reading Association. Reprinted by permission of Lois G. Dreyer and the International Reading Association.

3. *Instructional games.* These are designed to provide drill and practice in a challenging, intriguing manner.

4. *Simulation learning.* These programs simulate real experiences and allow students to role-play hypothetical situations.

5. *Tutorial experiences.* The purpose of these is to furnish more instruction than is found in drill and practice programs; for example, detailed explanations of how to accomplish an exercise, or explanations of why an answer is incorrect. Tutorials often feature branching, a technique allowing learners to bypass some instruction or spend additional time when appropriate.

6. *Story architecture programs.* Students build their own stories with the microcomputer's assistance.

7. *Telecommunication programs.* These use a modem and telephone line to access data from other computers.

8. *Utility programs.* In these, the teacher is able to select the information to be taught, for example, by entering a different set of spelling words into the program each week or by entering words to make up a crossword puzzle.

9. *Word-processing programs.* These can help young writers write, edit, read, and print material.

Here are some typical elements found in educational software:

1. The user's name is requested so the program can be personalized.

2. Decisions about other choices are sought, such as "Do you want sound effects?" and "Do you want instructions?" If the user requests help, explanatory statements then follow.

3. In some programs, the user may also select a level of difficulty and a rate of item presentation. (Dreyer, Futtersak, & Boehm, 1985, pp. 14–15)

There are many new computer programs in reading. While some older software was not highly recommended, better-quality software is becoming increasingly available. Two well-designed programs that provide sound practice are the *Playwriter* series (Woodbury Software) for elementary school students and *Reading Around Words* (Instructional/Communications Technology), used at the secondary level. *Book Brain* is designed to help students find books they would like to read; there are over 750 tempting book annotations on this database for grades 4 through 6 and 7 through 9. The *Muppet Slate* was designed to encourage writing in first- and second-grade children. *Read 'N Roll* is one of the better drill and practice programs.

Other software is cited throughout this text in relation to a variety of topics. Finally, there are resource books and lists of available programs, such as *The Educational Software Selector* (EPIE Institute) and *Computers and Reading Instruction* (Addison-Wesley), which specifies commercial and public-domain programs (public-domain software may be copied legally by anyone usually for the price of a computer disk).

A number of pros and cons have been voiced about reading programs designed for microcomputers. Some criticisms are that certain software is no more than a set of expensive workbook pages electronically displayed; that drill and practice programs especially supply no more than an electronic flashcard; and that uninspired program development leads to an inferior educational experience. On the other hand, high-quality software is now valued for supplementary instruction: it provides good practice, allows for instant feedback, serves as an effective tool for review, allows students to control the rate of presentation of material, and enables highly individualized teaching.

Most reading teachers believe that computers can promote students' thinking skills by engaging them in simulation programs, or through use of word processing programs to compose and edit. To make the best use of software programs, teachers should not view computers as a panacea. They should preview software before purchasing it, and they should integrate microcomputer teaching programs with teacher-directed instruction.

Teachers need to learn three major things about computers:

1. They must master the same computer skills their students should acquire, about component parts, operation, and special vocabulary.
2. To use computers efficiently, they need to recognize those times when less-expensive alternatives can serve the educational task just as well.
3. They should learn to manage a classroom program that integrates computer use.

In some cases, teachers may want to develop their own software so they can mold it to the specific needs of their students. For this, they will need to learn some programming skills.

Many books, magazines, and computer programs are available that provide inservice education to help educators stay abreast of the explosion of new developments in computer uses and technology. One such computer program is *The Computer Connection for Teachers* (Instructional Software); it is for teachers who know nothing about computers. A useful resource book is *Beyond Drill and Practice: Expanding the Computer Mainstream* (Council for Exceptional Children), which describes use of computers with students who have special learning needs. A helpful magazine is *Teaching and Computers* (Scholastic). And many professional journals now feature columns that give advice for teacher-created lessons, new uses for computers, and lists of recommended software.

Media.   Films, videos, and filmstrips add variety to reading lessons. Films can be obtained from commercial educational distributors and for free from public or school libraries. Three excellent films for encouraging writing and vocabulary development are *Let's Write a Story* (Churchill Films) and *Poems We Write* (Grover Films Productions), both for grades 3 through 6, and *The Red Balloon* (Brandon Films), for grades 1 through 12 (even the teacher will enjoy this last one).

Increasingly videos are being produced for use in reading classes and are available from a number of companies. One of these is the *Essential Word Roots Video* (EPS), which presents the most commonly occurring word roots and shows students how to pronounce, spell, and remember the meanings of the roots. Videos are also produced for parent training, such as *Parent Video* (Scholastic), which acquaints parents with the advantages of reading to their children and recommends routines for doing so.

Filmstrips are relatively inexpensive, so teachers may wish to start their own classroom collections. Many publishers have catalogs of filmstrips suitable for reading instruction. Available from the Learning Well Company are kits titled *Dinosaur World: Prehistoric Reptiles Invade Your Reading Program* and *Children's Literature Filmstrips;* books are included to accompany each filmstrip in these series.

Professional Books and Journals.   Carefully selected professional books and journal articles can provide a wealth of good suggestions for teachers to use in their own teaching. There should be a place on the classroom shelves for professional books and folders in file drawers for keeping articles from journals that have good teaching ideas.

The brief review in this section is provided to indicate the multiplicity of materials available to enhance reading instruction. Many other excellent choices for materials are available at both higher and lower reading levels.

Organizing the Classroom or Clinic to Teach

A well-organized classroom facilitates the use of a variety of materials, permits both individualized and group activities, and encourages on-task behavior of students. It also helps the teacher carry out functions efficiently.

Occasionally a remedial education teacher is assigned an odd little room in which to conduct classes, perhaps the janitor's former supply room, or the abandoned bell tower above the school attic. The reasoning seems to be that since these teachers don't work with a regular-sized class all at one time, they don't need a regular-sized class-room. Teachers forced to operate in such facilities must take the attitude that good teaching can occur anywhere—which is true—and that students can receive an excellent program even if space is scarce and the room is an architectural mongrel. Nevertheless, the following description assumes the more ideal condition of a normal-sized class-room; teachers with less space can, with ingenuity, make the necessary adaptations to have a well-organized room.

Physical Organization.   Arrange desks so that some students can work individually while other students are in a group with the teacher. Situate desks for small-group instruction near a chalkboard so it can be used for teaching. If you have a room with no chalkboard, ask for a portable one. Teachers also need a place to neatly display all the many books they should have in their room. A revolving metal rack for storing and displaying paperbacks, magazines, and newspapers is an excellent addition to the reading class; one source for bookracks is Scholastic. If possible, create a comfortable reading area, perhaps equipped with a small rug and a beanbag chair or two, near the book-shelves. Use a table or desk for a listening station area; place a tape recorder and earphones on the table and several chairs around it. Find a place to store games neatly so they are convenient for use. Ask that a pull-down screen be installed in the room for showing filmstrips, or that a portable one be made available. Find a place for neatly placing kits and mechanical devices so that they are accessible. Obtain a file cabinet and file folders for efficiently organizing tests, strategy lessons, information on teaching ideas, forms, and student records.

Devise attractive, organized ways to group supplies. Make supplies attainable to students who are working independently to minimize interruptions when the teacher is working with other readers.

Learning Centers and Writing Centers.   Find a place in your classroom for one or more learning centers. A **learning center** is a designated area where students can work independently on activities designed to help them concentrate on a specific knowledge, strategy, or skill area. Here are some points for developing learning centers:

1.   To begin, select a single skill, strategy, or knowledge area (for example, learning a word identification strategy, reading to predict outcomes, or editing stories). Develop or locate materials and media related to this area. These could include books, pens, pencils, dictionaries, games, teacher-made or commercial audio-tapes, a tape recorder and earphones, a filmstrip, a table-top filmstrip projector, activity cards, newspapers, a flannel board, a magnet board, and so on. (A cookie sheet makes a good, inexpensive magnet board.)

2.   To develop a comprehensive learning experience for the topic chosen for focus at the center include a variety of response opportunities such as reading, manipulating, observing, writing, creating, comparing, researching, orally answering questions into a tape recorder, or typing into a computer.

3.   Whenever possible, devise ways for students to self-correct.

4.   Organize materials at a table or desk maintained permanently for student use. Provide space on that table for students to work.

5.   Post clear and simple instructions at the learning or writing center so students can complete their activities independently until direct teacher assistance is available.

6.   Devise a system for keeping records of what students accomplish. Maintain a scheduling calendar for assigning students to the center.

The design and construction of a learning center requires much thought and effort. Because this process takes time and often requires trial and error solutions to unique problems, it is best to develop a single, successful learning center before attempting to start others. Many books are available to assist the teacher in this task. One of these is *Center Stuff for Nooks, Crannies, and Corners* (Incentive Publications).

Bulletin Boards.   Devise bulletin boards that teach. There are several functional levels of bulletin boards. The least useful are those that merely provide a colorful visual display in the room, for example, the one that says "It's Spring!" accompanied by cut paper flowers. A second type presents information, for example, pictures about the American Southwest with labels beneath them giving facts. A third, and more productive, bulletin board is the one around which a learning activity can take place. This third

A learning center is a designated area where students can work independently on activities designed to help them concentrate on a specific knowledge, strategy, or skill area.

type enables the teacher to teach lessons to small groups of students using the materials displayed.

In addition, the bulletin board can serve as a kind of learning center: students may use it independently to manipulate materials or otherwise engage in activities that have been arranged there. This is a good solution for teachers who would like to have a learning center but cannot because of space limitations. Another excellent way to use a bulletin board is to give it over to the students. They can display work of their own choosing, for example, perhaps the final versions of stories they have composed, after they have completed their cycle of editing and rewriting.

A Pleasant Place to Learn.   Make the classroom attractive. A bright and pleasant atmosphere seems to students more conducive to learning than a dreary room. When students or visitors come to the classroom, their response should be, "It is certainly evident that reading is taught here!" and "This would be a nice place in which to learn!"

The basic organizational procedures, equipment, and supplies cited here apply to reading clinics as well as classrooms. Clinics, however, should include more areas reserved for one-to-one instruction, because most teaching in the clinic setting is carried out in this manner. Individual study carrels are generally used for this purpose.

Classroom organization should be flexible, allowing the teacher to vary group instruction with individual instruction and independent work. The choice of the teaching arrangement should fit the teaching goal and thus provide for optimal learning. Teachers may wish to see *Organizing for Instruction,* a special themed issue of the journal *The Reading Teacher* (April 1991), in which all articles suggest alternatives for organizing to teach reading.

Planning Schedules for Instruction

Two types of planning of instructional schedules are necessary: (a) devising an overall daily agenda and (b) carefully mapping out what will occur within each class period.

When generating a daily agenda, the teacher should usually group students with similar needs. Because of the seriousness and diversity of poor readers' problems, some individual work is often necessary or advisable, but when students have comparable instructional requirements, group instruction also can occur. Though working with groups of five to eight students during each class period is common practice, some research has shown that when groups becomes larger than six, learning diminishes (Payne, Polloway, Smith, & Payne, 1981). Avoid schedules in which reading class conflicts with an activity a student considers highly enjoyable; and if the remedial class is arranged as a "pull-out" program, students should be scheduled into the class so that they do not miss relevant reading experiences in their regular classrooms.

Within each class period, reading teachers should follow certain basic guidelines:

1.   At least a third of *every* class period should be devoted to reading in connected text *by students*. This means they should read meaningful, written language with a developed beginning, middle, and end—for example, whole chapters, stories, articles, or short books. (It does not mean reading single sentences, isolated words on flashcards, or individual paragraphs in workbooks.) Time may be devoted to silent reading and to oral reading. The reading time also may be allotted in variable segments (for example, 5 minutes at the beginning of the period, 10 minutes during the middle, and 5 minutes more at the end). However it is achieved, the goal is to assure that one third of the time students spend in

remedial reading classes is spent in reading connected text. The only acceptable variation to this rule is to add more reading time.

2. Allocate time so that all reading is followed by comprehension responses. This can be accomplished by asking questions, by inviting students to retell the selection, or in a diversity of ways. (See the comprehension chapter later in this book.)

3. Activities should be based on assessed needs and should be varied throughout the period. A long period of concentrated effort might be followed by an academically relevant game. In addition, routines and materials should be changed from day to day to prevent boredom.

4. Provide students opportunities to make choices within tasks. For example, *you* may decide that Charles should spend the first 10 minutes of the period reading silently, but *he* may choose from three suitable stories the one he prefers to read. Research has shown that activities are more effective when students are offered some choices within the teacher-selected structure.

5. Spend some time during each class period reading aloud to students or have them listen to taped stories. The many ways readers profit from this exposure have already been noted.

6. Daily lesson plans should be modified if students are not demonstrating appropriate progress.

Planning instructional schedules for students enrolled in reading clinics is similar to planning for reading classes. Activities scheduled for clinical reading programs need not be of a different, unusual, or peculiar nature. Clinical reading instruction should exemplify the best of any reading instruction, with rich and meaningful experiences in abundance. Clinical programs incorporating current learning theory do not resort to materials that are different, nor to artificial instructional procedures that too often have only meager relation to authentic reading tasks. In Figures 8–9 and 8–10, two consecutive days' lesson plans are seen for a hypothetical student enrolled in a reading clinic.

CONCLUSION

Although students' needs differ, the principles reviewed in this chapter apply to all delayed readers. For example, a student who requires opportunities to practice word identification and one who needs help with comprehension strategies will both benefit from Principle Nine: "Provide Cues, Modeling, and Explanations"; and both will profit from the precept that says "Let the Students Read"; and feedback and correction (Principle Ten) will be advantageous for both; and this is the case with all principles cited. It is wise for teachers to review the principles in this chapter regularly to compare them with programs they are developing to determine if all important ideas are being incorporated.

Students enrolled in high-quality, well-organized remedial programs usually demonstrate learning far exceeding their previous development. Bliesmer (1962), for example, reported that average gains made by students enrolled for 1 year in a public school reading clinic were 1½ times their previous rates of progress, while the average gains of students in a second clinic were 3 times their preclinic percentages. These results are fairly typical.

FIGURE 8–9

The first of two consecutive days' lesson plans for a hypothetical student enrolled in a reading clinic

---

Name: Jim Coyne
Age: 10
Approximate instructional level: 2.5
Date: October 31, 19___

9:00–9:10 *(CRT = 5 min.)	Jim and I will orally read Chapter 1 of *Max the Monkey* (reading level, approximately 2.5). This book was chosen because of his interest inventory. Jim said he "loves monkeys" and "I wish I could go to the zoo every week to see the monkeys." Since this is his first day with this book, I'll take turns reading with him (I'll read one page, he'll read the next, etc.) to ease him into it. By my doing this, he'll hear me pronounce some of the new vocabulary. He'll also begin to get a feeling for the story line so he can make predictions when he reads the book without this assistance from me. Also, by hearing him read orally from the first chapter, I'll be able to make some determinations about whether this book is really at the appropriate level for him.
9:10–9:15	Jim will retell the chapter we have just read and at the conclusion I will ask the following inference question: "What are two things that Max's new owner did that tell us he already knew a lot about monkeys?"
9:15–9:25 *(CRT = 10 min.)	Jim will silently read Chapter 2 of *Max the Monkey*. (While he reads I will silently read a book of my own to model reading behavior.)
9:25–9:30	I will ask him to orally answer four questions I have prepared ahead of time about Chapter 2. One of these is a factual question; one is related to a new vocabulary word whose meaning is implied in the chapter but not directly stated; and two require him to draw conclusions.
9:30–9:40	Jim and I will play a game to review the work we did yesterday on consonant digraphs. He may choose between "Digraph Dominoes" or a digraph bingo game. Then he will read six sentences I have written, each of which contains a word beginning with one of the digraphs in the game.
9:40–9:45 *(CRT = 5 min.)	Jim will orally read a one-page information selection on monkeys from the easy-to-read worktext series, *Learn About Your World*. During his reading I will stress the self-correction strategies we have been working on.
9:45–9:50	He will answer the three multiple-choice questions which follow the informational selection on monkeys.
9:50–10:00	I will read aloud to him chapter 1 of *Follow My Leader*, by Garfield. This is a book of realistic, contemporary fiction of high literary quality, and is also very popular with intermediate grade students. The book is written at about 4.0 reading level, which makes it too difficult for Jim to read by himself. He should have no difficulty understanding it, however, based on what I've observed of his listening comprehension. This book was chosen not only because of its interest level, but also because *Follow My Leader* is the story of a boy who is blind; it was chosen from many other good choices because a blind student is to be mainstreamed into Jim's room beginning next week. I'll read a chapter a day to him until the book is completed.

CRT = Amount of *connected reading time* engaged in by the student

FIGURE 8–10
The second of two consecutive days' lesson plans for a hypothetical student enrolled in a reading clinic

---

Name: Jim Coyne
Age: 10
Approximate instructional level: 2.5
Date: Nov. 1, 19___

9:00–9:10	Jim will complete a strategy lesson on predicting and confirming. I have prepared a cloze story and he will be asked to do the following:
	1. Read the whole story silently.
	2. Reread it silently and tell me each word that he would supply where words have been omitted; I will write the word in the blank.
	3. Orally read the story to me and make changes if any of the original words he supplied do not make sense.
9:10–9:20 *(CRT = 10 min.)	Jim will silently read chapter 3 of *Max the Monkey*. (I will read my own book as he reads.)
9:20–9:30 *(CRT = 10 min.)	He will orally read chapter 4 of *Max the Monkey*. I will help him use the word identification strategies we have been working on, but will not take turns reading with him.
9:30–9:40	As a comprehension check over chapters 3 and 4 of *Max the Monkey*, he will play a game I have devised. I have prepared 10 questions, all of which require him to draw an inference. He will have a gameboard in front of him that says "Find the Treasure." For each question he answers correctly he may move one space on the board toward the "treasure." When he reaches it, he can lift a flap where he will find something he can have: a silly-looking picture of a monkey I found in *Field and Stream* magazine.
9:40–9:50	I will read aloud to him chapter 2 of *Follow My Leader*. Afterward, I will ask Jim to orally summarize this chapter.
9:50–9:55	Jim will orally read a one-page story I wrote which contains 21 words that begin with consonant digraphs.
9:55–10:00	He will dictate a story to me about the Halloween party in his room yesterday. I will write down the story as he dictates and give it to him to take home. His parents have agreed to listen to him read any of his dictated stories that I send home and are filing them in a folder he decorated.

Unfortunately, what sometimes happens is that after students are dismissed from special instruction, they do not maintain this improved rate of growth. L. R. Johnson and Platts (1962), for example, reported that learning rates of less-skilled readers who received individual and small-group instruction were 2 to 3 times those of students who did not receive this special help; however, in a follow-up study 2 years after the students had been "graduated" from the program, while they had continued to make headway, it was at a slower pace, and they had again fallen behind their peers. Mullin and Summers (1983) also found maintenance of gains to a be a problem in certain compensatory programs.

There are four implications. First, students should be retained in special programs until they have accomplished horizontal as well as vertical growth. **Vertical growth** implies an increase in reading instructional level or the learning of new skills or strategies previously unknown. **Horizontal growth** is the establishment of the new behaviors as firm, *habitual* patterns of functioning. Immediately dismissing students as soon as they have attained a reading level commensurate with their potentials often does not allow time for new skills to become routine. Retaining students in the reading program for an additional semester, for example, may promote maintenance of early gains, as well as continued acceptable rates of progress.

Second, after students have been discharged from intensive remedial programs into the mainstream, supportive assistance may be advisable.

Third, one-to-one tutoring featuring knowledgeable and flexible teaching may provide some support for this problem. After some such programs, students not only have maintained the gains established in their special programs, but have continued to progress (see Wasik & Slavin, 1993).

Fourth, and finally, in the cases of *severely disabled readers,* it cannot be expected that any brief program of remediation will be sufficient to actualize the ability of students to sustain and continue their reading progress; long-term instructional programs will more than likely be required in these cases.

📖 REFLECTIONS

1. Based on the information you learned from the four preceding chapters on assessment, what are several other principles you would add to the list of those offered in the present chapter?
2. Bloom (1984) and his colleagues, as well as other investigators, have conducted studies to ascertain the contributions of various factors to student achievement. The results of this research highlighted the following variables and their relative effects.

- The variable having the greatest effect on student achievement: one-to-one or small-group (2 to 3 students) tutorial instruction
- The variable having the second greatest effect: provision of reinforcement
- Variables having the third greatest effect:
  a. feedback and correction
  b. cues and explanations
  c. student classroom participation
  d. students' time on task
  e. improved reading and study skills
- Fourth most important:
  a. cooperative learning
  b. *graded* homework
- Next most important:
  a. classroom morale
  b. having initial cognitive prerequisites
- Also important: home environment interventions (Bloom, 1984, p. 6)

  Discuss practical applications of each of these.

9

Word Recognition

Accurate, automatic, rapid word recognition has positive effects on independent reading and on interest in voluntary reading.

To the layperson, recognition of words *seems* to be the basis of reading. And it is! Although reading professionals know the *purpose* of reading is the construction of meaning (i.e., to comprehend), word recognition is a necessary (although not sufficient) condition for understanding text.

Word recognition refers to the recall of words in which the reader resorts to no obvious mechanisms to discriminate them (although the reader's brain is conducting a number of operations, the reader is not aware of them). When the reader automatically recognizes a word, he or she is able to say the word with little or no hesitation. **Word identification,** on the other hand, refers to those cases in which a reader directly calls into play one or more strategies to help in "figuring out" a word. For proficient readers, the strategies are employed effortlessly and usually go unnoticed by the reader; however, in developing readers, they may be overtly displayed as these readers use phonic analysis or structural analysis or context clues to figure out the word.

As you read this textbook, in the vast majority of cases, you are using *word recognition.* You instantly and accurately recognize almost all of the words. In some cases, however, I have used technical words that may be new to you. In an earlier chapter, the term *automaticity* was introduced. Unless you have read much literature on literacy or psychology, that may have been a novel expression for you. The first time you saw the word, you may have paused and reread for a moment to check the letters—especially, in this instance, at the end of the word—and to think about how the word would be pronounced; if you did that, you were using *word identification* strategies.

Many reading theorists maintain that readers must acquire both whole word recognition and word identification strategies—and that deficits in either of these areas causes reading difficulties. This position has been corroborated by research (e.g., P. Bryant & Impey, 1986; Freebody & Byrne, 1988; Vellutino & Denckla, 1991). The present chapter addresses word recognition issues and instructional suggestions; the following chapter will consider word identification.

The Importance of Recognizing Words at Sight

Competent reading requires the following progressive steps in word recognition:

1. First, words must be read *accurately.* Words must be recognized and distinguished from other words. This step is now quite easy for you, but early readers and those with reading disabilities must give conscious effort to reading words correctly in many cases.

2. Able reading also requires that words be recognized *automatically.* That is, to read proficiently, a reader must recognize the majority of words without conscious thought so that attention can be directed to the message of the material. Automatic word recognition—referred to by that word *automaticity*—occurs after *accuracy* is obtained, and after a number of exposures to the word. (For instance, the word *automaticity* by now is probably in *your* word recognition, rather than identification, range.)

3. Finally, in skillful reading, words must be recognized *rapidly.* Like automatic recognition, this helps comprehension, and allows the reader to read more text.

Sight Word Recognition in the Earliest Stages of Reading

Students in the earliest stages of word learning, often called the logographic and rudimentary-alphabetic stages (see pp. 256–257), *must* read words by sight because they do not yet have in place sufficient concepts and skills for reading words through phono-logical recoding systems; that is, they have not yet internalized the prerequisites to word identification strategies (Ehri, 1991). Indeed, not only does recognizing words at sight originate before identifying words through decoding, it is a more effortless way for youngsters in the very early period of reading acquisition to read words, even if the readers are in a classroom where instruction in phonics is being presented (Barr, 1974–75; Ehri, 1991).

Sight Word Recognition as a Prerequisite and Aid to Word Identification Strategies

What is more, it appears to be necessary to recognize some words by sight (and to know names of letters) in order to learn word identification strategies. Ehri and Wilce (1985), for instance, found that when students had mastered letter recognition and could read some words in isolation, then they were able to move to stages of word learning where they systematically, rather than arbitrarily, selected visual clues in words to remember them, and also were then capable of applying letter-sound relations to read words. Abilities in word recognition accelerate learning to read (Biemiller, 1977–78).

Furthermore, young and developing readers need to acquire a sight vocabulary because this is requisite to a word identification strategy employed by readers until they gain more proficiency: that strategy is use of context clues. As you remember, when implementing this strategy, readers use the other words in a sentence or passage to help them detect what the unknown word should be. Sometimes the use of context results in the reader's guessing the exact word used by the author. In other cases, context simply helps the reader come up with a reasonable alternative that, nevertheless, makes sense in the passage—in other words, the author's overall intended meaning is still intact, even though the author's exact word is not used. But in either case, some words must already be known to use this assistance effectively. Here are some examples:

> The dog ran to see what was in his house. He did not like what he saw. It was a big, white cat. The cat had jumped into the dog's bed. She was sitting there looking at the dog's _____. She was going to go over to it and eat his food!

> Elaine and her mother had just moved to the country. Elaine was lonely and missed her old friends. She was sitting in a chair with nothing to do one morning when suddenly someone _____ at the door.

In the these two examples, you can use the surrounding context to guess what the miss-ing word would be, and you may guess the author's exact word. Obviously the reader must have accurate recognition of the words surrounding the word he or she is attempt-ing to identify; otherwise, context provides no help.

Sight Word Recognition Promotes More Word Recognition

Automatic recall of words leads to increased ability to recognize words. This cyclical process is influenced by the fact that, when readers no longer must stop often to puzzle over unknown words, they can read more.

Clay (1967) reported in a study of first-graders that the good readers had read approximately 20,000 words in a year's time, but the poor readers had read only about 5,000 words. Similarly, Juel (1988) found that over the course of a year, beginning readers who had good word recognition abilities were exposed to twice as many words in the books they read as those who had low word recognition competence. We know that the amount of contextual reading and the number of opportunities for response are important to reading achievement. The good readers had more opportunity to practice responding to words and therefore became even better; the poor readers had much less practice on the very task on which they needed to gain skill.

As in the old saying "The rich get richer and the poor get poorer," in this case, the good reader gets better and the poor reader remains poor. Remember from Chapter 3 that this phenomenon has been referred to as "Matthew effects" (Stanovich, 1986), and is now believed to have a major role in the development and maintenance of reading disabilities. Research has shown that students' progress is maximized when they are using materials that produce low rates of miscues, as low as 2% to 5% (Gambrell, Wilson, & Gantt, 1981).

Increasing the number of words a student can instantly recognize saves the time that he or she would need to apply a strategy to identify these words; reading then becomes more fluent and more rapid, and therefore more can be read. In normally developing readers, increasingly larger numbers of words are recognized at sight as these readers move through the elementary school years (Backman, Bruck, Hebert, & Seidenberg, 1984).

Sight Word Recognition and "Irregular" Words

Another reason why extensive recognition of words at sight is important is that, while letter-sound correspondences in English are not arbitrary, they are not always consistent with familiar patterns or rules (Ehri, 1991; Venezky, 1970). Readers may be able to match sounds to letters to figure out many words, but for others they must actually know the word first before they know the sounds of the letters.

For example, the word *where* would be pronounced as *were* if one common phonics rule was applied, or *we're* if another customary rule was used. Of course, it is pronounced neither way; *where* is one of many "irregular" words in English. One must simply learn that a rule doesn't apply here and learn the word that the letters represent. Only then can one say that the letters *-ere* in the word *where* make a sound like /air/, instead of /er/ or /ear/.

English words that do not follow common letter-sound correspondences or phonics rules cannot be "sounded out." In some cases, context helps the reader identify such words, but often it does not. Words that do not follow standard pronunciations, such as *of, some, who, learn, they, to, the, other,* and many more in the English language, cause exceptional problems for unskilled readers (Vellutino & Denckla, 1991). Sight recognition of these words is needed.

Success for All (Wasik & Slavin, 1993), an effective reading program conducted in several urban school districts in the U.S., although a balanced curriculum treating all important facets of literacy instruction, specifically includes as one of its components assisting children to "build a strong sight vocabulary that will help in identifying words that are not decodable" (p. 188). (For more information on Success for All, see Chapter 15.)

Sight Word Recognition and Comprehension

Stanovich (1991b) states that

> while it is possible for adequate word recognition skill to be accompanied by poor comprehension abilities, the converse virtually never occurs. It has never been empirically demon-

strated, nor is it theoretically expected, that some instructional innovation could result in good reading comprehension without the presence of at least adequate word recognition ability. (p. 418)

Word recognition ability has shown very high correlations with comprehension, for example, .74 in one study (Juel, Griffith, & Gough, 1986). *Accurate* word recognition is understandably important to comprehension; Beebe (1980) found that, the more the subjects in her study substituted text words with other words, the more difficulty they had with understanding the intended meaning of the material. Furthermore, investigations by Biemiller (1970); Blanchard (1980); Calfee and Piontkowsky (1981); Chall (1989); Herman (1985); Juel (1988); Lesgold, Resnick, and Hammond (1985); Lomax (1983); Scarborough (1984); Stanovich (1985); and others confirm that *automatic* word recognition contributes to improved comprehension. Research has also shown that *speed* of word recognition is related to comprehension for readers as low as first grade (Lesgold & Resnick, 1982) and as high as college level (Jackson & McClelland, 1979).

Most reading authorities attribute these relationships to the extra concentration readers can give to meaning when they do not have to focus unduly on word identification processes (e.g., Juel, 1991; Perfetti, 1985). Attention can, instead, be given to integration of text information with background knowledge and reflection on the gist of what is read. Comprehension may also be enhanced because fluent word recognition allows one to read *much* text. On the other hand, if learners must stop often to try to recall a word or to apply word identification strategies to decode the word, their train of thought is disrupted and they may disregard the text message by having to focus on lower-level operations—and they will also read less. If it is believed that the ultimate goal of reading is attainment of meaning—as is accepted by all currently trained reading professionals—then, one cannot deny the crucial need to provide adequate attention to students' word recognition development.

At times, a false dichotomy is offered. Arguments arise about the importance of word recognition/identification instruction *versus* the criticality of comprehension. This dichotomy is false—as seen in all contemporary models of the reading process (e.g., Just & Carpenter, 1987; Rumelhart, 1976; Stanovich, 1980). (See Chapter 1.) Word knowledge and meaning interact to produce proficient reading. Stanovich (1991b) points out that "lack of skill at recognizing words is always a reasonable predictor of difficulties in developing reading comprehension ability" (p. 418).

Sight Word Recognition and Independent Reading Ability

Research has shown that a reader needs instant recognition of about 95% of the words in any given text to read the text independently (M. J. Adams, 1990a, 1990b). Students must eventually achieve the point where they do not need direct teacher assistance to read. Since there is also research evidence demonstrating that amount of independent or free-time reading is associated with reading growth, this, too, is a vital argument for attention to word recognition in reading instruction.

Sight Word Recognition and Interest in Reading

Finally, reading in which many words are not within a student's automatic recognition vocabulary is simply laborious. The student may not develop—and indeed may lose—the *desire* to read; for example, the student may elect not to read for free-time enjoyment. Being capable of reading words easily leads to greater interest in pursuing reading as a pastime and to more extensive reading. A crucial catalyst to easy, fluent reading is the recognition of "whole words, effortlessly, automatically, and visually" (M. J. Adams, 1990b, p. 14).

GOOD READERS VERSUS POOR READERS

Large numbers of students who are enrolled in reading clinics and classes, as well as in LD programs, are experiencing reading difficulties because of their limited word recognition or virtually nonexistent word identification strategies. Many of these students appear to have few problems with understanding text, if it is written at a level they can read—or even at much higher levels if selections are read to them; they respond with high-level interpretations and insights. Their stumbling blocks are unlocking words so that they can read more difficult texts themselves.

Gough and Hillinger (1980) state that "the most conspicuous difference between good and poor readers is found in the swift and accurate recognition of individual words" (p. 95). And, poor readers have inferior word recognition to that of good readers regardless of whether the words are in context or out of context (Perfetti, Goldman, Hogaboam, 1979; Stanovich & West, 1981). M. J. Adams (1990a, 1990b) points out that a prominent aspect of good readers' behaviors is that they sweep through material rapidly and easily, appearing to recognize whole words with merely a glimpse. Many poor readers do not.

Why do some students progress adequately with word recognition and identification and others find the lack of ability to recognize and identify words to be major hindrances to literacy attainment? Part of the answer lies with the prerequisite experiences brought to the task. Therefore, before we embark on a discussion of word learning in remedial programs, we will examine factors involved in emerging literacy.

Emergent Literacy

Emergent literacy is the term used to refer to reading and writing behaviors that evolve before formal instruction begins. There is growing awareness that these behaviors contribute later to successful literacy acquisition (Pinnell, Lyons, DeFord, Bryk, & Seltzer, 1994; Sulzby, 1989).

Recent perspectives see children maturing into literate individuals based on experiences as early as birth, with research showing the importance of informal learning in the home and in other social environments (e.g., in preschool programs). It appears to be particularly important that preschool children have opportunities to engage in purposeful literacy activities with adults, who provide them with direct guidance in their endeavors. This guidance should allow children to operate at their individual levels of development, but also should aim at helping children gain slightly higher levels of understanding—a process referred to as **scaffolding** (Vygotsky, 1978).

Studies of emergent literacy are of significance to teachers who work with poor readers because these studies contribute to our realization of what should have occurred during readers' formative years and where gaps may lie that should be confronted. Also, reading teachers and LD teachers may work with somewhat older students still functioning at emergent literacy stages.

A major literacy activity that ought to occupy much time in preschool years is listening to books and stories read aloud. Doing so for significant amounts of time does have a positive effect. However, during book sharing, those reading aloud should do

A major literacy activity that ought to occupy much time in preschool years is listening to books and stories read aloud.

more than just provide a story. They should highlight linguistic concepts (such as *word*: "Look at what this word says," or *sentence*: "Listen to what the bear says in this sentence"). When reading ABC books to preschool children, adults may focus on letters and the relationship between letters and sounds. Parents should stimulate their children to inspect print. Asking children questions related to understanding the text also is a particularly helpful interaction, as is relating concepts in books to children's existing background information.

Sulzby and Teale (1991) point out that a critical variable in the effects of reading aloud to children is how an adult (parent; preschool teacher) mediates the reading and encourages reactions. As children have more experience with interactive read-aloud sessions, the sophistication of their responses during discussions about content increases, as does their knowledge of conventions of print. M. J. Adams (1990a, 1990b), an educator, reports reading aloud to her preschool son 30 to 45 minutes a *day*. In contrast, Teale (1986) studied families who placed less value reading to children; on the average, these children were read aloud to only about 20 minutes per *month*. Disparities in the knowledge about print that children bring to school may be accounted for by their different backgrounds with reading.

From listening to repeated readings of favorite books, children frequently move to "pretend" reading where they repeat the words of the story in a "reading-like" manner—often called **independent reenactments** or **emergent storybook readings.** Although such readings may not be conventional (or "accurate") from an adult's point of view, most authorities believe they are important contributors to formal literacy acquisition. During progressive reenactments, children move from attending to pictures to attending to print as they read, and show other increasingly broader understandings of conventional reading.

Children also exhibit writing behaviors in preschool years. Encouragement of these emergent actions, again, has been linked to success in learning to read. Scribbling, writing strings of letters to represent words, copying, "inventing" spellings based on sounds they hear, and asking adults how to spell words all are important precursors to higher levels of conventional writing—and to reading, because the child is playing directly with letters and sounds. Encouraging children to write is important to emerging literacy understandings.

How do emergent literacy activities specifically contribute to word recognition? They do so in several ways. First, students must have a concept of what a "word" is. This understanding may not be as simple as it seems since in speech we run many words together so that the "breaks" between them are not obvious to a young child. During adult-guided reading to children the *concept of word* can be developed by pointing out and discussing words, and this can also transpire by assisting children with writing words. In addition, letter recognition can begin to emerge through these activities. *Knowledge of the names of letters is one of the strongest predictors of success in word learning in the beginning stages of reading* (M. J. Adams, 1990a, 1990b; Biemiller, 1977-78; Blackman, 1984; Chall, 1967; Walsh, Price, & Gillingham, 1988); what is more, this connection has been shown regardless of the method of reading instruction that is used. (This does not merely mean being able to recite the alphabet, but, rather, being capable of telling the name of a letter when it is seen in print.) These early literacy experiences also promote phonemic awareness, which as you remember from an earlier chapter is strongly related to word learning.

Similar prereading activities are instituted in kindergartens and first grades, especially for students who arrive at school without these experiences. While it is true that some poor readers *have* had literacy experiences but do not respond productively to them, it also is true that progress in reading is unlikely to occur if they are lacking. When children have this valuable background but appear not to have benefited from it, it is likely that they did not form intuitions on their own, and this means the teacher's responsibility is to provide direct instruction to advance the child's perceptions and abilities related to reading.

PHASES OF WORD LEARNING

Word learning theory has proposed *naturally* developing phases as students advance from prereading to fluent reading.

Phase 1

This is the phase in which word recognition is first activated. It has been called the **logographic** (Ehri, 1991; Firth, 1985) or **selective-cue** (Juel, 1991) phase. The term *logographic* is used because students employ the graphic features of words to read them (from the Greek *logos*, for "word" and *graph* for "writing"); the term *selective-cue* is used because only certain cues are employed—not all that would be useful. The logo-graphic/selective-cue phase is typified by the following student behaviors:

1.   The student is able to read a few words in a context-free situation (i.e., in iso-lation).

2.   The student heeds only minimal, gross clues to the word—such as its length or its shape—to recollect it. From word to word, different clues may be randomly selected.

3.   Often *letters* are not used as clues to recognize a word, even though for more advanced readers these are major clues to reading words.

4.   If consideration is given to letters, attention is directed only to certain ones. The student does not use the sequence of letters in a word to recall it. And letter clues may not be remembered from one encounter with the word to the next.

5.   *Sounds* of letters (i.e., letter-sound correspondences) are not used.

6.   Words are best learned when only a few are presented at a time; when larger sets are introduced, there is failure to learn.

7.   Students remember a word only when they have had a good deal of expo-sure to it—short-term exposure produces little maintenance.

Phase 2

The second phase in word learning has been referred to as a **rudimentary-alphabetic** (Ehri, 1991) or **visual recognition** (Mason, 1980) phase. The term *alphabetic* refers to the letter-sound associations that learners use to recognize words; these relationships begin to be applied in a rudimentary way in this phase. Word recognition behaviors of students at this time are characterized by the following:

1.   The student recognizes more words in context-free conditions than in the pre-ceding phase.

2.   Words are learned and remembered after fewer exposures than are necessary in Phase 1.

3.   There is analysis of words into letters.

4.   There is dependable recall of some letter clues.

5.   Beginning and ending *sounds* are sometimes used as an aid in word recognition.

6.   Words are predominately read by sight, rather than through application of sounds, but recognition is more accurate than in the previous phase because of improved use of letter cues.

Depending on students' literacy experiences, the word learning traits of Phases 1 and 2 are seen commonly and naturally in preschool or kindergarten children or in stu-dents in the early parts of first-grade reading instruction. They also may be found in somewhat older students who have reading disabilities. When such behaviors occur in older students, they should not be interpreted as idiosyncratic or odd; they are merely an indication that the older student is operating in a phase of development natural to all readers, albeit at a more advanced age than is the norm. A later section of this chapter furnishes instructional recommendations for helping less able readers to move into and through these first two phases of word recognition.

Phase 3

The next phase in reading development is what has been termed the **cipher** (Gough & Hillinger, 1980), **spelling-sound** (Juel, 1991), or **alphabetic** (Ehri, 1991) phase. In this period, the following types of performances are noted:

1.   Students begin to learn and use more letter-sound relationships (also called **grapheme-phoneme correspondences**).

2.   Initially, when students start to use more sound-related cues, they may decode words slowly letter by letter.

3.   Eventually, students progress to a phase in which words are decoded more swiftly.

4.   Many words are identified through sound-symbol decoding, but there is also holistic word recognition.

5.   There is a significant increase in the number of words a reader is able to learn in a given amount of time.

6.   Word recognition and identification are more consistently correct than in previous phases.

7.   When errors do occur, fewer nonsense words are produced; there are more real-word substitutions.

Phase 4

Phase 4 is designated the **orthographic** phase (Ehri, 1991). *Orthography* refers to the letters and their *sequences* in words. Students begin to see common sequences or spelling patterns, which helps them read words. This more advanced step of word learning typically appears in normally achieving readers in about second grade, with more control progressively gained through about fifth grade. The following occur:

1.   Because the student has read many words at this point in which the same letter sequences recur, by *analogy,* new words can be recognized. For example, after a reader knows *make, bake, take, cake, lake, rake,* and *wake,* he or she may generalize this familiar word unit to *shake, brake,* and *flake* without direct instruction or without resorting to slower letter-by-letter use of the corresponding sounds. You, for instance, can decode these nonsense words in the same way: *clake, prake, splake.*

2.   Through strategies learned in Phases 2 and 3—and through the ensuing increases in experiences with print—students accumulate enough exposure to the *spelling patterns* in words—sequences that they come to recognize as *typical units* of words. Familiar sequences can be pronounced on sight (such as *-ing, -pre, -un, -tion*). This allows the reader to decode words in bigger units than are used in the letter-by-letter decoding seen in Phase 3. In addition, and partially because of this, more *multisyllabic* words can be decoded easily and quickly.

    Try to read these nonwords for which you know the familiar orthographic units and in which you may apply analogies from common word parts well known to you: *undeanful, pregatted, mistavelyment,* or *renickeration.* On this last one, you were able to quickly decode a five-syllable "word" you had never seen before (since I made it up) because you have sufficient knowledge of English spelling patterns.

3.   During this phase, more words can be recognized by sight.

4.   Reading is more fluent because of the skills developed in the previous phases.

Instructional implications for Phases 3 and 4 of word learning will be addressed in Chapter 10.

Phase 5

Phase 5 may be thought of as the **automatic** stage (Chall, 1983). Most words are recognized at sight. The reader has stable control over a variety of ways to learn and recognize words, assimilated and practiced in the preceding phases, which can be brought into play in the exceptional cases when a word is unknown.

WORD RECOGNITION INSTRUCTION IN REMEDIAL PROGRAMS

Planning for instruction with students who exhibit limited word recognition must take into account students' developmental phases, as described above. It is vital to analyze the means that a student is using to process words at his or her present stage of development. Such an analysis will suggest instructional procedures to complement the mechanisms students currently use and identify those that students need in order to move into the next phase. This approach to designing word recognition programs has support in child development theories (e.g., Vygotsky, 1978) and in current theories of word learning (e.g., Ehri, 1991; Firth, 1985; Goswami, 1988; Juel, 1991; Stanovich, 1991b; Vellutino & Denckla, 1991).

MINICASE STUDY 1

Bridget was enrolled in a university reading clinic in the middle of first grade by her mother, an elementary school teacher, who noticed that her intelligent young daughter was not progressing at a normal rate in reading.

Synopsis of Assessment Information

Preintervention assessments indicated that Bridget was operating at a very early phase of word learning, even though she had had four months of first-grade reading instruc-

FIGURE 9–1
Phases of word learning

Stages of Word Learning
1.   Logographic/Selective Cue
2.   Rudimentary-Alphabetic
3.   Alphabetic
4.   Orthographic
5.   Automatic

tion. Bridget did understand the concept of "word." However, on an entry-level test consisting of lists of isolated words, in the set of the 12 easiest, she was able to pronounce only 3—and with major hesitations on 2 of these. When Bridget's word recognition was examined in context, 1 additional known word was found, but no others. Bridget could recite the alphabet, which her mother said she had initially learned through the "Alphabet Song," but she did not recognize all of the letters in their printed forms: she knew 18 capital letters and 16 lowercase ones. She knew no letter sounds.

In one study, Ehri and Wilce (1985) subdivided students into prereaders (those who know no words), novices (those who know a few words), and veterans (those who know several words). When taught a set of words by the researchers, "prereaders" recognized words by obvious visual (graphic) clues—for example, remembering that "this is the word *look* because it has two 'eyes' in the middle"—while "novices" and "veterans" showed they had begun to use alphabetic knowledge. Although Bridget did know, perhaps, 2 to 4 words, she was not able to use alphabetic knowledge effectively in word recognition because she could not identify about 35% of the letters of the alphabet, and her overt behaviors also indicated that she was using gross visual clues almost exclusively to recognize words.

Instructional Strategies

A program to acquaint Bridget with letter names, to teach her sight recognition of a number of basic words, and to help her focus on *letters* as cues to words was instituted as the initial phase of her instruction. She participated in 1-hour lessons, 3 times per week. Several steps were taken.

1. Bridget was taught to recognize those letters of the alphabet she did not know. Research demonstrates that awareness of letter names promotes recall of the forms of written words. This occurs because readers are prompted to view words as regular arrangements of letters—rather than trying to remember them by grosser clues, such as word shape or word length (M. J. Adams, 1990a, 1990b; Ehri, 1987).

   Letter recognition was taught explicitly in direct exercises. As one part of these lessons, Bridget practiced printing the letters. Research has shown that writing contributes strong assistance to letter learning (M. J. Adams, 1990a, 1990b); also this would help Bridget to develop a skill needed for writing independently. A good deal of attention was given to letters so that Bridget would be confident in her recognition of them; we wanted Bridget to have automaticity in letter recognition. These experiences also were expanded by calling her attention to letters in the context of connected text and writing.

   (Letter recognition also helps students later to learn sound associations of letters more easily, a task made more difficult if they are still trying to remember which letter is which; and it also seems to induce interest in playing with writing, with the accompanying curiosity to know letter sounds in order to spell words [Chomsky, 1979]).

2. Predictable books were used. Several factors may go into making a book predictable, for example, when subplots are repeated, as in *The Three Bears* or similar stories. Other books are predictable because words and phrases are repeated on every page. An example of the latter type—the type used with Bridget—is *Brown Bear, Brown Bear, What Do You See?* (Martin, 1983). In this predictable book, brightly illustrated by Eric Carle, the first pages say:

"Brown bear, bear, what do you see?"

"I see a red bird looking at me."

"Red bird, red bird, what do you see?"

"I see a yellow duck looking at me.

"Yellow duck, yellow duck, what do you see?"

"I see a blue horse looking at me."

"Blue horse, blue horse, what do you see?"

And the book continues in this pattern, providing much repetition of the same words.

Predictable books were a good choice for Bridget for two reasons: (a) words that are seen recurrently in text are more likely to be later recognized at sight since they have been frequently practiced (Carpenter & Daneman, 1981; Ehri, 1991) and (b) being in the logographic phase of word learning, Bridget needed many exposures to words in order to remember them. Gough, Juel, and Roper-Schneider (1983) found that students at this stage knew best the words they had been exposed to most and remembered least well those with which they had the fewest encounters. Remembering words that have been practiced *infrequently* is hard for logographic readers because primarily selecting prominent visual hints to a word's identity does not provide efficient clues for recalling it—or for distinguishing a word from similar words (for instance, *look* does have two "eyes" in the middle, but so do *took, book*, and *cook*).

The same predictable book was used repeatedly with Bridget for 3 days, but in a variety of ways, both to prevent boredom and to be commensurate with the type of practice selected to match Bridget's skill level with the book on each day. For example, (a) while Bridget followed along, the teacher read the book, pointing to each word (finger-pointing by the teacher or the child provides an assist during early word learning [Clay, 1985]); (b) the teacher read, pausing to let Bridget chime in when she remembered words; (c) Bridget and the teacher read in unison; (d) the book was recorded on audiotape, and Bridget read along orally or silently, pointing to each word; (e) the teacher read the left page of the book and Bridget read the right to the end of the story, then positions were reversed and Bridget read the left page and the teacher read the right; (6) Bridget read independently, with the teacher chiming in when Bridget was stumped; (7) pages of the book were printed on chart paper so that Bridget read them without the support of the pictures. M. J. Adams (1990b) indicates that "[r]epeated readings and repetitive texts set the stage for the acquisition of a broad sight vocabulary" (p. 69). At the end of the 3-day cycle, a new predictable book was selected.

3.   After Bridget had read several predictable books, each day thereafter she decided on one of her former favorites to read once again to the teacher. She simply read the book through, with the teacher assisting on words if necessary. This reading was in addition to the work with the book that was the instructional focus at the time.

4.   Augmenting the practice of words through the context of predictable books, some isolated word exercises also were presented. The words were chosen from the book Bridget was working on during that particular 3-day cycle. This was deemed a better procedure than introducing additional words. Furthermore, there was direct practice on only five words at a time (the first practice set with the Brown Bear book contained *see, bear, you, red*, and *a*), and until she showed

accurate recognition of these, no others were included in the exercises. Both of these latter procedures were in keeping with Bridget's stage of word learning—better recall is obtained in the logographic phase if there is concentration on *small sets* of words at a given time. Practice of these words outside of the book context was an important addition to the contextual reading because the redundant nature of these texts makes the books *easy* to memorize by bright children. In these cases, word recognition may appear to be occurring when it is not.

Specific word practice also involved contextual exercises. For instance, sentence building was used—that is, words written individually on cards were placed randomly on the desk and Bridget picked cards and arranged them to form short, but meaningful sentences. These incorporated known words as well as the immediate focus words. For example, since *I* was one of Bridget's previously known words, even with her first practice set, she could create these sentences:

I see a bear

you see a bear

The direct practice on words ensured that Bridget would transfer the words she was exposed to in the predictable book to other texts.

Some direct word practice exercises also took place *with* the book—in particular, **masking** was used, that is, a card with an open rectangle cut into it was placed on a page so that only one word could be seen; Bridget attempted to pronounce the word, but if she could not, the card was raised so that she could use the context of the remainder of the sentence to assist in word identification. See the illustration in Figure 9–2.

A different type of "masking" was used in other direct word practice. Words were printed on individual cards, and a blank card was placed on top of one of the words. The blank card was then moved carefully from left to right, exposing one letter of the word at a time; Bridget was to say the word only after all letters were shown. This was then done with the words on the other cards.

Many word practice activities that were used with Bridget, and that can be used with other students in the logographic or the rudimentary-alphabetic word learning phases (i.e., Phases 1 and 2), are seen in Table 9–1.

FIGURE 9–2
Using a mask in word practice activities

TABLE 9–1
Three categories of word practice activities

A few examples of word practice activities:

1. *Contextual Activities* (Used to promote transfer to connected text)
   - Reading short sentences composed of target words plus known words
   - Reading short paragraphs, then short stories written by teacher (as students progress)
   - Reading cloze sentences
   - Sentence building
   - Reading cooperative stories (stories for which the teacher reads most of the text, but that include brief, interspersed sections to be read by the student)
   - Guessing words written in "invisible ink" within the context of a sentence, paragraph, or story and coloring in the words to confirm the choice

2. *Focusing on Internal Features of Words* (Used to encourage reflective—rather than impulsive—behavior, and recognition of unique sequences of letters in words. These activities require conscious detection of distinctive and redundant visual and orthographic information.)
   - Spelling words with magnetic letters
   - Manipulating letter dice to form words
   - Linking letters printed on puzzle pieces in arrangements to spell words
   - Guessing missing letters in words written with "invisible ink" marking pens, then coloring these in to self-check the choice.
   - Writing words on a Magic Slate and lifting the paper to rewrite correctly if wrong
   - Writing words on small hand-held chalkboards
   - Filling in missing letters in hangman games
   - Tracing words

3. *Games and Manipulatives* (Used to increase attention and to provide a stress-free form of practice. Interest and willingness to take risks positively influence performance.)
   - Board games
   - Card games
   - Bingo games
   - Word hunts
   - Puzzles
   - Concentration games
   - Word wheels
   - Grab bag activities
   - Word checkers
   - Games involving play money

5. In *every* session, Bridget's teacher called attention to letters *in words.* The focus was most often on the beginning letter since this is believed to be the most helpful graphic cue in a word, but attention was also systematically directed to the sequence of letters in words. The latter is called *focusing on the internal features of words* or *focusing on orthographic features.* This was done during word practice activities, but also during connected text reading with the predictable books to ensure that Bridget generalized this word learning strategy to real text reading.

Moreover, when Bridget evidenced use of nonproductive cues ("I can remember that word is *monkey* because it has a tail"), the teacher switched her attention to more productive cues by saying something like, "Yes, it ends with the letter *y*. What letter does *monkey* begin with? Great! You notice that *monkey* begins with an *m*. Can you spell the letters of *monkey* for me?" Bridget was asked to name and count the letters in words she was working on (as suggested by Ehri & Wilce, 1985) and to engage in other comparable activities. All these procedures were used to shift Bridget's selection of word cues to a higher stage so that she would no longer try to exploit visual clues that actually have limited serviceability—"eyes" (*look*), "tails" (*monkey*), shape, and length—but, rather, would view words as stable arrangements of letters.

6.   Bridget dictated a short "story" each day. The teacher attempted to structure the dictation so that some of her focus words were used. For instance, on the first day of the Brown Bear book, the teacher said, "We have been reading about a *brown* bear. But let's suppose you saw a *red* bear! Use your imagination. What could you tell me about that *red* bear?" After a little thought, Bridget said, "The red bear ate a man." The teacher then wrote this sentence, with Bridget looking on, and spelled each word aloud as she wrote the letters. She asked Bridget, "What did the red bear say that he saw?" Bridget responded, "He said 'I see a man.'" Thus, four of her focus words appeared in the dictation (*red, bear, a, see*). The teacher wrote, while spelling out loud, the second sentence of Bridget's "story." Bridget then read back her dictation, having little difficulty even though some words were new to her. The teacher helped her to finger-point to each word as she read and assisted where necessary.

The next step was to help with more advanced composing skills. The sequence of the two-sentence "story" was discussed and it was decided that it would make more sense for the bear to see the man first and eat him after that. So, her two sentences were cut apart by the teacher, and they were rearranged by Bridget to show a more logical progression of events. The story now read:

He said I see a man.

The red bear ate a man.

The new version of the story was read by Bridget. More discussion ensued, with the teacher questioning, "Instead of saying '*He* said I *see* a man,' could we also say '*The red bear* said I *see* a man'?" Bridget readily agreed that this could be said. The teacher then cut each sentence apart into its separate words, and Bridget rearranged them so that the next revision read:

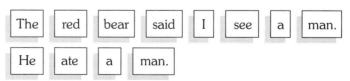

Bridget read the latest "draft" of her story. She thought it did sound good, and the teacher was satisfied that it was acceptable for now (even though in a more mature version, the *a* in the last sentence might have been substituted with the word *the*).

This activity contributed meaningful construction endeavors (by fostering explicit awareness that *the red bear* could be substituted for *he,* for example, and by supplying experiences with logical sequences in composing)—and gave Bridget many contextual reading response opportunities with some of her focus words. In addition, because the teacher spelled aloud *every* letter in each word as Bridget watched her write, this fortified the concept that words are made of a systematic ordering of letters.

7.   The teacher read aloud to Bridget for a few minutes *every* day from authentic texts. Most often attractive picture books were used, but poetry and stories from anthologies of famous fairy tales also were read. These habitually included words and sentence constructions slightly above her maturity level, as suggested from research for furthering learning (Chomsky, 1972; Vygotsky, 1978). Occasional word meanings were discussed. Once in a while, the teacher pointed to a word and said to Bridget, "You know this word now! Will you read it to me?" Bridget became attached to many of these books and took them home for her mother to read to her again.

Outcomes of Instruction

After approximately 30 hours of instruction over about 9½ weeks, Bridget could name and write all letters of the alphabet in their uppercase and lowercase forms, although she still occasionally confused lowercase *b* and *d;* she had accurate sight recognition of many more words, in and out of context; she was learning and maintaining words after shorter periods of exposure; and she attended to letter cues (and had become quite adept at playing the hangman game, which requires attention to orthographic sequences and positions of letters in words).

In short, she was operating rather well in Phase 2 of word learning—the rudimentary-alphabetic phase—with the exception that she was not using letter *sounds* in her word learning attempts. At that time, objectives for her instruction were changed. She was engaged in some direct phonemic awareness exercises, and the remainder of the goals for her were similar to those established for Daniel, who is described below. Particular attention was given to help Bridget write her own stories, using invented spellings, with much teacher guidance in assisting her to solidify perceptions about ways letters and sounds were associated.

MINICASE STUDY 2

Daniel's parents also referred him for clinical tutoring in January of first grade, after a conference in which his teacher had already broached the subject of retention at the end of that year because of Dan's limited word learning. However, Dan already had attained some reading concepts that Bridget did not have.

Synopsis of Assessment Information

Assessment showed that Dan knew the names of all letters and could print them in both their capital and lowercase forms.

During the assessment period, when asked if he would like to write a story, he eagerly agreed, having had experiences with this in his classroom where the teacher encouraged her first-graders to use invented spellings if they did not know conventional forms of words they wished to write. Dan's spellings showed preliminary understandings of letter-sound correspondences, for instance, spelling *monster* as *msr*, but with some letter *names* included in the spellings as well, for example, *seat* spelled *cet*. Most initial sounds in words were represented correctly, but the only words that had conventional spellings in their entirety were *to* and *I*. Dan seemed to like playing with writing and spelling.

On a test of phonemic awareness, Dan had respectable phonemic segmentation skills, but could not engage adequately in blending of sounds to form words. As seen in his writing, a word identification test confirmed that he knew *some* letter-sound correspondences, but when given simple unknown words to identify, he did not attempt to apply this knowledge in a systematic way by using all sounds he knew to decode the words. What he did do was to exploit his knowledge of one or two letter sounds and read words that shared these features (for instance, reading *cat* as *car* and *bug* as *big* and *fan* as *farmer*). Most often consonant sounds were noted at the beginnings of words and were correct, although the rest of the word was not. Occasionally, letter-sound associations in positions other than the beginning of the word also were seen (as in the ending letters of *bug/big*), but use of middle sounds was slight (for instance, he read *pick* for *pink*). When letter sounds were used, they most frequently were at the beginning of a word, and second most frequently the beginning *and* ending letters (called the **boundary letters**) were employed.

During preassessment, Dan was able to read more words by sight than Bridget, both in context and in isolation. He had solid recognition for about 10. There were several others that he recalled inconsistently, sometimes saying the word correctly, but sometimes confusing it with a similar word.

All these reading behaviors are manifestations of a student in the rudimentary-alphabetic phase of word learning (Phase 2).

Instructional Strategies

Daniel's initial program consisted of helping him increase his repertoire of sight words so he could have more comprehensive experiences in reading connected text, while at the same time introducing instruction that would enable him to make greater use of his rudimentary and emerging sense of letter-sound associations. His lessons included the following:

1.   Predictable books were used as one route to word learning with Dan, as they had been with Bridget, but he also read short, appealing, easy-to-read, high-interest books of about first, and later, second, preprimer level. He was shown two or three of these at a time and allowed to choose the book he wished to read on that day. Dan's self-selected book was read at the beginning of each period.

Before Dan began reading, some attention was directed at pictures that conveyed words found on the accompanying pages. In addition, a few words that were central to the story were highlighted prior to reading; routinely about two of these were pointed out to Dan, and their forms, sounds, and pronunciations emphasized. For instance, when a story about a lion and a mouse was to be read, both *lion* and *mouse* were presented in this way before he encountered them in text.

At the beginning of Dan's reading instruction, assisted reading was sometimes necessary; the teacher read a page first, each consisting of one sentence, finger-pointing as she did. Then Dan repeated the reading, also finger-pointing. During these assisted episodes, the teacher read with expression, and Dan and the teacher stopped to discuss pictures and events to enhance meaning and enjoyment as well as word learning. Because he did know a few words, Dan often jumped in to say a word during the teacher's reading. This strong assistance was required less as his sight word learning increased.

At times, when Dan missed a word for which he did know most letter sounds, the teacher paused to call attention to the sounds, modeling blending of these to form the word; for example, when *run* was misread as *ride,* she said, "You're correct. This word does begin with the *r* sound *(then saying the sound),* but you know the sound of *n,* too *(pointing to the* n *and saying its sound).* This word is *run (running her finger under the word as it was said, stressing and blending the sounds)."* Direct instruction is important, but to be most effective it should teach strategies as well as skills (Duffy & Roehler, 1987).

Other times when Dan miscalled words that he had correctly recognized on some other occasions, he was encouraged to use context—if the surrounding words or the story line did convey the word. For instance when *The chick said "There are two of us"* was read as *The chick said "There are two on us,"* he was asked to self-check for meaning by asking if what he had read made sense. Students should be taught to use strategies adaptably, according to the circumstances (Spiegel, 1992).

Sometimes the teacher pronounced words that were not yet in Dan's repertoire. This was done when unknown words were not amenable to letter-sound clues he knew, when they were irregular words, or when context did not aid in determining the word's identity. When told a word, Dan was asked to reread the sentence, pronouncing the word himself. Then, he simply got on with his reading.

Dan liked reading whole books—albeit short ones—seeming to feel pleased that he could do so.

2.   Next, direct practice on word learning was undertaken. Sets of 10 words were selected from books Dan had read, and these were the focus of practice until he consistently recognized them accurately, with some words moving out of the practice set before others and new target words moving in. An ongoing set of 10 was always maintained. Students in the rudimentary-alphabetic phase of word learning can work with slightly larger sets of words than those in the logographic phase (Ehri & Wilce, 1987). Words that were dependably recognized were placed in a file box called his "Words I Know!" Word Bank and were periodically taken out, reviewed, and counted to provide feelings of success.

Dan's word practice exercises included contextual activities; activities that focused on internal features of words; and practice with the words in isolation. The practice on words often incorporated games and manipulatives in order to boost Dan's attention and his willingness to take risks—and, in addition, because he found these to be fun while learning. Activities also used with Bridget, as seen in Table 9–1, often were employed.

Some care was taken not to include words in a learning set that were very similar, since inclusion of words that look very much alike in the same group to be studied increases the length of time to learn the words (Gough & Hillinger, 1980). For example, when *look* and *like* ended up in the same set, Dan had much confusion in sorting out the two, especially with his propensity to focus on beginning and ending letter-sound associations and to ignore the middles. More than the usual time elapsed before these two words went into his "Words I Know!" Word Bank.

Also, each set contained words for which it was *easy* to associate meanings, for example, nouns (*elephant, cake*) and imageable verbs (*jump, play*) and adjectives (*fast, pretty*). The meaningfulness of these types of words makes them comparatively easier to learn and remember than other words. However, many of the most frequently occurring words in written—and oral—language carry less concrete meanings. These are prepositions, conjunctions, and articles (called **function words**); because of their high frequency, they must be recognized automatically for proficient reading. Therefore, these were included in each set, too. There was an attempt to have a balance between meaningful words and function words in each set, usually five of each. Because the learning of function words is often difficult, it is useful to know that Ehri and Wilce (1987) discovered that having rudimentary-alphabetic readers *spell* function words helped students to learn them. In addition to this procedure, many of the activities listed in Table 9–1 under the heading "Focusing on Internal Features of Words" had the same effect—and also sped Dan's learning of meaningful words as well. Dan particularly liked to write his words on a small hand-held chalkboard or on a Magic Slate, and to form words by manipulating magnetic letters on a cookie sheet used as a magnet board.

Dan was able to retain words rather well after shorter exposure times than Bridget—probably because using *sounds* in combination with visual clues, as he was doing, makes it easier to recall words (Ehri, 1991). But, still, readers in the rudimentary-alphabetic phase need many practice opportunities for sight word reading to occur (Ehri & Wilce, 1987).

Many exposures to words also help students detect differences between similar words. Spring, Gilbert, and Sassenrath (1979) conducted a study in which one group of readers was presented with words that looked different from one another; this group learned the words relatively quickly, but later confused them with similar words. A second group was given sets of words in which similar words were included in the same set; they took longer to learn the words, but later had fewer confusions with other words. A third group had word sets like the first—none of the words looked very much alike, but they were given many more exposures to the words than the first group had been given. This third group did as well as the second group; they did not confuse the learned words with similar words. Although learning words initially is swifter when two words that look alike are not practiced at the same time, for students in early phases of word learning, these words can later be confused if they have not been overlearned to the point where there is automatic, accurate recognition. (Acquiring an adequate sense of letter-sound associations also helps students make distinctions between similar words [Vellutino & Denckla, 1991]. Therefore, as learners in the rudimentary-alphabetic phase and those in the alphabetic phase proper [Phase 3] gain greater control over these letter-sound relationships, differentiations between similar words become easier with fewer encounters.)

Word exposure is extended through contextual reading (Barr, 1984). However, Juel (1989) cites data demonstrating that achievement of students in early word learning phases depends on how well they read individual words. Only after they have acquired a fair amount of proficiency is word learning affected *simply* by connected text reading. For that reason, both connected text reading opportunities and direct practice with words were included in Dan's program.

3.   Following direct word practice, Dan was asked to reread a book he had read on a previous day. Although Dan selected the book for his first contextual reading

experience in each session, the teacher chose this book. This was done so a text would be used that either (a) included words he was currently practicing in his word learning set or (b) included ones that had progressed to his known-words word bank. This policy allowed more exposure to the words and prompted transfer to authentic texts. In addition, since function words occur frequently in all written material, any books used provided practice with those function words that were a focus of instruction for Dan.

Sometimes a book was picked because Dan now knew all words in the text. It was used to give him the opportunity for an eloquent, highly successful book reading experience. Other times a text was selected because it contained several words that he was confusing with similar words, and these, therefore, required more practice. Since occurrence of words in a context can at times help in identifying them, this practice was beneficial, allowing him to make correct responses. But in any case, customarily, Dan found rereading a book easier than the reading of his new book for the day. His rereadings were rather fluent and he moved through the book fairly quickly.

4. Dan wrote something for us every session. Usually he composed a story of about two or three sentences. He was encouraged to use invented spellings because this supported his evolving perspectives about letter-sound associations. These spellings were treated with appreciation by the teacher and praised, with good associations pointed out (for example, when *job* was spelled *jb*—Dan had written *GD JB!!!* at the top of his own paper—the teacher said, "You're right! *Job* does begin with the *j* sound," and then pronounced that sound for him).

Some research has shown that on tests of word recognition skill, students who have had experiences with inventing spellings perform better than those who have not (Baron & Treiman, 1980). In this research, that effect was seen more for *low-readiness* students than for high. It has been hypothesized that when students think about the connections between sounds they hear in words and the letters that could be written for these sounds, and then make active attempts to spell words themselves, their sense of letter-sound associations expands (M. J. Adams, 1990a, 1990b). These experiences are good precursors to more formalized instruction with word identification strategies, especially phonic analysis skills.

However, because we know that noting the order of letters in words also bolsters word recognition (Vellutino & Denckla, 1991), we wanted to use Dan's writing endeavors for this objective, too. Therefore, when he wrote a word he had been practicing in his word-learning sets, he was required to spell that word conventionally. To do so, he pulled his word card in front of him and copied the sequence of letters in the right order. Cards in his known-words word bank were placed alphabetically behind divider cards with lettered tabs for ease in finding the words. The current practice set was always available on the desk on which he was working. Examination of the effects of copying words shows that this exercise reinforces students' retention because it requires attention to the complete sequence of letters in these words (M. J. Adams, 1990a, 1990b; Whittlesea, 1987). Also, Dan sometimes asked for correct spellings of other words; although this was never required, when he asked, he was told.

5. At the end of each day's lessons, Dan and the teacher returned to the book that had been read at the beginning of the session. Dan read it again, with assistance as needed. Because this was the second time he read this book, he commonly showed better word recognition than earlier in the period, often *asking* for

"wait time" so he could pronounce words without assistance ("Don't tell me. I can get it"). **Wait time** refers to the time a teacher pauses to allow a student to reflect on a problem and to marshal known information and strategies to solve it. Wait time is critical for nourishing students' independence in using systems necessary for skillful reading.

Each of Dan's books was read at least three times: (a) an initial reading at the beginning of a session, (b) a rereading at the end of that period, in which growing adeptness was often seen, and (c) later when it was chosen by the teacher for the exercise of rereading a book.

If it was time to add words to his learning set, Dan was asked to help in selecting new additions from this book. However, since the goal was to equalize the numbers of meaningful words and function words in those sets, he was allowed to make choices from among those suggested by the teacher. For example, she might say, "Because you knew so many words today, we can add two more to your practice set. From this story shall we include *school* or *boy*?" After his first choice, she might ask "Should I put in your set, *in* or *for*?"

Outcomes of Instruction

After 5 weeks of one-to-one instruction, Dan had consistent, automatic recognition of about 40 words he had not known at the beginning of this period of his tutoring. There also were other words that he sometimes remembered, but did not always recall.

Dan was now reading short books with some success. Teacher prompts on words still were needed, but less so than in the initial part of his program. He was using context quite often in word recognition attempts. After successful experiences with books in his tutoring sessions, he liked to take them with him to read to his parents.

During his writing activities, he spelled more words conventionally, especially short words and ones that had been a part of his practice sets.

He was deliberately making more attempts at employing letter-sound associations to come up with accurate pronunciations of words; although more effective than previously, this was at times still unsuccessful—undoubtedly because, although he seemed to have internalized a few more letter sounds, he still did not know them all.

At this stage, more formal attempts to teach Dan word identification strategies were added to his lessons. These efforts will be described in Chapter 10 where his case study will continue.

MORE ABOUT EXPOSURES TO WORDS

Students learn what they practice. An important question when helping readers develop sight recognition of words is, How much practice is needed before a word is recognized automatically? The preceding sections indicated that this question must be considered in light of students' word learning phases. Basically, the earlier the phase, the more exposures that are necessary. With each progressive phase, readers learn to use cues and strategies that make recall of words more efficient.

Also you learned that the number of exposures needed for each word varies according to certain characteristics of the word itself. For example, the level of abstraction influences how easily it is learned—words that carry more highly apparent meanings (nouns—*horse*, imageable verbs—*run*, adjectives—*fast*) are generally easier to recall than function words (prepositions—*of*, conjunctions—*but*). The examples just given for the meaningful words actually are words that some students tend to confuse; for instance, these are fairly typical confusions: *horse/house, run/ran, fast/first.* And that is because of another reason noted earlier—the degree to which a word resembles a similar word also affects the number of exposures that are needed in order for accurate, automatic recognition to occur.

There is also research showing that we must be concerned about the number of practice opportunities provided according to a learner's intellectual functioning level. This is particularly important information for teachers who work with students who are developmentally disabled so that they can be sensitive to the needs of these learners in their classes. The general points of this research also have implications for all teachers. Gates (1931, p. 35) determined that these approximate numbers of repetitions were needed, on the average, by students in his study, as a function of intelligence levels:

Level of Intelligence	IQ	Required Exposures
Significantly above average	120–129	20
Above average	110–119	30
Average	90–109	35
Slow learner	80–89	40
Upper educable mentally retarded ranges	70–79	45
Middle educable mentally retarded ranges	60–69	55

These averaged results do not imply that a specific number of exposures is required in isolation—for example, 35 opportunities to say a word that is printed on a flashcard. Rather, it means total exposures of all kinds, including repeated exposures to the same word in a variety of regular, connected reading materials. The goal of the teacher should be to provide overlearning, not drill. *Drill* suggests that the student must do the same thing in the same way day after day. A common example of drill is the custom of limiting sight word learning to daily flashcard exercises *only. Overlearning,* on the other hand, implies that the student will have practice with the word in a variety of ways and in a variety of materials, including authentic texts. Overlearning facilitates generalization of word knowledge to all reading situations, not just to one (e.g., flashcards). Plainly, readers must recall a word in circumstances other than on a flashcard on which it has been practiced.

Gates's findings also are not intended to indicate the exact number of repetitions required by *every* student. It cannot be presumed, for example, that because Victor's intelligence quotient as specified on an accepted test of intellectual functioning is 88, that he will need exactly 40 exposures to every word. Obviously, some words may require more exposures and others less, especially in light of the other factors that make words easier or harder to remember. In addition, Victor may learn all words more rapidly or more slowly than another student of the same approximate intelligence level. It is the general conclusions of these findings that are informative, more so than the details.

Two general conclusions can be made from the study. First, all students, including those with high intelligence, need many exposures to a word before it becomes part of their sight vocabularies, especially beyond the accuracy level—that is, at the automatic and rapid recognition levels; three or four opportunities to practice a word are not enough. Second, the lower the student's intelligence quotient, the greater the likelihood that more practice will be required. For example, a student with average intelligence will probably need more opportunities to practice new words than will a student with above-average intelligence; a slow learner will probably need still more opportunities, and so on. Keeping these two main points in mind, teachers can avoid such statements as "I don't understand why Bob still doesn't know that word! We've worked on it for 3 days."

Related to the axiom of many exposures to a word is the notion of review. During the phases of initial learning, a single correct response to a word is not cause for the teacher to assume that the student knows the word and will recognize it accurately or automatically in future situations. The student must respond correctly and without hesitation several times before knowledge of the word can be assumed. Even then, to ensure maintenance (that is, long-term retention), the teacher should periodically provide occasions to review those words that have recently been learned.

MORE ABOUT CONTEXTUAL VERSUS ISOLATED PRACTICE

There has been much controversy over whether words should be taught in context or in isolation. Some have argued for contextual practice because this method more closely approximates recognition tasks in authentic reading; others maintain that context-free practice is important, pointing to the need for students to focus specifically on individual words so that they may attend carefully to the visual and sound characteristics that distinguish a word from others.

Even research about this issue seems to lead in contradictory directions at times and fails to provide definite evidence in favor of one side of this argument or the other. For example:

- Kibby (1989) reported research with 16 disabled readers enrolled in a reading clinic. These students were tutored individually, 4 days a week over a 4-week period in which they were taught word recognition as a part of a broader program. The average age of students in the study was 12 and on the average, they were 3 years behind their potentials in reading ability. Half the group were randomly assigned to be taught word recognition in context; the other half were taught words in isolation, focusing primarily on the distinguishing visual and sound features of the words. There were no significant differences between the two groups in age, reading ability, intelligence, or gender. Both groups learned and retained an equal number of words they had not known previously (average number = 64); however, the isolated-word group learned the words at twice the rate.
- On the other hand, Ceprano (1981) found that while introduction of words in context produced slower initial learning than when they were presented in isolation, the contextual introduction produced fewer errors later in real text reading.
- One type of contextual presentation may be useful and another kind may not, at least for certain types of words. In one investigation (Ehri, 1976), introduction of function words within the context of written sentences was supportive, but spoken sentences were not.
- Furthermore, Ceprano (1981) found that if students are to be assessed on words in isolation, practice on words in isolation may produce better results, but if they are to be assessed on words in context, it appears that practicing words in isolation or in context may work equally well.
- Another study by Kibby (1977) found that practice in isolation and practice in context were equally effective with his subjects for transfer of the word knowledge to reading in real contextual material.

These studies, plus the numerous ones reviewed earlier in this chapter, provide many reasons to use *both* contextual and context-free activities in instruction for word learning.

Here are some tentative conclusions about the results of presenting words in isolation:

1. Students better focus attention on letter-sound associations.
2. There is an increased rate of learning.
3. Studying words in isolation may be necessary at some word learning stages, because text coverage alone may not sufficiently develop word recognition.
4. Focus on words in isolation may be better in some word learning stages when it is helpful for students to concentrate on a few words at a time.
5. Students can more easily analyze words into their systematic ordering of letters.
6. Students develop phonemic awareness more readily.
7. Students can more readily focus attention on easily confused words.
8. Students can more easily work on blending,
9. Seeing words in isolation helps students with spelling.
10. Students' reading fluency increases.

Here are some tentative conclusions about the results of presenting words in context:

1. Students show increased interest.
2. Transfer of learning is promoted.
3. Seeing words in context helps students learn irregular words.
4. Reading words in context provides students assistance with learning function words.
5. There are opportunities for students to process many words.
6. Seeing words in context may be suitable for students in some word learning stages, in which words can be internalized from much text coverage.
7. In context, use of multiple cuing systems of language—for example, letters, sounds, and context—is possible.
8. Students can focus on word meaning, as well as recognition.
9. Students gain increased fluency.

There seem to be some things good about one approach and some things good about the other. However, there also is overlap in the positive aspects of each approach. For instance, students can also show interest in activities provided to help them in direct isolated word practice, and contextual experiences can facilitate phonemic awareness. In addition, there may be differences in positive attributes depending on whether use of context means use of whole books, stories, articles, and so forth, or whether it means a single-sentence context. Of course, there are those differences in student characteristics and word characteristics noted earlier that may make one type of word learning practice preferable in different cases.

The obvious conclusion is that both types of word practice are needed and desirable. Zealous arguments for the exclusion of either one in favor of the other present a false dichotomy. Furthermore, since students need many exposures to words for their recognition to be accurate, automatic, and rapid, combining the two approaches allows overlearning to occur.

Examples of how contextual practice and context-free word practice can be effectively combined were seen in Bridget's and Dan's programs. Many teachers as a rule of thumb follow this routine sequence: context, then isolation, then context again. For example

Step 1: *Context.* Each word to be practiced during a session is read in context.

Step 2: *Isolation.* A context-free activity is used to promote careful consideration of the distinguishing features of the words.

Step 3: *Context.* Students read the words in a new context.

MORE ABOUT SELECTING WORDS TO BE TAUGHT

We have been talking about recognizing words at sight; however, the term *sight words* is used in different ways. The following three common definitions were previously given in Chapter 6. The one we have been referring to thus far in the present chapter refers to *words the reader recognizes accurately and automatically.* When a word reaches this phase, the reader has no need to overtly use any word identification strategy (such as context clues or phonic analysis) because the word is recognized at "sight." Look at all of the words on this page. How many are unfamiliar to you? The answer is none. All of these words are part of your sight vocabulary under this definition. With only a glance, you recognize each one.

The term *sight words* has also been applied to *irregular words*—words that are phonetically irregular or have atypical spelling patterns. These words cannot be identified by applying knowledge of letter-sound correspondences and phonics rules, or, in more popular terminology, cannot be "sounded out."

Other times when educators use the phrase *sight words*, they are speaking of *core words*—words that arise with high frequency in all written language (and oral language, as well). Various lists of high-frequency words have been compiled as references for reading instruction. Because these words pervade written text, it is an important goal that students recognize them all, at sight, so that reading will be fluent and attention can be directed to higher-level reading processes. Therefore, when a teacher says, "He doesn't know his sight words," this teacher may often mean that the student does not have accurate recognition of the words on one of these rather widely used lists (the well-known Dolch List of 220 Basic Words, for example).

To add further confusion to the matter, the idea of sight words has served as the basis for a reading method. The **sight method** is a general approach to reading instruction that was popular in certain previous eras. In general, this method introduces words as "wholes" and places little or no emphasis on using phonics or other strategies to examine word parts to identify unknown words. The students are to look at the words, say them, and engage in various other holistic experiences with each word until it can be recognized at sight. The sight method was also called the whole-word method or the look-say method.

Very few reading programs today employ a sight method exclusively. Rather, learning whole words well enough to recognize them accurately and automatically is combined in a balanced way with the learning of various word identification strategies that can be used when unknown words are encountered. When students are taught strictly by a whole-word method, they often do begin to internalize some letter-sound concepts on their own, but not until they have developed a comprehensive sight vocabulary (Ehri, 1991). Research and experience have taught us that relying on a method that teaches reading strictly by sight or by a method that is devoted exclusively to word identification strategies is ineffective with many students. Although articles appear periodically in the popular press with titles such as "Look-Say Versus Phonics for Teaching Reading," these articles present debates that only attack a "straw man." This issue has long been settled in the reading education profession.

For many years, contemporary reading programs, with the exception of a very few that are not widely used, have not chosen one method to the exclusion of the other. Instead, they combine the development of sight recognition of words with the development of skills in phonics, knowledge of structural analysis, use of contextual strategies, and other effective word-learning strategies. It might be thought that an exception to this view of instruction is the currently well-liked whole language approach—with its focus on authentic texts and meaningful contexts. But in most instances, this is not the case. Because of influences of the burgeoning research on word recognition and word identification, balance is seen in most whole language classrooms (for example, see J. M. Newman & Church, 1990; Spiegel, 1992; Strickland & Cullinan, 1990).

Because the primary focus of this section is the issue of what words to teach, we will be directing our attention to *core* words. Teachers of students with reading problems must decide what words to choose for instruction when helping students extend their sight recognition vocabularies. What words should be taught first, and once these are learned which should be taught next?

Those words that have been identified as occurring frequently in all written text make up a large percentage of words in materials read at the primary, intermediate, secondary, and even adult levels. They also occur equally often in narrative and in informational selections. Obviously these words are very important for students to know. Some of the lists of high-frequency words that have been compiled are named and the references for locating each are found in Chapter 6, on assessing sight word vocabulary.

Several high-frequency word lists were compiled decades ago and some more recently, but examination reveals few differences among them. In other words, most words appearing on any one list are found on all the others.

In addition, all the lists are current for today's needs. While new words constantly are being added to our language (some fairly recent ones are *microwave oven, modem, space shuttle,* and *photocopy*), the basic function words (for example, *for, a, of, and, with, which, be, the,* and *that*) that occur with very high frequency, and therefore appear on these lists, remain the same. For example, one of the older and better known lists, the Dolch List of Basic Sight Words (Dolch, 1936), was analyzed by Mangieri and Kahn (1977) to see if it needed updating. They found that 66% of all words in primer through third-grade basal readers appeared on this list. These researchers concluded that it is still of critical importance for words from this list to be acquired by students if they are going to be successful in reading experiences. Equally high percentages of the words on this list (and other high-frequency word lists because they basically are duplicates of one another) have been found at other levels and for other types of materials, including library books (literature popular with young people). And although the preceding study was conducted in 1977, obviously the same words (*of, the, and, was, by, to, see, if, it,* and so on) are still found with high frequency in all written selections. In fact, I have just typed these example words into this text by looking at words in this very paragraph.

It does not matter very much which high-frequency word list teachers use since they contain essentially the same words, at least for the first couple of hundred of the most frequent words tabulated. Undoubtedly, words from these lists should be given high priority in a program to increase sight words.

However, since many words on high-frequency lists are prepositions and conjunctions, plus a few adjectives, pronouns, and verbs, it is quite difficult to write or read materials using just these words. For this reason, many other words, such as nouns, must also be learned early in order for students to read meaningful material. Therefore, merely having students memorize the words on a high- frequency list is inadequate; other words must be taught simultaneously. These other words may be "story-carrying" words—nouns and other words from stories students are attempting to read. The introduction of high-interest words stimulates secondary students, in particular, to learn to read material needed for their daily lives. In the process they pick up many high-frequency words that can in turn enable them to read other material. Just one example of how basic core word vocabulary can be learned in this way is seen in Figure 9–3, which provides a list of high-

FIGURE 9–3

Highway signs requiring instant recognition of words

All Cars (Trucks) Stop	Exit Only	Merge Left (Right)
	Exit Speed 25	Merge Left (Right)
Beware of Cross Winds		Merging Traffic
Bridge Out	Falling Rock	Minimum Speed
	Feet	
Caution	Fine for Littering	Narrow Bridge
C.B. 13 Monitored by Police	Flooded	Next Gas 15 Miles
Congested Area Ahead	Fog Area	Next Right
Construction Ahead	Food	No Dumping
Curve	Four Way Stop	No Left Turn
	Freeway	No Parking This Side
Danger Ahead		No Passing
Dangerous Curve	Gasoline	No Passing When Solid Line Is
Dangerous Intersection	Go Slow	Right of Center Line
Dead End		No Right Turn on Red Light
Deer Crossing	Hill—Trucks Use Lowest Gear	North
Detour	Historical Marker	Not a Through Street
Dim Lights	Hospital Zone	No "U" Turn
Dip		
Divided Highway	Ice on Bridge	One Way Do Not Enter
Do Not Block Walk	Information Center	One Way Street
Do Not Enter	Intersection	
Drive Slow	Interstate	Parkway
		Pavement Ends
East	Junction	Pedestrians,
Emergency Parking Only		Nonmotorized Traffic,
Emergency Vehicles Only	Maximum Speed 55	Motor-Driven Cycles,
End Construction	Mechanic On Duty	Prohibited
Entrance	Men Working	Pedestrians Prohibited
Exit	Merge into Single Lane	Peding

way signs that high school students wishing to obtain a driver's license should learn to read. This list also contains 101 exposures to words found on the Dolch list.

The recommendation to select words to be taught from materials students are reading at the time, as was done with Dan and Bridget, is also suggested for core words. Because core vocabulary is present throughout all texts, these words can be chosen for direct word practice in conjunction with any books used. Directly teaching with high-frequency word lists, then, is unnecessary. However, it would be wise for teachers to obtain one of these lists for reference and to familiarize themselves with the words that do have such high utility.

In sum, core words must be learned in order to read, but one cannot read with core words alone. Core words and meaning-carrying words both should be taught in contextual settings, and in context-free practice.

FIGURE 9–3 *(continued)*

Ped X Ing	School Zone When Flashing	Unloading Zone
Plant Entrance	Signal Ahead	Use Low Gear
	Slide Area	
Left Lane Ends	Slippery When Wet	Vehicles
Left Lane Must Turn Left	Slow	
Left Turn on Signal Only	Slower Traffic Keep Right	Warning
Litter Barrel	Soft Shoulders	Watch for Ice on Bridge
Loading Zone	South	Watch for Loose Gravel
Local Traffic Only	Speed Checked by Detection	Wayside Park
Loose Gravel	Devices/Radar	Weigh Station
Low Clearance	Speed Limit	Weight Limit 8 Tons
	Speed Limit 15 When Children	West
Police Jurisdiction	Are Present	Winding Road
Private Road	Speed Zone Ahead	Wrong Way
Put on Chains	Steep Grade	
	Stop	Yield
Radar Checked	Stop Ahead	Yield Right of Way
Railroad Crossing	Stop for Pedestrians	
Ramp Speed 25	Stop While School Buses Load	
Reduce Speed Ahead	or Unload	
Resume Speed		
Right Lane Must Turn Right	Truck Escape Ramp Unless	
Right Turn Only	Otherwise Posted	
Right Turn on Red After Stop	Truck Route	
Road Closed	Trucks and Combinations	
Road Construction	Trucks Entering Highway	
Road Ends Ahead	Trucks Over 11'6" Height	
Roadside Park	Two-Way Traffic	
School Bus Crossing	Unlawful to Block Intersection	

Source: From "Riding and Reading" by Lana McWilliams, *Journal of Reading, 22,* pp. 338–339. Copyright 1979 by the International Reading Association. Reprinted by permission of Lana McWilliams-Smith and the International Reading Association.

MORE ABOUT SPECIFIC TEACHING ACTIVITIES

Using Language Experience Stories

A word recognition program based of student-dictated stories can be instituted, as in the language experience approach. This technique can be used with secondary as well as elementary students; the major difference is simply in the choice of topics for story dictation. With the language experience approach, the student dictates a story, which the teacher writes down as it is dictated. Then the student reads the story.

Lessons are designed to ensure that students develop accurate recognition of words that occur in their dictated stories. Some or all words from the story are written on cards, with each word written in context on one side and in isolation on the other. For example, "I *am* a boy" may appear on one side of the card; *am* may appear on the other side. Initial work with the words on these cards is carried out in the context of the sentence. When the student is consistently recognizing the word in context, the other side of the card is used.

Each student may keep two word banks. A **word bank** can be any kind of a container (for example, a metal file box, a shoebox, or a manila envelope) in which a student's personal word cards are placed. Even if instructional procedures involve a group, students should keep individual files of words. One of the word banks can be labeled "Words I'm Working On" and the other "Words I Know."

Most high-frequency (core) words will occur in students' dictated stories because, once again, they are used so often in all *oral,* as well as written language. E. H. Henderson, Estes, and Stonecash (1971–72) confirmed this in a study of word acquisition in a program that used a language experience approach. These researchers found that in one week's sample of beginning readers' dictated stories, the average number of words per story was 54. Words from the stories were then compared with the Lorge-Thorndike Word List, and it was found that 45% of the students' dictated words were in that list's category of highest frequency.

If words a teacher wants a student to learn are failing to occur in the dictated stories, the teacher can structure a situation so that the word will be used. For example, suppose the word *green* is one the teacher wants Bradley to know, in one session the teacher might bring in several green items (a green leaf, a puppet with a green shirt, a green apple) and say to Bradley (or his group), "Today we are going to write our story about things that are green." If it is difficult to structure a story-dictation situation that will guarantee that the student will produce the desired word, the teacher can prepare a story in which the word occurs one or several times and say, "For many days we've been reading stories you've written. Today you have a holiday. I wrote the story." The teacher has again structured a situation to introduce a word through meaningful story material.

Words chosen for focus from student stories should, of course, include both high-frequency function words and more concrete meaning-carrying words. This allows students to build a base of words that will enable them to read published books.

If other words are learned incidentally or in other teaching situations (such as from signs, labels, and so on), these can be added to the student's word bank.

Throughout the beginning phase, a chart or graph showing the student's progress should be kept so there is a visual record of how many words have been learned. Figure 9–4 shows an example of such a chart. This chart or graph should be kept in a folder and be available to the teacher and student to use each day. *Visually* demonstrating progress is highly motivating to most learners.

If the student is at the appropriate phase of word learning, during the same time that sight vocabulary is being developed, the student may benefit from lessons that help in learning word identification strategies. This knowledge not only is necessary for identifying unknown words not yet in the student's sight vocabulary, but can actually assist in the initial learning of many sight words.

After the student has learned enough words to begin to read in published materials, his or her own dictated stories can be used in conjunction with these. First, check the words in the student's word bank labeled "Words I Know" against words in the stories found in beginning reading material. Compare the word bank words to, for exam-

FIGURE 9–4
Charts help students visualize
progress

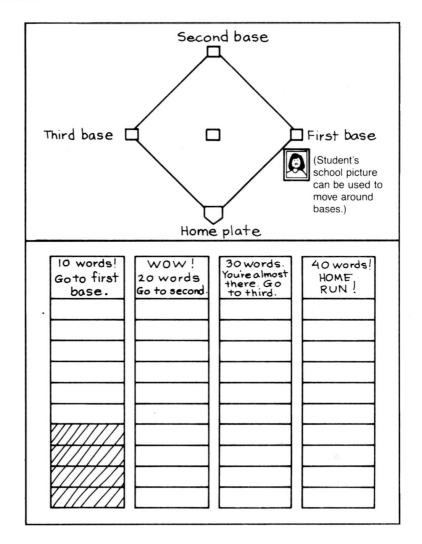

ple, a first preprimer in a basal reader series used in the student's regular classroom, or an easy-to-read, high-interest book being used in the special program. When the student's story-dictation experiences have helped him or her to know most words in the published story, have the student read it. This will provide practice with newly acquired words, an entrée into published material, and a success experience with a published text because the student learned the words before being asked to read it.

Eventually, most reading will occur in published materials. You may select words to be learned by perusing published material before the student reads it, anticipating the words that may present difficulty and preteaching these prior to the reading of the story. When students have finished reading the story, work with them on the words they found difficult, even if you did not anticipate a problem with these words.

Even after the student has progressed to reading published materials, you may wish to use dictated stories about once a week so that words in the student's oral language that may not occur in easy reading material but that may be of interest to the student can be added to the repertoire of sight words. Maintain the word bank system, using words from the published materials, as well as ones from the weekly dictated stories. File words in the "Words I'm Working On" word bank and use various practice activities until students can move words into the "Words I Know" word bank.

Other Specific Techniques for Student-Dictated Stories

Activities suggested in the following section may be used for introduction and initial learning of words and for practice.

1.   At the completion of a student's dictation and reading of a story, the teacher points to one sentence and asks the student to reread it. From the same sentence, the teacher randomly points to a word and asks "What is this word?" Upon eliciting a correct response, the teacher points to another word within the same sentence and again asks, "What is this word?" This procedure continues until the student has pronounced each word in the sentence. Using index cards, the teacher now writes one of the words from the sentence in isolation on one side of a card, pronounces it, turns the card over, and asks the student to generate another sentence using the same word. The teacher then incorporates the word into this new sentence on the second side of the card.

   The same procedure is used with each word from the dictated-story sentence until a pack of word cards can be assembled for the entire sentence. The cards are shuffled and the student is asked to read each sentence on the individual cards in which the words are written; if time permits during that session, other contextual and context-free activities for providing exposure to these words are used. (If it is appropriate for a particular student, words from more than one sentence may be selected from the dictated story for introduction during a single session.) At the conclusion of the session, the student files the new set of cards in a word bank labeled "Words I'm Working On."

   In the next session, the student reviews these words by reading them first from the contextual side of the card and then from the side where the word is written in isolation before engaging in other activities with the words.

2.   Prior to a session, the teacher writes each sentence from the previous day's dictated story on separate strips of colored construction paper.

My brother and I played softball.

My mother made chicken and potato salad.

On Sunday we had a picnic.

Our dog kept getting in our way.

During the session, the student rereads yesterday's story, and then is given the sentence strips in random order. The student reads the sentence strips orally and places the strips in the correct sequence. Then he or she rereads the story again from the rearranged strips.

On Sunday we had a picnic.

My mother made chicken and potato salad.

My brother and I played softball.

Our dog kept getting in our way.

FIGURE 9–5
Word practice based on a student-dictated story

1

Today I saw an owl.
Owls are birds. They
have big eyes. Owls
are pretty. I like owls.

During first session
student dictates a
story and reads it.

2

Before next session teacher prints story
on strips, sentence by sentence. These
are given in scrambled order for student to
read and arrange meaningfully.

3

Today I saw an owl.

Student cuts first sentence into
individual words. These are
scrambled. Student reads individual
words; arranges meaningfully; rereads.

4

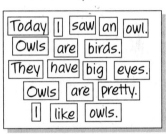

Student does the same with
the remaining sentences.

5

Today I saw an owl.
Owls are birds. They
have big eyes. Owls
are pretty. I like owls.

Student rereads whole story.

6

Keep a word bank of these words on
file. Add more for each story. Review
these every day.

Finally, word cards related to this story are taken from the student's word bank and shuffled. These are matched to words on the sentence strip story. For example, if the first word in the shuffled pack is *made*, the student finds *made* in the story, places the word card under it, and pronounces it.

A similar set of word practice exercises based on a student-dictated story is seen in Figure 9–5.

3.   Prior to a session, the teacher copies the students' previous day's dictated sto-ries onto another piece of paper. (Typing this copy may make it more appealing for older students.) After students have read the sentences and single words on the index cards in their word banks, they use these index cards to find each target word in the copy of the story and underline the target word with a colored mark-ing pen. They pronounce the word after underlining it. When all words have been found, they reread the whole story.

4.   The teacher prepares highly predictable material by repetitively using words and accompanying these with pictures. For example, the teacher might assemble a small book with one sentence and one picture to a page for the student to read. (Teachers can cut pictures from magazines or draw them themselves.) The pages in one such booklet might be:

I see a cat.

I see a boat.

I see a truck.

I see a hat.

I see a book.

I see a fish.

On the next day, the teacher may have a new booklet introducing an additional word.

I see a big fish.

I see a big truck.

5.   The teacher writes cloze sentences, leaving blanks where words on which the student is presently working would fit.

The student places word bank cards on a desk with the single words facing up. Next, the student reads the first cloze sentence and selects a word from the word bank cards that he or she thinks would fit the blank. Finally, the student places that card above the sentence and uses it as a model to write the word in the blank.

$$\boxed{\text{on}}$$

Get __on__ the bus.

6.   The teacher introduces new words through riddles. The riddle can be read, while finger-pointing, by the teacher from chart paper as the student follows along. The student supplies the word to answer the riddle and the teacher writes it on chart paper, chalkboard, or another convenient material. Afterward, these words are written on word bank cards, in context and isolation, and practiced using methods discussed earlier. Nouns are easiest to predict (guess) and provide concrete words to add to high-frequency prepositions and conjunctions in the stu-dent's word bank. Nouns may be chosen from a published story soon to be read, or they may be chosen to build upon a specific theme of words in the student's oral language.

7.   Published materials offer the teacher a variety of formats for introducing and reinforcing basic sight vocabulary. The *Read-A-Part* books (Houghton Mifflin) pro-vide students who are just beginning to develop a small sight vocabulary one

opportunity for contextual reading. These books consist of many short stories. The teacher reads the majority of each story as the student follows along. At certain points, the teacher stops and the student reads dialogue that is printed in speech balloons. The material that students read is made up of short sentences consisting primarily of high-frequency words. The reading by the teacher provides a strong context that prompts correct student responses when they read sentences. See Figure 9-6 for a sample page from these books.

The Janus Career Education series and the Janus Survival Guides (Janus) provide contextual material that can be used to introduce sight words needed for real-life reading. These materials provide initial learning experiences with words for reading want ads, job applications, supermarket food labels, and newspapers—a good choice with some secondary school students and adults.

8.   Use sentence building. Give the students several piles of word cards on which individual words are written. Place the cards randomly in each pile, but make sure that *each* pile contains words that when properly arranged *can* form a sentence. (For example, one set might include the words *fish, here, can, you;* another might include *will, go, you, where.*) Put rubber bands around each separate pile. The student selects a pile, removes the rubber band, places the cards on his or her desk, reads them, and then sequences them into a sentence. This sentence remains on the desk and he or she selects the next pile and follows the same procedure. When all sentences are "built," the teacher comes to each desk to check for corrections and hear students read the sentences (*You can fish here* or *Where will you go?*).

9.   Make blank bingo boards from oaktag, one for each student in the group. The squares on these cards should be drawn large enough so that an index card can be placed on each square. Each student places his or her own individual word bank cards (single word up) on the bingo board in a random order. (See Figure 9–7.)

Before beginning the game, the teacher prints cloze sentences on individual oaktag strips. (For example: This _____ not fun.) These are prepared so there are sentences for all students' word bank words (the group of words on which each student is presently working). The teacher places one cloze sentence strip on the chalkboard tray. Any student who has a word bank card that makes sense in the sentence raises his or her hand, points out to the teacher the word card on the bingo board that would fit, and reads the sentence pronouncing that word instead of the blank. If the student's word does make sense in the sentence, the student gets to remove that word card from his or her bingo board. This game is played like traditional group bingo, except that the student who first gets 5 empty bingo squares in a row or column wins. (If an easier or quicker bingo word game seems more appropriate for a given student group, the teacher can make 16-card bingo boards or even 9-card bingo boards.)

10.   If students miss a word they should know while reading a story or expository material, encourage them to use word identification to figure it out. If this is not possible at the student's level of word learning development, or if for any other reason the word remains unidentified, pronounce the word for the student and let him or her continue with reading. Afterward, however, provide practice with that word. The following is one example of how this might be done.

Mike does not recognize the word *off* when it is encountered twice in the story he is reading orally. At the completion of the story, the teacher asks him to think of some sentences that name things that can be turned off. The teacher asks

FIGURE 9–6
A page from the *Read-A-Part* series

Source: From *Getting Ready to Read-A-Part* from *Houghton Mifflin Reading* by W. Durr et al., Boston: Houghton Mifflin, 1974. Copyright 1974 by Houghton Mifflin. Reprinted by permission. This Read-A-Part selection was published as an ancillary for which Juanita Lewis, Paul McGee, and William E. Spaulding served as editorial advisers.

FIGURE 9–7
An example of a bingo board with sight-word cards from a student's word bank

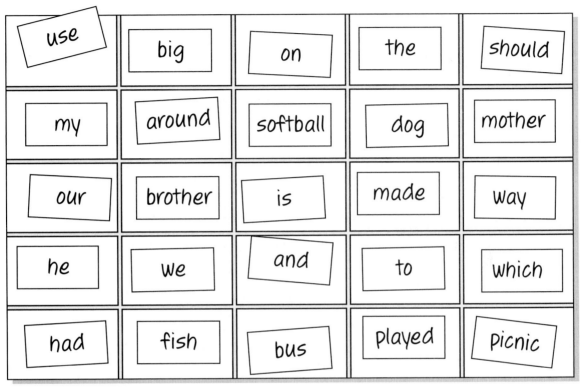

Mike to begin each sentence with "You can turn off _____." The teacher writes these sentences as Mike completes them, and underlines the word *off* each time.

You can turn *off* the stove.
You can turn *off* the air conditioner.
You can turn *off* the lights.
You can turn *off* the TV.

Mike observes as the teacher records the sentences and is then asked to read the sentences orally, finger-pointing to each word as he does. This usually produces successful recognition and response to the word *off* every time. To promote generalization of the correct response to other material, the teacher reopens the book Mike had been reading to the places where he had missed the word *off* and asks him to read the word in those sentences.

11.   Group games may be used even if students are working on individual words in their personal word banks. Prior to a game, one or two words are selected from each student's group of "Words I'm Working On." Students take turns teaching their words to the group. A student begins with the contextual side of the word card and then uses the side with the word in isolation to point out important graphic and sound features. All the words that all of the students have taught to the group are then included in a group game (a board game, rummy card game,

bingo, and so on). If a student has difficulty with another student's word during the game, the latter student assumes the role of teacher and gives instruction for identifying the word (showing the contextual side of the word card, calling attention to the beginning letters of the word, and so on). This provides an excellent learning experience for both the "teacher" and the "student." Secondary as well as elementary teachers have used this technique successfully in their classrooms.

ELIMINATION OF WORD CONFUSIONS

For many older disabled readers the problem with sight vocabulary is not one of needing initial learning experiences with words, but rather, one of confusing similar words. They do not look at a word such as *of* and simply block it because they do not know it at all. Instead they confuse it with another word that looks somewhat the same, like *if* or *off*. The following activities may be used to help students eliminate sight word confusions.

1.   Encourage the student to attend to meaning. In many cases in contextual material, words frequently confused cannot be read for each other and still result in a meaningful sentence. For example, here are some miscues that do not result in meaningful sentences:

use
It is fun for us to play in the park.

no
I can't play there on a school day.

May
My father is going in the car.

Came
Come here and look at this.

When a student produces miscues of this type, before calling attention to the graphic or sound clues of the word ask,"Did that make sense?" Teaching students to use the meaning and language clues the text has to offer will eliminate many word confusions.

2.   Goodman and Burke (1972) suggest placing both of two frequently confused words in a short teacher-written story in such a way that the correct choice of the two is unambiguous, that is, sentence structure and meaning clearly convey which word it is. Figure 9–8 contains such a story written for a fourth-grader who had a persistent sight word confusion with the words *so* and *some*.

After reading words in contextual material such as this, the student may be asked to visually discriminate between the two words he or she confuses. An example is an exercise in which the student circles all those words on a line that are identical to the first.

some	so	some	some	so
so	so	so	some	so	some

This lesson may end with another contextual activity in order to follow the rule of thumb of using context, isolation, and then context again in practice activities. Cloze sentences might be used for the final practice.

FIGURE 9–8
Example of a story that gives students many opportunities to practice frequently confused words

Michael was so glad that it was Friday! He knew that this was the day of the school Christmas party. Some of the other boys were going to stop by his house to walk to school with him today, so he had gotten up early.

The teacher had asked Michael and some of the boys to bring cookies from home, so they were going to go to school early so they could put the cookies on plates and put them out on tables. Some of the girls had been asked to come early so they could make a bowl of punch.

When the other boys got to Michael's house, he went to get his cookies. Much to his surprise some little parts of some of the cookies had been eaten away! He was SO mad!

Crumbs from the cookies were all around the plate. A small line of crumbs led to the edge of the table. Another line of crumbs led from the table to a place under some of the kitchen cabinets.

David and some of the other boys watched as Michael followed this line of crumbs to where they led. Michael got down on his knees. He saw a small hole under one cabinet. "So, that's it," he said. "Some little mouse has already had himself a party." David and some of the other boys laughed. David said, "That's okay. Christmas is for giving, and we just gave part of our party to a mouse."

a. He wanted _____ apples.
   so, some

b. She had grown _____ big that
   so, some
   I did not know who she was.

c. _____ boys like to play football.
   So, Some

3. Use S-S-S: Seeing, Sounding, Sensing. When two words are consistently confused, students may be asked to see how each one *looks* different from the other, to note the differences in the *sounds* of the two words, and to attend to the differences in the *sense* of each (that is, differences in meaning or grammatical function).

For example, if a student regularly confuses *on* and *in*, he or she is asked to name the letter at the beginning of each word, to note the difference in the sounds of the two initial letters, and, in order to sense the differences in meaning, to use each word in a sentence such as "My book is *on* the table," and "I rode *in* a car to come to the clinic." After the sentences are written and read, they should be discussed, and the lack of sense of each sentence pointed out if one were to substitute *in* or *on* for one another in the sentences. This procedure focuses on graphic and sound clues as well as the important clue of meaning. The ability to distinguish between the different graphic and sound clues of confused words is especially important when context (meaning) does not provide a clue to the word's identification. Research demonstrates that highlighting the visual characteristics of words is important whether the words are introduced in context or in isolation (see, for example, Arlin, Scott, & Webster, 1978–79, and Kibby, in Ceprano, 1981).

4.   Use "every-pupil-response cards" along with cloze stories. The purpose of every-pupil-response cards is to increase opportunities for individual responses when groups of children are engaged in the same activity. Each student is given several cards on which possible answers are printed. As the need for a response occurs, instead of one student being called on to give the answer, all students select from their cards the answer they believe to be correct, and then hold this card up. At a glance, the teacher can see who needs corrective feedback. To see how to use this group technique for eliminating sight-word confusions, let's look at an example. Three students are consistently confusing *which* and *with,* so the teacher prepares a cloze story on chart paper such as the one in this example.

I don't know _____ boys I want to go _____ to the fair. No matter _____ ones I choose, I know I'll have fun. When I go with Al and Bob, though, they never know _____ thing to do first. They can't decide if they want to go see the goats or go get one of those hot dogs _____ onions and peppers on it (_____ make me sick!)

Students are asked to print *which* and *with* on separate index cards and place these on their desks. The story is posted so everyone can see it and the teacher reads it out loud as the students follow along. The teacher pauses at each blank and each student quickly selects and silently holds up the word he or she believes to be the correct response. The teacher gives corrective feedback when necessary.

5.   The first one or two letters of a word often provide the most important graphic clue to that word. Lack of attention to the initial portion of a word can result in word confusions (such as *your/our, would/could, when/then,* and *where/here*) and in miscues commonly called **word reversals** (as in *was/saw* and *on/no*). To eliminate habitual confusions of this type, give students activities that require them to attend to the first letters of the confused words.

For example, students could be given words to alphabetize. (Alphabetizing necessarily causes a focus on the beginning portions of words.)

Another way to deal with these types of word confusions is to use maze exercises in which the possible alternatives differ only in their initial one or two letters so that the student must attend to the beginning of the word in order to make a choice.

I like to wear this old _____ .
(bat, hat)

_____ I'll get some new jeans,
(Then, When)

_____ I'll throw away these baggy pants.
(then, when)

WORD RECOGNITION AND ORAL READING

Word confusions and other types of word recognition miscues are obviously more easily recognized during oral reading than during silent reading. When teachers' instructional responses to students' miscues during oral reading have been studied (Spiegel & Rogers, 1980), eight main classifications of teacher prompts have been observed, as follows.

1. *Tell.* The teacher simply tells students the correct words when words are read incorrectly.

2. *Visual.* The teacher instructs the student to look at the word more carefully.

3. *Visual/Context Clues.* The teacher repeats a few words that came before the student's error and says "What?" to indicate that the student is to use context, plus examine the word again. For example,

    Text: Listen to the kitchen clock.
    Student: Listen to the curtain—
    Teacher: Listen to the what?

4. *Sound.* The teacher prompts students to sound out words they read incorrectly.

5. *Spell.* The teacher spells the word read incorrectly. For example,

    Text: A bluebird is smaller than a robin.
    Student: A bluebird is smaller then
    Teacher: t-h-a-n

6. *Meaning.* The teacher asks if what was read makes sense.

7. *Structural analysis.* The teacher breaks the word into syllables for students or tells them to do this.

8. *Reference to prior use.* The teacher tells the student that the word was used before, for example, saying something like, "I used that word when I gave you your math assignment after recess."

Prompt 8 seems less than useful since it is little more than an obscure hint that will not lead the student to independence in word learning strategies. A similarly ineffective

One way to encourage self-correction is to have students mark their own miscues while listening to tapes of their oral reading.

prod is seen when the teacher points to an item to divulge the word; for instance, Louis misses the word *green* and the teacher happens to be wearing a green blouse, so she tugs at her blouse looking at Louis meaningfully until he gets the point and says *green,* or Maria confuses the word *tree* with *three* so the teacher looks out the window and gesticulates strongly at a tree she sees there until Maria guesses *tree.* Because the teacher cannot follow students around for the rest of their lives providing little tips to the identities of words, such weak prompts are best avoided.

The other seven types of corrective feedback designated above all can be used legitimately at various times, depending on the skill level of the learner, the word, and the surrounding context. M. J. Adams (1990a, 1990b) makes recommendations based on current research examining word learning, saying that contrary to previous opinion, the best prompt most often is *not* to direct the student to skip the word. Rather, students should be asked to pause and study, considering letters and sounds in order to internalize the word pattern for future recognition. If many of these word study pauses are necessary—to the extent that meaning is being seriously disrupted—then undoubtedly, the student is reading a selection at his or her frustration level; use easier material. Remember, learners should be working with text in which they recognize about 90% to 95% of the words.

While a variety of prompts are needed for students to develop multiple independent strategies, Spiegel and Rogers (1980) found that more than half the time teachers simply told students words when oral reading miscues occurred. For only 5 percent of the miscues were students prompted to use meaning clues. These results indicate an unfortunate tendency to view the only purpose of oral reading as one of correctly pronouncing each word on a page. Instead, oral reading should be viewed as a chance to help students develop efficient and independent reading strategies—and to practice using these in real texts. Spiegel and Rogers observe that when teachers perceive miscues as spontaneous instructional opportunities, their students show better word recognition and identification. Although there are certainly some occasions when merely telling the student the word is appropriate, used indiscriminately, this teacher response has little long-term value in aiding reading growth.

The immediateness of teacher response to miscues is another concern. Research by McNaughton and Glynn (1981), and others, has examined students' behaviors when teachers correct readers' miscues immediately as they occur. Students who were corrected at once employed fewer self-corrections, simply opting to rely on the teacher's input. Remedial reading teachers must be sensitive to students developing dependencies that are detrimental to reading progress. Some *wait time* allows readers to catch their own mistakes and puts them on the road to independence. Positive correlations between reading ability and use of self-corrections have been demonstrated (Clay, 1979; Pflaum & Bryan, 1980). Self-corrections not only provide an assist to word learning, comprehension also increases when self-corrections rise (Beebe, 1980). Unfortunately, students with reading disabilities have their miscues immediately corrected more often than do good readers (Allington, 1984b). Students need time to monitor their own reading.

An additional unprofitable practice is seen in group reading instruction when students are allowed to call out a word when one of their peers makes a miscue. This approach has been negatively correlated with progress (Brophy & Evertson, 1981): the very student who requires opportunities for word study is denied them.

Another way to encourage self-correction processes is to use tape recordings of students' oral readings to create awareness of miscues. To do so, first have a student read a story or informational selection independently into a tape recorder. Next, with the student, follow along in the book while listening to the tape. Have the student stop the recorder when a miscue must be corrected. The student works through the replaying activity, circling corrections that should be made on a copy of the reading selection.

At this point, it should be noted that some students correct their miscues internally during oral reading; that is, although they do not make a correction out loud, they have corrected it in their minds and, therefore, continue reading. This behavior is generally characteristic of more advanced rather than less advanced readers.

Reutzel, Hollingsworth, and Eldredge (1994) point out that the main purpose of oral reading in elementary classrooms has changed over time from instruction to assessment. This, too, is the case when working with students having reading delays. The major reason for employing oral reading in remedial and clinical programs is to provide on-the-spot diagnostic and remediation possibilities. Another purpose is to help students gain oral reading fluency. This, in turn, can assist the development of fluency in silent reading by giving students a feeling for the structure of language and its relationship to the spoken word. For both these reasons, even with secondary students, in remedial programs oral reading activity has been correlated with achievement (Stallings, 1980).

Teacher modeling can increase oral reading fluency. The student reads the first page in a new story orally. Then the teacher reads the next page orally with the student listening and following along. The teacher should read with normal fluency at just an average pace, not rapidly or dramatically, but approximating a nice flow of language that communicates with a listener. On page 3 of this story, it's the student's turn again. Usually the student's fluency begins to improve noticeably as the teacher's reading is imitated. The teacher and student can take turns throughout the story. (For some students, alternating after every paragraph instead of page by page may be more helpful.)

An additional activity for increasing oral reading fluency is the reading of plays, which may be legitimately read and reread so that students gain control of their parts. Sometimes Reader's Theater is used (S. A. Wolf, 1993) in which students can turn any story into a play by taking the parts of the story characters and reading the dialogue in a playlike fashion. To do so, one student assumes the role of "narrator," reading the portions of the text that are not spoken by the characters. These "plays" are *read* from books containing the stories, thus giving reading practice, which orally performing a play does not.

Another procedure conducive to fluency development is paired readings, in which learners work together on texts until accurate, fluent readings are produced; encouraging students to work together this way as a *community* of learners, sharing reading and writing tasks and goals, is viewed with increasing favor (Spiegel, 1992).

Walley (1993) suggests combining paired reading practice with the dramatization of books. Learners practice together before acting out the text. He also recommends choral reading, with selections practiced in unison, and use of cumulative stories that have repeated patterns, as aids to fluency enhancement.

Individual student's repeated readings of the same stories (Samuels, 1979), and using read-along commercially published cassette tapes with their accompanying books, in addition, assist fluency. Also, see the suggestions found in Chapter 14, which discusses recommendations for working with severely disabled readers and which supplies other suggestions for eliminating nonfluent, word-by-word reading.

CONCLUSION

Several commercial materials have been cited that are useful for helping students develop an extensive sight vocabulary. Many others are available. A sampling of these is

---

Teachers' Store D

Sight Vocabulary

1. *ETA Language Arts Program: Basic Vocabulary Kit* (Educational Teaching Aids)
2. *Reading Reinforcement Skill Text Series* (Charles E. Merrill)
3. *Filmstrips: Read On! Series II* (ACI Films)
4. *Common Words* (Charles E. Merrill)
5. *Vocabulary Laboratories* (Holt, Rinehart & Winston)
6. *LEIR—Language Experiences in Reading, Levels I, II, and III* (Encyclopedia Britannica Educational Corporation)
7. *Supermarket Recall Program* (William Orr)
8. *Sight Words for Survival* (Lakeshore Curriculum Materials)
9. *Reading Joy Gameboard Kits* (Reading Joy)
10. *Sight Word Labs: Set 1 and Set 2* (Developmental Learning Materials)
11. *Breakthrough to Literacy* (Longman)
12. *Cove School Reading Program* (Developmental Learning Materials)
13. *Sight Words* (ESP)
14. *Reading Cartoons* (Frank Schaffer)
15. *Picture Word Program* (Amidon)
16. *Dolch Puzzle Books* (Garrard)
17. *Word Cover* (Houghton Mifflin)
18. *Play 'N Read* (Little Brown Bear Learning Associates)
19. *High Action Reading for Vocabulary* (Modern Curriculum Press)
20. *The Little Big Box of Books* (Fearon-Pitman Learning Inc.)
21. *Dolch Phrase Card Game* (Garrard)
22. *Sight Words for Beginning Readers* (Audiotronics)
23. *The Monster Series* (Bowmar/Noble)
24. *Sight Word Memory Match* (Developmental Learning Materials)
25. *Ladder Games: Sight Word Builders* (Developmental Learning Materials)
26. *Strange and Silly Stories* (Frank Schaffer)
27. *Basic Word Skills* (Frank Schaffer)

---

offered in Teachers' Store D. Some published materials for improving oral reading fluency also are listed in Teachers' Store E.

As has been prominently noted throughout this chapter, there are interactions among word recognition ability, word identification skill, and understanding of text. Accuracy and automaticity with words, at least to a minimum degree, appear necessary in order for reading to progress into the phases where word identification strategies can develop—which, then, cultivates additional automatic word learning—which, in turn,

Teachers' Store E

Oral Reading Fluency

1. *Favorite Plays for Classroom Reading* (Plays, Inc.)
2. *Your First Adventure* (Bantam Books)
3. *Invitations to Read, A Read-Along Listening Program* (Noble & Noble)
4. *SCORE Reading Improvement Series* (Prentice-Hall Media, Inc.)
5. *Film Ways to Reading* (Palisades Educational Films)
6. *Voycom Card Reader* (American Guidance Service)
7. *Read-A-Part* (Houghton Mifflin)
8. *Language Master* (Bell & Howell)
9. *Double Play Reading Series* (Bowmar/Noble)
10. *Sounds of Language Readers* (Holt, Rinehart & Winston)
11. *Cassette/Book Combinations* (Scholastic)
12. *Read-Along Libraries* (Random House)

FIGURE 9–9
Some interactions among word recognition, word identification, and comprehension

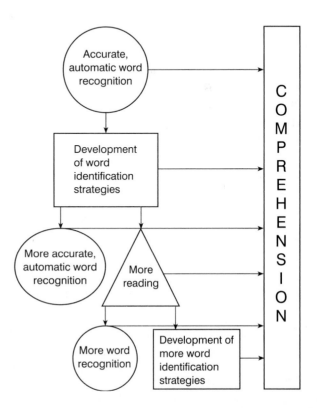

permits students to read more. And more reading leads to more word learning. And all of these lead to better comprehension. See the diagram in Figure 9–9.

📖 REFLECTIONS

1. Although not labeled "principles" in this chapter, nevertheless, a number of principles of word learning have been related throughout. Review these and make a list of word learning principles to which you can later refer.
2. Now select several of those principles and think of lesson components you could devise to enhance a student's word recognition achievement.

10

Word Identification

In the alphabetic phase of word learning, students show improved word identification strategies and more conventional spelling, as well.

C onsider this scene:

> Ten-month-old Eddie was extremely excited by the new puppy that his father had just placed on the floor in front of him. He waved his chubby arms wildly, stiffened up his body, sat up very straight, and pointing to the puppy said, "Ee-ya-ug!" His 7-year-old sister, Felicia, wanted to help him get the right words, so she looked at him seriously, and quietly but firmly said, "Sound it out."

The prod to "sound it out" obviously doesn't provide much help in oral language—and there has been much controversy about whether it is very helpful in "getting the right word" in written language. *Does* "sounding it out" help students to identify unknown words in written material? Apparently so. After decades of waffling back in forth between approaches that emphasize phonics instruction (or "sounding it out") and instruction that deliberately avoids phonics, and then back again to a stress on phonic analysis principles, and then again back to reading education that shuns phonics, it seems that we now have a large body of research that does confirm the utility of teaching learners to use letter-sound associations to read words. (See Figure 10–1.)

This chapter will discuss phonics instruction and this new research, as well as other word identification strategies. As you remember, in the last chapter, **word identification strategies** were defined as those procedures a reader employs when he or she does not recognize a word at sight. As a predecessor to these strategies, some rudimentary beginnings to using letter-sound associations arise in Phase 2 of word learning—as we saw with Dan in Chapter 9, although our other case study student, Bridget, had not advanced that far. In order for students to gain control of word identification strategies, they must have developed sufficient *phonemic awareness*.

FIGURE 10–1
History of attitudes toward phonics instruction

A Minihistory of Attitudes toward Phonics Instruction

- 1534 = Ickelsamer first suggested use of phonics to assist word identification
- Mid/late 1700s–1840 = ☺
- 1840–1890 = ☹
- 1890–1920 = ☺
- 1920–1930 = ☹
- Late 1930s–early 1940s = ☺
- Mid 1940s–mid 1950s = ☹
- Mid 1950s–1960s = ☺
- 1970–1990 = ☹
- 1990–present = ☺

PHONEMIC AWARENESS

As indicated in Chapter 3, where causes of reading and reading-related learning disabilities were discussed, a major characteristic distinguishing skilled readers from unskilled is poor readers' lack of sensitivity to phonemic features of words (Stanovich, 1994; Vellutino & Denckla, 1991). To benefit from word identification strategies instruction (particularly, learning letter-sound relationships and how to use these to identify unknown words), students need to obtain an adequate degree of **phonemic awareness**—that is, the awareness that spoken words can be broken down into their constituent sound units.

Tests to determine if students have phonemic awareness seek to determine if, for example, given single phonemic units, students can blend them into a word. (See Chapter 6, in the Assessment unit of this text.) You might ask if a specific student can respond correctly when requested to identify a word that begins differently when you orally pronounce a group of three or four words (e.g., "Which word begins differently: *fat, fell, sit, fog?*"), or, you might ask if the learner can break a sound from a word and say it in isolation (e.g., "Tell me the first sound you hear when I say *jump*"). You might also ask if the student can blend sounds together to form a word when you orally pronounce the individual *sounds* (e.g., for the word *got,* you might say to a student, "When I say /g/ /o/ /t/, what word is that?"), or you might ask if students can tap out the number of sounds heard, indicating they can break a word into its single phonemes (e.g., "Listen to this word: *mop.* Tap out the number of sounds you hear.") At a more advanced level of phonemic awareness, the learner should be able to manipulate phonemes (e.g., ask the student to "Say *has* without the /h/"). (You are, of course, pronouncing the sound the letter *h* stands for in the latter example—not the letter name—as indicated by the slash marks on both sides of the letter, a widely used convention introduced to you in an earlier chapter.) Skills demonstrated through these tasks are strong predictors of reading achievement (e.g., L. Bradley & Bryant, 1983; Liberman, Shankweiler, Liberman, Fowler, & Fischer, 1977; Lundberg, Olofsson, & Wall, 1980; Sweet, 1993; Vellutino & Scanlon, 1987).

If the student does not exhibit an awareness of phonemic analysis principles, then instruction to help students learn these linguistic concepts should be undertaken before beginning a program to teach explicit word identification strategies.

Understanding how phonemic awareness develops in normally achieving readers furnishes insights for intervention. It is common for phonemic awareness to mature in many children before they come to school. At home, in day-care centers, and in preschools, they (a) hear and memorize nursery rhymes under the auspices of adults who point out the features of rhymes (e.g., "Look! These words sound the same at the end: *jiggle, higgle, piggle!*"); (b) have stories read to them, again with adults pointing out words, letters, and sounds; (c) play at writing and ask for spellings of words; (d) manipulate magnetic letters into invented spellings of their own based on sounds they think they hear; and (e) participate in "lessons" from television programs for young children that include opportunities to play with sounds in language (e.g., *Sesame Street*). All these activities can be incorporated into teaching readers who have not developed ample phonemic awareness.

Advice for instruction also is obtained from research programs that have successfully trained children to increase their phonemic awareness. These investigations have been conducted with young children (e.g., Ball & Blachman, 1991), but also with students with reading disabilities—for example, Dewitz and Guinessey's (1990) work with third- through sixth-graders enrolled in Title I programs. In many cases, researchers deliberately designed their activities to be gamelike and playful to sustain children's interest. Most emergent literacy programs and beginning reading programs build this instruction from easiest to more complex, for instance, Lundberg, Frost, and Petersen (1988) used this sequence: (a) rhyming activities, including those that require learners to produce rhymes themselves; (b) hearing individual *syllables* in words; (c) hearing *initial sounds* of words; (d) hearing sounds *within* words. In remedial classes, the teacher should begin at the easiest level at which the student is unable to demonstrate phonemic awareness.

The following are a variety of exercises used by researchers.

1.   For *rhyme production* activities, explicitly point out that rhymes sound alike at the ends of words. Griffith and Olson (1992) advocated reading to students daily from rhyming texts, such as *Winter and Summer* (Livingston, 1958): "The winter/ is an ice cream treat,/ all frosty white and cold to eat" (p. 52). Or *Poem to Mud* (Snyder, 1969): "Poem to mud / Poem to ooze / Patted in pies, or coating your shoes" (p. 317). Students are to use poetry as springboards to orally create their own rhymes.

2.   To help students recognize that words may be made up of *separate syllables*, Lundberg et al. (1988) asked the teacher to pretend to be a troll with an unusual manner of speaking in which words were said syllable by syllable.

The troll had presents to give to the children, but to receive these the students had to figure out what item was being named—for example, when the troll said "lo-co-mo-tive" or "pen-cil."

For a nice addition, teachers might precede the activity by reading the story "The Three Billy Goats Gruff" to the children in order to ensure that they understand what a troll is.

3.   Ball and Blachman (1991) asked students to match pictures by alliteration (i.e., all those beginning with the same sound) to promote *awareness of likenesses and differences of sounds*.

4.   Yopp and her colleagues (1992) made good use of songs to develop various facets of phonemic awareness. For instance, to increase students' *recognition of isolated sounds* in words they sang lyrics, such as these, to the tune of "Old Mac-Donald Had a Farm":

What's the sound that starts these words:
Turtle, time, and *teeth?*

(*Children respond*)
/t/ is the sound that starts these words
Turtle, time, and *teeth.*
With a /t/, /t/, here and a /t/, /t/ there,
Here a /t/, there a /t/, everywhere a /t/, /t/.
/t/ is the sound that starts these words:
Turtle, time, and *teeth.* (p. 700)

5.   A variation of the troll activity (Lundberg et al., 1988) can be used to develop sensitivity to the principle that words are made up of a *sequence* of sounds. This modification requires students to mentally *blend* sounds to produce words. The troll's speaking pattern in this case would consist of pronunciations of the individual phonemes in a word (e.g., /m/ - /o/ - /p/, which the learners must combine to identify the word *mop*).

6.   To practice *segmenting words into phonemes*, students can be given a wooden dowel (or simply a pencil); after hearing a word pronounced, they men-

tally count and tap out the number of sounds it contains (Liberman, Shankweiler, Fischer, & Carter, 1973).

7. To refine *phonemic segmentation* principles, various adaptations of Elkonin boxes (1963) have been used (e.g., Ball & Blachman, 1991; Clay, 1985; Griffith & Olson, 1992). Examples are seen in Figure 10–2.

Prior to this activity, the teacher selects several simple pictures and places them on file cards. Boxes are drawn to represent each *sound* in a picture. Note in Figure 10-2 that a box is drawn only for the sounds, not for each letter; thus, there are 3 boxes drawn for the *second* example, *n-ai-l*.

Learners are given counters (e.g., plastic disks; pennies). They move a counter into each box as they hear each sound in a word the teacher slowly pronounces. For instance, as the teacher says *d-o-g*, a counter is moved into the first box as the /d/ sound is heard, into the middle box as the /o/ is heard, and into the last box to represent the /g/ sound.

FIGURE 10–2
Elkonin boxes that assist in phonemic segmentation activities

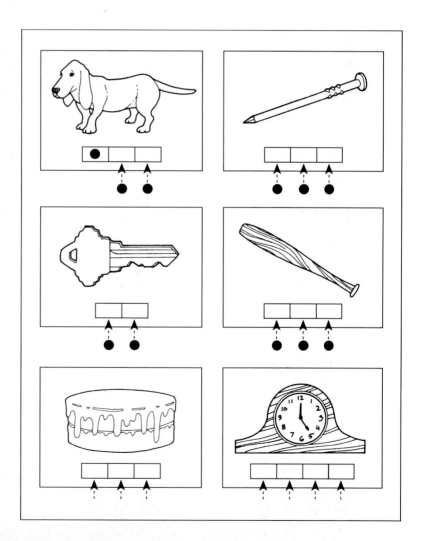

As students advance in their understanding, they can be requested to (a) pronounce the word with the teacher; (b) pronounce it by themselves as they manipulate the counters; and finally (c) write letters in the boxes instead of using counters.

These assignments aid students in hearing individual sounds within words, noting them in correct sequence, and associating them with printed letters. Teachers in some programs, for example, Reading Recovery (Clay, 1985), also have learners use Elkonin boxes during writing activities to assist them in spelling unknown words.

8.   Activities can be used to practice isolating and manipulating sounds through phoneme substitution and deletion tasks.

Yopp (1992) had students sing nonsense words, successively substituting beginning sounds (p. 701):

Fe-Fi-Fiddly-i-o
Ze-Zi-Ziddly-i-o
Bre-Bri-Briddly-i-o

In the same training program, students changed their own names to silly ones by *substituting* a different initial sound, for example, *Sandy/Tandy, Bobby/Tobby.*

Pictures can be used in phoneme *deletion* activities. For instance, learners may be directed to "Listen to the word *brake.* Think of the word that would be left if /b/ were taken away. Find the picture of the new word." The student selects from a series of pictures.

9.   Other exercises that researchers have used in programs to successfully accelerate students' phonemic awareness include (a) having students clap out syllables (or sounds) in words; (b) having students march to syllable patterns; (c) use of iteration (e.g., if students were to identify the initial sound in *kite,* the teacher said /k/ /k/ /k/ *kite*); (d) use of rhymed stories (e.g., certain Dr. Seuss books are useful); (e) having students categorize pictures by rhyme; (f) having students manipulate letter tiles consistent with sounds heard in words; (g) board games (such as bingo); (h) reading books with alliterative patterns to students; (i) using children's literature that playfully deals with sounds in language; and (j) employing riddles and guessing games focusing on sound units in words (Ball & Blachman, 1991; Griffith & Olson, 1992; Juel, 1991; Lundberg et al., 1988; Yopp, 1992).

10.   Combining phonemic awareness exercises *along with explicit instruction of letter-sound correspondences* has been found to be particularly effective (e.g., L. Bradley & Bryant, 1983). Once students begin noting sounds in words, and when they also recognize written letters, then associating *sound* cues with *visual* cues (letters) produces greater growth in phonemic awareness (Hohn & Ehri, 1983).

Linking phonemic awareness exercises with letter-sound association training also results in greater gains in one word identification strategy, phonics. For instance, Fox and Routh (1984) taught a group of students letter-sound correspondences (i.e., the sound of the letter *t;* the sound of the letter *m;* and so on); they taught a second group letter-sound correspondences plus skills in segmenting words into their phonemes; and a third group was instructed in both of these understandings plus skills in blending individual phonemes into words. The third group outperformed the others in learning to read words.

Using Writing Experiences to Develop Phonemic Awareness

As portrayed with Dan, one of our case study students in Chapter 9, writing experiences exploiting invented spellings serve learners by helping them "map" written language onto the spoken language they already know. Children develop increasing phonemic awareness as they try to spell words on their own (Clarke, 1988).

Teachers today no longer wait for students to gain some proficiency in reading before beginning writing activities. Instead, they encourage students to use their present level of letter-name and letter-sound knowledge to write words as they think they sound. Students' reading and writing abilities develop together (Sweet, 1993).

MOVING INTO PHASE 3 OF WORD LEARNING: THE ALPHABETIC PHASE

In the previous chapter, five phases of word learning were specified (including the one that *you* are in—Phase 5). Characteristics of readers in each of these phases also were enumerated. (It is recommended that you flip back to those descriptions and quickly review them now. Doing so will place what follows in perspective and convey its relevance to you—and you will, therefore, in addition, be more likely to recall the information at a later time. These phases are described on pages 256–269.

In the preceding chapter, we also examined the reading behaviors and instruction for a student in Phase 1 of word learning and for another in Phase 2. Our Phase 2 case study student was about to move into Phase 3 when we left him, ready to benefit from more explicit instruction in word identification strategies.

The Value of Word Identification Strategies

Skilled readers not only recognize large numbers of words at sight, they also know what to do when they come to words that are unknown to them. During developmental periods of learning to read, confronting many new words is typical, and doing so is necessary in order for learning to progress. Knowledge of strategies to employ when new words appear is critical for reading advancement.

When students have attained competency in use of word identification strategies, they can read unfamiliar words independently without the guidance of a teacher. Once students use these strategies, considerable strides are made in the number of words they can read (Juel, 1991). Therefore, like word recognition, the development of word identification strategies facilitates comprehension because students can read *more* (Daneman, 1991; Lesgold, Resnick, & Hammond, 1985; Stanovich, Cunningham, & Feeman, 1984; Tunmer & Nesdale, 1985). Furthermore, when readers have poor word identification abilities, they do not obtain satisfactory practice with higher-status comprehension processes (Daneman, 1991). There is also some evidence that when readers can associate sounds with the words they read, they can hold the words better in short-term and long-term memory, and thus they have improved recall of what they have read (Mann, Liberman, & Shankweiler, 1980; Mark, Shankweiler, Liberman, & Fowler, 1977). Systematic instruction on word identification strategies is not incompatible with comprehension, but rather is supportive of it.

Reliable word identification strategies also make recall of words at sight easier. One reason this occurs is because learners have expanded opportunities for exposures

Skilled use of word identification strategies assists comprehension.

to words, and this helps them internalize the forms of more words (Daneman, 1991). They also make errors less frequently when they read words by sight (Ehri, 1991) and because they require fewer exposures to new words to establish their identities, their sight word recognition vocabularies are rapidly extended (Vellutino & Denckla, 1991).

Knowledge of word identification strategies even helps somewhat with deciphering irregular words, because *portions* of these words *are* regular (Stanovich, 1991b). Vellutino and Denckla (1991) give this example: based on knowledge of regular spelling patterns, one might expect that *have* would be read so that it rhymes with *gave* and *save,* which is not the case, and therefore in terms of common **spelling patterns,** the word *have* is an irregular word. But the sounds for *h* and *v* in this word are not irregular—they are the sounds that these letters most typically stand for. As a result, the regular segments of the word can help the reader get at least within the recognition range of this word—if those sounds are known.

Skill in word identification accelerates reading acquisition (Jorm & Share, 1983; Rayner & Pollatsek, 1989; Stanovich, 1991b). Differences in word identification abilities lead to deviations in reading achievement for young readers and for students in secondary schools (Daneman, 1991; Frederiksen, 1982; Jorm, 1981).

And, students with dependable word learning strategies *spell* with fewer errors (Juel, Griffith, & Gough, 1985).

Word Identification Strategies in the Alphabetic Phase of Word Learning

Although there are various word identification strategies that must be assimilated to attain competence in reading, during Phase 3 of word learning, the focus is on **phonological recoding** (also called **decoding**). To "phonologically recode" a word means that you look at the letters in the word and turn them into (or, *recode* them into) their sounds—that is, the visual code (the letters) is recoded into a phonological code (the sounds); then these sounds are matched with the pronunciation of a word you already have stored in your memory—stored there because you have heard it in *oral* language (Daneman, 1991). For example, we will pretend that you do not know this word—*swift*—but that you are well established in the alphabetic phase of word learning (Phase 3) and have learned the sounds of all the letters in that word. Therefore, by saying the sounds of the letters ("sounding the letters out") and *blending* these sounds, you are able to come up with the correct pronunciation of the word, and because you have heard this word before, it clicks!

You now become aware that the word spelled *s-w-i-f-t* is that word *swift,* which you know because you have heard people say it before, or because you heard it when a story was read to you, or because you even have used it yourself. This takes care of that word for now, and you can get on with your reading. With enough pairings of *s-w-i-f-t* with the realization that "Oh, that's right, this is *swift,*" the word will also become established in your memory as a written word you know. This is another reason *sight word* reading increases rather dramatically when control is gained of word identification strategies—remembering words is less complicated because students can translate the letters that spell a word into a pronunciation of the *known* word and store this as one whole item, rather than using the more difficult approach of storing all of the individual letters (Ehri, 1991); learning letter-sound relationships decreases what must be recalled.

In order to make those kinds of associations, though, you must have some important prerequisite information—you must know the sounds of letters and you must have had practice in blending sounds, both of which are not particularly easy concepts to acquire.

Sequential decoding is learned first, followed by hierarchical decoding (Ehri, 1991). In **sequential decoding,** students learn simple one-to-one correspondences between letters and the sounds that the letters typically stand for—for example, that the sound associated with *f* usually is the sound heard at the beginning of *fat*; that the sound for *n* is usually the sound heard at the beginning of *nap*; and so on. Understanding of sequential decoding concepts may begin in the rudimentary-alphabetic phase (Phase 2) and are expanded and solidified during the alphabetic phase of word learning (Phase 3).

In **hierarchical decoding,** more complicated understandings are developed, such as the concept that sometimes letters cue the sounds of other letters, as in certain common spelling patterns. For example, many times when a word—or syllable—ends with an *e*, the vowel preceding it is long, as in "I *made* an attempt to *fade* my jeans in the washing machine, but my mother would always *hide* them because the *price* of *those* jeans was so high she did not want me to *fake* the *fade,* so I had to wear bright ugly jeans on my *date* when I went with *Abe* to get a *Coke* at the *Cave,* the *place* that all our friends go to when we do not have to be *slaves* to our books." The words I have highlighted in this sentence end with *e* and in all cases the vowel preceding it has the sound that we commonly refer to as "long"—or as we sometimes say to students, "it says its own name." You will also notice, though, that the words *machine* and *have* in this sentence do not conform to the rule. Students begin to use hierarchical decoding later in the alphabetic phase.

Instructional Procedures

To gain command of phonological recoding processes, students must have

1. developed phonemic awareness

2. learned letter-sound relationships
3. had practice with blending (Ehri, 1991)

Many ways to expedite phonemic awareness have been recommended above. We will now address procedures for learning letter-sound relationships. This is one primary objective when teachers instruct students in phonic analysis strategies. Being able to divide words into their separate sounds is important to word identification (M. J. Adams, 1990a, 1990b; Stanovich, 1991b; Vellutino & Denckla, 1991; J. P. Williams, 1980).

There have been vigorous disputes about whether illustrating sounds of letters to students *in the context of words,* or whether demonstrating the sounds *in isolation,* best facilitates learning. One approach to teaching letter-sound associations is labeled **implicit phonics instruction,** also called *analytic phonics.* When this method is used, letter sounds are never produced separately. Instead, students are given examples of words in which a targeted sound is heard, with the intent that they gain a sense of this sound from hearing many exemplars. For example, the teacher might say that "The sound of *h* is the one we can hear at the beginning of *house, horse, had,* and *hi,*" often with the targeted sound stressed somewhat when the example words are given. Those who subscribe to this method of presentation maintain that letter sounds should be produced only within the context of words because some sounds are difficult to pronounce in isolation (e.g., *b* is always followed by a vowel sound in an isolated pronunciation). There is concern that the distortion in sound will confuse students when they try to apply the sounds to the decoding of a word.

A different approach is designated as **explicit phonics instruction,** also called *synthetic phonics.* In this type of program, letter sounds are taught initially by the teacher articulating them in isolation and with students practicing them in isolation, as well as in the context of words. For production of those sounds for which a precise segregated pronunciation is difficult, an attempt to minimize the accompanying vowel sound is made by slightly *subvocalizing* (a fancy word for *whispering*) the letter sound and refraining as much as possible from drawing out that pesky vowel that follows along. Many consonant sounds can be pronounced in isolation without that accompanying vowel (for example, *f, h, l, m, n, r, s, t, v, x, z*), and all vowel sounds can be enunciated separately. Those who advocate this procedure for teaching letter sounds contend that illustrating sounds only *within* words does not provide students with information that is definitive enough for them to distinguish the sounds readily and then to be able to use them.

So which is best? We can turn to research for the answer. This research shows that implicit phonics instruction is less productive than explicit instruction, and that with the implicit phonics method, students find it harder to learn the separate sounds and to learn to blend them (M. J. Adams, 1990a, 1990b; R. C. Anderson, Hiebert, Scott, & Wilkinson, 1984; D. D. Johnson & Baumann, 1984). It appears that implicit phonics instruction does not convey phonemic details about letters sufficiently for many students to infer the sounds, and actually can lead to confusions. After a review of the research related to these two dissimilar approaches, M. J. Adams (1990a, 1990b) concluded that the advantages to pronouncing and initially practicing letter sounds in isolation outweigh the disadvantages. These research findings substantiating the superiority of explicit phonics instruction—in which students are taught and practice sounds in isolation—may come as a surprise to some, because at certain periods of time in many teacher-training programs, always teaching sounds in context was recommended.

Some students are able to learn word identification strategies incidentally; for example, even though strategies have not been specifically taught during reading lessons, after fairly extensive reading experiences they infer certain word learning principles themselves, or they learn these concepts from spelling instruction. However, many students require formal instruction to grasp the understandings necessary to apply letter-sound associations and other reading strategies (Mason, 1980). This is especially so with poor readers (Barr & Dreeben, 1983; Juel, 1991). For these students, intentional, precise phonics instruction moves students into and through the alphabetic phase of word learning (Ehri, 1991; Gough & Hillinger, 1980).

What, then, can you do to help students learn to decode letters to sounds? A systematic program for learning sounds, as well as explicit instruction in learning to blend sounds, is often necessary. Much practice is needed to obtain automaticity with these concepts (Juel, 1991).

Although it may be a good idea to introduce letter sounds in isolation, and although it is supportive to provide some practice so that the knowledge of letter sounds can enter into a student's word learning repertoire, exercises on letter sounds should be viewed as helpful but not sufficient. Students must also be given the opportunity to apply these new understandings in the reading of words and to the reading of real text. As with many routines in high-quality instruction, this is not an either-or matter. Systematic instruction in word identification strategies must always be accompanied with abundant opportunities for students to read worthwhile connected material. This, too, furnishes practice opportunities, allowing the student to try out and perfect newly learned perceptions about print reading strategies. Balancing word identification strategy instruction with reading in meaningful text leads to accelerated progress in unskilled readers (M. J. Adams, 1990a, 1990b).

Also, the value of writing experiences must not be forgotten. The influences of these opportunities were enumerated rather carefully in Chapter 9, when dealing with the topic of word recognition. These, too, apply here. Providing occasions for writing in daily lessons hastens students' control of word identification strategies in a number of ways, including helping to cultivate and strengthen consciousness of letter-sound patterns (M. J. Adams, 1990a, 1990b). Use of invented spellings and/or conventional spellings provides an assist with phonological recoding abilities. The reverse is also true. Learning more about reading supports spelling and writing. With more practice in reading, students begin to unconsciously note standard letter systems, for instance, that *e* comes at the ends of many English words even though it is not heard; that a *u* always comes after a *q*; that certain letter combinations are rarely used—for example, *sf* or *dl* (Nagy, Osborn, Winsor, & O'Flahavan, 1992).

Some specific practice activities are suggested below, exercises that should be incorporated into lessons that also include reading authentic texts and writing.

Consonants.   Consonant sounds are introduced before vowel sounds in most programs because consonants provide the framework of words. Try to read this sentence.

W_   h__rd   h_r   wh_n   sh_   y_ll_d   _t   h_r   br_th_r.

Although there are no vowels given, you were probably able to determine easily that the sentence says "We heard her when she yelled at her brother." Now try this one.

_e_ _   _ou_   _i_e_   _a_ _   _ _e   _i_e_.

Consonants provide important graphophonic clues to words, while vowels and their sounds provide relatively little assistance, as just demonstrated. If you were unable to read the second sentence, try the same one now, when you may use the consonant sounds instead.

H_lp   y_ _r   s_st_r   w_sh   th_   d_sh_s.

Using consonant clues makes it easy to determine that this sentence says "Help your sister wash the dishes."

When teaching consonant sounds, one must consider the issue of what to do about multiple sounds that certain consonants stand for—for example, the *c* sound is sometimes designated as "hard," as in *call* and other times is "soft" as in *city*. The sound for *g* can also be hard (*got*) or soft (*gem*). Both sounds of these two consonants occur often enough that some attention to each is relatively profitable. It appears that the best course of action in presenting these is to teach one of the alternatives, for instance the hard sound, and when the student has reasonable familiarity with it, then to acquaint the student with the other option, the soft sound. Teaching both at the same time has the potential to perplex learners, but if too long a delay elapses before the introduction of the second sound, then the first may have become so firmly established that it causes difficulties for students to add another sound for the same letter (Beck & McCaslin, 1978).

Many published activities, games, booklets, manipulatives, kits, audiovisuals, and other materials are available to help students recognize, practice, and internalize consonant sounds. A sampling of these is found in Teachers' Store F, along with materials suitable for use when students are rehearsing other word identification strategies.

Teachers also like to devise their own activities for teaching phonic analysis skills. Here are some for providing practice with consonants.

1. *Composing alliterations. Alliteration* occurs when all words or most of the words in a phrase or sentence begin with the same letter (for example, *Tiny Tommy tied two toads together*). As a first step, alliterative sentences may be read to the students, asking them to identify the consonant sound heard at the beginning of each word. Next, students are asked to compose their own alliterations. Older students, as well as younger, seem to think work with alliterations is fun. This task gives practice with consonant sounds in such a way that it is not viewed as "babyish" by more mature students. If students produce the alliterative sentences orally, they should then be written by the student or by the teacher. To make the best use of any phonic analysis activities, some part of the exercise should always deal with *written* words or letters (Stahl, 1992).

2. *Using a Language Master.* A Language Master (Bell & Howell) may be used to practice consonant sounds. (See Chapter 9 for a description of this mechanical device, which allows the recording and playback of information.) The teacher orally records statements on each of several cards, such as "On your paper, print the letter for the sound you hear at the beginning of *pumpkin*" and "Print the letter for the sound you hear at the beginning of *magic*." The teacher prints the correct letter on the back of each card.

   The students are given a pack of these cards and do the following: they sit at the Language Master, run the first card through the machine to hear the teacher's directions, print their responses on a piece of notebook paper, remove the card from the machine, and self-check their answers by turning the card over to see the answer the teacher has printed there.

3. *Self-correcting matching games.* Collect small boxes (some teachers use plastic margarine containers). On the outside of each, print a different single consonant sound with a felt-tip pen. On a large index card, paste four small pictures, each beginning with the same sound (old workbooks are a good source of small

Teachers' Store F

Word Identification Strategies

1. *Consonant Soup Cans* (Gamco)
2. *Group Word Teaching Game* (Garrard)
3. *Corrective Reading* (Science Research Associates)
4. *Rainbow Word Builders* (Kenworthy)
5. *Jumbo Phonics Cassette Program* (EBSCO)
6. *Phonic Rummy Card Games* (Kenworthy)
7. *Building Words* (Lakeshore Curriculum Materials)
8. *Programmed Phonics, Books 1 and 2* (Educators Publishing Service)
9. *Lessons in Vowel and Consonant Sounds* (Curriculum Associates)
10. *Individualized Reading Skills Program* (Science Research Associates)
11. *Sounds, Words, and Meanings* (Steck-Vaughn)
12. *Creature Teachers* (Bowmar/Noble)
13. *Language Lollipop* (Kids & Co.)
14. *Go Fish* (Remedial Education Press)
15. *Sound and Symbol Puzzles* (Developmental Learning Materials)
16. *Blank Gameboards* (Developmental Learning Materials)
17. *The College Reading Skills Series* (Jamestown)—the *Olive* set of this series is written at sixth-through eighth-grade reading levels and is suitable for use with high school students.
18. *Turn and Read* (Childcraft)
19. *Doghouse Game* (Kenworthy)
20. *Blend and Build* (Robert Rosche)
21. *Consonant Flip Book* (Developmental Learning Materials)
22. *Game Tree Kits* (Xerox)
23. *Reading Spectrum: Word Analysis* (Macmillan)
24. *HITS* (High Interest Teaching System)
25. *Sound Phonics* (Borg-Warner)
26. *Learning with Laughter* (Prentice-Hall)
27. *A Word Recognition Program* (Barnell Loft)
28. *System 80* (Borg-Warner)
29. *Help Your Child Learn Phonics: Consonants* (Frank Schaffer)
30. *Whatchamacallit* (Gamco)
31. The filmstrip "Suffixes" in the set, *What's the Word*, from the Reading-for-Meaning Series (Houghton Mifflin)
32. *Tutorgrams* (Gamco)
33. *The Frank Schaffer Gameboards* (Frank Schaffer)

pictures). Make a card with four pictures for *every* consonant sound you wish the students to practice. Turn each index card over and draw a simple picture on the back; the picture should be different on each card and should cover most of the back of the card. Now turn the cards back over and cut the cards into four parts so each picture is separate. (See Figure 10–3.)

Mix up all the pictures from all the cards and have the students sort the pictures according to the consonant with which each one begins. Then they should place each one in the container labeled with that consonant.

Students can check their work by taking the sorted cards from the container, turning them over, and arranging them to form the picture drawn by the teacher. Mistakes are immediately apparent because the picture will not make sense if incorrect letters and sounds are mixed together.

4. *Playing Guess and Poke.* Prepare flashcard-sized pieces of oaktag. Each card should have a small picture pasted or drawn at the top. Below the picture, make three holes with a hole punch. Print a consonant letter above each hole. (See Figure 10–4.) On the back, draw a red star around the hole of the correct answer.

Students are given a pile of cards prepared in this way, plus a knitting needle (or pencil or similar object). They pick up the first card, look at the picture, decide on the consonant with which it begins, and poke the knitting needle through the hole labeled with that consonant. Without removing the knitting needle, they turn the card over. If the knitting needle is through the hole with the star, the answer is correct. They continue in this manner with each card in the pack.

FIGURE 10-3
Materials for a self-correcting matching game

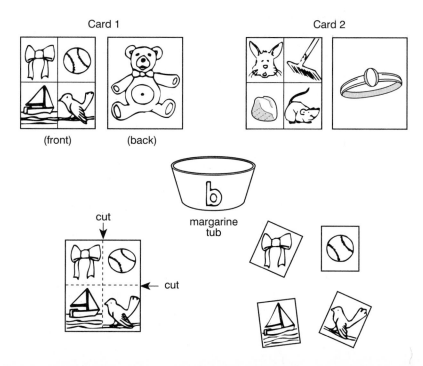

FIGURE 10-4
An example of a card used in Guess and Poke

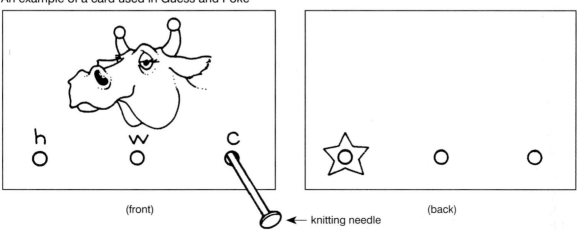

(front)   ← knitting needle   (back)

Short Vowel Sounds. The "short" vowel sounds are represented in the following words:

$$\breve{a} \ (at), \ \breve{e} \ (egg), \ \breve{i} \ (it), \ \breve{o} \ (on), \text{ and } \breve{u} \ (up).$$

Many programs introduce short vowel sounds before long vowels because the short sounds occur somewhat more frequently in words found in beginning reading materials. Knowing these allows students to combine what they have learned about consonants to read many words that appear in simple texts. In fact, since words cannot be read without vowel sounds (all words have at least one vowel), frequently a short vowel or two is introduced at the same time consonant sounds are being learned. In any case, most programs teach short vowels early in the instructional sequence (M. J. Adams, 1990a, 1990b).

Students often have difficulty learning short vowel sounds, although they may have learned consonant sounds more quickly. Much and varied practice, therefore, may be needed to facilitate learning of these sounds.

1. *Practicing vowel sounds in connected text reading.* It is important to choose the right words for practice. In connected text reading, words with varied patterns are encountered, and students will come across words that contain sounds and patterns that they have not yet learned. However, certain books will have more words that can be decoded with the sounds a student has presently learned. For example, some of the Dr. Seuss books such as *Hop on Pop,* would allow a reader who was practicing consonant and short vowel sounds to apply his or her budding knowledge.

2. *Direct-practice activities.* In direct-practice activities in a lesson, in addition to rehearsal of sound-letter associations alone, the associations should also be incorporated into words to give students practice in applying the targeted sounds in ways that will facilitate transfer to real text reading. This, in addition, furnishes occasions to engage in that difficult but important skill of blending separate sounds to form words. Modeling the latter skill is vital so that students are supported in this complex act.

Research shows that working with onsets and rimes provides much important assistance in word identification.

Onsets and Rimes.   Onsets and rimes are parts of syllables. The *onset* is the part of the syllable that comes before the vowel (in the one-syllable word *chat*, the *ch* is the "onset"). The *rime* is the remainder of the syllable (in *chat*, the *at* is the rime).

Helping students recognize and practice reading words using onsets and rimes is increasingly viewed as important (M. J. Adams, 1990a, 1990b; Nagy et al., 1992). When students have some experience with a rime, they can figure out other words that end with the same combination. For example, if they have had sufficient exposures to the words *got, hot, not,* and *pot*—and have been shown the connections among these (the rime *ot*)—they may be able to determine on their own, by analogy, the words *cot, dot, lot,* and *rot*. Students can also make analogies between beginning parts of words that are similar, but research has shown that making analogies between ending word parts (such as rimes) is easier for youngsters to make and occurs sooner in the developmental word learning sequence (Goswami, 1986). Having control over a number of rimes helps students quickly expand their repertoires of reading vocabulary (Willows, Borwick, & Hayvren, 1981).

Teachers actually have had students work with onsets and rimes for some time, but they have called rimes, **phonograms.**[1] (Phonograms are also sometimes called "word families.") They have had students practice adding consonants (or consonant clusters or consonant digraphs) to the phonograms, calling the process of adding these onsets, **consonant substitution.** The word families commonly used in this type of practice are word parts of two or three letters that appear in many different English words. For example, the phonogram (or rime) *-ill* appears in *fill, hill, pill, will,* and *chill.* Phonograms are quite regular from word to word and large numbers of words can be

---

[1]The word *phonogram* is pronounced so that the first *o* is long.

formed from the same phonogram; both of these factors make the learning of phonograms a significant objective (M. J. Adams, 1990a, 1990b).

Figure 10–5 lists some common phonograms, plus several words containing each. This information can be helpful when teachers are preparing practice activities.

Learning phonograms should involve using them in whole words, but substituting the initial portion of the word. For example, if students know the words *sat* and *hat,* and also know consonant sounds, they can be taken through the following steps:

1. The student reads the known word *sat.*

FIGURE 10–5
Phonograms that occur frequently in common words

-at	hall	*-in*	test	*-ore*	bran	drew	top
bat	mall	fin	vest	bore	clan	flew	crop
cat	tall	pin	west	core	plan	grew	drop
fat	wall	sin	zest	more	scan		flop
hat	small	tin	crest	pore	than	*-ick*	stop
mat	stall	win	chest	sore		kick	chop
pat		grin		tore	*-ay*	lick	shop
rat		skin	*-ell*	wore	bay	pick	
sat	*-ing*	spin	bell	score	day	quick	*-oke*
vat	king	chin	cell	snore	gay	sick	coke
brat	ring	shin	fell	store	hay	tick	joke
flat	sing	thin	sell	swore	lay	brick	poke
scat	wing		tell	chore	may	click	woke
slat	bring		well	shore	pay	slick	broke
spat	cling	*-ap*	yell		ray	stick	smoke
splat	fling	cap	dwell	*-ink*	say	trick	spoke
chat	sling	gap	smell	link	way	chick	stroke
that	spring	lap	spell	mink	clay	thick	choke
	sting	map	swell	pink	gray		
	string	nap	shell	rink	play	*-im*	*-ug*
-ed	swing	rap		sink	pray	dim	bug
bed	thing	tap	*-ear*	wink	slay	him	dug
fed		clap	dear	blink	spray	rim	hug
led	*-et*	flap	fear	drink	stay	brim	jug
red	bet	scrap	gear	stink	stray	grim	mug
wed	get	slap	hear	think	sway	skim	rug
bled	jet	snap	near		tray	slim	tug
fled	let	strap	rear	*-an*		swim	drug
sled	met	trap	year	can	*-ew*	trim	plug
sped	net	chap	clear	fan	dew		
shed	pet		smear	man	few	*-op*	*-ip*
	set	*-est*	spear	pan	mew	cop	dip
-all	vet	best		ran	new	hop	hip
ball	wet	nest		tan	blew	mop	lip
call	yet	pest		van	crew	pop	nip
fall		rest					

FIGURE 10–5   *(Continued)*

rip	fill	rot	crate	*-ide*	*-ock*	*-old*	*-ave*
sip	hill	plot	plate	hide	dock	bold	cave
tip	kill	slot	skate	ride	hock	cold	gave
zip	mill	spot	slate	side	lock	fold	pave
clip	pill	trot	state	tide	rock	gold	rave
drip	will	shot		wide	sock	hold	save
flip	drill		*-ent*	bride	block	mold	wave
grip	grill	*-ice*	bent	glide	clock	sold	brave
skip	skill	dice	cent	pride	flock	told	grave
slip	spill	lice	dent	slide	stock	scold	slave
strip	still	mice	lent		shock		shave
chip	chill	nice	rent	*-ight*		*-ash*	
ship		rice	sent	fight	*-ank*	cash	*-ab*
whip	*-it*	price	tent	light	bank	dash	cab
	bit	slice	vent	might	rank	hash	dab
-ake	fit	spice	went	night	sank	mash	jab
bake	hit	twice	spent	right	tank	rash	lab
cake	kit			sight	blank	crash	tab
fake	pit	*-ob*	*-ack*	tight	crank	flash	blab
lake	quit	bob	back	bright	drank	slash	crab
make	sit	cob	hack	flight	prank	smash	drab
quake	wit	job	lack	fright	spank	splash	flab
rake	grit	mob	pack		thank	trash	grab
sake	skit	rob	quack	*-eam*			scab
take	slit	sob	rack	beam	*-ade*	*-ace*	slab
wake	spit	blob	sack	seam	fade	face	stab
brake		slob	tack	team	jade	lace	
flake	*-ot*	snob	black	cream	made	pace	
snake	cot		crack	dream	wade	race	
stake	dot	*-ate*	smack	gleam	blade	brace	
shake	got	date	snack	scream	grade	grace	
	hot	gate	stack	steam	spade	place	
-ill	lot	hate	track	stream	trade	space	
bill	not	late	shack		shade	trace	
dill	pot	mate					

2. The student is asked to change the *s* to *h*, and read the known word *hat*.
3. The teacher points out that words ending with the same group of letters—such as *-at* in these two words—usually rhyme, and this can be a clue to identifying unknown words.
4. The student is asked to change *h* in *hat* to *r*, to think of the sound for *r*, and to combine it with the sounds for *-at* heard in the two words already known (*sat* and *hat*) to determine the unknown word *rat*. Teacher modeling of this process is often advantageous, and necessary, when the principle is initially being learned.

5. Several initial consonants are substituted for one another to make various words (*bat, fat, mat, cat, pat,* and so on).

Here are three additional activities for phonogram presentation and practice.

1. *Phonogram tic-tac-toe.* Make many small tic-tac-toe boards from oaktag. Each board should feature a different phonogram. Laminate the boards. Give the two students who will play each game different-colored washable marking pens. Student A thinks of a word that includes the phonogram and writes in the appropriate consonant to form the word using a green (for instance) marking pen. Student B makes another word by writing in the initial portion of a word with a blue marking pen, and so on. When there are three words in the same color in a row, that student wins.

  (Since the boards have been laminated and washable pens have been used, after the game they can be wiped off so that other students may use them.)

2. *Create a crazy story.* Give students a story that has several words containing phonograms. Underline these. Tell the students to make a "crazy" story by changing the first part of the underlined words to another letter or letters. Then they can illustrate their new and crazy version. (Since drawing pictures contributes nothing to learning to read, preparing illustrations to accompany reading activities is always best assigned as a "fun" homework activity. Students can return with their pictures the next day and they can be displayed on a classroom bulletin board.) (See Figure 10–6.)

3. *Play with hink pinks.* Cunningham (1991) suggests use of phonograms (rimes) with varied consonants (onsets) to make silly but meaningful descriptions.

FIGURE 10–6
Imaginative activities giving students opportunities to practice consonant substitution in an enjoyable way

Make a Crazy Story

Mary went for a walk with her ᵇc̶at. They sat in the park for awhile and played with a little red ʷb̶all. Mary decided to go to the hotdog ᵇs̶tand and bring back something for her ᵇc̶at to eat.

Going for a walk with her bat.

Girl and bat playing with a small red wall.

A hotdog band.

Each combination of two words must end with the same phonogram. Here are some examples to start students on their own hink pinks:

fat cat   quick lick   hot pot   back pack
red bed   nice mice   best nest   tan man
top cop   fake cake   mob job   light fight
mash hash   king ring   pay day   joke poke
bug hug   late date   pace race   jet set
pet net   near year   bent cent   new dew

Be certain that students write these words or that you write them for the students to see so they attend to the rimes in written form. When they are viewing the words, the teacher should ask the learner to tell the phonogram they see in both words, underlining that word part to emphasize it.

Cunningham had her students make up riddles about their hink pinks ("What do you get when it rains on your dog?" A wet pet) and also to illustrate them.

Consonant Clusters and Consonant Digraphs.   A *consonant cluster* (sometimes called a *blend*) is two or more consonant letters that commonly appear together, but even when in this combination, each retains its own sound. It is not uncommon for learners to be challenged when they must hear separate sounds in clusters and blend these with subsequent word parts: many have a tendency to invert the sequence of the letters—for example, attempting to pronounce *splash* as *slpash*. Guided practice may be required. Some common clusters are listed in Figure 10–7.

A *consonant digraph* is two consonant letters that commonly appear together, but do not retain their own individual sounds. For example, in the consonant digraph *sh* (as found at the beginning of *ship*), neither the usual sound of *s* nor the usual sound of *h* is heard; rather, the sound that corresponds to these two letters when they appear in combination is an entirely different sound. Some common digraphs are listed in Figure 10–7.

FIGURE 10–7
Some common consonant clusters and consonant digraphs

Consonant Clusters					
bl-	(*blond*)	gr-	(*great*)	sp-	(*spit*)
br-	(*brain*)	pl-	(*plate*)	spl-	(*splash*)
cl-	(*clock*)	pr-	(*practice*)	spr-	(*sprain*)
cr-	(*crown*)	sc-	(*scat*)	squ-	(*squirrel*)
dr-	(*drum*)	scr-	(*scram*)	st-	(*step*)
dw-	(*dwarf*)	sk-	(*skate*)	str-	(*straight*)
fl-	(*flower*)	sl-	(*slide*)	sw-	(*swim*)
fr-	(*from*)	sm-	(*small*)	tr-	(*train*)
gl-	(*glad*)	sn-	(*snail*)	tw-	(*twin*)

Consonant Digraphs					
ch-	(*chair*)	gh-	(*rough*)	th-	(unvoiced *path*) (voiced *this*)
sh-	(*shoot*)	ph-	(*phone*)	wh-	(*wheel*)

If students can now decode simple words using consonants and short vowel sounds, their prowess will be expanded when they are able to associate consonant clusters and consonant digraph sounds with those corresponding letters. For example, if they can decode *cat*, this additional knowledge will enable *scat* to be read—and the sentence *Scat, cat!* If they can read *win*, they will now be able to decode *thin*, and so on. Consonant clusters and consonant digraphs can also be applied to phonograms to further increase the number of words that may be decoded. For example, if the student knows the phonogram *-ick* and the sounds of individual consonants, then he or she can read *kick, lick, pick, sick, tick*; and when there is familiarity with consonant clusters, then *brick, click, slick, stick,* and *trick* may be recognized; when the consonant digraphs are known, then *chick* and *thick* may be determined.

Teaching activities suggested for working with consonant sounds may also be used by students when they are learning consonant clusters and consonant digraphs. In addition, here are several other ideas.

1.   *Word sorts.* Use word sorts to call attention to blends and digraphs during the introductory phases of learning these letter combinations. Give students a pack of cards in which words beginning with single consonant sounds are intermixed randomly with words beginning with clusters and digraphs. If, for example, the digraphs *ch* and *sh* have been introduced, students may be given the following packs of words to sort.

Pack 1: champ, can, chick, cat, cap, cut, chip, can't, chat
Pack 2: ship, shed, shot, sat, sick, shack, sink, sell

Have students sort cards into piles according to the beginning feature of the words (in other words, according to whether they begin with a single consonant or a cluster or digraph). Next, have students pronounce each word to the teacher and use each one orally in a sentence.

2.   *Group-response activity.* The teacher prints consonant clusters or digraphs on flashcards, with a different one on each. A line is drawn after the cluster/digraph to indicate that a word is to be filled in. On the back of each card, the teacher writes several statements, each of which describes a word beginning with the cluster/digraph on the front side. For example, for the *str-* cluster card, some statements on the back might be:

She wore braces; now her teeth are _____.

He is not weak, he is _____.

A zebra has black and white _____.

To carry out the activity, the teacher chooses one cluster/digraph card, holds it up so the front side showing only the targeted letters is seen by the students, reads statements from the back side, and the students call out a word that is a response to each statement and that begins with the appropriate cluster or digraph. After each word is guessed, the teacher quickly writes the word on the board, underlining the cluster or the digraph, so students can see the sound within a written word.

Long Vowel Sounds.   Long vowel sounds are those represented in the following words:

$$\bar{a} \ (ate), \ \bar{e} \ (eat), \ \bar{\imath} \ (ice), \ \bar{o} \ (oat), \text{ and } \bar{u} \ (use).$$

Because vowels are essential to words and syllables, they must be learned, just as the more easily distinguishable consonants and consonant combinations must be. Fortunately, students seem to find it easier to learn long vowel sounds than to learn the short sounds of vowels, probably because the sound that each long vowel represents is the same as the letter name. Learning these will continue to extend the numbers of words the student can read through phonological recoding processes, since long vowels as well as short vowels occur in high-frequency words (M. J. Adams, 1990a, 1990b).

Suggestions for working with short vowel sounds apply here as well: introduction and direct practice in isolation are perfectly acceptable, but long vowel sounds should also be practiced in words, with accompanying assists with blending. The Elkonin boxes suggested earlier for phonemic awareness training can be used for blending practice during this phase as well.

And, of course, experiences in applying the new knowledge while reading in real books are vital. By this time, the students should be able to read many more words, so the possibilities for appropriate books will have multiplied.

Writing activities should, by this point, supply generous opportunities to help students clarify the many letter-sound associations they are now making. Writing should be a part of the learning and reinforcement program.

Many of the materials listed in Teachers' Store F are also serviceable for working with both short and long vowel sounds.

R-Controlled Vowels.   Some students who have experienced a dabbling of phonics instruction but who have not had a systematic program seem to think that vowel sounds are either long or short. Actually there are other sounds as well.

When a vowel is followed by an r, often the sound is neither long nor short, but instead results in a special sound called an **r-controlled vowel.** R-controlled vowel sounds are those represented in the following words: *ar* (*star*), *er* (*cover*), *ir* (*circus*), *or* (*for*), and *ur* (*fur*). Note that the *er, ir,* and *ur* sounds are the same.

One reason vowel-sound concepts are hard to learn is that the same letters have so many variations in sounds. And conversely, the same sounds can be represented by so many letters. For example, the *e* in *bead* is long, but the *e* in *bread* is short, although they both are part of the letter pattern *ea*. Or, as another example, the short *a* sound is represented by a single *a* in *had*, by *au* in *laugh*, and by *ai* in *plaid*.

R-controlled vowel sounds, on the other hand, are comparatively regular. In studies to determine how often words encountered in reading materials actually conform to the rules that students are taught about sounds, three separate investigations found that in a large percentage of words, the sound heard is the one conventionally taught for each r-controlled vowel. Clymer (1963) found that for primary material, in 78% of the words that contained a vowel followed by an r, the "regular" r-controlled sound was heard; M. H. Bailey's (1967) investigation of reading material through sixth grade found 86% of the words with r-controlled vowels to be regular, and Emans (1967), in a study of words selected from *The Teacher's Word Book of 30,000 Words* (Thorndike & Lorge, 1944), found that there was 82% regularity for r-controlled vowels in these words.

1.   *Reading stories incorporating the patterns taught.* One suggested activity for helping students become familiar with r-controlled vowels is to prepare stories with many words containing these vowels. Have students circle all the words containing r-controlled vowels and then read the story silently using the r-controlled sounds to aid in identification of the words. When students have completed these

activities independently, they should be asked to read the story to the teacher. Here is an example of a teacher-prepared story containing many words with r-controlled vowel sounds.

The worn-out old witch stirred the ugly mess in her old pot. "Heh, heh, heh," she laughed horribly. "I need just one more ingredient, and it must be a living creature!" I shivered as I sat behind a large bush watching her. Then suddenly she pointed her wrinkled finger in my direction. I was stiff with fright. She came closer . . . but she pulled a half-dead bird from off a branch of that bush and dropped it into the boiling pot. I was shocked and wanted to help the poor bird. But just then I was surprised to see the witch's black-furred cat spring up and pull the bird from the pot. I was glad to see that the bird was still alive. The bird flew off through the forest. The cat ran off through the field. And I fell out of bed.

2. *A matching activity.* Another r-controlled activity has students complete words with r-controlled vowels. The teacher prepares strips with sentences that include a word that is to be completed with an r-controlled vowel. The teacher then punches holes in the strip and attaches them with paper fasteners onto colored posterboard. (See Figure 10–8.)

To the left of each strip, punch another hole and put in another paper fastener; attach a length of colored yarn to each of the fasteners at the left. On the right side of the posterboard, list r-controlled vowels with a paper fastener in front of each. The student is to read each sentence, then attach the yarn to the paper fastener by the r-controlled vowel that would complete the word.

Since the sentence strips are attached with paper fasteners, one set may be removed and others placed there after all students have had an opportunity to participate.

FIGURE 10–8
An example of teacher-prepared materials for an activity to help students distinguish among r-controlled vowels

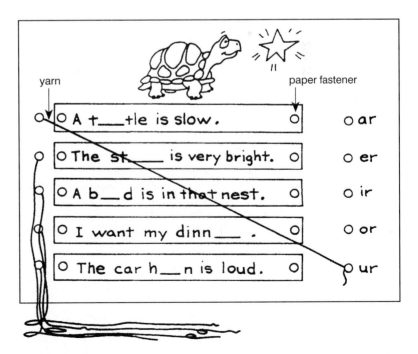

Special Vowel Combinations.   In reading programs of the past, students were often required to practice and learn many different diphthongs and vowel digraphs. A **diph-thong** is a vowel combination that begins with one sound and moves to another sound in the same syllable, such as *oy* in *toy*.[2]

Some vowel diphthongs[3] and digraphs taught in programs of the past are not included in most programs today because research has shown that many of these occur infrequently and/or have many exceptions to the rules about their sounds (e.g., Clymer, 1963). Today, diphthongs and digraphs usually are not even taught as separate categories. Instead, a small group of these, which do occur fairly frequently and have fewer exceptions, is selected for teaching and given the generic label *special vowel combinations*. Studies by M. H. Bailey (1971) and others indicate that these special vowel combinations are important to teach: *au* (*caught*), *aw* (*raw*), *oi* (*boil*), *oy* (*toy*), *oo* (*cool*), *oo* (*foot*), *ou* (*out*), and *ow* (*cow*) or *ow* (*snow*).

One set of commercial materials that may be used to practice these sound-symbol correspondences is the duplicating-master booklet titled *Special Vowels* (Frank Schaffer). Each lesson is illustrated with charming cartoonlike drawings; practice is provided for special vowel combinations plus r-controlled vowels.

Phonic Generalizations.   When students have comprehended a sufficient number of principles of sequential decoding, the more complex generalizations of hierarchical decoding can be presented. With this approach, students are helped to recognize the circumstances in which certain letter sounds often occur. Learning these generalizations can acquaint readers with common spelling patterns found in English words, and we have already seen that this is an important assist to reading. However, in addition to calling attention to the generalizations, it is important to provide opportunities to read many words that conform to the generalizations so that the patterns can be internalized rather than memorized.

Large numbers of these generalizations involve "vowel rules." Some commonly taught generalizations are the following:

1. When one vowel is between two consonants, that vowel is short, as in *cat*.
2. When there are two vowels side by side, the long sound is heard for the first and the second is silent, as in *mean*.
3. When a word ends with an *e*, the *e* is silent and the vowel preceding it is long, as in *make*.

Here are some other rules that are sometimes taught:

4. In the special vowel combination *ie*, the *i* is silent and the *e* is long, as in *shield*.
5. When the letter *g* is followed by *i* or *e*, it sounds like /j/, as in *gin*.
6. In a multisyllabic word containing the letter *v*, the *v* stays with the preceding vowel to form a syllable, as in *riv/er*.
7. When *a* is preceded by *w* it has the schwa sound, as in *was*. (The schwa sound is represented in dictionaries by an upside down *e*, and is pronounced like a short *u* sound regardless of the vowel it depicts.)

---

[2]Vowel digraphs are formed like consonant digraphs: they are pairs of vowels representing a single sound, such as *ea* in *heat*.

[3]Teachers sometimes mispronounce the word *diphthong*. Notice the consonant digraph *ph* in this word. As you know, *ph* represents the /f/ sound—as in *phone*. Therefore, the word is pronounced /dif'thong/.

8. When *w* is preceded by *e,* the sound is the same as that represented by the special vowel combination *oo* in *shoot,* as in *few.*

As can be seen, many of these rules are cumbersome, and, as might be expected, students often have difficulty learning them.

Even when only a few of these generalizations are taught, although students may be able to repeat the rules to the teacher, they may not apply them unless (a) teachers prompt them to do so (e.g., the student has difficulty with the word *held* and the teacher says,"Look, there is one vowel between two consonants, so what sound would the vowel make?") or (b) students are given a specific practice activity that stresses the relevant generalization (e.g., directions on a worksheet might say, "When a word ends with an *e,* the vowel in the middle of that word is usually long. Mark all the vowels that are long"). When reading independently in regular, connected materials, students may not stop to consciously apply a phonic generalization if they cannot identify a word.

Another obstacle to teaching vowel rules is that many English words are exceptions. For example, note these exceptions to the rules just listed:

Rule 1: told	Rule 5: get
Rule 2: bread	Rule 6: over
Rule 3: gone	Rule 7: way
Rule 4: friend	Rule 8: sew

Several researchers have investigated the usefulness of the phonic generalizations often taught in primary and intermediate reading programs. They have found that many phonics rules have so many exceptions that they have low utility. Clymer (1963), for example, found only 45% utility for the generalization that "when two vowels are side by side the first is long and the second is silent." That is, 55% of the words in the four widely used primary reading programs he examined were exceptions to this rule. Another way to say this is that in more than half the attempts by a student to apply this rule to an unknown word, the rule would not work! When M. H. Bailey (1967) applied the same vowel rule to words found in eight basal reader series through grade 6, only 34% utility was found. In short, some of the rules taught in primary reading programs are even less useful when applied to more difficult words found in higher-level reading selections. The percent of utility found in Bailey's study for the commonly taught rules listed earlier in this discussion were the following: Rule 1, 71%; Rule 2, 34%; and Rule 3, 57%. Further, of the 45 generalizations taught in major reading programs and examined by Bailey, only 27 were useful at least 75% of the time.

The preceding discussion indicates that some phonics generalizations may be comparatively useful, while others are not very helpful in identifying unknown words. Although it is important for students to internalize the spelling patterns of words and while practice with some phonic generalizations may be a useful interim step to assist with these understandings (Stahl, 1992), many exposures to common word patterns appear to also be productive for this purpose. Therefore, students should be given much experience with many words containing those patterns so that they may inductively form generalizations about them. Furthermore, practice with onsets and rimes may add much to grasping these concepts and may be easier for students than learning many phonic rules (M. J. Adams, 1990a, 1990b). The human brain appears to have greater facility for detecting patterns than for applying rules (Cunningham, 1992).

Stahl (1992) suggests these rules of thumb for presenting phonic generalizations:

1. Point out generalizations to emphasize specific spelling patterns, but do not require students to memorize the rules.
2. Be certain that learners understand that these generalizations may help in identifying a word sometimes, but that there are exceptions. (This is the reason the qualifier "usually" is employed when reciting these rules—"When a vowel is between two consonants, the vowel is *usually* short.")
3. Highlight only those generalizations that have comparatively high utility.

Some Final Notes.   Many myths have been built up around phonics instruction. Don't fall prey to these. One myth is that learners can become skilled readers by direct-practice activities in phonic instruction alone. Remember that even when students are studying phonic analysis skills, the emphasis should be on the total context of reading. Not only should students have many opportunities to read in authentic texts, when practicing letter sounds and pronunciations of words that include these sounds, students should have opportunities to read the words in contextual material (M. J. Adams, 1990a, 1990b). For example, in a session in which consonant substitution and work with the phonograms *-ake* and *-ill* have provided practice in identifying the words *bake, cake, make, take,* and *shake,* and *fill, will, spill,* and *still,* the lesson might conclude by having the student read a short passage the teacher has written, such as

> Jason has a birthday today, so his mother will bake him a big cake. She is going to fill a cup with milk and add it to some eggs and flour. Then she will take some salt and shake it in. She hopes she won't spill the sugar like she did last time. Sometimes the cakes she makes look funny, but they still taste good!

A second myth is that instructional programs that teach students decoding and the whole language programs enjoying popularity today are the antithesis of each other. This is not true and, indeed, most up-to-date whole language approaches do recognize and teach phonemic awareness, the alphabetic principle, and phonological recoding skills (e.g., see Freppon & Dahl, 1991; Holdaway, 1979). Often these skills are treated through writing, rather than reading activities, but increasingly it is being recognized in current whole language procedures that some students, especially low-skill readers, need direct instruction with phonics concepts in their reading lessons as well (e.g., see Spiegel, 1992; Winsor & Pearson, 1992).

It also should be noted that there are some myths about phonics instruction with middle school and high school students that should be avoided. When older students have severe difficulties with word identification, sometimes it has been said that "if they haven't learned phonic analysis strategies by now, they never will." This, fortunately, is not the case. If mature students are seriously inept at phonic analysis, this may mean that they need phonemic awareness training to facilitate their abilities to learn and apply these strategies. It also may mean they have not had a program that has provided *explicit, systematic* instruction and sufficient practice with these principles.

There is also the misconception that instruction with phonics is only for the brighter student. Again, research contradicts this belief. Studies show that slow learners find phonics instruction as advantageous as do other students (M. J. Adams, 1990a, 1990b; Bateman, 1979; Chall, 1967).

Finally, the last myth: reading professionals should recognize that phonics is not, nor should it be, considered "the method" for teaching reading. Rather, phonics is one of several cuing systems available to the reader to assist in identifying unknown words.

A RETURN TO DAN'S CASE STUDY

In Chapter 9, we examined a reading program for Dan, who, when he entered the special reading program, appeared to be operating in the rudimentary-alphabetic phase of word learning. After 5 weeks of individualized instruction, he had progressed to the point where it was believed that he was entering the alphabetic phase.

To promote his breakthrough into that critical phase, explicit teaching of letter sounds that Dan had not learned incidentally through his previous reading and writing activities was now included in his lessons. The sequence for introduction of letter-sound associations discussed above was used, as well as many of the practice activities that were described. He was taught letter sounds explicitly and given direct practice in blending these into words. A good deal of attention also was given to applications with onsets and rimes, helping him to compare patterns to words he already knew. He was also given some experiences with a few useful phonic generalizations.

In addition to the specific phonic analysis practice, writing projects were still used to increase Dan's attention to internal features and order of letters in words. Zutell and Rasinski (1989) showed that spelling variables are significantly related to students' word reading accuracy and fluency. In Dan's writing, his invented spellings were considered acceptable, but more attention to correct spellings began to be emphasized. The teacher planned to assist with conventional spelling of several words in each of Dan's stories. The words chosen had spellings that were consistent with the letter sounds Dan was focusing on in his direct practice lessons.

However, after a few days of teacher prompting, Dan began to initiate some of these procedures himself. He would pause and thoughtfully consider the letters to write for some of these words. This is not to say that all spellings were correct; they were not. But his stories began to exhibit a healthy mix of conventional spelling along with some invented spellings, partly because of teacher reminders of sounds he now knew and partly because of Dan's seeming pleasure in gaining control of these understandings. Furthermore, even words that were spelled incorrectly began to reflect his growing awareness of orthographic conventions as he advanced to higher stages of spelling development. Direct practice in sounding out words, experiences with onsets and rimes, and writing and spelling practice all contribute to awareness of common patterns in words (Stahl, 1992).

An exercise that complemented both his reading and writing activities is one designed by Cunningham and Cunningham (1992). They call this activity "Making Words." After Dan had some experiences with letter-sound relationships, the teacher used the "Making Words" practice with him about once a week. To prepare for the word-making exercise, the teacher decided on a word of several letters (perhaps five or six), and then determined other smaller words that could be formed from the letters of this word.

For example when *plates* was the word for the day, other constituent words were *pets, pat, pest, late, pleat, pale, at, ate, last*. Dan was given magnetic letters for each of the letters in the long word in a random order. He arranged these on a cookie sheet in response to the teacher's directions. For example, the teacher might say "Spell the word *at.*" Then, "What letter would you add to that word to make it *ate*? Now, add a letter to make the word *late*. Which of your letters would you use to spell *pets*? How can you rearrange the letters of that word to spell *pest*?" And so on. Generally the progression was to build up words from short ones to the longest one. These maneuvers helped Dan to focus very carefully on letter sounds (for example, think of the careful distinction that must be made to turn *pets* into *pest*).

As Cunningham and Cunningham rightly say, this activity make learners quite conscious of the importance of letter sequences in words. It also highlights some phonics generalizations without the memorization of the rules (for example, the silent *e* at the end of *ate* influencing the change in the vowel a from short to long). Making words was a popular endeavor with Dan. (This activity should not be confused with asking students to find small words in big words, which leads to more confusions than enlightenments. For instance, sometimes a teacher habitually prods students to look for a small word or words in a longer word they are having trouble identifying. This is less than helpful in many words; for instance a reader may find that the little words *fat* and *her* or *at* and *he* in *father* do not help with identifying that word at all.)

Dan also read authentic, connected texts every day. He read one or two new books or stories in each of these sessions and did a repeated reading of another. During his readings of new books, when words caused him difficulty, the sounds were pointed out to him if they were ones he had worked with in his exercises. He was thus given much opportunity to practice what he was learning in other portions of his lessons, and to do so in the context of what the other practice was all about—namely, text reading. Dan showed increasing use of letter-sound associations, though in the beginning he sounded out many words quite slowly—a naturally occurring behavior in the early part of the alphabetic phase. As time went by, he decoded words more quickly and began to recognize, at sight, words that previously had required him to apply decoding processes. When he was directed to sound out a word using his developing knowledge, he was also asked to check to see if the word he decided on made sense in the context of the selection he was reading. He did make some word substitutions, but he was not satisfied with nonsense words, and when real words he pronounced did not make sense, he returned to the word to try again. Teacher assistance continued to be necessary, but as Dan practiced more sound-symbol relationships, this support became less frequent. Dan sometimes tried to guess words from context without attempts to decode them and at times these inferences were correct. When they were not, he was requested to examine the word for letter-sound associations and commonplace word patterns.

Dan's repeated-reading experience was given more structure than previously. Following the procedures recommended by Samuels (1988), he read a short story and the teacher graphed the accuracy and fluency of his reading each day until he reached a criterion of 85 words per minute for his reading rate. Reading fluency and accuracy increased each session for every story he read for this repeated-reading activity. When the criterion was reached, usually after about 3 days, a new story was introduced. The intent of this procedure was to continue to increase Dan's automatic recognition of words, which ultimately would allow him to focus on the meaning of text he read. The repeated-reading procedure, as well as all others in his program, seemed to contribute to his learning more words more quickly than had previously been the case. Increasingly his word recognitions and identifications were correct.

Dan's teacher continued to read aloud to him for 5 or 10 minutes of his 1-hour sessions. Excellent books of narrative and expository selections were used to nurture his motivation to become an independent reader.

Dan worked in the reading program for about a year. At the end of that time, he was skillful at decoding words, was reading at his grade level, and never had any difficulties with comprehension. He had read an enormous amount of connected text by the time he was "graduated" from the program, and loved books, with certain favorites for specific periods of time. As he progressed, in addition to the sound-symbol relationships that were a focus of much of his early instruction, structural analysis concepts were introduced. Structural analysis principles, also important to word learning, are considered on page 324 in relation to our discussion about Phase 4 of word learning.

MOVING INTO PHASE 4 OF WORD LEARNING

Typical attributes of readers in Phase 4 of word learning, the orthographic phase, were listed in Chapter 9. You may wish to review those now. Another student will serve as an example of a learner moving from the alphabetic to the orthographic phase—a student named Neal.

Neal's Case Study

Neal was a fourth-grade boy of average intelligence who was reading material at approximately a third-grade level with teacher assistance, and at about a second-grade level independently. Like a number of the learners seen at the university-based reading clinic he was attending, he demonstrated no problems with comprehension. His knowledge of word meanings in oral language was quite advanced; one basis for his elevated meaning vocabulary was probably because his parents had read aloud to him consistently since he was a toddler.

Neal had a good grounding in letter-sound relationships and was successful in applying these to many words. His decoding of most words was reasonably rapid and he had a sizeable stock of words that he recognized at sight—accurately, automatically, and swiftly.

He also identified common word patterns and was aware of their usefulness in decoding new words. For example, in an early lesson when the word *snug* caused him to pause and puzzle a moment, the teacher supplied this hint: "Look at this word. (The teacher wrote *bug*.) If you removed the *b* and placed the *sn* there, that would be this word." Almost before the explanation had been finished, Neal jumped in, said "snug," and continued reading fluently along. He also appeared to use this strategy without prods, stumbling for a moment over certain words, but then rather quickly blending the beginning sound of the word with the ending part. This behavior was seen for words such as *splat, chore, strip, trot, jade,* and *scrap*. In short, he was able to read many words by analogy to other words that were known to him. Though it seemed doubtful that Neal could verbalize the principle he was implementing in these cases, he had apparently had enough prior experience with overt and incidental attention to word configurations that he naturally engaged in these word identification behaviors.

Neal's functioning with printed text, as described above, was typical of students in Phase 4, the orthographic phase of word learning. However, what was not characteristic of this phase were his difficulties with multisyllabic words. He pronounced words of one or two syllables rather fluently, but longer words stumped him. Even when he correctly applied common word parts to decode shorter words, very frequently these same word patterns were read incorrectly. And when he encountered words of three syllables or more, he did not use word parts at all as an aid to decoding. For instance, in one story Neal read during assessment, he was noticeably bothered when he strived to decipher the word *unwilling* and could not do so—though in the very same story he read with no complications the words *unlace, unbent, will, paying,* and *hearing,* indicating that he knew all of the individual word parts that made up *unwilling*. He also did not recognize some frequently occurring word patterns, particularly certain prefixes and suffixes. His general fluency in reading was disrupted when he came to multisyllabic words. The serious obstacles he experienced with multisyllabic words was preventing him from moving into fourth-grade selections.

It was thus decided that Neal needed instruction (a) in specific structural analysis concepts and (b) in how to *use* skills and knowledge he already possessed to decode "longer" words.

Let's turn now to just what it means to provide instruction in structural analysis as a word identification strategy.

STRUCTURAL ANALYSIS PRINCIPLES AND PROCEDURES

Structural analysis is a strategy in which attention is given to meaningful word parts so that an unknown word may be identified. Like phonic analysis, the aim is to examine the inner structure of unidentified words. In phonic analysis, the focus is on letter sounds; in structural analysis, the focus is often on larger word parts. Structural analysis helps with word identification, with spelling, and with determining word meanings. It also facilitates speed of recognition; if learners become quite familiar with certain word parts (e.g., *-tion, -less, re-*), words containing these parts can be identified more quickly (Nagy, Anderson, Schommer, Scott, & Stallman, 1989). Instruction in structural analysis deals with (a) inflectional endings, (b) recognition of words when their spellings have changed because an ending has been added, (c) contractions, (d) compound words, (e) prefixes, (f) suffixes, and, at times, (g) syllabication.

Some work with structural analysis should occur concurrently with instruction in phonic analysis; other structural analysis concepts may be better understood after the student has obtained some understanding of the alphabetic principle. Structural analysis is a major element in skilled reading, allowing learners greater command of the many new words they confront in reading texts. Coaching in use of structural analysis principles should furnish precise explanations about *how* and *when* to employ them (Nagy et al., 1992).

Instructional Procedures

Inflectional Endings.   **Inflectional endings** are affixes that are added to the ends of words (**affixes** are word parts that are added, or "affixed," to words). Inflectional endings form plurals (*cats, dishes*); third person singular verb present tense (*runs, washes*); past tense (*jumped*); present participle (*talking*); possessives (*Mary's*); and comparisons in adjectives and adverbs (*smaller, smallest*).

To teach inflectional endings, the teacher simply presents a known root word[4], and the same root word in an inflected form. For example, "Here is one duck" and "Here are two ducks." The student is asked to note the word element that changes the word. Practice with many other similar examples, using known words plus inflectional endings, is given. Most inflectional endings are taught early in a word identification program, and generally are easily learned.

One useful manipulative for practicing inflectional endings is the word slide. (See Figure 10–9.)

To make a word slide, cut four slits in a colored 5-inch by 8-inch file card. (You may wish to laminate the card for durability.) Next, make sets of strips containing known root words and inflectional endings. The student inserts the strips into the slits and slides them through attempting to form words. The student reads each pair silently. If the student thinks it does form a word, he or she says so and pronounces the word.

For young students, colorful drawings can be added to the basic file card to make the material appealing. (See Figure 10–9.) After the word has been presented using a

---

[4]In structural analysis, the terms *root word* and *base word* are used synonymously.

FIGURE 10–9
An example of a word slide, with an alternate suggestion suitable for younger students

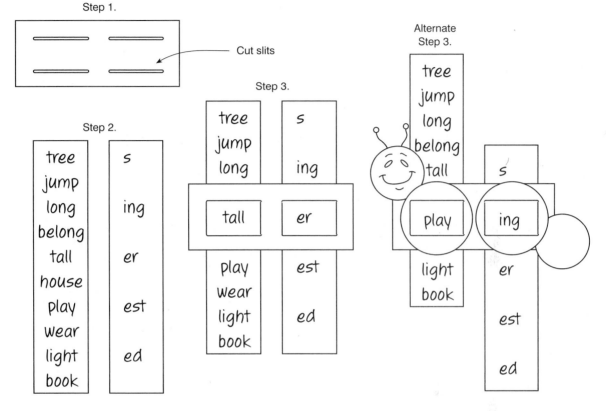

word slide, each inflected form should be presented in a sentence so the student may read the word in context.

Recognition of Words When Their Spellings Have Changed Because an Ending Has Been Added. Although poor readers may recognize a root word, they may not recognize it as a known word when an inflectional ending (or suffix) is added, particularly if a spelling change occurs in the root word. For example, Iris may know *dry* and may know the ending *-ed*, but because the *y* is changed to an *i* to make *dried,* it may not be apparent to her that this is a known word plus a familiar ending.

Students often need explicit instruction in the principles of spelling changes when inflected forms are added to their roots—for example, doubling final consonants (*hopping, hitter, wrapped, bigger*); changing *y* to *i* before adding an ending (*married, busily, tried, happily*); dropping the final *e* before adding an ending (*hoping, lived, releasing, freezer*). After initial instruction with these ideas, here are two practice activities you may wish to have students use.

1. *A board game.* To practice recognition of known words when the spellings have changed before an inflectional ending, have students play board games such as the one in Figure 10–10.

FIGURE 10–10
A board game for practicing a structural analysis word identification strategy

In some words, you must double the final consonant before adding an ending.

Which words are right and which are wrong? If you land on a word that is wrong, you lose your turn.

running | siting
claping
bating | getting | hitting
runing
cuting
wrapped | putting | canned | runner
beged
geting
clapping | FREE SPACE | puting | pating
caned
patting | sitting | begged | hiting
cutting
THE WINNER! | runer | wraping | batting

2. *Group ball toss.* Another group game can be played with a plastic ball. On a piece of foam or felt, draw a target and write root words with an indelible marking pen. Obtain a lightweight plastic ball of about golf-ball size. Glue a strip of velcro around the ball. Mount the target on the chalkboard, using masking tape. Beside the target write inflectional endings on the chalkboard. (See Figure 10–11.)

To play the game, students are divided into teams. Students take turns throwing the ball at the target in the same way they would throw a dart; the velcro causes it to stick to the target. After the student has determined which root word

FIGURE 10–11
Game for practicing structural analysis

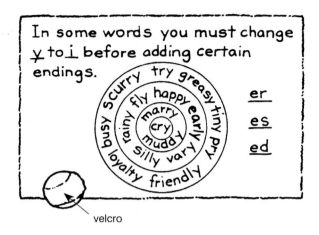

In some words you must change y to i before adding certain endings.

busy Scurry try greasy tiny pry rainy fly happy early loyalty marry cry muddy silly vary friendly

er
es
ed

velcro

the ball has hit, he or she goes to the chalkboard and writes a new word by combining the root with one of the inflectional endings. This is written under the appropriate ending already on the board. To score a point for a team, the student must remember to change *y* to *i* or double the final consonant, and so on, when writing the word.

Contractions. Although contractions occur frequently in oral language, and most contemporary reading programs introduce contractions in early first-grade materials, many students still find them confusing. Perhaps this is because the word form itself is unusual, with its use of an apostrophe. Direct practice in recognizing contractions and their relationships to the words from which they derive often is needed in remedial programs. Some commonly occurring contractions are listed in Figure 10–12.

One set of self-correcting commercial materials for practicing identification of contractions is Contraction Boards (Developmental Learning Materials). These boards are designed so students can work independently. All contractions are taught in the context of simple sentences with this set of activities.

FIGURE 10–12
Commonly occurring contractions

he's	you've	weren't	you'll
she's	we've	shouldn't	he'll
it's	they've	wouldn't	she'll
I'd	we're	couldn't	it'll
you'd	you're	isn't	we'll
he'd	they're	hasn't	they'll
she'd	let's	haven't	I'm
we'd	don't	hadn't	
they'd	won't	didn't	
I've	that's	I'll	

Compound Words.   There are three types of compound words. The type teachers most often describe to students are those formed when "two small words are put together to make a longer word" (e.g., *butterfly, into*). Hyphenated words are also often compounds (e.g., *self-correction*). The third type are those words not physically connected, but having a special meaning when used jointly—a meaning different from those of the individual words when they are not together. *Ice cream,* for example, means something distinct from just *ice* plus *cream.* In this latter example, although the words are not combined when conveyed by ink marks on paper (i.e., the surface structure of the language unit), they do function as one meaning unit (i.e., in deep structure) and are therefore considered to be a compound word. Here are two exercises for practicing compound words.

1. *Compound dominoes.* An activity students enjoy when practicing recognition of compound words is Compound Dominoes. The teacher writes compounds on oaktag strips, drawing a line between the two word parts (e.g., *bath/house, coat/room, fly/ball, game/bird, light/house*). Students try to match compound words so a new compound word is formed from the word parts of two other compounds. For example, matching *lighthouse* with *flyball* produces the compound *housefly,* matching *flyball* with *gamebird* produces *ballgame,* and so on. The longest sequence of matches wins.

light/house   fly/ball   game/bird   bath/house   coat/room

2. *Twister.* Use masking tape to attach oilcloth or butcher paper to the floor. Draw stepping-stones all over this "playing field" and write parts of compound words in them, with the first part of the compound on one stone and the second on a different one.

   A student from Team 1 places one foot on the beginning of a compound and the other foot on the ending. Then the students places one hand on the beginning of another compound and the other hand on its ending. If both words are correct, the student stays in this position, while a student from Team 2 does the same on the same playing field.

   Then another Team 1 member joins them, and so on. Soon students have to twist and turn through each other's arms and legs to reach their word parts. Points are lost if a wrong choice is made or students fall down in a happy pile.

Figure 10–13 presents a list of some compound words that teachers can use when preparing exercises for compound words.

Prefixes.   A **prefix** is a meaningful word part affixed to the beginning of a word, for example, the *un-* in *unhappy.* Work with prefixes should include recognition of prefixes; identification of words when prefixes are added to known root words; and attention to meanings of prefixes and the meaning changes that occur when prefixes are added to words.

   Because prefixes are meaning units, for instructional purposes, teachers often group those with like meanings. For example, introduction of prefixes might begin with *un-* and *dis-,* because both are "negative" prefixes: they mean "not," as in *unsure,* or "the opposite of," as in *untie.*

   Stauffer (1942) identified the 15 most commonly occurring prefixes in the English language. These are listed in Figure 10–14. Effective instruction incorporates these frequently seen prefixes before those that are used less often. However, some of the pre-

FIGURE 10–13
Some compound words

afternoon	downhill	mailbox	seaplane
airplane	downtown	mailman	shoeshine
backbone	downstairs	maybe	shoestring
barnyard	driveway	moonlight	snowball
baseball	drugstore	necktie	snowfall
basketball	everyone	neighborhood	snowflake
bathtub	everything	newspaper	sometimes
bedroom	eyebrows	nightgown	sunrise
beehive	firecracker	notebook	sunset
billboard	firefly	outlaw	sunshine
blackout	firehouse	overboard	surfboard
bookcase	fireplace	overcoat	tablecloth
bookmark	flashlight	pancake	toothbrush
bulldog	football	playground	typewriter
chalkboard	fullback	playhouse	underline
checkerboard	goldfish	piecrust	uphill
classroom	hallway	quarterback	waterfall
coffeeshop	headlight	railroad	watermelon
cookbook	highchair	rainbow	whirlpool
cowboy	highway	raincoat	wildlife
cupcake	homesick	rowboat	without
deadline	horseshoe		

fixes cataloged by Stauffer are absorbed prefixes while others are active prefixes. An **absorbed prefix** is a syllable that functioned at one time in the English language as a prefix but no longer does so (Durkin, 1976); these prefixes have been "absorbed" into words—examples are *ad-* in *adjacent* and *com-* in *combine.* An **active prefix,** on the other hand, is one that still functions as a prefix in the manner in which prefixes are generally defined, that is, they are word parts that are added to complete root words (such as *re-* in *repay,* or *sub-* in *subzero*). When the goal of teaching is to emphasize the identification of words, the majority of instructional time should be devoted to those that are active prefixes. When the objective is to add sophistication to the strategies that students use to determine word meanings, some attention to absorbed prefixes is appropriate.

Several activities that may be used when working with prefixes follow.

1.   *Divide words into parts.* Use worksheets that help students discern word parts. The exercise shown in Figure 10–15 is an example. Students are to write the prefix and the root in the two separate columns.

2.   *Play group games.* On file cards, print prefixes. Pass these out to students. Write root words on oaktag strips. Place one of the root word cards on the chalkboard tray. A student who has a prefix that will fit with the root word comes up and places it in front of the root word card. If it is correct and the student can pronounce the new word, the student may take the root word. The student with the most root word cards at the end of the game is the winner.

FIGURE 10–14
The most commonly occurring English prefixes

a- or *ab-*	atypical, amoral, abnormal	*in-*	(meaning *not*) incomplete, inaccurate, invisible, informal, inconvenient, inexcusable, inexpensive, incapable, infrequent, inactive, inadequate, inaccessible, inadvisable, inconsiderate
ad-	adjoining		
be-	beside, befriend, beloved, befitting, bemoan, besiege, becalmed, bedazzled, bedeviled	*pre-*	preschool, prehistoric, precooked, prepaid, prefix, prearrange, pretest, prepackaged, preview, precaution, presuppose, premature, prejudge, prerevolutionary
com-	compatriot, compress, commingle		
de-	dethrone, decontaminate, degenerate, dehumanize, dehumidify, deactivate, decode, decompose, decentralize, decompress, debug, de-escalate	*pro-*	prowar, pronoun, prolong, pro-American, prorevolutionary
		re-	repay, retie, recook, rewrite, reread, reappear, remake, replace, reload, reopen, reentry, review, repopulate, recall, repack, redraw, rearrange, rejoin, reactivate, react
dis-	disobey, disapprove, disagree, disrespectful, dishonest, disconnect, distrust, disarm, disuse, disability, disadvantage, disappear, disbelief, discomfort		
en-	encircle, enable, endanger, enforce, entangle, enslave, enclose, entwine, enrobe, enact, enfold, enthrone, encamp, encode	*sub-*	submarine, subzero, subtropical, subheading, subsoil, subdivision, substandard, subcommittee, subhuman
		un-	unfair, unhappy, uncooked, unlock, untie, uncover, unable, unlucky, untrue, unwrap, uninvited, undress, unfinished, uncertain, unreal, unripe, unwise, unlawful, untruthful, unconscious, unpopulated, undisturbed, unload, unwilling, unsold, unwashed, unspoken
ex-	ex-president, ex-wife, ex-husband, exterminate		
in-	(meaning *into*) ingrown, inbreed, incoming, inlay, input, inset, intake		

FIGURE 10–15
Worksheet for students learning prefixes

	PREFIX	ROOT
1. disobey	dis	obey
2. enclose		
3. repay		
4. incomplete		
5. prehistoric		

3. *Find prefixes in published stories.* Select a story from a sports magazine or any other magazine that might have appeal for your students. Have the students circle with a fine-point red marking pen all prefixes they can find. Give points for each one found. Give additional points for correct pronunciation of each of the words containing a prefix. Then read the article together.

Suffixes. As you know, a suffix is a word part affixed to the end of a root word or base word. Objectives for teaching suffixes are similar to those used for teaching prefixes. Instruction should include recognition of suffixes; identification of words when suffixes are added to known root words; and attention to meanings of suffixes and the meaning changes that occur when suffixes are added to words.

FIGURE 10–16
Some English suffixes

-able	enjoyable, comfortable, enviable	*-ion*	suggestion, graduation, creation, discussion
-age	shortage, leakage, wreckage, breakage	*-ity*	stupidity, humidity, sincerity, productivity
-al	musical, personal, original, removal	*-ive*	productive, expensive, excessive, destructive
-ance	appearance, performance	*-ize*	alphabetize, dramatize, colonize, symbolize
-ant	contestant, attendant, informant	*-less*	spotless, sleeveless, nameless, friendless
-ary	imaginary, summary, boundary, missionary	*-ly*	consciously, quickly, friendly, officially, slowly
-ation	confirmation, information, starvation, relaxation	*-ment*	refreshment, amazement, punishment, enjoyment
-active	informative, talkative, administrative, imaginative	*-ness*	completeness, wholeness, sickness, darkness
-ence	existence, persistence	*-or*	sailor, actor, inventor, inspector, translator
-ent	excellent, insistent, correspondent	*-ous*	joyous, famous, dangerous, nervous, courageous
-er	helper, teacher, player, farmer, miner, follower	*-th*	growth, truth, warmth, width, fourth
-ery	bakery, bravery	*-ty*	loyalty, safety, cruelty
-ful	delightful, careful, cheerful, truthful, plentiful	*-ward*	homeward, toward, westward, eastward
-fy	classify, beautify, falsify, simplify, purify	*-y*	rainy, windy, noisy, gloomy, curly, snowy

Suffixes, like prefixes, can alter the meanings of words, but they also often change a word's grammatical function. The latter are called *derivational suffixes* (Schumm & Saumell, 1994). For example, the suffix *-ness* changes adjectives to nouns, such as in *dark/darkness* and *happy/happiness*. A listing of some English suffixes is found in Figure 10–16.

Activities used for instruction with prefixes can also be used for work with suffixes. Here are some additional suggestions.

1.   *Use flip strips.* On colored strips of construction paper, print root words on the front left-hand side. On the back, print suffixes so the back can be folded over to form a new word with the suffix. (See Figure 10–17.) When a new suffix is introduced, packs of flip strips can be prepared so that the same suffix is used over and over with different root words, as in example A in the figure. After readers have become acquainted with several suffixes, flip strips can be prepared with many different suffixes being added to the same root word, as in example B. This demonstrates to students how their repertoires of known words have been substantially extended. Flip strips may also be used for practicing identification of words in which the spelling of the root has changed when an ending has been

FIGURE 10–17
Flip strips for practicing suffixes

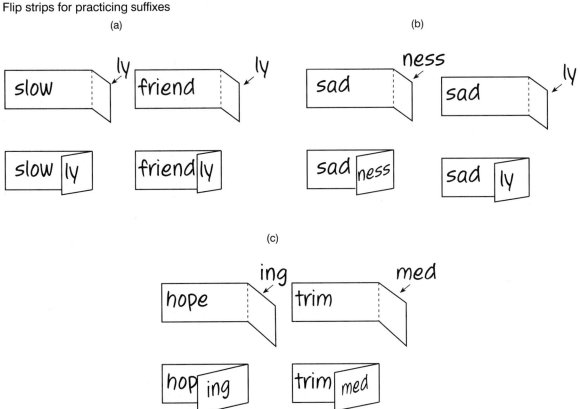

added, as in example C. After students have read each flip strip from a set, have them read or write each word in a sentence.

2.   *Root word tree.* Draw a tree on a large sheet of paper. Attach index cards labeled with root words to the roots (where else!) of the tree by stapling the ends of small strips of oaktag to the tree's roots and simply slipping the index cards behind the strips. (See Figure 10–18.) Write suffixes on index cards and place these in a pile facedown. Students take a card from this pile and attempt to match it with a root word. If the match is correct, the root word is removed from the roots and attached with the suffix to the leafy part of the tree.

Working With Prefixes and Suffixes.   After suffixes as well as prefixes have been introduced, give students practice with multisyllabic words that contain both. Students can be asked to identify and write each part of the word, as in Figure 10-19.

FIGURE 10–18
Root word tree for practicing suffixes

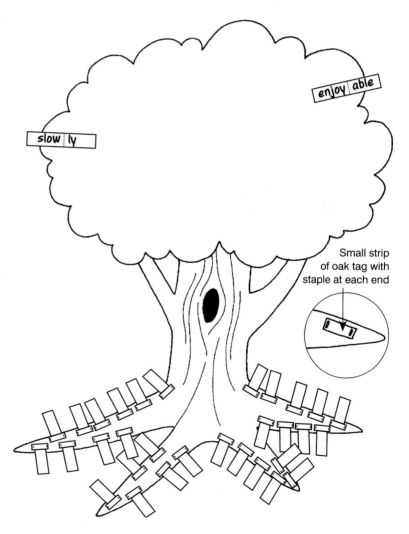

enjoy able

slow ly

Small strip
of oak tag with
staple at each end

FIGURE 10–19
Worksheet for students working
with prefixes and suffixes

	PREFIX	ROOT	SUFFIX
1. unbreakable	un	break	able
2. disgraceful			
3. refillable			
4. previewer			
5. dishonorable			

Or, they can be asked to form new words, as in this exercise.

Prefix	+	*Root*	+	*Suffix*	=	*Word*
re	+	fresh	+	ment	=	refreshment
un	+	sound	+	ness	=	
un	+	success	+	ful	=	
re	+	settle	+	ment	=	
un	+	law	+	ful	=	

When students have been introduced to both prefixes and suffixes they can also be helped to see the relationships of words that are similar to others by building word trees:

joy
enjoyable
  joyful
enjoyment
  joyous
rejoice

This not only highlights known word parts as assistance to word identification, but it also stresses interrelatedness of word meanings.

Syllabication.   Syllabication, or dividing words into syllables, is considered a part of phonic analysis instruction in some programs, but a part of structural analysis in others. In the former, the focus is on units of sound, and work with syllabication is believed to be crucial because the ways in which words are divided into syllables are clues to sounds of vowels. In programs that use syllables for phonic analysis, students are taught syllabication rules. Here are some commonly taught rules:

1.   When there are two like consonants, divide between them (for example, *pup/py*).
     Exception: When *-ed* is added to a word ending in *d* or *t,* it forms a separate syllable (*add/ed*).

2.   When there are two unlike consonants, divide between them (for example, *wal/rus*).
     Exception: Do not divide between consonant clusters or digraphs (*be/tween*).

3. When a consonant is between two vowels, divide after the first vowel (for example, *si/lent*).

    Exception: When the consonant between two vowels is *x,* divide after the *x* (for example, *ex/am*).

4. Prefixes, suffixes, and inflectional endings are separate syllables (for example, *re/state/ment*).

    Exception: When *-ion* is added to a word that ends in *t,* the *t* joins with the *-ion* to form the final syllable (for example, *ac/tion*).

5. When a syllable ends in a vowel, the vowel is long.

6. When a syllable ends in a consonant, the vowel in that syllable is short.

By applying a combination of these rules, presumably a reader would be aided in identifying vowel sounds, and, ultimately, unknown words. For example, by applying rule 3 and rule 5 the *i* in *silent* would be pronounced as its long form, which would expedite the identification of the word if it was unknown.

However, some students have difficulty learning these rules, and even when they do, they may only use them for specific workbook or teacher-directed exercises on syllabication. Because they are moderately complex and because of their exceptions, students may not employ the rules in authentic word identification tasks.

On the other hand, in programs where syllabication is considered a part of the structural analysis component, the purpose of showing students how words can be divided is to demonstrate that a long and possibly intimidating word may be analyzed in terms of its smaller word parts, and thus identified. The focus is on frequent spelling patterns. For example, when a poor reader first encounters in print such words as *enlargement* or *irreplaceable,* the student's first reaction may be, "I don't know that word and I'll never be able to figure out one that big." On the other hand, the word can seem quite manageable if the student has developed the habit of dividing the word up and looking for familiar word parts. For example, the student might go through these steps to identify the word *enlargement:*

"Oh, it begins with *en-*. We worked with a prefix like that. It's /en/."

"The middle of the word is *large*."

"The end is just that suffix, *-ment*."

"*En-large-ment. Enlargement.* 'I'll need to make an enlargement of this picture,' the photographer said."

The emphasis in syllabication in these programs is on looking for known word parts and not on memorizing rules. In such a program, the following activities would occur.

Step 1: Students are told that many long words can be divided into smaller parts to aid identification. This is demonstrated by removing inflectional endings from words (e.g., *entering = enter/ing; darkest = dark/est*). The term and concept of "syllable" is applied to each of these smaller parts.

Step 2: Step 1 is repeated, this time with prefixes (e.g., *disgrace = dis/grace; unselfish = un/selfish*).

Step 3: Step 1 is carried out again, this time with suffixes (e.g., *importantly = important/ly; enrollment = enroll/ment*).

Step 4: Step 1 is carried out with both prefixes and suffixes (e.g., *un/rest/ful; dis/appear/ance*).

Step 5:   Students are told that there are some other ways to divide long words and are given brief practice in dividing words based on a few of the most useful rules. The emphasis at this time remains on looking at common word parts. Memorization of the rules is not required. (Knowledge of syllabication rules may actually be more helpful for writing than for reading so that correct conventions of written language usage may be applied when a word is hyphenated at the end of a line.)

A RETURN TO NEAL'S CASE STUDY

Now that we have examined some structural analysis concepts, let's see how these pertain to Neal. Neal, our fourth-grade student, with a reading instructional level of approximately third grade, had had more exposures to print than the two other case study students, Bridget and Dan, whom we previously considered in regard to their word learning delays. He had also benefited from direct instruction in phonic analysis and structural analysis strategies in his regular school program. As a result of all these factors, he was familiar with some typical units in words. He recognized, at sight, common inflectional endings; knew all contractions; and had a concept of compound words, easily reading most of those he encountered in the selections that were part of his daily lessons. In addition, spelling changes when affixes were added usually did not confuse him. He recognized certain prefixes and a few suffixes, but there were a number of frequently occurring ones that he did not know. And he had not yet grasped how to break a long word into its salient parts, nor was he using what he already did know when he met multisyllabic words.

Many of the strategies for presenting and practicing prefixes and suffixes, discussed above, were employed with Neal. The teacher began by focusing on those prefixes and suffixes that are used most often in English words. Neal was given teacher-guided, rather than independent, practice with the use of these affixes. The teacher delivered explicit information about the pronunciations of prefixes and suffixes, and he had many opportunities to add the prefixes and suffixes he was working on to known root words before he was asked to apply them to unknown words.

In addition, Neal received a great deal of assistance for dividing words into syllables or known word parts. Readers' skill at reading multisyllabic words with ease relies on their deftness at separating long words into syllables (M. J. Adams, 1990a, 1990b). Again, Neal applied these principles and understandings to words he knew, prior to practicing them with new words. For example, the notion that words can be broken into parts was expedited by using the knowledge he already possessed about compound words. The teacher showed him compounds that were familiar to him, had him say the separate parts, write the parts separately, and then write the word back into its consolidated form. Neal also worked with Word-Building Notebooks (see Figure 10-20). Next, the same sequence was followed with two-syllable words that he already recognized. Then longer, unknown words were tackled in exactly the same manner. Word-Building Notebooks were used in this practice, but in this case with prefixes, roots, suffixes, and parts of multisyllabic words on the cards.

As with all students, Neal's use of new concepts in real text reading was considered critical. He spent one third to one half of his hour-long sessions reading in connected text that did include words with prefixes and suffixes and words having three or more syllables. A particular emphasis was placed on teacher-modeling to show him how to apply known information to multisyllabic words during his reading of stories and

FIGURE 10–20
A word-building notebook for practicing compound words

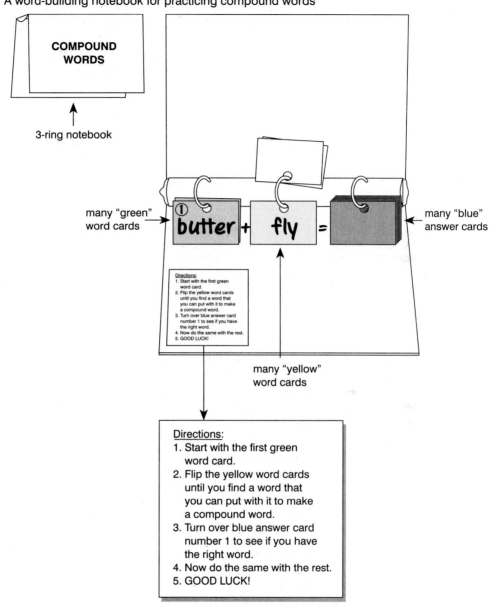

informational selections, as well as during his direct-practice exercises. He was also instructed to use what he already knew about letter-sound relationships when structural analysis strategies were not helpful in specific words, and was taught to use context to self-check the sense of the word his analysis had produced. His good oral language vocabulary aided him in making decisions about whether words he decoded fit into the context.

At the end of one academic term (approximately 9 weeks of instruction), Neal had made considerable progress. Still there were a few prefixes and suffixes that he was not readily recalling. In addition, although he now definitely understood the process of dividing long words into parts to identify them, he was not yet fluently carrying out this skill. He was retained in the clinic for an additional quarter to firm up his understandings and to provide more rehearsals with his newly learned concepts, especially through practice in contextual materials. By the middle of the next term, he was able to read fourth-grade materials and became progressively skillful in handling them. At the end of the second 9-week period, special instruction was no longer deemed necessary. His classroom teacher agreed with this assessment, having seen a major change in Neal's word recognition and word identification abilities in his work with her. She agreed to continue instruction in the manner that he had been experiencing. When Neal's progress was checked at the end of his fourth-grade year, he was to be promoted to the next grade level with the confidence that he could read the materials necessary for success in fifth grade.

CONTEXT CLUES AS A WORD IDENTIFICATION STRATEGY

Use of context clues as a prime strategy for identifying unknown words has been emphasized in recent years. Teachers were frequently advised to direct students' attention to the context surrounding a word *before* prompting other word identification tactics, or sometimes, *in lieu of* use of any other systems. Students were routinely asked to skip unknown words, read to the end of the sentence, and then to attempt to guess a word that would fit in that place in the sentence; they were to make these speculations based on their knowledge of language and their background experiences. For a time, it was assumed that proficient readers predicted what unknown words should be by using expectancies based on their knowledge of words and background knowledge.

For both skilled and unskilled readers, context clues were presumed to be the most valuable aid to word identification. While this theory seemed to hold some logic and was certainly well meaning, much to the surprise of many reading authorities, when research investigated widely held assumptions about the value context clues, this did not prove to be the case (e.g., M. J. Adams, 1990a, 1990b; Daneman, 1991; Ehri, 1991; Juel, 1991; Stanovich, 1991b). Proficient readers do not use context as the primary word identification strategy; rather, identifications are based on visual and phonemic information in the words themselves. And while it is true that context may assist with confirming the meaning of a word that has multiple definitions and therefore could be ambiguous, this occurs only *after* the word is identified. Context also may help a competent reader use word pattern information more quickly, but it does not replace the need to use letter and sound knowledge.

When research with developing readers investigated the benefits of using context clues, it was found that the strategy is used most by the students who are least skillful (e.g., Allington & Fleming, 1978; Perfetti, 1985; Pring & Snowling, 1986; Stanovich, 1994; Stanovich & West, 1981). And, those readers who make the least headway tend to remain in a stage where use of context is the central way to attempt to read words (Biemiller, 1970). Biemiller (1970) summarized these findings by saying that "the longer [a student] stays in the early, context-emphasizing phase without showing an increase in the use of graphic information the poorer the reader he is at the end of the year" (p. 95). In fact, use of context clues is now considered to be a compensatory strategy

(Stanovich, 1980), since it has been found to be used as a compensation because the reader does not yet have control of more productive methods of word recognition and identification (e.g., L. Carnine, Carnine, & Gersten, 1984; Daneman, 1991; Stanovich, 1994; Stanovich, West, & Feeman, 1981).

Investigations have also shown that context clues do not provide the support once believed. The easiest words to predict from context are function words (Gough, 1983). These are the words that occur most often in print—and, therefore, are the ones that students are most likely to recognize at sight, making use of context unnecessary. Individual content words occur less frequently, making it more probable that there will be greater challenge in identifying them. However, content words are the words most difficult to determine from context—and thus for the very words for which a word identification strategy may be needed, context may not be helpful (M. J. Adams, 1990a, 1990b). Quite a number of studies have shown that natural text is not especially predictable (Stanovich, 1991b). The chance that a reader can guess the next word in a passage turns out to be about 20% to 35% (e.g., see Gough, 1983; Stanovich, 1991b), and for content words, this percentage may be even less. Gough (1983) found content words, those which carry the meaning of a passage, could be predicted only about 10% of the time. Juel (1991) notes that no matter how imperfect letter-sound relationships are, they still are more reliable than context in word identification.

One major criticism of encouraging students to use context to the exclusion of other systems is that the student will not study a word's letters and sounds and, therefore, will not have any information to recognize the word the next time it is encountered. This would not be a problem if context habitually conveyed the unknown word, but since it doesn't, this is a significant issue. Another reason for teachers to refrain from prompting poor readers to use context clues as their chief word identification strategy is that for context to operate productively, the reader must know well the words surrounding the unfamiliar word, and this often is not the situation with unskilled readers (Ehri, 1991).

Use of context does have some value. Until readers are adept at using visual and sound information to determine the identities of many words, there *are* times when context will provide a clue to an unfamiliar word (though this may be less often than once was believed). Context can also limit the possibilities of what a word might be when a student is trying to identify it; for example, when students are reading independently and their identification strategies lead them to believe a word is one of two similar words but they are not sure which, then context may solve this dilemma. Furthermore, context provides a check on words that have been produced through use of other word identification systems, and this is indeed a valuable function. Moreover, the use of context to assist comprehension has been upheld by research (e.g., Baker & Brown, 1984). However, context clues are no longer regarded to be as helpful as once was supposed for learning or recognizing words.

CONCLUSION

A major problem for large numbers of students in remedial reading programs is their lack of automatic word recognition and in deficiencies in word identification strategies. A focus on any single approach for the remediation of these difficulties to the exclusion of others is detrimental to student progress. The nature of English words and English text structure requires use of a variety of clues as unknown words are encountered. Consideration of a student's phase of word learning must also be given consideration.

Proficient readers, like poor readers, may also encounter unknown words in their reading. Capable readers, however, have multiple strategies at their disposal. This fact should be an indicator to teachers that it is necessary to teach a variety of word learning systems to their students.

Finally, don't let the tail wag the dog. Remember that the real reason for work on word identification is to enable students to read and understand regular, connected reading material. Care should be taken to ensure that any emphasis on word identification training does not consume so much of a session that students have no time left for reading.

📖 REFLECTIONS

1. Consider this question: Why have many educators been fiercely pro or con in their views about the value of phonics instruction?
2. Based on what you have learned in Chapters 9 and 10, what clues for instruction are obtained by determining a student's phase of word learning? List as many specific implications as you can.

11

Knowledge of Word Meanings

Using structured overviews or semantic mapping aids both vocabulary development and comprehension.

Read Paragraph A:

(A) Apprehension of the semantic fields of morphological units is pivotal for deriving semantic content when reading. This seems to be consummately plausible and most preceptors' ripostes to this attestation would predictably be, "Inexorably so."

You may have had some difficulty getting the gist of that paragraph since it was written with words whose meanings are not commonplace. Paragraph B says the same thing but uses words more frequently found in the meaning vocabularies of the average college student. Now try it again.

(B) Knowledge of word meanings is important for reading comprehension. This seems to be quite logical and most teachers' responses to this statement would probably be, "Of course."

The contrasting examples in these paragraphs show that ease of comprehension is affected by knowledge of specific word meanings—in Paragraph A the point of the two sentences may have been hidden unless you stopped, reread, and mulled them over somewhat, and even then you may not have understood the full message. On the other hand, Paragraph B was as clear as a bell to you; with no conscious effort at all, you got the central idea.

Research has confirmed that students' performances on measures of vocabulary knowledge have solid correlations with reading comprehension achievement, and that an individual's understandings of word meanings is powerful evidence of how satisfactorily that person will comprehend text (e.g., R. C. Anderson & Freebody, 1981; Curtis, 1987; Kameenui, Carnine, & Freschi, 1982; Marks, Doctorow, & Wittrock, 1974).

It would seem, then, that instructional programs designed to teach learners word meanings would make vital contributions to the improvement of comprehension. However, the relationship between vocabulary and comprehension is a bit more complex. Investigations have tested the proposition that enhancing students' knowledge of word meanings will also bring about heightened comprehension. But, initially research brought a surprise: results from study to study were conflicting. Sometimes knowledge of new word meanings positively affected comprehension, but sometimes it did not! As the number of these inquiries expanded, a pattern began to arise. This pattern showed that, for the establishment of new word meanings to have any subsequent effect on comprehension, students had to know the meanings of the words *well*. Knowing a word well means having *breadth* and *depth* of information about the word. This finding has some very important implications for instruction and gives indicators about what can be effective instruction and what will not be, as we will see in this chapter.

An individual's **meaning vocabulary** is defined as the number of words for which that person knows one or more meanings. However, Beck and McKeown (1991) point out that what it means to "know" a word is a complicated concept. Word knowledge can really be expressed on a *continuum,* ranging from (a) words that are completely unknown, to (b) words that the learner has had some exposure to but for which he or she is unable to specify a meaning, to (c) words for which there is a general sense of the meaning if the text also provides some clues, to (d) words well established in the reader's understanding and that therefore can be readily used in context to assist comprehension and that also can be defined out of context. (See Figure 11–1.)

Word knowledge may develop first in an individual's oral language and then be extended to words in print. Many attempts have been made to estimate the number of word meanings children know when they come to school at ages 5 or 6. Beck and McK-

FIGURE 11–1
A continuum of word knowledge

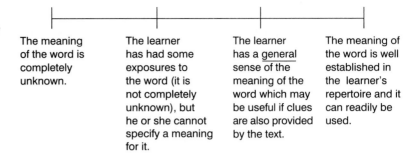

| The meaning of the word is completely unknown. | The learner has had some exposures to the word (it is not completely unknown), but he or she cannot specify a meaning for it. | The learner has a general sense of the meaning of the word which may be useful if clues are also provided by the text. | The meaning of the word is well established in the learner's repertoire and it can readily be used. |

eown (1991) suggest that the best approximation is between 2,500 and 5,000. Research also seems to show that during the school years, the average student adds a surprisingly large number of words to his or her meaning vocabulary each year; calculations vary, but most agree that the number is between 2,000 and 3,000 words (Dale, 1965; Nagy & Herman, 1987). In the preschool years, word meanings are obtained from oral language interchanges with parents and peers, from hearing stories read (Leung, 1992), from television and other media, from illustrations in books and magazines, and even from various print sources. These same sources account for word learning during the school years, along with specific instruction.

In particular, print sources become increasingly important in the school years and beyond. Or to put it another way, individuals who read a lot develop more extensive vocabularies than those who do not, and in some cases, word meanings develop in print before they are used in oral language. An example of the latter may be part of *your* experience: if you read a great deal—and what college student can get away with not doing so!—you may read words that you have seen in print many times, words for which you have at some time in the past determined their meanings. But because words found in the reading material of a sophisticated reader may not be typically used in oral language, you may have never heard some of these words said orally. The first time you do, you may react, "Oh, so that's how you pronounce that word!" Or, the first time you bravely say one of these words aloud, you may pronounce it incorrectly—even though you know perfectly well what it means. Knowing more words in print than you use in oral language is a characteristic of a competent reader.

Roelke's (1969) research showed that important aspects of vocabulary knowledge affecting comprehension are the following:

1. The sheer number of words for which a student knows meanings

2. Knowledge of multiple meanings of words; for example, knowing that *light* can mean "not heavy" as well as a shade of color (as in "*light* pink"), free from worry (as in "*light*hearted"), a source of illumination (as in a "bright *light*"), moderate (as in a "*light* meal"), or a small quantity (as in "*light* rain")

3. Ability to select the correct meaning of a word having multiple meanings in order to fit a specific context

To these, recent researchers have also added the insight that perceptions of a word's meaning must be adequately *thorough* to have an effect on comprehension. There must be a precise understanding of the concept underlying the word, not a mere parroting of a definition; in addition, there must be recognition of the word's relationship to other concepts and words (Herman & Dole, 1988). Partial or hazy conceptions of word meanings are not as useful in producing the degree of understanding typically necessary for depth of comprehension. Nagy (1988) contrasts rich awareness of word meanings with the fragmentary word knowledge produced by some typical types of instruction and says, "There is a big difference between being able to say what a word means and being able to use it" (p. 24).

These findings and insights give clues about what instruction must look like to provide effective learning of word meanings. Here are conclusions supported by current research:

1.   Instruction should *combine several methods for presenting meanings* if a complete understanding is to be obtained. For example, simply supplying a definition for a word is not robust enough for students to retain and use words. Neither is introducing words in the context of a teacher-prepared sentence, if this is all that is done. Combining these two modes of instruction, however, may furnish some assistance to help students learn well-developed word meanings, especially if they are accompanied by examples (Stahl & Fairbanks, 1986).

2.   Instruction should *include activities that encourage deep processing* of the meanings of the targeted words. Students should be actively engaged in sorting out relationships between the words and their prior knowledge, and between the targeted words and other words. They must be involved in seeing connotations (the implied sense of a word), as well as denotations (the literal meaning of a word), and "go beyond the superficial act of memorizing definitions" (Herman & Dole, 1988, p. 42).

3.   Students must have *many exposures* to words to gain thorough understandings of them (Mezynski, 1983). Stahl and Fairbanks (1986) contrasted studies in which learning new word meanings had an effect on comprehension and those that did not. They found that the ineffective programs furnished students with only one or two exposures to a word's meaning—which was not enough to have any lasting consequences. Most especially, only a sole encounter with a word is unlikely to be productive when the words are conceptually complex, even if explanations are given of the concepts during this single exposure (Nagy, Anderson, & Herman, 1987). Repetition is also important so that readers can identify a word's meaning speedily and effortlessly when it is encountered in reading (Nagy, 1988).

Many analyses have established that, in general, unskilled readers have meager meaning vocabularies in comparison with those of skilled readers (e.g., see Daneman, 1991). Since an adequate meaning vocabulary is important for reading comprehension, remedial teachers must be concerned with this area of instruction. If poor readers have not attained an adequate level of vocabulary acquisition, attention to the development of meaning vocabulary must occur as part of their programs.

Three ways students can increase their meaning vocabularies are (a) through direct instruction, (b) through independent word learning from texts, and (c) through learning words from oral language encounters.

DIRECT INSTRUCTION

Authorities do not agree on all aspects of how word meanings are most likely to be learned; however, there is one matter about which there is strong consensus. Based on their research and their interpretations of the studies of others, it is hard to find an authority in this area who is not convinced of the value of direct instruction to facilitate in-depth understanding of word meanings.

Meaning vocabulary knowledge is enhanced through thought-provoking activities, direct teacher guidance, and instruction that is systematic and continuous.

Beck and McKeown (1991) describe "direct instruction" as including teacher-guided lessons on vocabulary, as well as teaching in which students work individually with print materials that are specifically designed to present vocabulary information. Direct instruction of vocabulary is in contrast to situations in which word meaning knowledge evolves incidentally through students' interactions with written and oral language.

Hittleman (1983) reported that successful programs that incorporate vocabulary development have the following features:

1. A small number of words is taught intensively in a given lesson rather than many words being presented in a more cursory fashion.
2. The instruction is systematic and continuous. Students are exposed to the same word in many different contexts.
3. Gamelike activities are incorporated into the schedule to stimulate students to study vocabulary.
4. Any technique is employed that calls attention to the meanings of word parts.
5. Context, the dictionary, and the derivations of words are studied as means of obtaining word meanings.

If only a few words are to be taught in order to allow for intense instruction, how does the teacher decide on which words these are to be? Nagy (1988) advises that teachers examine the text students are to read and select those words that are the most *conceptually complex*. Another way to say this is, based on prior experiences—of this particular group of students—will it be difficult for them to derive the meaning of the words on their own? These are words that will benefit from a teacher's illustrations and direct explanations so that readers can see relationships and say "Ah ha! I get it."

Beck and McKeown (1991) suggest that other criteria to be used are *present and future utility*: (a) Will understanding of the passage be dependent on knowing this word's meaning? and (b) Is the word one that is likely to be useful to know in future situations? Highlighting conceptually difficult words that have only trifling significance for comprehending the material to be read, or that are rarely met in other written or oral language situations is not very worthwhile. Since limited time is available in any school day, efficient instruction considers the usefulness of a word as well as its complexity. If the present utility of a word is high, but the future utility is comparatively low, this gives an indication about the amount of attention that should be allotted to instruction of the word. That is, the word cannot be ignored if its presence will hinder comprehension of the immediate reading assignment, but it may not be a candidate for further, more protracted activities.

Since constructive teaching of word meanings involves focusing on a limited number of words at a time—that is, an emphasis on quality not quantity—what about the other words which a student might not know in a given selection? The good news is that a learner does not need to know the meaning of every word in a passage in order to understand it. Research has taken a look at how many unknown words a typical reader can encounter and still maintain an ample understanding of connected text. Marks, Doctorow, and Wittrock's (1974) probe demonstrated that 15% of word meanings could be unknown without loss of comprehension. Also many words in any selection will already be known by most readers—that is, these are words common in oral language usage.

Direct instruction always includes introductory transactions, in which the student is initially acquainted with the word; often direct instruction should also involve rich development of word meanings.

Introductory Transactions

Introducing new words—how should this be done? Some typical initial presentations result in more stable acquisition of words than others.

Use Context—Carefully.   Sometimes students learn words during the natural act of reading without direct instruction. That is, through exposures to a word (usually several of these), the context of the material ultimately conveys the meaning. This is normally referred to as **incidental learning** of word meanings. Incidental learning will be discussed in a later part of this chapter, but that is not what is being addressed here.

The present section, instead, considers what Herman and Dole (1988) call **pedagogical context** or **instructional context.** This type of context is exemplified when the teacher introduces the meaning of a new word by placing the word in a sentence or paragraph that is fashioned to communicate the word's definition. The words surrounding the unknown word are expected to assist the student in gaining a sense of the word's definition.

Use of pedagogical context can provide only a relatively vague sense of the meaning of a word, unless sentences are very carefully constructed to provide enough information so the meaning *can* be derived from the surrounding words. Here is an example: To introduce the meaning of the word *matted,* the teacher writes this sentence on the chalkboard, "The girl's *matted* hair looked dirty and messy," underlines *matted*, and asks the students to guess what *matted* means. *Matted* in this case refers to hairs that are tangled in a dense mass. But even with the use of "messy" in this sentence, that meaning is not really clear if the student has no familiarity with the term whatsoever. *Matted* in this context *could* refer to the words *black, blond, red, unwashed, thick, thin, long, short, permed, bleached, frosted,* or many other choices. For the teacher who already knows the meaning of *matted*, the context may seem sufficient, but for a person unfamiliar with the word, the meaning of the word may not be apparent at all from the context.

For this reason, many authorities contend that pedagogical context as an initial presentation method must be supplemented with other aids, such as definitions or multiple contexts for the same word (e.g., Herman & Dole, 1988; Nagy, 1988; Stahl & Fairbanks, 1986).

This is not to say that context is never helpful. But not only must there be a very strong and narrowed suggestion of the word's meaning in the sentences, furthermore, different types of context clues may supply more powerful hints than others. Dale and O'Rourke (1971) identify the following types of context clues:

1. *Synonyms.* "A martin is a *bird.*"
2. *Antonyms.* "The plastic dish won't *break*, but the glass one probably will *shatter.*"
3. *Apposition* (use of a word or phrase that explains another word and that is set off by commas). "Florida is a peninsula, *a body of land surrounded on three sides by water*, and has many beaches."
4. *Comparison.* "A newsreel is *like a short motion picture* that shows news events."
5. *Contrast.* "A story that *rambles on and on is not concise.*"
6. *Description.* "Flying lizards are *found in Asia and can spread winglike membranes out from the sides of their small bodies so they can sometimes be seen gliding through the air.*"
7. *Example.* "A task force is a temporary grouping of forces, *for example, a military unit that has been called up to achieve a specific objective.*"
8. *Origin.* "The Italian word for *fresh* is *fresco, which gives us the name of a painting done on fresh plaster.*" (Dale & O'Rourke, 1971, p. 34)
9. *Formal definition.* "Lightsome *means buoyant, graceful, light, or nimble.*"

Carnine, Kameenui, and Coyle (1984) found that synonym-type context clues provided the most help for intermediate grade students when compared with types that required learners to make an inference. Determination of meanings also was improved if the clue word or words were placed close to the unlearned word rather than farther away in the text.

Gipe (1978–79) had some success with using pedagogical context to teach word meanings when she combined this method with providing definitions and when the targeted words were presented in multiple sentences. She also strengthened the method by having students generate example statements. Gipe compared this approach with three other techniques. Here is a description of the four word-learning techniques in Gipe's study:

1. In the *context method*, students read a paragraph in which the target word appeared in each of three sentences, two of which used context clues to convey a meaning, with the third furnishing an actual definition. Students then wrote something that related the word to their own experiences.

2. An *association method* required students to associate new words with a synonym they already knew, or with a short, written definition. Four such associations

were memorized each day and then students wrote them from memory. For example,

wretched = unhappy

barbarian = a cruel, mean person

3.   In her *category method,* words were listed by various categories that included descriptive words and nouns. Students read these and then added their own words to each category. For example (Gipe, p. 630):

Bad People	*Things You Can Write With*
mean	pencil
cruel	graphite
barbarian	marker
robber	chalk

Write your own words:	*Write your own words:*

Next, students were given a list of all target words in random order, plus category titles. They were to list target words under the correct category without referring to their study sheet listing words under categories.

4.   In a *dictionary method*, the students looked up each word in the dictionary, wrote its definition, and wrote it in a sentence.

Of the four methods, the "context method" and the "association method" augmented vocabulary learning, but the "category method" and the "dictionary method" were not helpful.

Use the Dictionary—Judiciously.   Dale (personal communication, November 17, 1974) once conducted a survey asking students which of all activities in school they liked least. The winner of this dubious honor was the exercise of looking up of a list of words in a dictionary and writing their meanings.

Should use of a dictionary even be used as a route to vocabulary learning? Herman and Dole (1988) summarize from research answers to that question: (a) if a word embodies a complicated or difficult concept about which learners have minimal or no prior knowledge, just looking it up likely will not unravel the mystery; (b) if the students possess a fair amount of understanding of the underlying ideas and know other words that may be used to define it, a dictionary can be useful in pinpointing a word's meaning; (c) if thorough understanding of a word is needed to comprehend a passage, other procedures than obtaining a dictionary definition are preferable; (d) if the word is of only slight importance for understanding text to be read, then the partial understanding that may be obtained from looking it up in a dictionary can suffice (p. 44).

Here is an example of ineffective dictionary use. Suppose an article your students will read is about a certain time period in geologic history. As such it prominently and frequently includes the unfamiliar, potentially difficult word that names it, the *Archeozoic* period. You know this article is going to be of interest to your students because of its content, but this is a brand-new topic area for them. Since you certainly want the readers to understand the article they will be using, you write the word *Archeozoic* on the board and tell them that they should each look it up in their desktop dictionaries before they begin to read. The students pull their dictionaries in front of them and dutifully begin to thumb through to find the word. As they locate the word, they find that the definition says:

> **Archeozoic**—Of or denoting the earliest of two customary, but arbitrary, partitions of the Precambrian era.

After students have found and read the definition to themselves, they do as you have asked and start to read the article. But, what has this definition told the student who has no prior experience in learning or reading about geologic periods? Almost nothing. Teacher explanations would serve the purpose much better than a trip to the dictionary in such cases. Such explanations could involve a brief discussion of the ancient age of the earth and the fact that scientists have divided the time the earth has been in existence into periods in order to study what has gone on at various stages. A geologic map (readily available in most schools) on which time periods have been marked could be briefly shown, pointing out especially the times during which dinosaurs existed and when humans have lived (since these two points of information are more likely than others to have references in the prior knowledge of learners). The introductory activity might be ended with the statement that the article will show what was happening during one geologic time period, the Archeozoic. With questions peppered throughout this explanation to enhance student involvement and with predictions elicited at the end, this tactic for developing the meaning of a complex, unfamiliar term would be more powerful in building understanding than merely "looking it up."

A second example of a futile dictionary exercise may be one you have experienced yourself at some time in your learning career. Students go to the dictionary and discover that the meaning they are seeking contains a word *in the definition* that they do not know. If they truly need to understand the term, they then look up the other unknown word—only to find that it is defined with yet another term about which they don't have a clue.

For instance, Ronnie's teacher wants him to see the nuances of difference between the words *pity* and *compassion* because the theme of a story he will be reading hinges on the contrast between the two. Ronnie begins by looking up the word *pity,* intending to compare the definition with that of *compassion* as the teacher has directed. He finds that the word is defined as "a sympathetic, but sometimes slightly contemptuous sadness for the distress of another." Ronnie doesn't know what *contemptuous* means, so sighing, he wades through the dictionary to find its explanation, which is "a feeling of contempt." "Rats!" Ronnie says. "What is *contempt?*" He looks it up (easy this time since it is on the same page as *contemptuous*) and sees that it means "disdain." "Now, what does *disdain* mean?" mutters Ronnie to himself. "This activity is dumb, or I'm dumb." But, being incredibly motivated, he searches the dictionary for *disdain,* only to see that the word is defined as "a feeling of contempt; scorn." "Oh, no," grieves Ronnie, "that word *contempt* again—and what is *scorn?*" Although this is taking up much of the time allotted for reading the story that the procedure is supposed to facilitate, blowing a loud noise through his nose, Ronnie forges on to find *scorn*; the definition states, "vigorous contempt; disdain." "That's it!" he whimpers. "I give up!" And he closes the dictionary with a loud smack.

It is obviously impossible to ferret out meanings that are this circuitous. Plainly, before assigning dictionary work, teachers should look up—*in the dictionary students will be using*—words they plan to designate for investigation. In such cases as this one, a method other than finding dictionary definitions would be more effective.

On the other hand, here is an example where dictionary work could easily help to clarify a distinction. The students are reading *Call It Courage* (Sperry, 1968), the story of a Polynesian boy who has a fear of the sea. A question comes up about the difference between a bay and a lagoon—or are these really just the same thing? The readers already have a concept about different types of bodies of water from their social studies lessons; they know how a lake is different from a river and how both are different from oceans and seas. When they examine the dictionary definition for *bay,* they find it is "a body of water partly enclosed by land but with a wide opening to the sea," while the definition for *lagoon* is "a body of water separated from the sea by sandbars or coral reefs." The distinction is forthright and easy to grasp for students who have the underlying concepts.

"Looking it up" also may be an efficient way to handle a quick question about a word that is of interest, but that does not particularly merit a well-developed set of lessons to instill its meaning. In a story one class was reading, a young Appalachian girl, Katy O'Toole, was tormented by the teasing of other children in her school when she moved to a big city in Ohio. Among other taunts they called her a katydid ("Katydid! Katydid! You aren't nuthin' but an old katydid" a couple of boys chanted at her at various times in the book). A visit to the dictionary not only told the students reading this story that a katydid is a green insect related to a grasshopper and a cricket—one that makes a special kind of noise when it rubs its wings together—it also provided a small but nice photograph so they could see what this insect looked like. Satisfied, they were able to understand what the silly taunts based on Katy's name had frivolously meant, and they moved ahead to concentrate on the important ideas in the narrative.

In short, it is necessary to use dictionary activities judiciously in vocabulary development programs. Certainly, giving long lists of words unrelated to anything, and asking students to write out their definitions, is not recommended. There are other cases in which various techniques are more productive than dictionary work, but there also are circumstances when time with the dictionary is well spent.

Use Teacher Explanations.   There is no reason at all not to simply *tell* learners what a word means. Consulting an authority is one way to obtain information. This is, of course, optimally productive when the explanations of the authority (the teacher) are rich with examples and illustrations. Telling a brief anecdote to elucidate the meaning, showing a visual aid (a picture, map), and pointing out similar words that students have in their vocabularies are enriching ways to fortify verbal explanations. The example given above in which the teacher explains the meaning of *Archeozoic* shows the constructiveness of this tactic over some weaker introductory transactions.

Help Students Integrate New Word Knowledge With Text.   In a study conducted by Kameenui et al (1982), two techniques were found to be effective to present words. The first involved introducing words and their meanings written on index cards and conducting the following intensive procedures (pp. 375–376).

1. The teacher, then the students, pronounced the word (e.g., *altercations*).
2. A student read the word's meaning from the card (e.g., *fights*).
3. The teacher posed questions designed to illustrate the word's meanings and how these meanings related to use (e.g., "Do you have altercations with your teacher?" "Do you have altercations with a tree?").
4. The students were asked to specify a definition of the word again.
5. The teacher presented a second and third card and instruction employed the same steps.
6. After instruction on the third word, a review was conducted: students were asked questions about each to determine if meanings were understood. If not, the relevant card was shown and the student was asked to respond to additional questions.

7. Following this cumulative review, all of the above steps were carried out with three additional words.

While this highly structured procedure, including repetition, definitions, and contextual use, was found to facilitate comprehension of passages containing the instructed words, students who were exposed to a second technique scored even higher. The second technique consisted of all the steps used in the first one, but, in addition, students were taught to "integrate" the meanings of the words during passage reading. "Integration" meant that during text reading, the teacher asked the students to pause when they encountered one of the words they had practiced, to say the word's meaning, and to answer a quick question asked by the teacher, requiring understanding of the word's meaning.

Rich Development

Some words simply require a brief mention and a passing exchange with your students to confer enough about their function in a text. An introductory transaction may suffice in these cases, but other words deserve (because of their importance) or need (because of their complexity) deeper development.

General Features of an Intensive Program of Word Development. In-depth development of word meanings entails varied experiences and different levels of clarification, reflective and dynamic operations with connotations and denotations of words, and substantial practice. Such a method incorporates definitions, but also involves students in employing words in a variety of contexts, active use of the words in student-created situations, and seeing relationships with other words (Beck & McKeown, 1991).

A vocabulary program McKeown and Beck (1988) conducted for middle graders exemplifies this type of richness. They describe their approach in the following way (p. 43). Instruction focused on one set of words each week—about 8 to 10. Each set contained terms that were semantically related in order to facilitate useful activities; for instance, one group was based on the theme of "moods" and contained, among others, the words *enthusiastic, indignant,* and *jovial.* Introductory transactions involved simply relating the words to their meanings. However, each subsequent part of the weekly activities required successively deeper processing. In one activity, students worked with text that gave examples, actions regularly connected with the words, or consequences. This sample was given:

> Maria decided that she didn't want to play with Terry anymore. Terry was always being nasty about other people. She'd make a big joke out of the way other people looked or talked. What did Terry do to other people? (McKeown & Beck, 1988, p. 43)

Students were to connect their practice word *ridicule* with this description. The students next generated their own text about focus words based on engaging questions from the teacher, with teacher modeling of response initially employed. For example, to the challenge "What might a *hermit* have a nightmare about?" the teacher gave a response before the students prepared theirs in order to show how logical answers could be derived from the meanings they were beginning to understand about the target word. In state-of-the-art instruction, modeling is considered a crucial support for literacy learning (Sweet, 1993).

In a later activity, readers were asked questions that combined two of their target words and that required that they think about the meanings they had been practicing.

One question asked "Can a *tyrant* be a *miser?*" and another "Would you *berate* a person who had *inspired* you?" and another "Would you *baffle* someone who tried to *snare* you?" (McKeown & Beck, 1988, p. 43). Learners were required to give reasons for their answers to ensure that their processing was explicitly related to the focus words.

Such thought-provoking exercises, along with active discussion of answers, extends sensitivities to a word's connotations. Moreover, this approach conforms with a principle suggested by Nagy (1988)—that target words be subjected to meaningful *use.* Nagy underscores the need to encourage learners to make inferences about focus words. This produces a higher level of learning than merely requiring a definition to be stated. When a student decides that a *tyrant* and a *miser* are not the same thing, but then discussion with peers leads to the conclusion that one person *could* be both, deeper processing necessarily must occur than would result from simple instruction on definitions. Using words actively facilitates recall of the word's meanings at a later time.

Beck and McKeown (1991) state the following about rich development of word meanings:

> A common thread running through these examples of instruction that encourages active processing is that activities do not merely call for entering new information in memory. Rather, students are required to use information by comparing it to, and combining it with, known information toward constructing representations of word meaning. (p. 807)

Some Specific Activities That Require In-Depth Processing. Much interest has emerged recently about the direct instruction of meaning vocabulary. As a result many interesting ideas have been tested and a number have shown good results. Some of those are described here.

1. *Involve students in process-oriented semantic mapping.* Oral or written tasks that help students preview material can aid their vocabulary knowledge. One way to conduct an oral preview is to use a *semantic map* (G. Freedman & Reynolds, 1980; D. D. Johnson, 1984). Terms employed by some authorities for similar activities are use of *structured overviews* (Vacca, 1981), *conceptual vocabulary maps* (Haggard, 1985), *group mapping activities* (Davidson, 1982), *cognitive mapping* (Ruddell & Boyle, 1984), or *word maps* (Schwartz & Raphael, 1985). All these terms refer to the same basic idea. There are two broad categories of semantic maps. One type is process-oriented and the other is product-oriented. Both are designed to help students understand terminology and concepts related to narrative or informational materials.

In a **process-oriented semantic map,** there is group discussion before a story or informational material is read. The discussion is illustrated in some graphic manner by the teacher, often focusing on important concepts related to vocabulary. Process-oriented semantic maps are, in effect, advance organizers (Ausubel, 1960). Here is an example of this type of semantic map and how it is built.

Teacher: The story you're going to read tells you what happens when a boy uses sarcasm and people think his remarks are serious. What do you think *sarcasm* is?

David: A way of talking that's not serious.

Craig: Smart-alecky talk.

Albert: It seems to me it's being mean.

Teacher writes on board:

Sarcasm—Talk that is:
–Not serious
–"Smart alecky"
–Being mean

Jana: I had this Girl Scout leader once who would say sarcastic things to
           us if we didn't do things the way she tried to teach us.
Teacher: How about you, Kimberly? What do you think sarcasm means?
Kimberly: I don't know.
Michael: Sometimes kids say sarcastic things to you on the playground just to
           act big.

Teacher adds to information on board:

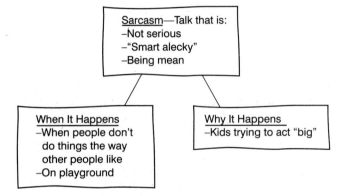

Teacher: Who can think of other times or reasons people have been sarcas-
           tic?
David: My dad has been sarcastic to me.
Teacher: When? And why do you think he was?
David: Like he gets tired of me arguing back when he tells me to do stuff,
           so he says,"Okay, Mr. Big Shot! No more arguing. Just do it."

Teacher writes more information on board:

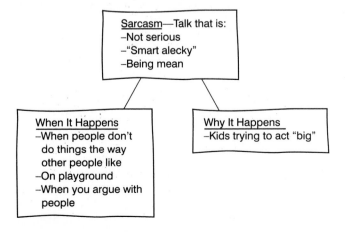

Teacher: Why do you think David's dad said something sarcastic when David argued with him?

David: It's his way of getting me to do it in a kind of joking way, but letting me know he means business.

Teacher: Why do you think Jana's Girl Scout leader sometimes made sarcastic remarks?

Albert: Maybe she's mean.

Jana: She wasn't really mean to us, but my mother said she was impatient.

Teacher completes diagram on board:

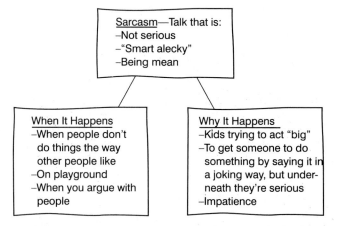

Barron (1969) calls this type of discussion a **visual-verbal presentation.** It is particularly effective with remedial students for whom mere explanation of concepts before reading material may not be sufficient to enable them to relate ideas to their own backgrounds. It also allows the input of many group members, which may in turn extend students' limited notions about concepts.

At the conclusion of a dialogue such as this, the teacher points to each part of the diagram the students have developed and directs them to make some forecasts about what they are about to read in relation to the ideas they have contributed. For instance, for the example just given, students may be asked to predict whether the boy in the upcoming story will be sarcastic because he is "smart alecky" or because he is mean. The students may also be asked to note whether *when* and *why* the boy was sarcastic are similar to any of the reasons they have suggested. After students read the story, they make these comparisons in a follow-up discussion.

2.   *Employ product-oriented semantic maps.* To use a **product-oriented semantic map,** Pachtman and Riley (1978) suggest that before a lesson, the teacher should select a concept to be emphasized from a selection that will be read. Vocabulary and/or ideas related to the concept are identified and, for student use, the teacher writes each of these on separate cards.

After reading the selection, students develop a product by working in small groups to arrange the cards into a semantic map, which can show relationships among terms and concepts. Figure 11–2 provides an example of a semantic map students used after reading an article on the history of money. Finally, the teacher and students engage in whole-group discussion, examining and critiquing one

FIGURE 11–2
A semantic map based on concepts and vocabulary from a reading selection on the history of money

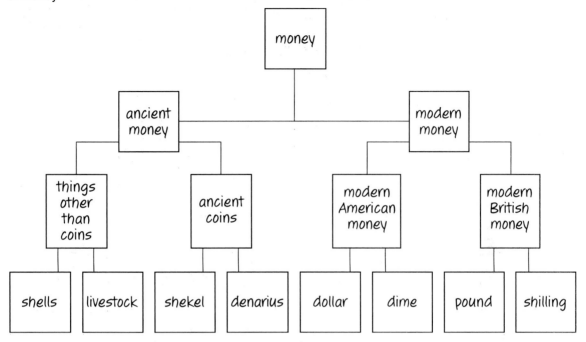

another's completed semantic maps. Justifications for differences are offered and revisions made when deemed important.

The product developed by students in this activity provides a reinforcement of vocabulary terms, additional exposures beyond those encountered in the connected text, and also helps students see the interrelationships among ideas. In this case, the product itself is referred to as a *semantic map*, while in a process-oriented semantic map, the whole procedure is referred to as *semantic mapping*.

Use of either type of semantic map is particularly helpful before or after reading books in which the concept load is heavy, such as science, history, or other textbooks.

3. *Use word maps for different parts of speech.* Duffelmeyer and Banwart (1993) described ways to adapt word maps so they relate purposefully to terms that embody various parts of speech. Figure 11–3 depicts three word maps to exemplify models for words that are nouns, adjectives, and verbs. In each of these maps, the focus word is placed in a center box in the drawing, and terms that suggest attributes and examples of the word are placed in surrounding boxes to fit specific categories. These categories vary according to the part of speech of the focus word.

4. *Engage learners in semantic feature analysis.* Bos and Anders (1990) had readers compare and contrast groups of semantically related words. With junior high school students who had learning disabilities, they employed semantic feature analysis.

FIGURE 11–3
Three word maps

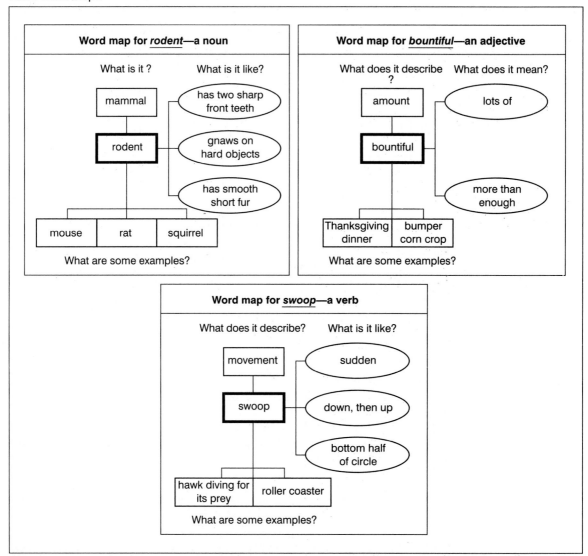

Source: From "Word Maps for Adjectives and Adverbs" by Frederick A. Duffelmeyer and Beth Husman Banwart, Dec. 1992/Jan. 1993, *The Reading Teacher, 46.* Copyright 1993 by the International Reading Association. Reprinted by permission of Frederick A. Duffelmeyer and the International Reading Association.

In **semantic feature analysis** (D. D. Johnson & Pearson, 1984), readers are helped to see associations and differences between semantically linked words through use of a "relationship matrix." (See Figure 11–4.) A list of semantically similar words is placed along the left side of the matrix. At the top, semantic features are listed. **Semantic features** are properties or meanings that the words listed to the left may share. The task is to determine which are shared and which

FIGURE 11–4

A relationship matrix used in a semantic feature analysis activity

	unknown	unexplained	unfamiliar	unusual	old-fashioned
strange	+	+	+	+	−
peculiar	−	+	−	+	−
quaint	−	−	+	+	+
outlandish	−	−	+	+	?
eccentric	−	+	+	+	?

are not. After discussion, pluses or minuses are placed in the columns to indicate group decisions. The value of the activity is, of course, in the discussion. Through these deliberations, readers must think through their ideas, and argue, and defend, and learn from one another precisions in denotations, as well as nuances of words—a process that leads to complete, rather than vague, definitions. In Bos and Ander's (1990) study, use of semantic feature analysis increased students' knowledge of word meanings, and reading comprehension, on both short-term and long-term measures.

Figure 11–4 shows how one group of learners filled in a relationship matrix for a set of words, after much discussion and examples offered by members of the group. The decisions might be slightly different with other students, depending on the illustrations offered by participants and the degree to which particular students have a propensity to split hairs (the latter being a positive behavior and one on which this procedure is designed to capitalize). Most decisions will closely agree with conventional meanings, and, in any case, the discussion is the important part of the learning episode.

5.   *Have learners develop Venn diagrams.* Nagy (1988) suggests having students develop Venn diagrams. These display semantic connections, but, in addition, exhibit features that are not shared by two concepts. Figure 11–5 shows a Venn diagram for comparing and contrasting two terms found in geography texts. In the

FIGURE 11–5

An example of a Venn diagram comparing two geographical terms

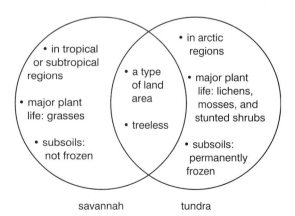

- in tropical or subtropical regions
- major plant life: grasses
- subsoils: not frozen

- a type of land area
- treeless

- in arctic regions
- major plant life: lichens, mosses, and stunted shrubs
- subsoils: permanently frozen

savannah   tundra

space where the circles of the diagram overlap, shared features of the two words are listed. In the outlying spaces above each term, the features that are different are itemized.

6.   *Provide experiences with synonyms and antonyms.* Gipe's (1978–79) study, cited earlier, shows that direct practice with words and their synonyms is an effective procedure. Gipe's synonym practice, called the *association method,* was a drill procedure.

An introductory exercise that is a manipulative activity for practicing synonyms can be made from 8½" by 11" pieces of colored construction paper. Draw two sets of lines across each piece with a marking pen. (See Figure 11–6.) Write known words on the left-hand lines of each construction paper "board" (for example, *name, tight, grumpy, winding, sparkle, useless, hothouse*). Cut strips of plain oaktag to a size that will fit on each of the right-hand lines. Write a synonym on each oaktag strip for one of the listed known words (for example, *sinuous, designation, taut, conservatory,* and so on). Place one set of these construction paper "boards" plus the accompanying synonym strips in each of several manila envelopes. Label the envelopes #1, #2, and so forth. Give each student one manila envelope set and a dictionary. Have students use their dictionaries to determine which words are synonyms and then place the oaktag strips next to the matching words on their "board."

A commercial game for practicing synonyms as well as antonyms is Swap (Steck-Vaughn).

Examining and substituting words in written materials can move practice with synonyms beyond the introductory level. (Vocabulary used in these exercises should be selected from focus sets where meanings have already been introduced.)

1. Mark the word that would *best* substitute for the underlined word:

Jim's <u>clever story</u> was entertaining everyone when I walked into the room.

_____ funny

_____ intelligent

✓_____ witty

Here is another example of a synonym exercise. This exercise is designed to move word use from a lower to a more sophisticated level. Afterward, ask students *why* one synonym is better than another.

FIGURE 11–6
A synonym board

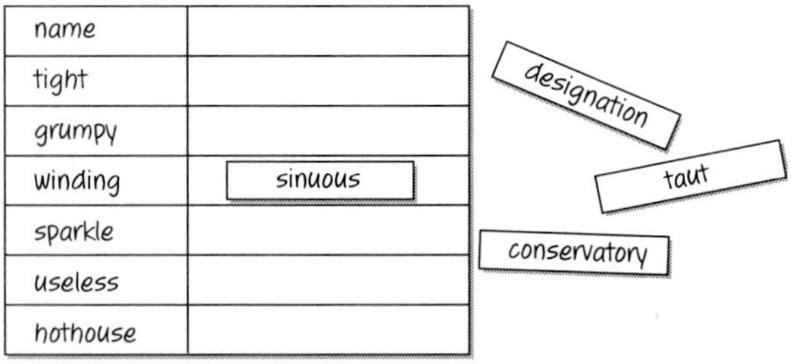

name	
tight	
grumpy	
winding	sinuous
sparkle	
useless	
hothouse	

designation

taut

conservatory

2. Choose the word that would *best* fit the blank.

As the wind _____ through the huge sails, all the sailors shuddered with fear.

(howled)   blew   moved

It is a good time to familiarize students with a thesaurus when they are working with synonyms. Many simplified versions of this functional reference tool are now available for use in elementary classrooms, and abridged paperback editions can be purchased for secondary programs.

Here is one activity for introducing the contents and value of a thesaurus that will get students thinking. Choose a theme, such as Halloween or pioneers or basketball, and ask students to tell you *every* word they can think of related to that topic. As students contribute words, write them on the chalkboard. When they have exhausted their suggestions and the chalkboard is quite full, tell them they are each to write a short story about this topic—but they may not use any of the words listed on the board! The task entails using the thesaurus to locate synonyms for any words on the board they wish to use in their stories. Not only is this fun and challenging, the resulting stories are usually quite interesting.

Writing haiku can also be a stimulus for using a thesaurus, as well as for adding new synonyms to vocabularies. Haiku is a form of Japanese poetry written in only 3 lines and having exactly 17 syllables in each poem. The syllables must follow a prescribed pattern: there must be 5 syllables in the first line, 7 in the second line, and 5 in the third line. If students wish to use a word in their poems to express a thought, but it doesn't have the right number of syllables, they use the thesaurus to find a word expressing the same thought but with the right number of syllables.

Many types of practice conducted with synonyms can also be carried out with antonyms. Edgar Dale (personal communication, February 22, 1984) stated that when a person can specify the opposite of a word he or she truly understands its meaning.

Antonym cards may be prepared by the teacher for students' independent practice. Following are directions for preparing cards for a matching activity that students can correct themselves. On index cards, print single words. Next, write their antonyms on an equivalent set, one antonym to a card. Turn pairs of antonyms over so they are placed next to one another. Paste a paper sticker on the cards so half of the sticker is on one card and half on the other. With scissors, snip the cards apart. Do the same with all pairs. As students practice with the antonym cards they should attempt to line them up by pairs on their desks. At the completion, each pair should be turned over to see if the two half pictures (forming the snipped sticker) on the backs fit together to make a whole; if not, a wrong choice has been made and the student should restudy the cards.

After students have used the cards described in the preceding paragraph, use the same basic set of antonyms, writing them into a short story. The learners are to revise your story by turning each of the focus set of antonyms into a word of an opposite meaning, thus producing a contradictory version. For example, where you may have used the word *bizarre*, they might use *normal*; where you have used *continuous*, they might use *sporadic*. Then, have them develop such stories with the focus set to exchange with each other, and engage in the same activity.

7. *Provide exposures to multiple meanings of words.* The difference between the meaning vocabularies of skilled and unskilled readers is often found in the number of meanings each is able to provide for a specific word. Paul and O'Rourke (1988) suggest that poor readers may require direct and imaginative teaching of multi-meaning words.

Frequently, a poor reader can give only the most common meaning of a word. And students in remedial programs need work, not only with words they encounter in narrative, story-type material, but also with multiple meanings of words that have specialized meanings in content area fields. For example, although Joe certainly knows the meaning for *mouth* when one is talking about the opening in the head used for eating and talking, he may have no understanding of its meaning when his geography book refers to the *mouth* of a river. Having students draw pictures of right and wrong meanings of such terms helps them remember less familiar definitions of words with multiple meanings.

Discussion of differences in shades of meaning also can help students develop precision in word usage. For example, questions such as the following might be asked.

What is the difference between *soft* fur and *soft* fruit?

What is the difference between *soft* light and *soft* pink?

Games, too, can be used for practice with multiple meanings. One example is the game illustrated in Figure 11–7 called "multiple meaning bingo." This game helps students become familiar with a number of meanings for the same word and gives practice in selecting the correct meaning to fit a specific context. To make this game, the teacher first consults a dictionary to compile a list of different meanings for a single common word. Number and list these meanings as shown in the bottom portion of Figure 11–7. On paper, draw a bingo board as shown in the upper portion of Figure 11–7, and write sentences for each of the listed definitions, writing one sentence in each square. Students are then given a photocopy of the bingo board together with a piece of oaktag of the same size. They are to quickly cut apart each square of the photocopy so there are 25 separate squares. These are to be placed on the piece of oaktag in random order—*not* in the same sequence as on the original paper copy—so that each student has squares in different places on the oaktag, but with five in a row horizontally and five vertically (as in typical bingo games). Students are also given 25 numbered markers for covering squares.

To begin the game, the teacher reads definition number 1; each student then selects a marker numbered "1" and places it on the sentence whose context is thought to indicate a match for the meaning given. When a student has five squares covered in a column or row he or she says "bingo!" The teacher uses the numbered markers to check the covered sentences against the numbers of the respective definitions on the teacher's master copy, and these must match for the student to win.

8. *Increase vocabulary learning through writing.* Cudd and Roberts (1993–94) report a successful approach with both poor and average readers to increase precision in use of word meanings. Students were helped to write better stories by focusing on sentence expansion and on interesting words from their reading texts, literature books, and content area material.

Teachers wrote sentence stems that students expanded and illustrated. The sentence stems used challenging vocabulary and syntactic structures students had

FIGURE 11–7

A game for practicing multiple meanings

(Student's materials)

After praying the man saw the light.	It i̶ ligh̶ [1]	He is one of the brighter lights of American literature.	Evelyn is a light eater.	He gave her a light to start the fire.
His daughter is the light of his life.	The sweater is light blue.	We will get up at first light.	Her eyes lighted up with liveliness.	Her light movements across the ice won her the championship.
He was in the light brigade.	We got a light snow last night.	LIGHT (free space)	Th̶ lig̶ [2]	The football missed the goalpost because it was a light kick.
I hate sitting in the dark; I wish it was light.	The Taming of the Shrew is light comedy.	I hope you can shed some light on the subject.	After the good news, Karen felt light at heart.	She felt light-headed.
Her piecrust is always light.	On November 1, 1918 he first saw the light of day.	She now saw things in a different light.	I think that butcher gave me a light pound.	Those women spend their lunch hours .engaging in light chatter

(Teacher's materials)

1. illumination	13. adored by another
2. not heavy	14. entertainment that is not serious
3. dawn	15. a distinguished person
4. daylight	16. free from worry
5. of less than correct weight	17. an expression of the eyes
6. means for igniting a fire	18. suffering from faintness
7. less than normal force	19. to be born
8. spiritual awareness	20. moving quickly and easily
9. having less quantity	21. to provide information
10. a way of regarding something	22. carrying little military arms or equipment
11. moderate	23. color mixed with white
12. insignificant	24. a flaky texture

already encountered in their reading. For example, the teachers wrote stems such as "During Alberto's *perilous* journey across the Sahara Desert, _____ " (p. 347), and the students discussed ways to complete the sentences. They then wrote their own sentence endings and illustrated the completed sentences. For instance, one third-grader finished the stem "While Stephanie *toiled* furiously to repair the spaceship, _____ " with the clause "the aliens were partying" and drew a picture of five aliens dancing around the spaceship saying "We love to party! Gooogley, woggley, yahoo!" (p. 346).

After practice with this technique, more complex structures and vocabulary began to appear in the students' original writings, as seen in comparisons between stories written in the first month of school with those written by the fourth month. This activity follows well the principle of active use of vocabulary words.

Teachers' Store G lists some commercial materials that may be useful supplements to a word-meaning study program.

INDEPENDENT WORD LEARNING FROM TEXT

Incidental Learning

Authorities do not agree about the effectiveness of learning new word meanings incidentally simply from reading text. Some educators question the productiveness of incidental learning of vocabulary. They point to studies showing that when learners read text containing unfamiliar vocabulary, they later are able to give meanings for only a small percentage of these words; this is believed to be an indication that students do not easily infer vocabulary meanings from connected narratives or informational material (Jenkins, Stein, & Wysocki, 1984). Further, poor readers appear to be less facile at gaining the sense of words from contextual selections than are skilled readers (McKeown, 1985). Finally, it is argued that natural text—that is, text that has not been purposely

---

Teachers' Store G

Meaning Vocabulary

1. *Vocabulary Building* (Zaner-Bloser)
2. *Words Are Important* (Hammond)
3. *SRA: Structural Analysis* (Science Research Associates)
4. *Prefix Puzzles* (Developmental Learning Materials)
5. *Suffix Puzzles* (Developmental Learning Materials)
6. *Cloze Practice Sheets* (Opportunities for Learning)
7. *Developing Structural Analysis Skills* (Educational Record Sales)
8. *Verbal Classifications* (Midwest Publications)
9. *Words in Context* (Opportunities for Learning)
10. *Be a Better Reader* (Prentice-Hall)
11. *The Vocabulary Development Series* (Macmillan)
12. *Vocabulary Drills* (Jamestown)
13. *Vocabulary Building Exercises for Young Adults* (Dormac)
14. *Idioms* (Dormac)
15. *Many Meanings* (Dormac)
16. *Word Power* (Developmental Learning Materials)
17. *Vocabulary Development* (Frank Schaffer)
18. *Vocabulary Building: A Process Approach* (Zaner-Bloser). (Professional material for teaching meaning vocabulary)

Some word meanings can be learned through independent reading.

structured to provide a supportive context—does not readily convey word meanings (Schatz & Baldwin, 1986).

On the other hand, other authorities counter that some studies of incidental word learning fail to show large gains in word meaning knowledge because readers do not internalize vocabulary understandings from single or brief encounters with words in context. (Jenkins et al. [1984], for example, compared connected text encounters when students were exposed to specific unknown words either 2 times, 6 times, or 10 times; words were learned incidentally from context only in the cases where there were 6 or 10 confrontations with the words.) That learners can derive vocabulary understandings simply from wide reading is accounted for by these educators from the immense number of words that are processed through natural text reading experiences (e.g, Nagy, 1988). Thus, it is believed that the more one reads, the more one's vocabulary grows. In addition, they regard not only reading that occurs in school as a vehicle to development but also reading that takes place in other settings as well. For example, quantity of free-time reading has been found to strongly predict maturation in word meaning knowledge (Fielding, Wilson, & Anderson, 1986).

In rebuttal to the concern that less skilled readers do not glean meanings easily from contextual reading, authorities who place strong stock in the effects of incidental word learning suggest that this is so because poor readers do not read as much as adept readers, and that a serious emphasis must be placed on arranging the environment so that these students read more. Further, they believe poor readers must be explicitly taught how to derive word meanings from connected text. These educators concede that natural narratives and expository materials do not always furnish needed information to learn word meanings. These authorities contend that the solution is to teach learners that context has limitations—that it sometimes provides a contribution to understanding vocabulary meanings and sometimes it does not; in the latter cases, other sources must be used.

Another argument that is made in defense of the power of incidental word learning from text is based on reports of the large numbers of vocabulary meanings school-age children and youth learn each year—numbers far greater than words taught directly (e.g., see Herman & Dole, 1988). A contradictory argument, however, is that the strongest influence on vocabulary learning in the preschool years is based on oral language encounters. Since students have access to these same sources during their school years, there is no reason to suppose that some of this remarkable growth is not accounted for from incidental learning from oral language, as well.

Currently research does not allow clear answers about the degree to which incidental learning from connected text affects the development of a meaning vocabulary. While some authorities argue that incidental learning plays an indispensable role in vocabulary growth, others contend that the effects of incidental learning are diluted by other factors. However, most acknowledge that there is value in promoting extensive reading, and a good amount of the disagreement concerns the *degree* to which ample reading affects the learning of new words. In brief, certain educators would claim that not as many words are learned from incidental learning as are often suggested, but that certainly some are (e.g., Beck & McKeown, 1991). This group would assert that comprehensive reading experiences do promote vocabulary advancement, but would caution that all readers may not be able to depend exclusively on this route to learning. Others would assert that most words are learned from incidental learning, but that certainly many are learned from direct instruction (e.g., Nagy et al., 1987). The bottom line, then, seems to be that most authorities support both direct instruction and incidental learning, but to different degrees.

It appears, then, that while knowledge of word meanings can improve reading, interestingly, the converse also is true—reading can improve knowledge of word meanings. Individuals who read voraciously usually have rich vocabularies that are larger in quantity of known words and broader in quality than the vocabulary of individuals who do not read extensively. This effect is not only seen with common words, but also for technical words and concepts needed to read content area texts (Farris & Fuhler, 1994). Wide reading also increases knowledge of multiple meanings of words for which previously only the common meanings were known. It seems then that one effective way to help students improve their word meaning knowledge is to stimulate them to read an abundance of books, magazines, articles, newspapers, and any other type of connected text. It is, therefore, reasonable for a remedial teacher to spend a portion of instructional periods motivating student interest in varied types of authentic reading materials.

Ironically, those poor readers who have conspicuous deficits in meaning vocabulary are often the very ones who do not like to read. Many other poor readers are often delighted to read—if given books and materials at an appropriate level so they *can* read them, and within such a classroom context, they will choose reading for pleasure over other activities. Too often this is not the case with the student who has a particularly meager meaning vocabulary. The teacher, then, must find ways to activate interest in reading, prompting this learner to view reading as a worthwhile activity. The following ideas are suggested.

1. *Explore students' interests through interviews and interest inventories.* See Chapter 7 for tools for assessing interests. Start a student's reading programs with short, easy books targeted to his or her interests. Use short magazine and newspaper articles, as well as books.

2. *Provide time for sustained silent reading (SSR).* During SSR, students *may read anything they wish,* but no other activity except silent reading is allowed. The teacher uses a timer, keeping the interval for reading on the first day quite short, usually about 5 minutes. The timer is placed facing the teacher—so you don't have a room full of clock-watchers instead of readers—and students read until the timer rings. Every few days the amount of time is increased by a minute or two until students are sustaining their silent reading from about 15 minutes (in elementary level remedial classes) to 30 minutes (in secondary level programs).

The technique works best if the teacher also reads a book of his or her choice to serve as a model for students. Teachers sometimes post a DO NOT DISTURB sign on the door during SSR, and students as well as teachers often begin to look upon this time period as the best of the day.

In the early phases of an SSR program, very reluctant readers may initially be disinclined to read, and instead, sit staring at an open page. After a while, this behavior simply becomes too boring, and they begin to look at pictures in the text. If there are captions, they may next be induced to read a few of these. Eventually, previously diffident readers are seduced into the reading material. Thereafter, these students usually participate willingly in SSR. Hilbert (1993) calls this giving them a nibble and watching their appetites grow. Motivation to read is simplified somewhat because the student is permitted to choose anything at all to read, no matter how easy or short, as long as there is enough text to sustain reading for the duration of the activity.

Although comic books, magazines, and joke books serve legitimate objectives for enticing unwilling readers into SSR, after the incentive to read has been awakened, the teacher may challenge the students to select a book that it will take a week to complete, a book with chapters, for instance.

Arranging some time after SSR for students to share what they have read breeds curiosity about books that peers have enjoyed and may impel students to select longer books or materials of different genres. This can be a rather informal discussion period or may involve more structured projects. For example, several youngsters who have read the same book could make simple stick puppets to dramatize the story to others. Such puppets can be made easily by having students paste tongue depressors on the backs of pictures they have drawn of characters from the book. Preparation of the puppets could occur outside of reading class (a fun homework assignment) so that class reading time will not be used.

Another way to augment interest is to have students write brief book reviews. To do this, create a group file box for index cards on which students are to write the names of books they've read, along with two or three observations about each book. Colored file cards and white file cards should be available. If students really like a book, they "review" it on the colored file cards. If their reaction is that the book was just so-so, the information goes on the white cards. When students want to choose a new book, they can refer to the file box and read the reviews on the colored cards.

3. *Read aloud to students who are at first reluctant to read themselves.* In addition to its other positive effects, reading to students is one of the best ways to get them interested in reading. Have similar books available so that once learners become absorbed with a topic, author, or genre, they can read a comparable text themselves.

Not only does reading to students inspire desire to read on their own, it is a direct route to vocabulary learning. A good principle to follow when reading aloud to students is to read material slightly above the level they could read for themselves. For example, reading aloud to urban sixth-graders from seventh grade materials resulted in vocabulary gains of approximately 7% in one study (Stahl, Richek, & Vandevier, 1991). Some have also found that having learners retell a story immediately after reading it to them also assists the learning of new word meanings—probably because students tend to use some of the words they have just heard when giving their own renditions (e.g., Leung & Pikulski, 1990)— and they also could be prompted to do so. Studies also show that reading aloud tends to most affect words that are already slightly familiar—students enlarge their understandings of these words, becoming able to use them with greater exactness (e.g., Leung, 1992).

If time is short, poetry is a good choice for the teacher to read aloud; it takes only a few moments to read a poem or two or three. An excellent book for this purpose is *An Invitation to Poetry* (Addison-Wesley) because it includes poems that genuinely engage students. The limerick section of this book is particularly popular. *Where the Sidewalk Ends,* by Shel Silverstein (Harper & Row), is another poetry book enjoyed enormously by most students. If this anthology is highlighted for reading aloud over a period of time, have another Silverstein book of poems, *The Light in the Attic* (Harper & Row), handy for readers to choose to read on their own.

Some books to read aloud to students who initially do not want to be read to are listed in Table 11–1. These books have routinely been found to be engrossing by even the most unenthusiastic students.

Table 11-2 suggests books for reading aloud to middle school students.

TABLE 11–1
Some books to read aloud to reluctant students

The Ghost Rock Mystery	Grades 4, 5, 6	Really scary. Leaves you "hanging" at the end of each chapter as something awful is about to happen. A good one to start the year with. Also available in paperback.
The Snake Who Went to School	Grades 3, 4, 5, 6	Funny. A snake gets loose in the school, isn't captured for several days, and is the cause of a number of wild happenings.
Casey, the Utterly Impossible Horse	Grades 3, 4, 5, 6	Ridiculously funny; a horse that talks.
All Pippi Longstocking books: *Pippi Longstocking; Pippi in the South Seas; Pippi Goes on Board*	Grades 3, 4, 5, 6	Even the teacher will laugh while reading these books. Pippi's father is the king of a cannibal island and her mother is dead, so she lives alone in a house in Sweden with her horse, her monkey, and a chest full of gold. And she does *anything* she wants to do.
Julie of the Wolves	Grades 5 and 6	Newbery Award Winner. Exciting, interesting, scary. An Eskimo girl is saved from starvation when a pack of wolves allows her to share their food and shelter. Realistic.
The House of the Sixty Fathers	Grades 5 and 6	Frightening, but realistically told story that takes place during the Japanese occupation of China during World War II when a boy becomes separated from his family and attempts to find them. Runner-up for the Newbery Award.
The Matchlock Gun	Grades 3, 4, 5, 6	A picture book for older children. Very exciting story and dramatic pictures. A settler's cabin is attacked by Indians during the French and Indian Wars. A Newbery Award Winner.

TABLE 11–2
Some books to read aloud to middle school students

Some of the books suggested here are most suitable for reading aloud to younger middle school students; some are better for use with older middle school pupils; others are suitable for any student of middle school age. Teachers should skim the first chapter of the book and read the information presented on the dust jacket to determine if a suggested book is suitable for the learners in their classes.

1. *Best Short Shorts,* Eric Berger, Editor (Paperback available from Scholastic. Every story has a surprise ending. Because selections are short, this book would be good to use when there is only a little time for reading aloud to students.)
2. *How to Eat Fried Worms,* Thomas Rockwell
3. *Fifty-two Miles to Terror,* Ruth and Robert Carlson (Nine tension-packed short stories)
4. *Encyclopedia Brown Takes a Case,* Donald Sobel
5. *Passport to Freedom,* Dorothy Bonnell
6. *Ben and Me,* Robert Lawson
7. *Out of the Sun,* Ben Bova
8. *Kareem! Basketball Great,* Arnold Hano
9. *The Wonderful Flight to the Mushroom Planet,* Eleanor Cameron
10. *New Sound,* Leslie Waller
11. *Julie of the Wolves,* Jean George
12. *Follow My Leader,* James B. Garfield
13. *Old Yeller,* Fred Gipson
14. *The Lost Ones,* Ian Cameron
15. *Island of the Blue Dolphins,* Scott O'Dell
16. *The Hornet's Nest,* Sally Watson
17. *Earthfasts,* William Mayne
18. *Trouble for the Tabors,* Barbara Goolden
19. *The House of the Sixty Fathers,* Meindert De Jong
20. *Hunger for Racing,* J. M. Douglas
21. *Incident at Hawk's Hill,* Allan Eckert
22. *Pippi Longstocking,* Astrid Lindgren
23. *Journey Outside,* Mary Q. Steele
24. *Bully of Barkham Street,* Mary Stolz
25. *The Phantom Tollbooth,* Norton Juster
26. *My Name is Pablo,* Aimee Somerfelt
27. *The Forgotten Door,* Alexander Key
28. *Escape To Witch Mountain,* Alexander Key
29. *A Wrinkle in Time,* Madeline L'Engle
30. *Funny Bananas,* Georgess McHargue
31. *The Witch of Blackbird Pond,* Elizabeth George Speare
32. *The Sound of Coaches,* Leon Garfield
33. *Eskimo Boy,* Pepaluk Fruchen
34. *The Gift,* Peter Dickinson
35. *The Yearling,* Marjorie Rawlings

4.   *Use movies of children's and adolescents' books to excite interest in reading the book itself.* Movies based on children's books may be obtained from many public libraries. Also, most school districts have central audiovisual libraries from which teachers may select films. Two well-known picture books for which movies have been produced are *Andy and the Lion* and *The Camel Who Took A Walk.* The original illustrations are depicted as the stories are read in these films. A movie that will make intermediate grade youngsters laugh is *The Doughnut Machine,* a funny episode from the popular book *Homer Price.*

   Again, have one or more copies of these books available for students to read after they have viewed the movie. On the face of it, it might seem that once students have seen a movie and know the story, they wouldn't be interested in reading it in a book, but in fact, the opposite effect occurs. A text based on a film a class has enjoyed often becomes the most popular book in the room for a time; even learners who struggle against your enticements to read will sign up for their turn with this book.

Filmstrips of books may be used in the same ways as movies. These are often available in the school media center.

5. *Cassette/book combinations are available to elicit interest in reading.* Cassettes accompanying books are available commercially (e.g., Scholastic). The books are often in paperback and so are relatively inexpensive. As a result, it is frequently feasible to purchase multiple copies of the books. Students may listen to the tape as a group and then the book is offered to students who wish to read it.

6. *Use commercial audiotapes.* Audiotapes have been prepared in which dramas of well-known books are presented, complete with sound effects. One teacher's successful experience with older students in a remedial reading class involved the group listening to a taped drama of the popular H. G. Wells's classic *The Time Machine.* When easy-to-read versions of this electrifying story were offered to the group afterward, almost all students chose to read the book. Check the school district's central audiovisual library or the public library for similar tapes.

7. *Have the students join a book club.* Scholastic and other companies sponsor such clubs from which students may order paperbacks monthly at a reasonable price. In a remedial class, a typical occurrence is for only a few students to order books the first month. To change this, on the day the books arrive the teacher makes a showy display of opening the package, removing the books one at a time, and passing them out to each student who ordered one. This is accompanied by enthusiastic comments about how interesting this one looks, about how that one is one of your own personal favorites, how this one really looks funny, and perhaps reading a page from one or two, or showing pictures. During that class period, students who have received new books are allowed to just sit and read them for the duration of the session. Thereafter, larger numbers of students become enthused with ordering—and reading—their own books.

8. *Use books that particularly lend themselves to lessons on word meaning.* The Amelia Bedelia series (Harper & Row), for example, has funny plays on words that students can enjoy and learn from. Amelia is a conscientious, but confused maid who misinterprets the written directions her employer leaves for her. When told to "dust the furniture," Amelia zips about with a box of powder and a powder puff covering the tables, chairs, and couch with a heavy dose of dusting powder. When told to "be sure to put out the lights," she hangs light bulbs on the clothesline with clothespins. When told to "dress the chicken," she sews a little dress complete with bows and tucks it around the uncooked roasting hen in the refrigerator. These books may be read just for the fun of it to provoke interest in reading, but follow-up lessons related to the word concepts will be easily tolerated because the books are delightful.

9. *Fill shelves with books that students can check out.* Books should be selected so reading levels appropriate for all students in the class are represented. If students are going to read them on their own, books should be available on their independent reading levels. If there are funds for purchasing books, the Hi-Lo paperbacks (Bantam) are a good choice for adding to a bookshelf collection for very low-achieving high school students. Reading levels in this series range from

second through third grade, while the subject matter is of interest to many contemporary teens. Some titles from the series are *Village of Vampires* and *The Bermuda Triangle and Other Mysteries of Nature.*

Fostering Independent Learning

The topic addressed here is somewhat of a cross between *direct instruction* and *incidental learning.* To foster independent learning, teachers provide direct guidance, striving to boost learning when students are on their own.

Teaching Students About the Uses of Context When Reading Independently. Previously in this chapter, use of context was described as an only moderately useful strategy for introducing words to students in direct instruction activities. Also, it's only moderately useful for deriving word meanings when reading independently—and for the same reasons. Sometimes context helps, but sometimes it doesn't. Still, when students are operating independently, it may give an assist on some occasions. Proficient readers do use context when it is productive to do so. Therefore, some attention to use of context is in order.

Nagy (1988) suggests that teachers model how to use context to get word meanings. First, find some examples in a book where context does indeed convey an understanding of a somewhat difficult word. Tell students that sometimes the text hints at what a word means. Then, using an example from the selected text, "think aloud" how you would use the surrounding words to derive an interpretation of the one that is unfamiliar. Next, have students take up the modeling role and think aloud for their peers how they might do this with other words in the connected text examples you have selected.

Provide other practice activities for gleaning word meanings from context. Here is one. A teacher-made activity can be assembled by cutting manila file folders into four folding strips. A sentence providing context for an underlined target word is written on the *outside* of each of the strips. The meaning of the target word is written *inside* each strip. Students are given a pack of these, asked to read the sentence on each, guess the meaning of the underlined word from context, and then open up the file folder piece to find the answer. This activity can be carried out independently and is self-correcting.

For variety, teachers may also prepare games to practice determining words from context before a story is read. For example, develop a card game by printing words, along with context sentences to illustrate the word meanings, on separate index cards (for instance, *hut—He was so poor that he lived in a small, poorly built hut*). Prepare a second pack of cards on which only the word appears. Put both packs together and shuffle them. Deal five cards to each student and leave the remainder on the table as an extra pile. The game is played like rummy; students must obtain pairs of matching cards (one with the word alone, and one with the word in a sentence) by drawing and discarding. Before students are allowed to keep a pair to count toward winning the game, they must tell the meaning of the word. To determine the meaning, they use the context of the sentence written on one card of the pair.

Helpful commercial materials include the *Using the Context* booklets from the Specific Skills Series (Barnell Loft). These booklets, in versions for beginning and advanced readers, provide students with practice in using context for identifying pronunciations of unknown words and for deriving word meanings.

Whether or not texts help in providing interpretations of vocabulary depends on the complexity of the concept the word is representing (Nagy et al., 1987). The strength of a particular context is also a factor. Beck, McKeown, and McCaslin (1983) actually found that some contexts were deceptive, leading readers to derive a wrong explanation of a word! Other contexts are neutral, equipping the student with no clues at all. Somewhat serviceable are those which give a general sense of the word, and, of course, the most supportive are contexts that steer the learner to a correct, precise meaning. Obviously, students derive more word meanings from reading when the latter two types are available.

Students should be made aware of the limitations of context use and know that at times they must use a different strategy.

Increasing Dictionary Skills.   When context doesn't help, the dictionary may. Certainly no educated person can operate in a literate environment without the skills to use this reference source. We want learners to be *able* to use the dictionary when it would be profitable, and to be *willing* to do so. One reason students shy away from using a dictionary is that their speed in locating words is slow.

Gamelike activities can provide practice to increase their speed in finding words in a dictionary. Try this one. Prepare a list of index cards to be used by the teacher. On each card, write one word for which it is likely that no student in the group will know the meaning, and then write a question about the word, along with three possible answers. Here is an example:

If you had a *timbrel*, would you:

1. serve soup in it,
2. plant it in your garden, or
3. play it in a band?

A dictionary should be placed on each student's desk. To begin the game, the teacher selects a card and reads it to the group. The students must vote. For example, the teacher would say, "How many would serve soup in it?" "How many would plant it in their gardens?" and "How many would play it in band?" The teacher then declares, "All right. Look it up!" Because they've made a commitment to one of the choices, students dive for their dictionaries and try to locate the word rapidly. Giggles begin to be heard from students who made choices number 1 or 2 when they find that a timbrel is a musical instrument like a tambourine. After all have read the meaning, the teacher directs them to close their dictionaries and reads from the next card.

To give practice with the pronunciation key of a dictionary, use jokes or riddles with the answers or punch lines written in dictionary respellings. Here are examples:

A Joke: *Mrs. Hastings:* Robert, I would like to go through one whole day without having to punish you.

Robert: Yü hav mi pərmishən.

A Riddle: One day two fathers and two sons went fishing and each one caught a fish. Only three fish were caught, however. How could this be?

Answer: Ā bȯi, hiz fäthər, and grandfäthər wər thə tü fätherz and tü sənz, sō thaar wər ōnlē thrē fishərmən.

Poindexter (1994) suggests a way to combine use of context and use of the dictionary. With middle school students, she used the following procedures: (a) difficult words from a text were listed on a chart and students predicted what these words were going to mean in an upcoming story, and their guesses were printed next to the words; (b) the teacher read the story to the class and when each of the words appeared, students tried to guess from context what each word did, in fact, mean, and a column of guesses from context was added to the chart; (c) the dictionary was consulted and definitions were added to the chart for each word. Comparisons were made of the three columns and decisions made about the actual meaning of each word in the text that had been read. Students showed interest in word study during these lessons, likely because of the predictions they had offered (always a good way to engender interest) and because of the active and collaborative nature of the lesson.

Working With Important Roots and Other Word Parts. Another beneficial procedure in a word study program is to choose a few roots and word parts to be learned. Knowing these will help students determine meanings of any words in which these word parts appear. Many authorities (e.g., Dale & O'Rourke, 1971; Nagy, Osborn, Winsor, O'Flahavan, 1992) suggest this as one approach to increasing knowledge of word meanings because of its efficiency. They point out that attempting to learn many unrelated words is a great deal more time consuming than learning several carefully selected roots and word parts that may then be applied to many more words. It also can be of assistance when readers are working independently.

Culyer (1978) estimates that Greek and Latin roots, for example, appear in about one fourth of the words in an English dictionary. One set of word parts often suggested for learning under this approach is the set of number prefixes. These are:

mono, uni	one
bi, di	two
tri	three
quad	four
quint, pent	five
sex, hex	six
sept	seven
oct	eight
novem	nine
dec	ten

Students may be asked to write words they already know that begin with each of these prefixes, such as *monorail, bicycle, bimonthly, tricycle,* or *triplets.* Then meanings of the words should be discussed and additional words added to each list. An interesting activity for working with number prefixes has been devised by Dale and O'Rourke (1971) and may be seen in Figure 11-8.

Point out other Latin and Greek roots that appear in many English words. The list in Figure 11–9 is suggested by Voigt (1978, p. 421). See Chapter 10 for additional ideas for working with meanings of other word parts, such as prefixes and suffixes.

Although structural analysis is an important strategy for identifying pronunciations of words, it is likewise productive in discovering word meanings (Nagy et al., 1992).

Promoting Out-of-Class Extensions. In three studies, using out-of-class extensions of in-class work has been shown to be a powerful procedure for students to learn vocabulary (Beck, Perfetti, & McKeown, 1982; McKeown, Beck, Omanson, & Perfetti, 1983; McKeown, Beck, Omanson, & Pople, 1985). McKeown and Beck (1988) describe how this was done in these studies. Rules were established for accomplishing vocabu-

FIGURE 11–8
Learning number prefixes

The Greek and Latin prefixes from one to ten are (1) mono-, uni-; (2) bi-, di-; (3) tri-; (4) quad-, tetra-; (5) quint-, penta-, pent-; (6) sex-, hex-; (7) sept-, hept-; (8) octo-; (9) novem-; (10) dec-. If you have learned these number prefixes, you can easily complete the prefix problems that follow.

Example: mono + uni = b_____   *Answer*: bi

1. sex + bi = o_____
2. bi + di = q_____
3. penta + quad = n_____
4. tri + di = q_____
5. quad + bi = h_____
6. quad + uni = p_____
7. quint + mono = s_____
8. bi + di = t_____
9. tri + quad = s_____
10. tetra + hex = d_____

11. penta + di = h_____
12. mono + bi = t_____
13. quad + tetra = o_____
14. bi + tri = p_____
15. octo – quad = t_____
16. tri x tri = n_____
17. bi ÷ di = m_____
18. octo – di = h_____
19. sex ÷ hex = u_____
20. dec ÷ penta = b_____

Source: From *The World Book Complete Word Power Library* (Volume 2). Copyright 1981 by World Book-Childcraft International Inc. Used by permission of World Book, Inc.

lary tasks outside of the classroom for which learners would be rewarded. Specifically, students earned points by being a "word wizard," that is, the student who could either (a) locate and report a word that had been studied in the classroom which he or she had seen or heard outside of school or (b) use the focus words in his or her assigned writings. The benefits from this extra practice were seen when students in a group who had rich instruction plus participation in the word wizard program performed more effectively on tasks involving speed in identifying word meanings than those who had traditional instruction or rich instruction alone.

McKeown and Beck (1988) believe that fostering independent word practice in this way may be particularly beneficial for some poor readers who do not have sufficient opportunities for the stimulus of word learning in their homes. They also attested to students' enthusiasm for this activity. This and similar out-of-class extensions are recommended (see also the suggestion below related to oral language development).

Using Computer Programs.   Today, as more and more educational technology finds its way into classrooms, teachers may wish to use the computer for enhancing students' word knowledge. Because students are frequently willing to engage in computer activities, use of the computer may provide some impetus for independent word learning.

Commercially prepared programs for vocabulary development are available. One such program is *The Game Show* (Computer Advanced Ideas). This program is based on the television program *Password* and is designed for reading levels 2 through 8. The game is used by two students at a time or by two teams, and features vocabulary on a variety of topics.

FIGURE 11–9

Common Greek and Latin roots

Meaning	Root	Meaning	Root
above	super-	across	trans-
after	post-	again	re-
against	anti-	against	contra-
before	pre-	I believe	credo
between	inter-	book	liber
both	ambi	capable	-able, -ible
to carry	port-	city	urbs
study, science	logos	disease	-itis
distant	tele-	enough	satis-
for	pro-	instead	vice-
I lead, led	duco, ductus	life	bios
light	photos	I make, made	facio, factus
not	in-	out of	ex-, e-
people	demos	play, I play	ludus, ludo
power	kratia	right	dexter
ripe	maturus	ship	navis
short	brevis	single	monos
small	micros	star	aster
stone	lithos	suffering	pathos
through	per-	under	sub-
windpipe	bronchos	writing, drawing	graphe
written	scriptum	two	bi-
cycle	circle	foot	ped

Another software program is *Dictionary* (Microcomputers and Education). Designed for reading levels 2 through 4, this set of activities provides practice in locating words in a dictionary.

Stickybear Opposites (Weekly Reader Family Software) is a cartoonlike program in which appealing brown bears teach young children such opposite concepts as "high" and "low." This software was designed by an author and illustrator of children's books and is accompanied by a hardcover book, a poster, and stickers. (See Figure 11–10.) Teachers can investigate other computer programs to use in their word study activities.

Instilling an Interest in Words. Helping students learn to love interesting aspects of language can assist them in developing a growing awareness of words that will lead to a richer vocabulary. One excellent booklet that will help teachers instill an interest in words is *Growing From Word Play Into Poetry* (Professional Educators Publications). The author of this booklet has included creative classroom activities for using words, such as word choirs, word trading cards, and poetry computers.

Cleary (1978) had her secondary students engage in Phobia Day to stimulate interest in words. First, students completed a worksheet like the one shown in Figure 11–11. Next they were allowed to invent phobias based on Latin roots (one example: *barbaphobia,* meaning "a fear of whiskers"). Finally, they each chose a phobia and for

FIGURE 11–10
Example of a computer software
program used in a word study
program

Source: From *Stickybear Early Learning Program* by
R. Hefter, S. Worthington, and J. Worthington, 1983,
Middletown, OH: Weekly Reader Software. Reproduced by
permission.

an entire class period exhibited behavior that would be typical of an individual having
that phobia. At the end of the class, of course, students tried to guess which phobias
were being dramatized by their classmates.

Many teachers also find that introducing students to information about word ori-
gins stimulates interest in vocabulary. A number of books are available that describe the
history and origin of words, such as *The Abecedarian* (Little, Brown).

LEARNING WORDS FROM ORAL LANGUAGE ENCOUNTERS

Another potentially effective and lasting way to increase students' meaning vocabulary
is through participation in new experiences. Not only does direct participation in new
experiences increase vocabulary, but when students discuss the new experience, this
develops precision in word knowledge and rectifies misconceptions. The "experiences"
can be firsthand or indirect.

Real Experiences.   When teachers consider providing new experiences for students,
one of the first thoughts to come to mind is probably the field trip. However, practical
considerations involving time and transportation often make frequent trips of the usual
type less than feasible. Teachers, therefore, should rethink just what a "field trip" is. If
any brief excursion away from the confines of the classroom is considered a "trip," then
many practical possibilities present themselves.

Using this expanded definition of a field trip, one teacher simply took her students
outside to examine the school building in ways they had never done before. One of several things noted during this trip was the block above the front door in which a sentence
had been carved: new words such as *motto* and *lintel* (the block above the door)
emerged. Before each new school year, another teacher makes it a point to drive

FIGURE 11–11
Worksheets to develop meaning vocabulary can be interesting

PHOBIA: fear, dislike, aversion

The root *phobia* is itself a complete word. Children may have "school phobia" or "ghost phobia" or "lion phobia." Their fear may be real or imagined. Likewise, adults may have a phobia of the dark, a phobia of responsibility, or a phobia of death.

Check the dictionary to determine whether phobias are rational or irrational. (Underline your choice.)

Is a phobia a mild dislike or extreme fear? (Underline your choice.)

Write a definition for *phobia*: _____

_____

Phobia is the root of each of these ten words. Use a dictionary to define them.

acrophobia   _____

agoraphobia   _____

Anglophobia   _____

claustrophobia   _____

Germanophobia   _____

hydrophobia   _____

monophobia   _____

phobia   _____

photophobia   _____

xenophobia   _____

Exercise: Complete each of the following sentences.

1. You wouldn't expect a mountain climber to have _____

2. As we grow up, we overcome our childhood _____ of the dark.

3. His _____ prevented him from swallowing liquids.

Source: From *Thinking Thursdays* (p. 40) by D. M. Cleary, 1978, Newark, DE: International Reading Association. Copyright 1978 by the International Reading Association. Reprinted by permission of the International Reading Association.

around the neighborhood of the schools in which she teaches. Her purpose is to locate places of interest within walking distance of the school. This has resulted in walking trips to a doughnut-making shop and an agency that trains guide dogs for the blind, among others. On occasion, she takes a video camera and films a portion of the experience. After the steps in making doughnuts were filmed and then viewed in the classroom, lessons on vocabulary and following a sequence of events were developed based on the film.

A second way to capitalize on real experiences without the impracticalities of frequent or elaborate excursions is to use experiences students have had in common outside of school. For example, if many of your secondary students attend hockey or football games, their interests can be the basis of vocabulary development activities. Discuss the activity and then have them dictate a group story that you write on the board. Challenge the students to revise the first "draft" that you have written by thinking of synonyms for common words (*Jones moved so fast across that ice*— can be changed to *Jones moved so swiftly across that ice*—). The advantage of a collaborative effort for the story is that students will hear words their peers suggest, each potentially adding some new thoughts about words that may previously have been only in the "partially known" category of word knowledge of other students.

Some real experiences teachers can organize within the classroom include the following.

- cooking
- food-tasting parties
- bringing in objects (e.g., a weather balloon that fell in your yard; a starfish Ken got on his vacation in Florida)
- science experiments
- displays (e.g., of clothing, artifacts, or art objects from other countries)
- inviting people to the classroom for demonstrations (e.g., of musical instruments or of origami making)

Following all such experiences, words that describe these experiences must be used in discussion. Furthermore, in all cases when oral language activities can be followed by or accompanied with the words in written form, the learning experience is strengthened. After all, the ultimate goal is that students be able to use these word meanings to enhance comprehension of written texts. If teachers fail to take this follow-up step, students will not end up with any more useful words than before.

Teachers must also remember the importance of time on task, and the specific purpose for providing new experiences, which is to help students expand their meaning vocabularies through development of new concepts and the acquisition of new labels (words) for old concepts. For example, if four reading-class sessions are devoted to an experience but only 20 minutes of follow-up for the development of related vocabulary are provided, this would be an inappropriate division of time. Better planning would call for a briefer experiential activity (perhaps 30 minutes, or a single class session) and more time devoted to work with related words.

Vicarious Experiences. It is not possible for students to experience everything directly. Few people, for example, have actually seen a volcano erupt or flown in a helicopter. Nevertheless, they can understand many things about these events and processes, can visualize them, and can use words to discuss them (e.g., *lava, ash, rotary blade, altimeter*). They know these things because they have had vicarious experiences that have helped build concepts.

A **vicarious experience** is an indirect experience. For example, although you probably have never directly seen a volcano erupt, you may know quite a lot about eruptions from viewing a film about volcanoes when you were in elementary school, reading about them in a magazine or a high school science book, or seeing TV news clips of erupting volcanoes. All these experiences are vicarious because they are indirect. Nevertheless, they can teach a great deal.

In remedial classes, vicarious experiences can be provided in many ways and can be used to develop meaning vocabulary. Pictures may be shown to develop concepts before students read a story or article. If, for example, the story to be read includes a horse and mentions its "forelock," the teacher may pull from a picture file a photograph of a horse, point to its forelock so that students will see what it looks like, and talk about the meanings of *fore* and *lock*, (*fore*, meaning "in front of," combined with *lock*, as in "lock of hair," equals a tuft of hair at the front of the horse's head). Learners should be encouraged to participate in the discussion, suggesting ways the word they see depicted in the picture could be used in oral sentences, offering other words that begin with *fore-* (e.g., *forehead, foreground, forearm, forecast*) and describing the uses of these words. The connection to written language takes place when the learners read the story.

Picture sets designed to help students explore and use new words are on the market (for example, from Bowmar). Or, teachers can make their own collections from magazine pictures. Slides can also be shown in conjunction with follow-up worksheets and discussions that require students to practice the words that were presented when the slides were viewed.

Filmstrips, movies, and records with sound effects all may be employed in the same way (Combs & Beach, 1994). TV programs that students watch at home can also provide an opportunity for enhancing knowledge of word meanings. The teachers may ask students to watch a particular program (one that many students might watch anyway, or one for which enough interest exists so that students *will* view it); then they bring in one word from the program to share with the class. These words are discussed—and to make the connection with written language, are listed on a chart, along with their meanings and synonyms, and examples of their uses.

It is critical that students *use* the words they have been exposed to through vicarious experiences. If the words are to become a part of their meaning vocabularies, just hearing them is not sufficient. Students should be induced to employ these new words in their own oral language, and ultimately in written activities through reading printed text—either published material or teacher-developed selections.

CONCLUSION

Which of the strategies suggested here might be most fruitful in generating gains in meaning vocabulary knowledge? Summarizing the results of research on increasing meaning vocabulary, Beck and McKeown (1991, p. 805) give four principles to keep in mind:

1. All teaching approaches yield greater vocabulary growth than no instruction.
2. No one tactic has been found to be invariably better than others.
3. There is a benefit to instruction that includes a diversity of techniques.
4. Repeated exposures to words are profitable.

Weak strategies are those in which only one type of encounter is involved (e.g., vocabulary "learning" consists of looking up 20 words in the dictionary every Friday and writing out their definitions) and those that are vague (e.g., guessing words from ambiguous or indeterminate contexts). Strong strategies are generally teacher-guided and require depth of processing for a few carefully selected words at a time.

📖 REFLECTIONS

- - - - - - - - - - - - - - - - - - -

1. Why do *you* read? What incentives make you pick up a book to read it? What implications might this have for your work with reluctant readers?

2. What strategies have helped you to learn word meanings? How can these be used with students you teach?
3. This has been another chapter in which "principles" have been offered—principles for effective instruction of meaning vocabulary. Some of these were enumerated and listed. Others are incorporated within the connected narrative. Could you specify these principles for another teacher?
4. Developing activities that encourage depth of processing and rich understandings of word meanings provides some absorbing challenges for teachers. What suggestions do you have for such activities *beyond those given in this chapter?*

12

Comprehension of Narrative Text

Comprehension instruction should go beyond only asking questions after material is read; it should also incorporate learning events that occur before and during reading.

E verything we do in reading instruction should be aimed at helping students comprehend written material. It matters not a bit whether students can instantly recognize *every* word on a page if they cannot understand the message those words are conveying. Being able to read orally with "expression" has no value if the student has missed the meaning. Increasing a student's rate of reading is purposeless if comprehension suffers in the process. Knowing how to identify difficult words is important only if the resulting word identification leads to comprehension of the words, sentences, and passages a student must read. Ensuring that readers comprehend is central to reading instruction.

Although few people would disagree with the premise that the purpose of reading is comprehension and although since 1970 there has been a flurry of comprehension research, the findings of the research have not always sifted down to teachers in the schools. As a result, sometimes instructional procedures used by remedial specialists have been based only on "what has always been done," even though those procedures have not always been very effective.

So, let's take a look at some of the more recent information on comprehension and how it can help you help your students better understand what they read.

COMPREHENSION PROCESSES

Having some understanding of *how* we comprehend helps in seeing the relevance—or irrelevance—of common and/or recommended comprehension instructional strategies. In order to comprehend, current theory says we employ both our knowledge of language and our knowledge of the world (the latter often being referred to simply as background information). We employ this knowledge to use *propositions,* to use *schemata,* and to use *mental models.* And we also use inferences to help with these processes—inferences that are based on the text as well as inferences that can be made based on our own prior knowledge (prior knowledge is another name for background information) (R. C. Anderson, 1977; K. S. Goodman, 1970; Kintsch, 1974; F. Smith, 1982). (See the definitions of some terminology used in association with comprehension processes and instruction found in Table 12–1.)

Propositions are the smallest units of text information that can stand separately and be tested as true or false (Kintsch, 1974). They are *ideas,* not the words themselves (McNamara, Miller, & Bransford, 1991).

Here is an example:

Ralph went into the autumn woods, which were golden in color.

This sentence has three propositions:

1. Ralph went into the woods.
2. It was autumn.
3. The woods were golden in color.

In order to comprehend, we consider the propositions in the written text. Sometimes this is done rather unconsciously and at other times with more deliberation.

We also employ background information—and yet another name for this is **schemata.** When we know something about a topic, we activate, or pull up, or think about (usually unconsciously, but sometimes intentionally) our schemata about that topic to understand what we read. Suppose, for instance, that Carolyn is reading a story about basketball. This is a topic she is quite familiar with because she plays on the girls' basketball team at her neighborhood recreation center and also watches games on TV.

TABLE 12–1
Definitions of comprehension-related terms

Terms Used in Recent Writings About Comprehension	Terms More Familiar to Teachers
Bottom-up processing	Comprehension based on what is in the book—not on the reader's individual experiences (at least not very much); the reader goes from the part to the whole
Text-driven processing	Same as bottom-up processing
Data-driven processing	Same as bottom-up processing
Top-down processing	Comprehension based on what is already in the reader's head, i.e., background information, that helps the reader make intelligent guesses about events, and so on, in material, and to understand relationships about them
Concept-driven processing	Same as top-down processing
Interactive processing	Comprehension is based on both bottom-up and top-down processing—the reader and the book work together so that student gains meaning
Schema	Background information
Schemata	Background information (plural of *schema*)
Prior knowledge	Background information
Schema availability	The familiarity of the topic to the student
Surface structure	The printed words on the page and how they are arranged within sentences
Deep structure	The meaning conveyed by printed words on a page
Microstructure	1. In regard to surface structure, the words *within* a sentence and how they are arranged 2. In regard to deep structure, the details in a passage
Macrostructure	1. In regard to surface structure, how ideas are arranged *among* sentences to make up the organization of a passage 2. In regard to deep structure, the main idea of a passage
Text structure	How material has been organized by the author into main ideas and supporting details, how these are sequenced, and how they are interrelated
Cohesion, or cohesiveness in text	The way parts of printed text are linked by certain words or statements within and between sentences so the text seems to "hang together" or is seen to be related by the reader
Anaphora	Words that refer to or provide a link to previous words; pronouns, for example, often have anaphoric relationships with nouns, such as in the sentence, "When *Tom* was asked if *he* liked to run, *he* said *he* did" (the noun—*Tom* in this case—is called a pronoun antecedent)
Proposition	The smallest units of text information that can stand separately and be tested as true or false

TABLE 12–1 *(continued)*

Terms Used in Recent Writings About Comprehension	Terms More Familiar to Teachers
Proposition density	The number of propositions (or ideas) in a given piece of written material
Concept load	The same as proposition density
Density	Same as proposition density
Textual features	Things in printed text that relate to reading ease or difficulty, such as vocabulary difficulty, cohesiveness, and density
Textual analysis	Analysis of the things in printed text that relate to reading ease or difficulty (see textual features)
Superordinate units	Sentences
Subordinate units	Words
Lexical item	A word
New information	Ideas with which the reader is unfamiliar
Old information	Information already in the reader's background knowledge
Reconstructing the author's message	Slightly modifying the author's intended meaning to conform to information already in the reader's background knowledge
Explicit information	Directly stated facts
Implicit information	Information that is not directly stated; it must be inferred since it is only implied
Imagery	Imagining mental pictures of what is read
Mental models	Constructing in our thoughts something similar to what is stated in text
Advance organizers	Material or activities (such as previewing or summarization) presented *before* students read material to help them understand it
Structured overview	A type of advance organizer (see advance organizers) in which vocabulary or ideas are visually related by drawings or diagrams
Hierarchical summarization study strategy	Outlining
Cognition	The process of reasoning
Metacognitive skills	Skills that help students "learn to learn"
Chunk	To organize small pieces of print into larger pieces (e.g., letters into words, or words into phrases)
Prediction strategy	Use of knowledge of language structure and meaning to anticipate words that are upcoming in the text; also, guessing about ideas that will follow, based on prior knowledge about the topic
Retrieval from long-term memory	Remembering
Introspective reporting	Students report the thought processes that occurred when they were reading material

When she reads that "Judd dribbled the ball but then was called for traveling," she does not think that someone called him on the phone in the middle of the game about his travel plans for vacation. She activates her existing schemata about basketball games and knows just what the author was relating.

Many of the new ideas about comprehension have been based on *schema theory.* (The singular for *schemata* is *schema.*) This theory says that what you already know or don't know about a topic can greatly influence your comprehension. This notion was originally advanced by Bartlett (1932), and later developed by R. C. Anderson (1977), Rumelhart (1981), and others. It suggests that when readers recognize words on a printed page, they think and react based on their background information (or schemata).

In this view, comprehension is the *active construction* of meaning (Sweet, 1993). That is, the reader is not an empty vessel into which some words from the page are poured and out comes understanding! Instead, readers actively work to integrate information in a text with what is already stored in their prior knowledge. (Again this may be done unconsciously—or, it may be a fairly conscious effort, if the text is difficult for a specific reader.) In summary, we must combine old and new information to be good comprehenders. The old information comes from our brains and the "new" information is what we are dealing with from the written text.

Kintsch (1979) has proposed one model (or explanation) of comprehension that is based on schema theory. This model says that the amount of difficulty students have in comprehending a text is related to how much searching of their memories they must undertake to find a schema that closely matches the words the author has presented. If they are quite familiar with the topic, little searching is necessary. If they are not very familiar with it, much searching is required—or they may match incoming information with the wrong schema, or they may not be able to find a match at all. In these circumstances, comprehension is diminished or even absent.

According to Kintsch, readers must make two kinds of matches to understand what they read:

1. Schema matches with the microstructure of the text (**Microstructure** means the details in a passage and the terms and relationships within sentences that help readers understand the details, such as the individual words or the order in which words are arranged.)
2. Schema matches with the macrostructure of the text (**Macrostructure** means the main ideas, or topic, of a passage and how ideas are arranged among sentences to make up the organization of the passage.)

If a reader has difficulty comprehending a text, the problem can be in the material or in the reader. When the microstructure (words, sentence structure) is too difficult for the readers so that they cannot find matches in their schemata even though they understand the concept, then the problem is in the material. For instance, Jocelyn reads, "Don't forget to use apostrophes." Jocelyn knows what apostrophes are, has heard the word in oral language, and has used them since first grade when she was taught to spell contractions; but she has never seen the word in print and does not recognize it. She cannot match *a-p-o-s-t-r-o-p-h-e-s* with anything she has stored in her schemata of known words. Therefore, she does not get the meaning of the message. Therefore, without understanding that microstructure element, she does not understand the text. As we once again see, word recognition and knowledge of word identification strategies are interactively involved with reading comprehension.

When students have no schema stored in their memories, or only a partial one, for the ideas being presented in a text, and cannot understand the message because the information is "too new" for them, then the "problem" lies with the reader. In such a case, the reader has no old information or too little of it to use in comprehending what the author wrote. This is a problem with macrostructure. Read the following paragraphs and try to answer the questions.

> They were obviously Maglemosian, as was evident since the culture was Mesolithic. Given these clues, any budding archaeologist can guess the area of the world in which these shards were found.
>
> 1. To what does the term *Maglemosian* refer?
> 2. Where were the shards found?

> A magnetron tube is of the thermionic type. Its electron beam generates microwaves that are high powered, and is influenced by electromagnetic fields.
>
> 1. Write a one paragraph description of a magnetron tube using terminology that can be understood by the general public.
> 2. Given the information about the obvious advantages of thermionic tubes, suggest their possible uses.

If you have some feelings of unease about the correctness of your answers to these questions, this is undoubtedly due to your lack of schema to match the topics. While an electrical engineer may be able to answer questions about the second paragraph, the same engineer might have considerable difficulty answering questions about word identification strategies in reading—a topic for which you should have, at this point, stored information (or schemata).

The two factors that Kintsch refers to as problems in the reader and problems in the material have been called by Pearson and Johnson (1978) "factors inside the head" and "factors outside the head." They say that factors inside the student's head that influence comprehension are

- what the student knows about language
- motivation
- how well the student can read (recognize words)
- interest (pp. 9–10)

Factors outside the head are

- elements on the page, such as how difficult the material is and how well it is organized to help the reader (e.g., providing subheadings, and so on)
- the quality of the reading environment, such as what the teacher does to facilitate comprehension—before the student reads, while the student is reading, and after the student reads

What other practical implications are available from schema theory for remedial reading teachers? First, we can conclude that wide *experiences* (direct and vicarious) are important for good comprehension. If students do not have sufficient experiences, prereading discussions become very important in supplying information. Second, *wide reading* on any topic will increase students' comprehension about that topic because over time students will have more and more old information in their schemata to help them understand new information. Engaging in a great deal of reading will make better readers, not only in terms of word recognition, but also in terms of comprehension. Wide experience and wide reading relate to what has been called **intertextuality,** a term that refers to use of connections with past written texts to interpret the present text, as well as to the use of the "texts" of our past experiences (Short, 1992). Third, one reason for poor readers' failure to comprehend may well be their lack of attempt to *use* the background information they *do* have to comprehend what they read. Therefore, teachers must instruct them about the need to use their prior knowledge—and show them *how.* A number of instructional procedures suggested later in this chapter and the next are based on these premises.

Readers may resort to another process if they find no close match in their schemata for the incoming information from text. To understand unfamiliar topics, it is hypothesized that we can use **mental models,** especially when we read narratives (i.e., stories). When we employ this process, we construct something in our thoughts similar to what is presented in the text. Often we, in effect, try to see in our minds what is being described in the selection. This has been characterized as akin to producing frames on a movie film and then flashing by to other frames as we move through the story. In doing so, readers also update, or sometimes revise, their mental models as the story changes.

A mental model consists of parts (called **mental tokens**) that represent things in the narrative (e.g., people and objects), and these are arranged in the "frames" to portray what is discussed in the material (McNamara et al., 1991). *Images* can be perceived, as in the cases just given (characters, objects), but other things can be contained in the mental model as well, for example, *ideas about causes* that link events between frames.

There are some things about which it is easy to form mental models and some things for which it is not. When it is difficult to form mental models, readers often rely on propositions instead—in other words, they rely more heavily on text structure. In addition, mental models preserve *ideas* in memory, not exact words; if the idea is what is needed, readers may use mental models. But, if, on the other hand, they need to remember text verbatim, they may use propositions, relying again more heavily on text structure.

When readers update or revise their mental models as they read a story, they can rely on information found in the selection but also on stored knowledge in their

Wide reading increases comprehension because information is added to the reader's schemata.

schemata, making inferences as they do. Or, to put this in another way, they infer certain things that are not actually stated in the text, basing these inferences on their prior knowledge. Here is an example of how this might be done. Suppose Sheila reads the statement, "On the first night of the camping trip, Tom sat cross-legged under a huge sycamore tree watching a small red squirrel scamper in and out of the hole at the end of the branch." Although Sheila is not familiar with all that she reads here, the author's words may trigger a match with her prior knowledge so that she can fill in her mental model in the following manner.

1. Sheila has not been on a camping trip herself, but from talking with her friend, Theresa, who has, Sheila knows that these trips are often to wooded areas away from a city.
2. She has been to a park with lots of trees and bushes, and she remembers the general impression.
3. She sometimes sits cross-legged herself on her living room floor when she is watching TV, and knows the look and feel of the action.
4. She does not know what a sycamore tree is, but there is a huge old oak in her grandmother's backyard and she visualizes it.
5. She has not seen a red squirrel, but there are gray squirrels all around her neighborhood, and she knows what they look like when they scamper on the ground and on a tree trunk.
6. She has not seen a hole in the end of a tree branch, but she has seen a picture in her science book of a hole in a tree trunk with owls peering out.

Sheila has thus developed several schemata that she can match with the words she has just read to get a sense of the meaning of this sentence.

But as can be seen, discrepancies may arise. First, because Sheila's schemata are not parallel to the author's, her mental images may lack precision (for instance, gray squirrels are larger than red squirrels; therefore, the squirrel she visualizes may be larger than what the author intended). Second, readers interpret written words differently according to their varied background experiences. Thus, while Sheila may have visualized an oak tree when she read sycamore, if the only large tree Lindsey has seen is an Austrian pine, she might call up that memory from her tree schema; a third reader with greater knowledge about trees, meanwhile, may call upon a schema of exactly what a sycamore tree looks like and, therefore, her understanding is more likely to agree with what the author meant to convey.

The degree of "closeness" of the schema of the reader to that of the author affects the quality of comprehension as the reader "constructs" meaning. In the squirrel and tree examples given here, this is presumably a "so what" situation—it probably does not matter how precise a mental model is formed for these minor details, but if the discrepancy involved a major construct of the story, then comprehension could be hampered. A possible cause of poor comprehension is forming inappropriate or meager mental models, which can therefore result in errors in reasoning (Johnson-Laird, 1983). McNamara et al. (1991) say that comprehension instruction should focus on meaning construction and propose that one way to do this is to link text with pictures; they believe that this procedure also has transfer value—what is learned in order to understand a specific account can add to the knowledge base to be drawn upon to interpret other material.

Actually, another process can occur when readers apply their schemata to words they read—their schemata can change. Returning to Sheila's schema for squirrels, perhaps squirrels came in only one color (gray) prior to her reading about Tom and the red squirrel. Now she knows that squirrels can also be red; thus, her schema has been altered and expanded. There is an interactive, two-way mechanism: schemata allow the reader to understand material that is read, and reading new material often changes schemata.

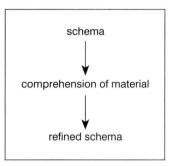

Comprehension, therefore, is an active endeavor that involves "inference making." In this case, inference making is not meant as a specific skill (as in "drawing inferences"), but as a process that permeates all aspects of reading. Inference making is necessary even when attending to single words, such as in deciding on the specific meaning of a word like *run,* which has multiple meanings. Using propositions, schemata, and mental models, and employing inferences to hold these processes together, provide the foundation of comprehension.

NARRATIVES

This chapter deals with the comprehension of narrative selections and the next chapter with the understanding of expository materials. What is meant by a narrative? **Narratives** are descriptions of events that can be fictional or nonfiction and can be written or oral. Usually we think of stories as narratives (realistic fiction, myths, fairy tales, plays, fables, historical fiction, and legends, as examples), but biography, a nonfiction genre, also can be considered a narrative. Since our purpose here is to address reading instruction, the present chapter will center primarily on comprehension of written, rather than oral, narratives. Narratives are often written to entertain. Expository material, on the other hand, is designed specifically to impart new information to readers. The textbook that you are reading at this moment is exposition, for example, but the mystery novel you plan to read during your next vacation is a narrative.

In actuality, many instructional procedures that facilitate comprehension of narratives also expedite interpretation of expository text, and vice versa. However, there are some special features of each text type that seem to merit separate consideration. Graesser, Golding, and Long (1991) suggest that there are characteristics of narratives that make them easier to comprehend than exposition because topics they cover may be more familiar than those in, for instance, textbooks. Often readers can read narratives more quickly than expository text without comprehension being hindered.

The structures of these two types of text, which should be learned to aid understanding, differ, and the written language in narrative material is often closer to that of oral language than that found in informational text. In addition, research on certain comprehension instructional strategies seems to have been more recurrently directed at either one of these types than the other. Still, a good deal of what you learn about furthering students' comprehension of narratives in this chapter also applies to expository readings, and much that is reported in Chapter 13 is not exclusively recommended for exposition, but, in addition, is helpful for story reading as well.

COMPREHENSION INSTRUCTION: NARRATIVES

Although more students are enrolled in remedial reading programs because of word recognition and identification problems than for any other reason, sizable numbers also are referred because of comprehension difficulties. Students who are identified as having comprehension difficulties often have experienced no undue obstacles with attaining word-learning strategies and often can orally pronounce words in a printed text with facility and fluency. Although not lacking intelligence, these learners exhibit major problems with understanding stories or content area selections, or both.

A Minicase Study: Frederick

Frederick is presented here as a an example. After Freddy's first day in a reading clinic, his tutor rushed to the clinic supervisor saying she believed he had been "misreferred." During this first session, in addition to activities designed to gain background information about Freddy and to learn something about his interests, the tutor had given Freddy two short tests focusing on word recognition in and out of context. She also had taken to the lesson a book of high-quality children's literature that she planned to read aloud to him. Much to her surprise, Freddy demonstrated a perfect performance on the word recognition tests. And, when she began to read to this third-grader from the fourth-grade book she had chosen, he wanted to read it to her instead—and did so with no difficulties of any importance!

Having seen such circumstances before, the supervisor asked the tutor if Freddy had been asked to retell the story after reading it, or had been asked questions, or had in any other way communicated his degree of understanding of what he had read. This had not been done and so the tutor was counseled to wait until she had more formal and informal appraisals of Freddy's reading abilities.

After the second session, the tutor was still perplexed. Freddy's performance on a test of word identification strategies showed excellent competence in phonic and structural analysis skills. Again he read orally for the tutor from an authentic text, doing so exceedingly well and with enjoyment of the activity. On that day, the tutor did ask Freddy to summarize what he had read and he was able to give a brief, literal retelling of events and remembered the main characters. But, no follow-up probes were made to assess higher-level understandings. The tutor agreed that this must be the next avenue of exploration.

Over the next two sessions, Freddy (a) read silently and completed the comprehension portion of a standardized test; (b) orally read a story for a Reading Miscue Inventory (RMI), which he retold and for which he was presented teacher probes designed to assess higher-order interpretations; (c) read from authentic narrative texts, after which he was questioned about details and asked to make inferences and draw conclusions; and (d) read from two well-written expository articles, followed with a variety of question types. A consistent pattern emerged. Freddy had no apparent difficulties with word recognition, and he was able to give some of the literal meanings from all types of materials, although even on these lower-level tasks, information was not complete.

When higher-level reasoning was required, Freddy made almost no adequate responses. When asked questions for which there were no directly stated answers in the text, he appeared confused by the task, saying that he didn't "think that was in there."

When asked to use information in his "own good head" to figure out what the answer could be, he drew conclusions that were far too broad for the question being asked or were erroneous, seeming to pull out information from the text not directly related to the question at hand. When given tasks in which he was expected to explain the general point or significance of the piece, he often focused on ideas of interest to him rather than the main ideas, suggesting that he had concentrated on details of lesser significance. Sometimes his answers to inferential probes merely reflected literal facts, with no reasoning or integration of text details with prior knowledge, thus producing what appeared to be illogical inferences. Often a question would spur Freddy into an anecdotal reply based on something that he had experienced, but that was only tangentially related to the author's intended theme; this resulted in an answer that was clearly unconnected to what was being asked.

Many of Frederick's responses to higher-level comprehension tasks were similar to those found in a study exploring reasons for disabled readers' faulty answers to inference questions (McCormick, 1992). In this investigation, the written answers of 80 fifth-grade students enrolled in a federally funded reading program were analyzed. Students responded to questions for different stories and expository articles they read each week over a period of 20 weeks, answering two inference questions for each. A variety of reasons for unsatisfactory replies were discovered (see Table 12–2). Some sources of substandard answers were more prevalent than others. After reading narratives, students made wrong responses most often because they (a) lacked appropriate strategies for integrating text information with prior knowledge, (b) had difficulty with recall of significant text material, (c) misread the question or misread words in the story, (d) gave answers unrelated to major points in the selection—answers that instead reflected a concentration on more trivial details, and (e) had difficulty in writing out responses that did portray what they intended to say. (Examine Figure 12–1; comparing this with Table 12–2, you can see which error sources most often caused poor readers problems.)

Freddy's score on the standardized test was dismally low in comparison with his oral reading word recognition abilities. On the RMI, his views of the story's plot were simply irrelevant to its significant points, and he was unable to respond to probes designed to determine his understanding of the story's theme. He demonstrated some literal recall of information in the RMI story, but not all important details were given or all characters remembered. For the stories read from children's literature books, his performance was similar to that on the RMI. On the expository selections, he was able to give answers requiring facts and to two questions assessing knowledge of word meanings, but he did not draw appropriate conclusions and did not link causes to events.

Frederick had not been misreferred. Although he could give a good imitation of an adept reader, his lack of true proficiency became evident when evaluations went beyond word reading. Freddy's school records indicated a measured intelligence solidly within the average range, yet deriving usable meanings from text was a task baffling for him. He did need a program of special reading assistance, and fortunately recent research gives many clues about how to help students such as Freddy.

Principles of Good Comprehension Instruction

Pearson and Fielding (1991) offer a bottom-line description of what good comprehension instruction should be: instruction that *is* in fact instructive. This means that teachers must go beyond asking a few insignificant questions after a student has read in order to judge whether the student has understood the text. Such procedures may do little more than provide a test; they are inconsequential in helping readers learn *how* to comprehend.

TABLE 12–2
Sources of errors in answers to inference questions

A. Reading the Question
    A–1:   Obviously misread question (omitted word, which made question read differently; substituted one tense for another; didn't read entire question, thereby cuing another question; substituted one word for another)
    A–2:   Misinterpreted question, thinking that a word referred to a different instance, concept, or object

B. Recalling Text Information
    B–1:   Apparent that only a part of the text information was recalled
    B–2:   Did not recall text information that would have cued that the answer was wrong
    B–3:   Incorrect recall of sequence of information caused incorrect inference
    B–4:   Answer obviously unrelated to major points in selection

C. Selecting Correct and Sufficient Cues from the Question and the Text
    C–1:   Selected correct, but incomplete, text information to answer the question
    C–2:   Misinterpreted question so that answer referred to the overall problem in the selection rather than the specific instance to which the question was referring
    C–3:   Selected wrong cues from text to answer this specific question
    C–4:   Did not use written text information; rather, drew inference based on a picture
    C–5:   Selected wrong cues from the question (focused on less important words in the question)
    C–6:   Answer suggested recall of information from a different selection
    C–7:   Responded to only a portion of the question

D. Selecting Relevant, Accurate, and Sufficient Background Knowledge
    D–1:   Background information selected was inaccurate (an overgeneralization; incorrect concept for a word)
    D–2:   Information selected was not entirely incorrect, but was too specific and therefore did not reflect the more global or inclusive constructs representing the best answers
    D–3:   Did not use all available background information in attempt to infer

E. Integrating Text Cues with Background Knowledge
    E–1:   Too heavy reliance on background knowledge (substantial or complete dismissal of text information in favor of prior knowledge; interpreted text content to conform to prior knowledge; answer given was an opinion rather than an inference)
    E–2:   Too heavy reliance on text information (substantial or complete dismissal of background information in favor of text information; failure to relate text information to background information that would have cued answer; literal response given with no inference drawn)

F. Writing Responses to Accurately Reflect the Intended Answer
    F–1:   Words used in written response lacked semantic preciseness, precluding judgment of correctness of answer
    F–2:   Appeared that student may have inferred correctly but determination could not be made because of lack of specificity in writing response
    F–3:   Appeared to know answer, but transposed words in written response resulting in incorrect statement
    F–4:   Answer not fully developed (partially correct, but in writing answer did not provide sufficient information)

G. No Analysis of Response Possible
    G–1:   Response totally illegible
    G–2:   No response (answer section left blank; responded "I don't know")
    G–3:   Merely restated question
    G–4:   Response incoherent (grammatical order did not approximate English; semantically anomalous)

FIGURE 12–1

Erroneous responses for narrative selections

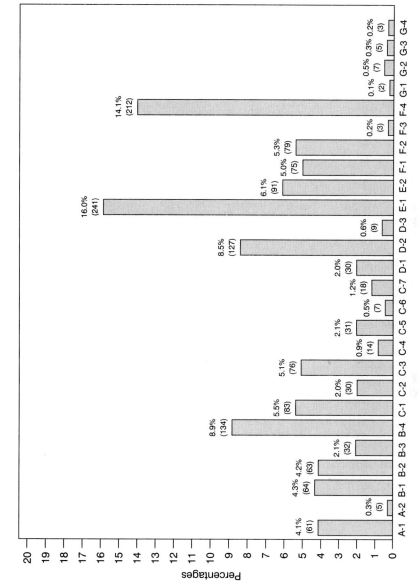

Note: Numbers in parentheses represent total number of incorrect responses for all students for all tests.

Source: From "Disabled Readers' Erroneous Responses to Inferential Questions: Description and Analysis," by S. McCormick, 1992, *Reading Research Quarterly, 27,* pp. 54–77. Copyright 1992 by the International Reading Association. Reprinted by permission of the International Reading Association.

When students are learning new strategies, precise explanations and guided practice usually are needed before they are able to practice the strategy independently.

Certain principles about the nature of good reading comprehension instruction have evolved from current research. Comprehension is a matter of *constructing meaning.* Instruction must emphasize activities that require depth of processing, as with instruction of word meanings. Students should be actively involved in learning events before, during, and after reading text—events that will amplify students' ability to obtain meanings.

A good deal of contemporary research comes out steadfastly in favor of **explicit instruction,** that is, instruction that fully and clearly expresses what must be done. This research does show that extensive reading is important for building rich stores of background information. However, considerable reading, alone, may not furnish sufficient practice with the strategies necessary for exploring deeper meanings, especially for poor readers. Teachers should offer students guidance on *how* to comprehend, supplying them wisdom and hints for interpreting texts—and teachers need to do this in a systematic way. An approach for explicit instruction is emerging in many effective programs and is exemplified by four steps recommended by Pearson and Gallagher (1983):

1. The teacher gives *precise explanations* about a comprehension strategy, frequently modeling or thinking aloud how the strategy is carried out.
2. The readers are given *guided practice* with the strategy.
3. Readers engage in *independent practice* on use of the strategy in specific exercises.
4. The strategy is *applied to regular, connected text.*

This model of explicit instruction is characterized by a gradual release of responsibility— the teacher's role diminishes and students take a more active role in their own learning as their skill develops. It is not that instruction for poor readers should be different; rather, it should be more explicit and guided.

Closely related to explicit teaching are *cognitive apprenticeships* (J. S. Brown, Collins, & Duguid, 1989), *instructional conversations* (Tharp & Gallimore, 1989), *instructional scaffolding* (Palincsar, 1986), and *responsive teaching* (Tharp & Gallimore, 1989). In all these, which are different names for similar approaches, students are given something to do that is slightly difficult for them; but as a result of teacher assistance, they are pulled up to higher levels of thinking. The teacher engages in reflective instruction, noting at any given moment what is puzzling a student or what is contributing complexity to the task for that learner. Students are required to be quite active in the learning events: teachers solicit much dialogue, but teacher coaching is also evident. As with explicit teaching, the teacher's share of duties is transferred to the learners as they grow more adept with a strategy.

The watchword *helping students become strategic readers* is a guide for comprehension instruction. This means that not only is it important to teach students tactics for interpreting text, students also must actually be willing to *use* these tactics (which implies motivation) and they must know how to choose the *right ones* for different situations. In order to describe this process, to J. R. Anderson's (1976) notions of **declarative knowledge** and **procedural knowledge,** Paris, Lipson, and Wixson (1983) added the category of **conditional knowledge.** These ideas were discussed in Chapter 8 in the section on assessment of metacognition, but to review them here: declarative knowledge refers to *what* a strategy is; procedural knowledge relates to *how* a strategy is carried out; and conditional knowledge means knowing *when* and *why* it is profitable to apply the strategy.

It is the attainment of conditional knowledge that allows a learner to be a "strategic" reader. A strategic reader is one who is savvy enough to grasp the importance of applying what he or she has been taught when confronting a complicated text (and to have had enough practice with the strategy so that it is not too laborious to use) and to pick the right one to employ. In conjunction with these concepts is the differentiation between (a) comprehension instruction that is necessary for understanding the immediate story and (b) comprehension instruction that teaches tactics learners can apply to a wide variety of reading activities, including during independent reading. While instruction on how to understand the immediate story is often required, a good comprehension program does not neglect instruction on reading strategies. Strategic readers know how to apply useful comprehension strategies with diverse texts. Strategic readers exhibit use of metacognition (Paris, Wasik, & Turner, 1991).

Introductory Transactions

Comprehension instruction should begin *before* students read a narrative. One goal before reading may be to build background information about the topic of the story, if learners' backgrounds are likely to be lacking or scanty. Lack of comprehension of a specific text can be due to lack of knowledge about an area of significance in the narrative (Voss, Fincher-Kiefer, Greene, & Post, 1985). Or, an alternate objective may be to activate students' prior knowledge, that is, making them think about their prior knowledge and helping them associate it with the upcoming selection.

This background building and activating of prior knowledge can consist of any activities that help readers make connections with the narrative, such as discussion, showing pictures, role-playing ideas, and relating examples to already familiar concepts (Weech, 1994). Some implications from research for introductory transactions—those activities that can be undertaken before a student reads—are presented here.

Assistance with the Immediate Text. To help students understand a specific text, the teacher can develop a number of procedures to use before students read in order to promote their comprehension.

1. *Previewing.* Research has shown that written previews can increase comprehension of narratives. One such study was conducted with middle school students who were reading disabled (Graves, Cooke, & Laberge, 1983). In that program,

previews were used before students read short stories. The teaching activity consisted of the following steps.

a. The teacher gave each student a written preview of the story. (See Figure 12–2 for a sample preview.)

b. The teacher read to the students the statements and questions found at the beginning of the preview. These were designed to (1) arouse interest and (2) link the story to something familiar in the students' backgrounds. The teacher led a brief discussion about these and about the story's topic.

c. The teacher read a summary of the story, which consisted of the middle portion of the written preview, to the students. The summary included the setting, general statements about the characters, and a brief description of the plot up to the ending.

d. Students were asked to look at the chalkboard, where the teacher had previously listed the characters and a short statement about each of them. These were read to the students.

e. Student attention was redirected to the written preview. This final portion defined three or four difficult words they would encounter in the story.

f. The previews were put away and students silently read the story on which the preview was based.

As a result of this procedure, students' recall of facts directly stated in the stories increased by 13% and their higher-level comprehension by 38%. In addition, scores on a test of recall of information, given after several days had elapsed, were significantly higher than when no written previews were used. And, important for poorly motivated readers, an attitude survey showed students liked the technique.

Although the type of previewing just described is conducted in much more depth than the suggestions found in most reading materials, it takes only about 10 minutes to implement. Other studies have shown that written previews are also effective with elementary and senior high school students (Graves & Cooke, 1980; Graves & Palmer, 1981).

2. *Emphasizing predictions.* In two investigations, one with average readers (J. Hansen, 1981) and a follow-up study with poor readers (McCormick & Hill, 1984), students' comprehension was boosted when teachers used a systematic method of focusing on predictions before stories were read—which Hansen had called the Strategy Procedure.

For the experimental groups, the teacher selected three main ideas from each of the stories students were to read. Two questions were written about each main idea, one always requiring the students to relate something in the upcoming text to their own background experiences, and the second asking students to make a prediction about what might happen in the story. For example, suppose a story concerned two boys who were such good friends they decided to change places for a few days, but the results were not as positive as either boy had anticipated. Based on the theme of the narrative, one of the main ideas the teacher might wish the students to infer could be:

Things aren't always as good for another person as they may seem.

In this case, the *background question* might be this:

Have you ever wished or pretended you were someone else—if so, who and why?

And the *prediction question* that followed might be this:

FIGURE 12–2
A written preview for a short story

Preview for "The Signalman"

It seems sometimes that life is full of dangers! Would you agree? Nearly every day an accident or a disaster of some kind happens somewhere. A plane crashes, an earthquake occurs, or cars pile up on the freeway. Can you think of some accidents or disasters that have happened lately?

Many times before a disaster occurs a warning is given. For example, lights might blink on the instrument panel of an airplane, or instruments might pick up tremors in the earth that predict an earthquake is about to occur. Can you think of other types of warnings? Were warnings given for the disasters we just talked about?

Some people believe that they are warned of dangers in supernatural ways. They believe in spirits, or voices, or maybe even ghosts guiding them to do—or not do—something. Have you ever heard of someone being warned like this? What did that person say?

Maybe you've been warned about something. For example, have you ever awakened from a dream thinking that what you dreamed would happen? And then—did it? Have you ever had a feeling something bad was about to happen? and then—did it happen? Can you think of any examples?

The story you will read today is about a man who often gets warnings. But, the warnings this man gets don't come from dreams or his mind. The man gets warnings of bad things about to happen from a ghost, or specter. It seems that the ghost always appears before something terrible happens, as if he is trying to warn of danger.

The story takes place in a very lonely and gloomy spot, hidden away in the mountains. The man you will read about lives alone in a hut which is on a railroad line and near a tunnel. The hut has many things the man needs—such as a desk, a record book, an instrument to send telegraphs, and a bell.

The man is a signalman. His job is to signal the trains, watch for danger on the tracks, and warn passing trains of trouble ahead. The signalman works very hard at his job and is quite exact in all his duties. He is nervous, though, because he has seen many people die in train accidents near his post. He wants to be sure that he signals the trains of any danger.

You will learn about what the signalman does and says through the man who tells the story. This man visited the signalman at two different times and learned much about him. The story you will read is the story the visitor tells after meeting the signalman.

The story opens as the visitor calls "Hello! Below there!" to the signalman. He wants to know how to reach the signalman's hut from where he is at the top of a cliff. The signalman hears the man call to him but doesn't answer. He is afraid and looks down the railroad line instead of up to the man.

What does the signalman think he will see? Why is he afraid? Read to find out.

Before you read the story, I want to show you a list of some of the people in it. They don't have names and are described by who they are or what they do. The signalman is the man who lives in a hut near the railroad. The visitor is the man who visits the signalman and who tells the story. Another character is the ghost.

There are also some words I would like to define for you. The signalman is a dark, *sallow* man, with a dark beard and heavy eyebrows. *Sallow* means that he looks sickly and pale.

The signalman's hut is also called a *post* because it is where he is stationed to do his job.

The ghost is also called a *specter*.

Source: From "Effects of Previewing Difficult Short Stories on Low Ability Junior High School Students' Comprehension, Recall, and Attitudes" by M. Graves, C. Cooke, and M. LaBerge, 1983, *Reading Research Quarterly, 18*(3), p. 267. Copyright 1983 by the International Reading Association. Reprinted by permission of the International Reading Association.

If two children changed places, what kinds of things, good or bad, do you think might happen?

The three main ideas were never shown or stated directly to the students: they simply served as a way to help the teacher devise important questions. However, the two questions written for each of the main ideas were thoroughly discussed by the group prior to their reading the story. Group discussion was considered critical because (a) students who at first could think of no responses to the questions often were able to respond after hearing other students' comments; (b) students sometimes modified their original responses after hearing and thinking about other students' answers; and (c) students could use many persons' ideas— not just their own—from which to draw inferences later during reading.

Instead of the systematic prediction exercises before reading, students in other groups did activities after reading, discussing answers to one higher-order question and five questions based on details specifically described in the text.

Students in the groups emphasizing predictions before reading performed significantly better on weekly tests of higher-level comprehension than those who did not engage in the carefully constructed prediction discussions.

3. *Using story impressions: a writing activity.* McGinley and Denner (1987) developed a combination prediction-writing activity that had favorable results on poor readers' story comprehension. Their research was conducted with children both in primary grades and at the middle school level. This method is called "using story impressions" and is implemented before students read.

To prepare for the lesson, the teacher selects words or phrases that represent important characters, settings, and key elements of the plot for a narrative students will read. The students then use these to compose their own stories, which are to represent a guess or prediction of what the upcoming story will be about. The point of the instruction is not that the learners duplicate the author's story, but rather that they are engaged with the ideas they will encounter in the upcoming reading. This activity is said to activate schema; and it is very likely that it also promotes interest, as students read and compare the actual story with their own. Figure 12–3 shows a sample of one student's story "guess," written in response to a set of words the teacher had presented before the middle school students read an adaptation of Edgar Allan Poe's "The Tell-Tale Heart." The clue words are listed in the sequence in which they occur in the published narrative and the arrows between words in the figure are the teacher's indication of the direction in which the action is to flow.

Before learners engage in use of story impressions independently, it is recommended that group stories be produced with the teacher's guidance, brainstorming ideas about ways to logically connect the words and phrases.

Development of Strategies That Can Be Used with a Wide Variety of Texts.   In addition to building and activating background knowledge necessary for reading specific narratives, prereading activities may focus on strategies that will be useful in many reading situations. These are "prepractice" exercises that give students opportunities to work with a strategy under teacher guidance before they apply the strategy independently. The objective is to make the text more accessible for students during later real connected reading.

1. *Using listening activities to practice complex skills.* Helping students gain a sense of just what certain strategies entail, and doing so within a context that sim-

FIGURE 12–3

Story impressions (prereading) activity based on Poe's "The Tell-Tale Heart"

Story Impressions Given to A Class	A Remedial Eighth-Grader's Story Guess Written From the Story Impressions
house ↓ old man ↓ young man ↓ hatred ↓ ugly eye ↓ death ↓ tub, blood, knife ↓ buried ↓ floor ↓ police ↓ heartbeat ↓ guilt ↓ crazy ↓ confession	There was a young man and his father, an old man. They lived in a house on a hill out in the bouniey's. The old man hated his son because he had an ugly eye. 　　The young man was asleep in his bedroom when he was awakened by screaming. He went to the bedroom and saw his father laying in the tub. There was blood everywhere and a knife through him. 　　The young man found a tape recording hidden behind the door on the floor. He turned it on there was screaming on the tape. The young man started to call the police, but then he stopped and remembered what his mother had told him. She had told him that he had a split personality. So he called the police and confessed to being crazy and killing his father. His heartbeat was heavy as he called.

Source: "Story Impressions: A Prereading/Writing Activity" by W. McGinley and P. Denner, 1987, *Journal of Reading, 37*, p. 250. Copyright 1987 by the International Reading Association. Reprinted by permission of W. McGinley and the International Reading Association.

plifies the task, can set students on the road to applying these while reading any text. Two relatively complex strategies that may profit from this type of prereading treatment are drawing conclusions and drawing inferences.

Drawing conclusions involves use of statements expressed in a text; although the conclusion is not directly stated, all information needed to reach the desired deduction is contained in the material. In contrast, **drawing inferences** is required when part of the knowledge necessary to derive the response is found in the selection, but part of it is not. When making inferences, students must search their schemata to find additional information and combine this with that reported in the story. Generating conclusions and constructing inferences both require interpretive thinking, and the two strategies are closely related. Further, both processes form the basis of, and are interrelated with, other higher-level comprehension skills.

Arriving at conclusions and making inferences may at times necessitate fairly intricate thinking. The process may appear particularly enigmatic for some disabled readers, unless they are given explicit instruction. When C. Hansen and Lovitt (1977) examined performances of students with learning disabilities on literal, sequential, and inferential questions, their scores were lowest when required to draw inferences. Furthermore, Wilson's (1979) study indicated that the differences in effectiveness between average readers and those with reading disabilities were greater on inferential than on literal questions.

Teachers can provide occasions for students to prepractice drawing conclusions and inferences during listening comprehension exercises. Studies have shown that reading comprehension and listening comprehension are related (e.g., Dreyer & Katz, 1992; Hoover & Gough, 1990). In listening exercises, the teacher does the reading while students devote their energies to thinking. Teachers should write or locate short passages, read these to the students, then ask them to draw an inference or conclusion. Here is one example of the kind of paragraph to be used:

Joe's toothache was making him feel awful. He tried many times to yank the tooth out himself, but he just couldn't do it. He made a big decision. He put on his coat and walked slowly downtown. He came to a building, stopped, sighed, and bravely went up the steps. What was his purpose?

After they have given their response, the teacher should ask students if the correct answer was *stated* in the paragraph, have them name all clues in the text that helped them arrive at the answer, and ask them to tell things from their own experiences (i.e., background information) that helped them determine their reply. This type of practice may be used even with very young students.

Pictures can also be exploited to give students practice with inferring and with drawing conclusions. See the example in Figure 12–4. In this example, the student is to draw a picture in the empty box depicting what occurred between pictures 1 and 3.

Nontextual practice (listening activities and working with pictures, for instance) should be used only as an introduction to the concept of inferring or drawing conclusions, the goal being simply to give learners a sense of what is

FIGURE 12–4
Preliminary practice in drawing inferences or conclusions can employ pictures: What happened between pictures 1 and 3?

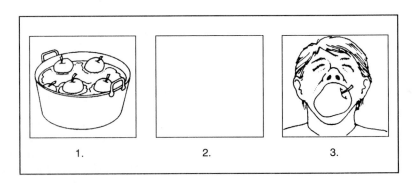

1.   2.   3.

called for in these strategies. Nontextual exercises should be followed by students' applying the strategy to written material.

2. *Guiding selection of main ideas.* The **main idea** of a passage is the most important idea the author has given about a topic; it is the idea to which most other information in the passage refers or relates. Determining the main idea of what has been read is also called finding the central thought; it is the process of deciding on the general significance of the material. Sometimes this has been referred to as getting the *gist.*

Individual paragraphs in expository (informational) material rather consistently contain a main idea. On the other hand, single paragraphs in narratives may not, because in stories the main ideas sometimes run across several sequential paragraphs (H. A. Robinson, 1983).

At times, main ideas are directly (that is, *explicitly*) stated, as in topic sentences. However, in other cases, the main idea must be inferred from a number of facts that are given; in those circumstances, it is said that the main idea is *implicit*—it's there but not specifically expressed, so the reader must figure it out. In either case, determining the main idea is considered a higher-level comprehension skill because it requires making a generalization. Even when a topic sentence states the main idea, the reader must decide that this statement, and not others, is the central thought.

Learning how to distinguish the main idea of a passage is a valuable strategy because it helps readers identify what is important to know—and to remember. In addition, details are more easily remembered if they are related to a more general point.

Less-skilled readers sometimes have difficulty understanding what is meant by a "main idea." Asked to specify the main point of a passage, they respond with a single, small detail. When the response is deemed inaccurate, they insist, "It does too say that here." They fail to distinguish between factual but less-inclusive supporting information and an idea of significance for the whole selection. The teacher must often illustrate the concepts of "main," "major," and "the most important" in a direct way before learning can progress.

To guide main idea selection, instruction typically begins with single paragraphs. At this stage, teachers should choose paragraphs in which the topic sentence is directly stated. Since authors may place a topic sentence in any of three locations in a paragraph, practice should be given in identifying this main idea statement in each position: at the beginning, at the end, and somewhere in the middle. Teachers should be actively involved to give students immediate feedback about the correctness of responses and to provide direct assistance in deciding why an answer is right or wrong. This is in contrast to many published activities designed for practicing the skill of determining main ideas. Too often the latter do little to teach *how* to ascertain major points, especially if students work the exercises independently. For example, in a typical published lesson, learners read single paragraphs and then answer multiple-choice questions that are later marked right or wrong by the teacher. This is an instance of an activity that is merely a test and does not enlighten students about the processes necessary for identifying central thoughts.

In the second phase, students work with paragraphs in which main ideas are not explicitly presented. Direct teaching, collaborative learning activities, and discussion are important at this stage. All of these can furnish "instruction that is instructive."

Here are some appropriate activities to help students determine main ideas of selections.

1.   *Use heuristic devices.* **Heuristic devices** are tools or mechanisms that guide or help learners discover concepts. At times, these take the form of a visual demonstration. For example, to teach main idea selection, you could demonstrate visually the relationship between the main idea and supporting details by drawing a tree with trunk and branches on an overhead projector transparency. After students have read a paragraph, they are asked to offer suggestions for the main idea and details. The teacher writes the main idea on the trunk and the details on the branches. The teacher should try different writing arrangements on the tree to determine which one makes sense. (Use a water-based felt tip pen for marking on the transparency; when answers are to be changed, dip a tissue in water and erase the previously written answer.)

2.   *Collaboratively outline paragraphs.* Have students work together to outline several single paragraphs to recognize the relationships between main ideas and the details that support them. To introduce the principle, before students read a paragraph, the teacher writes the main idea and each supporting detail on separate oaktag strips. After they read, students arrange the strips in outline fashion to show the main idea and the details.

Abby's measles were making her miserable.

- Abby hated the funny-looking spots on her body.
- Her measles were making her itch.
- The measles made her feel like she had a rash.
- She could not go places she wanted to go because measles are contagious.

Following several such experiences, inaugurate more formal outlining techniques. After learners have read a paragraph, through collaborative discussion, have them decide on the main idea. Next, the teacher writes a Roman numeral I on the board (using typical outlining format), followed by the statement selected as the main idea. The teacher asks for the details that prove or support the main idea. These are listed below the main idea, again in outlining format. This procedure is followed for several paragraphs.

Both categories of outlining practice (informal and formal) reinforce the concept that there are distinctions between major points and supporting points—that all ideas are not of equal significance.

3.   *Ask key questions and have students combine the answers to arrive at implicit main points.* The Who? What? When? and Why? questions employed so often in literal comprehension exercises can be used to focus students' attention on main points. They are particularly helpful for paragraphs in which the main idea is not explicitly stated. If a short phrase is written to answer each wh-question, these often can be combined into one statement that reflects the main idea that is not explicitly stated. For example,

Steven was planning to run away from home. He had decided that if on this birthday, his parents didn't get him the dog he had asked for year after year, that night he would take the Greyhound bus from the station downtown and go off to live on his own.

Who: a boy, Steven

What: planning to run away

When: on his birthday

Why: if his parents didn't get him a dog

Main idea statement: A boy, Steven, was planning to run away on his birthday if his parents didn't get him a dog.

4. *Collaboratively compose paragraph titles.* The teacher can work collaboratively with students to write titles for untitled paragraphs. Revisions can continue until the best title is developed.

Up to this point the discussion has centered on finding the main idea in single paragraphs. Of course, the next phase in the program should promote transfer of this skill to longer pieces of discourse, that is, material longer than one paragraph. All of the activities suggested above may be used, some with slight adaptations. For example, with *visual heuristics,* the main ideas of individual paragraphs become the supporting details for the main idea of the whole passage. When oaktag strips are used in *manipulative outlining activities,* the same strips used for main ideas of the individual paragraphs can be physically moved to the slots for supporting details in the passage outline. To ease the way into *formal outlining* of longer passages, the teacher may wish to print partially completed outlines on the board with the details already given for each paragraph and only the main idea slot for each one left blank. The blank slots are to be filled by the students after group discussion. When asking students to *compose titles for passages,* teachers can cut headlines off newspaper articles and have them write their own. If students are unable to read the regular community newspaper, any of the easy-to-read newspapers now available, such as *Know Your World* (Xerox), may be used.

Baumann (1984) had excellent success in teaching sixth-graders to select main ideas of both narrative and expository materials using many of the principles and procedures described above. Working with paragraphs and then short passages, and with explicit main idea statements and then implicit main ideas, students were instructed within a model that embraced the ideas of (a) clear and complete teacher instructions, (b) guided practice, (c) independent practice, and (d) and application to real materials. Students were exposed to heuristics (a table with the main idea written on it and supporting details on the legs that supported the table; a main idea umbrella with details beneath, and so on); constructed simple two-level outlines; and wrote out main ideas rather than merely selecting them. In addition, Baumann directly taught students how to paraphrase. Readers who participated in this program performed significantly better on main idea selection than those who were trained through regular basal reader manual suggestions.

Schunk and Rice (1992) taught fourth- and fifth-grade students with learning disabilities and with severe reading difficulties a strategy for determining main ideas of passages. They added to the instructional procedures a component that emphasized the *benefits* of employing the strategy, providing feedback that showed learners how their improved performance was tied to their *use* of the strategy they had been taught. These students employed the strategy more and generalized its use to other readings more than students who had not had the value of the strategy demonstrated to them. Including an element stressing the value of the strategy is in line with principles for developing strategic readers—readers who not only know how, but why they are to use a learning tactic. Furthermore, in a second experiment, this research team showed another group how to modify the main idea selection strategy for different tasks, and they, too, performed better than a control group who had not received this additional training.

The presentation, here, of recommendations for guiding selection of main ideas is to serve as an example of ways prepractice can be built to prepare youngsters for using complex skills in later connected text reading. Comparable practice activities with other comprehension strategies produce positive outcomes.

On-Line Assistance

What procedures can help a reader interpret text *during* reading? Recommendations from research investigations follow.

Assistance with the Immediate Text. Some techniques are designed to heighten understanding of a specific story students are reading, but in some cases, systematic use of these strategies builds tactics that readers can employ independently with other selections.

1. *Involving students in a DRTA.* The acronym DRTA stands for Directed Reading-Thinking Activity (Stauffer, 1975). DRTA is a carefully organized procedure designed to improve students' comprehension of narrative material and is directed by the teacher. It resembles a generic lesson plan. The steps for these lessons are as follows.

a. The first step consists of preparing students for what they will be required to do *during reading of a text.* Have them survey the material by reading the title and looking at pictures. Ask them to predict events in the first portion of the story. To encourage predictions, pose questions such as, "What do you think will happen?" or "After reading the title and looking at these two pictures, what do you think this section is going to be about?" Set a purpose for reading by telling students to check their predictions: "Read to find out if you're right" or "Read to find out who's right."

b. Have students read a beginning portion of the story silently.

c. Stop to verify (or reject) through discussion the predictions made before reading. Prediction questions are particularly effective when students compare their guesses with what actually takes place in the text (Fielding, Anderson, & Pearson, 1990).

d. Ask for new predictions before reading the next section. In many cases, these predictions will now be based on what has been previously read in the passage.

e. Continue with a cycle of predicting, reading, and confirming or rejecting through discussion until the material is completed.

DRTA teaches students to consider information, form hypotheses, suspend judgment, find proof, make decisions, and develop critical reading skills. Research has shown that DRTAs help students learn to monitor their own comprehension (Baumann, Seifert-Kessell, & Jones, 1992) and that the quality and quantity of students' answers are better than when using traditional questioning procedures found in basal reader manuals (e.g., see Reutzel & Hollingsworth, 1991). DRTA can be used for listening comprehension lessons, as well.

2. *Accentuating content-specific story discussions.* During guided reading of narratives, teachers commonly ask students to pause in their reading at various logical points to discuss events that have transpired so far. Research suggests it is advantageous for these discussions to accentuate story-specified content.

An example is seen in studies conducted by Harker (1988) and Golden (1988): when a teacher and learners engaged in substantial amounts of *content-focused* dialogue including discussion of story theme and when students answered intricate questions based on the story, often with teacher assistance, students remembered considerably more important information than when this was not the case. Readers recalled significantly fewer critical ideas when discussion simply focused on similarities of children's experiences to those of story characters, with students telling personal anecdotes related to experiences described in the text.

This is not to say that self-expression is to be denigrated, but this is an example of getting what you teach. If the objective is deep understanding of story information and themes, then emphasizing story information and themes during the reading of narratives is more valuable than less-focused discussion.

Development of Strategies That Can Be Used with a Wide Variety of Texts.   The suggestions here are used during the reading of a specific story, but demonstrate strategies students can "take with them" to subsequent texts they read.

1. *Using think-alouds.* Thinking aloud, or "making thinking public" (Paris, 1986) has been suggested previously in this text, for instance, as a mechanism for assessing students' reading processing. As you remember, a **think-aloud** is a self-report of one's own thinking operations. Think-alouds were also recommended for helping students as they try to employ word identification strategies while reading text. *Instructional* uses of think-alouds vary from the manner in which they are employed in assessment.

In instruction, the teacher is the first person to engage in a think-aloud. The teacher models how to approach a text metacognitively. The teacher states aloud those thinking processes he or she is using. Wade (1990) suggests the following. The teacher (a) *makes predictions* before beginning to read, stating these aloud (From looking at the title and this first picture, I think this story will be about witches"); (b) *demonstrates analogy use* ("What is being described here makes me think of some things I've been seeing on TV lately about what it's like to live through a hurricane"); (c) *admits*—or for purposes of instruction, simulates—*confusions* ("This doesn't quite make sense to me here"); (d) *specifies fix-up strategies* ("I think I'd better go back to that other part and reread for a moment to see if I can figure out why I don't understand this" or "Maybe if I read ahead this will become more clear"); and (e) *describes visual images* ("As I read this I can see in my mind the way that ferocious dog must have looked to Alex, with its teeth bared and its short, wiry hair bristling on its neck as it prepared to attack").

At the onset, focus is on just one strategy at a time, for example, one day the teacher models and asks for analogies—"What does this seem like that you already know about?" with a number of group members offering suggestions about various episodes or descriptions in the story. And, in another lesson, the teacher solicits visual images that different readers have called up as they read, and so on.

To promote generalization of these strategies to independent, as well as teacher-guided, reading of other texts, have readers engage in collaborative learning, using the procedures they have been practicing in daily lessons. Students take turns reading, suggesting their thoughts; others in the group are allowed to add additional, and contrasting, ideas as they prompt one another through their reading of the text.

Then the teacher puts it all together, asking the learners to follow silently the beginning portion of a story while he or she reads orally, role-playing all five strategies specified above (and perhaps others). After the teacher has illustrated the behaviors of a strategic reader, a student is called on to handle another portion of the narrative in the same manner, and then another student for a next small portion, and so on.

Furthermore, the teacher employs think-alouds as the need arises. When a learner evidences confusions, the teacher may say "Well, this is how I would figure that out. I would say to myself—let's see, that idea was talked about in the second part of the story; I'll look back there and see what I may have forgotten" or "I know they did not give the answer to that question in the book. But I can figure it out if I use what Bobby told Amy about the parrot, and, if I think about what I know parrots can do. Parrots can talk, so . . . Ah ha! The answer must be that it was the parrot who said that crazy thing, and not the man!" This has been called "sharing secrets with students"—sharing the ways *you* have learned to figure out text information. Share secrets with learners; don't just "test" their comprehension. In addition, when students show insightful thinking about a question they have answered well, ask them to tell *how* they arrived at their answers.

Studies have shown that even elementary school children can learn to think aloud (e.g., Baumann et al.'s [1992] work with fourth-graders) and that this helps them detect errors in reasoning. In Baumann et al.'s research, readers who had been taught through think-alouds outperformed, in depth and breadth of comprehension monitoring abilities, students who had not received the instruction.

2.   *Promoting visual imagery.* Because of the difficulties that some young readers and slower learners may have with forming visual images, as you may suggest that students do during your think-aloud demonstrations, a special word will be said about that strategy. Being able to form visual images seems critical to evoking mental models to comprehend texts.

When most people read a story, they are likely to "see" pictures in their minds of the events they are reading about as they progress through a text. Some poor readers, however, report that they do not see images as they read—perhaps because of exaggerated concern with pronunciation of words or lack of interest in reading. Several studies have shown that when students do form mental pictures of the message in a text, both comprehension and recall are aided (e.g., Gambrell, 1982; Sadoski, 1983; N. L. Williams, Konopak, Wood, & Avett, 1992).

In Sadoski's (1983) study, for example, the role of imagery was shown to be related to higher-level comprehension, which requires deeper levels of the processing of meaning than is required by literal-level comprehension. In this study, fifth-graders who reported forming a visual image of a critical part of a story scored better on higher-level comprehension tasks, such as telling the theme of the story, than did students who did not report visual imagery.

It has also been suggested that visual imagery is particularly helpful when students are reading about situations that are new to them. Forming images in these cases serves as a problem-solving strategy to comprehend the unfamiliar event or information (McNamara et al., 1991).

Imagery training has helped some poor readers increase their higher-level comprehension achievement. Several suggestions for this training follow.

a. Before students read a story, specifically direct them to try to form pictures in their minds, attempting to "see" the objects and events they are reading about, And tell them why: because it will help them understand and remember what they read.

b. Read the first paragraph of the story *to* students. Prior to beginning, ask them to close their eyes and attempt to form a mental picture of what they hear as you read. Afterward, discuss these images. Poetry is also a good choice for this purpose. Direct students to form pictures in their minds as they read the remainder of the story. At the conclusion, ask for images they "saw."

c. Read the first paragraph to students, again asking them to form a mental image of what they hear. Afterward, request that they quickly draw pictures of what they saw (a very quick sketch, perhaps using stick figures is what is called for here). Briefly compare and discuss the pictures. Lesgold, McCormick, and

Golinkoff (1975) reported a study in which third- and fourth-graders were trained for 4 weeks to draw cartoons about portions of selections they read; after the training period, students recalled more of the stories as a result of this imagery practice.

d. Have students read a paragraph of the story silently themselves. Proceed as in item b. And, with another paragraph, they—rather than you—have read, proceed as in item c. Direct them to attempt to construct the same kinds of images in their minds as they read the rest of the text. Tell them they should try to "see" what the author has described in all stories they read.

e. Have students carry out suggestions b through d, but with sections of the story longer than a paragraph.

f. Ask students to act out the first portion of a story. Engaging in short dramatizations necessarily induces "seeing" what must be acted out. L. C. Henderson and J. L. Shanker's (1978) study showed that this activity improved comprehension of students in primary grades more than workbook exercises designed to aid comprehension. Of course, students cannot act out everything they read, but they can "act it out" in their heads. Tell them to try to do this with the rest of the story.

g. Some teachers have assembled stories in this manner: a page of text, followed by a blank sheet of paper; another page of text, followed by another blank page; and so on. The empty sheet is a signal for students to pause and form a mental image of what they have just read on the preceding page.

h. To promote transfer of strategy use, assign a story for students to read independently. Ask that they draw a series of pictures to show the images they formed in their minds as they read. Share and compare these as a group activity.

3. *Engaging students in the ReQuest Procedure.* In this activity, originally developed in a reading clinic by Manzo (1969), students are helped to monitor their understanding through asking questions, listening to teacher modeling, and setting purposes for reading.

When a new story is introduced, students and teacher read the title and first sentence and examine illustrations found on the first page. The students are then to ask the teacher as many questions as they can pose about this introductory information. After the teacher answers these, it's the teacher's turn to question. He or she, too, asks questions over the same content, attempting to focus student attention on the major intent of the author and on a purpose for reading.

Next, a small portion more of the story is read followed with the students querying the teacher, asking as many questions as they can about it. Again, when the teacher has answered all of these, he or she directs questions to the students about this section.

The mutual asking and answering continues for approximately a 10-minute period, with the teacher leading the students to frame questions about the purpose and major ideas of the narrative through the types of questions modeled.

Students are then invited to read the remainder of the story silently, and at the conclusion, the teacher inquires "Did we read for the right purpose?" and asks more questions. In addition to aiding understanding of the current story, the ReQuest Procedure is believed to help students learn to monitor their thinking processes for later independent reading.

4. *Using text sets.* **Text sets** are groups of books that are conceptually related. For instance, in one study (Short, 1992), students read assortments of books based on shared character types (e.g., specific animals, such as stories about pigs); shared

genres (e.g., folktales); shared author (all written by the same individual); shared settings (e.g., stories set in Japan); and shared topic, but different rendition (e.g., various versions of the Cinderella story from around the world).

The advantage in using sets of several related books for a period of time is that story discussions can center on relationships among books, allowing students to draw upon what they have learned from one book to enhance their interpretations of others. This provides opportunities for analysis and comparison—and the deep processing of text that true understanding requires.

In this procedure, each day during story reading and discussion, the teacher has students focus on connections between the current book and any from the set they have previously read. They should also be guided to look for contrasts as well as likenesses. Correspondences and differences between themes as well as specifics should be included in the discussions. Short (1992) believed that collaboratively establishing connections is a positive feature since readers can springboard from one another's insights to realize more complex links among books and ideas. Teacher guidance can help learners build the connections with some depth.

Understandings should broaden as students read additional books in a set, understandings that can carry over into independent reading of narratives.

Culminating Events

Instructional events *after* students read can be more than the usual "testing" with a few literal questions. Studies of effective comprehension instruction suggest the following approaches.

Assistance with the Immediate Text.   Certain culminating experiences can strengthen immediate understandings.

1. *Asking questions: general principles and procedures.* For some teachers, a comprehension "program" hinges mainly on asking questions. Morrison (1968), for example, found that teachers ask as many as two questions per minute in a typical reading session. Is all this questioning really useful for improving comprehension? The answer to this depends on the quality of the teacher's "asking behaviors" and on the types of questions asked.

"Asking behavior" refers to how teachers foster the environment for question-and-answer sessions. For example, allowing active turn taking by all members of a group has a beneficial effect on learning (R. C. Anderson, Wilkinson, & Mason, 1991). Some good ways and poor ways to set the question-and-answering climate in remedial and clinical reading programs are listed in Table 12-3.

The quality of students' comprehension performance is also influenced by the types of questions asked. Obviously, important rather than trivial questions should be the focus. Avoid questions such as "What color was Mary's dress?"—questions that focus on irrelevant details. Emphasize information of significance.

Although there is much concern among reading educators that too little emphasis is placed on higher-order questions, and too much on those at a literal level, it is not unusual in remedial programs to find students who also seem challenged by this latter type of usually less difficult comprehension.

Literal-level comprehension is another name for reading for directly stated facts. If the story that students have read states that "Pam was the frog in the class play," and the teacher asks, "What role did Pam have in the class play?"

TABLE 12–3
Asking questions of students

Effective Asking Behaviors	Poor Asking Behaviors
Give students time to think before answering. Also, if they hesitate in mid-answer, be patient.	Demand immediate responses. Call on another student when an immediate response is not forthcoming. Allow other students to sit with hands raised while the first student is trying to think.
When a student gives a correct answer, take it a step further—ask the student to explain how he or she knows it is the correct answer.	When a correct answer is given, always move immediately to the next question.
Ask all students to respond, and to respond as often as possible, during any given session.	Only call on students who volunteer.
Require all students to pay attention during answering by another student. When appropriate, involve other students in the answering—for example, by saying something like, "Phillip, do you agree with Judy?" or, "How would you support the correct answer that DeMerrill has already given?"	When one student is answering a question, allow other students to be off-task (looking around the room, talking, working on something else).
If a student doesn't understand the question, rephrase it, break it down into parts, or in some other way assist the student in arriving at the correct response. Researchers (e.g., Guszak, 1967) have found that wrong responses often result because teachers ask questions that are too difficult.	If a student doesn't understand the question, blame the student and call on another person.
When an incorrect answer is given, take time to *teach*: model how *you* would determine the answer; ask the student to think of a previous answer; explain; give additional information; illustrate. Teach the student *how* to answer questions.	When an incorrect answer is given, immediately call on another student.

the teacher is asking them to respond on a literal level. If the geography book states that corn is one of the main farm products of Nebraska and the students are asked, "What is one of the main farm products of Nebraska?" this is an example of literal-level comprehension being required for expository material. In some cases, a literal-level question may be answered by merely restating the exact words found in the text; in other cases, the information must be paraphrased. However, in both situations the information is in the book. Literal-level comprehension *is* important because it provides the basis for higher-level comprehension.

Students are exposed to, and have practice with, literal-level questions and comprehension more than any other type. Guszak (1967) and several other researchers have observed and tabulated teachers' questions to determine the kinds of comprehension tasks required of students. Consistently, the researchers found that about 70% of all questions asked by teachers address the literal content of reading assignments. Since students have much practice with this type of comprehension, the teacher should consider several reasons if students persistently have difficulty comprehending directly stated facts.

The first reason a teacher should consider is whether the student is placed in material that is too difficult. While the teacher may have administered a test and determined the student's approximate instructional level, remember, tests are not infallible. Try the student in material that is slightly easier and see if literal comprehension is better. Incorrect placement can also be the fault of an inaccurate readability level assigned to the specific selection the student is reading. At best, readability formulas provide a ballpark figure of reading levels. And some publishers simply make educated guesses about the levels of their materials. Assess the student's literal comprehension with other books. The fault may be in the material, and not in the student.

A second question the teacher should ask is, "Does the student have an unusual lack of familiarity with the topic being presented in this selection?" If difficulty is seen with literal-level questions and if lack of knowledge of the subject appears to be the root of the problem, the implication is that the teacher must spend more than the usual time to build students' background information. To determine if students' problems in comprehending directly stated facts do result from lack of familiarity with the topic, students should be asked to read several selections (at the same reading level) on topics about which the teacher is certain they have knowledge. Students should be asked literal questions on these selections to determine if there may be other causes of their difficulties.

Of course, an emphasis should be placed on higher-level questions, as well. More students of average ability and below-average achievement do encounter greater obstacles with higher-order comprehension questions than with literal ones. Our case study student, Frederick, is a good example. Frederick's attention to literal details was not as well developed as it should have been, but his major impediments arose from his lack of ability to make complex interpretations of the text he read.

In 1992, the United States National Assessment of Educational Progress (NAEP) was administered nationwide to approximately 140,000 youngsters in grades 4, 8, and 12, and it was generally found that students showed less proficiency with higher-order comprehension skills than with literal interpretations. In fact, each time the NAEP has been conducted in recent years, this same area of weakness has appeared across all age levels. Therefore, a major concern of teachers of both average readers and students with reading disabilities has come to be higher-level understandings of written text.

Higher-level comprehension involves use of interpretive thinking, and, in some cases, evaluative or creative responses. It includes (a) drawing conclusions and inferences, (b) determining the main ideas of passages, (c) determining cause-and-effect relationships, (d) following a sequence of events, (e) using imagery, and (f) using critical reading skills.

Many different types of questions should be asked about any one story. Higher-level questions ask students to call on their background information, encourage them to seek out the important information conveyed by a story (main ideas), stimulate them to recall directly stated facts, and expand their vocabularies.

Since students must learn how to *recall* answers (with the book closed) as well as to *locate* answers, practice should be given in answering questions involving both types of tasks.

2. *Motivating effort for higher-level thinking.* On occasion, games may provide an alternative to traditional questioning after stories and motivate reluctant learners to expend the effort necessary for higher-level thinking as well. Effective com-

prehension games involve written text and require concentration on in-depth thinking.

Figure 12–5 shows a board game that focuses on higher-order questions. To play this game, students use a spinner with 1, 2, and 3 on its face. After spinning, the student moves his or her game piece according to the number of spaces indicated by the spinner. The square on which a student lands directs him or her to draw from one of three piles of cards: *question cards*—identified on the game board by a question mark—contain questions that require a conclusion or an inference to be drawn, *creativity cards* ask for a creative answer, and *evaluation cards* request an evaluative response. Sample questions for each set of cards are shown in Figure 12–5. Students attempt to answer the question on each card they draw, and then the next student takes a turn. Some questions, such as those that require students to make judgments about character traits or to give an opinion about the most important event in a story, while termed evaluative responses, also involve inferring and drawing conclusions. Teachers should require students to defend their answers with reasoning based on text information or their own background knowledge. As can be seen from examining the questions for this game, as found in the figure, this specific game is generic in nature and could be used after any story.

3.   *Combining "grand conversations" with teacher questions.* Studies with average readers show that students can involve themselves in higher-level comprehension tasks without teacher guidance. For example, McGee (1992) had students in regular classrooms engage in "grand conversations" after a story had been read, conversations in which students took the lead without a teacher's questions for the first half of the sessions. The grand conversations consisted of exchanges among the learners about their responses to a narrative. During this part of the lesson, teachers did not launch subjects for discussion; they simply asked "What do you think?" following the reading of the story and then made encouraging remarks, such as "That's a good idea" or "Interesting comment" as students talked about the book in an open-ended fashion.

The resulting discussions revealed inferences and evaluations that were primarily reader-focused reflections, that is, in which students offered personal reactions to the narrative, including beliefs, evaluations, and emotions. Voicing reactions certainly is important, particularly for engendering interest in reading. During the second half of the session, the discussion centered on an interpretative question that the teacher asked to summon higher-order thinking about the meaning of the narrative as a whole. This question was text-focused and attempted to promote inferences, identification of the importance of characters, events, and themes, or, in general, story understanding above the literal level. While student-led discussion did produce interpretations in all conversations, the teacher-posed question drew higher percentages of interpretive responses than open-ended discussions. Supplementing student-initiated responses with teacher-guided thinking appears to have positive effects with students of average ability, and this would likely prove to be true with students with reading or learning disabilities, also.

Development of Strategies That Can Be Used with a Wide Variety of Texts.   Certain culminating experiences can strengthen immediate *and* future comprehension.

1.   *Asking questions: general principles and procedures.* There are some particulars to be considered in regard to asking questions that apply to all texts read, not

FIGURE 12–5

A board game that can be used with any story to encourage higher-level comprehension

| ? | ? | Creativity card | ? | ? | ? | ? | Evaluation card |

Think and Enjoy

Evaluation card

Creativity card

Read another book | Evaluation card

Begin

Sample Question Cards	Sample Creativity Cards	Sample Evaluation Cards
1. Did anything happen in the story that was unbelievable? Why or why not? If so, what?	1. How would you have solved the problem in the story differently?	1. What character do you like best? Why?
2. Who do you think was the second most important character in the story? Why?	2. What do you think might have happened to the main character after the story was over?	2. What do you think was the one most important thing the main character did. Why do you think so?
3. What kinds of feelings do you think the main character had at different times in the story?	3. How would this story have been different if it had occurred 100 years in the past or 100 years in the future?	3. Choose one character. Tell what kind of person you think this character really is. Why?
4. Choose one of the characters. Tell something this character learned.	4. Make up an ending for the story that is completely different from the one the author wrote.	4. Did you like the story? Why or why not?
5. Was the story fiction or non-fiction? Cite three things from the story to support your answer.	5. Add a character to the story. What would he or she do to change the events in the story?	5. Tell the two events in the story that you think were most interesting. Why?

just the text with which students are engaged at the moment. If learners are having little luck with producing suitable responses, here are two questions you might ask.

The first is, "Do the students know they are supposed to be attending to the meaning of the material?" Some students in remedial programs look upon reading as a word-pronunciation task, as in "I said all the words right this time. You mean you wanted me to pay attention to what the words meant, too?" When readers have this attitude, a teacher's effort must be aimed at getting them to understand that the purpose of reading is to gain meaning. For a time, everything these students read should be followed by oral questions posed by the teacher. In addition, specific activities aimed at comprehension of written material—not just word recognition—should be used. An example of a published game teachers can employ for this purpose is Reading For Details (Gamco). This is a board game accompanied by 72 story cards. There are two editions of the game, one written at second-grade level and one at fourth-grade level. To advance along the race track on this board, players draw a story card, read it, and answer one of four questions. The four questions require a *who, what, when,* or *where* answer. A spinner is used to determine which of the four questions a student must answer. Although games are certainly ancillary exercises, they may serve as a supplement to show reading as a meaning-gathering venture if they are used instructionally in a teacher-guided lesson.

If students have *written* their answers to questions that have been posed, a second query should be, "Does the problem lie in the form of students' written responses—and not in their actual understanding?" If students' comprehension is evaluated based on written replies (e.g., on workbook pages and to questions found at the ends of chapters), the teacher must take care to separate their skills and their motivation in *writing out* an answer from their true understanding of the material. When left to their own devices to read and respond independently, some students read the questions before reading the material, search through the material until they find a sentence containing several words also found in the question, and mechanically copy down that sentence for their reply, whether it is a logical answer to the question or not. Suppose, for example, that the question was, "How did the rooster get caught by the fox?" A student may find a sentence in the story that says, "The rooster hoped that he would not get caught by the fox." Note that seven words in this statement are identical to words in the question. Therefore, although this sentence does not respond to the question at all, the student may nevertheless write it down as his or her reply.

To help students dispense with this unproductive habit, teachers can arrange for group discussions, using questions and statements such as these:

A. What did Mr. Hastings do the next morning?
   1. Mr. Hastings could hardly wait for the next morning.
   2. At dawn Mr. Hastings got out his golf clubs.
B. Describe these two kinds of stores: retail stores and wholesale stores.
   1. Retail stores sell to people like you and me, but wholesale stores sell to people who own retail stores.
   2. There are two kinds of stores: retail stores and wholesale stores.

The teacher reads the questions. Students are be asked to underline those words in each of the possible answers that are identical to words in the question. Count the number of such words for each possible response. Point out the right reply and discuss why the other answer does not resolve the question, despite the number of words the question and the statement have in common. Have the students note that the number of identical words is not necessarily relevant when answering a question.

Another issue regarding evaluation of written responses to comprehension questions is brought out in McCormick's (1992) study of erroneous replies to inference questions. One of the foremost causes for getting answers wrong was that students' written statements did not convey what they meant them to. Because the poor readers in this investigation also had somewhat deficient writing skills—a not untypical circumstance for students with reading difficulties—they left words out of sentences, used words that did not mean what they intended, wrote seriously incomplete statements, and evidenced other similar problems, so that what they started out to say was not said—even when they appeared to know the correct answers if asked to discuss their meanings orally. This raises questions about the wisdom of evaluating understanding of a text based on written responses for students who lack sufficiently developed writing skills. It also spotlights the need for functional writing competencies to be treated in literacy programs. The 1992 National Assessment of Educational Progress (NAEP) reported that teachers were relying less on multiple-choice questions to judge comprehension (likely a good thing!), and more on having students write paragraphs about what they read. However, it seems that some caution should be exercised with this latter policy of using writing to assess comprehension, particularly with disabled readers. Greater emphases on discussion and reflective observation may be advisable to make accurate evaluations of comprehension.

2.   *Using story maps.* Beck, Omanson, and McKeown (1982) suggest that teachers use story maps to develop good questions. A **story map** is a sequential listing of the important elements of a narrative and is based on simplified versions of what linguists call **story grammars.** A story grammar is in effect a list of "rules" for writing narratives. The "grammar" of narratives consists of the events, ideas, and motivations that direct the movement of stories, and, interestingly, the same elements are found to occur in stories across many countries and cultures.

A story usually has the following components:

- Characters
- Setting
- A problem and a goal to resolve it
- Events to solve the problem
- Achievement of the goal

Having a sense of this typical story structure is believed to aid understanding and recall.

Before writing questions, teachers use this list of story elements as a guide to determine the story map for the specific selection to be read by students. For instance, here is a story map for The Three Little Pigs. (There are various versions of this famous narrative. I will use a kinder rendition in which no one gets eaten or boiled.)

- *Characters:* Three pigs and a wolf
- *Settings:* A straw, stick, and brick house
- *Problem and goal to resolve it:* The wolf keeps bugging these pigs by blowing down their houses, and this has to be stopped!
- *Events to solve the problem:* When the wolf blows down the straw house in which they are living, they build a stronger one of sticks

- *Achievement of the goal:* When the straw house is also huffed and puffed down, the pigs finally realize they must build a *very* strong house and one of bricks does the trick

One or more questions is written for each element in a story's map. The questions should be sequenced in the order in which each aspect occurs in the story. This does not mean that only literal questions based on directly stated information are used; higher-level questions should also be written about each element.

In the study conducted by Beck et al., when questions systematically focused on central story content in this way, students showed better comprehension. In fact, the less-skilled readers who answered questions based on story maps did as well on comprehension performance as skilled readers who answered less-focused questions found in basal reader manuals.

What is more, the best news was that this technique had *transfer* value. That is, after students had experiences with answering questions based on story maps, they showed better comprehension of new stories where the story maps were not used.

So, although teacher's use of story maps to develop questions has a decided effect on comprehension of the immediate text, this procedure also influences development of mental sets learners may enlist with a variety of narratives.

A different way to structure a story map is by using "story frames." See Figure 12–6 for an example of a story frame.

Questions based on story maps apparently help students gain some *intuitive* sense of the important story elements on which to focus their attention. This understanding is viewed as useful enough so that some authorities also suggest *direct instruction about the structures of stories,* that is, teaching students the standard elements in story grammars. Idol and Croll (1987) found these procedures induced and maintained comprehension with readers with learning disabilities.

3. *Retelling as a route to understanding story structure.* Having readers retell a selection after they have read it is usually thought of as an assessment technique; however, some researchers have used this procedure instructionally. Morrow, Sisco, and Smith (1992) taught students with learning disabilities *how to retell,* and one of the outcomes was increased awareness of story structure.

In this program, learners in an experimental group had training in retelling stories from picture books. For all 12 books used, the teacher provided guidance by helping students tell the narratives in the correct sequence and, in addition, asking specific questions to focus their retellings on elements related to settings, plot episodes, resolution, and theme. During the retelling of the first four stories, students used the book, letting the pictures assist them. For the next four, they used props that represented characters and events as they retold. The last four narratives were retold without the book or props to support them. In contrast, students in a control group drew pictures after story reading about each of the 12 books.

When posttests were administered using another story, learners in the experimental group performed significantly better when asked to retell the story than the control-group students. Students who had experienced mediated story retellings included more information on setting, plot episodes, and resolution, and sequenced the story more appropriately as well. There was no difference in the two groups' abilities to give the theme of the story (admittedly a difficult concept).

FIGURE 12–6

Sample story frame for *Cinderella* by Charles Perrault

The story takes place ___*in a make believe kingdom where Cinderella*___

lives with her stepmother and sisters in a nice house .

Cinderella, a stepsister, _____ is a character in the story

who ___*has to do all the chores around the house like a servant*___ .

The fairy godmother _____ is another character in the

story who ___*does magic and helps Cinderella go to the ball*___ .

A problem occurs when ___*Cinderella is hurrying home at midnight and*___

drops one of her glass slippers at the ball .

After that, ___*the handsome prince searches in the kingdom for*___

a young lady who can put on the glass slipper and have it fit,

and ___*the shoe doesn't fit any of the young ladies who try it on*___ .

The problem is solved when ___*Cinderella tries on the glass slipper,*___

and it fits perfectly .

The story ends with ___*the handsome prince and Cinderella getting*___

married right away, and they live happily ever after .

Source: From "Sample Story Frame for Cinderella by Charles Perrault," *Responses to Literature: Grades K–8* by J. Macon, D. Bewell, and M. Vogt, 1991. Copyright 1991 by the International Reading Association. Reprinted by permission of the International Reading Association.

As another part of the posttest, children's listening comprehension was measured; although there was not a difference on general questions, on those related to important story structure components, again the experimental group scored higher.

It appears that use of mediated story retellings has potential. When teachers ask students to retell as a culminating event after narratives are read, the activity can be made instructionally richer by directing their focus to sequence and to significant story elements, and would be preferable to less structured retelling that may be used merely as an assessment of ability to read with comprehension.

4. *Clarifying question-answer relationships (QARs).* Different strategies are needed for answering different kinds of questions. To distinguish task requirements for various question types, Raphael (1986) devised a way to teach students what she called QARs, or question-answer relationships. In this procedure, four subtypes of QARs are described and practiced with students:

a. *Right There* (or what teachers would call literal questions). Students are told that for these question types the answer is right there in the book, often stated in one sentence, for example:

Question: "Where did Jimmy find the missing jewel?"
Answer as stated in the text: "Suddenly, Jimmy saw the missing jewel hanging in the chandelier among the pieces of carved glass."

b. *Think and Search* (questions that require a conclusion to be drawn). Students are told that the information needed to answer this type of question is found in the story, but statements given in more than one place must be linked; using these accounts, it is possible to conclude an appropriate answer. Teachers often describe this as being a "detective," finding and matching clues to reach a solution.

c. *The Author and You* (questions for which inferences must be drawn based on text details plus the reader's prior knowledge). For this QAR, learners are told that some of the information is found in the text, but some must come from information they already know; the two must be connected to determine the answer. Such an explanation is an important revelation for many students who have wondered where in the book those other kids were finding the answers they gave, because they had looked and looked to no avail.

d. *On Your Own* (several question types are implied, e.g., evaluative questions, background questions, creative questions). This category of QARs describes those questions for which most of the response, though associated with the text, is derived from the reader's own experiences or feelings (e.g., *evaluative question:* "Which character did you think was most interesting?"; *background question:* "In a moment we're going to read a story about some animals that showed up in the backyard of a family who lived near a woods. Other than pets, what animals have you seen in your yard?"; *creative question:* "In *Sarah, Plain and Tall,* Sarah's life changes when she moves to a place where she had not lived before and marries a man she had not known previously. How might her life have been different if she had not made those decisions?").

5. *Focusing questions on complex reading strategies.* J. Hansen (1981) developed a procedure that significantly improved the inferential comprehension of average readers. This procedure was also tested by McCormick and Hill (1984) in 12 classes of students having reading disabilities with the same positive results. The procedure, called the Question Technique, was based on the hypothesis that students typically do poorly in drawing inferences because they get very little practice with this type of comprehension. (Recall that several researchers have found that about 70% of questions teachers ask are literal.)

Throughout the several weeks that these research projects were being conducted, students in the experimental group were asked *only inference questions* after they read stories in their daily lessons. In contrast, students in a control group were asked only one inference question for *every* five literal questions, a typical practice in many classrooms. In weekly comprehension tests, the students in the experimental group scored significantly higher on inferential comprehension than did the control group.

An implication for remedial teachers is that they must provide their students with much more practice in drawing inferences than is usually given. For students who have a weakness in this area, teachers might select only those questions from commercial materials that require students to infer, or they may write their own inference questions to supplement these materials.

One reason students may be exposed infrequently to questions that require them to use inferences or to draw a conclusion is that such questions are often hard to write! It is even more difficult to think of a good inferential question on the spur of the moment to ask orally while working with a group. Therefore, these types of questions should be planned in advance to be ready for use.

Another reason teachers may ask fewer higher-level questions is that eliciting appropriate answers often takes considerably more time than is demanded for answers to literal questions. When a literal question is asked, students can usually answer quickly. Even when an incorrect answer is given, students may not need much time to locate the correct answer in the text. Questions requiring students to draw conclusions and inferences are not handled so quickly. Students may need to be reminded of, and directed in, an appropriate comprehension strategy. In addition, when a wrong response is given, it is not so easily resolved: much attention and time may be required to sort out the relevant information in the text, discussions of applicable background experiences may have to ensue, and so on. As a result, a teacher may cover 10 or so literal questions in the same amount of time as only two or three higher-level questions. Teachers must recognize that the challenges that inferential questions present are not valid reasons for avoiding them. Spending time in thoughtful—though prolonged—development of higher-level strategies is one of the most valuable forms of comprehension instruction. For many students, time spent in answering two or three higher-order questions thoughtfully may be more instructionally useful than responding to 10 or more literal questions.

6.   *Using character maps.* Character maps are heuristics that provide an additional way to focus students on making inferences. Understanding characters' attitudes and traits opens windows to interpreting actions that occur in stories. Typically authors tell the reader certain snippets of detail about a character, but reveal other attributes in more subtle ways—through actions, conversations, and thoughts expressed openly as inner dialogue for the reader to "listen" in on.

Understanding qualities of characters when the information is not directly stated as facts, but instead must be inferred, can be challenging for at-risk readers. Richards and Gipe (1993) had good results using character maps to address this need.

After students read a story, the teacher produced a "map" with four circles on it, each with a different label. The first, marked "Facts About the Character," was used to record statements from the text about one of the main personalities in the narrative. This was a literal-level task.

The teacher modeled ways to determine information to write in the second circle, labeled "What I Know About the Character's Actions." To do so, the teacher helped students point out places in the text where actions were described and showed how these were clues that could help them infer something about the person. For instance, if a narrative describes the character as preferring to spend his Saturdays helping his father who is a carpenter instead of playing games with other boys on his street, the teacher might say that "I suspect from Andy's actions that he likes to build things, because on Saturdays when I have a choice about what I do, I send my time doing things I like." They would write information based on this inference in the second circle along with inferences offered by the students based on other character actions.

The third circle was tagged "What I Know About the Character's Conversation" and the fourth, "What I Know About the Character's Thoughts." These circles in the map were filled in similarly, using text dialogue and information about thoughts to infer character traits and qualities that had not been directly discussed by the author.

This exercise teaches readers conventions authors use to reveal characters and provides the necessary practice to draw inferences needed to interpret underlying meanings. After several sessions of collaborative effort, Richards and Gipe (1993) found readers were ready to do this on their own. They also recommend extending the project to comparing characters within and between stories, and for learners to use to plan the stories they write themselves.

CONCLUSION

Comprehension is quite obviously a vital concern in reading instruction. For this reason, two chapters of this text are devoted to the topic. This chapter has provided information to help teachers make instructional decisions to help students read and comprehend narrative texts, offering specific suggestions for working with problems in literal-level and higher-level comprehension tasks. Many of the strategies presented provide a framework for, and can be infused within, a variety of comprehension lessons. The next chapter will extend the discussion of text comprehension to expository materials.

📖 REFLECTIONS
- - - - - - - - - - - - - - - - - - -

Which sections of the present chapter were the hardest for you to understand? Based on what you have learned about comprehension, what do you think were the reasons those segments were more challenging for you than others? Based on what you know about comprehension now, what could you do about it?
- -

13

Comprehension of
Expository Text

During reciprocal teaching, the teacher first models strategies; then students, in turn, assume the role of teacher, teaching their peers, as the group works through a section of text.

In the last chapter, the discussion of comprehension centered on one text type—narrative. In this chapter, we will explore instructional approaches for helping students read and learn from expository text, including a bit of attention to studying expository materials. Finally, to tie up the two chapters on comprehension, we will end with some more thoughts about metacognition, since use of metacognitive strategies applies to both the reading of narratives and the reading of exposition.

EXPOSITORY TEXT

Expository text is composed to communicate information. While readers may learn new ideas from narratives, that normally is not their primary intent; instead, the main reason narratives are read is for pleasure. Exposition has as its main goal, however, to transmit new facts and ideas (although at times, this also may be a source of enjoyment).

Textbooks read by elementary, middle school, and high school students to learn about science, history, geography, and other content subjects, as well as texts, professional journals, and research reports used by college students, are examples of expository text. Even math books require reading—to follow directions, to understand written descriptions of procedures, and to read word problems (Muth, 1993). In the workplace, adults may have to read training manuals—another type of exposition. In everyday life, there are numerous examples of nonnarrative reading, for example, reading newspapers, tax forms, and business letters.

Certain text structures occur with high frequency in expository texts, and some are unique to expository selections. **Text structure** refers to the way concepts are connected in written material to impart meanings. Expository text structures include patterns of cause and effect, sequence, comparison and contrast, classification, and others. See Figure 13–1 for a listing of some specific types of text structures often found in informational materials. At times, there are embedded definitions, explanations of technical processes, sequences of logical argument, or procedural descriptions (examples of the latter are instructions on how to connect a printer to a computer, how to assemble a piece of furniture that arrives distressingly in many unassembled pieces, or how to conduct a science experiment). Some nontextual layouts may have to be "read" as well, such as iconic diagrams (i.e., labeled pictorial drawings), schematic diagrams, graphs, and charts (Hegarty, Carpenter, & Just, 1991).

FIGURE 13–1
Some types of expository text structures

Analysis
Cause and effect
Classification
Comparison and contrast
Definition
Description
Enumeration
Identification
Illustration
Problem and solution
Sequence

Since text structure does influence comprehension, reading exposition may require some processes not used with narrative discourse (Bovair & Kieras, 1991). As with narratives, familiarity with expository text structures aids comprehension of important information (Weaver & Kintsch, 1991) and, conversely, lack of sensitivity to the way ideas are organized may hinder understanding. Expository structures are commonly more difficult to comprehend than story grammars, and, in fact, studies have shown that some content area materials can be made more "reader friendly" by altering them to what is called "soft expository text," that is, text that combines narration with exposition (see Guzzetti, Snyder, Glass, & Gamas, 1993).

Background information (remember schemata?) also is as important in reading expository discourse as it is in reading narratives, and, indeed, lack of sufficient background information may be a source of difficulty even more often. Expository texts are written specifically to convey new information. Therefore, it only stands to reason that readers may have less prior knowledge to bring to bear on an expository selection than with stories (which tend to deal with notions more common in the readers' life and environment). To be a good comprehender of exposition, a student is helped by already having some specific information about the content that is addressed—a rather cyclical problem since the student is reading the material to learn something new in the first place. In addition, the most refined reading strategies will not be of much assistance if the passage treats a completely alien topic (Weaver & Kintsch, 1991). Therefore, the amount of background information that the reader is able to "take to the text" can have a critical effect on how easy that text is for a person to understand.

Another factor that may make the reading of informational texts difficult is the specialized vocabulary found in all content area books. Specialized vocabulary can be an obstacle because many of these words are not present in the typical student's oral language vocabulary and because the technical words are often essential for understanding the passage. Furthermore, new words are not introduced at the moderate pace to which students are accustomed in basic reading instruction, and the words more often represent difficult concepts.

To complicate matters, students are not only expected to comprehend informational materials, but also to retain more of the specific facts than is generally necessary in story-type selections. Most textbooks have high density; **density** refers to the number of facts given in a specific amount of text. Density is also referred to as *proposition density, compactness,* or *concept load.* It may be necessary for students who are reading high-density material to understand and remember the facts presented in *every* sentence so they can comprehend each subsequent sentence and, therefore, understand a paragraph. In addition, the significance of each preceding paragraph must be comprehended to understand the next one.

Broad and abstract concepts, prevalent in certain types of exposition, add to students' difficulties, and in some content area materials, symbols and abbreviations must be read (e.g., math, science). In a recent survey of classroom teachers, 70% said that content area books were more difficult for their students than stories because of complex and unfamiliar ideas, students' lack of word knowledge, text characteristics—and students' lack of interest (Olson & Gee, 1991).

These problems exist for all readers, but are particularly vexing for poor readers. In addition, the complexities inherent in reading expository materials are exacerbated by the high readability levels of some content area texts. At times, unfortunately, content area books are written at levels higher than the grade for which they are used. In these cases, a good deal of students' reading problems may be due to the *material,* and not to the students.

Beginning at about the fourth-grade level, students are actually required to spend more of their reading time in expository materials than with narratives. Reading informational text will continue to take up much of their time in school—and in life. Since many of the students we work with find these materials especially demanding, attention to skills and strategies necessary to read this text type is as much a part of a reading teacher's responsibilities as is the need to aid comprehension of narrative text. Table 13–1 lists typical characteristics of some content area texts.

COMPREHENSION INSTRUCTION: EXPOSITORY TEXT

The key principles of excellent comprehension instruction hold regardless of whether the targeted texts are expository or narrative; for example, explicit teaching, fostering strategic reading, and that bottom-line item: instruction that is instructive—and not merely flimsy question asking. Furthermore, many of the same areas of concern—for example, selecting important ideas, drawing conclusions—are similar in reading expository materials and narrative texts, and a number of the instructional methods introduced in Chapter 12 also are applicable here. What the present chapter will do is to report additional teaching suggestions that research has offered when focus has been directed particularly on expository texts. Many of these, of course, can be adapted to narratives. Students should use strategies for constructing meaning *before, during,* and *after* reading (Sweet, 1993).

Introductory Transactions

As with comprehension instruction with narrative materials, teacher guidance with expository reading tasks should begin with activities that occur *before* the text is read.

Assistance with the Immediate Text. It may be even more critical to evoke students' existing background knowledge for reading expository text than it is for narratives, since there is likely to be more that is new to them in the expository materials. Background knowledge is particularly influential in determining the relative *importance* of some information in contrast to others. In addition, it may be necessary to build some *new* knowledge sets before reading. Some instructional suggestions for building background knowledge and activating prior knowledge follow.

1. *Employing K-W-L.* The acronym *K-W-L* represents words for phases of an instructional strategy conceived to activate prior knowledge and to promote a mental set for forthcoming expository text so that the reader can interpret and construct meanings. Devised by Ogle (1986), this teaching model develops active reading by involving readers in three steps. The first two are undertaken before students read the targeted text. The last occurs after reading. Here are the three steps:
   a. *Assessing what I **K**now.* Students brainstorm what they already know about the subject they will encounter in the selection to be read; their ideas are classified into categories.
   b. *Determining what I **W**ant to Know.* With the teacher's assistance, the students create questions they want to have answered when they read the text; they also predict what they expect the author to convey.
   c. *Checking what I **L**earned from my reading.* In order to reinforce information gained, after the material has been read, readers examine what they learned by organizing new knowledge into outlines, semantic maps, and the like.

TABLE 13–1
Content area texts: characteristics and teaching implications

Social Studies	1.　Embedded directions
	Texts often have directions to follow within a paragraph (e.g., "The Amazon is the longest river in South America. *Turn now to page 67 and trace the Amazon's route through Brazil*.")
	Teaching implications: Ask disabled readers to follow these directions rather than ignore them. Carrying out tasks specified by the direction will help students visualize, conceptualize, and remember text information. Do this *with* them so they see the benefits.
	2.　Pictures, graphs, and maps
	Teaching implications: Show students *how* to use these illustrative materials. Graphs are relatively easy to read, but many students overlook this source of information. Don't assume that students know how to use map legends or how to learn from maps—teach them how.
	3.　Specialized vocabulary
	Teaching implications: Encourage classroom teachers to select some words for preteaching before the selection is read. In addition, teach students how to use context clues. Follow other suggestions given in Chapter 11.
	4.　Cause and effect patterns
	Teaching implications: This pattern occurs more frequently in social studies than in other subject areas. Follow suggestions given later in the present chapter.
	5.　Comparative data (e.g., the text may ask students to compare the climate, amount of population, and major sources of income in two countries, such as Canada and Mexico)
	Teaching implications: To aid *recall*, show students how to prepare charts on "likenesses and differences." To aid *interpretative comprehension*, involve students in a discussion on implications of the similarities and contrasts. Have them show their charts and provide their background information.
	6.　Time sequences
	Teaching implications: Encourage classroom teachers to have students develop a time line throughout the year in conjunction with their study of topics such as American or world history. Displaying the time line prominently in the classroom will help students gain a perspective about time sequences. As an individual rather than class activity, poor readers can be shown how to develop time lines to be kept in their notebooks.
Science	1.　Specialized vocabulary
	Teaching implications: See the suggestion in this table under "Social Studies." Also, have students in your remedial class keep a vocabulary notebook of content-related words,

Jennings (1991), among others, has found that K-W-L provides a scaffolding to help learners build links between their existing background knowledge and important text concepts when they are reading content area materials. (K-W-L also can be used as an informal comprehension assessment procedure [McAllister, 1994].)

2.　*Using audiovisuals* before *reading*. Teachers often use movies and filmstrips during the study of a topic or at the end of a unit to serve as a culminating activ-

TABLE 13–1 *(continued)*

divided by topics such as science or social studies. The reading teacher can obtain text-books from regular classroom teachers and help students select words for upcoming lessons to discuss, list, define, and (when appropriate) illustrate words in this notebook.

2. Broad, abstract concepts

Teaching implications: Writers of science texts sometimes incorrectly assume students have more background information than they do. In addition, abstract ideas often are presented without sufficient concrete examples. Alert classroom teachers to these problems and suggest that films and other audiovisuals be used to supplement students' existing background knowledge and provide actual, specific instances of generalized topics.

3. Density

Teaching implications: Science material is noted for its density—more facts line for line than in other texts. Since comprehension requires understanding of the most important statement as well as each idea that supports this statement, teach poor readers how to prepare simple outlines after reading.

4. Explanations of technical processes (e.g., the workings of an internal combustion engine are explained)

Teaching implications: Students should be told that technical information must be read slowly. (Reading rates used for story-type reading are seldom appropriate.) Since these texts often have diagrams, help students develop the habit of studying these diagrams before, during, and after reading the explanatory passage.

5. Cause and effect patterns

Teaching implications: This pattern, found most often in social studies texts, is also found in science material. Again, use the suggestions found in this table under "Social Studies." Working *with* students to help them conduct experiments suggested in science books not only concretely illustrates cause-and-effect relationships but also gives practice in following directions, another skill needed for science reading.

6. Classification

Teaching implications: This writing pattern categorizes information, such as dividing animals into mammals, birds, amphibians, and so on. Teach students the concept of categorization, that is, how some ideas or facts can be subgroups of others. Outlining is also helpful.

Mathematics   1. Specialized vocabulary

Teaching implications: Specialized vocabulary is a characteristic of all three types of texts discussed. The most prevalent difficulty for poor readers within all content areas is that of

---

ity. With students who have reading disabilities, it is more effective to allow them to view these audiovisuals *before* they actually start to read the written text.

When reading teachers help students learn to learn from expository materials, the purpose, of course, is to give them assistance for future use—in their classrooms, for example, as well as in everyday expository reading activities. Because of the complexity of content area materials, remedial teachers may wish to provide prereading experiences with assignments their students will face in their regular classrooms in coming days. For instance, if a conference with the geography

TABLE 13–1 *(continued)*

dealing with difficult or unusual vocabulary. In math, however, the vocabulary is even more specialized. How often, for example, do students use words such as *minuend* and *subtrahend* in their everyday oral language, or find such words in anything else they read? Context clues don't help much in identifying vocabulary in math texts. All of this implies that direct teaching of mathematics vocabulary is needed, in terms of both word identification and meaning. If the classroom teacher does not do this, the reading teacher can assume this responsibility.

2.   Symbols and abbreviations

Teaching implications: Disabled readers must be taught to read symbols and abbreviations embedded in text. For example, "Solve this problem: $3 + 4 = \Delta$" is read, "Solve this problem: Three *plus* four *equals what*;" "3% of $39.14 is _____ " is read, "Three *percent* of thirty-nine *dollars and* fourteen *cents* is *what*;" and "$A = \pi r^2$" is read, "*The area equals pi times the radius squared*." In addition, abbreviations such as *in., ft., rd.,* and *yd.* must be read in problems such as "How many feet of fencing are needed to enclose a garden that is 48 ft. 3 in. long and 28 ft. 7 in. wide?" or, "What is the perimeter of a rectangle having the following dimensions: Length = 236 rd., width = 87 rd.?" While these reading tasks may seem quite obvious to most, for students who think reading is what they do in stories, such tasks may be quite difficult.

3.   Density

Teaching implications: Like science texts, math material is characterized by density. Readers cannot skip unknown words and still obtain meaning, as is sometimes possible with narrative writing. In addition, the reading rate must be slow.

4.   Unusual writing style

Teaching implications: Vos (cited in Ferguson & Fairburn, 1985) suggested that one language-related factor affecting performance on math story problems (sometimes called thought or word problems) is that their writing styles are different from other prose. He pointed out that story problems lack the continuity of ideas from paragraph to paragraph found in other writing. Practice can be given to familiarize students with this writing style. In Botel and Wirtz's research (cited in Kahn & Wirtz, 1982), students who practiced making up their own story problems did significantly better on these types of math applications than did those who lacked such practice.

Source: Complied from information in Ferguson & Fairburn, 1985; Kahn & Wirtz, 1982; McCormick, unpublished materials; Piercey, 1976; Santeusanio, 1983; and N. B. Smith, 1967.

teacher discloses that the class will read a chapter about South America soon, in the reading class, you may show a film or filmstrip about this topic, thus *building background* that students might otherwise lack, doing so through the visuals, the vocabulary, and the opportunity for discussion that your instruction provides.

     This strategy is most likely to aid the poor reader whose difficulties lie in the area of comprehension. However, it can also provide some help to those who have word recognition and meaning vocabulary deficits. These students can *hear* vocabulary associated with information they are viewing on films, and, in the case of filmstrips with captions, also *see* the printed form of these words; thus, they are more likely to recognize and attach meanings to the words when they read the text. (For this reason, teachers who have experience working with poor readers usually prefer filmstrips with captions to those without or to films.)

The regular classroom teacher might choose to adopt the procedure of using audiovisuals before reading text for the whole class, since they give everyone a preview of the subject, aiding comprehension and introducing new vocabulary. Because classroom teachers often ask the reading teacher or the LD teacher for suggestions to aid students with reading disabilities mainstreamed into their classes, this is a recommendation you can offer.

3.   *Prequestioning.* There has been some interest in the use of text questions or teacher's questions *before* students read expository material. A number of educators have seen this as a way to boost comprehension, rather than to merely test it, as is often done with questions used *after* reading.

In prequestioning, teachers have used the questions commonly found at the ends of chapters in content area books, examining these with learners beforehand, or have prepared questions of their own about details and impressions they want their students to comprehend and retain. Sometimes teachers may transform the questions into a small pretest; after reading, the students address the same questions as a posttest. The belief is that readers' prior awareness of the kinds of information considered to be important will help focus their attention and, thus, support meaning construction. In other words, if you want students to learn something, tell them what it is!

Tierney and Cunningham (1984) reviewed the research related to effects of teacher or text prequestions and concluded that prequestions do enhance learning in the following circumstances. Prequestions can be beneficial if

a. the text is difficult to understand
b. the questions are written about the most significant information in the selection
c. the concern is that students learn the *specific* information targeted by the prequestions

In contrast, if the goal is to obtain a more global sense of the information presented, use of prequestions may have a narrowing effect. That is, learners may center on the items in the prequestions to the detriment of gaining overall implications of the text.

The conclusion for teachers is that prequestions, in some cases, may be quite helpful, but the specific goals at the time must be considered—for the learners and for the particular text. Wade and Trathen (1989) did find that prequestions accomplished favorable results with poor readers.

Development of Strategies That Can Be Used with a Wide Variety of Texts.

In addition to strategies to promote familiarity with potentially unfamiliar topics, it seems particularly useful with expository text to heighten students' awareness of common text structures and patterns. A number of studies have supported this supposition (e.g., Armbruster, Anderson, & Meyer, 1991; Armbruster, Anderson, & Ostertag, 1989). Good readers use text structure, as well as their prior knowledge, to determine what is important in text selections, which, in turn, also aids recall (Dole, Duffy, Roehler, & Pearson, 1991).

Promoting familiarity with text structure includes helping students see how material is organized by an author into key ideas and supporting statements, how these are sequenced to explain a point, and how they are interrelated. Many good readers appear able to note and use text structure either intuitively or as the result of reading more extensively. Poor readers, on the other hand, do not seem to recognize how the organization of material helps them comprehend, unless they receive direct instruction in the special ways written text is structured to convey ideas.

Because interpretation of expository text relies heavily on recognizing and understanding how to follow certain patterns, some attention to the most prevalent patterns *before* students read provides knowledge that may be used later during reading.

1.   *Providing prepractice with the cause-and-effect pattern.* The cause-and-effect pattern is found recurrently in history books, geography books, and science books; it is also found in narratives. This pattern, hence, will be used as our first example of providing prepractice activities directly related to familiarizing students with text structure. Determining causes and effects involves understanding the "why" in relationships, as well as the results of actions and events. In some cases, the significant point to determine is the cause, in others it is the effect, and in still others it is both.

Determining causes and effects can be difficult for students because a number of other higher-level comprehension skills underlie this process; for example, being able to draw a conclusion, infer, determine the main idea, predict outcomes, and follow a sequence of events.

To complicate matters, sometimes a passage may relate a single outcome that has more than one cause or a single cause that results in more than one effect. Or, sometimes a chain reaction is described in which a cause produces an effect, but that effect in turn becomes a cause resulting in another effect, and so on.

Cause $\longrightarrow$ Effect

$\quad\quad\quad\quad\quad$ (Cause) $\longrightarrow$ Effect

$\quad\quad\quad\quad\quad\quad\quad\quad\quad\quad$ (Cause) $\longrightarrow$ Effect

Furthermore, in longer pieces of discourse, the cause may be stated in one paragraph and the effect or effects in another.

Authors often use signal words to alert readers to cause and effect relationships; words such as *because, if, therefore, so, so that, since, then, as a result of, unless, hence,* and *in order that* can help students see the tie between causes and effects. However, sometimes no signal words are used.

There are additional reasons why this comprehension skill is complex. Sometimes both the cause and the effect are directly stated; but sometimes although they are both stated, the relationship between the two is not, and, therefore, readers must find the relationship themselves; and finally, there are times when only the cause or the effect is stated, but the other is implicit and, therefore, must be inferred by the reader. Students need practice in dealing with passages that exemplify all three cases.

Some specific instructional suggestions for providing prepractice in recognizing the cause-and-effect concept and patterns follow.

a. Begin with causes and effects students already know to promote awareness of the cause-effect *concept.* Write several "causes" on the chalkboard and have students tell you the effects. List these effects. For example, you may write these sentences:

Water spills in your lap.

A car runs out of gas.

Your students may suggest these effects:

Your clothes get wet.
The car stops.

Then, reverse the process, write a series of familiar effects on the board, and have students suggest causes.

b. Use television programs students watch at home to emphasize the concept of cause-and-effect relationships. Discuss situations in a TV show routinely viewed by your students that indicate these relationships. In addition, bring in examples of statements from commercials that specify cause and effect, for example, "strained muscles due to exercise" (cause); "aching shoulders and neck" (effect); "Taking Whizzy-Fizzy Aspirins (cause) relieves the pain (effect)."

c. Prepare cards, some with causes on them and some with effects on them. Mix the cards up. Have students place the appropriate cards under a label that says *Causes* and then have them match the correct effect card to each, placing these under a label that says *Effects*. For example,

Causes	*Effects*
forest fires	destroy thousands of trees in a short time
meat kept in warm places	often spoils

d. Next, move to selecting causes and effects in text. Have students read paragraphs that contain causes and effects. As with the preceding exercises, these should, at first, be based on experiences familiar to students. Have students locate the statements of cause, underlining these in red. Have them do the same with statements of effects, underlining them in blue.

e. Follow the suggestion in item d, but this time give paragraphs in which only a cause is explicitly specified. After students have underlined the cause in red, have them write the effect on a line below the paragraph. Next do this when only an effect is given.

f. Use exercises like the one in Figure 13–2 in which the learners must decide if statement 1 (an event) did or did not cause statement 2 (an effect).

g. Interactive stories, such as shown in Figure 13–3, can be used to help students perceive cause-and-effect relationships. With these special stories, students choose the path they wish the story to take at certain junctures in the episodes. The path they select causes specific effects to ensue. Rereading and taking different routes reinforces the point even more strongly.

h. Give students practice with signal words that indicate cause-and-effect relationships. A sample exercise of this type is given in Figure 13–4. The Reading Spectrum series (Macmillan) also has excellent exercises for this kind of practice in its vocabulary books.

i. By this time, students should have a sense of the cause-effect concept. Now it is time to promote transfer to the real tasks they will confront in reading. Follow the suggestions in the items above, using topics in which causes or effects are less familiar to students. Through dialogue, help them discover and then relate these causes and effects.

j. Display cause-and-effect relationships by cutting arrows from oaktag strips and affixing these to the chalkboard. After reading a passage with less familiar material, print causes on each arrow and have students write corresponding effects directly on the chalkboard next to the arrow.

FIGURE 13–2
Exercise that helps students distinguish cause and effect

The library opens at 10:00. When the clock on the wall said 🕘 , the doors were opened and the children came in. Brian went to the picture book section, while Kerry looked through magazines. Brian found two books that he took to the table. He looked through these. He liked the second one better than the first, so he put the first book back on the shelf. He took the second one to the librarian and asked to check it out.

A. 1. The library opens at 10:00.
    2. When the clock says 🕘 the doors are opened and the children come in.

                            Yes   No
    Does #1 *cause* #2?   ❑   ❑

B. 1. Brian went to the picture book section.
    2. He only checked out one of the two books he looked at.

                            Yes   No
    Does #1 *cause* #2?   ❑   ❑

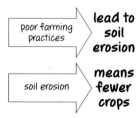

k. One commercially available set of texts, The Neighborhood Stories series (Jamestown), separates exercises for inferring causes from those for inferring effects. This gives students practice for those situations in which only the cause or the effect is given and they must infer the other. Reading levels of these materials range from third through fourth grade, but the selections are written to appeal to unskilled readers in grades 4 through 6.

l. Continue to provide students with opportunities to predict outcomes. Predicting outcomes can help students infer indirectly stated causes and effects.

m. Occasionally you may wish to use a game for students to practice determining causes and effects. For example, a commercial board game from Gamco, available in second- or fourth-grade editions, includes 96 story cards and 24 cause-and-effect cards. This specific game provides a considerable amount of text reading, as well as practice with an important text pattern.

n. Computer simulations can help students understand the concept of cause and effect and learn about story structure. Simulations allow students to manipulate story events, thus changing causes and consequences. Students make the decisions that determine the direction in which the plot evolves. One such computer program is EAMON (Kuchinskas, 1983). If a computer is available for the remedial classroom or clinic, investigate other story-environment simulations to employ in your program. Information on computer use in reading

FIGURE 13-3
Interactive stories used to enhance students' understanding of cause and effect

giant crickets. Earth crickets were noisy enough, thought Hal. But these giant insects could make sounds that would break his eardrums. Lynn waved her arms at them and mouthed the words. "Stop. Quiet! Please." At once they stopped.

Then, as Hal gazed at the giant crickets, he seemed to hear a voice. But it wasn't really a voice. It was more like someone thinking inside his mind. *Welcome to the Land of the Insects. We are sorry our greeting was too loud for you. Were you sent to help us with our problem?*

Hal glanced at Lynn. "Are you getting their message too?"

She nodded, wide-eyed. "Let's beam our thoughts back to them and ask what their problem is."

Our problem is our growth. Each time we double in size, our mass becomes greater but our strength does not increase. So we can hardly carry our weight. You are from a planet where insects live. Can you help us? We can no longer move as fast as we need to.

Hal frowned. "That's quite a problem. We haven't come up against that one on Earth. All our insects are small."

"But maybe we can still help," said Lynn. She aimed her thought question at the nearest cricket. "Do you have termites here?"

Yes.

"And do you have trees?" Lynn went on.

Yes.

Lynn clapped her hands. "Then maybe we can help you invent the wheel."

Hal stared at her for a moment, puzzled. Then he broke into a big smile. "Now I get it. Termites can chew through wood. Maybe tree trunks can be chewed into wheels. And insects that are too heavy to carry themselves can ride. It's a long shot, but . . ."

The cricket leader broke in and finished Hal's thought.

It's worth a try. Thank you. You helped us, so you are welcome to come out and explore our land.

Lynn and Hal climbed out of their spaceship as the giant crickets hopped away. Soon they were approached by . . . .

A GREEN MONSTER	FLYING CIRCLES	STATUES ON THE MARCH
continued on page 17	*continued on page 19*	*continued on page 21*

continued on page 17   *continued on page 19*   *continued on page 21*

TAKE YOUR CHOICE

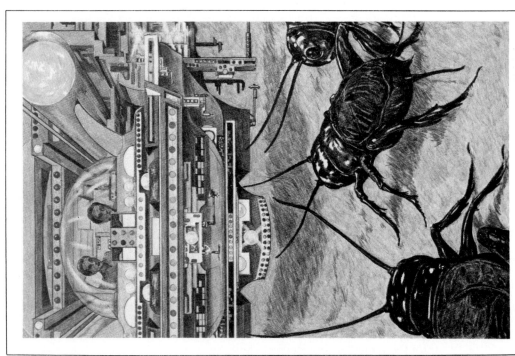

GIANT CRICKETS

Source: From "Star Trip" in *Attention Span Stories* (pp. 10–11) by L. Mountain, 1978, Providence, RI: Jamestown Publishers. Copyright 1978 by Jamestown Publishers. Reprinted by permission.

430

FIGURE 13–4

Exercises on signal words that indicate cause-and-effect relationships

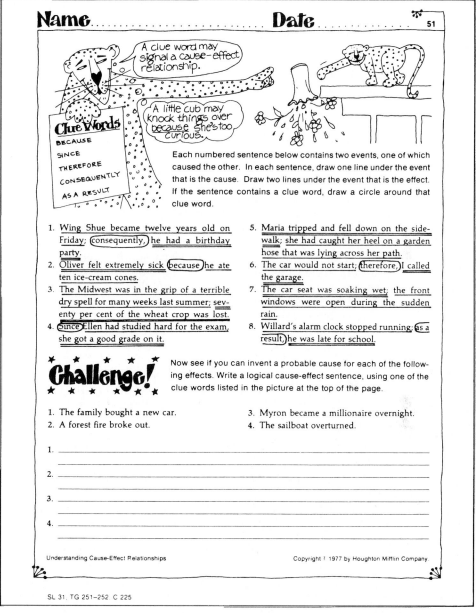

Source: From *Reading Bonus Duplicating Masters, Level L* (p. 51), 1977, Boston, Houghton Mifflin. Copyright 1977 by Houghton Mifflin. Reprinted by permission.

classes may be found in the journal *Computers, Reading, and Language Arts,* as well as in other journals.

Of course, students need to apply the concepts gained *during actual reading of texts* if the foregoing activities are to have any worth. And it should not be expected that transfer will automatically occur. The teacher must direct and guide students, reminding them of the pattern that they have been practicing when they encounter it in materials they are reading. Show students how to use their new knowledge to understand principles and facts that appear in their books. Demonstrate how using this new knowledge helps.

2.   *Providing prepractice with the sequence pattern.* As an additional example of prepractice to promote understanding of the relevance of text structure, we will look at the sequence pattern. Another frequently occurring textual organization, this text structure is seen in social studies books in the form of temporal (time) sequence. In science and mathematics materials, it appears often—in explanations of a technical process and in directions for conducting an experiment or computing a problem. Understanding the significance of sequence is important for reading narratives as well, since noting sequence aids the interpretation of relationships of events and characters. Perception of chains of events is also an important aid to recall.

The inability to follow a sequence and its effects often first becomes apparent when a teacher asks students to retell a story or expository selection they have read. Some readers will choose an event that occurs anywhere in the material and begin their retelling there—not because it is the beginning of the important information, but because the event is of interest to them. They may then return to an earlier portion of the selection, next jump ahead to a later event, and then swing back again to an earlier one. Often these students begin to make comments like, "No, he really did that before she said . . ." or, "No, that's not right, I think maybe he was the one who . . ." As the scrambled retelling progresses, the student forgets more and more of the relationships, causes, and actors in an episode. Inability to follow a sequence can be particularly detrimental when reading informational material—for example, when following the explanation of a scientific process or the directions for executing a math problem.

As a preliminary step to heighten awareness of the importance of sequences, have students talk through common events and the consequences that would follow incorrect sequencing. Ask them, for example, "What would happen if you put on your shoes and then put on your socks?" or "What would be the problem if you went to the stove to fix your breakfast, broke an egg over the burner, then put on the pan? What could you do to prevent this predicament?" Have students act out several of these garbled sequences so they can see the results.

After establishing this groundwork, you might further instill the relationship between sequence and sense—and move the point to the text realm—by giving to students the sections of a cartoon strip you have cut apart and mixed up. (See Figure 13–5.) Ask learners to read each section and then sequence the frames correctly.

Before students read a content area selection (for example, from a history book), list the important events in single sentences on paper, mixing up the correct sequence. Reproduce the list for each student. After students have read the material, they are to cut the list apart and rearrange the sentences to match in the order of events in the text. This provides opportunity for the teacher to supply immediate feedback and corrective suggestions as he or she moves about the classroom,

FIGURE 13–5
Learning to identify the proper sequence of events is a skill students need to understand causes and effects and to follow explanations and directions in informational material.

noting students needing support and extending assistance *while* students are working. Comments such as these can promote learning: "Chad, think about it. Does it make sense for this to have happened before that?" or, "Holly, I think you need to reread the third paragraph. Then rearrange your sequence and I'll come and check again."

Closely related to following a sequence of events is following written directions—an important academic skill, but also one used in daily life. When instructing students in this area, you are wise to kill two birds with one stone: many instructional materials you use should include directions students may actually be required to follow in some school activity. Select the directions they will have to read in their spelling book next week, or choose a science experiment they must complete for an upcoming chapter in their regular classroom. What follows is a prototypical activity for practicing following directions:

a. Copy directions for a science experiment on chart paper. Post these where they can be seen by the group. (See Figure 13–6.)

b. Read the first sentence aloud to the students and ask, "Does that statement give us a direction to follow?" If they decide that it does, use a colored marking pen to write a large "1" in front of the sentence.

c. Read the next statement and ask the same question. If it is indeed a direction to follow, number it "2." Continue through the information on the chart; number sentences that give a specific direction, but do not number filler statements often found intermingled with directions. Have students note the many statements interspersed with the instructions they are to follow; this type of writing style, in which authors' comments are mixed among directions (frequently found in textbooks), is difficult for poor comprehenders. Note in Figure 13–6

FIGURE 13–6
Give students practice following written directions with exercises similar to tasks they can expect to do in their regular classroom.

(1) Take a pan of water. (2) Dip an empty bottle into the pan. You will see bubbles rising from the bottle. These are bubbles of air. Air is all around us and fills any empty space—like an empty bottle. When the water goes into the bottle it pushes the air out. (3) Take the bottle from the water and (4) turn it upside down: (5) let all of the water run out. What is in the bottle now? Right— air. (6) Repeat the experiment by pushing the bottle back into the pan of water.

the number of statements that are actually directions to follow and the number that are not.

d. Encourage students to find and number (lightly with a pencil so marks can be erased) specific direction statements in their own textbooks when they must follow written directions of any kind.

Practice may also be given in following directions by having students actually construct or assemble something in the classroom. (Figure 13–7 illustrates one activity of this type.) Invest in some inexpensive paperbacks designed to involve students in "making and doing," such as these from Scholastic:

- *Easy Costumes You Don't Have to Sew:* how to make a dragon and other nifty costumes
- *Easy to Make—Good to Eat:* easy-to-follow recipes
- *Ed Emberley's Drawing Book of Animals:* step-by-step directions for making animals from various shapes
- *Fun and Easy Things to Make:* directions for using household objects to make puppets, bookmarks, and other items

FIGURE 13—7
Example of students making something by following written directions

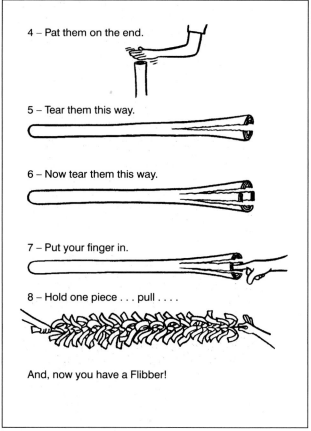

Source: From *The Beginner Book of Things to Make* by Robert Lopshire, 1964, New York: Random House. Copyright 1964 by Random House. Reprinted by permission.

The two sections above provide examples of prepractice activities to help students gain control of certain widespread text structures. There are other expository text organizations that benefit from explicit attention (see Figure 13–1 and the earlier discussion). The examples here are representative of the types of activities and the degree of specificity you should consider when designing instruction with other expository patterns.

On-Line Assistance

Probably more than with narratives, poor readers need assistance *during* their reading of expository text.

Assistance with the Immediate Text. If content area texts used in your students' regular classrooms are not too far removed from their instructional reading levels, it is often productive to use these actual texts in conducting the following approaches in which you support comprehension *during* students' reading.

1. *Using a hierarchical summarization strategy.* After a review of research on strategies designed to assist expository text reading, Pearson and Fielding (1991) concluded that positive support could be found for almost any type of text structure instruction. B. M. Taylor and Beach (1984) addressed the problem by helping students attend to text cues such as headings and subheadings. They called their approach a **hierarchical summarization strategy** and found that its use significantly improved understanding and recall of social studies material by middle school students. This strategy was useful when students were reading about topics that were quite unfamiliar to them. Hierarchical summarization, an adapted form of outlining, helps students gain sensitivity to text structure, and therefore, to the pertinence of specific information, in the following way. (See Figure 13–8 for a sample of a hierarchical summary.)
   a. An outline is begun by drawing a line at the top of the chalkboard. (The line is not filled in at this time; a heading representing the key idea of the entire passage is written there later.)
   b. A letter is written for each subheading found in the selection.
   c. Students begin by reading the first section (as designated by the first subheading), and then decide on a main idea for that section. The teacher writes the main idea in the outline next to the letter for that section.
   d. Two or three important details about the main idea are listed under the main idea.
   e. This is done as learners read all sections of the assigned lesson.
   f. Then topic headings are selected and these are written in the left margin, along with lines connecting main ideas related to the same topic. (See Figure 13–8 to see how this is done.)
   g. The key idea for the entire selection is chosen and written on the blank line at the top of the chalkboard.

   After a few sessions, students work independently, completing a hierarchical summary on their own. When individual summaries have been completed, collaborative discussion, in which the summaries are critiqued, should follow. Additionally, paired learning can be employed: students work as partners, each telling the other as much as they can about their summaries, as well as other information they remember from the selection.

   Using this strategy for one hour per week, students in B. M. Taylor and Beach's study (1984) improved their comprehension of unfamiliar topics more

FIGURE 13–8
Example of a hierarchical summary for a three-page social studies text segment with one heading and six subheadings

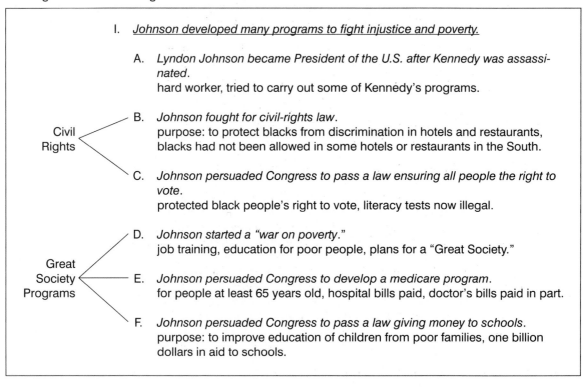

I. *Johnson developed many programs to fight injustice and poverty.*

A. *Lyndon Johnson became President of the U.S. after Kennedy was assassinated.*
hard worker, tried to carry out some of Kennedy's programs.

Civil Rights

B. *Johnson fought for civil-rights law.*
purpose: to protect blacks from discrimination in hotels and restaurants, blacks had not been allowed in some hotels or restaurants in the South.

C. *Johnson persuaded Congress to pass a law ensuring all people the right to vote.*
protected black people's right to vote, literacy tests now illegal.

D. *Johnson started a "war on poverty."*
job training, education for poor people, plans for a "Great Society."

Great Society Programs

E. *Johnson persuaded Congress to develop a medicare program.*
for people at least 65 years old, hospital bills paid, doctor's bills paid in part.

F. *Johnson persuaded Congress to pass a law giving money to schools.*
purpose: to improve education of children from poor families, one billion dollars in aid to schools.

than a control group not having the instruction. However, if the assigned topic was familiar, this fairly complex strategy was no more productive than the more traditional procedure of simply having students write answers to questions about main ideas and details after reading the selection.

2. *Inserting questions in text.* In the chapter on narrative comprehension, we discussed the use of teacher's oral questions interspersed during students' readings of stories. Some suggestions were made for the structure of those questions.

Teachers may also want to try the technique of inserting *written* questions within informational material. This is done by providing students with typed copies of text passages with questions written in at logical junctures. These questions are highlighted by setting them off from the remainder of the prose, for instance, like this:

> When the settlers arrived in the Northwest Territory many Native Americans were resentful of their presence. The French had come first for furs, believing that it gave them some claim to the land because they were the first Europeans to arrive there. Then the English came to live permanently. Since they were developing permanent settlements, they thought this gave them a right to the area. The Native Americans felt they had to protect their homes, hunting grounds, and their way of life.
>
> *** When more than one group of people believe they have claim to the same land, what can happen?**

Certain Native American tribes tried to make a stand for their lands. Attacks by these tribes against the settlers made life difficult in some parts of the Northwest Territory. In addition, the French and English had been fighting in Europe and they now carried that fight to the New World.

*What would have been the reason for the French and English to declare war against one another in the Northwest Territory?

Newcomers who had come to the Ohio Country and other Northwest Territory regions may have at times wished that they had never left the East as they fought the Native Americans and the French, who both wanted the land. The Native Americans had lived in the area for many, many years and it was, in truth, their homeland. Whether the French had a greater right to any part of that land than the English or vice versa seemed an unimportant issue to the Native Americans.

The inserted questions can prompt a prediction of upcoming text information (as in the first question seen above) or promote a reflection on details previously given (as in the second question), helping students to synthesize ideas.

There is research support for use of inserted questions. Tierney and Cunningham's (1984) review of several such studies concluded that literal questions inserted in text help students respond better to those questions after reading. Apparently this directs their attention to statements and ideas of importance. Positive benefits were also seen when higher-level questions were interspersed; in this case, better comprehension at the conclusion of reading is seen for information related both to those questions *and* to other questions.

Development of Strategies That Can Be Used with a Variety of Texts.   Although used during the reading of a specific text, the ideas in this section also have the purpose of helping learners obtain strategies they can apply to texts they will read in the future— and, indeed, research has shown that they do so.

1.   *Engaging students in reciprocal teaching.* This instructional approach involves teacher modeling and has most often been applied to expository text. In this online technique, first the teacher and then the students are responsible for leading the lesson—a lesson composed of definite sequences of learning events. Palincsar and Brown (1984) successfully used these steps with poor readers whose decoding skills were adequate but whose comprehension levels were 2 to 3 years below their grade levels:

After students have read silently the beginning section from a longer piece of discourse, the *teacher*

   a. explains parts of the beginning section that are difficult to understand
   b. demonstrates how to summarize the information in the section
   c. shows how to develop important questions about that material
   d. makes a prediction about what will be found in the section that follows

"Reciprocal" means shared. Next, students share the instructional responsibility. For subsequent sections, *students* are assigned a portion of the text (usually a paragraph) and, in turn, each assumes the teacher's full role and applies these same four steps to the part they are accountable for, teaching others in the group about their assigned piece: (a) explaining difficult ideas, (b) summarizing the section, (c) asking important questions about their portion, and (d) making a prediction about the upcoming part— before turning the teacher's role over to a peer for the next segment of the text.

If adequate summarization of a section does not occur, then fix-up strategies are used, such as rereading or clarifying. Teachers *and* students give feedback to each other. In the original research with this technique, students self-graphed their successes. Graphing is a powerful motivator because it provides a visual demonstration of the benefits of the strategies to the students. All practice takes place in the context of actual text reading. Students are consistently reminded to practice these activities while reading independently.

In the Palincsar and Brown study (1984), dramatic increases were seen in students' selection of important ideas for their oral summaries and their questions, significant increases occurred on standardized reading comprehension test scores, and the results were maintained. Excellent success has been obtained by many other researchers and by many teachers using reciprocal teaching with readers at many grade levels. For example, M. E. Bruce and Chan (1991) employed this technique in a pull-out program with 11- and 12-year-old students having reading difficulties and found that students applied the strategies learned in the resource room to their social studies class. Comparable results have been found by the original researchers and by others.

2.   *Designing and using schematic diagrams and charts of text structure.* In the hierarchical summarization strategy, described above, students' attention is called to cues such as headings and subheadings as a way of highlighting the relevance of text structure. Also, discussed earlier were prepractice activities to familiarize students with certain patterns that are prevalent in informational text. In addition, a number of educators have used various types of schematic and pictorial diagrams and charts to help students gain control of expository structures and to conceptualize ideas presented in expository materials (e.g., Armbruster et al., 1991; K. K. Miller & George, 1992; Naughton, 1993–94).

One example is use of *semantic mapping.* In Chapter 11, semantic mapping was discussed as a previewing process for increasing understanding of word meanings. Mapping, likewise, has value when students are reading informational text. In the description in Chapter 11, the focus was for students to understand concepts underlying words. You may want to review the semantic map in Figure 11–2 on page 355.

As a facilitator of comprehension of whole texts, semantic mapping focuses on broader constructs so that students have deeper understandings of the topic. It also has proved a viable method for visualizing important points and subordinate ideas to assist with text comprehension. Mapping has been one of the most widely researched content area text reading strategies (Swafford, 1990).

Schematics and charts are often designed to accent specific text patterns. Teaching students to organize information from comparison and contrast structures onto comparison-contrasts charts is relatively simple. (See Figure 13–9.) *Venn diagrams,* also introduced in Chapter 11, are particularly useful to compare and contrast likenesses and differences (see Figure 11–5 on page 357 to review the structure and use of a Venn diagram).

Classification boxes are similar to comparison-contrasts charts (see Figure 13–10) and concretely depict the relationship of ideas in text.

A heuristic for a sequence pattern might be stair steps (depicting the steps in the sequence), as in Figure 13–11. As the students read and come upon statements relating the sequence of occurrences, they write these on the *sequence stair steps,* one statement on each step. For instance, in the sample in Figure 13–11, after reading the first bit of information about the formation of glaciers, students would be asked to write on the bottom step, "Winters turned particularly cold," or a similar idea conveying the essence of the details given. As they read farther, and

FIGURE 13–9
Comparison-contrast chart

	CANADA	MEXICO	Similar or different?
Population			
Climate			
Products			
Size of country			

1. The main ways the countries are similar
   are _____
   _____
   because _____
   _____ .

2. The main ways they are different are
   _____
   _____
   because _____
   _____ .

find the next occurrence, they pause and write that on the next step—with the statements on the steps ultimately leading to the outcome, written at the top. The outcome can be placed at the top of the steps before the sequences leading to it are determined or placed there at the end when the conclusion is drawn that it is the consequence of this set of sequences.

As may be apparent, at times, a diagram of a sequence structure fits nicely with examination of cause-and-effect patterns—in the example in the figure, stu-

FIGURE 13–10
Classification boxes

	REPTILES	MAMMALS
Characteristics	• cold blooded • young born live or from eggs • •	• warm blooded • young born live • •
Examples	• snakes • alligators • • •	• humans • cats • • •

FIGURE 13–11
Sequence stair steps

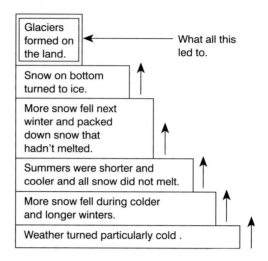

dents could be directed to write in the terms "cause" and "effect" at appropriate places on the stair steps after they have organized the sequence (the bottom step might have "cause" written above the statement, with an arrow pointing upward to the next step; the second step might have "effect" written below the statement, with an arrow pointing to the statement and "cause" written above the same statement with an arrow pointing upward toward the third step; and so on).

Figure 13–12 shows a problem-solution web, used to represent this common expository structure. When the problem is discovered in the text, it is written in the

FIGURE 13–12
Problem-solution web

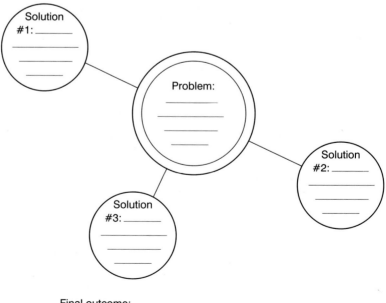

center circle. As solutions are proposed in the reading material, they are written in the ancillary circles. In some texts, all solutions are intermeshed to solve the problem; in others, one of the possible solutions is selected. When the solution becomes clear in the passage, students write the final outcome on the bottom line. Creating a diagram illustrating key concepts and connections facilitates understanding and retention.

Armbruster, Anderson, and Ostertag (1987) used another type of instructional graphic to convey the problem-solution pattern as applied specifically to social studies material—a pattern in which three items are commonly reported: (a) problem of a person or group, (b) the attempt to solve the problem, and (c) the results. Since some social studies material can resemble stories (i.e., in history books), it is not surprising that this structure resembles the elements in a story map. Armbruster et al. used the frame in Figure 13–13 to advance students' understanding of this particular problem-solution pattern. The frame visually portrays the form of the significant information in this text structure.

FIGURE 13–13
Problem-solution frame

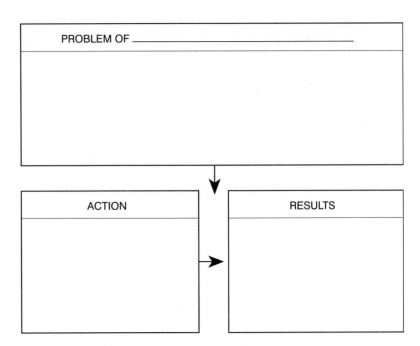

PROBLEM = something bad; a situation that people would like to change

ACTION = what people *do* to try to solve the problem

RESULTS = what happens as a result of the action; the effect or outcome of trying to solve the problem

Source: From "Does Text Structure/Summarization Instruction Facilitate Learning Expository Text," by B. Armbruster, T. Anderson, and J. Ostertag, 1987, *Reading Research Quarterly, 22*, pp. 54–77. Copyright 1987 by the International Reading Association. Reprinted by permission of the International Reading Association.

Fifth-graders were taught to follow three steps with each lesson: (a) while reading silently, they were to search for information that should be included in the problem-solution frames they had been given; (b) they wrote this information in the appropriate boxes in the frame diagram; and (c) they wrote a paragraph based on the information they had recorded in the frame. Teaching students to do this occurred in daily lessons over a 2-week period in which principles of explicit instruction were followed (teacher modeling, guided practice, teacher monitoring and feedback, and independent practice). Then students were evaluated on the ability to comprehend new social studies materials that employed a problem-solution pattern. Trained students scored significantly higher on comprehension of passages they had not previously read than learners who had been exposed to traditional postquestions instead. The differences were seen for grasping main ideas in the selections and for writing paragraphs that included more ideas of importance about the text. No differences were seen between the two groups on recalling literal details, however. Armbruster et al. (1991) extended this study to include other types of frames, such as sequence flow charts and comparison boxes, which also were successful with intermediate grade students.

Many other schematic diagrams have been used. You can design additional ones to logically fit the structure and aim of a lesson, being certain that they focus on the central ideas of the reading selection. Sometimes student work with schematics serves as the culminating event after reading. However, often the best use is in on-line assistance as you work with the learners during reading, or that they use independently *while* reading silently. Collaborative group activity or partnerships (working in pairs) fits quite naturally with the task of completing instructional graphics. Berkowitz (1986) found that an excellent learning experience, also, is for students, themselves, to design a diagram that will fit the pattern and the notions in a written text.

Diagrammatic representations of information do expedite comprehension of the immediate text, but the major purpose of comprehension instruction is to provide strategies that can subsequently be used to conquer obscure or difficult material. Diagramming and charting pivotal elements in text seems to be such a strategy. By producing diagrams and charts, readers are given the opportunity to internalize processes for recognizing text structures and organization (and, thus, important ideas), and have tools to use to do this when they encounter new text.

Culminating Events

As with foregoing activities, the culminating events recommended in this section have a research base supporting their value in assisting comprehension.

Assistance with the Text of the Moment.   The first suggestion provided here is based on a more recent practice—journal writing. The second has been recommended by comprehension studies for some time.

1.   *Instituting learning journals.* Jennings (1991) formulated a procedure to be carried out after students read expository text—that is, having students write in learning journals. This was described as a way for students to "think on paper." In Jennings's program, students reacted to social studies text by writing journal entries. They were asked to think about what they had gained from the material just read and to engage in writing a personalized response to it. This was seen as a

way of bonding new schema with old information already known by the reader. In their learning journals, students simulated roles, made conjectures concerning incidents they had read, and wrote about other reflections on their learning episode. Learners shared their journal entries with peers, and the teacher wrote individual replies to the entries.

Jennings (1991) provided research evidence for the constructiveness of this reflective writing about what has been read in an expository text. Students participating in the learning journals activity scored higher than students receiving a more traditional method of instruction when assessed on immediate comprehension of the text (based on end-of-chapter tests), and as well, showed superior recall on a measure of their knowledge after a time had passed (on a test over all chapters in the social studies unit).

Positive results of writing in learning journals was believed to be grounded in the interest bred from personal writing (in contrast to writing responses to teacher-produced tasks) and to the speculations about events students engaged in and the personal viewpoints they brought to occurrences, the latter thought to help tie old and new information.

2. *Generating questions.* This means *students* generating questions—not teachers. Asking students to generate questions after they have read text has become quite a popular idea and is believed to enhance recall because students focus on ideas that they think teachers will judge to be important. Generating questions has been suggested as a way to facilitate comprehension of informational material (Dole, Duffy, Roehler, & Pearson, 1991) and as a study skill (T. H. Anderson & Armbruster, 1984).

Choosing ideas about which to write questions prompts student attention to the principal information in a text, if the teacher directs notice toward this aim. Having to select important facts and concepts increases students' cognitive effort and thoughtfulness about the text. Several of the instructional methods recommended thus far in this chapter have included procedures for student-generated oral questions before reading (e.g., as with K-W-L) and during reading (e.g., in reciprocal teaching). When students write their own questions after reading exposition, meaning construction can be promoted (Schmeltzer, 1975).

However, there is one caveat: students must be taught *how* to generate questions. Some investigations have shown positive advantages of student-generated questions after reading and some have not—the difference often being whether this training was provided. To explore this issue, Andre and Anderson (1978-79) had one group of secondary school students write their own questions after being taught how to generate questions that were appropriately significant, another group creating questions but with no training, and a third who did not write questions. Both groups who wrote questions did better than those who did not, but readers with low- and middle-level skills did not experience the benefit unless they had been taught how to write questions that focused on important ideas. Comprehension increases in this study were related to the gist of the material. In J. R. King, Biggs, and Lipsky's (1984) research, positive effects on literal interpretations were found as the result of student-generated questions.

Development of Strategies That Can Be Used with a Wide Variety of Texts. Independent reading is a fact of life, in school and through adulthood. Students are asked to read silently in their classrooms and are later called upon to answer oral questions about what they read. Students are sent to study hall to read a chapter from a geography book and to write answers to the questions found at the end of the chapter. In home-work assignments, when textbooks must be read and questions must be answered, students are usually on their own, receiving little help from their parents or peers.

When reading income tax forms, reports, or other material, adults usually do not have the luxury of another person to guide and prompt them through what may at first seem incomprehensible. The majority of comprehension strategies taught to students should be aimed, therefore, at enabling them to internalize those strategies to be used when reading on their own.

1. *Teaching students to summarize.* Summarizing, a traditional task that has been assigned to myriads of students over years past, has recently come to interest reading authorities because, under certain conditions, this has proved to be a powerful way to help students improve comprehension of expository texts.

One condition that influences positive outcomes is training learners how to summarize. A. L. Brown and Day (1983) developed plans for teaching summarization that have been tested with readers of many age levels and with a variety of content area texts. Good results have been found for enhancing comprehension of the immediate material (e.g., Carr & Ogle, 1987); and, presumably because of the awareness of text structure that is built, positive effects have also carried over to comprehension of other selections (e.g., Rinehart, Stahl, & Erickson, 1986). When readers have been asked to summarize after reading but have not been explicitly taught how to do so, these favorable findings have not followed (T. W. Bean & Steenwyk, 1984).

Another condition on which success depends relates to the type of comprehension to be emphasized. Training and practice in summarizing seem to spawn improved understanding of main ideas or the general significance of a passage rather than recall of minor facts (Rinehart et al., 1986).

To teach your students the rules A. L. Brown and Day devised about summarization, do the following:

a. Show learners how to omit *insignificant* information from material they are summarizing.
b. Demonstrate how to omit *redundant* details.
c. Help them develop an *overarching, general label* for specifics (e.g., "deciduous trees" used in place of "oaks, maples, sycamores, hickories, beeches, ashes, and buckeyes").
d. Help them determine main ideas the author has stated and use these in the summary.
e. Teach them how to express the main ideas when the author has not stated these *explicitly*.

To the K-W-L technique recommended above, Carr and Ogle (1987) later added another feature, resulting in a K-W-L-Plus framework in which learners, additionally, wrote summaries based on their outlines or semantic maps; as with K-W-L, this expanded form of the method led to positive outcomes with comprehension.

For those with reading disabilities, use of a graphic organizer may help with summary writing. As noted above, instructional graphics can assist students in choosing ideas of importance in a selection and in understanding the relationships among them (as one example, in recognizing the appropriate sequence of the ideas). In a clinical setting with students who had reading and learning disabilities, Weisberg and Balajthy (1990) trained learners how to use graphic organizers. They taught them to underline important statements in text with colored pens and to construct organizers about the passages before writing summaries. Summaries improved after the readers had learned to use the graphic aids.

2. *Helping readers compose extended summaries.* After learners have conquered the basics of summarizing and can do so with a single portion of text (e.g., a short chapter), practice with extended summaries can help students determine interrelationships among several associated subjects (e.g., several chapters). For example, content area texts often structure chapters into units of similar topics. Pulling together overlying meanings can broaden understanding.

An extended summary can be composed by summarizing the component parts of targeted text and then, in effect, summarizing the summaries. Using a "Super Summary Form" organizes the process. See Figure 13–14.

3. *Looking back.* Strategies that may seem obvious to good readers and that they derive intuitively may not be so apparent to less skilled readers. A point in case involves what have been called "text lookbacks" (Garner, Wagoner, & Smith, 1983), or more formally "text reinspection." A **text lookback** simply means looking back in the material when a question cannot be answered.

When you need to respond to a question whose answer is given in a selection you've read, but you don't recall the particulars necessary for your reply, what do you do? You *look back* and see what it said there, of course! Some unskilled readers do not use this fairly simple solution. In some cases, they may believe checking back into the text is a "forbidden" resolution to their problem—they

FIGURE 13–14
A super-summary form

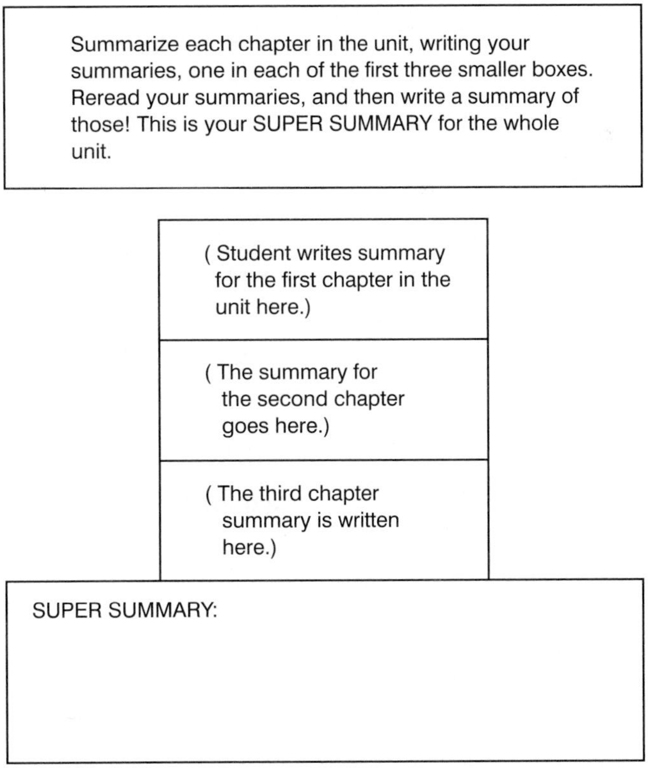

Summarize each chapter in the unit, writing your summaries, one in each of the first three smaller boxes. Reread your summaries, and then write a summary of those! This is your SUPER SUMMARY for the whole unit.

(Student writes summary for the first chapter in the unit here.)

(The summary for the second chapter goes here.)

(The third chapter summary is written here.)

SUPER SUMMARY:

think they are required to "remember" the details that they have read. Or they may have experienced previous trial-and-error attempts to reinspect text for answers, only to find that the random search method they have employed is unproductive. Or they may have previously used an inefficient approach in which they simply began at the beginning reading *everything* all over again until they found the answer—and this seems too great an effort to expend. As with many other comprehension strategies, it may be necessary to directly teach those with reading disabilities to systematically look back.

Table 13–2 shows results from a lookback study with fourth- and sixth-graders by Garner et al. (1983). The results of this study have implications for the instruction of students with poor comprehension strategies. A three-phase approach to such instruction follows.

a. Select a short, expository selection. Have students read it. Next, ask five literal questions. They should be of sufficient difficulty to require students to look back at the text for at least some questions. When a student is "stumped," ask what should be done to get the answer. Encourage the response, "Look back at the page where the answer is found." Praise this response, and have the students do it. After several sessions in which lookbacks are practiced, move to the second phase.

b. In the second phase, students must learn to distinguish between questions for which a text lookback will do the trick (e.g., literal-level questions), and those for which only their own background information can be used. Again present short passages followed by five questions—some literal and some that require the student's prior knowledge to obtain a correct response. Through discussion, aid students in deciding which is which. Confirm their decisions by looking back in the text and underlining the answers to literal questions, while noting when there is no answer to underline for the background-dependent questions. Have the students answer the questions. Practice these activities for several sessions before moving to the third phase. (Recall the exercises with

TABLE 13–2
Lookback study with fourth- and sixth-graders

	Good Comprehenders	Poor Comprehenders
Looked back in text for unknown answers	Often	Seldom
Looked back at the right time: a. did look back when answer was in text b. did not look back if answer had to be determined from student's own background information	Good differentiation was made	Poor differentiation was made
Knew how to sample text when they looked back (i.e., they looked back to the specific area where answer could be found and did not just reread whole passage until answer appeared)	Yes	No

Source: Adapted from information in "Externalizing Question-Answering Strategies of Good and Poor Comprehenders" by R. Garner, S. Wagoner, and T. Smith, 1983, *Reading Research Quarterly, 18,* 439–447.

QARs described in Chapter 12; those may also be in order here since for some questions text information and background knowledge must be combined.)

c. Follow the next sets of material by asking only literal-level questions. Tell students all these questions can be answered by looking at the passages. The questions should again be written at a difficulty level requiring students to engage in at least some text lookbacks. In this phase, however, before each lookback, tell students that looking through the whole passage takes too much time. They should be asked to try to remember where the answer occurred and be required to guess where they will find it (e.g., near the beginning middle, or end; right after the part about . . .). Category selection also is important here ("Since the article is divided into sections on religion of the Aztecs and social life of the Aztecs, and the question asks about Aztec gods, in which section should we look?"). Dreher (1992) reports that many students have difficulties with category selection during a text search. Points can be awarded for a correct guess about where to locate the specific information needed to answer a question. Practice this strategy for several sessions.

Until the strategies are firmly internalized, and to ensure generalization across other materials, prompt students to use them whenever appropriate and remind students about the strategies before they read independently. When students have missed or forgotten details, text lookbacks do a remarkably good job of repairing the problem. Reviewing a number of studies, Garner (1987) found the lookback strategy to have a beneficial effect on reading comprehension.

A comparable procedure, which also may be profitable in encouraging student use of text lookbacks, is the routine Herber and Nelson (1975) have suggested for learners who are having difficulty answering literal questions based on informational text:

a. Ask a question, and then *tell students the answer.* Next, *tell students where the answer may be found in the book,* and have them find it. After several practice sessions of this type, proceed to step b.

b. Ask a question, and *tell the answer;* do not tell where the answer is located in the material, but have the students find it.

c. Next, ask a question, but do not tell the answer; *do give the location of the answer,* and have the students find it.

d. Ask questions only. Students must find locations and answers.

e. Finally, Herber and Nelson (1975) suggested that students be required to make up questions about the material themselves.

4. *Teaching critical reading concepts.* **Critical reading** is defined as "the process of making judgments in reading" or "an act of reading in which a questioning attitude, logical analysis, and inference are used to judge the worth of what is read according to an established standard" (T. L. Harris & Hodges, 1981, p. 74).

Critical reading of expository material means judging the believability of what has been read. Poor readers often believe that anything presented *in print* is true or correct. As adults, they may be bilked or misled by vague or misleading language found in advertising and news articles. They can be influenced adversely because they do not trust their own judgments if they find ideas opposed to theirs in print.

Baker and Brown (1984) consider neglecting to read critically to be one type of comprehension failure. They say this failure occurs when readers construe text in a way an author wishes, instead of weighing other possibilities. They point out

To teach critical reading skills, have students read several newspaper accounts of the same incident and contrast the details reported.

that good comprehension involves realization that text is written with different goals in mind and that authors may utilize propaganda techniques to persuade readers to a certain view.

Critical reading concepts are no more difficult to grasp than other higher-level comprehension understandings. And, very important, the reasoning and thinking exercises employed to teach critical reading may positively affect other types of comprehension tasks. It has also been suggested that instruction in critical reading concepts, because of the emphasis on evaluation skills, may facilitate the important metacognitive strategy of monitoring reading (Baker & Brown, 1984).

Many teachers begin a program of teaching critical reading concepts by providing practice in recognizing the seven propaganda techniques identified by the Institute of Propaganda Analysis (H. M. Robinson, 1967). Here is a list of them:

a. *Bad names.* Name calling designed to cause dislike. ("Americans are capitalist imperialists.")
b. *Glad names.* Using "names" or descriptions of people to generate positive feelings. ("The candidate can be trusted. He was a Boy Scout in his youth.")
c. *Transfer.* Suggesting approval because other people purportedly approve. ("Use Acid-O Aspirin. Nine out of ten doctors do.")
d. *Testimonial.* Using public figures to endorse ideas or products. ("Melvin Mish, pole vaulting champion in the Olympics, drives the new Ford Taurus.")
e. *Plainfolks.* Suggesting that an important person is just like the average person, and, therefore, can be trusted, or indicating that average folks (just like you) prefer a certain product or idea. ("Senator Kitten's campaign manager says he spent Sunday at the family farm where he ate a fried chicken dinner and played with the dog.")
f. *Stacking the cards.* Not giving the full truth by omitting details or focusing attention on one detail. (The Chinese press reports the American system is on the verge of collapse because unemployment is high.)

g. *The band wagon.* Suggesting that since "everybody" is doing something you should too. ("Over 1 million people have bought the Higglely Pigglely screwdriver.")

To acquaint students with propaganda devices, teachers use expository materials such as newspapers, magazine articles, and ads. After students read these, they attempt to identify statements representing the various devices. Students are guided to make inferences about the believability of the statements, their purposes, and their relevance to the point being made.

Work with critical reading concepts should not be limited to practice in recognizing propaganda techniques, however. Other important abilities and skills include the following.

- Understanding that because something is found in print does not necessarily mean it's true (Practice in recognizing propaganda devices is a beginning, but developing this understanding should be carried further—for example, by examining several newspaper accounts of the same incident, some of which may report contradictory information; or by reviewing several different reports of an event in history, such as might be found in an encyclopedia or textbook in contrast to a work of historical fiction.)
- Identifying fact versus opinion
- Detecting faulty generalizations
- Detecting overgeneralizations
- Identifying the effects of quoting out of context
- Detecting false causality
- Discerning writers' purposes—and biases (Do they want to inform—or influence?)
- Asking questions about the writer's qualifications (Does the author of an article about learning disabilities in a women's magazine have the background and expertise for his or her statements to be believable?)
- Learning to ask these questions: Where's the proof? What facts support this? What data back this up?

Because there has been some debate about whether critical thinking can be taught or is a result of natural reasoning powers, one group of researchers set out to determine if critical reading could be improved through explicit instruction (Patching, Kameenui, Carnine, Gersten, & Colvin, 1983). They compared two instructional approaches. Fifth-graders in one group received workbooks containing lessons for learning three critical reading concepts. After students completed exercises, the teacher marked right and wrong answers and gave them back to the students. This method did not prove to be very effective—not a major bombshell.

A second approach, a systematic instruction method, did prove valuable, however. Teachers worked directly with the students during each lesson, employing principles of active teaching, providing feedback about responses, and guidance to help readers deduce logical responses. At the end of the program, students who engaged in the systematic instruction method scored significantly higher on a critical reading test than did the group using the workbook method. Furthermore, the systematic instruction method was most effective with the poorer readers in the group.

The important implication of this study for the remedial teacher is that students (including poor readers) can develop critical reading concepts, but the specific method chosen may well determine success or failure. Students who frequently participate in discussions about what they are reading are more likely to become critical readers than those who do not (Sweet, 1993).

STUDYING

Studying is certainly related to comprehension. It involves the interpretation and construction of meaning based on what the author has told the reader and what knowledge the reader can bring to the text. Unlike typical reasons for reading narratives, the focus of studying is on recall for some purpose—to take a test, to write a paper, to carry out an experiment correctly, to give an oral presentation, or to use the information in real-life needs, as for example, in one's profession. Often studying is done with expository materials.

The major concern of most remedial teachers is with the encoding process, that is, teaching learners how to gain the meanings of text. To accomplish this goal, much instruction is teacher-guided—and should be. However, in many study situations, students must learn independently. And additionally, student attention must be not only on *gaining meanings,* but also on *retention* of the understandings obtained. For some students, receiving direction about studying may significantly contribute to their school success.

When focusing on aspects of studying, many distinguish between learning skills and learning strategies. For example, Reynolds and Werner (1993–94) define **learning skills** to include skill in reading, locating and organizing information, and writing, while **learning strategies** are the processes of selecting and using appropriate skills. Throughout these last two chapters on comprehension, you have read suggestions for helping learners develop comprehension strategies that can be used with a wide variety of reading materials. Many of these suggestions can be useful approaches in interpreting and recalling information (for example, summarizing, employing text lookbacks, diagramming and charting). The present section extends these discussions to common study techniques.

Research on the most common study routines has produced many conflicting results, and the conclusion to be drawn from research findings is that there is simply no one system that is better than another. Some investigations show, for instance, that a technique works well and other studies show that the same study method is no better than several others the student could use. The difference in whether a study behavior is successful depends in part on the recall response the student must later produce. For instance, certain circumstances necessitate understanding and retention of specific data—in some science learning, for example, or in introductory information in texts and courses in many subject areas. Other situations require retention of the main ideas only, and in others, both the main ideas and the details are of importance.

Another factor on which success of the study system hinges is the *depth of processing* called into play. As with learning word meanings and with approaches that truly influence comprehension, deep processing is a key. Some study techniques, or specific versions of these, induce the learner to concentrate and expend more cognitive effort, both of which are associated with greater recall of information than a single reading of material (T. H. Anderson & Armbruster, 1984).

Here are some examples:

1. *Note taking.* In some investigations, note taking has been no more productive than other study procedures. However, when students *paraphrase* the author's words or *reorganize* the author's text, rather than recording words verbatim, the

process is effective (Bretzing & Kulhavy, 1979). Paraphrasing and reorganizing require deeper levels of processing.

2. *Outlining.* Outlining does require reorganization of the author's presentation, and as such, has been one of the more constructive study techniques according to a number of studies—but not all. One difference here seems to hang on whether the readers have been *trained* to outline. So, once again we see comparable results with other comprehension research: to be effective many of the most functional strategies must be taught directly—and fully—for worthwhile consequences to occur. When there is no training in selecting ideas of importance, although students may employ outlining *formats,* they may process information only superficially and therefore not recall significant information (T. H. Anderson & Armbruster, 1984).

Further, what the student does with the outlined material is important. Baker and Brown (1984) report that students who use effective study techniques concentrate first on the main ideas and, once sure these are understood and can be remembered, they then focus on the important details. Those who are less efficient place all attention on the main ideas, continuing to center on these even when they are well under control, not moving on to studying significant facts.

3. *Underlining.* Underlining is carried out simply by the student marking lines in a book (or highlighting with transparent pens). Why would this study routine help? Perhaps it is because critical details are signaled. With this hypothesis in mind, investigators have tried underlining portions of passages *before* giving them to students—emphasizing essential facts or concepts. But this has not proved to be helpful. Thus, it has been concluded that when students do their *own* underlining (and must necessarily make choices about the importance of text statements to underline), deep processing is encouraged (T. H. Anderson & Armbruster, 1984; Rickards & August, 1975).

4. *Using study guides.* Use of study guides is not entirely an independent study procedure because the teacher must supply the guide, but good results have been seen when they are used. You might confer with classroom teachers about the value of these aids and encourage their use—especially for the poor readers with whom you work. Herber (1992) suggests that study guides are most effective when they serve both content learning and strategy learning, that is, when they help students understand the subject addressed at the time and, as well, teach general ways for ferreting meanings out of text that can be used in the future. When this is the case, they also are suitable for remedial teachers to implement in strategy lessons for reading expository text. An example of such a study guide is seen in Figure 13–15.

Many new types of study guides are currently being developed, with some of these based on the effectiveness that has been found for using schematic diagrams to enhance comprehension. An investigation by D. A. Hayes and Reinking (1991) showed that use of graphic aids in combination with adjunct study materials was beneficial to both good and poor readers. Research shows that study guides are excellent resources, but not a cure-all for problems with learning from text. Study guides should be used during reading, not afterward; and though more often applied in independent study, they are particularly well suited for collaborative learning activities.

Wood, Lapp, and Flood (1992, pp. 73-74) provide these guidelines for using study guides:

FIGURE 13–15
Sample of a study guide

Fossils

Names _____   Date(s) _____

_____

Strategy Codes:
   RR — Read and retell in your own words
   DP — Read and discuss with partner
   PP — Predict with partner
   WR — Write a response on your own
  Skim — Read quickly for purpose stated and discuss with partner
  MOC — Organize information with a map, chart, or outline

Self-Monitoring Codes:
  ✓   I understand this information
  ?   I'm not sure if I understand.
  X   I do not understand and I need to restudy.

1. ____ PP   pp. 385–392. Survey the title, picture, charts, and headings. What do you expect to learn about this section?

2. ____ WR   As you are reading, jot down three or more new words and definitions for your vocabulary collection.

3. ____ RR   pp. 385–86, first three paragraphs.

4. ____ DP   pp. 386–87, next three paragraphs.
     a. Describe several reasons why index or guide fossils are important.
     b. How can finding the right type of fossil help you to identify it?

5. ____ MOC Map pp. 387–89. Make an outline of the information.

1. _____   2. _____   3. _____
   a. _____   a. _____   a. _____
   b. _____   b. _____   b. _____
   c. _____   c. _____   c. _____

6. ____ Skim p. 390, first three paragraphs
        Purpose: To understand the role of the following in the formation of fossils
          ____ a. natural casts
          ____ b. trails and burrows
          ____ c. gastroliths

7. ____ DP   pp. 390–91
        As an amateur fossil collector, describe:
     a. where to find fossils
     b. what to use to find them
     c. how to prepare them for display

8. ____ WR   p. 392, next to last paragraph
        Define pseudofossil. Jot down three other words that contain the prefix "pseudo." Use the dictionary if necessary.

9. ____ DP   Examine the fossil collection being passed around and list eight things you have learned by analyzing it.

Source: From "Helping Students Comprehend Their Textbooks" by K. D. Wood, 1987, *Middle School Journal, 18*(2), pp. 20–21. Reprinted by permission.

    a. Have students skim the guide and the text before reading.
    b. Explain and model.
    c. Sometimes encourage paired or group work with the guide; this is especially productive in beginning stages.
    d. Circulate and monitor as students work; supply feedback and assistance.
    e. Encourage strategic reading.
    f. End the guide with an activity that requires a mental and written review of the content.
    g. Follow with discussion; don't simply have them "turn in the guide for a grade."

See Test Bank J for three instruments to assess students' study skills.

Another critical issue related to study is that of transfer—that is, whether students, at a later time in texts studied for other classes, use strategies that have been taught in special programs. Frazier (1993) found that students taught to use a text-marking annotation strategy did not use it often and, when they did, had problems applying it to real texts. None of the students in this study reported using the strategy without prompting. Schumm and Saumell (1994) remind us that we also must determine what actually motivates students to put effective study strategies into play.

METACOGNITION

Metacognition has been discussed earlier in this book, particularly in relation to assessment, but the topic will be revisited and expanded here. As you recall, **metacognition** refers to two things: (1) *knowledge* individuals have about their own thinking and (2) *control* (or regulation) individuals have over their own thinking (Baker & Brown, 1984).

Knowledge implies that you are aware of basic characteristics of your thinking and literacy processes ("When I read a physics text, I usually have to read more slowly and carefully than when I read a history text"; or "I can write a paper more easily than my roommate because I seem to have a sense of expressing things through structures that

---

Test Bank J
Tests of Study Skills

Name	For Grades	Type of Administration	Time for Administration	Publisher
CAI Study Skills Test (SST). (Microcomputer edition also available)	College-bound students	Group	55 minutes	Effective Study Materials
Diagnostic Test of Library Skills	5–9	Group	30 minutes	Learnco
Survey of Study Habits and Attitudes. (Spanish edition available)	7–14	Group	20–25 minutes	Psychological Corporation

communicate easily"). It also refers to being aware of what you are thinking and mentally doing at any given time—that is, that you monitor your reading. "Awareness" may not always occur at a conscious level—if you are "getting it," you just move on through the reading. For the good reader, awareness may migrate to the conscious level only when understanding breaks down—you may say "Huh! What was that? Let's read that again!"

Control means doing something about those thinking processes, if there is a need to. And you must have strategies to do that something.

Some metacognitive strategies involve planning:

1. Thinking about the purpose ("The reason I'm reading this is to determine if dinosaurs existed in what is now the United States"; or "When I'm reading this, I can't just understand it, I also have to remember it for that quiz.")
2. Determining and focusing on what is important and not trivial ("This is important information for figuring out what I need to know so I'd better attend to this part carefully.")

Some metacognitive strategies involve *monitoring:*

1. Being alert to when understanding occurs but also to problems ("I get it, so I can read on"; or "That doesn't make sense to me!")
2. Taking corrective action ("That doesn't make sense to me, so I'd better reread this"; or "Let me see if I can mentally say what he's saying here in this paragraph because it's a little confusing.")

As can be seen, some metacognitive strategies mesh very closely with what we have been calling comprehension strategies. It can also be seen that readers need an awareness not only of their own thinking but also of the specific text and task requirements. A study conducted by Wade, Schraw, Buxton, and Hayes (1993) provides an example of how readers can relate awareness of text and task requirements with their own thinking processes. The skilled readers in this investigation spent more time and more effort when they thought ideas they were reading were important *and* would be difficult to remember; these competent readers expended less effort and time when the concepts, though believed to be important, were also deemed easy to recall. Poor readers often do not make such adjustments, reading all text at the same rate and making no discriminations about where more attention should be given and where less.

A good deal of interest in metacognition has arisen recently—and some controversy, as well. While educational psychologists have pursued the topic of metacognitive activity for quite some time, literacy professionals only began addressing the subject seriously in the 1980s. This concern arose along with new views of comprehension, which recognize that readers must not only acquire certain skills, they must also learn and use processes of "problem solving" to ferret out messages in text.

Metacognition requires complex processes. Research, not surprisingly, has shown that poor readers are inferior to good readers in metacognitive activity (e.g., August, Flavell, & Clift, 1984; Brown, Armbruster, & Baker, 1986). And, younger readers are less skilled than older. Daneman (1991) and others believe that some LD students' lack of metacognitive awareness may be one cause of their inadequate comprehension.

Early research cast some doubt about whether metacognition could be trained. These studies seemed to show that students could be taught to apply metacognition to specific tasks, but that students did not continue to do so once they were no longer prompted through the training program to exercise the skill or that they did not generalize what they had learned to new types of texts. Later research has identified the problem—that is, because of their complexity and the effort required for metacognitive skills to be internalized, there must be a lengthy training program. When researchers and teachers work with students over an extended period, provide much opportunity for practice, and furnish careful explanation of the value of the activity, metacognitive strategies have been learned, maintained, and employed in new situations (Day, 1980; Derry & Murphy, 1986; G. E. Miller, 1987; Palincsar & Brown, 1984; Schunk & Rice, 1987).

It is also important for less skilled readers (and younger ones) that metacognitive instruction be explicit and direct, with many examples given (Baker, 1984; Day, 1980; Paris & Meyers, 1981). In other words, these populations do not learn metacognitive strategies intuitively, simply from general opportunities with reading of connected text. Not only must we teach poor readers basic strategies for approaching a text in such a way that it is possible to construct meaning, Paris, Wasik, and Turner (1991) say that teachers must dramatize "troubleshooting routines" for them.

Metacognitive Strategies

A variety of suggestions for increasing students' metacognition can be found in the professional literature. A number of general strategies have been proposed, with many authorities contending that students should be taught them. You will see some familiar entries in the discussion below because some of these recommendations are incorporated in many of the successful comprehension strategies you have learned in this chapter and the previous one; others are of a broader nature and relate to any type of intentional learning. These strategies should be applied in both narrative and expository text reading.

Before Reading

1. Survey the materials before you read by looking at the title, pictures, and headings.
2. Think about your purpose for reading each specific selection; allot time for reading based on this.
3. Think about the topic; allot time and select strategies to be used based on your familiarity with the topic.
4. Be aware of your strengths and weaknesses; if you are not interested in the topic, plan strategies to keep yourself on task.
5. Predict what you think the text will tell you.
6. Think about what you already know about the topic.
7. Think of some questions you'd like answered by the selection.

During Reading

1. Relate what is being read to something you already are familiar with.
2. Use visual imagery; try to picture in your mind what the text is describing.
3. Use visual aids supplied in the text (don't just skip over them); relate these to the written information.
4. Think about the text cues. How can these help you understand? (Are main points numbered? Are there words and ideas printed in bold and italics?)
5. Think about text structure. (Is it important to remember the sequence? Are things compared to one another to help you understand?)
6. Keep making predictions; ask yourself if your guesses so far are right or wrong.
7. Notice when questions you asked before reading are answered.
8. Pause to think about important points; part way through stop and try to retell main points made so far.

To practice use of metacognitive strategies, students may work as partners.

9. When encountering something you don't understand, select a strategy to resolve this difficulty. For example:
   a. Slow down; reread the difficult part.
   b. Look back in the text and reread (text reinspection).
   c. Temporarily read ahead to see if difficult concepts are clarified.
   d. Work with a partner; talk through your understandings and confusions.
   e. Underline the parts you don't understand; consult an external source (e.g., the teacher).

After Reading

1. Think about your predictions. Which were correct?
2. Summarize the selection to aid in noting important information and in recalling it.
3. Attend to main ideas; when these are "mastered," fill in the significant details.
4. Try to think of questions that could be asked about the selection; focus questions on important rather than trivial information. Try to answer the questions to evaluate your understanding, and to aid later recall. Try to think how you would "prove" to someone that your answers are correct.
5. If questions are asked in the text or by the teacher, think about the *type* of question being asked. Think of the specific strategy needed to answer that type.

All of these strategies would, of course, be overwhelming if you tried to teach them in their entirety to poor readers at one time. Instead, you should select one or two that seem to be of particular relevance for a student or group. Make these strategies the focal point of lessons until students are comfortably operating with them. Then introduce another one or two. The optimistic news is that disabled readers *have* been taught to approach text metacognitively and thus with skillful teaching, your students, too, can achieve proficiency.

CONCLUSION

Comprehension is the aim of reading. The information in this chapter reflects current understandings about comprehension instruction directed to a difficult and common task—reading expository text. Because educators are continually expanding their understanding of, and developing their ideas about, how to assist students with comprehension problems, teachers should read their professional journals to stay abreast of new findings.

Once again a number of principles have been delineated that have potential to improve the comprehension of poor readers—principles that suggest instruction that varies from typical practices in the past. Some examples of specific teaching suggestions have been offered based on research data that is available now to guide practice. It is impossible in any one text to compile all research-based recommendations, but using the principles discussed in this text provides a frame for teacher-designed instruction. Much has been said in this book about one of those principles—the importance of feedback. However, feedback can also be seen as a two-way street: feedback from teacher to student and feedback from student to teacher. The latter means that as we observe students' responses to instruction, we reflect on them and flexibly adapt our teaching to students' confusions or needs. Nowhere may this be more crucial than in comprehension instruction.

📖 REFLECTIONS

Much of the information in the two preceding chapters should be helpful to college students studying and learning from text. Which of these strategies do *you* intuitively use or have you learned to employ? Which might you want to try in the future?

	Already Use	A Strategy to Try
1. Previewing a chapter before reading.	_____	_____
2. Establishing a purpose before beginning to read (e.g., for the present chapter, one purpose should be to learn instructional procedures you can use in your own teaching to help poor readers who have difficulties with comprehension. However, another immediate, practical purpose might likely be to remember information well enough to discuss it on a test or in a paper your instructor asks you to prepare).	_____	_____
3. Meshing your own background information with text information (e.g., What do you already know about the material given in the text? How does the text information apply to actual situations you know of with children or adolescents?)	_____	_____
4. Stopping at the ends of major sections to put the information in your own words.	_____	_____
5. Summarizing the entire chapter by thinking of the major points that were conveyed.	_____	_____
6. Reinspecting the text for important details omitted in your summarization attempt.	_____	_____

Reinspect the section on metacognition now. What other strategies suggested there could you experiment with to see if they increase your understanding and recall?

Other Strategies I Want to Try

1. _____

2. _____

3. _____

READING INSTRUCTION FOR SPECIAL POPULATIONS

14

The Severely Delayed Reader and the Nonreader

Greater explicitness may be necessary when instructing severely delayed readers.

Disabled readers are not all cut from the same cloth. There is great diversity among students enrolled in remedial reading programs and learning disability programs in their characteristics and needs. One way they vary is according to the severity of their difficulties with literacy attainment.

Figure 14–1 depicts the relative proportion of students who have some troubles with reading, according to the seriousness of their delays. The majority of students with reading problems face challenges that are fairly *mild*. In fact, they may never be in a remedial program; instead, when the classroom teacher supplies them with perceptive, individualized attention, the students are able to progress. The second largest group are those whose difficulties may be described as *moderate*. They make up a fairly substantial portion of the learners who are considered "poor" readers. Most students, at any grade level, who are receiving special instructional services in remedial reading classes, in learning disability programs, and in reading clinics are those experiencing moderately serious obstacles in learning to read. More research and program development has been directed to meet the learning requirements of this group than to any of the others represented in Figure 14–1.

A third group is much smaller in number—perhaps only about 3% of the reading disabled population: these are individuals whose lack of reading achievement constitutes a decidedly *severe* delay in learning. How a "severe" disability is defined differs with different authorities, with different agencies providing services, and with different organizations concerned with the interests of these individuals. When this specification is *discrepancy-based* (that is, based on differences between actual level of reading and expected level), some have suggested a lag in reading level that is 3 years or more below the individual's potential; others specify two standard deviations below the "norm" on standardized measurement instruments and the like. There also have been difficulties in defining the precise parameters of a severe reading disability when *learning characteristics* have been examined. For instance, H. G. Taylor, Satz, and Friel (1979) report a study of assumptions about severe reading disability inherent in a definition of "specific, developmental dyslexia" proposed by the World Federation of Neurology; the 80 severely disabled readers in their research did not conform to this organization's proposed characteristics and learning behaviors. Originally learning disability programs were established to serve this bottom 3% of students with reading and learning disabilities but in common practice today, many students enrolled in these classes fall within the moderate range of needs. Some research attention has been given to the instructional predicaments of severely delayed readers, but not nearly so much as given to those with moderate difficulties.

The smallest group—but those with the gravest problems—are *nonreaders* who make up, perhaps, 1% or less of the reading disability group. Obviously, they too are

FIGURE 14–1
Proportions of students with literacy problems

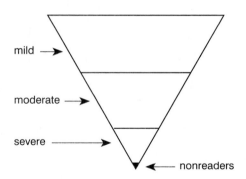

severely disabled, but these learners make up a special segment of those with the most severe problems because they can read almost nothing at all. Although few in number they represent the most needy students we serve and without special care are quite likely to grow up to join the ranks of the "unexplained" adult illiterate. Research on instruction for nonreaders has been exceedingly scant.

Assessing students' needs by examining the severity of the problem may be a constructive way to gain insights for program planning because it does seem that somewhat modified routes to learning are needed by severely delayed learners—and most particularly for nonreaders—versus those for students with more moderate limitations. This is not to say that outlandish instruction is called for with the more serious cases (like walking balance beams or tossing bean bags or other such approaches to promoting reading sometimes suggested in times past, which are totally unrelated to the reading task). However, instruction for severely delayed learners may need to focus on developing certain prerequisites over which moderately disabled readers have typically already gained control (e.g., letter recognition; phonemic awareness), to provide more than the usual number of opportunities for practice, to be even more explicit than is usually required for other learning-delayed readers, and to provide more than the typical amount of direct guidance since in the earliest stages these students seem to learn little incidentally. Furthermore, since the problems of severely delayed readers customarily lie with word recognition and identification, it is particularly crucial to consider their stages of word learning. And finally, lack of motivation, bred from persistent failure, can cripple instructional efforts if this variable is not given attention along with cognitive concerns. The present chapter focuses on instruction with the two groups of most serious cases—severely delayed readers and nonreaders.

SOME GENERAL CHARACTERISTICS OF SEVERELY DISABLED READERS AND NONREADERS

Some typical general characteristics of both severely delayed readers and nonreaders are the following:

1. Their problems may result from multiple and differing causes.

2. They are found in all IQ ranges, but most have average intelligence.

3. Some are unusually reticent about making attempts at reading, likely due to feelings of insufficiency and embarrassment. They *do* have a desire to learn to read, although their overt behaviors often belie that conclusion. Initially, they may avoid reading, exhibit off-task behaviors, and sometimes are uncooperative with attempts to instruct them.

4. Habitually they are demoralized, believing they *cannot* learn to read. Many have acquired this belief as the result of statements and actions of well-meaning but misinformed individuals and of past experiences. For example, Eric, a university football player referred to a college of education reading clinic, said to the staff at the first meeting, "I *can't* learn to read. They told me at the medical facility I have dyslexia." Eric was nevertheless asked to try to read a short selection, which he was able to handle, although with some difficulty. After reading he was told, "You can learn to read; you just don't recognize some long words. We'll teach you how to figure those out." Later assessment determined that Eric was reading at about fifth-grade level. This is certainly an indication of a severe delay for a college student, but it also indicates that he did not have some malady that made it

impossible to read. Further evaluation demonstrated he had little difficulty with word meanings or comprehension. Eric, a mature young man with average intelligence who wanted to read better, was delighted to find he wasn't "dyslexic" and cooperatively engaged in activities suggested for remediation.

5.   They usually require one-to-one instruction. Frequent remedial sessions are needed, and the typical severe reading disability case must be enrolled in a program for an extended period of time.

6.   They can learn to read. It is not unusual for these students to make consistent, but relatively slow progress during early remedial instruction; then a breakthrough occurs, and growth is rapid for a period. "Plateaus" are reached periodically, however, during which progress continues but slows considerably. These plateaus are followed by periods of return to rapid learning. Recognition of this cycle in learning rate is important to establish realistic expectations, prevent discouragement, and ensure continued motivation to persevere.

A GENERAL PRINCIPLE: INSTRUCTION SHOULD APPROXIMATE THE REAL ACT OF READING

This principle that reading instruction should approximate authentic reading certainly holds true for all students, but deviation from it has most often occurred with nonreaders and severely disabled readers. When students face uncommonly serious barriers to learning, some programs have advocated activities far removed from the act of reading. These approaches have employed body management and perceptual training, including activities such as visual tracking practice, walking balance beams, lateral dominance exercises, discriminating the left sides of their bodies from their right, visual-motor integration drills, crawling, jumping, climbing, hopping, rolling on the floor, and eye-hand coordination workouts such as throwing bean bags or drawing lines. The stated purpose of this training is to provide a prereading perceptual-motor foundation that ultimately will foster reading. Yet, whatever the intended goal may be, research has shown these procedures provide no assistance to academic learning of any kind for those with reading disabilities and learning disabilities or with developmentally disabled students. The Council for Learning Disabilities has adopted a position statement opposing measurement or training of perceptual and perceptual-motor functions as part of remedial programs; this position was based on the large volume of research discounting the value of such assessment and instruction ("Measurement and Training," 1986).

In addition, certain kinds of visual discrimination activities that have been used in prereading programs are not prerequisites for reading. One such activity requires students to visually discriminate between shapes and pictures. A typical exercise of this type asks students to look at the first shape or picture and find all others in a line that look the same or to find all the shapes or objects of one type in a picture. Numerous studies have shown that matching shapes and pictures as preliminary instruction for letter and word discrimination is useless (e.g., Barrett, 1965; Gates, 1926; and others). If we want students to visually identify the distinguishing features of letters and words, the exercises should include letters and words (not nonword forms).

Similar findings have resulted from research on certain types of auditory discrimination training. These studies have shown that instruction with *nonverbal* sounds does not transfer to the phonemic skills needed for reading. Training with nonverbal sounds may consist of exercises in which students are asked to distinguish between environmental noises, for example, by asking them to close their eyes while the teacher taps on several objects (such as a desk, the chalkboard, and a window) and then to guess the object being tapped; or by having them listen to tape recordings of an alarm clock, lawn mower, or bird call and to guess each sound. Such exercises simply do not have any relation to reading. These activities should be distinguished from phonemic awareness training that is helpful, that is, involving discrimination of phonemic elements of letters and words. Phonemic awareness activities, as specified in Chapter 10, have support from research, but auditory discrimination training with nonverbal sounds does not.

To choose instructional activities for severely delayed and nonreaders, you should ask, "How close to the real act of reading is this?" If it is suggested that your students walk balance beams, cry "Hogwash!" and have them dictate and read a story instead. If it is recommended that your students complete exercises to discriminate between shapes of triangles and ovals, whisper "Balderdash!" and instead give them opportunities to discriminate orthographic features of words. Appropriate instructional decisions prevent waste of learning time.

SEVERELY DELAYED READERS

Predicting the precise needs of severely delayed readers is not possible without knowing the learner. The term "severely delayed" is a rather general designation that can describe a wide range of differences. For example, a severely delayed high school student with an instructional level of, let's say, approximately third grade, may have advanced through the alphabetic stage of word learning, but not yet be reading words orthographically (or neither of these statements may describe this specific student's reading behaviors). On the other hand, a severely delayed sixth-grade student reading at beginning second-grade level may just be making his or her way through the alphabetic stage (or this may not be the case with this particular student).

When word recognition and identification is a source of the problem, as is most commonly the case, considering the word learning stage of the student yields clues for teaching. These stages suggest the reader's current *strengths* (how he or she can best learn words at this point in time) and *needs* (what he or she needs to learn to proceed into the next stage). Both should be taken into account for the most effective instruction. The description of typical reading behaviors associated with each stage, given in Chapter 9, can serve as a checklist for estimating word-learning level. (You may want to again review the stages of word learning presented in Chapter 9 since these will play a role in the discussion throughout the rest of this chapter. Having clear recall of these will increase your understanding of critical information presented here—time to do a text lookback!)

Although less frequent with severely delayed readers, another student with an extreme reading discrepancy may have grade-appropriate word recognition knowledge, but show acute deficiencies in comprehension. There may also be differences in how you would need to work with a student whose reading attainment is 3 years below his or her expected achievement versus one who is 5 years, or 6 years, or 8 years delayed—differences not only directly related to instructional focus, but also to issues of motivation. In any case, individual assessment is requisite for determining needs of severely delayed readers and for structuring beneficial programs.

Instructional Suggestions for Word Learning

Although many hypotheses have been proposed about causes of severe reading delays, a far too insufficient body of research is available to inform our instruction of severely delayed readers. Some of the limited number of instructional studies that do exist will be reviewed here. These studies have primarily investigated the merit of specific teaching techniques for promoting word learning.

Some of the investigations have been directed to word recognition and identification or error correction instruction with severely delayed readers at the *elementary school level*. These are discussed immediately below. (A discussion of investigations with middle school and high school students and adults follows.)

Word Self-Selection.   A motivational element was a factor in a word-learning program with severely reading delayed students in a laboratory clinic, which was evaluated by Noble (1981). Intermediate grade students with good oral language skills, but seriously limited reading vocabularies, participated in a plan based on a well-known word self-selection concept used earlier by Sylvia Ashton-Warner (1964) with Maori children in New Zealand. Students, whom the researcher described as being discouraged from being "left out and left behind," selected some of the words they wanted to learn, a procedure that was intended to profit from the learners' interest in those words.

The instructional approach was as follows: the young students orally read short passages at their instructional levels and the teacher recorded unknown words. Each student selected a few of the unknown words he or she wanted to learn, and the teacher chose an equal number of these to be studied. Word study took up 10 to 20 minutes in each session. Each word was written in isolation on one side of an index card and in context (using the sentence from the reading material) on the reverse side. After initial instruction using what the researcher described as "appropriate techniques for teaching sight vocabulary" (p. 387), words were reviewed through games and flashcard activities.

The majority of students learned more of the words they had chosen than those selected by the teacher, although with a few students no difference was seen. For students who are reluctant to try after repeated failure, the researcher suggested word self-selection as a motivating procedure.

No information was given on the specific words chosen by the students versus those selected by the teacher, although a partial list of one student's *combined* group of words was provided as an example; these were *then, while, came, exhibit, forced out, complete* (p. 386). Knowing if the student's choices had more easily distinguished characteristics than those picked by the teacher—or not—would make it easier to evaluate the power of this approach. The word *then,* for instance, might be harder to discriminate (because of similar words such as *than, them,* and *when*) than a phrase like *forced out* or a word with some distinctive letters and more concrete meaning like *exhibit*. Still, with excessively reluctant learners who have endured many failures, the approach of "self-selection" might prove to have some usefulness.

Analogy Use.   Wolff, Desberg, and Marsh (1985) obtained positive results by teaching analogy strategies to fifth-grade, learning disabled students who were reading 3 grades below their actual grade placements (i.e., at about second-grade reading level). Learners were taught to compare unknown words with words already known and make comparisons about letter combinations (e.g., the unknown word *fight* might be recognized by comparing it to the known word *light*). The learning disabled students in the study gave many indications of being in the rudimentary-alphabetic stage of word learning (they guessed at words using letter name cues and partial sound cues—using only a first letter or two; they seldom employed more complete, sequential decoding or use of sound-symbol generalizations). As you noted in your review of the word learning stages in Chapter 9, analogy use often begins at about second-grade level, but usually not by those who haven't yet reached the orthographic stage. These researchers saw their instruction as a way of "speeding up" reading development. They believed that while competent readers may develop analogy use intuitively, severely delayed readers must be systematically taught the strategy.

One of their two procedures was effective. The following steps helped students learn analogy use and to generalize the strategy to new words:

1. Students were shown an unknown word and directed to think of a word that would look like it, if the first letter were changed. (If they could not recall such a word, they were given three examples and then asked to think of a word of their own.)
2. They were directed to pronounce the unknown word like the known word they had given, changing only the sound of the first letter.

Here is the procedure that did *not* work:

1. A known word that had been written in red by the teacher was pronounced by the student.
2. An unknown word with a similar letter pattern with the exception of the first letter, written in blue, was then to be pronounced by the student.

Can you already guess what made the difference in the two procedures? It's that same old theme—the importance of depth of processing. The researchers credited the superior effectiveness of the first set of procedures to students' *generating their own words* in contrast to merely reading words that had been supplied by the teacher. They believed this helped the learners form better mental sets for generalizing the strategy to new situations.

It should be noted, however, that severely delayed readers would be able to use this strategy only with letter-sound associations they knew. This is because the technique described earlier called "consonant substitution" must be employed (e.g., substituting the /f/ sound for the /l/ sound when *light* is changed to *fight*). All common consonant letter-sound associations would have to be known for the strategy to be most effective.

Some aspects of this program seem reminiscent of the Glass Analysis approach (Glass & Glass, 1978), although the latter approach was not a part of this research effort. The Glass Analysis method has at times been recommended for use with severely delayed readers because of its focus on frequently occurring word parts larger than single letters. It is believed to be a simpler avenue to decoding than some other conventional systems that involve smaller phonic elements and somewhat cumbersome phonics rules. This program is based on letter clusters that are for the most part phonograms (see Chapter 10 for a list of phonograms), although a few clusters represent other types of letter combinations.

Instruction begins with one cluster. A number of words containing the cluster are analyzed, centering first on letters that stand for certain sounds and then on sounds heard for certain letters (for the cluster *ing* the following might occur: "Here is the word *rings*. What letters make the /ing/ sound? What letter makes the /r/ sound? What letter makes the /s/ sound?" and conversely, "What sound does *ing* make? What sound does *r* make? What sound does *s* make?" Then other words containing the *ing* phonogram are analyzed in this same way). Although suggested by a number of authorities, currently there is no research available to confirm the actual effectiveness of the Glass Analysis method. Rather, Glass based the approach on his observations with children and believed it to be valuable when used with students who had chronic reading problems.

Self-Correction of Errors Based on Meaning.   Pflaum and Pascarella's (1980) work involved students with learning disabilities in the primary and intermediate grades as well as some of middle school age. These were students who were reading 3 years below their actual grade levels despite normal intelligence. Learners were taught procedures aimed at inducing self-correction of oral reading errors based on meaning of passages read. In 24 lessons, students did the following:

1. First, they listened to tape recordings of another reader and underlined oral reading errors—first in lists of sentences, then in paragraphs, and then in stories.
2. They listened to their own taped readings and did the same.
3. They underlined errors made by another recorded reader, underlining twice when the errors changed the intended meaning, underlining once when they did not.
4. They did the same with their own taped readings.
5. Next, the focus moved from simply noting errors to self-correction. To introduce this, students marked with a small *c* those errors that were corrected by a recorded reader.
6. Some attention was given to using letter cues plus context to correct errors.
7. Learners corrected the errors made by a recorded reader, using the sense of the passage.
8. In paired learning situations, students worked together to correct errors on a worksheet prepared by the teacher.
9. Students recorded and analyzed their own reading. They stopped the tapes when they heard a miscue and corrected it.

Students receiving this instruction were contrasted with another group who were given phonics instruction in which they were taught individual sounds of letters and how to blend these sounds together to decode words.

The self-correction instructional procedures used with the first group represent a fine example of systematic, carefully sequenced, intensive instruction. And they worked—for students whose reading levels were second grade and above. For that group of students, posttest scores on word recognition and comprehension were significantly higher for students taught to self-correct than for students receiving the phonics instruction. However, for the students reading below second-grade level, the phonics group scored higher. This points again to the fact that the reader's level of word learning must be taken into account. What is most constructive instruction for students in earliest stages may not be for those in later stages—and vice versa. This is true although all the students may be deemed as severely reading disabled, each having a significant delay between his or her own expected achievement and actual attainment. One can assume that there may be differences in what is appropriate as instructional techniques for a seventh-grader reading at fourth-grade level, for example, and a fourth grader reading at first-grade level, although both have a 3-year lag in learning.

Certain investigations have been concerned with older learners, *middle-school, high-school, and adult severely disabled readers.*

Programming Based on Psycholinguistic Principles.   While some of the subjects in Pflaum and Pascarella's group study (1980, described above) were of middle school age, Eldridge (1985) focused on one middle school student, providing an in-depth case study of instruction and learning of a severely delayed reader in seventh grade. The student was of average intelligence but with a seriously restricted word recognition vocabulary; he was reading at about first-reader level, able to use materials customarily read by children near the end of first grade. This student had received instruction in learning disability classes since first grade with obviously limited success, and the school had concluded that he was "unable" to learn.

Eldridge's plan was to modify the instruction the boy had previously received by basing lessons on psycholinguistic theories of reading. **Psycholinguistic processes** are those that combine thinking processes with language knowledge. In the reading field, approaches based on psycholinguistic research emphasize meaning as a means and an end to reading and generally advocate instruction based on a whole language orientation. (The term *psycholinguistic* is used differently by educators in special education, where it once referred to training involving body management and perceptual activities—radically different instruction from that used by Eldridge.)

Eldridge's program consisted of (a) emphasizing the axiom that reading should make sense (and stressing the correction of errors based on meaning); (b) demonstrating to the reader that he could combine several sources of information to read—visual and orthographic cues (including the spelling of the word), semantic clues (meaning), and syntactic cues (sentence structure); and (c) ensuring that the boy read copious amounts of connected text material at his instructional level, carried out orally in the early stages. Eldridge also provided one-to-one instruction for 2 hours per day.

Some specifics of Eldridge's program in the early stages of the lessons included (a) use of a language experience approach, having the student dictate and read his own stories, and while reading, finger-point to individual words; (b) when difficulties arose, the teacher reading sentences followed by the student reading (sometimes called *echo reading*); (c) words targeted for learning based on those in the student's stories; (d) words always practiced in the context of stories or sentences, never in isolation; (e) the student writing out copies of his dictated sentences; (f) many rereadings of the same story, with the student being prompted to use various strategies with unknown words or sometimes simply told the word.

All these tactics together gave the student many exposures to the same sets of words. Stanovich (1986) and others have provided evidence that frequent exposures positively affects word recognition accuracy and latency. (A **latent period** in psychological research refers to the interval between a stimulus and a response; in plain language, *latency* simply means how quickly the reader recognizes a word after it is seen. If a student must pause and study before recalling a word, the period of latency is likely longer than desired. A shorter period is the goal—i.e., the ultimate objective is automatic word recognition.)

Later, Eldridge used "integrated" stories. Words from the student's dictations were written into new stories by the teacher and read by the boy. Eldridge's goal in doing this was to give the student repeated encounters with the words in a variety of contexts; this also precluded the student's simply memorizing his own dictated stories, and thus making it appear that the student had attained word recognition when he had not. Writing continued to be emphasized throughout the program, permitting the student to focus on distinctive features of words.

Fluency was promoted through rereading of the same stories, and as well as with timed one-minute readings of short passages, where the aim was rapid recognition of words. (See a description of timed repeated readings given below.) Eldridge noted that automatic recognition of words was fostered in these ways.

At the next stage, the student read commercially prepared stories, which were introduced when he had gained enough sight vocabulary from working with his own stories to use published materials. Over the 3-year period during which Eldridge worked with him, the student eventually progressed to reading short novels at his increasingly higher instructional levels. When these "chapter books" were first introduced, shared reading was employed—the student read some and the teacher read some, each taking turns throughout the lesson. Eldridge also had a rule of thumb called the 50-page limit; the student had to stick with the novel for 50 pages, then if he did not like it, a new novel was selected. Gradually expanded amounts of silent reading were included in the sessions.

At the end of the 3-year program, this severely delayed reader attained scores on an informal reading inventory indicating a word recognition level of 6.5; scores on a standardized test were equivalent to a fifth-grade level.

This was an excellent success story for a reader who previously had profound difficulties. No doubt, the amount of instruction available to him—2 hours per day of one-to-one instruction—was an influential factor. However, quality of instruction is also a crucial ingredient in learning. The procedures employed by Eldridge were sound and would be recommended by most contemporary reading educators. What occurred through the instruction indisputably affected this student's life in positive ways. The school had believed this boy was destined to be an adult "functional nonreader"; after this instructional experience, that no longer would be the case. And he had shown clear evidence that he was "able" to learn.

Still, after 3 years of instruction, this student would have been a tenth-grader and therefore a reading level of fifth or sixth grade continued to represent a severe lag between potential and achievement. Had he persevered with the program beyond the 3-year period, that may have resolved the difference. However, one also wonders if explicit instruction with sound-symbol correspondences would have hastened his learning. Given new information on the criticality of phonemic associations for adequate reading, it seems reasonable that such phonics instruction would have been a fruitful addition to the tutoring.

Teaching Functional Reading Skills.   Joynes, McCormick, and Heward (1980) taught high school students with severe reading delays a functional reading skill—how to read and complete job applications. Using explicit teaching procedures involving matching, recognizing, reading, and writing, students learned word identification and word meanings. The steps of this instructional procedure are described in the following chapter, Chapter 15, in the section on functional literacy.

Their study showed positive results with students who had serious reading delays, indicating that they could learn to read and write items to meet an important real-world requirement. It did not, however, investigate instruction of broader literacy development.

Instruction With Adult Severely Delayed Readers.   Bruner (1983), Watson (1982), and C. Meyer (1982) all targeted adult severely disabled readers in their research. Bruner reported step-by-step procedures of a technique that aided word identification for a 43-year-old man who had a critical sound-symbol decoding deficit; explicit instruction of letter-sound correspondences and their uses in word identification, as described in Chapter 10, were employed.

A 21-year-old intelligent college student with a severe reading handicap was the subject of Watson's (1982) work. Learning events and tenets of instruction were similar to those described above in Eldridge's program, with Watson designating this as instruction based on whole language principles. After 10 months of one-on-one instruction with reading and writing activities, the student showed improvement.

Adults reading at an elementary school level were aided in C. Meyer's study (1982) by a technique she called Prime-O-Tec, an adaptation of the neurological impress method (the neurological impress method is described in a later section of this chapter); Prime-o-Tec produced significant gains in vocabulary recognition and in comprehension over gains made by a control group of adults not receiving this instruction.

Even with adults, stages of learning must be considered. Types of miscues made by severely delayed adult learners have been shown to vary with the degree of reading development—with major differences seen in error types between those adults who read at or above third- to fourth-grade levels and those who read below these levels (C. A. Norman & Malicky, 1987).

Instructional Suggestions for Developing Word Recognition Fluency

Word-by-word reading is a normal behavior in beginning reading. Average readers usually progress through four stages.

Stage 1: Initial reading sounds quite fluent, but students make many miscues and are seemingly unaware or unconcerned that their reading does not accurately represent the written text.

Stage 2: Students become conscious of matching their speech responses to words in the text and, therefore, begin to point to individual words and read in a staccato fashion.

Stage 3: Finger-pointing disappears but word-by-word reading continues as students consciously match their oral responses to each word.

Stage 4: Word-by-word reading disappears as students read in meaningful phrase units (Clay, 1967).

Only when students remain at the second or third stage of this sequence without advancing to the fourth does their nonfluent reading become a concern.

Because of the inordinate difficulties severely delayed readers have had with initial word learning, they may stay locked in Stages 2 and 3 when it no longer is necessary. Excessively slow and halting oral or silent reading limits the amount of reading that can be accomplished. Thus, the interest with fluency in relation to severely delayed readers is not one of concern for "good expression" or with reading to perform for others in such a way that the rendition "communicates" well. The point of fluency training is that the students' reading not be so plodding and laborious that they do not wish to read or that they are unable to cover much text because of their ingrained—but no longer necessary—nonfluent style. Automaticity in word reading also frees attention for comprehension.

The first consideration when dealing with nonfluent reading is to ensure that students are not being required to read materials at levels too difficult for them. If the learner encounters an undue number of unknown words in a passage, then slow and halting reading is to be expected. This is an altogether different problem. Word recognition must be accurate before it can become automatic.

Repeated Readings.   When suitable texts are used but a student's reading is still abnormally nonfluent, the method of repeated readings has been suggested. Timed and graphed readings of short selections have enjoyed widespread use since their applications were outlined by Samuels (1979). Rather than reading a new selection at each lesson, Samuels advocated **repeated oral readings** of the same selection until a criterion had been reached for words read per minute. With exceptionally nonfluent readers,

Samuels advised establishing the criterion at 85 words per minute. When that criterion is reached, a new passage is introduced. A half a dozen or so repeated readings of a selection is typical for students early on, but fewer readings are needed as more practice takes place. When fluency increases, a higher criterion level may be established.

While improved fluency is the primary objective for engaging in repeated readings, some positive side effects occur. Routinely, because many exposures to the same words are afforded, word recognition accuracy escalates. And, as well, comprehension of the passage typically improves with each rereading, probably because (a) word recognition becomes automatic and thus attention can be directed to meaning and (b) rereading the same passage allows opportunity to glean many ideas that might be missed in a single reading of the material. To emphasize reading as a meaning-gathering process, as well as stressing fluency, teachers often graph the reader's progress both for rate of reading and for comprehension. (See Figure 14–2.)

FIGURE 14–2

Sample graphs showing rate and comprehension for 14 lessons

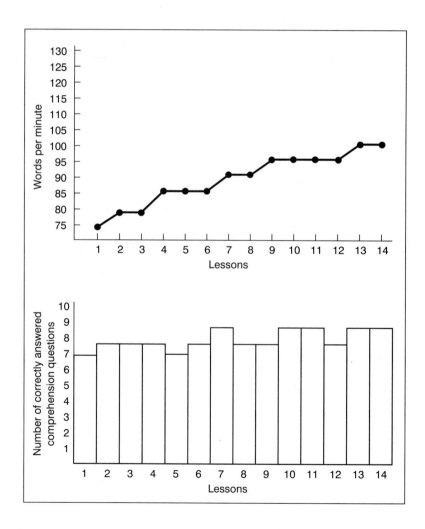

The Neurological Impress Method.   Developed by Heckleman (1966), the **neurological impress method,** or NIM, is a technique in which the teacher and student simultaneously read aloud from the same material. The student selects a book of interest from several the teacher has determined to be at an appropriate reading level. As the teacher and student read orally together, the teacher slides a finger under each line to center attention on the words being read—and to keep both readers at the same place. At first, the teacher reads *slightly* faster than the learner, just fast enough to move the student along at a reasonable pace. After the beginning stages, and when the student has demonstrated increased fluency, the student assumes the responsibility of sweeping a finger under the words being read and the teacher does not attempt to read at a faster rate. If the student misses a word, no attempt is made to use word identification strategies; instead, the teacher, who *has* read the word correctly, just keeps the student moving along by continuing to read.

NIM is a supplementary technique that requires no more than 15 minutes per session. This method has been used successfully with older as well as younger severely delayed readers. As can be seen, the program is not suitable for nonreaders since students must have at least a small sight vocabulary to read with the teacher in this fashion.

Heckleman has contended that NIM is effective because memory traces are strengthened from the procedure. With this technique, the student practices making quick response to words he or she knows. The student also receives immediate feedback on words about which he or she is not sure by hearing the teacher's reading. Moreover, the student processes a great deal of regular, connected reading material, more than might be the case if left to his or her usual inflexibly slow reading pace.

Nonreaders

Nonreaders are individuals who are unable to read any connected text. Despite normal intelligence, lack of sensory deficits, absence of obvious neurological defects—and much reading instruction–they have not learned to read.

Taken literally, the description *nonreader* would suggest that the individual can recognize no words. In some cases, however, by the time the student has been referred to a remedial program he or she has learned a word or two or even a few—but, not many. Students with extreme delays may recognize their own names, or a word or so they have picked up because of its frequent occurrence in their environment, such as *Boys* or *Girls* on restroom doors. As a result of instruction, some nonreaders may have spotty knowledge of several words typically taught in beginning reading programs, such as color words or a few function words from a high-frequency word list or a couple of words learned from a preprimer. However, recognition is occasional and recall is sporadic.

Experience has shown that the number of words known by a nonreader may range from about 2 to 50; however, because nonreaders know so few words and because of the nature of the words they do know, the words cannot be combined into any kind of meaningful reading. Take the case of Peter, an 8-year-old boy with a measured intelligence of 116 and a superior oral language vocabulary. Peter could distinguish 4 written words when he was enrolled in a university reading clinic during the summer after his second-grade year; in spite of 2 years of schooling, and above-average intelligence, the only words he knew were *I, a, and,* and *but.* Thomas, an 8-year-old, third-grader with a high average IQ of 107, recognized more words, 21, but most were function words such as *at, the, no, has, to, a, it, is, as,* and *in.* He had managed to learn these 21 with great effort over a 2½ year period of time, perhaps because of their frequent appearance in early reading lessons. In neither student's case, however, could the known words result in the reading of any kind of meaningful text, even simple sentences.

The term *nonreader* should be distinguished from the term *prereader.* **Prereaders** are individuals who cannot read, simply because they have not yet been exposed to reading instruction; for example, many 5-year-olds are prereaders. A nonreader, on the other hand, has had reasonably extensive instruction and still is unable to read in any meaningful sense. Older individuals who are often labeled as illiterates are sometimes nonreaders, but in other cases are really prereaders; that is, they do not read because they have not had the opportunity to learn. (The term *preliterate* is sometimes used synonymously with the designation *prereader,* especially if referring to an adult.)

Nonreaders also should be differentiated from students like Bridget and Dan, our case study students in earlier chapters. Bridget and Dan each had gotten off to a slow start in first-grade, and early intervention was instituted to prevent successively larger gaps in their reading growth. Nonreaders have had a good deal more instruction than the case study students. The description *nonreader* is not applied unless a student has had a minimum of one full year of instruction with virtually no reading development seen.

A typical route for nonreaders is a move to a remedial reading program after no increases in learning occur despite substantial assistance in their regular classroom work. When other students in the remedial reading class progress and the nonreader does not, he or she may be tested to assess eligibility for a learning disabilities program. With the continued lack of advancement after a year or so in an LD class, if a reading clinic is available, the student may be referred there. After much attention by a number of educators, the student still arrives at this clinic unable to read at all. Conversations with previous teachers who have worked with a nonreader generally uncover a variety of futile programming attempts to resolve the student's problems. The nonreader's difficulties seem highly resistant to instruction.

Can these students be helped? We are slowly learning more about how to set the learning environment for nonreaders in such a manner that they can learn to read. Special care must be taken to provide word study in ways that are appropriate to the students' stage of development and that takes into account the resistant behavior they may exhibit toward typical instruction. Furthermore, motivational factors must be considered. Because of recurring failures, many nonreaders cease to try. Not only may there be lack of task persistence (Friedman & Medway, 1987), but these students may simply refuse to engage in reading-related activities at all. All these factors should be considered in the design of early phases of programs for nonreaders to ensure positive outcomes.

Research concerned with nonreaders has most often been directed to issues of causation (for example, attempts to determine if visual perception aberrations are impeding their word learning or if brain malformations are the source of their problems—the latter usually assessed during autopsies, and therefore, a little late to do anything about it!) or to describing their learning characteristics (for instance, assessing their speed in naming letters or ability to read nonwords in comparison with the aptitudes of more competent readers). This is *not* to say that exploring causes for the nonreading enigma or the response behaviors of these individuals is without worth. At some time, these studies taken together may provide clues that will allow preventive efforts or that may suggest ways in which instruction should be structured. In the meantime, however, teachers need information on how to teach those who seem "unteachable." Sadly, *instructional* studies are exceedingly scarce—that is, research examining what does and what does not facilitate learning for nonreaders.

The Multiple-Exposure/Multiple-Context Strategy

Among the small amount of instructional research available on nonreaders are two studies investigating the Multiple-Exposure/Multiple-Context (M-E/M-C) Strategy (McCormick, 1991, 1994). In both, use of this program had positive results with nonreaders. The M-E/M-C Strategy consists of the following interventions:

1. A high-interest, easy-to-read book *series* is used for instruction, a series in which the easiest book is written at a simple preprimer level. Typically these books consist of a single short story divided into five or six small chapters. The same major characters often appear throughout the series, having different adventures in each succeeding book. Such series are intended for remedial work and although written at easy levels with new words introduced at a moderate pace, they focus on topics designed to appeal to somewhat older learners. A series of this type is used because stories intentionally repeat words from earlier books. Thus, when a student has completed one small book, he or she may move to the next and there find familiar words learned in previous stories in the series. This is preferable to using a number of different unrelated books in early stages of instruction with nonreaders. A very moderate rate of word introduction and many opportunities to review the same words is necessary for initial instruction with nonreaders.

2. The first chapter in the easiest book is used for a pretest. The student reads the chapter as best he or she can and the teacher records words that are unknown. To allay student anxiety, the teacher simply says "Don't worry about words you miss. I'll teach those to you later."

    Even a nonreader may know a few of the words (perhaps *I, a,* and one or two more). Each chapter at the easiest level in this type of series is notably short,

In the M-E/M-C Strategy, the first chapter of the book is read as a pretest.

with approximately 5 pages per chapter and 1 or 2 brief sentences per page. Chapters also are written so that only 10 or so different words are used. Therefore, even if the student does not know most of these, the number of unknown words that the student needs to learn is in an acceptable range.

3.   The teacher's task for the next several sessions is to teach the unknown words from the first chapter. Because the targeted words are tied directly to the book, once the student learns these words, he or she is able to successfully read a selection of connected text—a first-time occurrence in the life of a nonreader.

Word recognition is accomplished through providing students with *multiple exposures* to the words, but using techniques other than drill. Rather, the words are presented in *multiple contexts*. Although nonreaders require many occasions for practice, flashing word cards at them 40 or 50 times is not the path to learning.

Three major categories of practice are used to study words:

a. *Contextual activities.* Practice of words in context is undertaken to boost generalization from recognition of individual words to recognition of these in connected text. Practicing words in context is difficult in earliest stages since students know so few words, but simple sentences usually can be written by combining unknown words from the chapter and the few words the learner already knows, including, perhaps, his or her own name. Cooperative stories, as seen in Figure 14–3, are useful also; to use cooperative stories, the teacher reads most of the text and the student reads only the boxed material, which includes his or her practice words and known words. As more words are learned over time, contextual practice involves increasingly larger pieces of text, moving to paragraphs and short stories written by the teacher.

b. *Practice that focuses on the internal features of words.* This consists of writing, spelling, manipulating letters to form words, tracing words, and other activities that encourage attention to the orthographic elements of words.

c. *Use of games and manipulatives.* These are used to provide a stress-free form of practice and to motivate discouraged learners to expend maximum effort. Some of these activities offer contextual practice, but more afford exposures to words in context-free situations (i.e., in isolation).

A list of word practice activities is given in Table 9-1 in Chapter 9; these activities and word practice experiences similar to them are used in the M-E/M-C Strategy.

During the several days when unknown words from the first chapter are practiced, the lessons focus only on that small set of words (never more than 10). An attempt is made to include all three practice types at least once in each session (contextual practice; attention to the internal features of the words; use of games and manipulatives). Thus, the student has repeated practice with the words but in a variety of ways, each of which is designed to satisfy specific goals. Changing activities frequently throughout the lesson also maintains attention. Because of nonreaders' all too frequent reluctance to participate in any reading activities, capturing interest is important in the early lessons. This reluctance, born from previous failure, lessens when successes begin to occur. Moreover, identification of distinctive features of words under a variety of stimulus conditions has another advantage: transfer of learning is strengthened. It is more likely that a learner will recognize the word in another context than if all learning had been limited to one form of exposure (e.g., seeing the word many times on a flashcard).

A vital feature related to word study is the *visual demonstration of progress.* Throughout sessions, the student is helped to realize that gains in learning are

FIGURE 14–3

Sample of a cooperative story

Larry was running to Dan's house. Dan lived in a neighborhood where all the houses looked the same. Larry was in a hurry and wasn't thinking very carefully. As he scooted up to the gate in front of one house, he paused for a moment and said to himself:

- This is Dan's house.

Larry rushed through the gate, up onto the porch, and pushed the doorbell. When a woman appeared he did not recognize her, but thought maybe she was Dan's aunt. Larry wasn't sure, though, so he said:

- Is this Dan's house?

The unfamiliar woman said, "No. Dan lives next door." Down the steps and out the gate Larry ran, then into the next yard and up onto that porch. Another unfamiliar woman was sitting right on this porch, in the porch swing. Larry asked again:

- Is this Dan's house?

"Right!" said the woman. "Do you want me to call him?" "Yes," replied Larry.
"Dan!" the woman called. And in a moment or two a tall, baldheaded man with large muscles and a beard appeared. "Who are you?" asked Larry politely. "I was looking for Dan." The woman responded by saying:

- This is Dan.

Flustered, Larry sputtered, "Dan is a guy who plays softball with me." The baldheaded man laughed. He said:

- I work.

He went on to say, "I think you have the wrong house and the wrong Dan." But the woman quickly added with a smile and a twinkle in her eyes:

- This Dan plays, too.

She asked Larry, "Would you like to take him to your softball game instead of your friend?" Larry looked at the tall man with his large muscles and thought how neat it would be to have *him* on their team. They'd probably win every game. "Wish I could," said Larry, also with a twinkle in *his* eyes, "but the other team would never allow it. Guess I'd better find the right house and the right

- Dan .

occurring. Simply telling a nonreader that "You are doing well" is not a potent indicator to these students who never before have "done well." Being intelligent individuals, they are aware of their deficiencies when they compare themselves to peers. A verbal pat on the back in the form of statements, such as "You are doing a good job," simply may not be believed. Therefore, progress charts and graphs, the counting of newly learned words, and the like, are used abundantly. By self-charting the number of words known from one day to the next, a student can see that headway is being made. If the known words in a word bank are counted every day, the increase in number is plainly discernible to the student. Motivational incentives are considered critical in the M-E/M-C strategy and should not be overlooked.

In addition to word practice, one other element is included each day. The teacher reads aloud to the nonreader to provide exposure to real narratives or expository selections at a time when these students cannot yet access connected text themselves. A standard one-hour lesson may encompass 10 minutes of the teacher's reading aloud from a well-known book of children's or adolescent literature and 50 minutes of varied word practice. Figure 14–4 depicts three successive days of lessons with one nonreader when the M-E/M-C Strategy was inaugurated with her.

Following the plan outlined above, on the average, a nonreader learns the small set of words from the first chapter of a book in about 3 to 5 hour-long sessions. When words are known, the student returns to the chapter, reading it again, this time successfully! Early on, emphasis is placed on learning the words well before returning to the book to reread in order to demonstrate to the student that he or she can indeed learn to read. The effective chapter reading does just that. Although strong emphasis on word study is necessary to launch the reading effort, this method also allows a relatively quick return to connected text reading in comparison with some alternate approaches to teaching nonreaders.

4.   The second chapter of the book is approached in the same way—pretesting the words by a contextual reading of them, practicing the words repeatedly but in a variety of ways (some of which are highly appealing to disinclined readers), and rereading the chapter triumphantly when words are known. Each chapter of the first book is completed in this way.

5.   When all chapters in the book have been undertaken in this manner, the student rereads the entire book in one sitting. This is the first time a nonreader has conquered an entire book, and is a red-letter day!

6.   At this point the student is ready to move to the next book in the series. By this time, the student knows a reasonably sized corpus of words, which is composed of a variety of types (nouns and verbs, as well as function words, for example). Contextual practice activities have expanded and have begun to look very much like natural text. Rate of word learning accelerates as students proceed through the chapters of the books and fewer practice sessions are needed before returning to read the chapter. Furthermore, the student typically shows a will to try and exhibits less avoidance behavior.

7.   As the learner moves through the series, there comes a time when it is apparent that the strong support system of the M-E/M-C Strategy is no longer needed. The student is then moved into a more typical reading program with attention to sound-symbol correspondences, ample amounts of connected text reading every day, and instruction to meet other assessed needs.

FIGURE 14–4
Three M-E/M-C sessions

<u>Session 1 for Kerry</u>

<u>9:00-9:05</u> – Talk with Kerry about the events of her weekend.

<u>9:05-9:15</u> – Work on Kerry's 7 targeted words: (<u>house, this, Dan, work,
too, plays, is</u>). I have made flashcards with these words. For the 4
words that can be illustrated, I drew a picture for the word on one
side and put the word only on the other side:

(front)   (back)

The other 3 words will have no picture. To give success experiences I
included in the flashcard pack the 3 words Kerry already knows (<u>a,
and, I</u>). To provide a strong support system to introduce these words
we'll do the following:

<u>First</u> – She'll read the word (using the picture if one accompanies
it). I'll pronounce those without pictures and use each one
in a sentence before <u>she</u> reads it.
– She'll trace the word.
– She'll read the word again.
– She'll use each one in an oral sentence.

<u>Second</u> – I'll scramble the word cards.
– She'll read them all again.
– When she cannot, I'll pronounce those words and have her
trace again. I'll point out important features of the word
and have her say it once more.

<u>Third</u> – We'll go through the second step again; this time <u>one</u> of the
pictures will be turned over so she must read the word
without help from the picture.

<u>Fourth, Fifth, Sixth</u> – Same as step 2, but each time we'll turn over
one more of the picture words.

<u>9:15-9:25</u> – Continue practice on her targeted words: I have made a game
board with a track. The words are written on file cards. Correct
responses will allow Kerry to move along squares to the final goal.

<u>9:25-9:35</u> – I will read <u>to</u> Kerry: <u>Amigo</u> by Byrd Baylor (rdg. level = approx. 3.5).

<u>9:35-9:40</u> – I have written short sentences with Kerry's words. Examples:
Dan plays.
Dan and I work, too.
She will read these to me orally.

<u>9:40-9:50</u> – Kerry will play Word Bingo using her words and a blank bingo
board I have made. I will lay file cards with the words on the blanks.
Since she doesn't have enough words to cover all squares, some words
will appear more than once. I will call the words and she will cover them
with pennies.

<u>9:50-10:00</u> – End-of-session check:
1) Using words written on index cards, I will check Kerry's recognition
of the words at the end of this session.
2) Words she knows instantly will be placed on a word bank ring.
She will help me do this. We will count the number she has on the ring
today and talk briefly about trying to add more the next day.

FIGURE 14–4 *(continued)*

<u>Session 2 for Kerry</u>

<u>9:00-9:05</u> – We will talk about Kerry's success in the last session in getting some words on her word bank ring. For a beginning-of-the-session review I will have Kerry read the words already on the ring. I will show her two games I have made for word practice today and ask her to choose which game we play first. Game #1 = "Grand Slam;" Game #2 = "Rotten Apple."

<u>9:05-9:15</u> – We will play the game Kerry chooses to use first.

<u>9:15-9:20</u> – I have written a "cooperative" story which both Kerry and I will read. I will read most of it, but I have interspersed her words in brief sentences throughout. She will read these.

<u>9:20-9:30</u> – We will play the other game specified above.

<u>9:30-9:40</u> – I will read <u>to</u> Kerry <u>Once A Mouse</u> by Marcia Brown (rdg. level = approx. 3.0).

<u>9:40-9:50</u> – Play Word Hunt. I will write her words on red construction paper rectangles the size of a small file card. Before class I will hide these around the clinic materials room. Kerry will look around the room and find her word slips (I used red so finding them would be easy). As she finds each one she will bring it to me and READ it.

<u>9:50-10:00</u> – End-of-session check:
1) Using flashcards I will check her recognition of the words.
2) She will assist in adding those she recognized instantly to her word bank ring.
3) We will <u>count</u> these and make goals to add more tomorrow.

One study conducted with the M-E/M-C Strategy (McCormick, 1994) examined the learning of Peter, introduced on p. 473, who could read only 4 words after completing second grade. Peter's mother understood the importance of emergent literacy activities in the years before he came to school; as a result, experiences with hearing stories read, trips to the library, and the like had been an important part of his formative years. The usual good effects of these activities were not realized with Peter if measured in terms of his reading attainment—in his first 2 years of school he attained no reading competence at all. After experiences with a basal reading program, a language experience approach, an intensive phonics procedure, and the Fernald Method (described below) carried out by a classroom teacher, an LD tutor, and two reading clinicians—all to no avail, the M-E/M-C Strategy was tried as the frame for his instruction. Learning commenced quickly, and by the end of 16 weeks (56 hours) of one-to-one instruction, he had learned 170 words and was reading material at a second-grade level.

At that point, Peter's program was modified to one that is more standard in remedial instruction, and a follow-up study was undertaken to monitor his progress. The heavy emphasis on word recognition early on did not have adverse effects, but rather allowed him to learn. Peter had excellent comprehension throughout his participation in the clinic, learned decoding strategies, and eventually read with fluency. He read a large variety of narrative and expository materials, developing interest in different genres and topics as time went by. Peter participated in the clinic program for 3½ years in all, including the early period during which instruction was not effective, the time of the M-E/M-C Strategy application, and the follow-up period. He was "graduated" from the program at age 12, reading at a seventh-grade level.

FIGURE 14–4 *(continued)*

<u>Session 3 for Kerry</u>

<u>9:00–9:10</u> – I will read aloud to her <u>Frederick</u> by Leo Lionni (rdg.
level = approx. 3.0–3.5). Afterward I'll have Kerry compare
Frederick, the mouse, and the mouse in Marcia Brown's story I
read to her yesterday. How were they alike? How were they different?

<u>9:10–9:15</u> – For a beginning-of-the-session review Kerry will read the
words on her word bank ring to me. Yesterday all of her remaining
words were added except <u>this.</u> I think that after today's session of
word practice she will be ready to reread the first chapter of the
book tomorrow. Yesterday she even knew the word <u>this</u> after some
hesitation and a self-correction. Although she did <u>correctly</u> read all
of the other words when I checked her at the end of the period, there
was also a hesitation on a couple of these. I thought one more day of
practice on all of them was wise to be sure she really knows them so
she'll have a success experience with the book tomorrow.

<u>9:15–9:25</u> – Special work on the word <u>this</u>:
1) I will show the word on a flashcard and say it.
2) She will read it, trace it, and say it again.
3) We will compare <u>this</u> and <u>is</u> on 2 flashcards since she has often
   confused <u>this</u> with <u>is</u>. We will talk about differences in how the
   words look and she will use each one in an oral sentence.
4) I will give her sentences to read in which both <u>this</u> and <u>is</u> appear.
   The sentences will use her targeted words and sometimes
   pictures. Examples:

Is this Dan?

This is a house.

Is this a 🐱?

<u>9:25–9:35</u> – Practice with <u>all</u> words in her set: Since we have read about
mice for the last 2 days we will have a "mouse" game. In this game,
cloze sentence strips will be used. Kerry must say the correct word
that will fit into the context of the sentence, then match this word
with the correct one written on a construction paper mouse. Correct
responses allow these mice to move across a game board to a large
piece of cheese.

<u>9:35–9:45</u> – Special practice with the word <u>this</u>: Manipulate letters on
a magnet board. The purpose of this activity is to highlight the features
that distinguish <u>this</u> and <u>is.</u> After deciding which of these fits into
each of several cloze sentences I show her, she will spell it on the
magnet board.

<u>9:45–9:55</u> – Work with <u>all</u> of her words: Puzzle Activity. I have written
the words on puzzle pieces I made. She will read each word; when it
is read correctly she will fit it together with other pieces to form an
animal (a camel). After she identifies the animal, I will tell her that
tomorrow I'm going to read her a book called <u>The Camel Who Took A
Walk</u>.

<u>9:55–10:00</u> – End-of-session-check: Hopefully the word <u>this</u> can be added
to her word bank ring. To check for this I will lay out cards on the desk
with all her words on them. The word <u>this</u> will be placed somewhere
in the middle. I'll ask her to quickly read over them all.

Another research investigation with the M-E/M-C Strategy (McCormick, 1991) was undertaken with Thomas (p. 473), who before beginning the program recognized 21 function words (plus his first name, but not his last). Thomas, like Peter, came from a home where he enjoyed preschool years rich with books. He showed clear abilities in mathematics computation and logic, and although his speech development had been delayed, after its onset he had acquired a broad expressive vocabulary. Thomas also had several experiences with different methods of reading instruction, each instituted when he had not responded favorably to a previous one. In an early one, Thomas had opportunities for writing experiences, but he was not yet able to recognize or write most letters and was unable to profit from these opportunities to any productive degree. By the time he enrolled in a reading clinic, he did have control over letter recognition, but he scored below first preprimer level on an informal reading inventory (IRI), unable to read the easiest first-grade material, although he was in the middle of third grade.

While being instructed with the M-E/M-C Strategy, he completed a preprimer and primer-level book and learned automatic recognition of 90 words over a period of 11 weeks. Tests of word recognition in isolation and in context administered one month after the intervention had been terminated showed he had maintained knowledge of words he had learned. After approximately 10 additional months of clinical work, he progressed to third-grade reading before his mother removed him from the program. Five months later his parent reported that he had continued to progress.

The Fernald Approach

Probably the best-known clinical procedure for nonreaders is an approach developed in 1921 by Grace Fernald and Helen B. Keller, known as the Fernald Method. The method is carried out in four stages that employ the visual, auditory, kinesthetic, and tactile senses (from which come the acronym VAKT, which is also used to describe the method). Since a number of senses are involved, it is often referred to as a multisensory approach. The Fernald Method uses the following four stages.

Stage 1: Tracing. The program is begun with whole words, not letters. Students choose a word to learn. This can be a short word, long word, easy word, or hard word. The teacher prints the word on a card and the students trace it. As they trace, they say the *sounds* of the word parts (this does not mean spelling the word letter by letter). The process is repeated until the students can write the word without looking at it. If they cannot do this, they are given the card again and must repeat the original process. When they are able to write the word from memory, it is typed and they read it in typed form. Finally, the word on the card is filed alphabetically in a box for later review. After a number of words have been accumulated, the student uses these to write a story. The story is immediately typed to be read. Instruction in Stage 1 may occur for a few days or several weeks before it appears that the student can learn without tracing and can be moved to Stage 2.

Stage 2: Writing. The teacher prints the word on a card, saying the parts as this is done. Students observe the process. The students are given the card, study the word, try to visualize it with their eyes closed, and silently "say" it to themselves. Next they write the word without looking at the card, saying the word parts as they do. If an error is made, they are given the card again to compare the error with the correct form. They continue to study, visualize, and say the word until they can write a story using this word and those previously learned. The story is typed, and the students immediately read it silently and then orally.

Stage 3: Recognition from print. The teacher no longer writes the word on a card. Instead, the students choose a word from a book, are told its pronunciation, study it, visualize it, "pronounce" it silently to themselves, and then write it from memory. If they cannot do this, they study and pronounce the word until they can. Reading in first preprimers begins during Stage 3.

Stage 4: Recognition without writing. In this stage, each new word is not written. Instead the students are taught to study new words and note their similarities to familiar words. Silent reading precedes oral reading. During oral reading, if students do not know a word, it is pronounced for them. After the reading, only these "problem" words are pronounced and written by the student.

Research on the Fernald Method has produced contradictory findings, with some studies not indicating favorable results with the use of the method. In other studies, however, this approach has helped nonreaders—when a variety of other procedures had proved unsuccessful (S. Bryant, 1979; Hulme, 1981). However, it is a method in which progress sometimes seems to be rather slow. For this reason, other instructional plans might be tried before the Fernald method is implemented.

One factor that may contribute to the Fernald Method's lack of success with some nonreaders is the limited interest they have in the learning activities. Some aspects do not capture the attention of students who have developed antagonistic attitudes toward reading; they become quickly bored with the repeated tracing and sounding and visualizing and copying from memory—having some difficulty seeing the point of these procedures. Although you may know that doing this can lead to word learning, they are skeptical and do not think this is going to help them read books. After a session or two, students may exhibit avoidance behaviors, seem reluctant to engage in the activities, and make only half-hearted attempts, limiting the amount of practice they obtain and the serious attention they give to the words. No participation—no learning.

Remember who you are working with here. These are students who have met roadblocks in their *every* attempt at reading. Day after day, week after week, month after month, maybe year after year, they have been frustrated in their efforts to do what others around them can do. While they may believe that nothing is going to make the difference, give a game to the same students who are bored with less involving activities and they will participate for the fun of it whether they think it will help their reading or not—and in the meantime a little learning sneaks in. Give the same students a manipulative (arranging magnetic letters on a magnet board, for example), and they will concentrate because they are actively engaged with a concrete operation. Creative teachers probably can modify the procedures in the Fernald Method to provide for the greater need to figure motivation into the learning equation for nonreaders.

Reading Mastery: DISTAR Reading

The Reading Mastery: DISTAR Reading program employs a grapheme-phoneme method based on a synthetic phonics approach. It has often been used in classes for students with learning disabilities and developmentally disabled students. In general, its use had been bypassed by remedial reading teachers because the procedures are viewed by some to be undesirably mechanistic. Still, research with DISTAR has routinely produced favorable results (e.g., Haring & Bateman, 1977; L. A. Meyer, 1984). It is unclear whether students in some of the research investigations of this program consisted of severely disabled readers in the more general sense with serious delays of varying degrees or consisted of nonreaders, but it appears likely both categories have been included in the groups studied. The first stage of the program assumes the student is not reading.

In the initial stages, students learn the sounds of 40 symbols. These include the lowercase letters, certain letter symbols designed by joining letters that are sounded together such as *ng,* and long vowel sounds with their diacritical marks. Silent letters appear in small type. (Later in the program a transition is made to more conventional forms of print.) After learning the sounds of these symbols, students sequence and blend them to form words. Still later, two- and three-word sentences are read. One of the first of these is

hē rēads.

Eventually the students progress to reading stories.

One advantage of the DISTAR program is that an ample amount of instructional time is provided: (a) daily lessons are considered a basic requirement; if students miss a day, they must have two lessons the next; (b) lessons last for 40 minutes—twice the length of sessions in many beginning programs; and (c) procedures are conducted to ensure that every student responds during every lesson. Another advantage is that there is immediate feedback to each student response.

There is also a disadvantage to the DISTAR program. Instruction is begun with the abstract task of learning the sounds that letters stand for, and students do not read words until they have mastered the sounds. For some students, this means that it is a long time before they are in contact with meaningful material.

The Orton-Gillingham Approach

In 1966, Gillingham and Stillman developed a program for working with seriously delayed readers based on theories about causes of reading disability advanced in the late 1920s by Samuel Orton. This is generally known as the Orton-Gillingham Approach. In 1976, Slingerland proposed certain adaptations to the program. The adapted program is referred to as the Gillingham-Slingerland Approach or the Orton-Slingerland Approach. If the programs are followed as outlined, students receive instruction 5 days a week for a 2-year period. Sessions are 1-hour in length and the activities are changed at least every 10 minutes. This latter is a plus with off-task students, keeping them involved and the lesson moving. A grapheme-phoneme orientation is employed and includes four basic steps:

1. Students trace single letters and then learn the sounds they commonly stand for. An extended period of time is spent on working with letters and letter-sound associations.
2. Students are taught to blend consonants and short vowels into words that have a consonant-vowel-consonant pattern. They blend the first two letters and then add the last: /ma/+/t/. Finally, they spell the word.
3. Sentences composed of the resulting words are read.
4. Phonetically irregular words are learned through tracing.

Though Orton's theories are no longer considered tenable, some aspects of this program are consistent with more recent research indicating the need for development of phonics understandings. The advantage of the Orton approaches is that students obtain explicit instruction with sound-symbol associations and help with blending these to read words. A principal disadvantage is the lack of opportunity for students to read meaningful, connected text until after they have mastered a large number of skills. On occasion, the basic forms of the programs have been modified by various educators to incorporate additional principles and procedures that vary, or add to, the fundamental models.

As with DISTAR, the precise characteristics of the populations in research studies on these approaches are somewhat vague, but the programs in the studies direct their instruction in the beginning to students who are not reading. Although these programs have been successful with some students, Ruppert's (1976) research showed that the Orton-Slingerland Approach produced no better reading achievement than a more flexible, eclectic method when used with students who had been classified as learning disabled.

Using Predictable Books

Predictable books have become a common vehicle for instruction with beginning readers, and research has shown favorable results in sight vocabulary learning when they have been used with poor readers with more moderate barriers to reading acquisition (Bridge, Winograd, & Haley, 1983). Their use has been recommended with nonreaders.

A number of elements can make a book "predictable," and a variety of types have come under this rubric. When language patterns in books are very repetitive, when there are cumulative structures (that employ, for example, the adding of new lines to old in a systematic way, as in *The House That Jack Built*), if there are sequential episodes, or if there is rhythmic and rhyming language, the books all may be designated as predictable (Slaughter, 1993). When a book, like the classic *Three Billy Goats Gruff* for instance, has sequential episodes in a plot in which events repeat themselves with only a little variation, this helps students to predict story lines, which is often an aid to comprehension. However, this does not assist nonreaders with their basic problem—severe difficulties with word recognition. Thus, when predictable books are recommended for use with seriously delayed readers, the type of predictable book is an important consideration.

Predictable books that may provide assistance with word learning are those with very repetitive language. An example is *Brown Bear, Brown Bear, What Do You See?* (Martin, 1970); an excerpt from this book was presented in Chapter 9, where you may notice the high degree to which the same words are consistently repeated. Routinely, after initial use of a predictable book with emerging readers, the book is read over again several times in a variety of ways. The frequent repetition of words in the text and the rereadings of the book may foster word learning because of recurrent exposures student have to a limited number of words.

The positive effects of highly repetitive predictable books have been seen with students whose word learning difficulties are less extreme. With nonreaders, however, there have not always been good results. Perhaps this is because despite serious reading delays, nonreaders are usually very bright individuals, individuals who have learned alternative strategies to survive in academic and real-world environments. They have mastered a good deal of information through listening. When the teacher reads a predictable book to a nonreader, with its easy-to-discover pattern of words, and the learner then "reads" it in unison with the teacher, and he or she then "reads" it with teacher assistance, and so on, soon, as a result of all these readings, the student is able to give an excellent rendition of the book. It appears that the student is indeed reading the text because he or she says all the words correctly—the performance is even fluent. Unfortunately, when the student later confronts the same words in another text, the words are not recognized at all. Clues to what has occurred can be seen in the cases in which non-readers have had "read and reread" experiences with a predictable book and then recite the book word for word with perfect accuracy—while the book is closed, or even when it is in another room! They have learned the exceptionally uniform book pattern through listening, not through attending to the written words.

Remember, nonreaders usually are in the logographic phase of word learning (sometimes called the selective-cue phase): they have not found productive ways of attending to word clues. Something more than rereading of easily memorized books is needed to establish word knowledge that is functional—word knowledge that can be *used* in real reading of other books.

Becker (1994) has developed a plan for working with nonreaders using pre-dictable books. The multiple rereading of stories is maintained to provide many contextual exposures to words—as well as experiences with connected text in the early phases of their learning—but between each reading, direct attention is given to recognition of specific words found in the book, both through isolated and in-context practice exercises. In addition, explicit focus on word clues is promoted (i.e., centering on clues within words, such as letter sequences). During introductory reading of a text, the non-reader is directed to the illustrations, but, in addition to 6 repeated oral readings of the actual book in a variety of ways over a 3-day period, chart-story versions of the book are used. To do so, the teacher reproduces the exact story on chart paper for the student to read without the aid of illustrations; this procedure is used after the learner has had several contextual and noncontextual exposures to the words.

Many activities are employed with the predictable book in Becker's plan—dis-cussing concepts, the author, illustrator, and title; making predictions before reading based on illustrations; the teacher reading the text while the student follows along; finger-pointing; checking predictions and asking questions; word games; shared reading; visual cloze activities; assisted reading; matching word cards to text; looking for repeated words in the text; using masks or frames to focus on orthographic sequences or on specific words or phrases; matching sentence strips to the text; silently reading along while listening to the story on tape; independent oral reading of the book; and innovating on the text by adding, deleting, or substituting words and phrases to produce new sentences on the chart story. Given the inordinate difficulties of nonreaders, this plan has greater promise for developing generalizable word knowledge than plans in which learning is expected to occur incidentally from numerous rereadings alone.

One carefully conducted in-depth case study has been undertaken using these procedures with a nonreader (Becker, 1994). The participant was a second-grader who at the beginning of the program recognized only 15 words, most of which were function words (e.g., prepositions and conjunctions). After instruction with 10 predictable books following this plan, at the end of 10 weeks, the student had automatic recognition of 75 words. The researcher reassessed the student's knowledge of these words after a lapse of 1 month during which no intervention occurred, finding that the student had main-tained recognition of 71.

A myriad of predictable books are now published commercially and are widely available. Even among books for which "predictability" is grounded in very repetitive language structures, there still are differences in difficulty. Becker (1994) has made a careful analysis of recommended predictable texts and proposes a sequence to inaugu-rate a program with nonreaders. The sequence begins with books that have the fewest number of *different* words and progresses to those that have slightly more. (A book, for example, might have 90 total words, but only 9 that are different from one another.)

The 10 predictable books to establish reading behaviors with nonreaders suggested by Becker, and used successfully in her study, are the following in this order (numerals in brackets indicate the number of different words in the book): (a) *Have You Seen My Duckling?* (Greenwillow) [8]; (b) *Have You Seen My Cat?* (Picture Book Studio) [9]; (c) *I Went Walking* (Harcourt Brace Jovanovich) [28]; (d) *The Cake That Mack Ate* (Joy Street Books) [30]; (e) *Brown Bear, Brown Bear, What Do You See?* (Holt) [32]; (f) *The Chick and the Duckling* (Macmillan) [32]; (g) *Where's Spot?* (G. P. Putnam Sons) [33]; (h) *10 Bears in My Bed* (Random House) [34]; (i) *Polar Bear, Polar Bear, What Do You Hear?* (Holt) [36]; (j) *Dear Zoo* (Four Winds Press) [42].

Other Instructional Possibilities

In addition to research, the professional literature also includes *suggestions* from educators for instructing nonreaders. Although no supporting research is offered to confirm the effectiveness of the approaches, they are usually based on direct experiences in working with nonreaders and are, for the most part, in conformance with current educational thinking.

Cunningham's Method. Cunningham (1988) suggests combining language immersion, explicit and targeted sight vocabulary teaching, and phonemic awareness training in a program for nonreaders.

Following Chomsky's (1976) suggestion, Cunningham recommends that a nonreader listen to a book the teacher has taped until he or she has learned it well. Repeated listening/reading procedures are often referred to as **language immersion programs,** that is, the student is immersed in large amounts of oral and written language. Chomsky worked with very poor readers who had beginning reading skills, but who had failed to progress beyond the introductory level. She had students follow along in books while they listened repeatedly to taped stories. The students engaged in multiple listenings of the same narrative until they became familiar enough with the words to read the story orally with ease. Most students required about 20 listenings before they could fluently read their first narrative; but, thereafter, they were able to read each successive book with facility after fewer and fewer listening sessions. Not only did fluency increase, students participating in this program acquired confidence and increased interest in reading. Chomsky reported that one parent said her daughter, who had previously avoided reading, had begun to read with great frequency at home and that "[s]he even reads to the dog and cat" (p. 291).

Cunningham (1988) recommends language immersion with nonreaders and further proposes extending this experience by giving the learners a blank tape on which they record any small portion they can read themselves as they progress from learning by listening to the teacher's version.

In addition, specific words are selected for instruction. These are taught to mastery, using a variety of techniques, so they can be identified independent of the book. Furthermore, when the number of words learned reaches 25, these are used as a basis for phonemic awareness exercises and later phonic analysis training. The phonics instruction begins with the teacher selecting two of the learned sight vocabulary to serve as key words to letter sounds, slowly adding more as student understanding of decoding principles grows. Phonograms and consonant substitution also are introduced and are based on words from the fund of known sight words.

After earliest stages of the program, some silent reading is encouraged with short selections of text, allowing the student to engage in "mumble reading." **Mumble read-**

A language immersion technique is to have students follow along in books while they listen repeatedly to taped stories.

ing consists of saying the words quietly; this serves as an intermediate phase between oral reading and true silent reading.

Cunningham's method is founded on the premises that one learns to read by opportunities to engage in reading of real texts and that word recognition and letter-sound associations are best taught by linking them with something that is already known.

An Adapted Language Experience Approach.   One standard reading method, the Language Experience Approach (LEA), has been useful with some *severely delayed* readers (Eldridge, 1985 [see above]; Stauffer, 1970). Stauffer (1970) reported that certain students enrolled in the university reading clinic with which he was associated made progress with LEA. However, this often has not been the case with nonreaders.

LEA, based on student-dictated stories, does not seem to provide the support needed by many of the most delayed learners. Nonreaders typically have *well-developed oral language skills*. Thus, the stories they dictate tend to be lengthy, interesting, and difficult to read. There are too many words. Even if the teacher structures a situation so the story is maintained to a shorter composition, there are not enough repetitions of individual words for the nonreader to learn, remember, and retain them. Rereadings of the stories produce easy memorization, but not true word learning in which the knowledge of words transfers to any other situations.

Adaptations of the typical LEA program may be useful for nonreaders, however. To develop a functional program, short selections must be used; students must continue to work with the same story until words are known, in contrast to frequent dictation of new stories; and direct practice with individual words is necessary. Providing a strong reinforcement program to motivate the students through the difficult early phases of the process also is recommended. Reinforcement can come about from visual demonstrations of progress and small appropriate awards when short-term goals are met. (See Figure 14–5).

FIGURE 14–5
A bar graph charting the number
of words known by a student

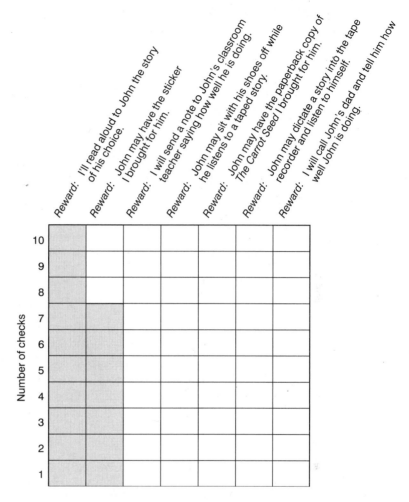

Other Concerns

There are certain specific teaching and learning problems that often occur with readers who are severely learning delayed, regardless of the general approach used. Suggestions for remediating these follow.

Letter Recognition. While not often a problem with older nonreaders, if students enter a program immediately after a year of first grade or even after a slightly more extended period of schooling, they may not yet have obtained accurate, not to say, automatic, recognition of all letters of the alphabet. The importance of this knowledge has been previously discussed. In summary, recent research indicates that "reading depends first and foremost on visual letter recognition" (M. J. Adams, 1990, p. 21). Large numbers of studies have shown that knowledge of letter names is the single best predictor of success in first-grade reading (see M. J. Adams, 1990; R. Johnson, 1969; Venezsky, 1975; Walsh, Price, & Gillingham, 1988). This is not to say that other factors are unimportant in the complex act of reading, of course; however, it is difficult for nonreaders to gain control of these other factors without letter recognition. The following descriptions of *f* and *g* suggest how cumbersome it would be to have to go through a student's instructional program referring to letters in ways other than by their names: "What sound does that upside-down candy cane with a line across it make?" or "Notice that this word begins with a ball with a tail."

But letter recognition is not easy. The task of letter recognition causes learners to grapple with a great many abstractions. For example, when learning the letter *r*, the student is expected to remember that a line like this |, and a line like this ⌒, placed together in just the right relationship (for example, not like this h or this ɿ), together have a name that people call by the nonsense sound "ar." And in addition, an "ar" has another form consisting of lines like these: | ⊃ \. And these lines also must be put together in just the right relationship, like this R, and not like this Я or like this ᴚ. And even though this looks different from the first letter, it's an "ar," too. Learning to attach nonsense names to lines and squiggles requires much abstract thinking and places a high demand on memory. Although most students have no difficulty learning letter recognition if given the right experiences, many poor readers have decided difficulty trying to memorize all the abstractions necessary to learn letters of the alphabet in their uppercase *and* lowercase forms.

The term **letter recognition** does not mean learning the correct alphabetical sequence (as in saying the alphabet), nor does it mean the sounds of the letters are known. It simply means a student is able to look at a letter, recognize it, and name it. Here are some suggestions for assisting students with letter recognition.

1. Being able to say the alphabet in order is helpful because written symbols can be tied to the names already known; the "Alphabet Song" is an easy way for young students to learn the alphabet sequence.
2. Many of the uppercase (capital) letters are easier to distinguish from one another than the lowercase (small) letters. Note the differences between the capital and lowercase forms of these often confused letters:

BD bd

For this reason, capital letters often are taught first to preschool children. However, once students are enrolled in school and face the task of reading, the preferred choice is usually to begin with lowercase letters because lowercase letters are encountered more frequently in printed text.

3. One of the best ways to help students learn names of letters is through writing. They learn to form each one and associate it with the name from the "Alphabet Song." Writing the letter calls the student's attention to its distinguishing features and fosters recall.
4. Another technique that will help students note the distinctive forms of individual letters is tracing while saying the name. Several variations of letter tracing that may be employed are tracing letters written on paper, tracing cardboard cutouts of letters (these may be purchased through a teachers' supply catalog), and placing a light layer of sand in a cafeteria tray and having students trace letters in the sand. Using several methods provides variety in lessons. It should also be noted that there has been some misunderstanding about the purpose of tracing activities.

Tracing is not used because certain students learn in some unusual manner; that is, it is not because they learn with their fingertips instead of their brains. Tracing is used simply because it aids students who might not attend to specific details if asked *merely to look at letters* as they are learning them.

5.   Relate lessons on letter recognition to other materials that are meaningful to students. For example, write Susan's name and call attention to the letter it begins with. Then have her find all the words in the day's lesson that begin with that letter.

6.   Work with only a few letters at a time—perhaps two or three—and introduce new letters only after these are learned.

7.   Help students eliminate letter confusions. When students confuse similar letters, this is often the result of a *reversal* of the left and right directions of letters (for example, confusing lowercase *b* and lowercase *d*). At other times, the confusion is an *inversion;* that is, the tops and bottoms of letters are inverted (for example, in confusing *b* and *p*).

In the past, when students mistook *b/d, n/u, d/p, M/W,* and so on, this was often attributed to a visual perception problem, mixed lateral dominance, or a neurological processing difficulty, and it was an easy way to get a student labeled as "dyslexic." Research in the fields of education, neurology, and psychology has shown these views to be incorrect. In the first place, reversals and other letter confusions are found in only about 10% of reading disability cases (L. Harris, 1970). In addition, letter confusions are as common with young average readers as with poor readers. Most educators today believe that these confusions simply result from inexperience with directionality as a way of making discriminations (Moyer & Newcomer, 1977). For identification of concrete objects like chairs, or pipes, or birds, or cars, the direction of the object does not affect its name. A chair facing right or a chair facing left, or a chair placed upside down, is still a chair. To discriminate among many similar letters, however, direction is important. A line with a circle on its right side is a *b,* but a line with a circle on its left side is a *d,* while an "upside-down" line with a circle on its right side is a *p.* With training in the importance of directionality, even preschool children can be taught to no longer confuse reversible and invertible letters.

Confusion of letters is a fairly typical behavior pattern during the early stages of learning to read. It should not be presumed to be a danger signal indicating some type of major or unusual problem. However, such confusions need not be ignored; instructional procedures can be implemented to ensure that they do not persist. Some suggestions for helping students eliminate letter confusions follow.

a.   If students confuse *b* and *d* (probably the most common reversal), prepare a capital *B* and a lowercase *b,* each cut from oaktag. Show students how the small *b* could fit on top of a capital *B.*

Tell them that if the letter they are looking at does not fit on top of the capital *B* correctly—it is not a *b.*

b.   Use file cards. Print *b*s on some cards and *d*s on the others, or do this with whatever letters are confused. Mix up the cards. Have the students sort all the *b*s into one pile and all the *d*s into the other. When they can do this accurately, then time them to see how quickly they can make the discriminations in order to build speed of recognition.

c. Make up worksheets containing rows of letters. Have the students circle all the *b*s, or *m*s, or whatever letter they are confusing. When they can do this accurately, time them to see how quickly they can do this correctly. For example:

w   o   h   w   (n)   s   o   (n)   u   p   l   o   (n)   g   i   u   l   (n)   u

p   r   u   t   u   o   v   (n)   k   a   b   t   z   (n)   h   u   j

The worksheet should contain both letters the students are confusing, for example *n* and *u*, but the students should be asked to circle only one of the two.

d. Have the students go over a page from a magazine and circle with a marking pen all of one of the letters in the pair they are confusing.

e. Don't forget the helpfulness of context once the student begins to read a bit. Suppose a student frequently confuses *b* and *d*. If the student is reading for meaning, context frequently will not allow these confusions. For example, reading *big* as *dig* would not make sense in this sentence:

That big dog ran away.

When context does provide a clue to letter identification, encourage learners by asking "Did that make sense?"

Phonemic Awareness and Orthographic Processing.   The critical role of phonemic awareness has been stressed at several places in this text. There is strong and convincing evidence that the root of the problem for many poor readers—even those with more moderate disabilities—is lack of phonemic understandings. Unquestionably assessment of phonemic awareness should be undertaken with nonreaders—and with other individuals with severe learning delays, as well. Practice activities proposed earlier for developing phonemic awareness very likely should be a part of the remedial interventions for a large number of delayed learners.

However, evidence is beginning to emerge that deficiencies in orthographic processing may be the locus of the problem for certain individuals (Solman & May, 1990; Stanovich, 1991). For these learners, deficits may lie heavily in the visual domain, not the phonological—although this group of learners may be much smaller in number. These learners have difficulties in recognizing words using visual and orthographic cues—that is, recognizing and remembering letters, noting and recalling sequences of letters in words, and using other productive cues that help them visually distinguish word patterns (Stanovich & West, 1989).

It is hypothesized that this subgroup of students may have complications in storing patterns of words in memory. On the other hand, they simply may not have learned the importance of doing so. Or they may have failed to learn prerequisite information that allows visual cues to be employed; for instance, it is difficult to remember the sequences of letters in a word if you don't know the letter names (let's suppose you were trying to do this with the word <u>word</u>, not knowing letter names, and said to yourself "This begins with that squiggly mark that has lines pointing downward, then there is a circle, then there is a squiggly mark that is a straight line with a little piece of curve at the top, then there is a circle with a long line stuck on the back of it."

And if you had to do that with very many words—whew! You might give up trying to read right then). Another hypothesis is that although words might be stored in memory, there may be unique difficulties in retrieving the patterns that have been stored.

Stanovich (1991a) cautions that these obstacles should not be confused with the "visual perception enigmas" that were once proposed as a cause of reading problems but that have since been refuted; it is not now suggested that students perceive print in any eccentric manner, but, rather, that learning the visual abstractions of writing and recalling word patterns is uncommonly troublesome for them.

Thus, it seems that a prevalent problem among many disabled readers is lack of phonological awareness. Also, there are some whose troubles seem to stem instead from orthographic processing problems. It is interesting to speculate about nonreaders. Perhaps the reason their reading delays are so abnormally pronounced is that they have *both* phonological *and* visual processing impediments.

Independent Activities for Nonreaders.   There are two reasons why nonreaders may be asked to work on activities independently. First of all, although instruction is best carried out individually with these students, a clinical reading program may not be available in the area where the student lives. Therefore, enrollment in a remedial program in which most instruction is conducted in a group setting may be the only recourse. Some instruction for the students may be undertaken individually, but there will be times when each student must work alone so the teacher can provide instruction to others. Second, nonreaders spend only part of the school day in the reading teacher's class; during the remainder of the day, they are in regular classrooms with many other students. Obviously, the regular classroom teacher cannot spend all of the day working on a one-to-one basis with any one student.

Appropriate independent activities are difficult to devise for nonreaders because there is so little they can read. Unfortunately, this results too often in students being given independent work that provides no assistance to academic learning (such as coloring pictures unrelated to any reading skill or activity).

The instructionally relevant activities that follow may be especially useful to special teachers in their reading programs, but also prove successful in the regular classroom. Most teachers are especially perplexed about how to handle students who read very little (if at all), and welcome good ideas for independent student activities. Reading teachers can make copies of these or similar suggestions and give them to classroom teachers who have students in the earliest stages of reading acquisition. Used in the regular classroom, these activities provide the nonreader with reading-related experiences to supplement those provided in the special clinical or remedial program.

1.   Ask a more skilled reader to record a story onto an audiotape. Have the nonreader listen to the story, using earphones. After the story is completed, the nonreader is to fold a piece of paper into four sections, then draw pictures about the story in four-parts that follow the sequence of main occurrences. This provides opportunity for seriously delayed readers and nonreaders to hear connected text and to focus on comprehension of what was heard.

2.   Place labels on objects around the room, for example, *clock, chalkboard, door, chair, desk.* Give the student index cards with the same words written on them, and ask the students to match the word cards with the labels around the room. Next, the student scrambles the cards and attempts to read each one without looking at the labels. After silently reading each word, the student checks it against the labels in the room. The student places the cards back in the pack and continues to practice until he or she feels confident of being able to correctly read

all cards without looking at the labeled objects. A peer tutor can listen to the words read and place those recognized correctly into a file box of known words. The other words are retained for more practice.

3. After hearing the teacher read a story to the whole group, the nonreader can use the tape recorder at the room's listening center and record retellings of the story. The student may be given different instructions at different times such as, "Be sure to tell something about all of the important characters," or "Tell the story exactly in the order things happened," or, "At the beginning, tell the main idea of the story, then give as many details as you can." At a later time the teacher listens to the taped retellings and provides feedback during the next individual session with the student.

4. Write words on one half of the front side of an index card. Place an illustration of the word on the other half of the card's front side. Make a cut between the word and its illustration, jigsaw-puzzle fashion. The cut should be slightly different for each card. Students are to try to read the words, but when they cannot, they match the illustration to the word by finding the jigsaw cut that fits. Students continue reading and matching until they can say each word without using the illustration. Here are two examples of such word-picture cards.

5. Have the student use a wordless picture book. A **wordless picture book** illustrates a story from beginning to end but contains no words. Many of these are available. A particularly delightful one is *The Chicken's Child* (Scholastic). The learner should be asked to study the pictures from beginning to end and silently develop his or her own stories. In the next individual session with the teacher, with the book used as an aid, the student dictates a story for the teacher to write. This story can be used as the focus of a language experience lesson for one or several days.

6. Have the student use a Language Master, as described in Chapter 8.

7. Ask the student to listen to a tape recording of an informational selection that the teacher or an aide has previously taped. Include questions on the tape about the selection and ask the student to draw answers. Example: "According to what you have just heard, which of these is a reptile: a bird, a dog, or a snake? Turn off the tape recorder now and draw a picture of the right answer. When you have finished, turn on the tape recorder again to hear the next question."

8.   Give the student a magazine along with an envelope labeled with a letter, such as *f.* Have student cut out all the pictures in the magazine he or she can find that begin with the sound of that letter and place them in an envelope to take home for parents to check. The teacher can talk with the parents or enclose a note so they understand the task. Also, it is important to set up a system, such as requiring a parent's signature on the envelope, for determining whether the check was made.

9.   Collect old reading books that can be cut apart. In one session, have a peer tutor read a story to the student from one of the books. Before the next session, cut out the pictures from the story. In the second session, during which the student works independently, give him or her the pictures in a scrambled order. Ask the student to sequence them correctly and paste them on hole-punched notebook paper, one picture to a page. By tying yarn through the holes in the paper, the student can assemble his or her own wordless picture book. In a third independent session, the student can use this "book" to dictate the story into a tape recorder to be checked later by the teacher for accuracy in remembering details.

10.   Cut pictures from old reading books or magazines so that there are pairs of pictures representing words that rhyme. Paste the pictures on colorful construction paper squares and give them to the student in random order; have the student match those that rhyme.

11.   Tape-record a series of word pairs, some of which begin with the same sound and some which do not. Prepare a worksheet like this:

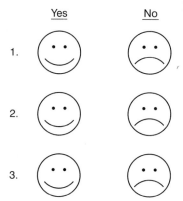

As students listen to the tape, they circle the happy face if the paired words begin with the same sound or the unhappy face if they do not.

12.   Paste two pictures on a card side by side and draw frames around each, cartoon-style. The pictures should be related to one another and placed to show a logical progression of events or action. (Old reading books are a good source for these.) Draw one more frame, following the other two, but leave this third frame blank. To aid in story prediction, ask the student to draw a picture in this frame depicting what might logically occur next.

The suggestions here are only a sampling of ideas for providing reading-related independent work for nonreaders. These ideas were selected to demonstrate a variety of alternatives to direct teacher intervention (by use of peer tutors, taped material, self-correcting materials, and so on) and to list ways in which nonreaders *can* respond (by drawing, circling happy faces, coloring, and so on). These suggestions were chosen to illustrate several different skill, strategy, and knowledge areas (following a sequence of events, developing a sense of story, recognizing words, relating reading activities to the real world, noting details and main ideas, relating words to concrete objects, using picture clues, recognizing the messages conveyed by books, making letter-sound correspondences, dictating stories, and gaining familiarity with the book language of narrative and expository material). Teachers can add to these suggestions and maintain a file of ideas for academically relevant, independent activities that can be used with nonreaders.

CONCLUSION

Working with severely delayed readers and nonreaders of any age can be one of the most rewarding of all tasks for the remedial teacher. With the right combination of features, instructional programs can be structured so that these students *can* learn. One way to continually increase your skill in this area is to read professional journals regularly for new insights on designing programs to ameliorate these students' puzzling problems.

📖 REFLECTIONS

1. Why do you think there have been so few instructional research studies focusing on severely delayed readers and nonreaders?
2. If you could design an *instructional* study with severely delayed readers or nonreaders, what would the study investigate?

15

Other Learners With Special Needs

For adults, literacy—both reading and writing—is needed to increase occupational knowledge, to attend to one's health needs, to be able to use community resources, and to understand government and law.

C atherine Gillie, Columbus, Ohio, wife of a judge, mother of four, part-time nurse, heard a radio commercial.

"It said seventy-seven thousand persons in central Ohio did not know how to read. I didn't believe there was anyone like that."

She and the judge took the four Saturday morning training sessions offered by the Columbus Literacy Council.

Mrs. Gillie: "Then I was assigned a student, and I called her. Her voice was so soft I could hardly hear her. It was obvious that I had awakened her, but when I said, 'I've been assigned to be your tutor' a shriek of joy came over that telephone.

"She was so delighted. Several times before, she had tried to get help. Once she even telephoned the Columbus Board of Education to say she couldn't read, and the secretary there wouldn't believe her. Because of her use of language and the way she presented her ideas so well, the secretary was sure she was a college graduate playing a prank."

The student was Betty Elliott, something over thirty years old (she isn't sure because there are no records), who was orphaned at three weeks and taken to New York City by a woman who wanted her to help around the house. She remembers having to stand on a chair to wash dishes and diapers. Whenever the truant officer came around, the woman would say, "Don't bother with her; she's not right, you know."

Never a day in school and not able to read a word. She recalls: "I get surprised when I think back to when I had to memorize things and wasn't able to put them down on paper."

What she did was fake it a lot. She "wrote" her name—but actually she drew the letters. She made reports at the end of her night shift as a cottage mother at Franklin Village, a children's home, by calling a friend and telling her what she wanted to say. Slowly the friend would spell out the letters, and laboriously Betty would print them in capitals.

"I had no idea you could picture letters because I didn't know what reading and writing were all about. Now I can close my eyes and see that a *and* b and you know, *that's marvelous.*"

Mrs. Gillie would go to the Elliott home for lessons: "We both cried a great deal at the beginning. We spent many sessions with not too much time reading but with her telling about her life. Never before, she said, had any individual been personally interested in her. Many friends, because she's a very friendly person, but never anyone that interested."

Elliott: "People think if you can't read or write, you're stupid."

To cover up, she learned numbers. She counted on her fingers and found how to make change. She couldn't read labels at the grocery, but she knew how to shake the cans. If the contents rattled, they were peas. If the can was heavy, it was fruit. She even could tell pears from peaches without pictures.

Gillie: "It's fascinating, the extent to which people learn to cope and work around the printed word. It takes immeasurable use of energy and brainpower and time and money, but to a small extent, it can be done.

"After two months, I asked her whether she was able to see any difference at work or anywhere else because she could begin to read. Betty answered: 'I notice now that when I look in the mirror, I'm smiling.' "

Over about three years, there were some eighty tutoring sessions, ninety or so minutes each, sometimes twice a week, sometimes only once a month when both were very busy.

Elliott: "Another surprise, when you see on paper the word that you have been holding up here in your mind and rattling it around, then you see it there and begin to make some sense out of it. It's surprise; it's happiness.

"The first day I was able to do one word, one word as I have in my book, to know that I could spell it out; it stood out so much for me, just to know I could spell it and hear it. That was so neat, the way the sounds came together. I can see it; I can hear the letters."

(The word was s-p-y.)

Gillie: "She's such an intelligent person, with such compassion, such wisdom. She could write a psychology book about working with children. And she accomplished all this with no models. A very wise, very smart person."

Elliott: "If I could just tell it all, if people only knew exactly how I felt then and also bring it up to now, it would be some story. It would be like—like it's not the truth. I have all intentions some day to write that for others to know."

Gillie: "I've been involved in all the things you do as your children are growing up, and I've thought they were good causes, and you put your shoulder to the wheel, and that's fine.

"But this is different, seeing a whole world open up to one person who had been seeing the world through a long tube without much light at the end. That's the most exciting thing that can happen."

Betty Elliott's book: the one from which she read her very first word, The New Streamlined English Series: In the Valley.

Happy ending: She won a prize for reading the most books of any student in the literacy program her first year. (Sabine & Sabine, 1983, pp. 49–51)

ILLITERACY AND FUNCTIONAL ILLITERACY IN OLDER YOUTHS AND ADULTS

The above real-life story furnishes a poignant example of illiteracy and the effect it had on one life. An **illiterate** individual is one who lacks the ability to read and/or write, resulting from having had little or no instruction or from not having learned from instruction. The term usually refers to older individuals rather than school-age students.

Functional illiterates, on the other hand, are older youths and adults who can read, but to such a limited extent that they cannot understand basic written information needed to function in adult daily life. They may, for example, be able to read easy primary-level stories, but be unable to cope with personal or business letters, traffic signs, writing found on packages, medicine bottle labels, bank statements, application forms, advertisements, bills, maps, telephone books, recipes, or newspapers. Probably because the effects are similar, the terms *illiterate* and *functional illiterate* are used interchangeably by many writers.

Job-related reading, which was found by Gutherie and Kirsch (1987) to constitute a large part of all reading by adults, offers another functional literacy problem. Literacy demands in some workplaces may actually be greater than those required in the daily reading of students in school. In many cases, students read less often in instructional settings than workers do on the job, and school reading frequently involves easier material that can be read with less depth than that required in the workplace. Occupational effectiveness may be determined by literacy level. Many businesses today are seriously concerned about advancing the reading competence of their lowest level of workers. In what has been called "concerned self-interest," businesses are inviting reading professionals and other literacy workers into their plants and companies to teach reading to their employees on-site (Levine, 1986). In addition, jobs requiring few reading skills are diminishing in availability. The U.S. Department of Labor estimates a considerable decline in opportunities for household help and laborers, but a projected growth for clerical workers, managers, nonhousehold service workers, and technicians—occupations requiring a considerable degree of literacy, and obviously not open to either illiterate or functionally illiterate persons.

Literacy, both reading and writing, is needed to increase occupational knowledge, to attend to one's health needs, to be able to use community resources, and to understand government and law. Many believe that increasing adult literacy levels would be accompanied by higher employment rates and by more individuals assuming civic responsibilities (P. Shannon, 1991). The 1992 Adult Literacy Survey in the United

States found that 40% of adults reading at the lowest levels had poverty-level incomes and that many fewer voted than those at middle and higher literacy levels (50% compared to 75% and 90%, respectively) (OERI Bulletin, 1993). It is one of America's National Educational Goals to eradicate illiteracy and functional literacy by the year 2000. Though some believe this to be an overly hopeful aspiration (e.g., Wagner, 1993), this federal educational initiative, along with the 1991 National Literacy Act aimed at adults, has raised awareness of the demand for solutions. Reading teachers are needed to work in this field.

Illiteracy Rates in the United States

The United Nations estimates that the illiteracy rate in the United States is approximately 4%, which is comparable to that of other industrialized countries (Wagner, 1993). Although this illiteracy level is much less than in developing countries, there also are individuals in the U.S. who are functionally illiterate. An often-cited guess at the incidence of functional illiterates in the U.S. is approximately 23 million. However, the exact number of illiterates or functional illiterates is difficult to ascertain because the criteria used to determine illiteracy are different for various organizations and authorities.

Reading Level.   Some definitions assume there is a reading level one must attain to read everyday printed matter successfully, but opinions vary about just what this level is. It has been suggested as fifth-grade level (L. Smith, 1977), fourth-grade level (Ahmann, 1975), sixth-grade level (Bureau of Census, 1971), and eighth-grade level (G. A. Miller, 1973). Obviously, the level chosen changes the number of illiterates or functional illiterates estimated. Some authorities believe there is a stage that must be attained for literacy to be self-sustaining, that is, a level adequate enough to allow sufficient practice opportunities so that literacy is maintained; UNESCO claims this to be fifth-grade level (Venezky, 1991).

Grade Completed.   A more questionable criterion for defining literacy is the number of years of schooling completed by an individual. For example, in Canada, literacy is assumed if a person has completed eighth grade (Rigg & Kazemek, 1985), and the United Nations has cited 4 years of schooling as the necessary requisite (L. Smith, 1977). However, as any reading teacher knows, the fact that students have completed a particular grade is not necessarily an indicator that they are reading at that grade level.

Skills Mastered.   Others define literacy in terms of ability to perform reading tasks associated with real-world experiences. These may include functional literacy skills needed in occupations, to attend to the economic necessities of life, and to use transportation. Suggested basic reading tasks have included (a) reading accounting statements, forms, and invoices; (b) reading letters, memos, and notes; (c) reading newspapers; (d) reading manuals and instructions at work; (e) reading information while shopping; and (f) reading signs when traveling. Table 15–1 is a list of some basic items for which reading is needed in everyday life.

The 1992 National Adult Literacy Survey sponsored by the U.S. Department of Education evaluated literacy according to three types of skills needed to use written material:

1. *Prose literacy*—being able to read fiction, poems, news stories, editorials
2. *Document literacy*—being able to read job applications, maps, tables, schedules for transportation

TABLE 15–1
Some basic literacy needs in everyday life

Completing job applications	Filling out forms at work
Reading bank statements	Reading labels on grocery items
Reading destinations on the front of a bus	Writing checks
Reading and completing income tax forms	Reading and writing letters
Reading directions for operating appliances	Reading road signs
Reading directions on medicine bottles	Reading driver's manuals
Reading advertisements	Reading loan agreements
Reading bills	Using the telephone book
Reading maps	Reading notices
Following recipes	Reading newspapers
Registering to vote	Completing applications for Social Security
Reading warranties and guarantees	Reading memos from a supervisor
Reading airline tickets	Reading danger warnings

3. *Quantitative literacy*—being able to use numbers embedded in written materials, such as order forms, restaurant checks, advertisements (OERI Bulletin, 1993).

Tests to Determine Literacy Levels

A number of tests have been developed to assess adult literacy. These are sometimes composed of items similar to reading tasks required to function minimally in daily life. One such test is R/EAL (Reading/Everyday Activities in Life). R/EAL (Westwood Press) is a criterion-referenced test that measures nine areas including reading application forms, directions, and maps. The Adult Performance Level Program (American College Testing Program) is also an assessment battery that focuses on basic tasks relevant to everyday living. Figure 15–1 is a sample item from one test used to assess functional literacy. Some tests of functional literacy are listed in Test Bank K.

Two tests that assess more general literacy skills are the Adult Basic Learning Examination (Psychological Corporation) and Reading Evaluation: Adult Diagnosis, 2nd edition (Literacy Volunteers of America). The Adult Basic Learning Examination is a series of tests to measure literacy and math skills. Reading Evaluation: Adult Diagnosis is designed for adults from nonreaders through fifth-grade reading level. The content of this test is written to conform with adult maturity levels, and it has three subtests: word recognition, word identification strategies, and reading/listening inventory.

Reviews of adult literacy tests can be obtained from the Northwest Regional Educational Laboratory. These reviews supply information on measurement issues related to content, reliability, and validity of the tests.

School-Based and Nonschool-Based Programs

Reading teachers may wish to pursue work in school-based adult literacy programs. Others may want to participate in, or begin, nonschool-based programs in their communities.

FIGURE 15–1
A sample item from one test of functional literacy

Look at the instructions. Circle the statements that tell all the names you should get if you are involved in an accident.

What to Do at Time of Accident

1. Do not admit responsibility and make no statement regarding the accident except to the police or claims representatives.
2. Do not reveal the amount or limits of your liability coverage to anyone.
3. Obtain names and addresses of all occupants of other car involved.
4. Obtain names and addresses of all witnesses.
5. Report all accidents immediately.
6. Consult your claim representatives for complete claim reporting instructions.

Source: From *Adult Functional Reading Study* (PR 75–2) by R. T. Murphy, 1975, Princeton, NJ: Educational Testing Service. Reprinted by permission.

School-based programs designed to fight illiteracy and functional illiteracy usually are composed of adult basic education (ABE) classes, authorized by the U.S. Adult Education Act, Public Law 91–230. These are administered by local school systems, state departments of education, or other organizations. Classes may be held in public or private school buildings but sometimes take place in other locations to lessen older students' adverse feelings about their earlier educational experiences. Typically more than 2 million persons enroll in these programs each year, with about half being out-of-

Reading teachers may be interested in working in school-based adult literacy programs; others may want to begin non-school-based programs in their communities.

Test Bank K
Tests of Functional Literacy

Name	For Grades	Type of Administration	Time for Administration	Publisher
Life Skills— Forms 1 and 2	9–12, and adults	Group	80–100 minutes	Riverside
Minimum Essentials Test	8–12, and adults	Group	45–50 minutes per subtest	American Testronics
Performance Assessment in Reading	6–9	Group	100 minutes	CTB/McGraw-Hill
Reading/Everyday Activities in Life (R/EAL)	Age 10 and up	Individually by tape recording	50–90 minutes	Westwood Press
Senior High Assessment of Reading Performance (SHARP)	9–12	Group	120–150 minutes	CTB/McGraw-Hill
SRA Survival Skills in Reading and Mathematics	7–12	Group	60 minutes	Science Research Associates

school older youths and adults ages 16 through 24. About a quarter are clients who are ages 45 or over, and the majority are usually female and Caucasian. Every year about 2 million additional individuals are added to the number of illiterates and functional illiterates in this country through refugee and immigration policies and through school dropouts. Considering these figures, the number of participants in school-based adult literacy classes is strikingly few.

Although most *nonschool-based literacy programs* use paid staff, sometimes consisting of professionals with backgrounds in reading disabilities or learning disabilities, these endeavors rely heavily on volunteers. Community-based ventures are rapidly expanding. Clients enrolled in nonschool-based programs usually consist of both illiterate and functionally illiterate persons, and tutors are required (professional or volunteer) who can work with reading, spelling, writing, and math. Individuals wishing to initiate such programs must take a number of administrative and instructional concerns into consideration:

Administrative Concerns

1. Can a combined staff of paid teachers and volunteers be used to coordinate and conduct the program?
2. What sources of funding are there for this literacy effort?
3. Where can volunteers be obtained?

4. How should volunteers be assigned?
5. How should the program's budget (if any) be allotted and managed?
6. What publicity will help illiterate individuals learn of the services?
7. What types of publicity can be used for fund–raising?
8. What administrative forms are needed?
9. What established programs can be contacted for advice to avoid stumbling blocks and growing pains?

Instructional Concerns

1. What training (both preservice and inservice) can be provided for teachers and volunteers?
2. What audiovisual materials are available for instructing those who will deliver services?
3. What testing practices are best for adult learners?
4. Which teaching methods are best?
5. What reference materials can volunteers use for ideas for instruction?
6. What reading strategy sequence is most appropriate for each client's needs?
7. What types of lesson plans most facilitate the teaching sessions?
8. Where can low readability materials be obtained?
9. How can instructional materials be cataloged so they can be used to best advantage?
10. How can the public library help?
11. What special considerations (psychological, occupational, and others) must be taken into account for adult learners?
12. What counseling services for older youths and adults are available in the community to supplement the literacy services being provided?

Regardless of the type of program (school-based or nonschool-based), it is important for educators to realize that successful programs are not short-term. At times, promises of unrealistically rapid acquisition of literacy are fostered by uninformed literacy program workers, materials developers, and the media. Those that promise quick results may raise false hopes, which rapidly develop into frustrations and program dropout. The most successful programs are gradual and long-term. Furthermore, in effective undertakings, teaching or supervision is provided by educational specialists with thorough training in reading instruction. In addition, the special learning needs of those who have experienced serious literacy difficulties over a prolonged period should be taken into account. Johnston (1985), working with adult male disabled readers, found many stress-related symptoms and other complicating variables, including (a) anxiety, (b) attributions of their difficulties to false causes, (c) maladaptive strategies for learning, (d) nonexistent or inaccurate conceptualizations about the reading process, and (e) low motivation.

Working With Illiterate Older Youths and Adults

Because of age, geographic isolation, unusual economic factors, immigration from an underdeveloped nation, or other reasons, illiterate older individuals have often been denied the intensive schooling enjoyed today by most youths in our society. Others have failed to benefit from educational experiences in their normal school years. In either case, reading instruction at the acquisition or very early stages is called for.

Use of "organic primers" is one avenue for providing early-level reading instruction to adults in a nonpatronizing manner (Amoroso, 1985). **Organic primers** are collections of stories written by the teacher reflecting the experiences and concerns of the students in the literacy class. To prepare organic primers, teachers write simple stories— using natural language structures—about basic themes of adult interest such as marriage or job-related concerns. Each story is slightly longer than the preceding one. After students have been in the classes a few days, stories are prepared so they are based on discussions with that specific group of clients. To use the primers, the following steps are undertaken.

1. The story content is discussed prior to reading it.
2. The teacher reads the story aloud *to* the students.
3. The teacher and students read and reread the story in unison until the learners are able to read it alone.
4. Students read the story individually.
5. Practice activities are employed to ensure that word recognition will generalize to other reading materials and to emphasize meaning as well as word identification strategies.

This technique has some similarities to language immersion techniques described for use with seriously delayed readers (see Chapter 14). In addition to the United States, introductions to reading with organic primers have been successful in literacy programs in developing countries such as Brazil (Freire, 1973) and Nicaragua (Cardenal & Miller, 1981).

The language experience approach (LEA) has also shown utility in literacy programs. A variation of LEA, using computers, was instrumental in reading growth in the Adult Literacy Project at the University of New Orleans (Wangberg, Thompson, & Levitov, 1984). Following introduction to reading through LEA, adults wrote their own stories on the computer, assisted by prompts programmed into it. After the computer lesson, the student took the story to a teacher station for reading and help in editing. The edited story was also entered into the computer and a resulting printout displayed the original story, the edited story, a list of words used by the student, and a set of follow-up activities. A composite list of words these adults used most frequently when writing language experience stories was developed as a spelling reference and made available to them. (Another helpful reference list for literacy programs is The Functional Reading Word List for Adults [Mitzel, 1966].)

Kazemek (1985) and others have used song lyrics in adult reading programs, and poetry has also proved to be particularly motivating to adult clients. Such language forms often have less negative associations than typical school reading instructional materials.

Reading strategies advocated throughout this book are appropriate for adult clients. Suitable *materials* used with adults may be different in format (e.g., no childlike pictures) and content (e.g., passages at higher maturity and interest levels), but adults must still learn to identify unknown words and comprehend the message. Many published instructional materials are currently available to use in literacy programs for older individuals. (See Figure 15–2 for an example.) These introduce word recognition and other basic reading strategies in formats suitable for the adult student. Some helpful programs, activities, and materials have been cited in previous chapters; others are listed in Teachers' Store H.

Working With Functionally Illiterate Older Youths and Adults

Functional literacy programs are often undertaken with individuals who have mastered the rudiments of beginning reading strategies but who need assistance with literacy tasks

FIGURE 15–2

Sample of published literacy materials with a reading selection of interest to adults

11

IS SCHOOL FOR ME?

Should I go back to school? Mr. Night asked himself. That thought was always going through his mind. Why should I go back to school? What would other people think if I did? Am I too old to go back? Mr. Night asked himself these things over and over again.

One day Mr. Night had to face himself. He looked at himself a long time. He didn't like what he saw. Here I am now in the same place that I have been in for years, he thought. I have done nothing to better my mind. I must get back in school. I could get better work. Mr. Night knew he should go to a school for adults. He knew it well, but he didn't like the thought of it at all.

Direct attention to the picture. Have students predict what the story may be about. Read the title and the story while students read along silently.

Source: From *Steck-Vaughn Adult Reading Program—1300* (p. 38), Austin, TX: Steck-Vaughn. Reprinted by permission.

Teachers' Store H

Illiteracy and Functional Illiteracy

For Use With Illiterate Individuals

1. *The Steck-Vaughn Adult Reading Program* (Steck-Vaughn)
2. *Adult Reading Improvement Series* (Monarch)
3. *Survival Vocabularies* (Janus)
4. *Programmed Reading Comprehension, Level I* (National Tutoring Institute)
5. *The Work Series; The Health Series; The Money Series* (Hopewell Books)
6. *Pacemaker Vocational Readers* (Fearon)
7. *Basic Education: Reading Book I* (Follett)
8. *News for You* (Laubach Literacy Council)
9. *Communications* (Follett)

For Use With Functionally Illiterate Individuals

1. *Practical Skills in Reading* (National Textbook)
2. *I Can Make It On My Own* (Good Year)
3. *Recipes for Learning* (Good Year)
4. *Survival Guides* (Janus)
5. *BesTeller Magazines* (Fearon)
6. *Essential Life Skills Series* (National Textbook)
7. *Cambridge Pre-GED Program, Introduction to Reading* (Cambridge Book Co.)
8. *Scope/Consumer Skills, Dollars and Sense* (Scholastic)
9. *Forms in Your Future* (Globe)

Professional Resources for Teaching Illiterate and Functionally Illiterate Older Youths and Adults

1. *Teaching and Learning Basic Skills: A Guide for Adult Basic Education and Developmental Education Programs* (Teachers College Press)
2. *Books for Adult New Readers*, 2nd Edition (Project LEARN)
3. *Teaching Reading in Adult Basic Education* (Wm. C. Brown)
4. *The Illiterate Adult Speaks Out* (National Institute of Education)
5. *Challenging Adult Illiteracy* (Teachers College Press)
6. *Adult Literacy* (International Reading Association)
7. *Adult Education* (a journal)
8. *Lifelong Learning* (a journal)
9. *TUTOR* (Literacy Volunteers of America)
10. *Tutor's Sampler* (Faculty Press)

encountered in their everyday environments—demands requiring decidedly more read-ing skill than they have attained. Instead of a more extensive program (focusing on gen-eral word recognition, multiple strategy use, universal comprehension abilities), func-tional literacy emphasizes direct teaching of the reading tasks that are dictated by specific needs.

An example of direct instruction of a specific functional literacy skill is shown in a program developed to teach students of high school age with severe reading disabilities and mild retardation to read and complete job applications (Heward, McCormick, and Joynes, 1980; Joynes, McCormick, & Heward, 1980). Both populations were residing in a residential facility for male delinquent youth. As a preliminary step to this program, a master employment application was developed by collecting real applications from employers who might hire functionally illiterate persons. The real applications were ana-lyzed to determine what types of items occurred and in what form. *Form* referred to instances where an item might be written in various ways on different applications, for example, "Social Security Number," "Soc. Sec. #," or "Social Security No." The items occurring with highest frequency and the forms of these items most often seen on real applications were selected to be placed on the Master Employment Application used in the training program. The Master Employment Application is seen in Figure 15–3. This job application was divided into four sections to teach students to read a few items at a time and to teach them to correctly fill in the requested information.

To ensure that all students had the opportunity to respond to all questions during instruction, every student had an overhead projector at his desk along with transparen-cies for answering the teacher's questions. Students' answers were projected on screens behind their desks so the teacher could give immediate corrective feedback. The teacher also had an overhead projector and screen for displaying items. The instruc-tional program required 11 class periods, 40 minutes in length, and had several steps:

1. The teacher showed an individual item from the job application, read it, and explained what it meant. Students found identical items in their sets of preprinted transparencies and placed these on their overhead projectors so that they showed on the screen.
2. The teacher showed a job application item, and students had to find a preprinted transparency showing the statements that would be used to fill in the required information.
3. The teacher showed an application item and students had to print the required information on a blank transparency.
4. Students filled in a transparency that depicted the entire master application.

Before the program, students were able to read and complete an average of 13 of the 35 items on the master application form. Afterward, correct reading and completion of items ranged from 29 to 35.

Abbass (1977) analyzed 50 commonly used forms and found that many of the words on them are not on high-frequency word lists used in basic reading programs and that the readability of the forms ranged from 8.0 to above college level. When the NAEP Assessment of Functional Literacy examined the performances of 17-year-olds, they scored more poorly on the reading of forms than on any other area except reading reference material. Programs such as the one described above for reading job applica-tions can also be used to train functionally illiterate individuals to complete other types of forms requiring biographic information, such as credit applications, Medicaid applica-tions, and income tax forms. A temporary survival strategy used with very low-function-ing individuals is to write basic information on the front and back sides of a small index

FIGURE 15–3
Master employment application using terms that often appear on actual application forms

MASTER EMPLOYMENT APPLICATION

Please print

PERSONAL

Name	Last	First	Middle		Date
Date of Birth	Age	Social Security Number			Sex ☐ M ☐ F
Married ☐ Yes ☐ No	No. of Dependents ___		Weight		Height
Are you a citizen of the U.S.?			Phone No.		
Present Address	No. Street		City	State	Zip Code
Previous Address	No. Street		City	State	Zip Code

PHYSICAL

Do you have any physical disabilities? ______ If yes, describe.

Have you had any major illness in the past 5 years? ______
If yes, describe.

In case of an emergency, notify, Name ______

Address Phone No.

EDUCATION

	Name of School	Attended From - To	Did you graduate?
Elementary			
High School			
College or University			
Other			
Other			

Do you plan to continue your education?

Last grade completed ______ Grade point average ______

Extracurricular activities ______

List any special office skills that you have. ______

EMPLOYMENT HISTORY

List below your last three employers:

Name and Address	Salary	Position	Date From - To
1.			
2.			
3.			

MILITARY

Have you ever served in the U.S. armed forces? ☐ Yes ☐ No

If yes, what branch? ______

Dates of Duty: From ______ To ______

Rank at Discharge ______

REFERENCES

List below three names of people not related to you, whom you have known at least one year.

Name	Address	Phone No.	Years Acquainted
1.			
2.			
3.			

Do you have any relatives in this company? ______

JOB PREFERENCE

Type of work desired ______

Date available ______ Hours available ______

Starting expected salary ______

Why do you want this job? ______

GENERAL INFORMATION

Have you committed any felonies or violations? ______

If yes, explain. ______

Are you a licensed driver? ☐ Yes ☐ No

List here any additional comments that you think are important to us in considering you for employment: ______

SIGNATURE

To the best of my knowledge the above statements are complete and are true. False statements may be cause for dismissal.

Date ______ Signature ______

Source: From "Teaching Reading Disabled Students to Read and Complete Employment Applications" by Y. D. Joynes, S. McCormick, and W. L. Heward, 1980, *Journal of Reading, 23,* pp. 712–713. Copyright 1980 by the International Reading Association. Reprinted by permission of the International Reading Association.

card, such as the correct spellings of the individual's street address, the Social Security Number, and so on. The card is then laminated and carried in a billfold to provide individuals with an aid in filling out forms.

Another direct instruction program was reported by Murph and McCormick (1985) when they taught severely reading disabled older youths to read road signs. Students were pretested on this task using the state driver's license manual. No student was able to read any of the signs prior to the training program. For instruction, signs were placed in two groups. One of these was called "worded signs" and included those on which words alone appeared, such as *Wrong Way* or *Road Construction Ahead*. The second group was composed of "combination signs" on which pictorial information appeared along with words, such as *School Crossing* or *Merge Left*. Students learned words on the signs using the following materials and procedures for *each word* on a sign:

1. *Use of cards with a single word printed on each.* The students were told the word, required to repeat it, and asked to use it orally in a sentence. If students could not do so, the teacher provided a sentence.

2. *Use of word strips on which the target word was printed along with two similar words.* Students selected the target word. If they were unable to do this, the teacher indicated the correct word and pointed out its distinguishing features.

3. *Use of sentence strips on which three different sentences were printed, each containing the same target word.* Students read all sentences. If unable to pronounce words other than the target word they were told these, and then they reread the sentence orally.

4. *Use of cardboard road signs.* Representations of signs constructed in the shape and color used in the students' home state were shown, and students read each one orally.

Road signs were taught to students on a one-to-one basis and in sets of three; students did not move to the next set until they had performed all tasks correctly on the current set. After the program, all students read all signs correctly when posttested with the driver's manual.

The major characteristic of the programs described here is that the necessary reading tasks were taught specifically and directly, rather than more generalized instruction being given, such as instruction in phonic analysis. Direct instruction, use of ministeps, careful sequencing of steps, and a moderately slow progression through steps are important factors when teaching minimally literate individuals. Figure 15–4 lists other

FIGURE 15–4
Commonly encountered words and phrases relating to household appliances

Switch	Instructions	Blade	Immerse	Filter
Turn	Avoid	Locked	Dial	Press button
High/low	Disconnect	Manual/automatic	Cord	Close door
Remove	Attachments	control	Plug	Empty
Caution	Left/right/rear/front	Temperature	Position	Fuses
		Cycle		

functional words that could be taught in a similar manner. Adults want to learn to read materials that have practical meaning for their everyday lives.

Elsewhere in this book, the advantages of cooperative learning have been discussed. This technique should also be considered for adult functional illiterates. Heath (1991) points out that many of the features of cooperative learning are those considered desirable in the workplace. Employers now want workers who can learn through exchanging information and solving problems through group collaboration.

The U.S. Armed Forces are using several computer programs to deal with functional literacy problems within their ranks. These include programs for sentence construction, vocabulary learning, problem solving, learning reading skills through job-related lessons, study skills, and paragraph organization. Research on one series of computer programs used by the Navy indicates that reading skill increased about as much as with noncomputer programs, but in about half the time (Blanchard, 1984).

Ideas for teacher-made activities for functional literacy programs can be found in *Survival Learning Materials: Suggestions for Developing* (Strine Publishing). Some published materials suitable for functional literacy classes are listed in Teachers' Store H. (See Figure 15–5 for one example of the latter.)

One of the issues in the field of adult education is the debate about whether the "functional literacy" approach is too narrow, since literacy has a much broader scope than does reading for specific kinds of tasks. The U.S. Armed Forces, in fact, have attempted two different approaches in their efforts with low-literacy enlistees—one that deals with general literacy and the other with on-the-job literacy (Blanchard, 1984). They have found that students in the general literacy programs retain about 40% of the material they have been taught, while those in the job-related reading courses retain about 80% of what they have learned (Sticht, 1981).

The goals of functional literacy programs are necessarily to develop reading skills to deal with immediate tasks; once these goals have been realized, students can be encouraged to participate in wider literacy goals to improve their overall abilities to deal with all dimensions of reading experience.

Intergenerational Literacy

Recently there has been much interest in combating low reading skills in families where recurring illiteracy cycles have been seen—parents (and probably grandparents) who have limited levels of literacy and their children also potentially growing to adulthood with the same debilitating condition. P. Shannon (1991) reminds us that illiteracy or very low literacy in one generation can set up preconditions for its continuance in the next. A number of efforts have been instituted to attack the reading problems of the older and younger generations together, and these are being called **intergenerational literacy programs.**

Intergenerational literacy efforts have been carried out in a number of ways—for example, with both parents and children attending a center in the evenings and on weekends where they all receive reading instruction—by different teachers and in different rooms—but with the whole family attending at the same time.

Another version of intergenerational literacy programs teaches low-literacy adults several basic reading skills and strategies, and then coaches them in how to tutor their young children in these areas. Thus, the children learn and the parents' learning is reinforced. Tutoring of the children may occur at the literacy center or at home.

In yet another variation, parents are taught how to work in their homes to promote emergent literacy. They are apprised of the value of activities that seem to foster

FIGURE 15–5
Literacy programs teach functional, as well as basic, reading
skills.

66   Schedules

This section of the book will help you learn to read schedules. Bus companies, railroads, and airlines all use schedules to show where they go and when. Schedules show a lot of information in a small area, so it is important to pay close attention to everything.

Study the schedule below. Then use it and the information in the questions to fill in the blanks.

Bus Schedule

CITIES	ARRIVALS and DEPARTURES	
Plains	Ar.	6:50a
	Lv.	7:00a
Largo	Ar.	7:32a
	Lv.	7:45a
Deton	Ar.	8:15a
	Lv.	8:30a
River City	Ar.	9:10a
	Lv.	9:25a

1. Some of the cities served by the bus company are given in a column on the left side of the schedule. What are

   they? ....

2. Look at the row for Largo. It is divided into two parts. The *Ar* means "arrive." the *Lv* means "leave." The *a* stands for "A.M.," or morning. At what time does the bus leave

   Largo? ....

3. Look at the row for River City. It shows the times of arrival and departure. The bus arrives at ....

   The bus leaves at ....

4. The bus from Plains to River City also stops in Largo and Deton. At what time does the bus arrive in Largo? ....

5. At what time does the bus arrive in Deton? ....

6. If you boarded the bus in Plains, at what time should you

   arrive in River City? ....

7. How long should the trip between Plains and Deton take?

   ....

Source: From *Steck-Vaughn Adult Reading Program—2700* (p. 84), Austin, TX: Steck-Vaughn. Reprinted by permission.

reading success. These parents are shown how to read aloud to their preschool children in ways that promote understanding, language development, and concepts about print. In addition, they are given tools and instructions for promoting writing activities as another way of fostering literacy.

A related area is *family literacy,* which deals more broadly with literacy events in any family—those in which reading problems are not seen, as well as those in which they are. Some issues that are treated within this arena are the roles preschools, as well as elementary and secondary schools, can play to positively affect circumstances within families to nurture literacy. Sometimes the terms *intergenerational literacy* and *family literacy* are used interchangeably.

There is currently much optimism about the potential of these programs, and they are spreading. One plan that has received funding from the U.S. government is called Even Start. The objective is to give children from families who have had high illiteracy rates an even start with other children when they enter school. In 1993, Native American groups in seven states, for example, received government support for Even Start intergenerational literacy programs. Participants are parents who are in need of adult basic education and their children from birth to age 7.

A federally funded program in Dade County, Florida, called Project Start, features a link between libraries and day-care centers for poverty-level children. Day-care workers are given training to conduct high-quality story time programs with children from ages 3 to 5. Kits are supplied by the libraries, each based on a theme, that include books, flannel board stories, finger plays, and cassettes with music. Materials are available in English, Spanish, and Creole. More than 100 day-care centers are participating and furnishing at-risk preschool children with a daily story time (OERI Bulletin, 1993).

Prison Literacy

An adult literacy problem about which there should be more concern is the large numbers of prison inmates who are exceedingly poor readers. Of the more than one million persons incarcerated in the United States, enormous numbers have low literacy levels and are school dropouts requiring additional literacy education if they are to be rehabilitated (Staff, 1993).

A. P. Newman, Lewis, and Beverstock (1993) describe this situation as one that is relatively unknown to educators and that most corrections professionals are not trained to deal with. This is an area ripe for attention from reading and learning disabilities teachers. A complicated assortment of considerations must be confronted for actual rehabilitation to take place. This offers a challenge and one that when met has the potential to make real differences for individuals and society.

Sources of Information About Established Literacy Programs

Here are some sources to which you can write or telephone to obtain more information about literacy programs:

Contact Literacy Center
P.O. Box 81826
Lincoln, NE 68501–1826

The Library Literacy Program
(202) 219-1315
(Promotes literacy projects in the inner city and delivers books by bookmobiles and vans)

Literacy Volunteers of America, Inc
404 Oak St.
Syracuse, NY 13203

The National Center on Adult Literacy
(215) 898-2100

The National Clearinghouse on Literacy Education
(202) 429-9292

The Public Library Services Program
(202) 219-1303

STUDENTS WITH LINGUISTIC AND CULTURAL DIFFERENCES

Today's teacher often provides reading instruction to students from cultural and linguistic backgrounds differing from the mainstream culture. Increased numbers of these students in school classrooms is a phenomenon across the country. Students with culturally diverse backgrounds include those who speak standard English, those who speak nonstandard English, those who are bilingual, and those who do not speak English at all. Culturally diverse students can come from any socioeconomic background, but many of those who speak nonstandard English, who are bilingual, or who speak no English also come from low-income homes. Some may have reading problems that are similar to those of students we have discussed earlier throughout this book—that is, they may have difficulties that are atypical and that would be designated as "true" remedial reading problems; on the other hand, some read perfectly well in another language, but not in English. (See Figure 15–6.)

Students for whom there may be special linguistic and cultural considerations are rural, African-American, Appalachian, migrant, Native American (Indian and Eskimo), Hispanic-American (Puerto Rican, Cuban, Mexican-American), recent Asian immigrants (Vietnamese, Laotian, Cambodian), and students who are new to our country as a result of the breakdown of the former U.S.S.R. In addition, in Hawaii, many different dialects may be found in single classrooms as well as a rich and diverse cultural heritage among the students. And there are, of course, other, smaller groups of foreign-born individuals who now make their homes in this country and who may require special attention from the reading teacher because of their linguistic and cultural backgrounds.

FIGURE 15–6
Because of the multicultural nature of North American society, reading teachers often work with culturally and linguistically different students

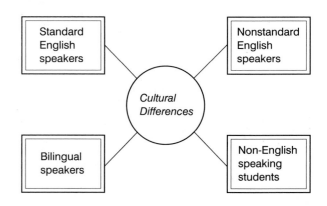

Linguistic Considerations

Because reading is language-based, when reading problems have arisen among students whose linguistic patterns are different from those of students in the majority culture, it has often been suggested that language differences may be at the root of the problem. In some cases, this may be true, but in others, it is not.

Nonstandard Dialects. Nonstandard dialects may be used by students whose only language is English and by bilingual students. Standard English is also a dialect, but it is the dominant one, used by most members of society.

Variations in the *phonological* aspects of language production are heard quite often throughout the United States (e.g., the differences in the pronunciation of certain vowels in the Southeast, Northeast, or Midwest may be referred to as a Southern "accent," New England "accent," or Midwestern "accent"). Vocabulary (semantic) variations are also prevalent; for example, speakers from different parts of the country may refer to the same beverage as "pop," "soda," or "a soft drink." These variations are not considered renditions of nonstandard English, but rather, regional dialect variations. Although there are some semantic and sound considerations, a nonstandard English dialect is most often perceived in terms of *grammatical* variation. When a student drops or adds morphological units (e.g., "He land on his feets" as opposed to "He landed on his feet"), uses archaic language forms (e.g., the Elizabethan English *ain't* instead of the modern English *isn't,* and double negatives such as "We don't have no more of them" instead of "We don't have any more of them"), or does not use standard subject-verb agreement ("Charles like it" instead of "Charles likes it"), the student is usually tagged as a nonstandard dialect speaker.

Most people have a positive attitude toward regional dialect differences, viewing them as interesting products of our diverse heritage ("You say to-ma-to, I say to-mah-to"; "What a charming Southern accent she has."). But, many standard English speakers have decidedly negative feelings about the grammatical (and sometimes semantic and sound) variations of nonstandard American dialects, probably because these are frequently associated with low socioeconomic levels. The attitude is that these sociocultural dialects should be changed (although this is considered unnecessary for regional dialect variations).

Pressure to adopt the standard dialect comes not only from speakers of standard English, but also from many nonstandard dialect speakers themselves; for example, the parents in homes where a nonstandard dialect is spoken who believe an important role of the school is to teach their children the "standard" manner of speaking as a prerequisite to job success and upward social mobility. This attitude indicates dual goals for teachers in relation to the *oral language* of nonstandard dialect speakers: although one purpose may be to help these students add a second dialect (standard English) for social reasons, the second purpose—of more importance to reading teachers—is to understand how nonstandard dialects should be handled so they do not adversely affect reading achievement.

Much research has been conducted about nonstandard dialect production. What this research shows is that nonstandard dialects are viable language forms in their own right with their own rules and complexities, just as in the dialect known as standard English. They communicate equally well. These dialects are not a deficient or substandard language form; they are only different.

There is no exact match between any oral dialect (including standard English) and written language. Therefore, it is not surprising that research has also shown that the lack of an exact match between the language forms of nonstandard dialects and the printed language found in reading material does not affect reading achievement, if handled appropriately by teachers. Attempts to change written materials to match students' dialect productions also have made no differences. For example, an effort several years ago at writing instructional materials such as basal readers in one or more of the various African-American dialects used in the U.S. failed to produce changes in reading ability of African-American dialect-speaking students (and also caused waves of protest from African-American parents who wanted their children's school exposure to language to be consistent with that of the mainstream culture). Likewise, rewriting standardized reading tests in African-American dialects has made no difference in scores obtained. Attempts to change the oral language of students to standard English have also failed to promote *reading growth*.

Nonstandard dialect speakers understand standard English even if they don't always produce it. They understand television. They understand their teachers and others who speak standard English. They can also understand printed English. In fact, when students orally read a printed form so that it conforms to their own oral speech, this is a clear indication that they do understand the author's message. Doing this is referred to as a *dialect translation*. For example, if the text reads, "She isn't at home," and a rural Appalachian student reads, "She ain't at home," the student has had to understand the printed sentence to translate its meaning to the spoken form of his or her own oral language.

The major implication from research is that teachers must distinguish between language differences and reading errors. Studies shows that teachers require students to correct meaningful miscues (those that do not affect the meaning gained from the page) more often when those miscues represent a dialect variation than when they do not. In these cases, teachers are confusing goals. In a language arts lesson designed to aid students in adding a second dialect to their language repertoires, discussing alternative ways to express meaning may be appropriate (e.g., pointing out that another way to make the statement "She ain't at home" is, "She isn't at home"). However, in the case of reading, the nonstandard English performance does not affect the purpose of reading—getting meaning. When oral reading during instructional lessons and on tests is evaluated, dialect renditions must be assessed for what they are—simply variations of the most common dialect—and not as mistakes. Dialect alternatives are not reading errors.

In sum, research does not show that structural differences between standard English and other dialects—those differences reflected in phonology, morphology, or syntax—are the cause of reading problems among nonstandard dialect speakers (Weber, 1991).

Language Interference   *Language interference* is the phenomenon of sounds, syntax, and vocabulary of two languages intruding on each other as they come into contact in the learner's oral language learning and reading experiences. Some educators have suggested that language interference is detrimental to the reading growth of non-English-speaking students as they learn English as a second language. This has also been suggested as a problem for nonstandard English speakers and bilingual students.

At the phonological (sound) level, English sounds may be perceived in terms of the sound system of the student's first language or dialect. In Spanish, for example, there are only five variations in vowel sounds, while in English there are many. Therefore, a Spanish-speaking student may pronounce some English vowels to make them sound like one of the vowel sounds of Spanish. Likewise, some African-American vernacular dialects employ other sound substitutions (e.g., /f/ for final /th/ as in *wreaf* instead of *wreath*). During *oral* English instruction, it may be appropriate to teach students to hear these differences, but the differences have little importance in understanding what is *read*. If an African-American student reads,"Tiny Tim hung the Christmas *wreaf*" (instead of *wreath*), the pronunciation does not change the author's intended meaning. If a teacher asks, "Did that make sense?" the student can rightfully say, "Yes." Teachers must maintain the attitude that there is more than one acceptable pronunciation of a word. It is important to be sensitive to the phonological differences in the student's primary language.

At the syntactic level, non-English-speaking students may face a special learning task as they attempt to gain control of English sentence structure because syntactic rules vary across languages. Spanish syntax, for example, is quite different from English. In addition, the order in which English syntactic and morphological rules become a part of the student's oral English varies according to the first language of the student, and it often differs from the order of acquisition by native English speakers. Special attention to English syntactic form is often necessary in oral language instruction for non-English-speaking students. Bilingual students may read more slowly in their weaker language because of the need to mentally reorganize syntactic forms to obtain their meanings. However, when the second language is fully developed (i.e., is not weaker than the first), this finding does not hold true.

Concerns of language interference at the semantic level are related to vocabulary. Bilingual speakers frequently intermingle English expressions with vocabulary from their primary language, resulting in polylinguistic expressions when *speaking* in either of their languages. Ziros (1976) gives the example, "Your mother is planching" in which the Spanish word *planchando,* which means "ironing," was anglicized to fit into an English sentence. However, Ziros points out that vocabulary switching in oral language does not hamper students' cognitive activities and is not detrimental to reading growth. In fact, research indicates that bilingualism may have a cognitive benefit (Hakuta, 1986).

Lack of Oral English.   Superior education in a multilingual classroom diverges in notable ways from outstanding instruction in a class composed of students who all are native speakers of English (Faltis, 1993). Currently there are three basic approaches for providing literacy education to non-English-speaking students who are enrolled in U.S. and Canadian schools. One is called *transitional bilingual education.* In such programs, initial reading instruction occurs in materials using the student's mother tongue, while during the same period, oral English is gradually introduced. The viewpoint of educators subscribing to this approach is that, while students need time to gain control of the second language (English), they *can* learn to read at a normal rate of progress if given the opportunity to do so in their first language—the language in which they already are proficient (Weber, 1991).

A second approach, adopting what is called a *submersion* program, introduces reading instruction in English immediately, and concurrently, with instruction in oral English. In these programs, no literacy instruction takes place in the context of the student's first language.

In *structured immersion programs,* the third general approach, there also is an immediate use of English in literacy instruction, but with the first language employed when deemed appropriate by the teacher. In these classrooms, English predominates in listening, speaking, reading, and writing activities because of the belief that students will become fluent speakers and readers of English more quickly if they are immersed in it— the view also held by proponents of submersion programs.

Research results on the effectiveness of these approaches are mixed. Willig (1985), for example, found faster rates in attaining English literacy skills among students who first learned to read in their mother tongue in transitional bilingual education classes, but Gersten's (1985) study showed higher achievement among students instructed in structured immersion programs. In any of these cases, students must eventually deal with the complicated tasks of moving across languages to become competent readers of English texts. Interestingly, young children have been shown to be able to use the knowledge they have of literacy in their native language to help themselves in literacy acts in the new language they are learning. This has been the case particularly in writing development (Edelsky, 1986), but in reading as well (Moll & Diaz, 1987), even when the student is not yet skillful in *speaking* English (Edelsky, 1986). However, in the middle grades successful reading achievement in English appears to be more strongly associated with proficiency in spoken English (Weber, 1991). What is more, English learned outside the school may not entirely suffice. Studies have shown that English used in classrooms differs in a number of ways from English learned in vernacular settings (Piper, 1993).

Many states now have laws that make oral English instruction mandatory for non-English-speaking and bilingual students. For example, Alaska requires that any school system with eight or more students whose first language is not English must provide special language programs. Many states also have mandated adaptations in assessment practices for such students (Bennett, 1987). (Interestingly, some educators have suggested that majority culture English-speaking students learn a non-English language at the same time minority students are learning English [e.g., Hakuta & Gould, 1987]).

To develop *oral* English, teachers use concrete objects and pictures to teach vocabulary for nouns and role-playing to develop knowledge of action words. To promote *reading,* games can be employed in which printed words are matched to pictures. Sentence scrambling and cloze activities are also helpful to assist students in gaining control of English syntax. Students need to use new vocabulary and syntactic forms frequently to have good retention of them. Some teachers use songs to promote retention. Teaching students songs and having them sing these every day provides repeated exposures to the second language. Puppets are helpful if young non-English-speaking students are shy about practicing their new language learning. Tape recorders are useful with both younger and older students. Opportunities to engage in extended discussions in English are important (Ramirez, Yuen, Ramey, & Pasta, 1990).

The language experience approach (LEA) has been widely adopted by teachers of English as a second language (ESL) to use when students are ready to make the switch from reading their first language to reading English. This approach is helpful because student-dictated stories or informational passages reflect the oral vocabulary students have mastered. Moustafa and Penrose (1985) suggest that teachers prepare limited-English-speaking students for an LEA lesson by adding new oral vocabulary and giving practice with sentence structure through discussions of pictures prior to each dictation. To do this, the teacher is to point to people, objects, places, and actions in pictures and ask that they be named. To reinforce oral language development, questions about the pictures should be repeated so that students produce names and answers to questions several times during the course of the lesson. To transfer these oral English words to print, key words about the picture are printed on cards and matched to that portion of the picture. Finally, students dictate information about the picture, and their statements are printed for (a) the teacher to read *to* them, (b) the teacher and students to read in unison, (c) the students to read as a group without the teacher, and (d) the students to read individually. Moustafa and Penrose found that LEA stories were longer and contained more appropriate English syntax when dictation was preceded by picture discussion.

It is also important to tie reading lessons to other language arts activities to reinforce new learning. After students have learned to read their own dictated stories successfully in English, then listening, reading, speaking, and writing may be developed simultaneously. Correlation of these language activities will support a smoother transition into the reading of published materials.

Gersten and Jiménez (1994) describe an effective "sheltered English" reading lesson using Big Books, the type of book that sits on an easel and is large enough for a group to see pictures and print. In the example they gave, the teacher read to the students using a slightly slower than normal pace, stopping after every two or three pages to determine students' knowledge of word meanings and understanding of ideas. Meanings of key words were *demonstrated* (e.g., for the word *pierce* the teacher pierced a hole in paper with scissors) and were related to known concepts (the teacher pointed out the pierced ears of the some of the girls in the class). Only vocabulary words particularly significant for understanding the story were highlighted rather than overwhelming the students with large numbers of words. Comprehension questions were interspersed throughout the reading, both at the literal level and the inferential level. After reading, the highlighted vocabulary was written on the chalkboard, and students used the words in context, writing in their journals. Finally, each student drew a picture based on the story and described it to the group—an activity designed to promote extended use of oral English.

Some special considerations for teaching reading to students who are only beginning to learn English, are the following.

1. Take special care to explain English idioms. Confusions result from literal interpretation of phrases like *she came out smelling like a rose, he escaped by the skin of his teeth, he bit her head off,* or *she had a bitter pill to swallow.* When idioms such as these appear in published reading material, discuss them.
2. After the common meanings of English words are learned, attention should be given to multiple meanings ("There are leaves under the tree"; "She put the leaves in the table").
3. Homonyms may also cause problems (*hair/hare; hole/whole*). Explain the differences when the words occur in oral language or reading instruction.
4. It often aids comprehension for students to engage in prereading activities designed to provide background information. Moreover, both knowledge of English syntactic structure and knowledge of English vocabulary affect comprehension.

Gersten and Jiménez (1994) studied reading instruction of language minority students in real classrooms to determine which procedures used were productive; the following practices were found to be most effective:

1. Promoting English vocabulary development
   a. Taking time out to determine students' understanding of important new vocabulary in stories
   b. Giving students opportunities to *use* the new vocabulary in meaningful ways
2. Providing mediation and feedback
   a. Paraphrasing students' statements (The teacher asks, "What did the mosquito do?" The student replies, "Buzz." The teacher says, "Yes, it buzzed in peoples' ears.")

        b. Prompting expanded replies

        c. Asking questions that necessitate elaborated answers to give practice in expressing ideas in English

   3. Presenting the same information in both oral and written forms (The teacher asks questions before students read. While they are reading, the teacher writes the same questions on the chalkboard for students to refer to.)

   4. Showing sensitivity to language needs

        a. Using oral language that is relatively consistent (minimizing use of synonyms during early stages of English development)

        b. Minimizing use of idioms early on

Furthermore, they found useful any activities with much student involvement that encouraged higher-level thinking, and that provided for extended discussion. These included many activities and approaches that have been stressed throughout this book for all students with special learning needs: having high, but reasonable, expectations; involving *all* students in activities; assigning tasks at which students *can* be successful and overtly noting students' successes; providing scaffolding through teacher modeling and thinking aloud; using visual organizers and story maps; teaching metacognitive strategies as well as skills; employing collaborative learning as an adjunct to direct instruction; incorporating students' first language when appropriate; and showing respect for cultural diversity.

    Teachers' Store I lists some materials that can be used with students when teaching reading through their first language and some for students who are in the stage where they are making a transition to reading in English. Several professional references also are listed for you to learn more about this topic. Ample reading material in students' first language should be available in the classroom—as well as in the school library.

Cultural Considerations

Considerations related to differences in cultural backgrounds of students that are relevant to reading instruction are diversities in value systems and differences in concept development based on experiences.

Value Systems.   As you may remember from your sociology courses, *mores* (moreaz) are accepted traditional customs and beliefs of cultural groups. Mores or value systems of individuals can affect how they learn best and how they perform in relation to school expectations. Earlier in this book, studies were cited showing that some Hawaiian children learned best when verbal interactions during reading lessons were like those of their oral language traditions and that certain Native American, as well as some African-American and Hispanic-American students, participate in group activities more readily than in individual activities because of their value systems.

    Most schools promote views consistent with the middle-class American mores of hard work, delayed gratification, achievement orientation, and meeting one's responsibilities on time. These values contrast with those of some other cultures whose children are educated in American schools. Culturally instilled beliefs of some groups, for example, are to maintain the occupational positions of one's parents rather than to strive for higher socioeconomic status; to value anonymity rather than recognition; to experience the joys of life each day rather than work to experience them at some later time; to work for the good of the group rather than strive for individual attainment; and to adopt

---

Teachers' Store I

Materials for Teaching Linguistically and Culturally Different Students

1. *Vietnamese/English Bilingual Readers* (National Textbook)
2. *The Spanish Oral Reading Test* (Paradox Press)
3. *Miami Linguistic Readers Series* (D. C. Heath)
4. *Bilingual Syntax Measure* (Harcourt Brace Jovanovich)
5. *Spanish Reading Charts* (Dissemination Center for Bilingual-Bicultural Education)
6. *Prueba del Desarrollo Inicial del Lenguaje* (PRO-ED)—the Spanish version of The Test of Early Language Development (TELD).
7. *El Gran Cesar* (Education Consulting Association)
8. *Primeros Pasos para Prepararse a Leer* (Highlights for Children); the Spanish version of *First Steps in Getting Ready to Read*.
9. *Maria Luisa* (Lippincott)
10. *Reading Adventures in Spanish and English* (Highlights for Children)
11. *I Am Here. Yo Estoy Aquí* (Franklin Watts Co.)
12. *Spanish-language audiovisual materials* (Proyecto LEER)
13. *Navajo and Zuni bilingual publications* (Gallup-McKinley County Public Schools, Gallup, New Mexico)
14. *Multilingual books and audiotapes in Vietnamese, Spanish, Korean, Cantonese, Mandarin, and Japanese* (Los Angeles City Schools, California)
15. *The Monster Series I and II* (Bowmar/Noble); Spanish version
16. *A test for determining language dominance in Indochinese students* (English/Vietnamese Bilingual Program)

Professional Resources for Teaching Linguistically and Culturally Different Students

Books

1. *Reading and the Bilingual Child* (International Reading Association)

---

an unhurried approach to meeting commitments rather than an approach based on respecting set times, being punctual, and making every minute productive.

Careful consideration of some of these values by harried, stress-ridden, middle-class Americans should cause one to see the good sense of alternate points of view. However, because these values are different from those of most professionals in the education system, problems can arise if teachers are insensitive to the traditions of the students they teach. Ogbu (1992) contends that groups whose cultural frameworks differ from the cultural frames of reference of mainstream society face genuine obstacles spanning cultural lines at school to learn.

To help students have successful learning experiences, teachers must respect differences in value systems, understand the specific values of groups within an individual classroom, help students acculturate to mainstream values within the school setting when their own values are detrimental to learning, and adapt teaching processes to the students' belief system when this facilitates learning. When attempting to adapt to stu-

---

Teachers' Store I (cont.)

2. *Literacy for America's Spanish-Speaking Children* (International Reading Association)
3. *When You Teach English as a Second Language* (Book-Lab)
4. *Hints for Dealing with Cultural Differences in Schools: A Handbook for Teachers Who Have Vietnamese Students in Their Classrooms* (Center for Applied Linguistics)
5. *Migrant Education* (International Reading Association)
6. *Reading and the Black English Speaking Child* (International Reading Association)
7. *Dialects and Educational Equity* (Center for Applied Linguistics)

ERIC Documents

1. "A Reading and Writing Program Using Language-Experience Methodology Among Adult ESL Students in a Basic Education Program" (ED 213 915)
2. "Providing Effective Reading Instruction for Refugee Students" (ED 217 373)
3. "A Haitian-Spanish Bilingual Program" (ED 200 696)
4. "The Challenge of the Multicultural Classroom" (ED 207 023)
5. "The Use of Games in Teaching a Second Language in the Classroom" (ED 225 357)
6. "Language Arts for Native Indian Students" (ED 238 630)
7. "A Review of Research on the Teaching of Reading in Bilingual Education" (ED 210 903)
8. "Chinese/Korean Bilingual Language Arts Resource Center" (ED 201 687)
9. "A Handbook for Teaching Vietnamese-Speaking Students" (ED 228 335)
10. "The Rock Point Experience: A Navajo School Program" (ED 195 363)
11. "Adult ESL Suggested Materials List" (ED 233 610)
12. "Language and Literacy Learning in Bilingual Instruction: Cantonese/English" (ED 245 572)

Audiovisual

The Children of Akiachak (Bureau of Indian Affairs, Fairbanks, Alaska); a film showing training techniques in bilingual education with young children.

---

dents' cultural differences, teachers should remember that there also are *differences among members of the same group or subgroup as well,* for example, between urban and rural low socioeconomic status (SES) African-Americans, among different Native American peoples, or among various Asiatic or Hispanic groups.

While teachers are selecting books for reading instruction with bilingual or bicultural students, they may also wish to select books to introduce their mainstream-culture students to a realistic understanding of the culture of these classmates. Books can help students avoid misleading overgeneralizations and distorted views. These books should realistically reflect the way of life of the group and avoid stereotypes. Second, they should seek to rectify historical omissions and distortions. Finally, they should contain illustrations that accurately reflect the diversity of the group.

One helpful resource for the teacher selecting these types of books is *Reading for Young People: The Southwest* (American Library Association). This is an annotated bibliography of books for students in grades K–12 about the Anglo, Native American, and

Spanish cultures of the American Southwest. Other annotated bibliographies of book titles for young people are *Shadow and Substance: Afro-American Experience in Contemporary Children's Fiction* (National Council of Teachers of English) and *Reading Ladders for Human Relations* (National Council of Teachers of English). See also Lankford and Riley (1986) for an example of a culturally relevant text for Native American students. Table 15–2 lists some excellent children's and adolescent literature representing diverse cultural groups.

Concept Development.   When students' backgrounds differ from those expected by the teacher, it may be found that they do not understand concepts presumed to be commonly known. For students who have always lived in this country, television has certainly filled some experiential gaps that might otherwise exist. Nevertheless, other subtle differences in vocabulary and concept knowledge often are seen. Students who have only recently moved to this country show greater disparities between their prior knowledge and that of the larger body of students in their schools. This is not to say that either of these groups has a deficiency of experience. Indeed, students from cultures other than middle-class American have rich backgrounds and vocabulary development specific to their own cultures that middle-class American students lack. Some of their concepts may be different from those routinely anticipated by teachers. The list that follows illustrates selected concepts or vocabulary that are common to certain cultural/regional groups within this country but less familiar to others:

Concept (Vocabulary)	Culture
chitterlings	African-American or Caucasian Southern rural
divan	Eastern rural
egg cream	Northeastern urban
hawk (not the bird)	African-American
lava tube	Hawaiian
poke salad	Appalachian
pollo	Southwestern Hispanic-American
salted soybeans	Hawaiian
scrapple	Eastern rural
volunteer corn	rural

TABLE 15–2
Some excellent children's and adolescent literature representing diverse cultural groups

And Now Miguel by Krumgold (Hispanic-American)
Blue Willow by Gates (Migrant families)
Hannah Elizabeth by Rich (Amish)
The Cornrows by Yarborough (African-American)
Child of the Owl by Yep (Asian-American)
When Thunders Spoke by Sneve (Native American)
First Snow by Coutant and Vo-Dinh (Asian-American)
When I Was Young in the Mountains by Rylant (Appalachian)
To Stand Against the Wind by Clark (Vietnamese refugee families)
Sing Down the Moon by O'Dell (Native American)
Plain Girl by Sorenson (Amish)
Where the Lilies Bloom by the Cleavers (Appalachian)
Tough Tiffany by Hurmence (African-American)
Judy's Journey by Lenski (Migrant families)

During reading instruction teachers should be alert to language and ideas that are based on experiences that may be unfamiliar to students who are not from mainstream America. These should be explained, experiences provided, opportunities for wide reading furnished, and vocabulary development activities offered. At the same time, the teacher should capitalize on the vocabulary and concepts culturally diverse students bring to the classroom by including these in reading lessons and activities. This latter strategy also allows majority-culture students to broaden their horizons.

Special Considerations for At-Risk Students

Students may be academically at risk for a number of reasons unrelated to linguistic and cultural differences, for example, because of physical impairments, emotional disturbance, drug abuse, or a myriad of other factors. However, many at-risk students served by reading specialists, especially Title I teachers, frequently are from nonmainstream groups with specific ethnic, racial, and linguistic identities, and often represent the urban or rural poor.

Differences That May Originate From the Home Environment.   Special considerations are needed when providing remedial or clinical reading instruction for students from low socioeconomic status (SES) backgrounds. Children from low SES homes may come to school with fewer of the experiences that promote rapid reading growth, and they may lack helpful support at home throughout their school years. A dual approach can be taken to help at-risk students overcome limitations that have originated in the home environment: educate parents and make adaptations at school.

One route to amelioration of the problems of these children is through *parent education*. This point has been touched on briefly in the discussion of family literacy. Some parents from low-income homes are willing participants in programs to help their children have school success. Others wish to do so, but have difficulty adding this responsibility to the mix of their other duties and problems. Efforts can be made by school professionals to help this latter group find at least limited ways to be of assistance. McConnell's (1989) report of work with Northern Cheyenne and Hispanic-American children concluded that parental involvement can have a pivotal influence on literacy accomplishments for minority students, as did Goldenberg's (1987) research with low-income Hispanic-American parents and children.

Teachers find it helpful when working with parents to provide information about home behaviors that have helped other at-risk children. Parents need to know that successful students

- are read aloud to by older brothers and sisters
- come from homes where discipline is evident, but fair
- come from homes rich in books
- come from organized homes
- have parents who are aware of local, national, and world events (and presumably model an interest in these for their children)
- have parents who read themselves
- have parents who show an interest in each of their children's needs and interests
- have parents who understand the value of education to their own lives and the lives of their children

There can also be adaptations at school. Some myths have arisen about the causes for reading failure in at-risk children. Teachers should be aware of these. For example, research has shown that factors unrelated to success or failure include absent fathers, the size of the family, attendance at many schools, and a working mother (Greenberg & Davidson, 1972). Not only does the school lack control over these conditions, but the data point out that school attempts to compensate for home-originated limitations should concentrate directly on educationally related variables. Some suggestions for adaptations within the school setting follow.

1. Have a classroom rich in books. There should be many books, a wide variety of types, and books of high appeal, including fiction and nonfiction that are easy, short, funny, colorful, scary, and a myriad of other engaging types. Ascertain students' interests, and be sure there are books related to them. Research has shown, for example, that at-risk students who are second-language learners have significantly improved comprehension when books are of interest to them (Elley & Mangubhai, 1983).

2. Structure your program so that independent activity time and free time are spent in reading (or even just looking at) books.

3. Set up learning centers with listening stations so students can hear taped books read to them as they follow the words and/or pictures.

4. Take students to the school library regularly to check out books (even if the books are sometimes lost). Use of the library significantly increases the number of books read by at-risk students who don't have books bought for them in the home (Rodriguez-Trujillo, 1986). Also, make a field trip to acquaint students with the services of the *public library*.

5. Help students acquire and own books. Use school or PTA/PTO funds to purchase inexpensive books and give them to students.

For at-risk students, it is important to encourage heavy involvement in authentic reading tasks, as opposed to an emphasis on workbook activities.

6.   Have magazines in your room intended for both young people and adults. Bring in your own magazines rather than discard them and give them to students to take home.

7.   During sustained silent reading (SSR), read so students see an adult reading. Talk to students about books you loved as a child; have them available for your students to read. Tell them about books you are reading and enjoying now.

8.   Read aloud to students—every day. Choose books of high-quality children's or adolescent literature. When doing so, provide interactions that encourage advanced conceptualizations. Even if your at-risk students have had home experiences in listening to books read, they may not have experienced the rich discussions that lead to advanced literacy success. Investigations (Edwards, 1989; Heath, 1982) have shown that mainstream parents scaffold information by comparing ideas from several books, as well as linking text to background experiences. However, nonmainstream parents tend to focus attention more restrictedly on the text at hand. Consistent text reading experiences of either type positively affect beginning reading acquisition, but only ones that incorporate scaffolding are associated with attainment in higher-level comprehension. Use story-comparison charts as seen in Figure 15–7; students write in comparisons of books they have shared as a group.

FIGURE 15–7
Story comparison charts

Books We Have Read About Mice			
Title	Once A Mouse by Brown	Frederick by Lionni	Mouse Tales by Lobel
Main characters	A mouse, a man	Frederick, the mouse	
Other characters	A bird		
Problem			
How the story ends			

Our Favorite Folk Tales			
Name	Country of origin	Human or animal characters?	Moral or lesson

9.   Capitalize on the rich (although sometimes different) backgrounds students bring to school. Use these as an impetus to read, write, share, and then compare with the experiences of others.

10.   Plan for copious amounts of connected text reading.

11.   Informally assess learning frequently, relying on careful and constant scrutiny of students' reading behaviors (sometimes called "kid watching").

12.   Teach students to self-monitor and to use other metacognitive strategies to empower them as learners.

13.   Allow students to engage in paired learning; process writing is a good example of this when students are involved in peer conferences for planning, revising, and editing their written work.

14.   Decrease the assignment of worksheets and workbooks; increase the amount of direct teacher instruction in authentic reading tasks.

15.   Establish an organized classroom; have set procedures and no wasted time; let every minute of the school day include interesting intellectual stimulation.

16.   Help students learn self-discipline and help organize their own tasks and time.

17.   Try to understand students' problems, but remember that the kindest thing you can do for at-risk students is to help them obtain a first-rate education. You do have control over what happens in your classroom, and education is the business of schools.

18.   If disruptive behavior occurs, be firm, consistent, and fair about refusing to accept those behaviors in an educational setting.

19.   Have successful individuals who have come from ethnic or racial backgrounds similar to your students talk to them to provide inspiration and models.

20.   Expand students' interests. Try to get them intrigued with things beyond their own homes or neighborhoods.

Problems That May Originate at School.   Problems in low SES students' learning can also be caused by attitudes of educational personnel. Unfortunately, some teachers and administrators hold lower expectations for these students than for their middle- and upper-class counterparts. Low expectations lead to low achievement. In contrast, Durkin (1982) reported, in a study of poor African-American children who became successful readers, that minority students from low-income homes were most likely to read at or above grade level when the school gave special attention to reading—and when it maintained high expectations for students. In discussing programs for at-risk students, Durkin (1982) stated that "children achieve what they are expected to achieve." Although teachers may find it necessary to provide compensatory and remedial activities for low SES students, their ultimate expectations for these students should equal those for others. A watered-down program or a willingness to adapt to a lower set of standards does an injustice to at-risk children.

Understanding cultural attitudes and predilections can also provide a basis for learning so students rise to meet your expectations. It has been pointed out earlier that many sociocultural groups value group participation and cooperation rather than a focus on the individual (Heath, 1991). Table 15–3 shows two important differences between what often is esteemed in mainstream cultures (expectations that may cause difficulties for at-risk students) and what is valued in many nonmainstream communities.

TABLE 15–3
Mainstream and nonmainstream expectations

Mainstream Expectations (Parents and School)	Expectations in Many Nonmainstream Communities
• Individual learning and displays of knowledge • Knowledge imparted by an "expert" (teacher/parent)	• Group learning and cooperative displays of knowledge • Knowledge gained through direct participation

These differences have implications for teaching at-risk students, and they suggest use of cooperative learning procedures. Cooperative learning activity places nonmainstream students at an advantage when they are allowed to create stories collaboratively, solve problems together, share information, and learn through participation.

In schools where large numbers of students come from populations that historically have not fared well in our educational system, reading teachers can take a leadership role in assessing the school reading program. Schoolwide efforts to adopt a goal of high achievement for all, and to provide a careful, systematic, and rich reading program in every classroom have had an appreciable impact in low-income areas.

The Success for All Program.   The Success for All Program (Slavin, Madden, Karweit, Dolan, & Wasik, 1992) is a specially conceived intervention effort in inner-city schools with high-risk students in six states. Begun in Baltimore, Maryland, this program is indeed providing success for many at-risk readers. The Success for All plan encompasses two components: (a) regular classroom reading instruction and (b) tutoring.

The *regular classroom instruction* is organized so that teaching occurs in groups of about 15 children in grades 1 through 3. Though grouped heterogeneously during the rest of the day, the children move to their special reading class—grouped so that students of only one reading level are in the room—where they receive instruction for 90 minutes, 5 days a week. Direct teacher guidance is employed throughout the period and no independent seatwork activities are used. Classroom teachers, Title I reading teachers, special education teachers, and tutors who are certified teachers all share the responsibility of teaching the reading sections; thus class size is kept at a reasonable level.

Instruction consists of (a) reading *to* students; (b) discussions of story structure; (c) development of oral language skills; (d) connected text reading, with an emphasis on oral reading in early stages; (e) systematic instruction with phonics, including work on phonemic awareness and on letter sounds and blending; (f) teaching error-correction strategies; (g) development of an instantly recognized sight vocabulary; (h) repeated reading of texts to promote fluency; (i) writing to facilitate word recognition and identification, as well as process writing; (j) attention to comprehension and to metacognitive strategy use; (k) partner reading and paired-practice activities (Wasik & Slavin, 1993).

Basal reading materials are used along with specially written stories that emphasize the phonic understandings being taught in class. For some time, reading researchers have called for texts in which there was a relation between phonics lessons and what students must read. This recommendation is based on studies showing the helpfulness of this practice (e.g., see M. J. Adams, 1990a, 1990b; R. C. Anderson, Hiebert, Scott, & Wilkinson, 1984). The trick is to write stories that are engaging and that have natural language structures, while at the same time including words that incorporate sounds and phonic generalizations learners have been practicing. This is what the Success for All program has tried to do.

Student progress is evaluated every 8 weeks. Parental involvement is a part of the program, including use of parent support teams. Parents oversee that students meet requirements, such as the assignment to read a library book at home each night for 20 minutes. There also is a part-day preschool program and a full-day kindergarten program as a part of Success for All.

Teachers are trained for the program for 2 days before school begins and receive an additional 4 days of training at a later time during the year.

The goal of Success for All is that all students learn to read "the first time they are taught" and that they not require remedial services at a later time. To assist with the achievement of this objective the second major component is a one-to-one *tutoring program* for students who are in the lowest 25% of their classes based on a battery of pretests. Tutoring is begun in first grade, and if needed, continued into second and third grades. The tutoring is a supplement to the reading instruction that children receive in the regular classroom program and is closely integrated with it. Tutoring occurs for 20 minutes, 5 days a week, and teachers in the classroom program use a communication system to let tutors know what the tutored children have been working on in the regular reading class. Tutors all are certified teachers who receive the same Success for All training as the other school personnel. The tutoring activities are based on the belief that one learns to read by reading, but specific attention also is given to skills and strategy work. The framework of each tutoring session is seen in Figure 15–8.

Excellent results have been attained with the Success for All program. Students participating in the intervention have scored significantly higher on reading measures at the end of the year. What is more, there has been a growing difference after each year the children have been in the program. This effectiveness has been seen for all learners, even those in the bottom one fourth of class (Wasik & Slavin, 1993). A school in Philadelphia has used Success for All with limited-English-proficient Cambodian refugee children with very positive effects.

FIGURE 15–8
Success for All: framework for a tutoring session

- The session begins with the student reading orally from a familiar story previously read in the regular reading class.
- This is followed by a 1-minute drill on letter sounds that are being practiced in the regular class.
- Most of the session is spent on the oral reading of specially designed "shared stories" that are written to be predictable and interesting. The stories contain phonemically controlled vocabulary written in large type and other words written in small type. The student reads the large-type words; the teacher reads the small. The teacher provides assistance with sounding out words when needed. The stories correspond to work in the regular class.
- Comprehension questions are asked and answered.
- Passages from the story are reread to promote fluency.
- The student engages in writing activities.

Source: Wasik & Slavin, 1993.

CONCLUSION

The problems of illiteracy and functional illiteracy and issues surrounding them have become widely discussed topics. They are, indeed, subjects about which reading and learning disabilities teachers, as well as the full educational community, should be fully informed. Illiteracy and functional illiteracy have negative effects on society as a whole: they are associated with unemployment, impoverishment, welfare costs, and increased crime rates. Equally important, the detrimental effects on the individual illiterate are well known; it is difficult in our society for anyone to lead a life of self-satisfaction and pro-ductivity without being able to read.

Solutions to reading problems need to be sought—and solutions implemented—in students' early years of schooling. Throughout the school years, programs should be set up to address the needs of those with reading disabilities. Enrollment in, and successful completion of, adult literacy programs should be dramatically increased for society's welfare and the welfare of low-literacy individuals.

This chapter also has been concerned with issues that are fundamental to working with students with ethnic, language, and social class differences. The United States is undergoing a change in demographics; by the year 2000, it is predicted that as high as 40% of school-age individuals will come from ethnically diverse groups that vary from present mainstream America. Remedial teachers must be as prepared to understand stu-dents' conceptions of language and culture as they are to understand the reading process. This necessitates a strong inclination on the part of the teacher to be concerned with the affective as well as the academic nature of the learning environment.

📖 REFLECTIONS

Linguistic and cultural diversity has always been a part of the United States. At the time the United States gained its independence, for example, many languages were spoken. Weber (1991) reminds us that not only were there speakers of English, but there were people speaking languages of the many countries from which the new United States was receiving immigrants, persons from the nearby New World colonies of Spain and France, and Native American speakers. Throughout the years, individuals, languages, and cultural practices have arrived from all over the world. Canada has had a similarly richly diverse cultural and linguistic history.

For both these countries, a willingness to accept immigration to strengthen the nation and to be responsive to human rights will continue to add this important contri-bution to life in the Americas.

Consider the following.

1. Why is it difficult for many people to accept differences? What are the responsibilities of educators in this regard?
2. What linguistic differences have you dealt with as a teacher (or individual)? What cul-tural differences?
3. What specifically can you plan to do as a teacher in regard to the linguistic and cul-tural differences experienced in classrooms?

Supplementary Test Bank: Intelligence Tests

T est banks have been placed throughout chapters of this book in relation to various topics that the tests relate to (e.g., reading inventories, writing skills). This Supplementary Test Bank lists intelligence tests that may be of interest to teachers.

		Intelligence Tests		
Name	For Ages	Type of Administration	Time for Administration	Publisher
Kaufman Assessment Battery for Children (K–ABC). Also available for hearing impaired and non-English-speaking children	2.5–12.5	Individual	35–85 minutes	American Guidance Service
Peabody Picture Vocabulary Test—Revised. Also available for Spanish-speaking students	2.5–adult	Individual	10–20 minutes	American Guidance Service
Stanford-Binet Intelligence Scale, Fourth Edition (S–B)	2 and up	Individual	30–90 minutes	Riverside
Wechsler Adult Intelligence Scale—Revised (WAIS–R)	16 and up	Individual	60–90 minutes	Psychological Corporation

Intelligence Tests *(continued)*

Name	For Ages	Type of Administration	Time for Administration	Publisher
Wechsler Intelligence Scale for Children— Revised (WISC–R). Spanish edition available	6–16	IIndividual	50–75 minutes	Psychological Corporation

B

Easy-to-Read, High-Interest, Content-Area Books

Many lists of easy-to read, high-interest story books are available to help remedial teachers. However, most reading teachers believe their responsibilities to disabled readers extend beyond the remedial classroom, resource room, or clinic. The books in this list will make poor readers more comfortable in their regular classes and better able to learn. Share this information about easy-to-read, high-interest, content-area books with other teachers. Some books listed here are suitable for upper elementary school students, but most are intended for students in middle school or senior high school.

B–1
English

Title and Publisher	Instructional Level	Reading Level
Get It Down in Writing (Xerox)	7–12	2.5–4.5
The Learning Language Skills Series: Language Arts (McGraw-Hill)	7 and up	1.5
Learning Our Language, Books One and Two (Follett)	7–Adult	5
Guidebook to Better English (Economy)	7–Adult	4.7
Getting Help (Skill area: language arts) (Xerox)	9–12	3.5–4.5
Write for the Job (Xerox)	9–12	3.5–4.5
Read It Right (Using reference materials) (Xerox)	7–12	2.5–4.5
Language Workshop: A Guide to Better English (Globe)	7–12	4–5
The World of Vocabulary Series (Globe)	8–12	2–7
Everyday English (Globe)	7–12	3–4
Writing Sense (Globe)	7–12	5–6
Writing a Research Paper (Globe)	7–12	5–6
Using Spelling, Capitalization, and Punctuation Packs (Holcombs)	7–12	2.5–3.5
The Business of Basic English (Holcombs)	7–12	4.5–5.5
English for Everyday Living (Holcombs)	7–12	3.0–4.0

B–1 *(continued)*

Title and Publisher	Instructional Level	Reading Level
Language Drills, Book 1—52 Duplicating Masters (Holcombs)	7–12	3.0–4.0
Language Drills, Book 2—50 Duplicating Masters (Holcombs)	7–12	3.5–4.5
Big Time Comics—Complete Collection (Written Expression: Paragraphs & Sentences) (Holcombs)	7–12	2.0–6.0
Letter Writing Learning Lab (Holcombs)	7–12	3.0–4.0
Writing Skills for Everyday Life—A Multimedia Program (Holcombs)	8–12	5.0–7.0
Spotlight on Writing (Reproducible activities) (Holcombs)	7–12	2.0–4.0
Letter Writing Skills (Reproducible activities) (Holcombs)	7–12	3.5–4.5
Writing to Others Program (Holcombs)	8–12	3.0–4.0
English for Employment (Holcombs)	8–12	4.0–5.0
English for Everyday (Holcombs)	7–12	3.0–4.0
How Do I Fill Out a Form? Duplicating Masters (Holcombs)	9–12	3.5–4.5
Basic Writing Skills: The Freddy Klinker Skill-Box Series (Holcombs)	7–12	3.0–5.5
Improve Your Writing for Job Success (Handwriting kit) (Holcombs)	7–12	3.0–4.0
Handwriting Legibility Kit (Holcombs)	7–12	2.5–3.5
Webster's Alphabetical Thesaurus (Holcombs)	7–12	5.5–6.5
Super Dictionary Activity Unit (Holcombs)	7–12	4.0–5.0
Using a Dictionary Duplicating Masters (Holcombs)	7–12	4.5–5.5
Library Strategies Learning Lab (Holcombs)	7–12	3.0–4.0
Libraries Are for Finding Out: Using the Encyclopedia (Holcombs)	7–12	3.5–4.5
Libraries Are for Finding Out: Using the Card Catalog (Holcombs)	7–12	3.5–4.5
Using Reference Skills Performance Pack (Holcombs)	7–12	3.5–5.0
Language Skills Crossword Puzzles Duplicating Masters (Holcombs)	7–12	3.0–5.0
Grammar for Adult Living (Holcombs)	9–12	3.0–4.0
English Exercises Duplicating Masters (Holcombs)	7–12	2.0–3.0
Spinning Grammar Game Set (Holcombs)	7–12	3.0–4.0
Spelling Rules and Problem Areas Learning Lab (Holcombs)	7–12	2.0–3.0
Spell Stumpers Duplicating Masters (Holcombs)	7–12	2.5–3.5
Basic Writing Game Module (Holcombs)	7–12	3.0–4.0
Right Your Writing Performance Pack (Holcombs)	7–12	3.5–4.5
Spotlight on Sentences (Holcombs)	7–10	2.5–3.5
Sentence Writing Learning Lab (Holcombs)	7–12	3.0–4.0
Paragraph Writing Learning Lab (Holcombs)	7–12	3.5–4.5
Descriptive Writing: Using Nouns and Verbs (Holcombs)	7–12	3.0–4.0
Sentences and Paragraphs Workshop (Holcombs)	7–12	3.0–4.0
Activities for Writing and Rewriting (Holcombs)	7–12	3.5–4.5
Outlining Skills Duplicating Masters (Holcombs)	7–12	4.5–5.5
Flub Stubs (Composition) (Holcombs)	7–12	2.5–3.5
Everyday Reading and Writing (New Readers' Press)	7–12	5–6
From A to Z (Handwriting) (Steck-Vaughn)	7–Adult	1
Using English (Steck-Vaughn)	10–Adult	3–4
Everyday English (Steck-Vaughn)	10–Adult	4–5
Learning Our Language Revised Books 1 & 2 (Steck-Vaughn)	7–Adult	6–8
English Essentials: A Refresher Course Revised (Steck-Vaughn)	11–Adult	8–10
Fundamental English Review (Steck-Vaughn)	11–Adult	8–12

B–2

History

Title and Publisher	Instructional Level	Reading Level
The New Exploring World History (Globe)	7–12	5–6
Exploring American Citizenship (Globe)	7–12	5–6
Cultures in Conflict (Globe)	7–12	5–6
Our Nation of Immigrants (Globe)	7–12	5–6
Inquiry: Western Civilization (Globe)	7–12	5–7
The Afro-American in the United States History (Globe)	7–12	5–6
Pollution of the Environment (Globe)	9–12	8
The New Exploring Our Nation's History (Globe)	7–12	6–7
United States Government (Bowmar/Noble)	7–12	4–6
The War Between the States (Educational Insights)	7–12	4
Frontiers West (Educational Insights)	7–12	4
American History Study Lessons Units 1–9 (Follett)	7–12	5
Study Lessons in Our Nation's History (Follett)	7–12	5
World History Study Lessons Units 1–9 (Follett)	7–12	5
Study Lessons in Civics (Follett)	7–12	6–9
The New Exploring American History (Globe)	7–12	5–6
Civilizations of the Past: Peoples and Cultures (Globe)	7–9	6
The United States: Its People and Leaders (Globe)	7–9	4
The Story of William Penn (Prentice-Hall)	7–12	3
William Penn: Founder of Pennsylvania (Wm. Morrow)	7	4–5
Human Cargo: The Story of the Atlantic Slave Trade (Garrard)	7	6
North to Liberty: The Story of the Underground Railroad (Garrard)	7–9	6
The American Revolution (Educational Insights)	7–12	4
Our Indian Heritage (Xerox)	7–9	4–5
Women in American Life (Xerox)	7–9	4–5
Youth Crime and Punishment (Xerox)	7–9	4–5
America Moves West (Xerox)	7–9	4–5
The Great Depression (Xerox)	7–9	4–5
Juveniles and the Law (Xerox)	7–9	4–5
The Labor Movement (Xerox)	7–9	4–5
Land of Immigrants (Xerox)	7–9	4–5
A Nation in Rebellion (Xerox)	7–9	4–5
Exploring Civilizations: A Discovery Approach (Globe)	7–12	5–6
The United States in the Making (Globe)	7–12	5–6
Our American Minorities (Globe)	7–12	3–4
(Benjamin) Franklin/(Martin Luther) King (Pendulum)	7–12	4–6
We Honor Them, Vols. 1, 2, 3, (Short biographies of African-Americans) (New Readers Press)	7–12	3–5
Insights About America (Educational Insights)	7–12	4
The Police and Us (New Readers Press)	7–12	3–4
Claiming a Right (Biography of 24 Indians) (New Readers Press)	7–12	3–4
Our United States (New Readers Press)	7–12	3–4
Government by the People (New Readers Press)	7–12	4–5
The Peoples' Power (New Readers Press)	7–12	4–5
Blacks in Time (New Readers Press)	7–12	4–5

B–2   *(continued)*

Title and Publisher	Instructional Level	Reading Level
I Am One of These (Real life stories of African-Americans, Caucasians, Mexican-Americans, Native Americans, Cubans, foreign-born citizens) (New Readers Press)	7–12	3–4
Martin Luther King (New Readers Press)	7–12	4–5
The Men Who Won the West (Scholastic)	7–12	4–7
Lincoln/Roosevelt (Pendulum)	7–12	4–6
Washington/Jefferson (Pendulum)	7–12	4–6
Crockett/Boone (Pendulum)	7–12	4–6
Lindbergh/Earhart (Pendulum)	7–12	4–6
Forts in the Wilderness (Children's Press)	7–12	4
Explorers in a New World (Children's Press)	7–12	4
Men on Iron Horses (Children's Press)	7–12	4
Pioneering on the Plains (Children's Press)	7–12	4
Settlers on a Strange Shore (Children's Press)	7–12	4

B–3
Math

Title and Publisher	Instructional Level	Reading Level
Daily Math Application Program (Holcombs)	10–12	4.5–5.5
Real-Life Math Program (Holcombs)	8–12	4.5–5.5
Using Checks and Charge Cards Learning Lab (Holcombs)	8–12	3.0–4.0
Survival Math Skills Program (Holcombs)	9–12	4.0–5.0
Using Money Wisely (Xerox)	9–12	3.5–4.5
Math for the Road (Xerox)	9–12	3.5–4.5
Checking Account: A Multimedia Kit (Holcombs)	9–12	5.5–6.5
Lakeshore Math Competency Performance Packs (Holcombs)	9–12	3.0–4.5
Math in the Marketplace Filmstrip Activity Library (Holcombs)	8–12	2.5–4.0
Basic Skills in Using Money (Holcombs)	9–12	4.0–5.0
Money Management Duplicating Masters (Holcombs)	8–12	4.5–5.5
Job Simulations Using Math (Holcombs)	9–12	4.0–5.0
Math for Employment 1 Skillbook (Holcombs)	9–12	4.5–5.5
Math for Employment 2 Skillbook (Holcombs)	9–12	4.5–5.5
Math for the Worker Skillbook (Holcombs)	9–12	4.5–5.5
Payroll Deductions Activity Unit (Holcombs)	9–12	5.5–6.5
Basic Buying Skills Duplicating Masters (Holcombs)	7–12	2.5–4.0
Using Consumer Math Competency Lab (Holcombs)	7–12	3.5–4.5
Consumer Math for Self-Defense (Holcombs)	7–12	5.0–6.0
Grocery Bills Skillbook (Holcombs)	7–12	2.5–3.5
Arithmetic for Grocery Shopping (Holcombs)	7–12	2.0–3.0
Consumer Math Strategies (Holcombs)	7–12	4.5–5.5
Newspaper Math Tasks (Holcombs)	7–10	4.5–5.5
Using Dollars and Sense Activity Book (Holcombs)	7–12	2.5–3.5
Everyday Math Survival Skills (Holcombs)	7–12	3.5–4.5

B–3 *(continued)*

Title and Publisher	Instructional Level	Reading Level
Mathematics and You: A Hands-On Approach (Holcombs)	7–12	4.5
Your Daily Math Skills Books 1 and 2 (Holcombs)	7–12	4.5–5.5
Math Marathon (Holcombs)	7–12	2.5–3.5
Math Puzzlers (Holcombs)	7–12	4.5–5.5
Metric Football (Holcombs)	7–12	4.0–5.0
Metric Puzzles Duplicating Module (Holcombs)	7–12	5.0–6.0
Measurement Learning Labs (Holcombs)	7–12	2.8–3.8
Money Makes Sense Activity Book (Holcombs)	7–12	2.0–3.0
Multi-Step Math Drill Cassettes (Holcombs)	7–12	2.5–3.5
Basic Math Facts Competency Lab (Holcombs)	7–12	2.0–4.0
Number Power Skillbook (Holcombs)	7–12	2.0–4.0
Back to Basics From Addition to Division (Holcombs)	7–12	2.5–4.5
Lifeskills Math Activity Book (Holcombs)	7–12	3.2–4.5
Veri-Tech: A Self-Check Basic Math System (Holcombs)	7–12	3.0–4.0
Sports Cards Math Kit (Holcombs)	7–12	3.0–4.0
Making Basic Math Easy (Holcombs)	7–12	4.2–5.5
Single Topic Math Duplicating Series (Holcombs)	7–12	4.5–5.5
Fractions Sequential Activity Card Set (Holcombs)	7–12	3.5–4.5
Lakeshore Learning Lab (Fractions and decimals) (Holcombs)	7–12	3.0–4.5
Decimals Sports Cards (Holcombs)	7–12	4.5–5.5
Figure It Out (Xerox)	5–9	2.5–3.5
The Learning Skills Series Arithmetic, 2/e (McGraw-Hill)	6–up	2–3
Understanding Word Problems Multimedia Kit (Holcombs)	7–12	4.5–5.5
How to Solve Word Problems Practice Cards (Holcombs)	7–12	3.5–4.5
Solving Word Problems Duplicating Masters (Holcombs)	7–12	4.5–5.5
High-Interest Math Duplicating Library (Holcombs)	7–12	3.0–3.5
Basic Math Operations (Holcombs)	7–12	2.5–3.5
Whole Number Operations (Holcombs)	7–12	3.5–4.5
Captain Quotient (Holcombs)	7–12	3.0–4.0
Mysteries of History (Multiplication) (Holcombs)	7–12	3.0–4.0
Arithmetic Drills Review (Holcombs)	7–10	2.5–4.5

B–4
Science

Title and Publisher	Instructional Level	Reading Level
Spaceship Earth/Life Science (Houghton Mifflin)	8–12	7
Spaceship Earth/Physical Science (Houghton Mifflin)	8–12	6–7
Spaceship Earth/Earth Science (Houghton Mifflin)	9–12	7–8
Edison/Bell (Pendulum)	7–12	4–6
Curie/Einstein (Pendulum)	9–12	4–6
Biology Workshop 1: Understanding Living Things (Globe)	9–12	4–5
Earth Science Workshop 1: Understanding the Earth's Surface (Globe)	9–12	4–5
Chemistry Workshop 1: Understanding Matter (Globe)	9–12	4–5
Physics Workshop 1: Understanding Energy (Globe)	9–12	4–5

B–4 *(continued)*

Title and Publisher	Instructional Level	Reading Level
Biology Workshop 2: Understanding the Human Body (Globe)	9–12	4–5
Earth Science Workshop 2: Understanding the Atmosphere and Oceans (Globe)	9–12	4–5
Chemistry Workshop 2: Understanding Mixtures (Globe)	9–12	4–5
Physics Workshop 2: Understanding Forces (Globe)	9–12	4–5
Biology Workshop 3: Understanding Reproduction (Globe)	9–12	4–5
Earth Science Workshop 3: Understanding Space (Globe)	9–12	4–5
Chemistry Workshop 3: Understanding the Chemistry of Metals (Globe)	9–12	4–5
Physics Workshop 3: Understanding Light and Sound (Globe)	9–12	4–5
What Is an Atom? (Benefic)	7–8	4
What Is a Cell? (Benefic)	7–8	4
What Is Energy? (Benefic)	7–8	4
What Is Gravity? (Benefic)	7–8	4
What Is Heat? (Benefic)	7–8	4
What Is an Insect? (Benefic)	7–8	4
What Is a Machine? (Benefic)	7–8	4
What Is a Magnet? (Benefic)	7–8	4
What Is Matter? (Benefic)	7–8	4
What Is a Solar System? (Benefic)	7–8	4
What Is Sound? (Benefic)	7–8	4
What Is Space? (Benefic)	7–8	4
What Is Weather? (Benefic)	7–8	4
What Makes a Light Go On? (Little, Brown)	7–up	3
The Bug Club Book: A Handbook for Young Bug Collectors (Holiday House)	7	4
What Colonel Glenn Did All Day (John Day)	7–up	4
Magic With Chemistry (Grosset & Dunlap)	7–up	4
This is Cape Kennedy (Macmillan)	7–up	3
Experiments for Young Scientists (Little, Brown)	7–up	3

B–5
Health

Title and Publisher	Instructional Level	Reading Level
Keeping Fit! (Xerox)	9–12	3.5–4.5
Health and Safety: Keeping Fit Multimedia Kit (Holcombs)	7–12	5.0–6.0
Human Body Activity Cards (Holcombs)	7–12	3.5–4.5
Your Life in Your Hands (Holcombs)	7–12	4.0–5.0
Health Resource Cards (Holcombs)	7–12	5.0–6.0
First Aid: Newest Techniques Multimedia Program (Holcombs)	7–12	3.0–4.0
Health Survival Skills Multimedia Kit (Holcombs)	7–12	3.0–4.0
Sigh of Relief: First Aid Guide for the Classroom (Holcombs)	7–12	3.0–4.5
Having a Baby Series (New Readers Press)	7–12	4
Be Informed on Drugs (New Readers Press)	7–12	4–5

B–5 *(continued)*

Title and Publisher	Instructional Level	Reading Level
Contemporary Reading Series (Seven books on topics such as drugs, alcohol, V.D., pregnancy) (Educational Activities)	7–12	4–5
Emergency Medical Care Worktext (Holcombs)	7–12	5.0–6.5
Health and Nutrition Reference Library (Holcombs)	8–12	5.0–7.5
Is It Safe to Eat Anything Anymore? (Holcombs)	7–12	3.0–5.0
The Basics of Nutrition, A Multimedia Program (Holcombs)	7–12	4.0–5.0
Nutrition Survival Kit (Holcombs)	7–12	4.5–6.0
Nutrition: Food vs. Health (Holcombs)	7–12	3.0–4.0
You and Food Additives Activity Unit (Holcombs)	7–12	5.0–6.0
Label Literacy: How to Read Food Packages (Holcombs)	7–12	2.0–3.0
Modern Human Sexuality (Houghton Mifflin)	7–9	4–5
The Body Machine: Parts and Functions (Xerox)	7–9	4.0–6.0
The Body Machine: Care and Maintenance (Xerox)	7–9	4.0–6.0

B–6
Careers

Title and Publisher	Instructional Level	Reading Level
Survival Skills for Work (Holcombs)	9–12	4.5–5.5
The Very Basics of Work Reading Series (Holcombs)	9–12	1.5–2.5
The Job Hunt Cassette Activity Program (Holcombs)	9–12	5.0–6.0
The Job Hunting Game (Holcombs)	9–12	3.5–4.5
Don't Get Fired Activity Book (Holcombs)	9–12	2.0–3.0
Job Applications Activity Book (Holcombs)	8–12	2.5–3.5
Job Interview Worktext (Holcombs)	8–12	2.5–3.5
You and Others on the Job Reading Series (Holcombs)	8–12	3.5–4.5
Janus Job Interview Guide (Janus)	7–12	2.5
Janus Job Planner (Janus)	7–12	2.8
People Working Today (Ten books about teenage workers) (Janus)	7–12	1.9
Get Hired! Thirteen Ways to Get Your Job (Janus)	7–12	2.5
Don't Get Fired! Thirteen Ways to Hold Your Job (Janus)	7–12	2.5
First Jobs Multimedia Program (Holcombs)	7–12	3.0–4.0
Your First Job Reading Series (Holcombs)	7–12	2.0–3.0
Career Exploration Resource Library (Holcombs)	7–12	5.5–6.5
The Info-Job Resource Center (Holcombs)	7–12	4.5–5.5
Real People at Work Library 1 (Holcombs)	7–12	2.0–4.0
Real People at Work Library 2 (Holcombs)	7–12	4.0–5.0

B–7

Geography

Title and Publisher	Instructional Level	Reading Level
The Earth: Regions and Peoples (Globe)	7–8	3
Homelands of the World: Resources and Cultures (Globe)	7	5
Exploring the Western World (Globe)	7	5
The New Exploring the Non-Western World (Globe)	7–12	5–6
Exploring the Urban World (Globe)	7–12	5–6
The Congo: River into Central Africa (Garrard)	7	5
The Niger: Africa's River of Mystery (Garrard)	7	5
The Nile: Lifeline of Egypt (Garrard)	7	5
The Ganges: Sacred River of India (Garrard)	7	5
The Indus: South Asia's Highway of History (Garrard)	7	5
The Yangtze: China's River Highway (Garrard)	7	5
The Rhone: River of Contrasts (Garrard)	7	5
The Seine: River of Paris (Garrard)	7	5
The Shannon: River of Loughs and Legends (Garrard)	7	5
The Thames: London's River (Garrard)	7	5
The Tiber: The Roman River (Garrard)	7	5
The Volga: Russia's River of Five Seas (Garrard)	7	5
The Amazon: River Sea of Brazil (Garrard)	7	5
The Mississippi: Giant at Work (Garrard)	7	5
The St. Lawrence: Seaway of North America (Garrard)	7	5
The Jordan: River of the Promised Land (Garrard)	7	5
The Colorado: Mover of Mountains (Garrard)	7	5
The Rio Grande: Life for the Desert (Garrard)	7	5
A World Explorer: Roald Amundsen (Garrard)	7	4

B–8

Literature

Title and Publisher	Instructional Level	Reading Level
Great American Library—Biography (Junior A + B, Senior A + B) (Scholastic)	7–12	3–7
		4–8
House of the Seven Gables (Globe)	8–12	6–7
An O. Henry Reader (Globe)	9–12	7–8
Short World Biographies (Globe)]	9–12	5–6
Profiles: A Collection of Short Biographies (Globe)	9–12	5–6
A Tale of Two Cities (Globe)	9–12	5–6
Moby Dick (Globe)	9–12	5–6
Jane Eyre (Globe)	8–12	4–5
An Edgar Allan Poe Reader (Globe)	8–12	6–7
Turning Point: A Selection of Short Biographies (Globe)	8–12	3
Lorna Doone (Globe)	8–12	5–6
Journeys to Fame (A series of short biographies) (Globe)	7–12	2–3
Modern Short Biographies (Globe)	7–12	5–6

B–8 *(continued)*

Title and Publisher	Instructional Level	Reading Level
Tales Worth Retelling (Rudyard Kipling) (Globe)	7–12	5–6
The Adventures of Sherlock Holmes (Globe)	8–12	6–7
Tom Sawyer (Globe)	7–12	3–4
Chitty Chitty Bang Bang (Scholastic)	7–12	6
Kidnapped (Globe)	7–12	5–6
The Odyssey (Globe)	7–12	5–6
Twenty Thousand Leagues Under the Sea (Globe)	7–12	4–5
Treasure Island (Globe)	7–12	5–6
American Folklore and Legends (Globe)	7–12	4
Legends for Everyone (Globe)	7–12	3
Myths and Folktales Around the World (Globe)	7–12	4
The Magnificent Myths of Man (Globe)	7–12	4–5
Scholastic Reluctant Reader Libraries (Junior A + B, Senior A + B) (Scholastic)	7–12	4–8
Their Eyes on the Stars: Four Black Writers (Garrard)	7–9	6

Two Outlines for Preparing Case Reports Based on Remedial Assessment and Instruction

CASE REPORT OUTLINE: EXAMPLE 1

This outline is used at The Ohio State Pyschoeducational Clinic, at Ohio State University in Columbus, Ohio.

The Case Study

A case study is a comprehensive report that integrates a student's case history and results of previous studies, as well as inferences about behavior observed during teaching and intensive analysis of patterns of behavior as revealed through achievement tests and observation. This type of report ordinarily relates the subject's behavior to a specific educational problem. Your case study must point toward recommendations, that is, toward what can be done to help the student.

The Outline

IDENTIFYING DATA

Name of Student: Quarter and Year:

Age: Grade: Tutor:

I. HISTORY
   A. Developmental
      1. Prenatal and postnatal health and medical history
      2. Speech and language development
      3. Other pertinent data obtained from parents
   B. Educational
      1. Age of school entrance, summary of progress in school, including retentions and areas of difficulty

The Case Study *(cont.)*

2. Summary of teacher's or principal's remarks concerning student's behavior and adjustment in school

II. RESULTS OF PREVIOUS TESTS OR DIAGNOSTIC EXAMINATIONS

If your student has previously attended this clinic, for the last quarter (semester) of attendance, list tests administered and summarize results.

If your student has attended the clinic for more than one quarter, make the following statement: " (Dave)   also attended the clinic during   (Winter)   and   (Spring)   Quarters of 19___. Case studies for those quarters are on file at the clinic."

If your student has not previously attended this clinic, simply say so.

III. GENERAL OBSERVATIONS

Summarize observations of student in the following areas:
A. Interpersonal response to the tutor
B. Perceptiveness
C. Attention and concentration

IV. TESTS ADMINISTERED DURING THE QUARTER

List the tests administered and for each state the scores and other descriptive classifications. If test results are questionable, give evidence and show reasoning. Analyze test items and patterns for best and poorest abilities, significant variability, and so forth.

V. INSTRUCTION DURING THE QUARTER

Include the following:
A. Objectives of instruction
B. Methods used *(This section is the most important section of the case study and should be comprehensive. Give specific information on* all *instructional activities.)*
C. Materials covered (with reading levels of materials)
D. Evidence of gain

VI. RECOMMENDATIONS

Make specific recommendations to help others understand and work with the problem (e.g., the classroom teacher or future tutors).

(Name) _____
Tutor

Approved by _____

Date: _____

CASE REPORT OUTLINE: EXAMPLE 2

This outline is used in the Reading Clinic at Norfolk State University, in Norfolk, Virginia. It is printed with permission of Professor Carmelita Williams.

CASE HISTORY RECORD FOR ANALYSIS OF LEARNING DIFFICULTIES
CASE STUDY

DATE _____

I. REFERRAL DATA

NAME _____ BIRTHDAY _____ SEX _____

PARENTS' NAMES _____ OCCUPATIONS _____

ADDRESS_____ TEL. NO. _____

_____

AGE (AS OF CURRENT DATE) YEARS _____MONTHS_____

SCHOOL_____ CITY _____

PRINCIPAL_____ LAST GRADE _____

TEACHER_____ REFERRED BY_____

SUMMARY OF THE HOME'S DESCRIPTION OF THE LEARNING PROBLEM:

SUMMARY OF THE SCHOOL'S DESCRIPTION OF THE LEARNING PROBLEM:

II. CAPACITY AND ACHIEVEMENT TEST DATA (LIST IN ORDER OF DATE ADMINISTERED)

A. TESTS OF CAPACITY

			VERBAL		NONVERBAL		TOTAL	
TEST	DATE	CA	MA	IQ	MA	IQ	MA	IQ
——	——	——	——	——	——	——	——	——
——	——	——	——	——	——	——	——	——

B. GENERAL TESTS OF ACHIEVEMENTS

SUMMARIZE PART AND TOTAL SCORES:

TEST	DATE	CA	AGE-GRADE EQUIVALENTS, ETC.
——	——	——	_____
——	——	——	_____

CORRECTIVE AND REMEDIAL TEACHING

C. READING SURVEY TESTS (SILENT)

TEST	DATE	CA	SUMMARY OF RESULTS
——	——	——	_____
——	——	——	_____

D. ORAL READING TESTS

TEST   DATE   CA   SUMMARY OF RESULTS

——   ——   ——   _____

——   ——   ——   _____

E. DIAGNOSTIC TESTS IN THE BASIC SKILL AREAS

TEST   DATE   CA   SUMMARY OF RESULTS

——   ——   ——   _____

——   ——   ——   _____

F. APPRAISAL OF TEST RESULTS (DISCREPANCIES NOTED; PUPIL'S BEHAVIOR IN TEST
SITUATION; CORRESPONDENCE OF TEST PERFORMANCE WITH FUNCTIONAL LEVELS;
FURTHER TESTING NEEDED)

III. PHYSICAL AND DEVELOPMENTAL DATA

A. DEVELOPMENTAL HISTORY

1. AGE OF FIRST SITTING_____   WALKING _____
USE OF FIRST WORDS _____
FIRST SENTENCES_____

2. PRESCHOOL LANGUAGE DIFFICULTIES_____
_____

3. ADEQUACY OF LANGUAGE DEVELOPMENT UPON ENTRANCE TO SCHOOL
_____
_____

4. EXPERIENTIAL DEVELOPMENT UPON ENTRANCE TO SCHOOL
_____
_____

B. HEALTH HISTORY _____
_____
_____
_____

C. PRESENT HEALTH _____
_____
_____
_____

D. VISION

   1. GLASSES _____ WHEN PRESCRIBED _____

   WHY _____

   WORN REGULARLY _____ DEGREE OF COMFORT _____

   LAST VISIT TO EYE SPECIALIST _____

   RECOMMENDATIONS _____

   2. EYESTRAIN _____ WITH OR WITHOUT GLASSES _____

   OCCURS ONLY WHEN STUDYING _____

   EVIDENCE OF EYESTRAIN IN READING _____

   _____

   3. OTHER DATA ON VISUAL EFFICIENCY _____

   _____

E. HEARING

   1. LOSS   L _____   R _____   HOW LONG _____   EFFECTS _____

   2. DISCRIMINATION

   INITIAL CONSONANTS _____

   MEDIAL VOWELS AND CONSONANTS _____

   FINAL CONSONANTS _____

IV. ENVIRONMENTAL DATA

A. HOME _____

_____

_____

B. PARENTS _____

_____

_____

C. SIBLINGS _____

_____

_____

D. FRIENDS _____

_____

_____

E. COMMUNITY ACTIVITIES _____

_____

_____

F. OUTSIDE WORK _____

_____

_____

G. OTHER ENVIRONMENTAL EFFECTS _____

_____

_____

V. EMOTIONAL AND PERSONALITY ADJUSTMENT DATA

_____

_____

_____

A. ATTITUDE TOWARD HOME _____

_____

_____

_____

B. ATTITUDE TOWARD SCHOOL _____

_____

_____

_____

C. RECREATION _____

_____

D. EMOTIONAL ADJUSTMENT _____

_____

_____

E. PERSONALITY CHARACTERISTICS _____

_____

_____

_____

VI. EDUCATIONAL DATA
   A. SCHOOL PROGRESS
      1. AGE ENTERING: NURSERY _____   KINDERGARTEN _____
         FIRST GRADE _____
      2. SCHOOLS ATTENDED   GRADES ATTENDED

      _____   _____

      _____   _____

      _____   _____

      _____   _____

3. SCHOOL GRADES: REPEATED _____   SKIPPED _____

4. AVERAGE SCHOOL MARKS: LOW_____   AVERAGE _____   HIGH _____

5. SUBJECTS: WEAK_____

STRONG _____

6. ATTENDANCE _____

B. STUDY HABITS _____

_____

_____

_____

C. ADJUSTMENT OF SCHOOL TO PUPIL'S NEEDS _____

_____

_____

_____

D. FUTURE EDUCATIONAL AND VOCATIONAL PLANS _____

_____

_____

_____

VII. READING DATA

A. READING READINESS

1. AGE WHEN READING FIRST INTRODUCED:_____   YEARS _____

MONTHS _____   GRADE_____

2. MENTAL READINESS _____

3. PHYSICAL READINESS _____

4. SOCIAL-EMOTIONAL READINESS _____

5. EXPERIMENTAL READINESS _____

B. HISTORY OF READING DIFFICULTIES _____

_____

_____

_____

C. SILENT READING

1. OBSERVABLE HABITS _____

_____

_____

_____

2. REPORTED HABITS _____

_____

_____

_____

3. INTERPRETATION _____

_____

_____

_____

4. INSTRUCTIONAL DIAGNOSIS_____

_____

_____

_____

D. ORAL READING HABITS
   1. DEFECTS AND ERRORS OBSERVED IN INFORMAL ORAL READING (CHECK).

   ___STUTTERING   ___FOREIGN ACCENT   ___SUBSTITUTIONS

   ___LISPING   ___HESITATIONS   ___INSERTIONS

   ___HARELIP   ___MISPRONUNCIATIONS   ___REPETITIONS

   ___CLEFT PALATE   ___OMISSIONS

   2. INTERPRETATIONS _____

   _____

   _____

   _____

E. CURRENT READING INTERESTS _____

_____

_____

_____

F. QUESTION: DOES THE STUDENT FEEL A REAL NEED FOR IMPROVING HIS OR HER
   READING?

_____

_____

_____

VIII. DESCRIPTION OF THE PUPIL'S PERFORMANCE IN THE OTHER BASIC SKILL AREAS:
INSTRUCTIONAL DIAGNOSIS OF TYPICAL PERFORMANCE IN AREAS OF DIFFICULTY

IX. APPARENT CAUSES OF THE LEARNING DIFFICULTY

X. SUMMARY AND EVALUATION OF TREATMENT

References

Abbass, M. (1977). The language of fifty commonly used forms. *Dissertation Abstracts International, 37,* 5655A. (University Microfilms No. 77–6197, 520)

Ackerly, S. S., & Benton, A. L. (1947). Report of a case of bilateral frontal lobe defect. *Proceedings of the Association for Research on Nervous and Mental Disease, 27,* 479–504.

Adams, M. J. (1990a). *Beginning to read: Thinking and learning about print.* Cambridge, MA: MIT Press.

Adams, M. J. (1990b). *Beginning to read: Thinking and learning about print: A summary.* Urbana-Champaign, IL: Center for the Study of Reading, University of Illinois.

Adams, M. J., & Huggins, A. W. F. (1985). *The growth of children's sight vocabulary: A quick test with educational and theoretical implications* (Tech. Rep. No. 330). Urbana-Champaign, IL: University of Illinois, Center for the Study of Reading.

Afflerbach, P., & Kapinus, B. (1993). The balancing act. The *Reading Teacher, 47,* 62–64.

Ahmann, J. S. (1975). An exploration of survival levels of achievement by means of assessment techniques. In D. M. Nielsen & H. F. Hjelm (Eds.), *Reading and career education.* Newark, DE: International Reading Association.

Allington, R. L. (1984a). Content coverage and contextual reading in reading groups. *Journal of Reading Behavior, 16,* 85–96.

Allington, R. L. (1984b). Oral reading. In P. D. Pearson (Ed.), *Handbook of reading research* (pp. 829–864). New York: Longman.

Allington, R. L. (1993). Michael doesn't go down the hall anymore. *The Reading Teacher, 46,* 602–604.

Allington, R. L., & Fleming, J. T. (1978). The misreading of high frequency words. *Journal of Special Education, 12,* 417–421.

Amoroso, H. C. (1985). Organic primers for basic literacy instruction. *Journal of Reading, 28,* 398–401.

Anania, J. (1982). The effects of quality instruction on the cognitive and affective learning of students (Doctoral dissertation, University of Chicago, 1981). *Dissertation Abstracts International, 42,* 4269A.

Anderson, G., Higgins, D., & Wurster, S. (1985). Differences in the free reading books selected by high, average, and low achievers. *The Reading Teacher, 39,* 326–330.

Anderson, J. R. (1976). *Language, memory, and thought.* Hillsdale, NJ: Erlbaum.

Anderson, R. C. (1977). *Schema-directed processes in language comprehension* (Tech. Rep. No. 50). Urbana-Champaign, IL: University of Illinois. Center for the Study of Reading. (ERIC Document Reproduction Service No. ED 142 977)

Anderson, R. C., & Freebody, P. (1981). Vocabulary knowledge. In J. Gutherie (Ed.), *Comprehension and teaching: Research reviews* (pp. 77–117). Newark, DE: International Reading Association.

Anderson, R. C., Hiebert, E. H., Scott, J. A., & Wilkinson, I. A. G. (1984). *Becoming a nation of readers.* Washington, DC: National Institute of Education.

Anderson, R. C., Wilkinson, I. A. G., & Mason, J. M. (1991). A micro-analysis of the small-group guided lesson: Effects of an emphasis on global story meaning. *Reading Research Quarterly, 26,* 417–441.

Anderson, R. W. (1966). Effects of neuro-psychological techniques on reading achievement. *Dissertation Abstracts International, 26,* 5216A. (University Microfilms No. 65–14, 796)

Anderson, T. H., & Armbruster, B. B. (1984). Studying. In P. D. Pearson (Ed.), *Handbook of reading research* (pp. 657–679). New York: Longman.

Andre, M. E. D. A., & Anderson, T. H. (1978–79). The development and evaluation of a self-questioning study technique. *Reading Research Quarterly, 14,* 605–623.

Andrews, G. R., & Debus, R. L. (1978). Persistence and the causal perception of failure: Modifying cognitive attributions. *Journal of Educational Psychology, 70,* 154–166.

Arlin, M., Scott, M., & Webster, J. (1978–79). The effects of pictures on rate of learning sight words. *Reading Research Quarterly, 14,* 645–660.

Armbruster, B. B., Anderson, T. H., & Meyer, J. L. (1991). Improving content-area reading using instructional graphics. *Reading Research Quarterly, 26,* 393–416.

Armbruster, B. B., Anderson, T. H., & Ostertag, J. (1987). Does text structure/summarization instruction facilitate learning from expository text? *Reading Research Quarterly, 22,* 331–346.

Armbruster, B. B., Anderson, T. H., & Ostertag, J. (1989). Teaching text structure to improve reading and writing. *The Reading Teacher, 43,* 130–137.

Ashton-Warner, S. (1964). *Teacher.* New York: Bantam.

Au, K. H., & Mason, J. M. (1981). Social organizational factors in learning to read: The balance of rights hypothesis. *Reading Research Quarterly, 17,* 115–152.

August, D. L., Flavell, J. H., & Clift, R. (1984). Comparison of comprehension monitoring of skilled and less-skilled readers. *Reading Research Quarterly, 20,* 39–53.

Ausubel, D. P. (1960). The use of advance organizers in learning and retention of meaningful material. *Journal of Educational Psychology, 51,* 267–272.

Ayres, A. J. (1972). *Sensory integration and learning disorders.* Los Angeles: Western Psychological Services.

Backman, J., Bruck, M., Hebert, M., & Seidenberg, M. S. (1984). Acquisition and use of spelling-sound correspondence in reading. *Journal of Experimental Child Psychology, 38,* 114–133.

Bader, L. A., & Wiesendanger, K. D. (1986). University-based reading clinics: Practices and procedures. *The Reading Teacher, 39,* 698–702.

Bailey, E. J. (1975). *Academic activities for adolescents with learning disabilities.* Evergreen, CO: Learning Pathways.

Bailey, M. H. (1967). The utility of phonics generalizations in grades one through six. *The Reading Teacher, 20,* 413–418.

Bailey, M. H. (1971). Utility of vowel digraph generalizations in grades one through six. In M. A. Dawson (Ed.), *Teaching word recognition skills.* Newark, DE: International Reading Association.

Baker, L. (1984). Spontaneous versus instructed use of multiple standards for evaluating comprehension: Effects of age, reading-proficiency, and type of standard. *Journal of Experimental Child Psychology, 38,* 289–311.

Baker, L., & Brown, A. L. (1984). Metacognitive skills in reading. In P. D. Pearson (Ed.), *Handbook of reading research* (pp. 353–394). New York: Longman.

Bakwin, H. (1973). Reading disability in twins. *Developmental Medicine and Child Neurology, 15,* 184–187.

Ball, E. W., & Blachman, B. A. (1991). Does phoneme awareness training in kindergarten make a difference in early word recognition and developmental spelling? *Reading Research Quarterly, 26,* 49–66.

Balota, D., Pollatsek, A., & Rayner, K. (1985). The interaction of contextual constraints and parafoveal visual information in reading. *Cognitive Psychology, 17,* 364–390.

Balow, B. (1971). Perceptual-motor activities in the treatment of severe reading disability. *The Reading Teacher, 24,* 513–525, 542.

Balow, B., Rubin, R., & Rosen, M. J. (1975–76). Perinatal events as precursors of reading disability. *Reading Research Quarterly, 11,* 36–71.

Bargantz, J. C., & Dulin, K. L. (1970). Readability levels of selected mass magazines from 1925 to 1965. In G. B. Schick & M. M. May (Eds.), *Reading Process and Pedagogy. Nineteenth Yearbook of the National Reading Conference* (pp. 26—30). Washington, DC: National Reading Conference.

Baron, J., & Treiman, R. (1980). Use of orthography in reading and learning to read. In J. Kavanaugh & R. Venezky (Eds.), *Orthography, reading, and dyslexia.* Baltimore: University Park Press.

Barr, R. C. (1974–75). The effect of instruction on pupil reading strategies. *Reading Research Quarterly, 10,* 555–582.

Barr, R. C. (1984). Beginning reading instruction: From debate to reformation. In P. D. Pearson (Ed.), *Handbook of reading research* (pp. 545–581). New York: Longman.

Barr, R. C., & Dreeben, R. (1983). *How schools work.* Chicago: University of Chicago Press.

Barr, R. C., Sadow, M., & Blachowicz, C. (1990). *Reading diagnosis for teachers: An instructional approach* (2nd ed.). New York: Longman.

Barrett, T. C. (1965). The relationship between measures of prereading visual discrimination and first grade reading achievement: A review of the literature. *Reading Research Quarterly, 1,* 51–76.

Barron, R. C. (1969). The use of vocabulary as an advance organizer. In H. Herber & P. L. Sanders (Eds.), *Research in reading in the content areas: First year report.* Syracuse: Syracuse University Reading and Language Arts Center.

Bartlett, F. C. (1932). *Remembering.* Cambridge, MA: Harvard University Press.

Bateman, B. (1971). The role of individual diagnosis in remedial planning for reading disorders. *Reading Forum* (NINDS Monograph II). Bethesda, MD: National Institute of Neurological Diseases and Stroke.

Bateman, B. (1979). Teaching reading to learning disabled and hard-to-teach children. In L. B. Resnick and P. A. Weaver (Eds.), *Theory and practice of early reading* (Vol. III, pp. 227–259). Hillsdale, NJ: Erlbaum.

Bates, G. W. (1984). Profile of university-based reading clinics: Results of a U.S. survey. *Journal of Reading, 27,* 524–529.

Baumann, J. F. (1984). The effectiveness of a direct instruction paradigm for teaching main idea comprehension. *Reading Research Quarterly, 20,* 93–115.

Baumann, J. F., Seifert-Kessell, N., & Jones, L. A. (1992). Effect of think-aloud instruction on elementary students' comprehension monitoring abilities. *Journal of Reading Behavior, 24,* 143–172.

Bean, R. M. (1992, June/July). Learning without labels: How one school handles mainstreaming. *Reading Today,* p. 28.

Bean, T. W., & Steenwyk, F. L. (1984). The effects of three forms of summarization instruction on sixth graders' summary writing and comprehension. *Journal of Reading Behavior, 15,* 297–306.

Beck, I. L., & McCaslin, E. S. (1978). *An analysis of dimensions that affect the development of code-breaking ability in eight beginning reading programs* (LROC Report No. 1978/6). Pittsburgh, PA:

University of Pittsburgh Learning Research and Development Center.

Beck, I. L., & McKeown, M. (1991). Conditions of vocabulary acquisition. In R. Barr, M. L. Kamil, P. Mosenthal, & P. D. Pearson (Eds.), *Handbook of reading research* (Vol. II, pp. 789–814). New York: Longman.

Beck, I. L., McKeown, M. G., & McCaslin, E. S. (1983). Vocabulary development: All contexts are not created equal. *Elementary School Journal, 83,* 177–181.

Beck, I. L., Omanson, R. C., & McKeown, M. G. (1982). An instructional redesign of reading lessons: Effects on comprehension. *Reading Research Quarterly, 17,* 462–481.

Beck, I. L., Perfetti, C. A., & McKeown, M. G. (1982). The effects of long-term vocabulary instruction on lexical access and reading comprehension. *Journal of Educational Psychology, 74,* 506–521.

Becker, E. (1994). *Using predictable books with a nonreader: Cognitive and affective effects.* Unpublished doctoral dissertation, Ohio State University, Columbus, OH.

Beebe, M. J. (1980). The effect of different types of substitution miscues on reading. *Reading Research Quarterly, 15,* 324–336.

Beed, P. L., Hawkins, E. M., & Roller, C. M. (1991). Moving learners toward independence: The power of scaffolded instruction. *The Reading Teacher, 44,* 648–655.

Beers, J., & Henderson, E. (1977). A study of developing orthographic concepts among first graders. *Research in the Teaching of English, 11,* 133–148.

Belmont, L., & Birch, H. G. (1965). Lateral dominance, lateral awareness, and reading disability. *Child Development, 36,* 57–71.

Bennett, W. J. (1987). *The condition of bilingual education in the nation: 1986* (A report from the Secretary of Education to the President and the Congress). Washington, DC: U.S. Department of Education.

Benton, C. D., & McCann, J. W. (1969). Dyslexia and dominance: Some second thoughts. *Journal of Pediatric Ophthalmology, 6,* 220–222.

Berkowitz, S. J. (1986). Effects of instruction in text organization on sixth-grade students' memory for expository reading. *Reading Research Quarterly, 21,* 161–178.

Berliner, D. C. (1986). In pursuit of the expert pedagogue. *Educational Researcher, 15,* 5–13.

Bertera, J. H., & Rayner, K. (1979). Reading without a fovea. *Science, 206,* 468–469.

Bettman, J. W., Stern, E. L., & Gofman, H. F. (1967). Cerebral dominance in developmental dyslexia. *Archives of Ophthalmology, 78,* 722–729.

Betts, E. A. (1940). Reading problems at the intermediate grade level. *Elementary School Journal, 15,* 737–746.

Biemiller, A. (1970). The development of the use of graphic and contextual information as children learn to read. *Reading Research Quarterly, 6,* 75–96.

Biemiller, A. (1977–78). Relation between oral reading rates for letters, words, and simple text in the development of reading achievement. *Reading Research Quarterly, 13,* 223–253.

Bishop, D., & Butterworth, G. (1980). Verbal-performance discrepancies: Relationship to both risk and specific reading retardation. *Cortex, 16,* 375–389.

Bittner, J. R., & Shamo, G. W. (1976). Readability of the 'Mini Page.' *Journalism Quarterly, 53,* 740–743.

Bjork, R. A., & Whitten, W. B. (1974). Recency-sensitive retrieval processes. *Cognitive Psychology, 6,* 173–189.

Black, W. F. (1974). Achievement test performance of high and low perceiving learning disabled children. *Journal of Learning Disabilities, 7,* 178–182.

Blackman, B. A. (1984). Relationship of rapid naming ability and language analysis skills to kindergarten and first-grade reading achievement. *Journal of Educational Psychology, 77,* 610–622.

Blanchard, J. S. (1980). Preliminary investigation of transfer between single-word decoding ability and contextual reading comprehension of poor readers in grade six. *Perceptual and Motor Skills, 51,* 1271–1281.

Blanchard, J. S. (1984). U.S. Armed Services computer-assisted literacy efforts. *Journal of Reading, 28,* 262–265.

Bliesmer, E. T. (1962). Evaluating progress in remedial reading programs. *The Reading Teacher, 15,* 344–350.

Bloom, B. S. (Ed.) (1956). *Taxonomy of educational objectives.* New York: Longman.

Bloom, B. S. (1984). The 2 sigma problem: The search for methods of group instruction as effective as one-to-one tutoring. *Educational Researcher, 13* (6), 4–17.

Bohline, D. S. (1985). Intellectual and affective characteristics of attention deficit disordered children. *Journal of Learning Disabilities, 18,* 604–608.

Bond, G. L., Tinker, M. A., & Wasson, B. B. (1979). *Reading difficulties: Their diagnosis and correction* (4th ed.). Englewood Cliffs, NJ: Prentice-Hall.

Bormuth, J. R. (1968). The cloze readability procedure. In J. R. Bormuth (Ed.), *Readability in 1968.* Champaign, IL: National Council of Teachers of English.

Bormuth, J. R. (1973–74). Reading literacy: Its definition and assessment. *Reading Research Quarterly, 9,* 7–66.

Bos, C. S., & Anders, P. L. (1990). Effects of interactive vocabulary instruction on the vocabulary learning and reading comprehension of junior-high learning disabled students. *Learning Disability Quarterly, 13,* 31–42.

Bovair, S., & Kieras, D. E. (1991). Toward a model of acquiring procedures from text. In R. Barr, M. L. Kamil, P. Mosenthal, & P. D. Pearson (Eds.), *Handbook of reading research* (Vol. II, pp. 206–229). New York: Longman.

Bradley, J. M. (1976). Evaluating reading achievement for placement in special education. *Journal of Special Education, 10,* 239–245.

Bradley, L., & Bryant, P. E. (1983). Categorizing sounds and learning to read—a causal connection. *Nature, 301,* 419–421.

Bradley, L., & Bryant, P. E. (1985). *Rhyme and reason in reading and spelling.* Ann Arbor: University of Michigan Press.

Brainerd, C., Kingma, J., & Howe, M. (1986). Long-term memory development and learning disability: Storage and retrieval loci of disabled/non-disabled differences. In S. Ceci (Ed.), *Handbook of cognitive, social, and neuropsychological aspects of learning disabilities* (Vol. I, pp. 161–184). Hillsdale, NJ: Erlbaum.

Bretzing, B. B., & Kulhavy, R. W. (1979). Note taking and depth of processing. *Contemporary Educational Psychology, 4,* 145–153.

Bridge, C. A., Winograd, P. N., & Haley, D. (1983). Using predictable materials vs. preprimers to teach beginning sight words. *The Reading Teacher, 36,* 884–891.

Brophy, J. E. (1983). Classroom organization and management. *Elementary School Journal, 83,* 265–285.

Brophy, J. E., & Evertson, C. M. (1981). *Student characteristics and teaching.* New York: Longman.

Brophy, J. E., & Good, T. L. (1970). Teacher communication of differential expectations for children's classroom performance: Some behavioral data. *Journal of Educational Psychology, 61,* 365–374.

Brown, A. L., Armbruster, B. B., & Baker, L. (1986). The role of meta-cognition in reading and studying. In J. Orasanu (Ed.), *Reading comprehension: From research to practice* (pp. 49–75). Hillsdale, NJ: Erlbaum.

Brown, A. L., & Day, J. D. (1983). The development of plans for summarizing texts. *Child Development, 54,* 968–979.

Brown, D. A. (1982). *Reading diagnosis and remediation.* Englewood Cliffs, NJ: Prentice-Hall.

Brown, J. I. (1976). Techniques for increasing reading rate. In J. E. Merritt (Ed.), *New horizons in reading.* Newark, DE: International Reading Association.

Brown, J. S., Collins, A., & Duguid, P. (1989). Situated cognition and the culture of learning. *Educational Research, 18* (1), 32–42.

Bruce, D. (1964). An analysis of word sounds by young children. *British Journal of Educational Psychology, 34,* 158–170.

Bruce, M. E., & Chan, L. K. S. (1991). Reciprocal teaching and transenvironmental programming: A program to facilitate the reading comprehension of students with reading difficulties. *Remedial and Special Education, 12,* 44–54.

Bruner, L. G. (1983). The remediation of a graphophonic decoding deficit in an adult. *Journal of Reading, 27,* 145–151.

Bryan, T. H. (1974). Learning disabilities: A new stereotype. *Journal of Learning Disabilities, 7,* 304–309.

Bryant, P., & Impey, L. (1986). The similarities between normal readers and developmental acquired dyslexics. *Cognition, 24,* 121–137.

Bryant, S. (1979). *Relative effectiveness of visual-auditory versus auditory-kinesthetic-tactile procedures for teaching sight words and letter sounds to young disabled readers.* Unpublished doctoral dissertation, Teachers College, New York.

Buckland, P. (1970). The effect of visual perception training on reading achievement of low readiness first grade pupils. *Dissertation Abstracts International, 31,* 1613A. (University Microfilms No. 70-15, 707)

Bureau of Census, Department of Commerce (1971, March). *Illiteracy in the United States: November 1969.* Current Population Reports (Series P-20, No 217).

Burke, A. J. (1984). Students' potential for learning contrasted under tutorial and group approaches to instruction (Doctoral dissertation, University of Chicago, 1983). *Dissertation Abstracts International, 44,* 2025A.

Burns, E. (1982). Linear regression and simplified reading expectancy formulas. *Reading Research Quarterly, 17,* 446–453.

Bush, W. J., & Waugh, K. W. (1982). *Diagnosing learning problems* (3rd ed.). Columbus, OH: Merrill.

Byers, R. K., & Lord, E. E. (1943). Late effects of lead poisoning on mental development. *American Journal of Diseases of Children, 66,* 471–493.

Calfee, R. (1993). Assessment, testing, measurement: What's the difference? *Educational Assessment, 1,* 1–7.

Calfee, R. C., & Hiebert, E. (1991). Classroom assessment of reading. In R. Barr, M. L. Kamil, P. Mosenthal, & P. D. Pearson (Eds.), *Handbook of reading research* (Vol. II, pp. 281–309). New York: Longman.

Calfee, R. C., & Perfumo, P. (1993). Student portfolios: Opportunities for a revolution in assessment. *The Reading Teacher, 46,* 532–537.

Calfee, R. C., & Piontkowski, D. C. (1981). The reading diary: Acquisition of decoding. *Reading Research Quarterly, 16,* 346–373.

Capobianco, R. J. (1967). Ocular-manual laterality and reading achievement in children with special learning disabilities. *American Educational Research Journal, 2,* 133–137.

Cardenal, F., & Miller, V. (1981). Nicaragua 1980: The battle of the ABCs. *Harvard Educational Review, 51,* 1–26.

Carnine, D., Kameenui, E. J., & Coyle, G. (1984). Utilization of contextual information in determining the meaning of unfamiliar words in context. *Reading Research Quarterly, 19,* 188–202.

Carnine, L., Carnine, D., & Gersten, R. (1984). Analysis of oral reading errors made by economically disadvantaged students taught with a synthetic-phonics approach. *Reading Research Quarterly, 19,* 343–356.

Carpenter, P. A., & Daneman, M. (1981). Lexical retrieval and error recovery in reading: A model based on eye fixations. *Journal of Verbal Learning and Verbal Behavior, 20,* 137–160.

Carr, E., & Ogle, D. (1987). K-W-L Plus: A strategy for comprehension and summarization. *Journal of Reading, 30,* 626–631.

Carroll, J. B., Davies, P., & Richman, B. (1971). *American Heritage word frequency book.* Boston: Houghton Mifflin.

Cartwright, C. A., & Cartwright, G. P. (1984). *Developing observation skills* (2nd ed.). New York: McGraw-Hill.

Ceprano, M. A. (1981). A review of selected research on methods of teaching sight words. *The Reading Teacher, 35,* 314–322.

Chall, J. S. (1967). *Learning to read: The great debate.* New York: McGraw-Hill.

Chall, J. S. (1983). *Stages of reading development.* New York: McGraw-Hill.

Chall, J. S. (1987). Reading and early childhood education: The critical issues. *Principal, 66,* 6–9.

Chall, J. S. (1989). Learning to read: The great debate 20 years later. *Phi Delta Kappan, 70,* 521–538.

Chall, J. S., & Squire, J. R. (1991). The publishing industry and textbooks. In R. Barr, M. L. Kamil, P. Mosenthal, & P. D. Pearson (Eds.), *Handbook of reading research* (Vol. II, pp. 120–146). New York: Longman.

Chang, T., & Chang, V. (1967). Relation of visual-motor skills and reading achievement in primary grade pupils of superior ability. *Perceptual and Motor Skills, 24,* 51–53.

Chinn, C. A., Waggoner, M. A., Anderson, R. C., Schommer, M., & Wilkinson, I. A. G. (1993). Situated actions during reading lessons: A microanalysis of oral reading error episodes. *American Educational Research Journal, 30,* 361–392.

Chittenden, E., & Courtney, R. (1989). Assessment of young children's reading: Documentation as an alternative to testing. In D. S. Strickland & L. M. Morrow (Eds.), *Emerging literacy: Young children learn to read and write* (pp. 107–120). Newark, DE: International Reading Association.

Chomsky, C. (1972). Stages in language development and reading exposure. *Harvard Educational Review, 42,* 1–33.

Chomsky, C. (1976). After decoding: What? *Language Arts, 53,* 288–296, 314.

Chomsky, C. (1979). Approaching reading through invented spelling. In L. B. Resnick & P. A. Weaver (Eds.), *Theory and practice of early reading* (Vol. 2, pp. 43–65). Hillsdale, NJ: Erlbaum.

Clarke, L. K. (1988). Invented vs. traditional spelling in first graders' writing: Effects on learning to spell and read. *Research in the Teaching of English, 22,* 281–309.

Clay, M. M. (1967). The reading behavior of five-year-old children: A research report. *New Zealand Journal of Educational Studies, 2,* 11–31.

Clay, M. M. (1979). *Reading: The patterning of complex behavior* (2nd ed.). Auckland, New Zealand: Heinemann.

Clay, M. M. (1985). *The early detection of reading difficulties* (3rd ed.). Portsmouth, NH: Heinemann.

Cleary, D. M. (1978). *Thinking Thursdays: Language arts in the reading lab.* Newark, DE: International Reading Association.

Clymer, T. (1963). The utility of phonics generalizations in the primary grades. *The Reading Teacher, 16,* 252–258.

Cohen, D. (1968). Effect of literature on vocabulary and reading. *Elementary English, 45,* 209–213.

Cohen, D. K. (1972). *The effects of the Michigan Tracking Program on gains in reading.* New Brunswick, NJ: Rutgers University. (ERIC Document Reproduction Service No. ED 064 700)

Cohen, S. A. (1969). Dyslexia. *Encyclopedia Americana, 9,* 516.

Coles, G. S. (1980). Evaluation of genetic explanations of reading and learning problems. *The Journal of Special Education, 14,* 365–383.

Combs, M., & Beach, J. D. (1994). Stories and storytelling: Personalizing the social studies. *The Reading Teacher, 47,* 464–473.

Committee on Nutrition of the American Academy of Pediatrics (1976). Mega-vitamin therapy for childhood psychoses and learning disabilities. *Pediatrics, 58,* 910–912.

Conley, M. W. (1986). Test review: Basic Achievement Skills Individual Screener. *The Reading Teacher, 39,* 418–420.

Cook, W. D. (1977). *Adult literacy education in the United States.* Newark, DE: International Reading Association.

Cooter, R. B. (1993). A think aloud on secondary reading assessment. *Journal of Reading, 36,* 584–586.

Cossu, G., Shankweiler, D., Liberman, I. Y., Katz, L., & Tola, G. (1988). Awareness of phonological segments and reading ability in Italian children. *Applied Psycholinguistics, 9,* 1–16.

Covington, M. V., & Omelich, C. L. (1979). Are causal attributions really causal? A path analysis of the cognitive model of achievement motivation. *Journal of Personality and Social Psychology, 37,* 1487–1502.

Craik, F. I. M., & Lockhart, R. S. (1972). Levels of processing: A framework for memory research. *Journal of Verbal Learning and Verbal Behavior, 11,* 671–684.

Critchley, M. (1970). *The dyslexic child* (2nd ed.). London, England: Heinemann Medical Books.

Culyer, R. C. (1978). Guidelines for skill development: Vocabulary. *The Reading Teacher, 32,* 316–322.

Cunningham, P. M. (1977). Investigating the role of meaning in mediated word identification. In P. D. Pearson & J. Hansen (Eds.), *Reading: Theory, research, and practice.* Clemson, SC: National Reading Conference.

Cunningham, P. M. (1988). When all else fails . . . *The Reading Teacher, 41,* 800–805.

Cunningham, P. M. (1991). *Phonics they use: Words for reading and writing.* New York: HarperCollins.

Cunningham, P. M. (1992). What kind of phonics instruction will we have? In C. K. Kinzer & D. J. Leu (Eds.), *Literacy research, theory, and practice: Views from many perspectives.* Chicago: National Reading Conference.

Cunningham, P. M., & Cunningham, J. W. (1992). Making words: Enhancing the invented spelling-decoding connection. *The Reading Teacher, 46,* 106–115.

Cunningham, P. M., Moore, S. A., Cunningham, J. W., & Moore, D. W. (1983). *Reading in elementary classrooms.* New York: Longman.

Curtis, M. E. (1987). Vocabulary testing and instruction. In M. G. McKeown & M. E. Curtis (Eds.), *The nature of vocabulary acquisition* (pp. 37–51). Hillsdale, NJ: Erlbaum.

Cziko, G. A. (1983). Another response to Shanahan, Kamil, and Tobin: Further reasons to keep the cloze case open. *Reading Research Quarterly, 18,* 361–365.

Dale, E. (1965). Vocabulary measurement: Techniques and major findings. *Elementary English, 42,* 895–901, 948.

Dale, E., & O'Rourke, J. (1971). *Techniques of teaching vocabulary.* Palo Alto, CA: Field Educational Publications.

Dale, E., & O'Rourke, J. (1976). *The living word vocabulary.* Elgin, IL: Dome.

Daneman, M. (1991). Individual differences in reading skills. In R. Barr, M. L. Kamil, P. Mosenthal, & P. D. Pearson (Eds.), *Handbook of reading research* (Vol. II, pp. 512-538). New York: Longman.

Daneman, M., & Carpenter, P. A. (1980). Individual differences in working memory and reading. *Journal of Verbal Learning and Verbal Behavior, 19,* 450–466.

Daneman, M., & Green, I. (1986). Individual differences in comprehending and producing words in context. *Journal of Memory and Language, 25,* 1–18.

Davidson, J. L. (1982). The group mapping activity for instruction in reading and thinking. *Journal of Reading, 27,* 52–56.

Day, J. D. (1980). Teaching summarization skills: Influence of student ability level and strategy difficulty. *Cognition and Instruction, 3,* 193–210.

Dearborn, W. F., & Anderson, I. H. (1938). Aniseikonia as related to disability in reading. *Journal of Experimental Psychology, 23,* 559–577.

DeFord, D. (1985). Validating the construct of theoretical orientation in reading instruction. *Reading Research Quarterly, 20,* 351–367.

Delacato, C. H. (1963). *The diagnosis and treatment of speech and reading problems.* Springfield, IL: Charles C. Thomas.

Derry, S. J., & Murphy, D. A. (1986). Designing systems that train learning ability: From theory to practice. *Review of Educational Research, 56,* 1–39.

Dewitz, P., & Guinessey, B. (December 1990). *The effects of phoneme awareness training and repeated readings on the oral reading of disabled*

readers. Paper presented at the meeting of the National Reading Conference, Miami, FL.

Diehl, W. (1978). A critical summary of Rumelhart's interactive model of reading. In W. Diehl (Ed.), *Secondary reading: Theory and application.* Bloomington, IN: Indiana University School of Education.

Dishaw, M. (1977). *Description of allocated time to content areas for the A-B period.* Beginning Teacher Evaluation Study. (Tech. Rep. No. IV–11a). San Francisco: Far West Regional Laboratory for Educational Research and Development.

Dolch, E. W. (1936). A basic sight vocabulary. *The Elementary School Journal, 36,* 456–460.

Dole, J. A., Duffy, G. G., Roehler, L. R., & Pearson, P. D. (1991). Moving from the old to the new: Research on reading comprehension instruction. *Review of Educational Research, 61,* 239–264.

Dreher, M. J. (1992). Predicting the location of answers to textbook search tasks. In C. K. Kinzer & J. D. Leu (Eds.), *Literacy research, theory, and practice: Views from many perspectives* (pp. 269–274). Chicago: National Reading Conference.

Dreher, M. J., & Singer, H. (1985). Parents' attitudes toward reports of standardized reading test results. *The Reading Teacher, 38,* 624–632.

Drew, A. L. (1955). Familial reading disability. *University of Michigan Medical Bulletin, 21,* 245–253.

Dreyer, L. G., Futtersak, K. R., & Boehm, A. E. (1985). Sight words in the computer age: An essential list. *The Reading Teacher, 39,* 12–15.

Dreyer, L. G., & Katz, L. (1992). An examination of "the simple view of reading." In C. K. Kinzer & D. J. Leu (Eds.), *Literacy research, theory, and practice: Views from many perspectives* (pp. 169–175). Chicago: National Reading Conference.

Dufflemeyer, F. A., & Banwart, B. H. (1993). Word maps for adjectives and verbs. *The Reading Teacher, 46,* 351–353.

Duffy, G. G., & Roehler, L. R. (1987). *Improving classroom reading instruction: A decision-making approach.* New York: Random House.

Dunn, L. M. (1973). Children with mild general learning disabilities. In L. M. Dunn (Ed.), *Exceptional children in the schools: Special education in transition.* New York: Holt, Rinehart, & Winston.

Durkin, D. (1976). *Strategies for identifying words.* Boston: Allyn & Bacon.

Durkin, D. (1978–79). What classroom observations reveal about reading comprehension instruction. *Reading Research Quarterly, 14,* 481–533.

Durkin, D. (1982). *A study of poor Black children who are successful readers* (Reading Education Report No. 33). Urbana-Champaign: University of Illinois, Center for the Study of Reading.

Durkin, D. (1984). Is there a match between what elementary teachers do and what basal reader manuals recommend? *The Reading Teacher, 37,* 734–744.

Durr, W. K. (1973). Computer study of high frequency words in popular trade journals. *The Reading Teacher, 27,* 37–42.

Dusek, J. B. (1980). The development of test anxiety in children. In I. G. Sarason (Ed.), *Test anxiety: Theory, research, and applications.* Hillsdale, NJ: Erlbaum.

Dweck, C. S., & Goetz, T. E. (1978). Attributions and learned helplessness. In J. H. Harvey, W. I. Ickes, & R. F. Kidd (Eds.), *New directions in attribution research* (Vol. 2). Hillsdale, NJ: Erlbaum.

Earle, R. A., & Sanders, P. L. (1977). Individualizing reading assignments. In W. J. Harker (Ed.), *Classroom strategies for secondary reading.* Newark, DE: International Reading Association.

Edwards, P. A. (1989). Supporting mothers attempting to provide scaffolding for bookreading. In J. B. Allen & J. Mason (Eds.), *Risk makers, risk takers, and risk breakers: Reducing the risks for young learners* (pp. 69–80). Portsmouth, NH: Heinemann.

Ehri, L. C. (1976). Word learning in beginning readers: Effects of form class and defining contexts. *Journal of Educational Psychology, 68,* 832–842.

Ehri, L. C. (1987). Learning to read and spell words. *Journal of Reading Behavior, 19,* 5–31.

Ehri, L. C. (1991). Development of the ability to read words. In R. Barr, M. L. Kamil, P. Mosenthal, & P. D. Pearson (Eds.), *Handbook of reading research* (Vol. II, pp. 383–417). New York: Longman.

Ehri, L. C., & Wilce, L. S. (1985). Movement into reading: Is the first stage of printed word learning visual or phonetic? *Reading Research Quarterly, 20,* 163–179.

Ehri, L. C., & Wilce, L. S. (1987). Does learning to spell help beginners learn to read words? *Reading Research Quarterly, 22,* 47–65.

Ekwall, E. E. (1975). *Corrective reading system.* Glenview IL: Psychotechnics.

Ekwall, E. E., & Shanker, J. L. (1983). *Diagnosis and remediation of the disabled reader.* Boston: Allyn & Bacon.

Eldridge, B. H. (1985). Reading in context: An alternative approach for the adolescent disabled reader. *Journal of Reading, 29,* 9–17.

Elkonin, D. B. (1963). The psychology of mastering elements of reading. In B. Simon & J. Simon (Eds.), *Educational psychology in the U.S.S.R.* (pp. 165–179). London: Routledge & Kegan Paul.

Elley, W. B., & Mangubhai, F. (1983). The impact of reading in second language learning. *Reading Research Quarterly, 19,* 53–67.

Emans, R. (1967). The usefulness of phonic generalizations above the primary grades. *The Reading Teacher, 20,* 419–425.

Estes, T. H. (1971). A scale to measure attitudes toward reading. *Journal of Reading, 15,* 135–138.

Evans, M. M. (1982). *Dyslexia: An annotated bibliography.* Westport, CT: Greenwood Press.

Ewoldt, C. (1981). A psycholinguistic description of selected deaf children reading in sign language. *Reading Research Quarterly, 17,* 58–89.

Faltis, C. J. (1993). *Joinfostering: Adapting teaching strategies for the multilingual classroom.* New York: Macmillan.

Farr, R. (1969). *Reading: What can be measured?* Newark, DE: International Reading Association.

Farr, R. (1992). Putting it all together: Solving the reading assessment puzzle. *The Reading Teacher, 46,* 26–37.

Farr, R., & Carey, R. F. (1986). *Reading: What can be measured?* (2nd ed.). Newark, DE: International Reading Association.

Farris, P. J., & Fuhler, C. J. (1984). Developing social studies concepts through picture books. *The Reading Teacher, 47,* 380–387.

Feitelson, D., & Goldstein, Z. (1986). Patterns of book ownership and reading to young children in Israeli school-oriented and nonschool-oriented families. *The Reading Teacher, 39,* 924–930.

Felton, G. S., & Felton, L. S. (1973). From ivory tower to the people: Shifts in readability estimates of American presidential inaugural addresses. *Reading Improvement, 10,* 40–44.

Ferguson, A. M., & Fairburn, J. (1985). Language experience for problem solving in mathematics. *The Reading Teacher, 38,* 504–507.

Feuerstein, R. (1979). *The dynamic assessment of retarded performers: The learning potential assessment device, theory, instrument, and techniques.* Baltimore: University Park Press.

Fielding, L. G., Anderson, R. C., & Pearson, P. D. (1990). *How discussion questions influence children's story understanding* (Tech. Rep. No. 490). Urbana-Champaign: University of Illinois, Center for the Study of Reading.

Fielding, L. G., Wilson, P. T., & Anderson, R. C. (1986). A new focus on free reading: The role of trade books in reading instruction. In T. Raphael (Ed.), *The contexts of school-based literacy.* New York: Random House.

Finucci, J. M., Gutherie, J. T., Childs, A. L., Abbey, H., & Childs, B. (1976). The genetics of specific reading disability. *Annals of Human Genetics, 40,* 1–23.

Firth, V. (1985). Beneath the surface of developmental dyslexia. In K. E. Patterson, J. C. Marshall, & M. Coltheart (Eds.), *Surface dyslexia* (pp. 301–330). London, England: Erlbaum.

Fisher, J. A. (1962). The use of out-of-grade tests with retarded and accelerated readers. *Dissertation Abstracts International, 1962, 22,* 2683A. (University Microfilms No. 61–5564)

Foster, J. M. (1966). Effects of mobility training upon reading achievement and intelligence. *Dissertation Abstracts International, 26,* 3779A. (University Microfilms No. 66–00, 336)

Fox, B., & Routh, K. D. (1984). Phonemic analysis and synthesis as word-attack skills: Revisited. *Journal of Educational Psychology, 76,* 1059–1064.

Fraatz, J. M. B. (1987). *The politics of reading: Power, opportunity, and prospects for change in American public schools.* New York: Teachers College Press.

Frazier, D. (1993). Transfer of college developmental reading students' textmarking strategies. *Journal of Reading Behavior, 25,* 17–41.

Frederiksen, J. R. (1981). Sources of process interaction in reading. In A. M. Lesgold & C. A. Perfetti (Eds.), *Interactive processes in reading* (pp. 361–386). Hillsdale, NJ: Erlbaum.

Frederiksen, J. R. (1982). A componential theory of reading skills and their interactions. In R. J. Sternberg (Ed.), *Advances in the psychology of human intelligence* (Vol. I, pp. 125–180). Hillsdale, NJ: Erlbaum.

Freebody, P., & Byrne, B. (1988). Word-reading strategies in elementary schoolchildren: Relations to comprehension, reading time, and phonemic awareness. *Reading Research Quarterly, 23,* 441–453.

Freedman, G., & Reynolds, E. G. (1980). Enriching basal reader lessons with semantic webbing. *The Reading Teacher, 33,* 677–684.

Freedman, S. W. (1993). Linking large-scale testing and classroom portfolio assessments of student writing. *Educational Assessment, 1*(1), 27–52.

Freire, P. (1973). *Education for critical consciousness.* New York: Seabury Press.

Freppon, P. A., & Dahl, K. L. (1991). Learning about phonics in a whole language classroom. *Language Arts, 68,* 190–197.

Friedman, D., & Medway, F. (1987). Effects of varying performance sets and outcomes on the expectations, attributions, and persistence of boys with learning disabilities. *Journal of Learning Disabilities, 20,* 312–316.

Fry, E. B. (1980). The new instant word list. *The Reading Teacher, 34,* 287–289.

Fuchs, L. S., Fuchs, D., & Deno, S. L. (1982). Reliability and validity of curriculum-based informal reading inventories. *Reading Research Quarterly, 17,* 6–25.

Fuchs, L. S., Fuchs, D., & Hamlett, C. L. (1989). Computer and curriculum-based measurement. *School Psychology Review, 18,* 112–125.

Gambrell, L. B. (1982). Induced mental imagery and the text prediction performance of first and third graders. In J. A. Niles & L. A. Harris (Eds.), *New inquiries in reading research and instruction.* Rochester, NY: National Reading Conference.

Gambrell, L. B. (1984). How much time do children spend reading during teacher-directed reading instruction? In J. A. Niles & L. A. Harris (Eds.), *Changing perspectives on research in reading/language processing instruction.* Rochester, NY: National Reading Conference.

Gambrell, L. B., Wilson, R. M., & Gantt, W. N. (1981). Classroom observations of task-attending behaviors of good and poor readers. *Journal of Educational Research, 24,* 400–404.

Garcia, G. E. (1991). Factors influencing the English reading test performance of Spanish-speaking Hispanic children. *Reading Research Quarterly, 26,* 371–392.

Gardner, H. (1975, August). Brain damage: A window on the mind. *Saturday Review,* 26–29.

Garner, R. (1987). *Metacognition and reading comprehension.* Norwood, NJ: Ablex.

Garner, R. (1992). Metacognition and self-monitoring strategies. In S. J. Samuels & A. E. Farstrup (Eds.), *What research has to say about reading instruction* (2nd ed.) (pp. 236–252). Newark, DE: International Reading Association.

Garner, R., Macready, G. B., & Wagoner, S. (1984). Readers' acquisition of the components of the text lookback strategy. *Journal of Educational Psychology, 76,* 300–309.

Garner, R., Wagoner, S., & Smith, T. (1983). Externalizing question-answering strategies of good and poor comprehenders. *Reading Research Quarterly, 18,* 439–447.

Garrigan, J. J., Kender, J. P., & Heydenberk, W. R. (1980). Reading disability and family dynamics. In D. J. Sawyer (Ed.), *Disabled readers: Insight, assessment, instruction.* Newark, DE: International Reading Association.

Gates, A. I. (1926). A study of the role of visual perception, intelligence, and certain associative processes in reading and spelling. *Journal of Educational Psychology, 17,* 433–445.

Gates, A. I. (1931). *Interest and ability in reading.* New York: Macmillan.

Gates, A. I., & Bennett, C. C. (1933). *Reversal tendencies in reading: Causes, diagnosis, prevention, and correction.* New York: Bureau of Publications, Teachers College, Columbia University.

Gentry, J. R. (1981). Learning to spell developmentally. *The Reading Teacher, 34,* 468–474.

Gersten, R. (1985). Structured immersion for language minority students: Results of a longitudinal evaluation. *Educational Evaluation and Policy Analysis, 7,* 187–196.

Gersten, R., & Jiménez, R. T. (1994). A delicate balance: Enhancing literature instruction for students of English as a second language. *The Reading Teacher, 47,* 438–447.

Gipe, J. (1978–79). Investigating techniques for teaching word meanings. *Reading Research Quarterly, 14,* 624–644.

Glaser, N. A. (1965). A comparison of specific reading skills of advanced and retarded readers of fifth grade reading achievement. *Dissertation Abstracts International, 25,* 5785A-5786A. (University Microfilms No. 65-2467)

Glass, G. G., & Glass, E. W. (1978). *Glass analysis for decoding only: Easy starts kits.* Garden City, NY: Easier to Learn.

Golden, J. M. (1988). The construction of a literacy text in a story-reading lesson. In J. Green & J. Harker (Eds.), *Multiple perspective analyses of classroom discourse* (pp. 71–106). Norwood, NJ: Ablex.

Goldenberg, C. N. (1987). Low income Hispanic parents' contributions to their first-grade children's word recognition skills. *Anthropology and Education Quarterly, 18,* 149–179.

Goodman, K. S. (1967). Reading: A psycholinguistic guessing game. *Journal of the Reading Specialist, 6,* 126–135.

Goodman, K. S. (1970). Behind the eye: What happens in reading. In K. S. Goodman & O. S. Niles (Eds.), *Reading: Process and program.* Champaign, IL: National Council of Teachers of English.

Goodman, Y. M., & Burke, C. L. (1972). *Reading miscue inventory manual.* New York: Macmillan.

Goodman, Y. M., Watson, D., & Burke, C. L. (1987). *Reading miscue analysis.* New York: R. C. Owen.

Goswami, U. (1986). Children's use of analogy in learning to read: A developmental study. *Journal of Experimental Child Psychology, 42,* 73–83.

Goswami, U. (1988). Orthographic analogies and reading development. *Quarterly Journal of Experimental Psychology, 40,* 239–268.

Gottlieb, J. (1974). Attitudes toward retarded children: Effects of labeling and academic performance. *American Journal of Mental Deficiency, 79,* 268–273.

Gough, P. B. (1983). Context, form, and interaction. In K. Rayner (Ed.), *Eye movements in reading* (pp. 203–211). New York: Academic Press.

Gough, P. B., & Hillinger, M. L. (1980). Learning to read: An unnatural act. *Bulletin of the Orton Society, 30,* 179–196.

Gough, P. B., Juel, C., & Roper-Schneider, D. (1983). A two-stage model of initial reading acquisition. In J. A. Niles & L. A. Harris (Eds.), *Searches for meaning in reading/language processing and instruction* (pp. 207–211). Rochester, NY: National Reading Conference.

Graesser, A., Golding, J. M., & Long, D. L. (1991). Narrative representation and comprehension. In R. Barr, M. L. Kamil, P. Mosenthal, & P. D. Pearson (Eds.), *Handbook of reading research* (Vol. II, pp. 171–205). New York: Longman.

Graue, M. E. (1993). Integrating theory and practice through instructional assessment. *Educational Assessment, 1,* 283–309.

Graves, M. F., & Cooke, C. L. (1980). Effects of previewing difficult short stories for high school students. *Research on Reading in Secondary Schools, 6,* 38–54.

Graves, M. F., Cooke, C. L., & Laberge, M. J. (1983). Effects of previewing difficult short stories on low ability junior high school students' comprehension, recall, and attitudes. *Reading Research Quarterly, 18,* 262–276.

Graves, M. F., & Palmer, R. J. (1981). Validating previewing as a method of improving fifth and sixth grade students' comprehension of short stories. *Michigan Reading Journal, 15,* 1–3.

Gray, W. S. (1920). The value of informal tests of reading achievement. *Journal of Educational Research, 1,* 103–111.

Greaney, V. (1980). Factors related to amount and type of leisure-time reading. *Reading Research Quarterly, 15,* 337–357.

Greaney, V., & Hegerty, M. (1987). Correlates of leisure-time reading. *Journal of Research in Reading, 16,* 3–20.

Greenberg, J. W., & Davidson, H. H. (1972). Home background and school achievement of black urban ghetto children. *American Journal of Orthopsychiatry, 42,* 803–810.

Greenwood, C. R., Delquadri, J. C., & Hall, R. V. (1984). Opportunity to respond and student academic performance. In W. L. Heward, T. E. Heron, D. Hill, & J. Trap-Porter (Eds.), *Focus on behavior.* Columbus, OH: Merrill.

Griffith, P. L., & Olson, M. W. (1992). Phonemic awareness helps beginning readers break the code. *The Reading Teacher, 45,* 516–523.

Guszak, F. J. (1967). Teacher questioning and reading. *The Reading Teacher, 21,* 227–234.

Gutherie, J. T., & Greaney, V. (1991). Literacy acts. In R. Barr, M. L. Kamil, P. Mosenthal, & P. D. Pearson (Eds.), *Handbook of reading research* (Vol. II, pp. 68–96). New York: Longman.

Gutherie, J. T., & Kirsch, I. (1987). Distinctions between reading comprehension and locating information in text. *Journal of Educational Psychology, 79,* 220–227.

Gutherie, J. T., Seifert, M., Burnham, N. A., & Caplan, R. I. (1974). The maze technique to assess, monitor reading comprehension. *The Reading Teacher, 28,* 161–168.

Guzzetti, B. J., Snyder, T. E., Glass, G. V., & Gamas, W. S. (1993). Promoting conceptual change in science: A comparative meta-analysis of instructional intervention from reading education. *Reading Research Quarterly, 28,* 117–155.

Haggard, M. R. (1985). An interactive strategies approach to content area reading. *Journal of Reading, 29,* 204–210.

Hakuta, K. (1986). *Mirror of language.* New York: Basic Books.

Hakuta, K., & Gould, L. J. (1987). Synthesis of research on bilingual education. *Educational Leadership, 44,* 38–45.

Hall, M. (1970). *Teaching reading as a language experience.* Columbus, OH: Merrill.

Hallgren, B. (1950). Specific dyslexia: A clinical and genetic study. *Acta Psychiatrica et Neurologica.* Supplement No. 65. Copenhagen, Denmark.

Hammill, D. D., Goodman, L., & Wiederholt, J. L. (1974). Visual-motor processes: Can we train them? *The Reading Teacher, 27,* 469–478.

Hammill, D. D., & Larsen, S. C. (1974). The effectiveness of psycho-linguistic training. *Exceptional Children, 41,* 5–15.

Hansen, C., & Lovitt, T. (1977). An applied behavior analysis approach to reading comprehension. In J. T. Gutherie (Ed.), *Cognition, curriculum, and comprehension.* Newark, DE: International Reading Association.

Hansen, J. (1981). The effects of inference training and practice on young children's reading comprehension. *Reading Research Quarterly, 16,* 391–417.

Hardyck, C. D., & Petrinovich, L. F. (1969). Treatment of subvocal speech during reading. *Journal of Reading, 12,* 361–368, 419–422.

Haring, N. G., & Bateman, B. (1977). *Teaching the learning disabled child.* Englewood Cliffs, NJ: Prentice-Hall.

Harker, J. O. (1988). Contrasting the content of two story-reading lessons: A propositional analysis. In J. Green & J. Harker (Eds.), *Multiple perspective analyses of classroom discourse* (pp. 49–70). Norwood, NJ: Ablex.

Harris, A. J. (1968). Five decades of remedial reading. In J. A. Figurel (Ed.), *Forging ahead in reading* (pp. 25-34). Newark, DE: International Reading Association.

Harris, A. J. (1970). *How to increase reading ability* (5th ed.). New York: David McKay.

Harris, A. J. (1976). *Ten years of progress in remedial reading.* Anaheim, CA: Paper presented at the meeting of the International Reading Association. (ERIC Document Reproduction Service No. ED 182 465)

Harris, A. J. (1981). What is new in remedial reading. *The Reading Teacher, 34,* 405–410.

Harris, A. J., & Jacobson, M. D. (1972), *Basic elementary reading vocabularies.* New York: Macmillan.

Harris, A. J., & Serwer, B. L. (1966). The CRAFT Project: Instructional time in reading research. *Reading Research Quarterly, 2,* 27–56.

Harris, A. J., & Sipay, E. (1980). *How to increase reading ability.* New York: Longman.

Harris, T. L., & Hodges, R. E. (Eds.). (1981). *A dictionary of reading and related terms.* Newark, DE: International Reading Association.

Hayes, C. S., Prinz, R. J., & Siders, C. (1976). Reflection-impulsivity and reading recognition ability among mildly retarded children. *American Journal of Mental Deficiency, 81,* 94.

Hayes, D. A., & Reinking, D. (1991). Good and poor readers' use of graphic aids cued in texts and in adjunct study materials. *Contemporary Educational Psychology, 16,* 391–398.

Healy, J. M. (1982). The enigma of hyperlexia. *Reading Research Quarterly, 17,* 319–338.

Heath, S. B. (1982). What no bedtime story means: Narrative skills at home and school. *Language in Society, 11,* 49–76.

Heath, S. B. (1991). The sense of being literate: Historical and cross-cultural features. In R. Barr, M. L. Kamil, P. Mosenthal, & P. D. Pearson (Eds.), *Handbook of reading research* (Vol. II, pp. 3–25). New York: Longman.

Heckleman, R. G. (1966). Using the neurological impress method of remedial reading instruction. *Academic Therapy Quarterly, 1,* 235–239.

Hegarty, M., Carpenter, P. A., & Just, M. A. (1991). Diagrams in the comprehension of scientific texts. In R. Barr, M. L. Kamil, P. Mosenthal, & P. D. Pearson (Eds.), *Handbook of reading research* (Vol. II, pp. 641–668). New York: Longman.

Heller, M. F. (1991). *Reading-writing connections: From theory to practice.* New York: Longman.

Henderson, E. H., Estes, T. H., & Stonecash, S. (1971–72). An exploratory study of word acquisition among first-graders at midyear in a language-experience approach. *Journal of Reading Behavior, 4,* 21–31.

Henderson, L. C., & Shanker, J. L. (1978). The use of interpretive dramatics versus basal reader workbooks for developing comprehension skills. *Reading World, 17,* 239–243.

Herber, H. L. (1992). Foreword. In K. Wood, D. Lapp, & J. Flood, *Guiding readers through text: A review of study guides* (p. V). Newark, DE: International Reading Association.

Herber, H. L., & Nelson, J. (1975). Questioning is not the answer. *Journal of Reading, 18,* 512–517.

Herman, P. A. (1985). The effect of repeated readings on reading rate, speech pauses, and word recognition accuracy. *Reading Research Quarterly, 20,* 553–565.

Herman, P. A., & Dole, J. (1988). Theory and practice in vocabulary learning and instruction. *The Elementary School Journal, 89,* 41–52.

Hess, R. D., & Holloway, S. (1984). Family and school as educational institution. In R. D. Parke (Ed.), *The family* (pp. 179–222). Chicago: University of Chicago Press.

Heward, W. L., McCormick, S., & Joynes, Y. (1980). Completing job applications: Evaluation of an instructional program for mildly retarded juvenile delinquents. *Behavioral Disorders, 5,* 223–234.

Hiebert, E. H., Colt, J. M., Catto, S. L., & Gary, E. C. (1992). Reading and writing of first-grade students in a restructured Chapter I program. *American Educational Research Journal, 29,* 545–572.

Hilbert, S. B. (1993). Sustained Silent Reading revisited. *The Reading Teacher, 46,* 354–356.

Hildreth, G. (1965). Experience related reading for school beginners. *Elementary English, 42,* 280–297.

Himelstein, H. C., & Greenberg, G. (1974). The effect of increasing reading rate on comprehension. *The Journal of Psychology, 86,* 251–259.

Hinshelwood, J. (1896). A case of dyslexia: A peculiar form of word-blindness. *Lancet, 2,* 1451–1454.

Hinshelwood, J. (1917). *Congenital word blindness.* London, England: H. K. Lewis.

Hirshoren, A., Hunt, J. T., & Davis, C. (1974). Classified ads as reading materials for the educable retarded. *Exceptional Children, 41,* 45–47.

Hittleman, D. R. (1978). *Developmental reading: A psycholinguistic perspective.* Chicago: Rand McNally.

Hittleman, D. R. (1983). *Developmental reading, K-8: Teaching from a psycholinguistic perspective* (2nd ed.). Boston: Houghton Mifflin.

Hochman, C. H. (1973). Black dialect reading tests in the urban elementary school. *The Reading Teacher, 26,* 581–583.

Hoffman, J. V., O'Neal, S. F., Kastler, L. A., Clements, R. O., Segel, K. W., & Nash, M. F. (1984). Guided oral reading and miscue focused verbal feedback in second-grade classrooms. *Reading Research Quarterly, 19,* 367–384.

Hohn, W., & Ehri, L. (1983). Do alphabet letters help prereaders acquire phonemic segmentation skill? *Journal of Educational Psychology, 75,* 752–762.

Holdaway, D. (1979). *The foundations of literacy.* Sydney, Australia: Aston Scholastic.

Hoover, W. A., & Gough, P. B. (1990). The simple view of reading. *Reading and Writing: An Interdisciplinary Journal, 2,* 127–160.

Horn, A. (1941). *The uneven distribution of the effects of special factors.* Southern California Education Monograph (No. 12).

Hoskisson, K., Sherman, T. M., & Smith, L. L. (1974). Assisted reading and parent involvement. *The Reading Teacher, 27,* 710–714.

Hulme, C. (1981). The effects of manual tracing on memory in normal and retarded readers: Some implications for multi-sensory teaching. *Psychological Research, 43,* 179–191.

Huttenlocher, R. R., & Huttenlocher, J. (1973). A study of children with hyperlexia. *Neurology, 23,* 1107–1116.

Hynd, G. W. (1986, April). *Neurophysiological basis of developmental dyslexia.* Paper presented at the meeting of the International Reading Association, Philadelphia, PA.

Hynd, G. W., & Hynd, C. R. (1984). Dyslexia: Neuroanatomical/neurolinguistic perspectives. *Reading Research Quarterly, 19,* 482–498.

Idol, L., & Croll, V. J. (1987). Story-mapping training as a means of improving reading comprehension. *Learning Disability Quarterly, 10,* 214–228.

Ignoffo, M. (1993–94). Theater of the mind: Nonconventional strategies for helping remedial readers gain control over their reading experience. *Journal of Reading, 37,* 310–321.

Inouye, R. (1981). *Dyslexia.* Unpublished manuscript.

Irwin, D. M., & Bushnell, M. M. (1980). *Observational studies for child study.* New York: Holt, Rinehart & Winston.

Jackson, M., & McClelland, J. (1979). Processing determinants of reading speed. *Journal of Experimental Psychology: General, 108,* 151–181.

Jackson, M. D. (1980). Further evidence for a relationship between memory access and reading ability. *Journal of Verbal Learning and Verbal Behavior, 19,* 683–694.

James, C. (1987). Book buying for and by children. *Proceedings of the Childrens' Market Symposium.* London: Publishers Association.

James, E. (1994). What is a reading resource specialist? *The Exchange: A Newsletter of the International Reading Association Secondary Reading Interest Group, 7*(2), 1–3.

Jenkins, J. R., Stein, M., & Wysocki, K. (1984). Learning vocabulary through reading. *American Educational Research Journal, 21,* 767–787.

Jennings, J. H. (1991). A comparison of summary and journal writing as components of an interactive comprehension model. In J. Zutell & S. McCormick (Eds.), *Learner factors/teacher factors: Issues in literacy research and instruction* (pp. 67–82). Chicago: National Reading Conference.

Johns, J. L. (1982). The dimensions and uses of informal reading assessment. In J. L. Pikulski & T. Shanahan (Eds.), *Approaches to the informal evaluation of reading.* Newark, DE: International Reading Association.

Johnson, D. D. (1971). A basic vocabulary for beginning readers. *Elementary School Journal, 72,* 31-33.

Johnson, D. D. (1984, May). *Two important approaches to vocabulary development: Semantic mapping and semantic feature analysis.* Paper presented at the meeting of the International Reading Association, Atlanta.

Johnson, D. D., & Baumann, J. F. (1984). Word identification. In P. D. Pearson (Ed.), *Handbook of reading research* (pp. 583–608). New York: Longman.

Johnson, D. D., & Pearson, P. D. (1978). *Teaching reading vocabulary.* New York: Holt, Rinehart & Winston.

Johnson, D. D., & Pearson, P. D. (1984). *Teaching reading vocabulary* (2nd ed.). New York: Holt, Rinehart, & Winston.

Johnson, L. R., & Platts, D. (1962). A summary of a study of the reading ages of children who had been given remedial teaching. *British Journal of Educational Psychology, 32,* 66–71.

Johnson, R. (1969). The validity of the Clymer-Barrett Prereading Battery. *The Reading Teacher, 22,* 609–614.

Johnson-Laird, P. N. (1983). *Mental models.* Cambridge, MA: Harvard University Press.

Johnston, P. H. (1983). *Reading comprehension assessment: A cognitive basis.* Newark, DE: International Reading Association.

Johnston, P. H. (1985). Understanding reading disability: A case study approach. *Harvard Educational Review, 55,* 153–177.

Johnston, P. H. (1992). *Constructive evaluation of literate activity.* New York: Longman.

Johnston, P. H., Afflerbach, P., & Weiss, P. (1993). Teachers' assessment of the teaching and learning of literacy. *Educational Assessment, 1,* 91–117.

Johnston, P. H., & Allington, R. (1991). Remediation. In R. Barr, M. L. Kamil, P. Mosenthal, & P. D. Pearson (Eds.), *Handbook of reading research* (Vol. II, pp. 984–1012). New York: Longman.

Johnston, P. H., Nolan, E. A., & Berry, M. (1993). Learning to listen. *The Reading Teacher, 46,* 606–608.

Johnston, P. H., & Winograd, P. N. (1985). Passive failure in reading. *Journal of Reading Behavior, 17,* 279–301.

Jones, M. B., & Pikulski, E. C. (1974). Cloze for the classroom. *The Reading Teacher, 27,* 432–438.

Jorm, A. F. (1981). Children with reading and spelling retardation: Functioning of whole-word and correspondence-rule mechanisms. *Journal of Child Psychology and Psychiatry, 22,* 171–178.

Jorm, A. F., & Share, D. L. (1983). Phonological recoding and reading acquisition. *Applied Psycholinguistics, 4,* 103–147.

Joynes, Y. D., McCormick, S., & Heward, W. L. (1980). Teaching reading disabled students to read and complete employment applications. *Journal of Reading, 23,* 709–714.

Juel, C. (1988). Learning to read and write: A longitudinal study of 54 children from first through fourth grades. *Journal of Educational Psychology, 80,* 437–447.

Juel, C. (1989, December). *The longitudinal study of reading acquisition: Grades 1-4.* Paper presented at the meeting of the National Reading Conference, Austin, TX.

Juel, C. (1991). Beginning reading. In R. Barr, M. L. Kamil, P. Mosenthal, & P. D. Pearson (Eds.), *Handbook of reading research* (Vol. II, pp. 759–788). New York: Longman.

Juel, C., Griffith, P. L., & Gough, P. B. (1985). Reading and spelling strategies of first-grade children. In J. A. Niles & R. Lalik (Eds.), *Issues in literacy: A research perspective* (pp. 306–309). Rochester, NY: National Reading Conference.

Juel, C., Griffith, P. L., & Gough, P. B. (1986). Acquisition of literacy: A longitudinal study of children in first and second grade. *Journal of Educational Psychology, 78,* 243–255.

Just, M., & Carpenter, P. (1987). *The psychology of reading and language comprehension.* Newton, MA: Allyn & Bacon.

Kagan, J. (1965). Reflection, impulsivity, and reading ability in primary grade children. *Child Development, 36,* 609–628.

Kahn, E., & Wirtz, R. W. (1982). Another look at applications in elementary school mathematics. *Arithmetic Teacher, 30,* 21–25.

Kameenui, E. J., Carnine, D. W., & Freschi, R. (1982). Effects of text construction and instructional procedures for teaching word meanings on comprehension and recall. *Reading Research Quarterly, 17,* 367–388.

Kamil, M. L., Smith-Burke, M., & Rodriguez-Brown, F. (1986). The sensitivity of cloze to intersentential integration of information in Spanish bilingual populations. In J. A. Niles & R. V. Lalik (Eds.), *Solving problems in literacy: Learners, teachers, and researchers* (pp. 334–338). Rochester, NY: National Reading Conference.

Kazemek, F. E. (1985). Functional literacy is not enough: Adult literacy as a developmental process. *Journal of Reading, 28,* 332–335.

Keogh, B. K. (1974). Optometric vision training programs for children with learning disabilities: Review of issues and research. *Journal of Learning Disabilities, 7,* 219–231.

Kephart, N. C. (1960). *The slow learner in the classroom.* Columbus, OH: Merrill.

Kibby, M. W. (1977). *The effects of context emphasis on teaching sight vocabulary.* Unpublished manuscript, State University of New York at Buffalo, Buffalo, NY.

Kibby, M. W. (1989). Teaching sight vocabulary with and without context before silent reading: A field test of the "Focus of Attention" hypothesis. *Journal of Reading Behavior, 21,* 261–279.

Kibby, M. W. (1993). What reading teachers should know about reading in the U.S. *The Reading Teacher, 37,* 28–40.

Killgallon, P. A. (1942). *A study of relationships among certain pupil adjustments in language situations.* Unpublished doctoral dissertation, Pennsylvania State University, University Park.

Kilty, T. K. (1976, March 17). Many are found unable to comprehend instructions on grocery store package. *The New York Times,* p. 49.

King, C., & Quigley, S. (1985). *Reading and deafness.* San Diego, CA: College-Hill.

King, J. R., Biggs, S., & Lipsky, S. (1984). Students' self-questioning and summarizing in reading study strategies. *Journal of Reading Behavior, 16,* 205–218.

Kintsch, W. (1974). *The mental representation of meaning.* Hillsdale, NJ: Erlbaum.

Kintsch, W. (1979). On modeling comprehension. *Educational Psychologist, 14,* 3–14.

Kirsch, I. S., & Jungeblut, A. (1987). *Literacy: Profiles of America's young adults.* Princeton, NJ: National Assessment of Educational Progress, Educational Testing Service.

Klesius, J. P., Griffith, P. L., & Zielonka, P. (1991). A whole language and traditional instruction comparison: Overall effectiveness and development of the alphabetic principle. *Reading Research and Instruction, 30*(2), 47–61.

Kroll, N. E. A., Parks, T., Parkinson, S. R., Bieber, S. L., & Johnson, A. L. (1970). Short-term memory while shadowing: Recall of visually and aurally presented letters. *Journal of Experimental Psychology, 85,* 220–224.

Kuchinskas, G. (1983). Twenty-two ways to use a microcomputer in reading and language arts classes. *Computers, Reading, and Language Arts, 1,* 11–16.

Kwolek, W. F. (1973). A readability survey of technical and popular literature. *Journalism Quarterly, 50,* 255–264.

LaBerge, D., & Samuels, S. J. (1974). Toward a theory of automatic information processing in reading. *Cognitive Psychology, 6,* 293–323.

Lahaderne, H. M. (1976). Feminized schools— Unpromising myth to explain boys' reading problems. *The Reading Teacher, 29,* 776–786.

Lankford, R., & Riley, J. D. (1986). Native American reading disability. *Journal of American Indian Education, 25,* 1–11.

Lee, N. G., & Neal, J. C. (1993). Reading Rescue: Intervention for a student "at promise." *Journal of Reading, 36,* 276–283.

Leland, C., & Fitzpatrick, R. (1993–94). Cross-age interaction builds enthusiasm for reading and writing. *The Reading Teacher, 47,* 292–301.

Lerner, J. (1981). *Learning disabilities* (3rd ed.). Boston: Houghton Mifflin.

Lesgold, A. M., McCormick, C., & Golinkoff, R. M. (1975). Imagery training and children's prose learning. *Journal of Educational Psychology, 67,* 663–667.

Lesgold, A. M., & Resnick, L. B. (1982). How reading disabilities develop: Perspectives from a longitudinal study. In J. P. Das, R. Mulcahy, & A. E. Wall (Eds.), *Theory and research in learning disability* (pp. 40-62). New York: Plenum.

Lesgold, A. M., Resnick, L. B., & Hammond, K. (1985). Learning to read: A longitudinal study of word skill development in two curricula. In G. E. Mackinnon & T. G. Waller (Eds.), *Reading research: Advances in theory and practice* (Vol. 4, pp. 107–138). New York: Academic Press.

Leung, C. B. (1992). Effects of word-related variables on vocabulary growth through repeated read-aloud events. In C. K. Kinzer & D. J. Leu (Eds.), *Literacy research, theory, and practice: Views from many perspectives* (pp. 491–498). Chicago: National Reading Conference.

Leung, C. B., & Pikulski, J. J. (1990). Incidental learning of word meanings by kindergarten and first-grade children through repeated read-aloud events. In S. McCormick & J. Zutell (Eds.), *Literary theory and research: Analysis from multiple paradigms* (pp. 231–239). Chicago: National Reading Conference.

Liberman, I. Y., Shankweiler, D., Fischer, F. W., & Carter, B. (1974). Reading and the awareness of linguistic segments. *Journal of Experimental Child Psychology, 18,* 201–212.

Liberman, I. Y., Shankweiler, D., Liberman, A. M., Fowler, C., & Fischer, F. W. (1977). Phonetic segmentation and recoding in the beginning reader. In A. S. Reber & D. L. Scarborough (Eds.), *Toward a psychology of reading* (pp. 207–225). Hillsdale, NJ: Erlbaum.

Livingston, M. C. (1958). *Whispers and other poems.* San Diego: Harcourt.

Lomax, R. G. (1983). Applying structural modeling to some component processes of reading comprehension development. *Journal of Experimental Education, 52,* 33–40.

Lomax, R. G., & McGee, L. M. (1987). Young children's concepts about print and meaning: Toward a model of word reading acquisition. *Reading Research Quarterly, 22,* 237–256.

Long, J. V., Schaffran, J. A., & Kellog, T. M. (1977). Effects of out-of-level survey testing on reading achievement scores of Title 1, ESEA students. *Journal of Educational Measurement, 14,* 203–213.

Lundberg, I. (August, 1984). Learning to read. *School Research Newsletter.* National Board of Education, Sweden.

Lundberg, I., Frost, J., & Petersen, O. P. (1988). Effects of an extensive program for stimulating phonological awareness in preschool children. *Reading Research Quarterly, 23,* 264–284.

Lundberg, I., Olofsson, A., & Wall, S. (1980). Reading and spelling skills in the first school years predicted from phonemic awareness skills in kindergarten. *Scandinavian Journal of Psychology, 21,* 159–173.

Lysakowski, R. S., & Walberg, H. J. (1982). Instructional effects of cues, participation, and corrective feedback: A quantitative synthesis. *American Educational Research Journal, 19,* 559–578.

MacGinitie, W. H. (1973a). An introduction to some measurement problems in reading. In W. H. MacGinitie (Ed.), *Assessment problems in reading.* Newark, DE: International Reading Association.

MacGinitie, W. H. (1993). Some limits of assessments. *The Reading Teacher, 36,* 556–560.

Madden, N. A., Slavin, R. E., Karweit, N. L., Dolan, L. J., & Wasik, B. A. (1991). Success for All: Ending reading failure from the beginning. *Language Arts, 68,* 47–52.

Mangieri, J. N., & Kahn, M. S. (1977). Is the Dolch Test of 220 Basic Sight Words irrelevant? *The Reading Teacher, 30,* 649–651.

Mann, V. A., Liberman, I. Y., & Shankweiler, D. (1980). Childrens' memory for sentences and word strings in relation to reading ability. *Memory and Cognition, 8,* 329–335.

Manzo, A. V. (1969). The ReQuest procedure. *Journal of Reading, 13,* 123–126.

Manzo, A. V., & Manzo, U. C. (1993). *Literacy disorders: Holistic diagnosis and remediation.* Fort Worth, TX: Harcourt Brace Jovanovich.

Mark, L. S., Shankweiler, D., Liberman, I. Y., & Fowler, C. A. (1977). Phonetic recoding and reading difficulty in beginning readers. *Memory and Cognition, 5,* 623–629.

Marks, C. B., Doctorow, M. J., & Wittrock, M. C. (1974). Word frequency and reading comprehension. *The Journal of Educational Research, 67,* 259–262.

Martin, B. (1983). *Brown bear, brown bear, what do you see?* New York: Holt, Rinehart, & Winston.

Marzano, R. J., Hagerty, P. J., Valencia, S. W., & DiStefano, P. P. (1987). *Reading diagnosis and instruction: Theory into practice.* Englewood Cliffs, NJ: Prentice-Hall.

Masland, R. L., & Cratty, B. J. (1971). The nature of the reading process: The rationale of noneducational remedial methods. *Reading Forum* (NINDS Monograph No. 11). Bethesda, MD: National Institute of Neurological Disease and Stroke.

Mason, J. (1980). When *do* children learn to read: An exploration of four-year old children's letter and word reading competencies. *Reading Research Quarterly, 15,* 203–227.

Matheny, A. P., Dolan, J. B., & Wilson, R. S. (1976). Twins with academic learning problems: Antecedent characteristics. *American Journal of Orthopsychiatry, 46,* 464–469.

Matthews, M. M. (1966). *Teaching to read: Historically considered.* Chicago: University of Chicago Press.

May, R. B., & Ollila, L. O. (1981). Reading sex-role attitudes in preschoolers. *Reading Research Quarterly, 16,* 583–595.

McAllister, P. (1994). Using K-W-L for informal assessment. *The Reading Teacher, 47,* 510–511.

McAloon, N. M. (1993). Our role in mainstreaming. *Journal of Reading, 36,* 328–329.

McConnell, B. (1989). Education as a cultural process: The interaction between community and classroom in fostering learning. In J. B. Allen & J. Mason (Eds.), *Risk makers, risk takers, risk breakers: Reducing the risks for young children* (pp. 47–56). Portsmouth, NH: Heinemann.

McCormick, S. (1977). Should you read aloud to your children? *Language Arts, 54,* 139–143, 163.

McCormick, S. (1981). Assessment and the beginning reader: Using student dictated stories. *Reading World, 21,* 29–39.

McCormick, S. (1983). Reading aloud to preschoolers aged 3-6: A review of the research. *Reading Horizons, 24,* 7–12.

McCormick, S. (1991). *Working with our most severe reading disability cases: A strategy for teaching nonreaders.* Paper presented at the meeting of the National Reading Conference, Palm Springs, CA.

McCormick, S. (1992). Disabled readers' erroneous responses to inferential comprehension questions: Description and analysis. *Reading Research Quarterly, 27,* 54–77.

McCormick, S. (1994). A nonreader becomes a reader: A case study of literacy acquisition by a severely disabled reader. *Reading Research Quarterly, 29,* 156–177.

McCormick, S., & Hill, D. S. (1984). An analysis of the effects of two procedures for increasing disabled readers' inferencing skills. *Journal of Educational Research, 77,* 219–226.

McCormick, S., & Moe, A. J. (1982). The language of instructional materials: A source of reading problems. *Exceptional Children, 49,* 48–53.

McCracken, R. A. (1962). Standardized reading tests and informal reading inventories. *Education, 82,* 366–369.

McGee, L. M. (1992). An exploration of meaning construction in first graders' grand conversations. In C. K. Kinzer and D. J. Leu (Eds.), *Literacy research, theory, and practice: Views from many perspectives* (pp. 177–186). Chicago: National Reading Conference.

McGinley, W. J., & Denner, P. R. (1987). Story impressions: A prereading/writing activity. *Journal of Reading, 31,* 248–253.

McKeown, M. G. (1985). The acquisition of word meaning from context by children of high and low ability. *Reading Research Quarterly, 20,* 482–496.

McKeown, M. G., & Beck, I. L. (1988). Learning vocabulary: Different ways for different goals. *Remedial and Special Education, 9,* 42–52.

McKeown, M. G., Beck, I. L., Omanson, R. C., & Perfetti, C. A. (1983). The effects of long-term vocabulary instruction on reading comprehension: A replication. *Journal of Reading Behavior, 15,* 3–15.

McKeown, M. G., Beck, I. L., Omanson, R. C., & Pople, M. T. (1985). Some effects of the nature and frequency of vocabulary instruction on the knowledge and use of words. *Reading Research Quarterly, 20,* 522–535.

McNamara, T. P., Miller, D. L., & Bransford, J. D. (1991). Mental models and reading comprehension. In R. Barr, M. L. Kamil, P. Mosenthal, & P. D. Pearson (Eds.), *Handbook of reading research* (Vol. II, pp. 490–511). New York: Longman.

McNaughton, S., & Glynn, T. (1981). Delayed versus immediate attention to oral reading errors' effects on accuracy and self-correction. *Educational Psychology, 1,* 57–65.

Measurement and training of perceptual-motor functions. (1986). *Learning Disabilities Quarterly, 9,* 247.

Mehegan, C. C., & Dreifus, R. E. (1972). Hyperlexia—exceptional reading ability in brain damaged children. *Neurology, 22,* 1105–1111.

Meyer, C. (1982). Prime-O-Tec: A successful strategy for adult disabled readers. *Journal of Reading, 25,* 512–515.

Meyer, L. A. (1984). Long-term academic effects of the direct instruction project Follow-Through. *Elementary School Journal, 84,* 380–394.

Mezynski, K. (1983). Issues concerning the acquisition of knowledge: Effects of vocabulary training on reading comprehension. *Review of Educational Research, 53,* 253–279.

Miller, G. A. (1973). *Linguistic communications: Perspectives for research.* Newark, DE: International Reading Association.

Miller, G. E. (1987). The influence of self-instruction on the comprehension monitoring performance of average and above-average readers. *Journal of Reading Behavior, 19,* 303–316.

Miller, K. K., & George, J. E. (1992). Expository passage organizers: Models for reading and writing. *Journal of Reading, 35,* 372–377.

Mills, R. E. (1970). *The teaching of word recognition.* Ft. Lauderdale: The Mills School.

Mitchell, J. V., Jr. (Ed.), (1985). *The ninth mental measurements yearbook.* Lincoln, NE: The Buros Institute of Mental Measurements.

Mitzel, M. A. (1966). The functional reading word list for adults. *Adult Education, 2,* 67–69.

Moll, L. C., & Diaz, S. (1987). Change as the goal of educational research. *Anthropology and Education Quarterly, 18,* 300–311.

Monroe, M. (1932). *Children who cannot read.* Chicago: University of Chicago Press.

Morais, J., Cluytens, M., Alegria, J., & Content, A. (1984). Segmentation abilities of dyslexics and normal readers. *Perceptual and Motor Skills, 58,* 221–222.

Morrison, V. B. (1968). Teacher-pupil interaction in three types of elementary classroom reading situations. *The Reading Teacher, 22,* 271–275.

Morrow, L. M., Sisco, L. J., & Smith, J. K. (1992). The effect of mediated story retelling on listening comprehension, story structure, and oral language development in children with learning disabilities. In C. K. Kinzer & D. J. Leu (Eds.), *Literacy research, theory, and practice: Views from many perspectives* (pp. 435–443). Chicago: National Reading Conference.

Moustafa, M., & Penrose, J. (1985). Comprehensible input PLUS the language experience approach. *The Reading Teacher, 38,* 640–647.

Moyer, S., & Newcomer, P. (1977). Reversals in reading: Diagnosis and remediation. *Exceptional Children, 43,* 424–429.

Mullen, F. A., & Itkin, W. (1961). *Achievement and adjustment of educable mentally handicapped children in special classes and in regular classes.* Chicago: Chicago Board of Education.

Mullin, S., & Summers, A. (1983). Is more better? The effectiveness of spending on compensatory education. *Phi Delta Kappan, 64,* 339–347.

Murph, D., & McCormick, S. (1985). Evaluation of an instructional program designed to teach minimally literate juvenile delinquents to read road signs. *Education and Treatment of Children, 8,* 133–155.

Muth, K. D. (1993). Reading in mathematics: Middle school mathematics teachers' beliefs and practices. *Reading Research and Instruction, 32,* 76–83.

Nagy, W. E. (1988). *Teaching vocabulary to improve reading comprehension.* Newark, DE: International Reading Association.

Nagy, W. E., Anderson, R. C., & Herman, P. (1987). Learning word meanings from context during normal reading. *American Educational Research Journal, 24,* 237–270.

Nagy, W. E., Anderson, R. C., Schommer, M., Scott, J., & Stallman, A. (1989). Morphological families in the internal lexicon. *Reading Research Quarterly, 24,* 262–282.

Nagy, W. E., & Herman, P. A. (1987). Depth and breadth of vocabulary knowledge: Implications for acquisition and instruction. In M. G. McKeown & M. E. Curtis (Eds.), *The nature of vocabulary acquisition* (pp. 19–35). Hillsdale, NJ: Erlbaum.

Nagy, W. E., Osborn, J., Winsor, P., & O'Flahavan, J. (1992). *Guidelines for instruction in structural analysis* (Tech. Rep. No. 554). Urbana-Champaign, IL: University of Illinois, Center for the Study of Reading.

Nassi, A. J., & Abramowitz, S. I. (1976). From phrenology to psychosurgery and back again: Biological studies of criminals. *American Journal of Orthopsychiatry, 46,* 591–606.

National Advisory Committee on Hyperkinesis and Food Additives (1975). *Report to the Nutrition Foundation.* New York: The Nutrition Foundation.

National Assessment of Educational Progress. (1975). *Functional literacy: Basic reading performance.* (Technical summary of an assessment of in-school 17-year-olds in 1974). Denver: National Assessment of Educational Progress.

National Assessment of Educational Progress. (1976). *Reading in America.* A perspective on two assessments. (Reading Report No. 06–R–01). Denver: National Assessment of Educational Progress.

National Assessment of Educational Progress. (1992). Reading Report card for the nation and the states. (Report No. 23–ST06). Washington, DC: National Center for Education Statistics.

Naughton, V. M. (1993–94). Creative mapping for content reading. *Journal of Reading, 37,* 324–326.

Neuman, S. (1986). The home environment and fifth-grade students' leisure reading. *Elementary School Journal, 86,* 333–343.

Newcomer, P. L., & Hammill, D. D. (1975). ITPA and academic achievement: A survey. *The Reading Teacher, 28,* 731–741.

Newman, A. P., Lewis, W., & Beverstock, C. (1993). *Prison literacy: Implications for program and assessment policy* (Tech. Rep. No. 93–1). Philadelphia: University of Pennsylvania, National Center on Adult Literacy.

Newman, J. M., & Church, S. M. (1990). Myths of whole language. *The Reading Teacher, 44,* 20–26.

Newsome, G. L. (1986). The effects of reader perspective and cognitive style on remembering important information from texts. *Journal of Reading Behavior, 18,* 117–133.

Noble, E. F. (1981). Self-selection: A remedial strategy for readers with a limited reading vocabulary. *The Reading Teacher, 34,* 386–388.

Norman, C. A., & Malicky, G. (1987). Stages in the reading development of adults. *Journal of Reading, 30,* 302–307.

Norman, D. A. (1984). Theories and models in cognitive psychology. In E. Donchin (Ed.), *Cognitive psychophysiology.* Hillsdale, NJ: Erlbaum.

O'Donnell, P. A., & Eisenson, J. (1969). Delacato training for reading achievement and visual-motor integration. *Journal of Learning Disabilities, 2,* 441–447.

OERI Bulletin (1993). *How literate are American adults?* [Fall issue]. Washington, DC: U.S. Department of Education, Office of Educational Research and Improvement.

Ogbu, J. V. (1992). Understanding cultural diversity and learning. *Educational Researcher, 21,* 5–14, 24.

Ogle, D. M. (1986). K-W-L: A teaching model that develops active reading of expository text. *The Reading Teacher, 39,* 564–570.

Olson, M. W., & Gee, T. C. (1991). Content reading instruction in the primary grades: Perceptions and strategies. *The Reading Teacher, 45,* 298–307.

Otto, W. (1986). Peter Johnston, we salute you. *Journal of Reading, 29,* 700–703.

Pachtman, A. B., & Riley, J. D. (1978). Teaching vocabulary of mathematics through interaction, exposure, and structure. *Journal of Reading, 22,* 240–244.

Palincsar, A. S. (1986). The role of dialogue in providing scaffolded instruction. *Educational Psychologist, 21,* 73–98.

Palincsar, A. S., & Brown, A. L. (1984). Reciprocal teaching of comprehension-fostering and comprehension-monitoring activities. *Cognition and Instruction, 1,* 117–175.

Paradis, E., Tierney. R., & Peterson, J. (1975). A systematic examination of the reliability of the cloze procedure. In G. H. McNinch & W. D. Miller (Eds.), Reading: Convention and inquiry. *Yearbook of the National Reading Conference.* Chicago: National Reading Conference.

Paratore, J. R., & Indrisano, R. (1987). Intervention assessment of reading comprehension. *The Reading Teacher, 40,* 778–783.

Paris, S. G. (1986). Teaching children to guide their reading and learning. In T. E. Raphael (Ed.), *The contexts of school-based literacy* (pp. 115–130). New York: Random House.

Paris, S. G., Calfee, R. C., Filby, N., Hiebert, E. H., Pearson, P. D., Valencia, S. W., & Wolf, K. P. (1992). A framework for authentic literacy assessment. *The Reading Teacher, 46,* 88–99.

Paris, S. G., Lipson, M., & Wixson, K. (1983). Becoming a strategic reader. *Contemporary Educational Psychology, 8,* 293–316.

Paris, S. G., & Myers, M. (1981). Comprehension monitoring, memory, and study strategies of good and poor readers. *Journal of Reading Behavior, 13,* 5–22.

Paris, S. G., Wasik, B. A., & Turner, J. C. (1991). The development of strategic readers. In R. Barr, M. L. Kamil, P. Mosenthal, & P. D. Pearson (Eds.), *Handbook of reading research* (Vol. II, pp. 609–640). New York: Longman.

Patching, W., Kameenui, E., Carnine, D., Gersten, R., & Colvin, G. (1983). Direct instruction in critical reading skills. *Reading Research Quarterly, 18,* 406–418.

Paul, P. V., & O'Rourke, J. P. (1988). Multimeaning words and reading comprehension: Implications for special education students. *Remedial and Special Education, 9,* 42–52.

Payne, J. S., Polloway, E. A., Smith, J. E., & Payne, R. A. (1981). *Strategies for teaching the mentally retarded* (2nd ed.). Columbus, OH: Merrill.

Pearson, P. D., & Fielding, L. (1991). Comprehension instruction. In R. Barr, M. L. Kamil, P. Mosenthal, & P. D. Pearson (Eds.), *Handbook of reading research* (Vol. II, pp. 815–860). New York: Longman.

Pearson, P. D., & Gallagher, M. C. (1983). The instruction of reading comprehension. *Contemporary Educational Psychology, 8,* 317–344.

Pearson, P. D., & Johnson, D. (1978). *Teaching reading comprehension.* New York: Holt, Rinehart & Winston.

Pearson, P. D., & Valencia, S. (1987). Assessment, accountability, and professional prerogative. In J. E. Readence & R. S. Baldwin (Eds.), *Research in literacy: Merging perspectives.* Rochester, NY: National Reading Conference.

Peck, C. V., & Kling, M. (1977). Adult literacy in the seventies: Its definition and measurement. *Journal of Reading, 20,* 677–682.

Perfetti, C. A. (1985). *Reading ability.* New York: Oxford University Press.

Perfetti, C. A., Beck, I., Bell, L., & Hughes, C. (1987). Children's reading and the development of phonological awareness. *Merrill Palmer Quarterly, 33,* 39–75.

Perfetti, C. A., Goldman, S., & Hogaboam, T. (1979). Reading skill and the identification of words in discourse context. *Memory and Cognition, 7,* 273–282.

Pflaum, S. W., & Bryan, T. H. (1980). Oral reading behaviors in the learning disabled. *Journal of Educational Research, 73,* 252–257.

Pflaum, S. W., & Pascarella, E. T. (1980). Interactive effects of prior reading achievement and training in context on the reading of learning disabled children. *Reading Research Quarterly, 16,* 138–158.

Phillips, S. U. (1972). Participant structures and communicative competence: Warm Springs children in community and classroom. In C. Cazden, V. John, & D. Hymes (Eds.), *Functions of language in the classroom.* New York: Teachers College Press.

Piercey, D. (1976). *Reading activities in content areas.* Boston: Allyn & Bacon.

Pinnell, G. S. (1989). Success of at-risk children in a program that combines reading and writing. In J. M. Mason (Ed.), *Reading and writing connections.* Boston: Allyn & Bacon.

Pinnell, G. S., Lyons, C. A., DeFord, D. E., Bryk, A. S., & Seltzer, M. (1994). Comparing instructional models for the literacy education of high-risk first graders. *Reading Research Quarterly, 29,* 9–39.

Piper, T. (1993). *Language for all children.* New York: Macmillan.

Poindexter, C. (1994). Guessed meanings. *Journal of Reading, 37,* 420–422.

Powell, W. R. (1971). Validity of the IRI reading levels. *Elementary English, 48,* 637–642.

Pratt, A. C., & Brady, S. (1988). Relation of phonological awareness to reading disability in children and adults. *Journal of Educational Psychology, 80,* 319–323.

Pring, L., & Snowling, M. (1986). Developmental changes in word recognition: An information-processing account. *Quarterly Journal of Experimental Psychology, 38A,* 395–418.

Pyrczak, F. (1976). Readability of instructions for Form 1040. *Journal of Reading, 20,* 121–127.

Ramirez, J. D., Yuen, S. D., Ramey, D. R., & Pasta, D. J. (1990). *Final report: Longitudinal study of immersion strategy, early-exit and late-exit transitional bilingual education for language-minority children.* San Mateo, CA: Aguirre International.

Rankin, E. F. (1978). Characteristics of the cloze procedure as a research tool in the study of language. In P. D. Pearson & J. Hansen (Eds.), Reading: Disciplined inquiry in process and practice. *Yearbook of the National Reading Conference.* Chicago: National Reading Conference.

Ransom, P. (1968). Determining reading levels of elementary school children by cloze testing. In J. A. Figurel (Ed.), *Forging ahead in reading.* Newark, DE: International Reading Association.

Raphael, T. E. (1986). Teaching question-answers relationships, revisited. *The Reading Teacher, 39,* 516–522.

Ratekin, N. (1978). A comparison of reading achievement among three racial groups using standard reading materials. In D. Feitelson (Ed.), *Cross-cultural perspectives on reading and reading research.* Newark, DE: International Reading Association.

Rauch, M., & Fillenworth, C. (1993). Learning through self-evaluation: Writing the essay answers. *Journal of Reading, 37,* 54–55.

Rayner, K., & Duffy, S. A. (1988). On-line comprehension processes and eye movements during reading. In M. Daneman, G. E. Mackinnon, & T. G. Waller (Eds.), *Reading research: Advances in theory and practice* (Vol. 6, pp. 13–56). New York: Academic Press.

Rayner, K., & Pollatsek, A. (1989). *The psychology of reading.* Englewood Cliffs, NJ: Prentice-Hall.

Razik, T. A. (1969). A study of American newspaper readability. *The Journal of Communication, 19,* 317–324.

Read, C. (1975). *Children's categorization of speech sounds in English.* Champaign, IL: National Council of Teachers of English.

Reed, J. C., Rabe, E. F., & Mankinen, M. (1970). Teaching reading to brain-damaged children. A review. *Reading Research Quarterly, 6,* 379–401.

Rekrut, M. D. (1994). Peer and cross-age tutoring: The lessons of research. *Journal of Reading, 37,* 356–362.

Reutzel, D. R., & Hollingsworth, P. M. (1991). Using literature webbing for books with predictable narrative: Improving young readers' prediction, comprehension, and story structure knowledge. *Reading Psychology, 12,* 319–333.

Reutzel, D. R., Hollingsworth, P. M., & Eldredge, J. L. (1994). Oral reading instruction: The impact on student reading development. *Reading Research Quarterly, 29,* 41–62.

Reynolds, J., & Werner, S. C. (1993–94). An alternative paradigm for college reading and study skills courses. *Journal of Reading, 37,* 272–278.

Ribovich, J. K. (1978). Teaching reading fifty years ago. *The Reading Teacher, 31,* 371–375.

Richards, J. C., & Gipe, J. P. (1993). Getting to know story characters: A strategy for young and at-risk readers. *The Reading Teacher, 47,* 78–79.

Rickards, J. P., & August, G. J. (1975). Generative underlining strategies in prose recall. *Journal of Educational Psychology, 67,* 860–865.

Rigg, P., & Kazemek, F. E. (1985). Professional books. *Journal of Reading, 28,* 569–571.

Rinehart, S. D., Stahl, S. A., & Erickson, L. G. (1986). Some effects of summarization training on reading and studying. *Reading Research Quarterly, 21,* 422–438.

Ringler, L. H., & Smith, I. L. (1973). Learning modality and word recognition of first grade children. *Journal of Learning Disabilities, 6,* 307–312.

Robbins, M. P. (1966). A study of the validity of Delacato's theory of neurological organization and reading. *Exceptional Children, 32,* 517–523.

Robinson, H. A. (1966). Reading: Seventy-five years of progress. *Proceedings of the 29th Annual Conference in Reading, Vol. 38.* (Supplementary Educational Monographs No. 96.) Chicago: University of Chicago.

Robinson, H. A. (1983). *Teaching reading, writing, and study strategies: The content areas* (3rd ed.). Boston: Allyn & Bacon.

Robinson, H. M. (1946). *Why pupils fail in reading.* Chicago: University of Chicago Press.

Robinson, H. M. (1966). The major aspects of reading. In H. A. Robinson (Ed.), *Reading: Seventy-five years of progress.* Chicago: University of Chicago Press.

Robinson, H. M. (1967). Developing critical readers. In M. L. King, B. D. Ellinger, & W. Wolf (Eds.), *Critical reading.* Philadelphia: Lippincott.

Robinson, M. E., & Schwartz, L. B. (1973). Visuomotor skills and reading ability: A longitudinal study. *Developmental Medicine and Child Neurology, 15,* 281–286.

Rodriguez-Trujillo, N. (May, 1986). *Effect of availability of reading materials on reading behavior of primary school students.* Paper presented at the meeting of the International Reading Association, Philadelphia.

Roelke, P. L. (1969). Reading comprehension as a function of three dimensions of word meaning. *Dissertation Abstracts International, 30,* 5300A–5301A. (University Microfilms No. 70-10, 275)

Rosenshine, B. V. (1980). How time is spent in elementary classrooms. In C. Dunham & A. Lieberman (Eds.), *Time to learn* (Publication No. 695–717). Washington, DC: U.S. Government Printing Office.

Rosenshine, B. V., & Stevens, R. (1984). Classroom instruction in reading. In P. D. Pearson (Ed.), *Handbook of reading research.* New York: Longman.

Royer, J. M., Cisero, C. A., & Carlo, M. S. (1993). Techniques and procedures for assessing cognitive skills. *Review of Educational Research, 63,* 201–243.

Ruddell, R. B., & Boyle, O. (1984). *A study of the effects of cognitive mapping on reading comprehension and written protocols* (Tech. Rep. No. 7). Riverside, CA: University of California, Learning from Text Project.

Rumelhart, D. E. (1976). Toward an interactive model of reading. In S. Dornic (Ed.), *Attention and performance,* VI. Hillsdale, NJ: Erlbaum.

Rumelhart, D. E. (1981). Schemata: The building blocks of cognition. In J. T. Gutherie (Ed.), *Comprehension and reading.* Newark, DE: International Reading Association.

Ruppert, E. T. (1976). The effect of the synthetic-multisensory method of language instruction upon psycholinguistic abilities and reading achievement. *Dissertation Abstracts International, 37,* 920A–921A. (University Microfilms No. 76-18, 223)

Sabine, G., & Sabine, P. (1983). *Books that made the difference: What people told us.* Hamden, CT: Library Professional Publications.

Sadoski, M. (1983). An exploratory study of the relationships between reported imagery and the comprehension and recall of a story. *Reading Research Quarterly, 19,* 110–123.

Salvia, J., & Ysseldyke, J. E. (1982). *Assessment in special and remedial education* (2nd ed.). Boston: Houghton Mifflin.

Sammons, R. B., & Davey, B. (1993–94). Assessing students' skill in using textbooks: The Textbook Awareness and Performance Profile (TAPP). *Journal of Reading, 37,* 280–286.

Samuels, S. J. (1977). Introduction to theoretical models of reading. In W. Otto, C. Peters, & N. Peters (Eds.), *Reading problems: A multidisciplinary perspective.* Reading, MA: Addison-Wesley.

Samuels, S. J. (1979). The method of repeated readings. *The Reading Teacher, 32,* 403–408.

Samuels, S. J. (1981). Characteristics of exemplary reading programs. In J. Gutherie (Ed.), *Comprehension and teaching: Reviews of the research.* Newark. DE: International Reading Association.

Samuels, S. J. (1988). Decoding and automaticity: Helping poor readers become automatic at word recognition. *The Reading Teacher, 41,* 756–760.

Sanders, N. M. (1966). *Classroom questions: What kinds?* New York: Harper & Row.

Santeusanio, R. P. (1983). *A practical approach to content area reading.* Reading, MA: Addison-Wesley.

Saphier, J. D. (1973). The relation of perceptual-motor skills to learning and school success. *Journal of Learning Disabilities, 6,* 583–591.

Sawyer, W. E. (1989). Attention Deficit Disorder: A wolf in sheep's clothing . . . again. *The Reading Teacher, 42,* 310–312.

Scarborough, H. S. (1984). Continuity between childhood dyslexia and adult reading. *British Journal of Psychology, 75,* 329–340.

Schatz, E. K., & Baldwin, R. S. (1986). Context clues are unreliable predictors of word meanings. *Reading Research Quarterly, 21,* 439–453.

Schmeltzer, R. V. (1975). The effect of college student constructed questions on the comprehension of a passage of expository prose (Doctoral dissertation, University of Minnesota). *Dissertation Abstracts International, 1975, 36,* 2162A. (University Microfilms No. 75–21, 088)

Schmitt, M. C. (1990). A questionnaire to measure children's awareness of strategic reading processes. *The Reading Teacher, 43,* 454–461.

Schreiner, R., & Tanner, L. R. (1976). What history says about reading. *The Reading Teacher, 29,* pp. 513–520.

Schumm, J. S., & Saumell, L. (1994). Learning the meaning of common English suffixes. *Journal of Reading, 37,* 390.

Schunk, D. H. (1981). Modeling and attribution effects on children's achievement: A self-efficacy analysis. *Journal of Educational Psychology, 73,* 93–105.

Schunk, D. H., & Rice, J. H. (1987). Enhancing comprehension skill and self-efficacy with strategy value information. *Journal of Reading Behavior, 19,* 285–302.

Schunk, D. H., & Rice, M. J. (1992). Influence of reading-comprehension strategy information on children's achievement outcomes. *Learning Disability Quarterly, 26,* 417–441.

Schwartz, R. M., & Raphael, T. E. (1985). Concept of definition: A key to improving students' vocabulary. *The Reading Teacher, 39,* 198–205.

Shanahan, T., & Kamil, M. L. (1984). The relationship of three concurrent and construct validities of cloze. In J. A. Niles & L. A. Harris (Eds.), *Changing perspectives on research in reading/language processing and instruction* (pp. 334–338). Rochester: National Reading Conference.

Shanahan, T., Kamil, M. L., & Tobin, A. W. (1982). Cloze as a measure of intersentential comprehension. *Reading Research Quarterly, 17,* 229–255.

Shankweiler, D., & Liberman, I. Y. (1972). Misreading: A search for causes. In J. F. Kavanagh & I. G. Mattingly (Eds.), *Language by eye and by ear* (pp. 293–317). Cambridge, MA: MIT Press.

Shannon, D. (1985). Use of top-level structure in expository text: An open letter to a high school teacher. *Journal of Reading, 28,* 426–431.

Shannon, P. (1991). Politics, policy, and reading research. In R. Barr, M. L. Kamil, P. Mosenthal, & P. D. Pearson (Eds.), *Handbook of reading research* (Vol. II, pp. 147–167). New York: Longman.

Shaw, N. (1989). *Sheep on a ship.* Boston: Houghton Mifflin.

Short, K. G. (1992). Intertextuality: Searching for patterns that connect. In C. K. Kinzer & D. J. Leu (Eds.), *Literacy research, theory, and practice: Views from many perspectives* (pp. 187–197). Chicago: National Reading Conference.

Sieben, R. L. (1977). Controversial medical treatments of learning disabilities. *Academic Therapy, 13,* 133–147.

Siegel, L. S. (1989). IQ is irrelevant to the definition of learning disabilities. *Journal of Learning Disabilities, 22,* 469–478.

Silberberg, N., & Silberberg, M. (1967). Hyperlexia: Specific word recognition skills in young children. *Exceptional Children, 34,* 41–42.

Sindelar, P. T., & Wilson, R. J. (1982, October). *Application of academic skills as a function of teacher-directed instruction and seatwork.* Paper presented at the meeting of the Applied Behavior Analysis in Education Conference, Columbus, OH.

Sipay, E. R. (1964). A comparison of standardized reading scores and functional reading levels. *The Reading Teacher, 17,* 265–268.

Slaughter, J. P. (1993). *Beyond storybooks: Young children and the shared book experience.* Newark, DE: International Reading Association.

Slavin, R. E., Madden, N. A., Karweit, N. L., Dolan, L., & Wasik, B. A. (1992). *Success for All: A relentless approach to prevention and early intervention in elementary schools.* Arlington, VA: Educational Research Service.

Smith, F. (1971). *Understanding reading.* New York: Holt, Rinehart & Winston.

Smith, F. (1978). *Understanding reading* (2nd ed.). New York: Holt, Rinehart & Winston.

Smith, F. (1982). *Understanding reading* (3rd ed.). New York: Holt, Rinehart & Winston.

Smith, H. P., & Dechant, E. V. (1961). *Psychology in teaching reading.* Englewood Cliffs, NJ: Prentice-Hall.

Smith, I. L., Ringler, L. H., & Cullinan, B. L. (1968). *New York University Learning Modality Test.* New York: New York University.

Smith, L. (1977). Literacy: Definitions and implications. *Language Arts, 54,* 135–138.

Smith, N. B. (1965). *American reading instruction.* Newark, DE: International Reading Association.

Smith, N. B. (1967). Patterns of writing in different subject areas. In M. L. King, B. D. Ellinger, & W. Wolf (Eds.), *Critical reading.* Philadelphia: Lippincott.

Snyder, Z. (1969). *Today is Saturday.* New York: Atheneum.

Solman, R. T., & May, J. G. (1990). Spatial localization discrepancies: A visual deficiency in poor readers. *American Journal of Psychology, 103,* 243–263.

Spache, G. D. (1976). *Investigating the issues of reading disability.* Boston: Allyn & Bacon.

Spache, G. D. (1981). *Diagnosing and correcting reading disabilities* (2nd ed.). Boston: Allyn & Bacon.

Sperry, A. (1968). *Call it courage.* New York: Macmillan.

Spiegel, D. L. (1981). *Reading for pleasure: Guidelines.* Newark, DE: International Reading Association.

Spiegel, D. L. (1992). Blending whole language and systematic direct instruction. *The Reading Teacher, 46,* 38–48.

Spiegel, D. L., & Rogers, C. (1980) Teacher responses to miscues during oral reading by second-grade students. *Journal of Educational Research, 74,* 8–12.

Spring, C., & French, L. (1990). Identifying children with specific reading disabilities from listening and reading discrepancy scores. *Journal of Learning Disabilities, 23,* 53–58.

Spring, C., Gilbert, N., & Sassenrath, J. (1979). Learning to read words: Effects of overlearning and similarity on stimulus selection. *Journal of Reading Behavior, 11,* 69–71.

Staff (1993, July). New releases. *National Center on Adult Literacy: Connections,* p. 2.

Stahl, S. A. (1992). Saying the "p" word: Nine guidelines for exemplary phonics instruction. *The Reading Teacher, 45,* 618–625.

Stahl, S. A., & Fairbanks, M. (1986). The effects of vocabulary instruction: A model-based meta-analysis. *Review of Educational Research, 56,* 72–110.

Stahl, S. A., Richek, M. A., & Vandevier, R. J. (1991). Learning meaning through listening: A sixth-grade replication. In J. Zutell & S. McCormick (Eds.), *Learner factors/teacher factors: Issues in literacy research and instruction* (pp. 185–192). Chicago: National Reading Conference.

Stallings, J. A. (1980). Allocated academic learning time revisited, or beyond time on task. *Educational Researcher, 9*(11), 11–16.

Stallings, J. A. (1986). Using time effectively: A self-analytic approach. In K. K. Zumwalt (Ed.), *Improving teaching.* Alexandria, VA: Association for Supervision and Curriculum Development.

Stanovich, K. E. (1980). Toward an interactive-compensatory model of individual differences in the development of reading fluency. *Reading Research Quarterly, 16,* 32–71.

Stanovich, K. E. (1985). Explaining the variance in reading ability in terms of psychological processes: What have we learned? *Annals of Dyslexia, 35,* 67–96.

Stanovich, K. E. (1986). Matthew effects on reading: Some consequences of individual differences in the acquisition of literacy. *Reading Research Quarterly, 21,* 360–407.

Stanovich, K. E. (1991a). Discrepancy definitions of reading disability: Has intelligence led us astray? *Reading Research Quarterly, 26,* 7–29.

Stanovich, K. E. (1991b). Word recognition: Changing perspectives. In R. Barr, M. L. Kamil, P. Mosenthal, & P. D. Pearson (Eds.), *Handbook of reading research* (Vol. II, pp. 418–452). New York: Longman.

Stanovich, K. E. (1993–94). Romance and society. *The Reading Teacher, 47,* 280–291.

Stanovich, K. E., Cunningham, A., & Feeman, D. J. (1984). Intelligence, cognitive skills, and early reading progress. *Reading Research Quarterly, 19,* 278–303.

Stanovich, K. E., Nathan, R. G., & Zolman, J. E. (1988). The developmental lag hypothesis in reading: Longitudinal and matched reading-level comparisons. *Child Development, 59,* 71–86.

Stanovich, K. E., & West, R. F. (1981). The effect of sentence context on on-going word recognition: Tests of a two-process theory. *Journal of Experimental Psychology: Human Perception and Performance, 7,* 658–672.

Stanovich, K. E., & West, R. F. (1989). Exposure to print and orthographic processing. *Reading Research Quarterly, 24,* 402–433.

Stanovich, K. E., West, R. F., & Feeman, D. J. (1981). A longitudinal study of sentence context effects in second-grade children: Texts of an interactive-compensatory model. *Journal of Experimental Child Psychology, 32,* 185–199.

Stauffer, R. G. (1942). A study of prefixes in the Thorndike list to establish a list of prefixes that should be taught in the elementary school. *Journal of Educational Research, 35,* 453–458.

Stauffer, R. G. (1969). *Teaching reading as a thinking process.* New York: Harper & Row.

Stauffer, R. G. (1970). *The language experience approach to the teaching of reading.* New York: Harper & Row.

Stauffer, R. G. (1975). *Directing the reading—thinking process.* New York: Harper & Row.

Stein, N., & Prindaville, P. (1976). Discrimination learning and stimulus generalization by impulsive and reflective children. *Journal of Experimental Child Psychology, 21,* 25–39.

Sticht, T. G. (Ed.). (1975). *Reading for working: A functional literacy anthology.* Alexandria, VA: Human Resources Research Organization.

Sticht, T. G. (1981). *Basic skills in defense.* Alexandria, VA: Human Resources Research Organization.

Strickland, D., & Cullinan, B. (1990). Afterword. In M. Adams, *Beginning to read: Thinking and learn-*

ing about print (pp. 425–434). Cambridge, MA: MIT Press.

Sulzby, E. (1989). Assessment of writing and children's language while writing. In L. Morrow & J. Smith (Eds.), *The role of assessment and measurement in early literacy instruction* (pp. 83–109). Englewood Cliffs, NJ: Prentice-Hall.

Sulzby, E., & Teale, W. (1991). Emergent literacy. In R. Barr, M. L. Kamil, P. Mosenthal, & P. D. Pearson (Eds.), *Handbook of reading research* (Vol. II, pp. 727–758). New York: Longman.

Swafford, J. (1990). A comparison of the effectiveness of content area reading strategies at the elementary, secondary, and postsecondary levels. In N. D. Padak, T. V. Rasinski, & J. Logan (Eds.), *Challenges in reading* (pp. 111–126). Provo, UT: College Reading Association.

Swalm, J. E. (1972). A comparison of oral reading, silent reading, and listening. *Education, 92,* 111–115.

Sweet, A. P. (1993). *State of the art: Transforming ideas for teaching and learning to read* (GPO Document No. 065-000-00620-1). Washington, DC: U.S. Department of Education, Office of Education Research and Improvement.

Taylor, B. M., & Beach, R. W. (1984). The effects of text structure instruction on middle-grade students' comprehension and production of expository text. *Reading Research Quarterly, 19,* 134–146.

Taylor, E. A. (1937). *Controlled reading.* Chicago: University of Chicago Press.

Taylor, H. G., Satz, P., & Friel (1979). Developmental dyslexia in relation to other childhood reading disorders: Significance and clinical utility. *Reading Research Quarterly, 15,* 84–101.

Teale, W. H. (1986). Home background and young children's literacy development. In W. H. Teale & E. Sulzby (Eds.), *Emergent literacy: Writing and reading* (pp. 173–206). Norwood. NJ: Ablex.

Tharp, R. G., & Gallimore, R. (1989). *Rousing minds to life: Teaching, learning, and schooling in social context.* New York: Cambridge University Press.

Thompson, L. J. (1966). *Reading disability: Developmental dyslexia.* Springfield, IL: Charles C. Thomas.

Thorndike, E. L., & Lorge, I. (1944). *The teacher's word book of 30,000 words.* New York: Columbia University Teacher's College.

Tierney, R. J., Carter, M. A., & Desai, L. E. (1991). *Portfolio assessment in the reading-writing classroom.* Norwood, MA: Christopher-Gordon.

Tierney, R. J., & Cunningham, J. W. (1984). Research on teaching reading comprehension. In P. D. Pearson (Ed.), *Handbook of reading research* (pp. 609–655). New York: Longman.

Timian, J., & Santeusanio, R. (1974). Context clues: An informal reading inventory. *The Reading Teacher, 27,* 706–709.

Torneus, M. (1984). Phonological awareness and reading: A chicken and egg problem? *Journal of Educational Psychology, 76,* 1346–1358.

Treiman, R., & Baron, J. (1983). Phonemic-analysis training helps children benefit from spelling-sound rules. *Memory and Cognition, 11,* 382–389.

Tunmer, W. E., Herriman, M. L., & Nesdale, A. R. (1988). Metalinguistic abilities and beginning reading. *Reading Research Quarterly, 23,* 134–158.

Tunmer, W. E., & Nesdale, A. R. (1985). Phonemic segmentation skill and beginning reading. *Journal of Educational Psychology, 77,* 417–427.

Uhry, J. K. (1993). Predicting low reading from phonological awareness and classroom print. *Educational Assessment, 1,* 349–368.

Underwood, N. R., & Zola, D. (1986). The span of letter recognition of good and poor readers. *Reading Research Quarterly, 22,* 6–19.

Vacca, R. (1981). *Content area reading.* Boston: Little, Brown.

Valencia, S. W., McGinley, W., & Pearson, P. D. (1990). Assessing reading and writing. In G. G. Duffy (Ed.), *Reading in the middle school* (2nd ed.). Newark, DE: International Reading Association.

Vellutino, F. R., & Denckla, M. B. (1991). Cognitive and neuropsychological foundations of word identification in poor and normally developing readers. In R. Barr, M. L. Kamil, P. Mosenthal, & P. D. Pearson (Eds.), *Handbook of reading research* (Vol. II, pp. 571–608). New York: Longman.

Vellutino, F. R., & Scanlon, D. B. (1987). Phonological coding, phonological awareness, and reading ability: Evidence from longitudinal and experimental study. *Merrill Palmer Quarterly, 33,* 321–363.

Venezsky, R. L. (1970). Regularity in reading and spelling. In H. Levin & J. Williams (Eds.), *Basic studies on reading.* New York: Basic Books.

Venezsky, R. L. (1975). The curious role of letter names in reading instruction. *Visible Language, 9,* 7–23.

Venezsky, R. L. (1991). The development of literacy in the industrialized nations of the West. In R. Barr, M. L. Kamil, P. Mosenthal, & P. D. Pearson (Eds.), *Handbook of reading research* (Vol. II, pp. 46–67). New York: Longman.

Visionhaler, J. F., Weinshank, A. B., Polin, R. M., & Wagner, C. C. (1983). *Improving diagnostic reliability in reading through training* (Research Series 176). E. Lansing: Michigan State University, Institute for Research on Teaching. (ERIC Document Reproduction Service No. ED 237 934)

Voigt, S. (1978). It's all Greek to me. *The Reading Teacher, 31,* 420–422.

Voss, J. F., Fincher-Kiefer, R. H., Greene, T. R., & Post, T. A. (1985). Individual differences in performance: The contrast approach to knowledge. In R. J. Sternberg (Ed.), *Advances in the psychology of human intelligence* (Vol. 3, pp. 297–334). Hillsdale, NJ: Erlbaum.

Vygotsky, L. S. (1978). *Mind in society: The development of higher psychological processes.* Cambridge, MA: Harvard University Press.

Wachs, T. D., Uzgiris, I. C., & Hunt, J. M. (1971). Cognitive development in infants of different age levels and from different environmental backgrounds: An exploratory investigation. *Merrill-Palmer Quarterly, 17,* 283–317.

Wade, S. E. (1990). Using think-alouds to assess comprehension. *The Reading Teacher, 43,* 442–451.

Wade, S. E., Schraw, G., Buxton, W. M., & Hayes, M. T. (1993). Seduction of the strategic reader: Effects of interest on strategies and recall. *Reading Research Quarterly, 28,* 93–114.

Wade, S. E., & Trathen, W. (1989). Effect of self-selected study methods on learning. *Journal of Educational Psychology, 81,* 40–47.

Wagner, D. A. (1993, July). Belief and reality in adult literacy. *National Center on Adult Literacy: Connections,* pp. 1, 6–7.

Wallen, N. E., & Wodtke, K. H. (1963). Relationships between teacher characteristics and student behavior—Part I (Report of Project No. 1217). Washington, DC: U.S. Office of Education.

Walley, C. (1993). An invitation to reading fluency. *The Reading Teacher, 46,* 526–527.

Walsh, D. J., Price, G. G., & Gillingham, M. G. (1988). The critical but transitory importance of letter naming. *Reading Research Quarterly, 23,* 108–122.

Wangberg, E. G., Thompson, B., & Levitov, J. E. (1984). First steps toward an adult basic word list. *Journal of Reading, 28,* 244–247.

Ward, M., & McCormick, S. (1981). Reading instruction for blind and low vision children in the regular classroom. *The Reading Teacher, 34,* 434–444.

Warwick, B. E. (1978). Cloze procedures (Ebbinghaus completion method) as applied to reading. In O. K. Buros (Ed.), *Eighth mental measurements yearbook* (Vol. II). Highland Park, NJ: Gryphon Press.

Wasik, B. A., & Slavin, R. E. (1993). Preventing early reading failure with one-to-one tutoring: A review of five programs. *Reading Research Quarterly, 28,* 179–200.

Watkins, S. (1993). Mail that letter! *The Reading Teacher, 46,* 621–624.

Watson, D. J. (1982). In college and in trouble—with reading. *Journal of Reading, 25,* 640–645.

Waugh, J. C. (1993). Using LEA in diagnosis. *Journal of Reading, 37,* 56–57.

Weaver, C. A., & Kintsch, W. (1991). Expository text. In R. Barr, M. L. Kamil, P. Mosenthal, & P. D. Pearson (Eds.), *Handbook of reading research* (Vol. II, pp. 230–245). New York: Longman.

Weber, Rose-Marie (1991). Linguistic diversity and reading in American society. In R. Barr, M. L. Kamil, P. Mosenthal, & P. D. Pearson (Eds.), *Handbook of reading research* (Vol. II, pp. 97–119). New York: Longman.

Weech, J. (1994). Writing the story before reading it. *Journal of Reading, 37,* 364–367.

Weiner, B. (1979). A theory of motivation for some classroom experiences. *Journal of Educational Psychology, 71,* 3–25.

Weisberg, R., & Balajthy, E. (1990). Improving disabled readers' summarization and recognition of expository text structure. In N. D. Padak, T. V. Rasinski, & J. Logan (Eds.), *Challenges in reading* (pp. 141–151). Provo, UT: College Reading Association.

Wendelin, K., & Zinc, R. (1983). How students make book choices. *Reading Horizons, 23*(2), 84–88.

Wepman, J. M. (1973). *Auditory discrimination test* (Revised ed.). Chicago: Language Research Associates.

Whittlesea, B. W. A. (1987). Preservation of specific experiences in the representation of general knowledge. *Journal of Experimental Psychology: Learning, Memory, and Cognition, 13,* 3–17.

Wigfield, A., & Asher, S. R. (1984). Social and motivational influences on reading. In R. Barr, M. L. Kamil, P. Mosenthal, & P. D. Pearson (Eds.), *Handbook of reading research* (Vol. II, pp. 423–452). New York: Longman.

Wilkinson, I., Wardrop, J. L., & Anderson, R. C. (1988). Silent reading reconsidered: Reinterpreting reading instruction and its effects. *American Educational Research Journal, 25,* 127–144.

Williams, J. (1984). Phonemic analysis and how it relates to reading. *Journal of Learning Disabilities, 17,* 240–245.

Williams, J. L. (1964). A comparison of standardized reading test scores and informal reading inventory scores. *Dissertation Abstracts International, 24,* 5262A. (University Microfilms No. 64-4485)

Williams, J. P. (1980). Teaching decoding with an emphasis on phoneme analysis and phoneme blending. *Journal of Educational Psychology, 72,* 1–15.

Williams, N. L., Konopak, B. C., Wood, K. D., & Avett, S. (1992). Middle school students' use of imagery in developing meaning in expository text. In C. K. Kinzer & D. J. Leu (Eds.), *Literacy research, theory, and practice: Views from many perspectives* (pp. 261–268). Chicago: National Reading Conference.

Willig, A. C. (1985). A meta-analysis of selected studies on the effectiveness of bilingual education. *Review of Educational Research, 55,* 269–317.

Willows, D. M., Borwick, D., & Hayvren, M. (1981). The content of school readers. In G. E. MacKinnon & T. G. Waller (Eds.), *Reading research: Advances in theory and practice* (Vol. II, pp. 97–175). New York: Academic Press.

Willows, D. M., & Ryan, E. B. (1986). The development of grammatical sensitivity and its relationship to early reading achievement. *Reading Research Quarterly, 21,* 253–266.

Wilson, M. M. (1979). The processing strategies of average and below average readers answering factual and inferential questions on three equivalent passages. *Journal of Reading Behavior, 11,* 235–245.

Winfield, L. (1986). Teacher beliefs toward academically at-risk students in inner-city schools. *Urban Review, 18,* 254–268.

Winograd, P. (1994). Developing alternative assessments. *The Reading Teacher, 47,* 420–423.

Winsor, P. J. T., & Pearson, P. D. (1992). *Children at risk: Their phonemic awareness development in holistic instruction.* (Tech. Rep. No. 556). Urbana-Champaign, IL: University of Illinois, Center for the Study of Reading.

Wixson, K. K., & Lipson, M. Y. (1991). Perspective on reading disability research. In R. Barr, M. L. Kamil, P. Mosenthal, & P. D. Pearson (Eds.), *Handbook of reading research* (Vol. II, pp. 539–570). New York: Longman.

Wixson, K. K., & Peters, C. W. (1987). Comprehension assessment: Implementing an interactive view

of reading. *Educational Psychologist, 22,* 333–356.

Wolf, K. P. (1993). From informal to informed assessment: The role of the classroom teacher. *The Reading Teacher, 46,* 518–523.

Wolf, S. A. (1993). What's in a name? Labels and literacy in Readers Theatre. *The Reading Teacher, 46,* 540–545.

Wolff, D. E., Desberg, P., & Marsh, G. (1985). Analogy strategies for improving word recognition in competent and learning disabled readers. *The Reading Teacher, 38,* 412–416.

Wood, K. D., Lapp, D., & Flood, J. (1992). *Guiding readers through text: A review of study guides.* Newark, DE: International Reading Association.

Worthington, J. S. (1977). The readability of footnotes to financial statements and how to improve them. *Journal of Reading, 20,* 469–478.

Yopp, H. K. (1988). The validity and reliability of phonemic awareness tests. *Reading Research Quarterly, 23,* 159–177.

Yopp, H. K. (1992). Developing phonemic awareness in young children. *The Reading Teacher, 45,* 696–703.

Ysseldyke, J. E., & Algozzine, B. (1982). *Critical issues in special and remedial education.* Boston: Houghton Mifflin.

Ziros, G. I. (1976). Language interference and teaching the Chicano to read. *Journal of Reading, 19,* 284–288.

Zola, D. (1984). Redundancy and word perception during reading. *Perception and Psychophysics, 36,* 277–284.

Zutell, J. (1978). Some psycholinguistic perspectives on children's spelling. *Language Arts, 55,* 844–850.

Zutell, J. (1985). Linguistic and psycholinguistic perspectives on brain mechanisms and language. In V. Rental, S. Corson, & B. Dunn (Eds.), *Psychophysiological aspects of reading and learning.* New York: Gordon & Breach.

Zutell, J., & Rasinski, T. (1989). Reading and spelling connections in third and fifth grade students. *Reading Psychology, 10,* 137–155.

Index

Author Biography

Before assuming a teaching position at a university, Sandra McCormick taught as a fourth- and fifth-grade classroom teacher in schools comprised primarily of at-risk youngsters; served as a Title I reading teacher for elementary and middle-school students; worked as a Reading Resource Teacher assisting teachers in inner-city schools with their classroom reading and language arts programs; and supervised a city-wide reading program that served 129 elementary schools in a large midwestern city. She also was a television reading teacher, teaching children in eight cities in Ohio via a PBS program aimed at students having reading disabilities.

After receiving her Ph.D. at The Ohio State University, Dr. McCormick joined the faculty in the College of Education at that university where she has taught courses on remedial and clinical reading assessment and instruction, and on methods for instructing students having learning disabilities. She also has supervised a university-based reading clinic for several years.

Dr. McCormick is the author or editor of several books in addition to this one, including *Remedial and Clinical Reading Instruction* and *Cognitive and Social Perspectives for Literacy Research and Instruction* (the latter with Jerry Zutell). She publishes articles frequently in journals such as *Reading Research Quarterly, The Reading Teacher, Journal of Reading, Journal of Reading Behavior, Journal of Educational Research, Exceptional Children, Journal of Learning Disabilities,* and *Language Arts.* Dr. McCormick was coeditor of the National Reading Conference Yearbook for three years and is on the editorial advisory review board for several journals. Her research interest, as might be expected, is with students having literacy problems. Though for several years her research focus was on comprehension instruction and reading/learning disabled students, currently she is investigating ways to facilitate word learning with severely delayed readers, including nonreaders.

Dr. McCormick has served as a member of the Board of Directors of the International Reading Association; was a distinguished finalist in 1990 for the Albert J. Harris Award presented annually for significant research on reading disabilities; and has been elected to Fellow Status in the National Conference on Research in English. Dr. McCormick is a frequent presenter at national and international conferences, and she regularly reviews research and development proposals for the United States Department of Education.